Exploring Writing

Exploring Writing
Sentences and Paragraphs
SECOND EDITION

John Langan
Atlantic Cape Community College

Mc Graw Hill

Connect
Learn
Succeed™

Published by McGraw-Hill, an imprint of The McGraw-Hill Companies, Inc., 1221 Avenue of the Americas, New York, NY 10020. Copyright © 2010, 2008. All rights reserved. No part of this publication may be reproduced or distributed in any form or by any means, or stored in a database or retrieval system, without the prior written consent of The McGraw-Hill Companies, Inc., including, but not limited to, in any network or other electronic storage or transmission, or broadcast for distance learning.

This book is printed on acid-free paper.

2 3 4 5 6 7 8 9 0 DOW/DOW 0 9

ISBN 978-0-07-337186-3 (student edition)
MHID 0-07-337186-6 (student edition)
ISBN 978-0-07-730317-4 (instructor's edition)
MHID 0-07-730317-2 (instructor's edition)

Vice President, Editor in Chief: *Michael Ryan*
Publisher: *David S. Patterson*
Senior Sponsoring Editor: *John Kindler*
Marketing Manager: *Jaclyn Elkins*
Director of Development: *Dawn Groundwater*
Development Editor: *Alyson Watts*
Editorial Coordinator: *Jesse Hassenger*
Senior Production Editor: *Karol Jurado*
Production Service: *Aaron Downey, Matrix Productions Inc.*
Manuscript Editor: *Dan Hays*
Design Manager: *Preston Thomas*
Text Designer: *Maureen McCutcheon*
Cover Designer: *Laurie Entringer*
Photo Research: *Emily Tietz*
Media Project Manager: *Vivek Iyer*
Senior Production Supervisor: *Tandra Jorgensen*
Composition: *11/13.5 Palatino by Macmillan Publishing Solutions*
Printing: *45# New Era Thin Plus, RR Donnelley & Sona*

Cover images: © Jo McRyan/Stone/Getty Images (top left); © White Packert/Stone/Getty Images (top right); © Michael Poehlman/Photographer's Choice/Getty Images (bottom left); © Jan Cobb Photography Ltd./Photographer's Choice/Getty Images (bottom right)

Credits: The credits section for this book begins on page 637 and is considered an extension of the copyright page.

Library of Congress Cataloging-in-Publication Data

Langan, John
    Exploring writing : sentences and paragraphs / John Langan. — 2nd ed.
      p. cm.
  Includes bibliographical references and index.
  ISBN-13: 978-0-07-337186-3 (alk. paper)
  ISBN-10: 0-07-337186-6 (alk. paper)
  1. English language—Sentences—Problems, exercises, etc. 2. English language—Paragraphs—Problems, exercises, etc. 3. English language—Rhetoric—Problems, exercises, etc. 4. Report writing—Problems, exercises, etc. I. Title.
  PE1441.L34 2009
  808'.042076—dc22

                                     2009004597

The Internet addresses listed in the text were accurate at the time of publication. The inclusion of a Web site does not indicate an endorsement by the authors or McGraw-Hill, and McGraw-Hill does not guarantee the accuracy of the information presented at these sites.

www.mhhe.com

John Langan has taught reading and writing at Atlantic Cape Community College near Atlantic City, New Jersey, for more than twenty-five years. The author of a popular series of college textbooks on both writing and reading, John enjoys the challenge of developing materials that teach skills in an especially clear and lively way. Before teaching, he earned advanced degrees in writing at Rutgers University and in reading at Rowan University. He also spent a year writing fiction that, he says, "is now at the back of a drawer waiting to be discovered and acclaimed posthumously." While in school, he supported himself by working as a truck driver, a machinist, a battery assembler, a hospital attendant, and apple packer. John now lives with his wife, Judith Nadell, near Philadelphia. In addition to his wife and Philly sports teams, his passions include reading and turning on nonreaders to the pleasure and power of books. Through Townsend Press, his educational publishing company, he has developed the non-profit "Townsend Library"—a collection of more than fifty new and classic stories that appeal to readers of any age.

BRIEF CONTENTS

Preface xxi

PART 1 Writing: Skills and Process 2

1. An Introduction to Writing 4
2. The Writing Process 16

PART 2 Writing Effective Paragraphs 44

3. Four Steps for Writing, Four Bases for Revising 46
4. Nine Patterns of Paragraph Development 85
5. Moving from Paragraph to Essay 126

PART 3 Sentence Skills 150

SECTION I Sentences 152

6. Subjects and Verbs 153
7. Fragments 162
8. Run-Ons 179
9. Sentence Variety I 195

SECTION II Verbs, Pronouns, and Agreement 209

10. Standard English Verbs 210
11. Irregular Verbs 220
12. Subject-Verb Agreement 231
13. Consistent Verb Tense 241
14. Additional Information about Verbs 245
15. Pronoun Reference, Agreement, and Point of View 252
16. Pronoun Types 263

SECTION III Modifiers and Parallelism 275

17. Adjectives and Adverbs 276
18. Misplaced Modifiers 283
19. Dangling Modifiers 289
20. Faulty Parallelism 295
21. Sentence Variety II 304

SECTION IV Punctuation and Mechanics 318

22. Paper Format 319
23. Capital Letters 324

24. Numbers and Abbreviations 334

25. End Marks 339

26. Apostrophes 342

27. Quotation Marks 354

28. Commas 365

29. Other Punctuation Marks 379

SECTION V Word Use 385

30. Dictionary Use 386

31. Spelling Improvement 395

32. Omitted Words and Letters 402

33. Commonly Confused Words 407

34. Effective Word Choice 423

PART 4 Readings for Writers 436

INTRODUCTION TO THE READINGS 438

GOALS AND VALUES 442

EDUCATION AND SELF-IMPROVEMENT 483

HUMAN GROUPS AND SOCIETY 537

APPENDIXES 585

A. Parts of Speech 586

B. ESL Pointers 597

C. Sentence-Skills Diagnostic Test 609

D. Sentence-Skills Achievement Test 614

E. Answers to Activities in Part 3 619

Credits 637

Index 639

CONTENTS

Preface   xxi

PART 1 Writing: Skills and Process   2

1. An Introduction to Writing   4

Understanding Point and Support   5
An Important Difference between Writing and Talking   5
Point and Support in Two Cartoons   6
Point and Support in a Paragraph   8
Writing as a Skill   10
Why Does Your Attitude toward Writing Matter?   10
Writing as a Process of Discovery   12
Keeping a Journal   13

2. The Writing Process   16

How Do You Reach the Goals of Effective Writing?   17
Prewriting   17
Technique 1: Freewriting   17
Technique 2: Questioning   20
Technique 3: Making a List   21
Technique 4: Clustering   22
Technique 5: Preparing a Scratch Outline   23
Writing the First Draft   25
Writing a First Draft: A Student Model   25
Revising   27
Revising: A Student Model   28
Editing and Proofreading   29
Editing Tips   30
Proofreading Tips   30
Editing and Proofreading: A Student Model   31
Tips on Using a Computer   32
Using a Computer at Each Stage of the Writing Process   33
Using Peer Review   35
1. Identification   35
2. Scratch Outline   35
3. Comments   36
Review Activities   36
Prewriting   37

Outlining, Drafting, and Revising   37

Taking a Writing Inventory   39

Chapter Review   40

PART 2 Writing Effective Paragraphs   44

3. Four Steps for Writing, Four Bases for Revising   46

What Are the Steps to Writing Effective Paragraphs?   47

Step 1: Make a Point   47

Step 2: Back Up Your Point   50

Step 3: Organize the Support   67

Step 4: Write Clear, Error-Free Sentences   73

Four Bases for Revising Writing   73

Base 1: Unity   74

Base 2: Support   75

Base 3: Coherence   76

Base 4: Sentence Skills   77

4. Nine Patterns of Paragraph Development   85

Important Considerations in Paragraph Development   86

Knowing Your Subject   86

Knowing Your Purpose and Audience   86

Patterns of Development   87

1. Exemplification   88

A Paragraph to Consider   89

Writing an Exemplification Paragraph   89

2. Description   92

A Paragraph to Consider   92

Writing a Descriptive Paragraph   93

3. Narration   97

A Paragraph to Consider   97

Writing a Narrative Paragraph   98

4. Process   100

A Paragraph to Consider   100

Writing a Process Paragraph   101

5. Cause and Effect   105

A Paragraph to Consider   105

Writing a Cause-and-Effect Paragraph   106

6. Comparison or Contrast   108

Two Paragraphs to Consider   109

Writing a Comparison or Contrast Paragraph   111

7. Definition 114
A Paragraph to Consider 114
Writing a Definition Paragraph 115
8. Division-Classification 117
Two Paragraphs to Consider 117
Writing a Division-Classification Paragraph 119
9. Argument 121
A Paragraph to Consider 121
Writing an Argument Paragraph 122

5. Moving from Paragraph to Essay 126
What Is an Essay? 127
Differences between an Essay and a Paragraph 127
The Form of an Essay 127
A Model Essay 128
Important Points about the Essay 129
Introductory Paragraph 129
Supporting Paragraphs 131
Transitional Sentences 131
Concluding Paragraph 132
Essays to Consider 132
Planning the Essay 135
Outlining the Essay 135
Form for Planning the Essay 136
Practice in Writing the Essay 136
Understanding the Two Parts of a Thesis Statement 136
Supporting the Thesis with Specific Evidence 137
Identifying Introductions 139
Revising an Essay for All Four Bases: Unity, Support, Coherence, and Sentence Skills 140
Essay Assignments 142

PART 3 Sentence Skills 150

SECTION I Sentences 152

6. Subjects and Verbs 153
A Simple Way to Find a Subject 154
A Simple Way to Find a Verb 154
More about Subjects and Verbs 157
Distinguishing Subjects from Prepositional Phrases 157
Verbs of More Than One Word 158
Compound Subjects and Verbs 159

7. Fragments 162

What Fragments Are 163

Dependent-Word Fragments 163

How to Correct Dependent-Word Fragments 164

-*ing* and *to* Fragments 167

How to Correct -*ing* Fragments 167

How to Correct *to* Fragments 168

Added-Detail Fragments 170

How to Correct Added-Detail Fragments 170

Missing-Subject Fragments 172

How to Correct Missing-Subject Fragments 172

8. Run-Ons 179

What Are Run-Ons? 180

A Warning: Words That Can Lead to Run-Ons 180

Correcting Run-Ons 181

Method 1: Period and a Capital Letter 181

Method 2: Comma and a Joining Word 184

Method 3: Semicolon 186

Semicolon Alone 186

Semicolon with a Transition 186

Transitional Words 187

Method 4: Subordination 188

Dependent Words 188

9. Sentence Variety I 195

Four Traditional Sentence Patterns 195

The Simple Sentence 195

The Compound Sentence 196

The Complex Sentence 197

The Compound-Complex Sentence 201

Review of Subordination and Coordination 202

SECTION II Verbs, Pronouns, and Agreement 209

10. Standard English Verbs 210

Regular Verbs: Dialect and Standard Forms 210

Present Tense Endings 211

Past Tense Endings 213

Three Common Irregular Verbs: Dialect and Standard Forms 214

11. Irregular Verbs 220

A Brief Review of Regular Verbs 220

List of Irregular Verbs 221

Troublesome Irregular Verbs 226

12. Subject-Verb Agreement 231

Words between the Subject and the Verb 232

Verb before the Subject 233

Indefinite Pronouns 234

Compound Subjects 235

Who, Which, and *That* 236

13. Consistent Verb Tense 241

Keeping Tenses Consistent 241

14. Additional Information about Verbs 245

Verb Tense 245

Present Perfect (*have* or *has* + past participle) 246

Past Perfect (*had* + past participle) 246

Present Progressive (*am, is,* or *are* + the *-ing* form) 246

Past Progressive (*was* or *were* + the *-ing* form) 246

Verbals 247

Infinitive 247

Participle 248

Gerund 248

Active and Passive Verbs 249

15. Pronoun Reference, Agreement, and Point of View 252

Pronoun Reference 253

Pronoun Agreement 255

Indefinite Pronouns 256

Pronoun Point of View 258

16. Pronoun Types 263

Subject and Object Pronouns 263

Subject Pronouns 264

Object Pronouns 265

Relative Pronouns 267

Points to Remember about Relative Pronouns 268

Possessive Pronouns 269

Demonstrative Pronouns 270

Reflexive Pronouns 272

Points to Remember about Reflexive Pronouns 272

SECTION III   Modifiers and Parallelism   275

17. **Adjectives and Adverbs   276**
    Adjectives   276
        What Are Adjectives?   276
        Using Adjectives to Compare   277
        Points to Remember about Adjectives   277
    Adverbs   279
        What Are Adverbs?   279
        A Common Mistake with Adjectives and Adverbs   279
        Well and *Good*   280

18. **Misplaced Modifiers   283**
    What Misplaced Modifiers Are and How to Correct Them   283

19. **Dangling Modifiers   289**
    What Dangling Modifiers Are and How to Correct Them   289

20. **Faulty Parallelism   295**
    Parallelism Explained   295

21. **Sentence Variety II   304**
    -ing Word Groups   304
    -ed Word Groups   305
    -ly Openers   306
    To Openers   308
    Prepositional Phrase Openers   309
    Series of Items   311
        Adjectives in Series   311
        Verbs in Series   313

SECTION IV   Punctuation and Mechanics   318

22. **Paper Format   319**
    Guidelines for Preparing a Paper   320

23. **Capital Letters   324**
    Main Uses of Capital Letters   325
        First Word in a Sentence or Direct Quotation   325
        Names of Persons and the Word *I*   325
        Names of Particular Places   325
        Names of Days of the Week, Months, and Holidays   325
        Names of Commercial Products   326
        Titles of Books, Magazines, Articles, Films, Television Shows,
        Songs, Poems, Stories, Papers That You Write, and the Like   326
        Names of Companies, Associations, Unions, Clubs, Religious and
        Political Groups, and Other Organizations   326

Other Uses of Capital Letters   327

Names That Show Family Relationships   328

Titles of Persons When Used with Their Names   328

Specific School Courses   328

Languages   328

Geographic Locations   328

Historic Periods and Events   328

Races, Nations, and Nationalities   329

Opening and Closing of a Letter   329

Unnecessary Use of Capitals   330

24. **Numbers and Abbreviations**   334

Numbers   334

Abbreviations   336

25. **End Marks**   339

Period (.)   339

Question Mark (?)   339

Exclamation Point (!)   340

26. **Apostrophes**   342

Apostrophes in Contractions   343

Four Contractions to Note Carefully   344

Apostrophes to Show Ownership or Possession   345

Points to Remember   346

Apostrophes versus Possessive Pronouns   348

Apostrophes versus Simple Plurals   348

Apostrophes with Plural Words Ending in -s   350

27. **Quotation Marks**   354

Quotation Marks to Set Off the Words of a Speaker or Writer   355

Indirect Quotations   358

Quotation Marks to Set Off the Titles of Short Works   359

Other Uses of Quotation Marks   361

28. **Commas**   365

Six Main Uses of the Comma   366

Commas between Items in a Series   366

Commas after Introductory Material   367

Commas around Words Interrupting the Flow of Thought   368

Commas between Complete Thoughts Connected by Joining Words   370

Commas with Direct Quotations   372

Commas with Everyday Material   373

Unnecessary Use of Commas   374

29. Other Punctuation Marks   379

Colons (:)   379

Semicolons (;)   380

Dashes (—)   381

Hyphens (-)   382

Parentheses ( )   382

SECTION V Word Use   385

30. Dictionary Use   386

Spelling   387

Syllabication   387

Pronunciation   388

Vowel Sounds   388

The Schwa (ə)   389

Accent Marks   389

Full Pronunciation   389

Other Information about Words   390

Parts of Speech   390

Principal Parts of Irregular Verbs   390

Plural Forms of Irregular Nouns   391

Meanings   391

Etymology   392

Usage Labels   392

Synonyms   393

31. Spelling Improvement   395

Step 1: Using the Dictionary   395

Step 2: Keeping a Personal Spelling List   396

Step 3: Mastering Commonly Confused Words   396

Step 4: Using a Computer's Spell-Checker   396

Step 5: Understanding Basic Spelling Rules   396

Step 6: Understanding Plurals   397

Step 7: Mastering a Basic Word List   399

32. Omitted Words and Letters   402

Finding Omitted Words and Letters   402

Omitted Words   403

Omitted -s Endings   403

33. Commonly Confused Words 407

Homonyms 407

Other Words Frequently Confused 414

Incorrect Word Forms 419

34. Effective Word Choice 423

Slang 424

Clichés 425

Inflated Words 426

Wordiness 428

PART 4 Readings for Writers 436

INTRODUCTION TO THE READINGS 438

The Format of Each Selection 438

How to Read Well: Four General Steps 439

1 Concentrate as You Read 439

2 Skim Material before You Read It 439

3 Read the Selection Straight through with a Pen Nearby 440

4 Work with the Material 440

How to Answer the Vocabulary in Context Questions 440

How to Answer the Reading Comprehension Questions 441

GOALS AND VALUES 442

Sister Helen Mrosla
All the Good Things 442

Paul Logan
Rowing the Bus 448

Rick Bragg
All She Has—$150,000—Is Going to a University 455

Mee Her
Bowling to Find a Lost Father 462

Rose Del Castillo Guilbault
The Conveyor-Belt Ladies 468

Firoozeh Dumas
The "F Word" 475

EDUCATION AND SELF-IMPROVEMENT 483

Ben Carson, M.D., with Cecil Murphey
Do It Better! 483

Janny Scott
How They Get You to Do That 492

Grant Berry
A Change of Attitude 501

Beth Johnson
Let's Get Specific 511

B. J. Penn
Stance   521

Natalie Goldberg
Baking a Cake   525

Robert S. Feldman
Why Go to College?   531

HUMAN GROUPS AND SOCIETY   537

Katherine Barrett
Old before Her Time   537

Amy Tan
The Most Hateful Words   546

Bill Wine
Rudeness at the Movies   551

Luis J. Rodriguez
Turning Youth Gangs Around   558

Maya Angelou
Reclaiming Our Home Place   566

Al Gore
Consume Less, Conserve More   572

Paul Boutin
A Grand Unified Theory of YouTube and MySpace   579

APPENDIXES   585

A. Parts of Speech   586

B. ESL Pointers   597

C. Sentence-Skills Diagnostic Test   609

D. Sentence-Skills Achievement Test   614

E. Answers to Activities in Part 3   619

Credits   637

Index   639

READINGS Listed by Rhetorical Mode

Note: Some selections are listed more than once because they illustrate more than one pattern of development.

EXEMPLIFICATION

All the Good Things,   Sister Helen Mrosla   442

How They Get You to Do That,   Janny Scott   492

Let's Get Specific,   Beth Johnson   511

The Most Hateful Words,   Amy Tan   546

Rudeness at the Movies,   Bill Wine   551

Stance,   B. J. Penn   521

Why Go to College?   Robert S. Feldman   531

Old before Her Time,   Katherine Barrett   537

DESCRIPTION

Rowing the Bus,   Paul Logan   448

The Conveyor-Belt Ladies,   Rose Del Castillo Guilbault   468

Old before Her Time,   Katherine Barrett   537

Rudeness at the Movies,   Bill Wine   551

NARRATION

All the Good Things,   Sister Helen Mrosla   442

Rowing the Bus,   Paul Logan   448

All She Has—$150,000—Is Going to a University,   Rick Bragg   455

Bowling to Find a Lost Father,   Mee Her   462

The Conveyor-Belt Ladies,   Rose Del Castillo Guilbault   468

The "F Word,"   Firoozeh Dumas   475

Do It Better!   Ben Carson (with Cecil Murphey)   483

Old before Her Time,   Katherine Barrett   537

The Most Hateful Words,   Amy Tan   546

A Change of Attitude,   Grant Berry   501

Turning Youth Gangs Around,   Luis J. Rodriguez   558

Reclaiming Our Home Place,   Maya Angelou   566

PROCESS

Let's Get Specific,   Beth Johnson   511

Baking a Cake,   Natalie Goldberg   525

Consume Less, Conserve More,   Al Gore   572

A Grand Unified Theory of YouTube and MySpace,   Paul Boutin   579

CAUSE AND EFFECT

Do It Better!   Ben Carson (with Cecil Murphey)   483

Old before Her Time,   Katherine Barrett   537

How They Get You to Do That,   Janny Scott   492

Why Go to College?   Robert S. Feldman   531

The Most Hateful Words,   Amy Tan   546

Rudeness at the Movies,   Bill Wine   551

Turning Youth Gangs Around,   Luis J. Rodriguez   558

COMPARISON OR CONTRAST

Rowing the Bus,   Paul Logan   448

Old before Her Time,   Katherine Barrett   537

The Most Hateful Words,   Amy Tan   546

A Grand Unified Theory of YouTube and MySpace,   Paul Boutin   579

DEFINITION

Rowing the Bus,   Paul Logan   448

Baking a Cake,   Natalie Goldberg   525

Reclaiming Our Home Place,   Maya Angelou   566

A Grand Unified Theory of YouTube and MySpace,   Paul Boutin   579

DIVISION-CLASSIFICATION

Rudeness at the Movies,   Bill Wine   551

Let's Get Specific,   Beth Johnson   511

ARGUMENT

Rudeness at the Movies,   Bill Wine   551

Turning Youth Gangs Around,   Luis J. Rodriguez   558

Consume Less, Conserve More,   Al Gore   572

A Grand Unified Theory of YouTube and MySpace,   Paul Boutin   579

Learning to write effective paragraphs and essays, master essential sentence skills, and read critically are turning points for writers; these skills will prepare them to tackle many types of writing in college and beyond. Along the way, however, there are many other important skills to explore and develop—using specific and concrete language to make a point and stick to it, selecting good supporting details to back up that point and create a convincing argument, organizing a paragraph in a way that best fits its purpose, and writing clear, error-free sentences to maximize the effectiveness of the writing. In *Exploring Writing: Sentences and Paragraphs*, I encourage new writers to see writing as a skill that can be learned *and* a process that must be explored. I refer to a set of four skills for effective writing as **the four bases:**

- **Unity:** Discover a clearly stated point, or topic sentence, and make sure all the other information in the paragraph or essay is in support of that point.

- **Support:** Support the points with specific evidence, and plenty of it.

- **Coherence:** Organize and connect supporting evidence so that paragraphs and essays transition smoothly from one bit of supporting information to the next.

- **Sentence skills:** Revise and edit so that sentences are error free for clearer and more effective communication.

The four bases are essential to effective writing, whether it be a narrative paragraph, a cover letter for a job application, or an essay assignment.

Highlights of the *Second Edition*

Real Students

Whether it is in the avatars (see the front cover foldout or jump online to meet a few) or the *Writer's Template* activities, *Exploring Writing* emphasizes meaningful writing across the curriculum and throughout life.

- **Avatars:** Throughout the margins of *Exploring Writing,* you will meet more than thirty characters who are experiencing various writing dilemmas. For instance, within the chapter on commas, we meet Amy, who is having trouble using commas correctly in her journal entries. Writers are prompted to visit these fellow students online to learn more about their stories and to complete the lessons that solve and correct each writing problem. NOTE: The easiest way to locate a specific character online is to go to the *Connect Writing* Web site at mhconnectwriting.com and enter the topic/subject area you are working on (for instance, *commas*) in the search box. This will bring up a link to the writing scenario for that particular character.

- **A Writer's Template:** The *Templates* showcase the writing of a student from a different course across the disciplines. Writers will read Quang's geography paper and Desmond's psychology writing assignment and will be asked to evaluate and edit them in terms of the four bases. My hope is that by allowing new writers to see how writing plays a significant part in their other college courses, it will help to validate the importance of learning how to write, and write effectively. In addition, they will learn how the four bases can be applied to the writing they do in their other classes as well.

Real Situations

Just as the avatars work to improve their writing in class, at home, and in the workplace, *Exploring Writing* offers *Beyond the Classroom* for students to explore how certain professionals in the workforce may utilize a particular mode of writing in their day-to-day tasks.

How Am I Improving?

Students often struggle to see their improvement as writers. To help, *Exploring Writing* offers *Reflective Activities* that invite students to consider what they've learned thus far, to note their progress as writers, and to take some pride in their growth. Similarly, the personalized *Learning Plan* online shows students the skills they have mastered and charts their progress toward new levels of attainment.

More Activities

With over 4,000 online activities and 350 more in print (50% of which are new to *Exploring Writing*) students have ample opportunity to practice their skills.

- **Collaborative Activity:** These activities give students a chance to collaborate as they develop stronger writing skills.

- **Introductory Activity:** These provide hands-on introductions to the topics covered in each chapter of Part 3.

- **Exploring Writing Online:** These writing prompts give students a chance to apply a chapter's lessons to a specific purpose—while learning to make use of the Internet at all stages of the writing process.

- **Responding to Images:** Throughout the text, images are used to help students visualize concepts (such as comparison or contrast and argument). Writing prompts are provided to get students thinking and responding critically to each image.

- **Writing Assignments:** The text includes a variety of writing assignments focusing on many new and interesting topics, such as racial profiling, returning to school after age 30, and how electronic devices enhance as well as interfere with our daily lives.

Some assignments are highly structured with suggestions for prewriting and revision; others are open-ended.

- **Review Test:** Chapter 2 and all chapters in Part 3 conclude with tests that cover all the content in that chapter; answers to these are available in the *Instructor's Manual* and the *Annotated Instructor's Edition,* but not in the student text.

Goals

Exploring Writing's diagnostics help students set individual learning plans and goals for their writing skills. Similarly, each part of the print text opens with a list of goals and an intriguing full-page visual accompanied by a related writing prompt to get writers writing—and thinking—immediately.

Readings for Writers

Part 4 has been carefully updated and expanded in the *Second Edition.* The new readings were selected based on recommendations from our panel of reviewers, and I am excited to include them in this edition. New selections range from Rose Del Castillo Guilbault's *The Conveyor-Belt Ladies* to Paul Boutin's *A Grand Unified Theory of YouTube and MySpace,* B. J. Penn's *Stance,* and Maya Angelou's *Reclaiming Our Home Place.* I have retained the more popular and thought provoking readings of the first edition, including Ben Carson's *Do It Better!* Katherine Barrett's *Old before Her Time, Let's Get Specific* by Beth Johnson, and *The Most Hateful Words* by Amy Tan. I hope you enjoy the new reading selections and that they prompt lively discussions in your classroom or chatroom.

Flexibility

Since no two instructors teach in exactly the same way and no two students have identical needs, I have designed *Exploring Writing* to be extremely flexible. Online, the lessons adapt to the needs of each individual student, while in print each of the book's four parts is color-coded along the outside margins so that instructors can turn quickly and easily to the skills they want to present. A sample syllabus is provided in the Instructor's Manual (available in the Exploring Writing Online Learning Center at www.mhhe.com/langan).

Acknowledgments

I am grateful to my McGraw-Hill editors, John Kindler and Alyson Watts, without whom this edition would not be possible. Editorial/marketing team members Jesse Hassenger, Dawn Groundwater, and Jaclyn Elkins also made valuable contributions to this text. Many thanks to the skilled production and design team—Karol Jurado, Laurie Entringer, Aaron Downey, Maureen McCutcheon, Emily Tietz, and Tandra Jorgensen. I'd also like to thank Paul Banks and Andrea Pasquarelli for their work on *Connect Writing.*

Finally, I'd like to express my thanks to the following professors of developmental English for their invaluable contributions to this text:

Donna T. Matsumoto, Assistant Professor of English and the Writing Discipline Coordinator at Leeward Community College in Hawaii (Pearl City). Professor Matsumoto has taught writing, women's studies, and American studies for a number of years throughout the University of Hawaii system.

Santi V. Buscemi, Professor of English and Chair of the Department of English at Middlesex County College in Edison, New Jersey, where he teaches reading and writing.

Maria Villar-Smith, Senior Associate Professor at Miami Dade College (Wolfson).

Joyce Stern, Assistant Professor at Nassau Community College and Assistant to the Chair in the Department of Reading and Basic Education.

Special thanks to the following reviewers who have contributed to this edition of the Exploring Writing *series through their helpful comments:*

Atlantic Cape Community College: Jay Peterson • **Belmont Technical College:** Cynthia Clarke, Karen Taylor • **Bergen Community College:** Leigh Jonaitis • **Broward College:** Carolyn Barr, Linda McCloud • **Bryant and Stratton College:** Christian Blum • **Bunker Hill Community College:** Patricia Colella • **Camden County College:** Elisabeth Bass • **Central Piedmont Community College:** Steven Mullis • **Century Community and Technical College:** Xuewei Wu • **Chandler-Gilbert Community College:** Caryl Terrell-Bamiro • **Citrus College:** Lisa Telesca • **Clark College:** Dena DeCastro • **College of the Desert:** Steven R. Acree • **Community College of Allegheny – South:** Joseph Scherer • **Community College of Denver:** Marta Brown • **Community College of Rhode Island – Flanagan:** Holly Susi • **Daytona Beach Community College – Daytona Beach:** Elizabeth Barnes • **Daytona State College:** Debbie Wilke • **Delaware County Community College:** Dawn Hayward • **Dixie State College of Utah:** Susan Ertel • **El Camino College:** Michael Jaffe • **El Paso Community College:** Mary Joyce Whiteside • **Elizabethtown Community and Technical College:** Beverly Dile • **Essex County College:** Rita Higgins, Paulette Longmore • **Florence-Darlington Technical College:** Kathleen S. Britton • **Germanna Community College:** Alexandra C. Campbell-Forte • **Greenville Technical College:** Lori Smalley, Ross Wagner • **Gulf Coast Community College:** Hank Smith • **Harper College:** James M. Andres • **Harrisburg Area Community College:** Valerie Gray • **Hawkeye Community College:** Crystal Stallman • **Hillsborough Community College:** Suzanne Lynch • **Hudson County Community College:** Angela Hebert • **Illinois Valley Community College:** Jennifer Bubb, Kaushalya Jagasia, Jeanette Maurice • **Iowa Western Community College:** Jim Fields • **Jackson State Community College:** Teri Maddox, Mark Walls • **Lonestar College – CyFair:** Anna Schmidt • **Longview Community College – Lees Summit:** Zoe Albright • **Lorain County Community College:** Heather Kichner • **Marshall Community and Technical College:** Susie Peyton • **McHenry County College:** Cynthia VanSickle • **McLennan Community College:** Jennifer Black, Linda Austin Crawford, Arthur Wellborn • **Mesa Community College:** Amy Lerman • **Miami Dade College – Kendall:** Billy Jones • **Miami Dade College – Wolfson:** Jessica Carroll, Maria Villar-Smith • **Milwaukee Area Technical College:** Helen Chester • **Minneapolis Community and Technical College:** Douglas Texter • **Montgomery College:** Ellen Olmstead • **Montgomery College – Takoma Park/Silver Spring:** Stephanie Sabourin • **Montgomery County Community College – Blue Bell:** Diane McDonald • **Nassau Community College:** Kristin Le Veness • **Northern Virginia Community College:** Carrie Dorsey • **Northwest Mississippi Community College:** Anne Smith • **Northwestern State University:** Sarah McFarland • **Nova Southeastern University:** Shanti Bruce • **Okaloosa-Walton College:** Deborah Fontaine, Julie Nichols, James Suderman • **Oklahoma City Community College:** Lori Farr • **Onondaga Community College:** Theresa Mohamed • **Pellissippi State Technical Community College:** Alexander Fitzner, H. L. Ford • **Pensacola Junior College:** Tracy Peyton • **Piedmont Technical College:** Claudia Edwards • **Pikes Peak Community College:** Jaquelyn Gaiters-Jordan • **Pulaski Technical College:** Leslie Johnston • **Queensborough Community College:** Manette Berlinger • **Quinsigamond Community College:** Betsy Zuegg • **Richland Community College:** Deborah Yaden • **Rio Hondo College:** Marie Eckstrom • **Rochester Community and Technical College:** Nikka Harris • **Rose State College:** Dianne Krob, Lori Morrow • **Sandhills Community College:** Donna-Marie Colonna • **Santa Barbara City College:** Sheila Wiley • **Seminole Community College:** Karen Feldman • **Sinclair Community College:** Karen Fleming, Sharyn Hunter, Teresa Prosser • **South Seattle Community College:** Laura Kingston • **Southern University at Shreveport:** Jennifer Green • **St. Louis Community College:** James Sodon • **St. Petersburg College:** Marjorie-Anne Wikoff • **State Fair Community College:** Cathy Clements • **Suffolk County Community College:** Shonda Wilson • **Tallahassee Community College:** Sharisse Turner • **Tarrant County College – South Campus:** Catherine Higdon • **Tyler Junior College:** Patti Casey, Desha S. Hill, Lee Nell W. Hill • **University of Arkansas Community College at Batesville:** Glenda Bell • **University of Cincinnati:** Amy England, Connie Kendall Theado • **University of South Alabama:** William Young • **University of Wisconsin – Parkside:** Christinie Tutlewski • **Valdosta Technical College:** Kelli Wilkes • **Wake Technical Community College:** Linda Shief • **Walters State Community College:** Christopher Morelock

Exploring Writing

Writing:
Skills and Process

CHAPTER 1
**An Introduction
to Writing**

CHAPTER 2
**The Writing
Process**

PART ONE WILL

- introduce you to the basic principles of effective writing

- present writing as both a skill and a process of discovery

- explain and illustrate the sequence of steps in writing an effective paragraph, including

  - prewriting

  - revising

  - editing

- ask you to write a paragraph

EXPLORING WRITING PROMPT:

Think about the kinds of things people write every day—grocery lists, e-mails to friends and coworkers, notes to family members, and text messages, for example. Keep track of the things you write for seven days. Each time you write something—even if it's only a few words—make a record of it in your journal or notebook. At the end of the week, make a list of all these items.

An Introduction to Writing

CHAPTER PREVIEW

Understanding Point and Support

Writing as a Skill

Writing as a Process of Discovery

Keeping a Journal

RESPONDING TO IMAGES

Do you think that Tiger Woods' prowess on the golf course is more a result of natural talent or hard-earned skill? What about Aretha Franklin's ability to write and perform multiple Grammy-winning hits? Take a few minutes to respond to these questions. In this chapter, you will find the answer as it pertains to one's ability to perform a skill.

Exploring Writing grows out of experiences I had when learning how to write. My early memories of writing in school are not pleasant. In the middle grades I remember getting back paper after paper on which the only comment was "Handwriting very poor." In high school, the night before a book report was due, I would work anxiously at a card table in my bedroom. I was nervous and sweaty because I felt out of my element, like a person who knows only how to open a can of soup being asked to cook a five-course meal. The act of writing was hard enough, and my feeling that I wasn't any good at it made me hate the process all the more.

Luckily, in college I had an instructor who changed my negative attitude about writing. During my first semester in composition, I realized that my instructor repeatedly asked two questions about any paper I wrote: "What is your point?" and "What is your support for that point?" I learned that sound writing consists basically of making a point and then providing evidence to support or develop that point. As I understood, practiced, and mastered these and other principles, I began to write effective papers. By the end of the semester, much of my uneasiness about writing had disappeared. I realized that competent writing is a skill that I or anyone can learn with practice. It is a nuts-and-bolts process consisting of a number of principles and techniques that can be studied and mastered. Furthermore, I learned that although there is no alternative to the work required for competent writing, there is satisfaction to be gained through such work. I no longer feared or hated writing because I knew I could work at it and be good at it.

Exploring Writing: Sentences and Paragraphs explains in a clear and direct way the four basic principles you must learn to write effectively:

1. Start with a clearly stated point that unifies your paragraph or essay.

2. Provide logical, detailed support for your point.

3. Organize and connect your supporting material, always aiming for coherence.

4. Revise and edit so that your sentences are effective and error-free.

This book explains each of these steps in detail and provides many practice materials to help you master them.

Understanding Point and Support

An Important Difference between Writing and Talking

In everyday conversation, you make all kinds of points, or assertions. You say, for example, "I hate my job"; "Sue's a really generous person"; or "That exam was unfair." The points that you make concern such personal matters as well as, at times, larger issues: "A lot of doctors are arrogant"; "The death penalty should exist for certain crimes"; and "Tobacco and marijuana are equally dangerous."

The people you are talking with do not always challenge you to give reasons for your statements. They may know why you feel as you do, they may already agree with you, or they simply may not want to put you on the spot, and so they do not always ask "Why?" But the people who *read* what you write may not know you, agree with you, or feel in any way obliged to you. If you want to communicate effectively with readers, you must provide solid evidence for any point you make. An important difference, then, between writing and talking is this: *In writing, any idea that you advance must be supported with specific reasons or details.*

Think of your readers as reasonable people. They will not take your views on faith, but they *are* willing to consider what you say as long as you support it. Therefore, remember to support any statement that you make with specific evidence.

Point and Support in Two Cartoons

The following two *Peanuts* cartoons will show you quickly and clearly what you need to write effectively. You need to know how to (1) make a point and (2) support the point.

Look for a moment at the following cartoon:

PEANUTS © United Feature Syndicate, Inc.

See if you can answer the following questions:

- What is Snoopy's point in his paper?

Your answer: His point is that _____

- What is his support for his point?

Your answer: _____

Snoopy's point, of course, is that dogs are superior to cats. But he offers no support whatsoever to back up his point. There are two jokes here. First, he is a dog, so he is naturally going to believe that dogs are superior.

The other joke is that his evidence ("They just are, and that's all there is to it!") is no more than empty words. His somewhat guilty look in the last panel suggests that he knows he has not proved his point. To write effectively, you must provide *real* support for your points and opinions.

Now look at this other cartoon about Snoopy as a writer.

PEANUTS © United Feature Syndicate, Inc.

See if you can answer the following questions:

* What is Snoopy's point about the hero in his writing?

Your answer: His point is that _____

* What is his support for his point?

Your answer: _____

Snoopy's point is that the hero's life has been a disaster. This time, Snoopy has an abundance of support for his point: The hapless hero never had any luck, money, friends, love, laughter, applause, fame, or answers. The remaining flaw in Snoopy's composition is that he does not use enough supporting *details* to really prove his point. Instead, he plays the opposites game with his support ("He wanted to be loved. He died unloved."). As readers, we wonder who the hero wanted to be loved by: his mother? a heroine? a beagle? To sympathize with the hero and understand the nature of his disastrous life, we need more specifics. In the final panel of the cartoon, Snoopy has that guilty expression again. Why might he have a hard time ending this paragraph?

Point and Support in a Paragraph

Suppose you and a friend are talking about jobs you have had. You might say about a particular job, "That was the worst one I ever had—a lot of hard work and not much money." For your friend, that might be enough to make your point, and you would not really have to explain your statement. But in writing, your point would have to be backed up with specific reasons and details.

The following is a paragraph written by a student named Mike Cornell about his worst job. A *paragraph* is a short paper of 150 to 200 words. It usually consists of an opening point called a *topic sentence* followed by a series of sentences supporting that point.

My Job at the Crescent Falls Diner and Truck Stop

Working at the Crescent Falls Diner and Truck Stop was the worst job I ever had. First, the work was physically very hard. During my ten-hour days, I had to carry heavy trays of food to the customers, and I had to clean the tables. I washed dishes and then unloaded the delivery truck, lifting sixty-pound cartons of food supplies. The second bad feature was the pay. I had to work at least sixty hours a week to afford next semester's tuition because I got only minimum wage, and I had to share my tips with the kitchen workers too. Finally, the working conditions were horrible. I had to wash dishes in a hot and steamy kitchen. Once, when unloading a truck, I hurt my back so badly I was out of work for a week, without pay! And the boss was a tyrant who hated me because I was a college student. He gave me terrible hours, ridiculed my clothes, and even made racist slurs to my face.

Notice what the specific details in this paragraph do. They provide you, the reader, with a basis for understanding *why* the writer makes this particular point. Through this specific evidence, the writer has explained and successfully communicated the idea that this job was his worst one.

The evidence that supports the point in a paragraph often consists of a series of reasons followed by examples and details that support the reasons. That is true of the previous paragraph: Three reasons are provided, with examples and details that back up those reasons. Supporting evidence in a paper can also consist of anecdotes, personal experiences, facts, studies, statistics, and the opinions of experts.

ACTIVITY 1	Point and Support

The paragraph about the Crescent Falls Diner and Truck Stop, like almost any piece of effective writing, has two essential parts: (1) A point is advanced, and (2) that point is then supported. Taking a minute to outline the paragraph will help you understand these basic parts clearly. Add the words needed to complete the outline that follows.

Point: Working at the Crescent Falls Diner and Truck Stop was the worst job I ever had.

Reason 1: _____

    a. Carried heavy trays while waiting on customers and busing tables

    b. _____

Reason 2: _____

    a. Got only minimum wage; had to share my tips with others

    b. _____

      _____

Reason 3: _____

    a. Kitchen was hot and steamy

    b. _____

    c. Manager was unfair and insulting

      1. Disliked college students; favored other workers over me

      2. Made insulting remarks about my appearance, race

Fill in the Blanks

ACTIVITY 2

See if you can complete the following statements.

1. An important difference between writing and talking is that in writing

    we absolutely must _____ any statement we make.

2. A _____ is made up of a point and a collection of specifics that support the point.

WRITING ASSIGNMENT 1

An excellent way to get a feel for the paragraph is to write one. Your instructor may ask you to do that now. The only guidelines you need to follow are the ones described here. There is an advantage to writing a paragraph right away, at a point where you have had almost no instruction. This first paragraph will give a quick sense of your needs as a writer and will provide a baseline—a standard of comparison that you and your instructor can use to measure your writing progress during the semester.

Here, then, is your topic: Write a paragraph on the best or worst job you have ever had. Provide three reasons why your job was the best or the worst, and give plenty of details to develop each of your three reasons.

Notice that the sample paragraph, "My Job at the Crescent Falls Diner and Truck Stop," has the same format your paragraph should have. You should do what this author has done:

- State a point in the first sentence.

- Give three reasons to support the point.

- Introduce each reason clearly with signal words (such as *First of all, Second,* and *Finally*).
- Provide details that develop each of the three reasons.

Write or type your paragraph on a separate sheet of paper. After completing the paragraph, hand it in to your instructor.

Writing as a Skill

A realistic attitude about writing must build on the idea that *writing is a skill*. It is a skill like driving, typing, or cooking, and like any skill, it can be learned. If you have the determination to learn, this book will give you the extensive practice needed to develop your writing skills.

People who believe that writing is a "natural gift" rather than a learned skill may think that they are the only ones for whom writing is unbearably difficult. They might feel that everyone else finds writing easy or at least tolerable. Such people typically say, "I'm not any good at writing" or "English was not one of my good subjects." The result of this attitude is that people try to avoid writing, and when they do write, they don't try their best. Their attitude becomes a self-fulfilling prophecy: Their writing fails chiefly because they have convinced themselves that they don't have the "natural talent" needed to write. Unless their attitude changes, they probably will not learn how to write effectively.

Many people find it difficult to do the intense, active thinking that clear writing demands. It is frightening to sit down before a blank sheet of paper or a computer screen and know that an hour later, little on it may be worth keeping. It is frustrating to discover how much of a challenge it is to transfer thoughts and feelings from one's head into words. It is upsetting to find that an apparently simple writing subject often turns out to be complicated. But writing is not an automatic process; for almost everyone, competent writing comes from plain hard work—from determination, sweat, and head-on battle. The good news is that the skill of writing can be mastered, and if you are ready to work, you will learn what you need to know.

Why Does Your Attitude toward Writing Matter?

ACTIVITY 3	**How Do You Feel about Writing?**

Your attitude toward writing is an important part of learning to write well. To get a sense of just how you feel about writing, read the following statements. Put a check beside those statements with which you agree. (This activity is not a test, so try to be as honest as possible.)

_____ 1. A good writer should be able to sit down and write a paper straight through without stopping.

_____ 2. Writing is a skill that anyone can learn with practice.

_____ 3. I'll never be good at writing because I make too many
            mistakes in spelling, grammar, and punctuation.

_____ 4. Because I dislike writing, I always start a paper at the last
            possible minute.

_____ 5. I've always done poorly in English, and I don't expect that
            to change.

Now read the following comments about the five statements. The comments will help you see if your attitude is hurting or helping your efforts to become a better writer.

1. **A good writer should be able to sit down and write a paper
    straight through without stopping.**
    The statement is *false*. Writing is, in fact, a process. It is done not in one easy step but in a series of steps, and seldom at one sitting. If you cannot do a paper all at once, that simply means you are like most of the other people on the planet. It is harmful to carry around the false idea that writing should be an easy matter.

2. **Writing is a skill that anyone can learn with practice.**
    This statement is absolutely true. Writing is a skill, like driving or typing, that you can master with hard work. If you want to learn to write, you can. It is as simple as that. If you believe this, you are ready to learn how to become a competent writer.

    Some people hold the false belief that writing is a natural gift that some have and others do not. Because of this belief, they never make a truly honest effort to learn to write—and so they never learn.

3. **I'll never be good at writing because I make too many mistakes
    in spelling, grammar, and punctuation.**
    The first concern in good writing should be *content*—what you have to say. Your ideas and feelings are what matter most. You should not worry about spelling, grammar, or punctuation while working on content.

    Unfortunately, some people are so self-conscious about making mistakes that they do not focus on what they want to say. They need to realize that a paper is best done in stages, and that applying the rules can and should wait until a later stage in the writing process. Through review and practice, you will eventually learn how to follow the rules with confidence.

4. **Because I dislike writing, I always start a paper at the last
    possible minute.**
    This is all too common. You feel you are *going to* do poorly, and then your behavior ensures that you *will* do poorly! Your attitude is so negative that you defeat yourself—not even allowing enough time to really try.

    Again, what you need to realize is that writing is a process. Because it is done in steps, you don't have to get it right all at once. Just get started well in advance. If you allow yourself enough time, you'll find a way to make a paper come together.

5. **I've always done poorly in English, and I don't expect that to change.**

   How you may have performed in the *past* does not control how you can perform in the *present*. Even if you did poorly in English in high school, it is in your power to make this one of your best subjects in college. If you believe writing can be learned, and if you work hard at it, you will become a better writer.

In brief, your attitude is crucial. If you believe you are a poor writer and always will be, chances are you will not improve. If you realize you can become a better writer, chances are you *will* improve. Depending on how you allow yourself to think, you can be your own best friend or your own worst enemy.

Writing as a Process of Discovery

In addition to believing that writing is a natural gift, many people believe, mistakenly, that writing should flow in a simple, straight line from the writer's head onto the page. But writing is seldom an easy, one-step journey in which a finished paper comes out in a first draft. The truth is that *writing is a process of discovery* that involves a series of steps, and those steps are very often a zigzag journey. Look at the following illustrations of the writing process:

Very often, writers do not discover just what they want to write about until they explore their thoughts in writing. For example, Mike Cornell had been asked to write about a best or worst job. Only after he did some freewriting on jobs he liked and disliked did he realize that the most interesting details centered on his job at a diner and truck stop. He discovered his subject in the course of writing.

Another student, Rhonda, talking afterward about a paper she wrote, explained that at first her topic was how she relaxed with her children. But as she accumulated details, she realized after a page of writing that the words *relax* and *children* simply did not go together. Her details were really examples of how she *enjoyed* her children, not how she *relaxed* with them. She sensed that the real focus of her writing should be what she did by herself to relax, and then she thought suddenly that the best time of her week was Thursday after school. "A light clicked on in my head," she explained. "I knew I had my paper." Then it was a matter of detailing exactly what she did to relax on Thursday evenings.

The point is that writing is often a process of exploration and continuing discovery. As you write, you may suddenly switch direction or double back. You may be working on a topic sentence and realize that it could be your concluding thought. Or you may be developing a supporting idea and then decide that it should be the main point of your paper. Chapter 2 will treat the writing process directly. It is important to remember that writers frequently do not know their exact destination as they begin to write. Very often they discover the direction and shape of a paper *during* the process of writing.

Keeping a Journal

Because writing is a skill, it makes sense that the more you practice writing, the better you will write. One excellent way to get practice in writing, even before you begin composing formal paragraphs, is to keep a daily or almost daily journal. Keeping a journal will help you develop the habit of thinking on paper and will show you how ideas can be discovered in the process of writing. A journal can make writing a familiar part of your life and can serve as a continuing source of ideas for papers.

At some point during the day—perhaps during a study period after your last class of the day, right before dinner, or right before going to bed—spend fifteen minutes or so writing in your journal. Keep in mind that you do not have to plan what to write about, be in the mood to write, or worry about making mistakes as you write; just write down whatever words come out. You should write at least one page in each session.

You may want to use a notebook that you can easily carry with you for on-the-spot writing. Or you may decide to type your journal entries on a computer or write on loose-leaf paper that can be transferred later to a journal folder. No matter how you proceed, be sure to date all entries.

Your instructor may ask you to make journal entries a specific number of times a week for a specific number of weeks. He or she may have you turn in your journal every so often for review and feedback. If you are keeping the journal on your own, try to make entries three to five times a week every week of the semester. Your journal can serve as a sourcebook of ideas for possible papers. More important, keeping a journal will help you develop the habit of thinking on paper, and it can help you make writing a familiar part of your life.

Using a Journal to Generate Ideas	**ACTIVITY 4**

Following is an excerpt from one student's journal. (Sentence-skills mistakes have been corrected to improve readability.) As you read, look for a general point and supporting material that could be the basis for an interesting paper.

October 6

Today a woman came into our department at the store and wanted to know if we had any scrap lumber ten feet long. Ten feet! "Lady," I said, "anything we have that's ten feet long sure as heck isn't scrap." When the boss heard me say that, he

---

continued

almost canned me. My boss is a company man, down to his toe tips. He wants to make a big impression on his bosses, and he'll run us around like mad all night to make himself look good. He's the most ambitious man I've ever met. If I don't transfer out of Hardware soon, I'm going to go crazy on this job. I'm not ready to quit, though. The time is not right. I want to be here for a year and have another job lined up and have other things right before I quit. It's good the boss wasn't around tonight when another customer wanted me to carry a bookcase he had bought out to his car. He didn't ask me to help him—he <u>expected</u> me to help him. I hate that kind of "You're my servant" attitude, and I told him that carrying stuff out to cars wasn't my job. Ordinarily I go out of my way to give people a hand, but not guys like him. . . .

If the writer of this journal is looking for an idea for a paper, he can probably find several in this single entry. For example, he might write a narrative supporting the point that "In my sales job I have to deal with some irritating customers." See if you can find another idea in this entry that might be the basis for an interesting paragraph. Write your point in the space below.

_____

WRITING ASSIGNMENT 2

Take fifteen minutes to write a journal entry on your own recent experiences at work or in school. What happened to you yesterday or even earlier this morning? On a separate sheet of paper, just start writing about anything that you have said, heard, thought, or felt, and let your thoughts take you where they may.

EXPLORING WRITING ONLINE

Visit each of the following Web sites. Then, for each site, write a sentence that states what its purpose, or main point, is.

eBay: www.ebay.com

Google: www.google.com

YouTube: www.youtube.com

MySpace: www.myspace.com

Wikipedia: www.wikipedia.org

USA.gov: www.usa.gov

RESPONDING TO IMAGES

A lot is happening in this photograph, but we are immediately drawn to one particular interaction. What is the focus (or central point), and how does the photographer guide our eyes and attention to it?

For additional materials on Chapter 1, visit **www.mhhe.com/langan**.

2 | CHAPTER

The Writing Process

CHAPTER PREVIEW

How Do You Reach the Goals of Effective Writing?

Prewriting

- Technique 1: Freewriting

- Technique 2: Questioning

- Technique 3: Making a List

- Technique 4: Clustering

- Technique 5: Preparing a Scratch Outline

Writing the First Draft

Revising

Editing and Proofreading

Tips on Using a Computer

Using Peer Review

Review Activities

RESPONDING TO IMAGES

Students often feel uncomfortable sharing their writing with others. How do you feel about letting classmates read your work? Do you feel differently when you post a message to a social blog or forum? Take a few minutes to jot down your responses to these questions. In this chapter, you'll learn about the benefits of having others read and respond to your written work.

How Do You Reach the Goals of Effective Writing?

Even professional writers do not sit down and write a paper automatically, in one draft. Instead, they have to work on it a step at a time. Writing a paper is a process that can be divided into the following steps:

- Prewriting
- Writing the first draft
- Revising
- Editing and proofreading

These steps are described on the following pages.

Prewriting

If you are like many people, you may have trouble getting started writing. A mental block may develop when you sit down before a blank sheet of paper or a blank screen. You may not be able to think of an interesting topic or a point to make about your topic. Or you may have trouble coming up with specific details to support your point. And even after starting a composition, you may hit snags—moments when you wonder "What else can I say?" or "Where do I go next?"

The following pages describe five techniques that will help you think about and develop a topic and get words on paper: (1) freewriting, (2) questioning, (3) making a list, (4) clustering, and (5) preparing a scratch outline. These prewriting techniques help you think about and create material, and they are a central part of the writing process.

Technique 1: Freewriting

When you do not know what to write about a subject or when you are blocked in writing, freewriting sometimes helps. In *freewriting*, you write on your topic for ten minutes. You do not worry about spelling or punctuating correctly, about erasing mistakes, about organizing material, or about finding exact words. You just write without stopping. If you get stuck for words, you write "I am looking for something to say" or repeat words until something comes. There is no need to feel inhibited since mistakes *do not count* and you do not have to hand in your paper.

Freewriting will limber up your writing muscles and make you familiar with the act of writing. It is a way to break through mental blocks about writing. Since you do not have to worry about mistakes, you can focus on discovering what you want to say about a subject. Your initial ideas and impressions will often become clearer after you have gotten them down on paper, and they may lead to other impressions and ideas. Through continued practice in freewriting, you will develop the habit of thinking as you write. And you will learn a technique that is a helpful way to get started on almost any piece of writing.

Freewriting: A Student Model

Mike Cornell's paragraph "My Job at the Crescent Falls Diner and Truck Stop" on page 8 in Chapter 1 was written in response to an assignment to write a composition on the best or worst job he ever had. Mike began by doing some general freewriting and thinking about his jobs. Here is his freewriting:

> I have had good and bad jobs, that's for sure. It was great earning money for the first time. I shoveled snow for my neighbor, a friend of mine and me did the work and had snowball fights along the way. I remember my neighbor reaching into his pocket and pulling out several dollars and handing us the money, it was like magic. Then there was the lawnmowing, which was also a good job. I mowed my aunt's lawn while she was away at work. Then I'd go sit by myself in her cool living room and have a coke she left in the refrigerator for me. And look through all her magazines. Then there was the job at the Crescent Falls diner and truck stop that I had after high school. That was the worst job that left me wiped out after my shift. I had to wait on customers and bus tables while listening to my boss complain. I only got minimum wage. I had to unload delivery trucks. The manager was a real creep, he enjoyed treating all the other guys much better than me. He wouldn't even give me a few days off to go to a wedding, and he made nasty comments about the way I look, my clothes and everything. Even my race. I thought I would make a lot in tips. Then, I find out I have to share them with the other workers. I will never work in a diner again!

At this point, Mike read over his notes, and as he later commented, "I realized that I had several topics. I said to myself, 'What point can I make that I can cover in a paragraph? What do I have the most information about?' I decided to narrow my topic down to my awful job at the diner and truck stop. I figured I would have lots of interesting details for that topic." Mike then did a more focused freewriting to accumulate details for a paragraph on this job:

The job I remember most is the worst job I ever had. I worked at the Crescent Falls diner and truck stop. I put in very long hours and would be totally beat after ten hours of work, six days a week. Most of time waiting on customers and cleaning tables, but also washing dishes in a kitchen that was unbearably hot and steamy, I even had to unload heavy cartons of food from delivery trucks. And I had to keep track of all the cartons I took off. I worked so much that I never had a social life. My boss was always complaining about my work—I didn't get my orders out fast enough, I didn't clean the tables as good as he wanted. I only got minimum wage. The manager was a real creep, he seemed to enjoy irritating me, treating all the other guys much better than me. After a while, I realized he just didn't like college kids. He envied them. He wouldn't even give me a few days off to go to a wedding, and he made nasty comments about the way I look, my clothes and everything. Even my race. I thought I would make a lot in tips. Then, I find out I have to share them with the other workers. Besides the tips, I only got minimum wage. So, I had to work sixty hours a week in that hell whole just to make enough for my first semester's tuition. I will never work in a diner again!

TIP   Notice that there are problems with spelling, grammar, and punctuation in Mike's freewriting. Mike was not worried about such matters, nor should he have been. At this stage, he just wanted to do some thinking on paper and get some material down on the page. He knew that this was a good first step, a good way of getting started, and that he would then be able to go on and shape that material.

You should take the same approach when freewriting: Explore your topic without worrying at all about being "correct." Figuring out what you want to say and getting raw material down on the page should have all of your attention at this early stage of the writing process.

ACTIVITY 1	**Freewriting**

To get a sense of the freewriting process, take a sheet of paper and freewrite about different jobs you have had and what you liked or did not like about them. See how much material you can accumulate in ten minutes. And remember not to worry about "mistakes"; you're just thinking on paper.

Technique 2: Questioning

In *questioning,* you generate ideas and details by asking as many questions as you can think of about your subject. Such questions include *Why? When? Where? Who? How? In what ways?*

Here are questions that Mike Cornell asked while further developing his paragraph:

Questioning: A Student Model

Questions	Answers
What did I hate about the job?	Very hard work
	Poor pay
	Unfair, nasty manager
	Bad working conditions
How was the work hard?	Carried heavy trays
	Unloaded heavy cartons from trucks, keeping track of what I took off washed dishes
Why was pay poor?	Earned minimum wage
	Had to share tips with coworkers
How was the manager unfair?	Favored coworkers over me when giving days off
	Didn't like college students
	Made insulting remarks about my appearance/race
In what ways were working conditions bad?	Kitchen hot, boss was overly critical of my work

> **TIP**   Asking questions can be an effective way of getting yourself to think about a topic from different angles. The questions can help you generate details about a topic and get ideas on how to organize those details. Notice how asking questions gives Mike a better sense of the different reasons why he hated the job.

Questioning

ACTIVITY 2

To get a feel for the questioning process, use a sheet of paper to ask yourself a series of questions about your best and worst jobs. See how many details you can accumulate in ten minutes. And remember again not to be concerned about "mistakes" because you are just thinking on paper.

Technique 3: Making a List

In *making a list,* also known as *brainstorming,* you create a list of ideas and details that relate to your subject. Pile these items up, one after another, without trying to sort out major details from minor ones, or trying to put the details in any special order, or even trying to spell words correctly. Your goal is to accumulate raw material by making up a list of everything about your subject that occurs to you.

After freewriting and questioning, Mike made up the following list of details.

Making a List: A Student Model

> **Diner and truck stop job—worst one I ever had**
>
> Manager was unfair and nasty
>
> Worked ten hours a day, sixty hours a week
>
> Waited on customers, bused tables, cleaned bathrooms
>
> Washed dishes in hot, steamy kitchen, unloaded heavy cartons
>   off delivery trucks
>
> Got paid minimum wage
>
> Had no social life
>
> Sometimes had to work overtime—no extra pay
>
> Boss always critical of my work
>
> Manager hated college kids, treated them worse than other workers
>
> Couldn't get a day off to rest or be with friends

continued

No real friends at this job—no social life

Asked for two days off to go to a wedding—no way!

Hurt my back

Had to work at least sixty hours a week to make tuition for
first semester in college

Boss was insulting, even made racial remarks

Ridiculed my hair, clothing

Had to share my tips with other workers in the kitchen and
cashiers—not just with other servers

T I P   One detail led to another as Mike expanded his list. Slowly but surely, more details emerged, some of which he could use in developing his paragraph. By the time you finish making a list, you should be ready to plan an outline of your paragraph and then to write your first draft.

ACTIVITY 3	**Listing**

To get a sense of making a list, use a sheet of paper to list a series of details about one of the best or worst jobs you ever had. Don't worry about deciding whether the details are major or minor; instead, just get down as many details as you can think of in five or ten minutes.

Technique 4: Clustering

Clustering, also known as *diagramming* or *mapping,* is another strategy that can be used to generate material for a paper of any length. This method is helpful for people who like to think in a visual way. In clustering, you use lines, boxes, arrows, and circles to show relationships among the ideas and details that occur to you.

Begin by stating your subject in a few words in the center of a blank sheet of paper. Then, as ideas and details occur to you, put them in boxes or circles around the subject and draw lines to connect them to each other and to the subject. Put minor ideas or details in smaller boxes or circles, and use connecting lines to show how they relate as well.

Keep in mind that there is no right or wrong way of clustering. It is a way to think on paper about how various ideas and details relate to one another. The following is an example of what Mike might have done to develop his ideas:

Clustering: A Student Model

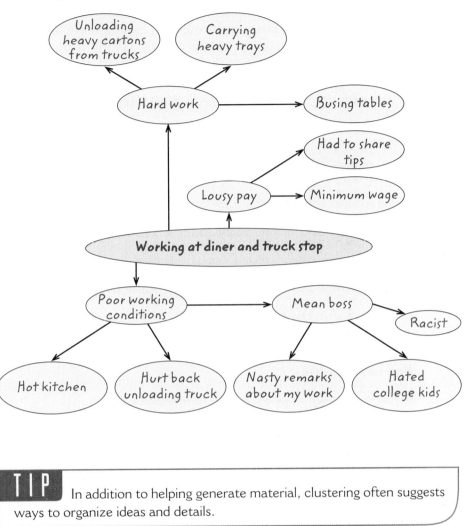

> **TIP**   In addition to helping generate material, clustering often suggests ways to organize ideas and details.

Clustering/Diagramming   **ACTIVITY 4**

Use clustering or diagramming to organize the details that you created for the previous activity about a best or worst job (page 22).

Technique 5: Preparing a Scratch Outline

A scratch outline can be the *single most helpful technique* for writing a good paper. A scratch outline often follows freewriting, questioning, making a list, or clustering, but it may also gradually emerge in the midst of these strategies. In fact, trying to make a scratch outline is a good way to see if you need to do more prewriting. If you cannot come up with a solid outline, then you know you need to do more prewriting to clarify your main point and its several kinds of support.

In a scratch outline, you think carefully about the point you are making, the supporting items for that point, and the order in which you will arrange those items. The scratch outline is a plan or blueprint to help you achieve a unified, supported, and well-organized composition.

Scratch Outline: A Student Model

In Mike's case, as he was working on his list of details, he suddenly realized what the plan of his paragraph could be. He could organize many of his details into one of three supporting groups: (1) the work involved in the job, (2) the pay, and (3) the working conditions. He then went back to the list, crossed out items that he now saw did not fit, and numbered the items according to the group where they fit. Here is what Mike did with his list:

Diner and truck stop job—worst one I ever had

3   Manager was unfair and nasty

2   Worked ten hours a day, sixty hours a week

1   Waited on customers, bused tables, cleaned bathrooms

1   Washed dishes in hot, steamy kitchen, unloaded heavy cartons off delivery trucks

2   Got paid minimum wage

~~Had no social life~~

~~A few times had to work overtime—no extra pay~~

3   Boss always critical of my work

3   Manager hated college kids, treated them worse than other workers

~~Couldn't get a day off to rest or be with friends~~

~~No real friends at this job~~

3   Asked for two days off to go to a wedding—no way!

3   Hurt my back

2   Had to work at least sixty hours a week to make tuition for first semester in college

3   Boss was insulting, even made racial remarks

3   Ridiculed my hair, clothing

1   I had to mop floors

2   Had to share my tips with other workers in the kitchen and cashiers—not just with other servers

1   When I interviewed, I didn't know I would also be unloading trucks, cleaning bathrooms

Under the list, Mike was now able to prepare his scratch outline:

The diner and truck stop was my worst job.

1. Hard work

2. Lousy pay

3. Poor working conditions

> **TIP** After all his prewriting, Mike was pleased. He knew that he had a promising composition—one with a clear point and solid support. He saw that he could organize the material into a paragraph with a topic sentence, supporting points, and vivid details. He was now ready to write the first draft of his paragraph, using his outline as a guide. Chances are that if you do enough prewriting and thinking on paper, you will eventually discover the point and support of your paragraph.

Making a Scratch Outline   ACTIVITY 5

Create a scratch outline that could serve as a guide if you were to write a paragraph on your best or worst job experience.

Writing the First Draft

When you write a first draft, be prepared to put in additional thoughts and details that did not emerge during prewriting. And don't worry if you hit a snag. Just leave a blank space or add a comment such as "Do later" and press on to finish the paper. Also, don't worry yet about grammar, punctuation, or spelling. You don't want to take time correcting words or sentences that you may decide to remove later. Instead, make it your goal to state your main idea clearly and develop the content of your paragraph with plenty of specific details.

Writing a First Draft: A Student Model

Here is Mike's first draft, done in longhand:

~~The crescent diner and truck stop job was the pit.~~ Working at the cresent falls diner and Truck Stop was the worst job I ever had. The work was physically very hard. During my ~~long~~ ten hour days I had to carry heavy trays of food to the

continued

custamers, and the tables had to be cleaned.. ~~Then~~, You would wash dishes and then go unload the delivery truck of food supplies. At the same time I had to keep track in my head of all the cartons I had unloaded. The second bad feature that made the job a worst one was the pay. The pay was lousey. I had to work at least sixty hours a week to afford next semester's tuition. I got only minimun wage, and I had to share my tips with the kitchen workers too. And the boss was a creep who hated me cause I was a college student, he gave me lousey hours. Even called me horrible names to my face. DETAILS!

> **TIP**   After Mike finished the first draft, he was able to put it aside until the next day. You will benefit as well if you can allow some time between finishing a draft and starting to revise.

ACTIVITY 6   Drafting

Working with a fellow classmate, see if you can fill in the missing words in the following explanation of Mike's first draft.

1. Mike presents his _____ in the first sentence and then crosses it out and revises it right away to make it read smoothly and clearly.

2. Notice that he continues to accumulate specic supporting details as he writes the draft. For example, he crosses out and replaces "long" with the more specific _____. When talking about his pay, he adds _____.

3. There are various misspellings—for example, _____. Mike doesn't worry about spelling at this point. He just wants to get down as much of the substance of his paragraph as possible.

4. There are various punctuation errors, especially the run-on and the fragment near the *(beginning, middle, end)* _____ of the paragraph.

5. Near the close of his paragraph, Mike can't think of more details to insert, so he simply prints _____ as a reminder to himself for the next draft.

Revising

Revising is as much a stage in the writing process as prewriting, out-lining, and doing the first draft. *Revising* means that you rewrite a paragraph or paper, building upon what has already been done in order to make it stronger. One writer has said about revision, "It's like cleaning house—getting rid of all the junk and putting things in the right order." It is not just "straightening up"; instead, you must be ready to roll up your sleeves and do whatever is needed to create an effective paper. Too many students think that a first draft *is* the final one. They start to become writers when they realize that revising a rough draft three or four times is often at the heart of the writing process.

Here are some quick hints that can help make revision easier. First, set your first draft aside for a while. You can then come back to it with a fresher, more objective point of view. Second, work from typed or printed text, preferably double-spaced so you'll have room to hand-write changes later. You'll be able to see the paragraph or paper more impartially if it is typed than if you were just looking at your own familiar handwriting. Next, read your draft aloud. Hearing how your writing sounds will help you pick up problems with meaning as well as with style. Finally, as you do all these things, write additional thoughts and changes above the lines or in the margins of your paper. Your written comments can serve as a guide when you work on the next draft.

There are two stages to the revision process:

* Revising content
* Revising sentences

Revising Content

To revise the content of your paragraph, ask the following questions:

1. Is my paragraph **unified?**
   * Do I have a clear, single point in the first sentence of the paragraph?
   * Does all my evidence support my opening point?

2. Is my paragraph **supported?**
   * Are there separate supporting points for the opening point?
   * Do I have *specific* evidence for each supporting point?
   * Is there *plenty of* specific evidence for the supporting points?

3. Is my paragraph **organized?**
   * Do I have a clear method of organizing my thoughts?
   * Do I use transitions and other connecting words?

Revising Sentences

To revise individual sentences in your paragraph, ask the following questions:

1. Do I use *parallelism* to balance my words and ideas?

2. Do I have a *consistent point of view?*

3. Do I use *specific* words?

4. Do I use *active* verbs?

5. Do I use words effectively by *avoiding slang, clichés, pretentious language,* and *wordiness?*

6. Do I *vary my sentences* in length and structure?

Part 3 of this text will give you practice in revising sentences.

Revising: A Student Model

For his second draft, Mike used a word-processing program on a computer. He then printed out a double-spaced version of his paragraph, leaving himself plenty of room for handwritten revisions. Here is Mike's second draft plus the handwritten changes and additions that became his third draft:

　　　Working at the cresent falls diner and Truck Stop was the worst
　　　　　　First of all
job I ever had. The work was physically very hard. During my ten

hour days I had to carry heavy trays of food to the custamers, and
　I had to clean the tables　　I
~~the tables had to be cleaned~~. ~~You~~ would wash dishes and then go
　　　　　　　　　　　　sixty-pound
unload the delivery truck, lifting ~~heavy~~ cartons of food supplies.

~~At the same time I had to keep track in my head of all the cartons I~~

~~had unloaded~~. The second bad feature ~~that made the job a worst one~~

was the pay. ~~The pay was lousey~~. I had to work at least sixty hours
　　　　　　　　　　　　　　　because
a week to afford next semester's tuition, I got only minimun wage,
　　　　　　　　　　　　　　　　　Finally
and I had to share my tips with the kitchen workers too. The working
　　　　　　　in a hot and steamy kitchen
conditions were horrible. I had to wash dishes. Once, when unloading

a truck, I hurt my back so badly I was out of work for a week without
　　　　　tyrant
pay! And the boss was a ~~creep~~ who hated me cause I was a college
　　　　　　　terrible　　　　　　　　*made racist slurs*
student, he gave me ~~lousey~~ hours. Even ~~called me horrible names~~

to my face.

> **TIP** Mike made his changes in longhand as he worked on the second draft. As you will see when you complete the following activity, a revision should serve to make a paragraph more unified, supported, and organized.

Revising a Draft

Fill in the missing words.

1. To clarify the organization, Mike adds at the beginning of the first supporting point the transitional phrase "_____" and he sets off the third supporting point with the word "_____."

2. In the interest of (*unity, support, organization*) _____, he crosses out the sentence "_____." He realizes that this sentence is not a relevant detail to support the idea that the work was physically hard.

3. To add more (*unity, support, organization*) _____, he changes "heavy cartons" to "_____"; he adds "_____ _____" to his sentence about washing dishes.

4. In the interest of eliminating wordiness, he removes the words "_____" and "_____."

5. To achieve parallelism, he changes "the tables had to be cleaned" to "_____."

6. For greater sentence variety, Mike combines two short sentences beginning the second part of the sentence with "_____."

7. To create a consistent point of view, Mike changes "You would wash dishes" to "_____."

8. Mike becomes more specific by changing "called me horrible names to my face" to "_____."

9. Finally, he replaces the somewhat vague word "creep" with the more precise word "_____."

Editing and Proofreading

The next-to-last major stage in the writing process is editing—checking a paper for mistakes in grammar, punctuation, usage, and spelling. Students often find it hard to edit a paper carefully. They have put so much work into their writing, or so little, that it's almost painful for them to look at the paper one more time. You may simply have to *will* yourself to carry out this important closing step in the writing process. Remember that eliminating sentence-skills mistakes will improve an average paper and help ensure a strong grade on a good paper. Furthermore, as you get into the habit of checking your papers, you will also get into the habit of using sentence skills consistently. They are an integral part of clear, effective writing.

The checklist of sentence skills on the inside back cover of the book will serve as a guide while you are editing your paper.

Here are tips that can help you edit the next-to-final draft of a paper for sentence-skills mistakes:

Editing Tips

1. Have at hand two essential tools: a good dictionary (see Chapter 30) and a grammar handbook (you can use Part 3 of this book).

2. Use a sheet of paper to cover your writing so that you can expose only one sentence at a time. Look for errors in grammar, spelling, and typing. It may help to read each sentence out loud. If the sentence does not read clearly and smoothly, chances are something is wrong.

3. Pay special attention to the kinds of errors you tend to make. For example, if you tend to write run-ons or fragments, be especially on the lookout for these errors.

4. Try to work on a typed and printed draft, where you'll be able to see your writing more objectively than you could on a hand-written page; use a pen with colored ink so that your corrections will stand out.

Proofreading, the final stage in the writing process, means checking a paper carefully for spelling, grammar, punctuation, and other errors. You are ready for this stage when you are satisfied with your choice of supporting details, the order in which they are presented, and the way they and your topic sentence are worded.

At this point in your work, use your dictionary to do final checks on your spelling. Use a grammar handbook (such as the one in Part 3 of this text) to be sure about grammar, punctuation, and usage. Also read through your paper carefully, looking for typing errors, omitted words, and any other errors you may have missed before. Proofreading is often hard to do—again, students have spent so much time with their work, or so little, that they want to avoid it. But if it is done carefully, this important final step will ensure that your paper looks as good as possible.

Proofreading Tips

1. One helpful trick at this stage is to read your paper out loud. You will probably hear awkward wordings and become aware of spots where the punctuation needs to be changed. Make the improvements needed for your sentences to read smoothly and clearly.

2. Another strategy is to read your paper backward, from the last sentence to the first. This helps keep you from getting caught up in the flow of the paper and missing small mistakes—which is easy to do since you're so familiar with what you meant to say.

Editing and Proofreading: A Student Model

After typing into his word-processing file all the revisions in his paragraph, Mike printed out another clean draft. He then turned his attention to editing changes, as shown here:

My Job at the Crescent Falls Diner and Truck Stop

Working at the cresent falls diner and Truck Stop was the worst
job I ever had. First of all, the work was physically very hard. During
my ten hour days, I had to carry heavy trays of food to the customers,
and I had to clean the tables. I would wash dishes and then go unload
the delivery truck, lifting sixty-pound cartons of food supplies. The
second bad feature was the pay. I had to work at least sixty hours a
week to afford next semester's tuition because I got only minimun
wage, and I had to share my tips with the kitchen workers too. Finally,
the working conditions were horrible. I had to wash dishes in a hot
and steamy kitchen. Once, when unloading a truck, I hurt my back so
badly I was out of work for a week without pay! And the boss was
a tyrant who hated me cause I was a college student; he gave me
terrible hours, Even made racist slurs to my face.

TIP   You can make your changes (as Mike did) in longhand right on the printout of your paper. To note Mike's changes, complete the activity that follows.

Editing and Proofreading a Draft   ACTIVITY 8

Fill in the missing words.

1. As part of his editing, Mike checked and corrected the _____ of two words, *customers* and *minimum*. He also added a _____ between the compound adjective "ten-hour."

2. He added _____ to set off an introductory phrase ("During my ten-hour days") and an introductory word ("Finally").

3. He corrected a run on ("_____

_____") by replacing the comma with a period between the two sentences and by capitalizing the first word of the second sentence.

4. He corrected word use by changing "cause" to "_____." He eliminated wordiness by changing "I would wash dishes and then go

unload . . ." to "_____."

5. He corrected _____ by changing "crescent falls diner" to "Crescent Falls Diner."

6. Since revision can occur at any stage of the writing process, including editing, Mike makes one of his details more vivid by adding the

descriptive words "_____."

At this point, all Mike had to do was to enter his corrections, print out the final draft of the paper, and proofread it for any typos or other careless errors. He was then ready to hand it in to his instructor.

Tips on Using a Computer

- If you are using your school's computer center, allow enough time. You may have to wait for a computer or printer to be free. In addition, you may need several sessions at the computer and printer to complete your paper.

- Every word-processing program allows you to save your writing by pressing one or more keys. Save your work file frequently as you write your draft. A saved file is stored safely on the computer or network. A file that is not saved will be lost if the computer crashes or if the power is turned off.

- Keep your work in two places—the hard drive or network you are working on and, if you have one, a backup USB drive. At the end of each session with the computer, copy your work onto the USB drive or e-mail a copy to yourself. Then if the hard drive or network becomes damaged, you'll have the backup copy.

- Print out your work at least at the end of every session. Then not only will you have your most recent draft to work on away from the computer, but also you'll have a copy in case something should happen to your electronic copy.

- Work in single spacing so that you can see as much of your writing on the screen at one time as possible. Just before you print out your work, change to double spacing.

- Before making major changes in a paper, create a copy of your file. For example, if your file is titled "Worst Job," create a file called "Worst Job 2." Then make all your changes in that new file. If the changes don't work out, you can always go back to the original file.

Using a Computer at Each Stage of the Writing Process

Following are some ways to make word processing a part of your writing.

Prewriting

If you're a fast typist, many kinds of prewriting will work well on the computer. With freewriting in particular, you can get ideas onto the screen almost as quickly as they occur to you. A passing thought that could be productive is not likely to get lost. You may even find it helpful, when freewriting, to dim the screen of your monitor so that you can't see what you're typing. If you temporarily can't see the screen, you won't have to worry about grammar or spelling or typing errors (all of which do not matter in prewriting); instead, you can concentrate on getting down as many ideas and details as possible about your subject.

After any initial freewriting, questioning, and list-making on a computer, it's often very helpful to print out a hard copy of what you've done. With a clean printout in front of you, you'll be able to see everything at once and revise and expand your work with handwritten comments in the margins of the paper.

Word processing also makes it easy for you to experiment with the wording of the point of your paper. You can try a number of versions in a short time. After you have decided on the version that works best, you can easily delete the other versions—or simply move them to a temporary "leftover" section at the end of the paper.

If you have prepared a list of items during prewriting, you may be able to turn that list into an outline right on the screen. Delete the ideas you feel should not be in your paper (saving them at the end of the file in case you change your mind), and add any new ideas that occur to you. Then use the cut and paste functions to shuffle the supporting ideas around until you find the best order for your paper.

Writing Your First Draft

Like many writers, you may want to write out your first draft by hand and then type it into the computer for revision. Even as you type your handwritten draft, you may find yourself making some changes and improvements. And once you have a draft on the screen, or printed out, you will find it much easier to revise than a handwritten one.

If you feel comfortable composing directly on the screen, you can benefit from the computer's special features. For example, if you have written an anecdote in your freewriting that you plan to use in your paper, simply copy the story from your freewriting file and insert it where it fits in your paper. You can refine it then or later. Or if you discover while typing that a sentence is out of place, cut it out from where it is and paste it wherever you wish. And if while writing you realize that an earlier sentence can be expanded, just move your cursor back to that point and type in the added material.

3. Comments

Under the outline, write the heading "Comments." Here is what you should comment on:

- Look at the spots where your reading of the paragraph snagged: Are words missing or misspelled? Is there a lack of parallel structure? Are there mistakes with punctuation? Is the meaning of a sentence confusing? Try to figure out what the problems are and suggest ways of fixing them.

- Are there spots in the composition where you see problem with *unity*, *support*, or *organization*? (You'll find it helpful to refer to the checklist on the inside back cover of this book.) If so, offer comments. For example, you might say, "More details are needed to back up your main point" or "Some of the supporting details here don't really back up your point."

- Finally, make note of something you really liked about the paragraph, such as good use of transitions or an especially realistic or vivid specific detail.

After you have completed your evaluation of the composition, give it to your partner. Your instructor may provide you with the option of rewriting a piece of work in light of this feedback. Whether or not you rewrite, be sure to hand in the peer evaluation form with your composition.

REFLECTIVE ACTIVITY

1. Has your understanding of the writing process changed since reading Chapter 2? In what ways?

2. Of the four prewriting techniques (freewriting, questioning, making a list, and clustering), which one seems best for the way you might approach a writing assignment?

Review Activities

You now have a good overview of the writing process, from prewriting to drafting to revising to editing. The chapters in Part 2 will deepen your sense of the four goals of effective writing: unity, support, organization or coherence, and sentence skills.

To reinforce much of the information about the writing process that you have learned in this chapter, you can now work through the following review activities:

- Prewriting

- Outlining, drafting, and revising

- Taking a writing inventory

- Chapter review

Prewriting

These activities will give you practice in some of the prewriting strategies you can use to generate material for a paragraph. Although the focus here is on writing a paragraph, the strategies apply to writing an essay as well. See if you can do two or more of these prewriting activities.

Freewriting

REVIEW ACTIVITY 1

On a sheet of paper, freewrite for several minutes about a success or failure in your life. Don't worry about grammar, punctuation, or spelling. Try to write, without stopping, about whatever comes into your head concerning your success or failure.

Questioning

REVIEW ACTIVITY 2

On another sheet of paper, answer the following questions about the success or failure you've started to write about.

1. When did this success or failure occur?

2. Where did it take place?

3. What is one reason you consider this experience a success or failure? Give specific details to illustrate this reason.

4. What is another reason for this success or failure? What are some details that support the second reason?

5. Can you think of a third reason for this success or failure? What are some details that support the third reason?

Clustering

REVIEW ACTIVITY 3

In the center of a blank sheet of paper, write and circle the word *success* or *failure*. Then, around the circle, add reasons and details about this experience. Use a series of boxes, circles, or other shapes, along with connecting lines, to set off the reasons and details. In other words, try to think about and explore your topic in a very visual way.

Making a List

REVIEW ACTIVITY 4

On a separate piece of paper, make a list of details about the success or failure. Don't worry about putting them in a certain order. Just get down as many details about the experience as you can. The list can include specific reasons why the experience was a success or failure and specific details supporting those reasons.

Outlining, Drafting, and Revising

Here you will get practice in the writing steps that follow prewriting: outlining, drafting, revising, editing, and proofreading.

REVIEW ACTIVITY 5 | Scratch Outline

On the basis of your prewriting, see if you can prepare a scratch outline made up of your main idea and the three main reasons for your success or failure. Use the form below:

I experienced success or failure when I _____.

Reason 1: _____

Reason 2: _____

Reason 3: _____

REVIEW ACTIVITY 6 | First Draft

Now write a first draft of your paragraph. Begin with your topic sentence, stating the success or failure you experienced. Then state the first reason to support your main idea, followed by specific details supporting that reason. Next, state the second reason, followed by specific details supporting that reason. Finally, state the third reason, followed by support.

Don't worry about grammar, punctuation, or spelling. Just concentrate on getting down on paper the details about your experience.

REVIEW ACTIVITY 7 | Revising the Draft

Ideally, you will have a chance to put your paragraph aside for a while before writing the second draft. In your second draft, try to do all of the following:

1. Add transition words such as *first of all, another,* and *finally* to introduce each of the three reasons why your success or failure occurred.

2. Omit any details that do not truly support your topic sentence.

3. Add more details as needed, making sure you have plenty of support for each of your three reasons.

4. Check to see that your details are vivid and specific. Can you make a supporting detail more concrete? Are there any persuasive, colorful specifics you can add?

5. Try to eliminate wordiness (see pages 428–429) and clichés (see pages 425–426).

6. In general, improve the flow of your writing.

7. Be sure to include a final sentence that rounds off the paragraph, bringing it to a close.

Editing and Proofreading

When you have your almost-final draft of the paragraph, proofread it as follows:

1. Using your dictionary, check any words that you think might be misspelled. Or use a spell-check program on your computer.

2. Using Part 3 of this book, check your paragraph for mistakes in grammar, punctuation, and usage.

3. Read the paragraph aloud, listening for awkward or unclear spots. Make the changes needed for the paragraph to read smoothly and clearly. Even better, see if you can get another person to read the draft aloud to you. The spots that this person has trouble reading are spots where you may have to do some rewriting.

4. Take a sheet of paper and cover your writing so that you can expose and carefully check one line at a time. Or read your writing backward, from the end of the paragraph to the beginning. Look for typing errors, omitted words, and other remaining errors.

Don't fail to edit and proofread carefully. You may be tired of working on your paragraph at this point, but you want to give the extra effort needed to make it as good as possible. A final push can mean the difference between a higher and a lower grade.

Taking a Writing Inventory

Your Approach to Writing

This activity is not a test, so try to be as honest as possible when answering the following questions. Becoming aware of your writing habits can help you make helpful changes in your writing.

1. When you start work on a paper, do you typically do any prewriting?

    _____ Yes   _____ Sometimes   _____ No

2. If so, which of the prewriting techniques do you use?

    _____ Freewriting   _____ Clustering

    _____ Questioning   _____ Scratch outline

    _____ List making   _____ Other (please describe)

3. Which prewriting technique or techniques work best for you or do you think will work best for you?

    _____

4. Many students have said they find it helpful to handwrite a first draft and then type that draft on a computer. They then print out the draft

and revise it by hand. Describe your own way of drafting and revising a composition.

_____

5. After you write the first draft of a composition, do you have time to set it aside for a while so you can come back to it with a fresh eye?

6. How many drafts do you typically write when doing a paper?

_____

7. When you revise, are you aware that you should be working toward a composition that is unified, solidly supported, and clearly organized? Has this chapter given you a better sense that unity, support, and organization are goals to aim for?

_____

8. Do you revise a paragraph for the effectiveness of its sentences as well as for its content?

_____

9. What (if any) information has this chapter given you about prewriting that you will try to apply in your writing?

_____

10. What (if any) information has this chapter given you about revising that you will try to apply in your writing?

_____

Chapter Review

REVIEW ACTIVITY 10   **The Writing Process**

Answer each of the following questions by filling in the blank or circling the answer you think is correct.

1. *True or false?* _____ Writing is a skill that anyone can learn with practice.

2. An effective paragraph or essay is one that
   a. makes a point.
   b. provides specific support.
   c. makes a point and provides specific support.
   d. none of the above.

3. The sentence that states the main idea of a paragraph is known as the

   _____ sentence.

4. Prewriting can help a writer find
   a. a good topic to write about.
   b. a good main point to make about the topic.
   c. enough details to support the main point.
   d. all of the above.

5. One step that everyone should use at some stage of the writing process is to prepare a plan for the paragraph or essay known as a(n) _____.

6. When you start writing, your first concern should be
   a. spelling.
   b. content.
   c. grammar.
   d. punctuation.

7. The words *first, next, then, also, another,* and *finally* are examples of signal words, commonly known as _____.

8. A computer can help a writer
   a. turn a list into an outline.
   b. find just the right words to express a point.
   c. add and delete supporting evidence.
   d. all of the above.

WRITING ASSIGNMENT

All of us have come to various crossroads in our lives—times when we must make an important decision about which course of action to follow. Think about a major decision you had to make (or one you are planning to make). Then write a paragraph on the three reasons for your decision. Start out by describing the decision you have reached. Each of the supporting details that follow should fully explain the reasons for your decision. Here are some examples of major decisions that often confront people:

Enrolling in or dropping out of college

Accepting or quitting a job

Getting married or divorced

Breaking up with a boyfriend or girlfriend

Having a baby

Moving away from home

EXPLORING WRITING ONLINE

In this chapter, you learned that writing is a multistep process. Using your favorite search engine, such as Google, type the words "writing process." Find at least three Web sites that provide helpful information about how to approach writing in this way.

RESPONDING TO IMAGES

1. What process is being illustrated in this image? Translate the steps into written, rather than visual, instructions.

2. How would you illustrate the steps of the writing process visually?

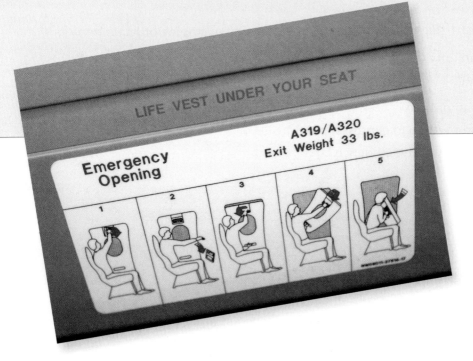

For additional materials on Chapter 2, visit **www.mhhe.com/langan**.

As a college student, you will do a lot of writing. The writing that you do will often involve making a point and supporting that point with reasons and details. Keep this in mind when you read the first draft of the following paragraph written by Desmond for a psychology course, and then answer the questions that follow.

What Do Psychologists Do?

Psychologists study human behavior and the way the mind works. When psychologists conduct experiments, they look for patterns to understand and predict behavior. When psychologists work with people, they ask questions about thoughts, feelings, and actions. Lastly, when psychologists work with people, they also help them change unproductive habits.

Desmond, the writer of the previous paragraph, provided three reasons to support his opening point but not much else. Together with a classmate, complete the following outline by providing two specific supporting details for each of Desmond's three reasons.

Title: What Do Psychologists Do?

Topic sentence: Psychologists study human behavior and the way the mind works.

1. When psychologists conduct experiments, they look for patterns to understand and predict behavior.

   a. _____

   b. _____

2. When psychologists work with people, they ask questions about thoughts, feelings, and actions.

   a. _____

   b. _____

3. Lastly, when psychologists work with people, they also help them change unproductive habits.

   a. _____

   b. _____

Using your outline, revise Desmond's paragraph.

COLLABORATIVE ACTIVITY

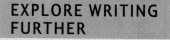
EXPLORE WRITING FURTHER

PART

Writing Effective Paragraphs

CHAPTER 3
Four Steps for Writing, Four Bases for Revising

CHAPTER 4
Nine Patterns of Paragraph Development

CHAPTER 5
Moving from Paragraph to Essay

PART 2 SHOWS YOU HOW TO

- begin a paper by making a point of some kind

- provide specific evidence to support that point

- organize and connect specific evidence

- revise so that your sentences flow smoothly and clearly

- edit so that your sentences are error-free

PART 2 WILL ALSO

- introduce you to nine patterns of paragraph development

- explain and illustrate the differences between a paragraph and an essay

- show you how to evaluate paragraphs and essays for unity, support, coherence, and sentence skills

EXPLORING WRITING PROMPT:

In Part 2, you will learn to make a point and to back it up in paragraphs and essays by using various patterns of development. Among these are (1) exemplification and (2) comparison or contrast.

Consider the following topics:

1. The students I have met since coming to college are, for the most part, _____.

2. The expectations of high school teachers and college professors differ in that _____.

In each blank, write a main point that turns the topic into a central idea. Then write a paragraph that develops each point fully. For topic 1, use examples to support your point, and you will be writing an exemplification paragraph; for topic 2, illustrate how the teachers and professors differ, and you will be writing a comparison or contrast paragraph.

3

Four Steps for Writing, Four Bases for Revising

CHAPTER PREVIEW

What Are the Steps to Writing Effective Paragraphs?

- Step 1: Make a Point
- Step 2: Back Up Your Point
- Step 3: Organize the Support
- Step 4: Write Clear, Error-Free Sentences

Four Bases for Revising Writing

- Base 1: Unity
- Base 2: Support
- Base 3: Coherence
- Base 4: Sentence Skills

RESPONDING TO IMAGES

Has anyone misunderstood something you wrote? What happened? What did you write to make that person get the wrong idea? Take a few minutes to recount your experience. In this chapter, you'll learn how to write clearly so that others don't misinterpret your point.

What Are the Steps to Writing Effective Paragraphs?

To write an effective paragraph, you should begin by making a point, and then go on to support that point with specific evidence. Finally, end your paper with a sentence that rounds off the paragraph and provides a sense of completion.

Step 1: Make a Point

It is often best to state your point in the first sentence of your paragraph, as Mike does in his paragraph about working at a diner and truck stop. The sentence that expresses the main idea, or point, of a paragraph is called the *topic sentence.* Your paragraph will be unified if you make sure that all the details support the point in your topic sentence.

It is helpful to remember that a topic sentence is a *general* statement. The sentences that follow it provide specific support for the general statement.

Understanding the Paragraph	**ACTIVITY 1**

Each group of sentences in the following activity could be written as a short paragraph. Circle the letter of the topic sentence in each case. To find the topic sentence, ask yourself, "Which is a general statement supported by the specific details in the other three statements?"

Begin by trying the following example item. First circle the letter of the sentence you think expresses the main idea. Then read the explanation.

EXAMPLE

    a. CNN.com provides market trading information.

    b. CNN.com is a good source of national and world news.

    (c.) CNN.com has a lot to offer its readers.

    d. There are many video clips and podcasts available on CNN.com.

> EXPLANATION: Sentence *a* explains one important benefit of CNN.com. Sentences *b* and *d* provide other specific advantages of CNN.com. In sentence *c*, however, no one specific benefit is explained. Instead, the words "a lot to offer" refer only generally to such benefits. Therefore, sentence *c* is the topic sentence; it expresses the main idea. The other sentences support that idea by providing examples.

1. a. Food and toiletries can be purchased at bulk prices.

    b. The price of gasoline is cheaper at a warehouse club.

    c. My family and I enjoy shopping at warehouse clubs.

    d. My children love the food samples.

2. a. Instead of talking on the telephone, we send text messages.
    b. People rarely talk to one another these days.
    c. Rather than talking with family members, we sit silently in front of the TV or computer all evening.
    d. In cars, we ignore our traveling companions to listen to the radio.

3. a. Once I completely forgot to study for a history final.
    b. During finals week, something awful always happens.
    c. The city bus was twenty minutes late on the day of my English final.
    d. Another time, the battery in my calculator died during my math final.

4. a. Today's retail environment relies on a variety of technologies.
    b. Cash registers operate on point-of-sale software.
    c. Merchandise is tracked through hand-held barcode scanners.
    d. Anti-shoplifting devices help reduce retail theft.

5. a. The submission techniques in MMA were developed from jujitsu and judo.
    b. Mixed martial arts (MMA) is an evolution of different fighting techniques.
    c. Kickboxing and karate provided MMA with striking techniques.
    d. The clinching techniques in MMA were taken from wrestling and sumo.

Understanding the Topic Sentence

An effective topic sentence does two things. First, it presents the topic of the paragraph. Second, it expresses the writer's attitude or opinion or idea about the topic. For example, look at the following topic sentence:

Professional athletes are overpaid.

In the topic sentence, the topic is *professional athletes*; the writer's idea about the topic is that professional athletes *are overpaid*.

ACTIVITY 2	Topic Sentences

For each topic sentence that follows, underline the topic and double-underline the point of view that the writer takes toward the topic.

EXAMPLES

Living in a small town has many advantages.

Cell phones should be banned in schools.

1. The apartments on Walnut Avenue are a fire hazard.

2. Losing my job turned out to have benefits.

3. Blues is the most interesting form of American music.

4. Our neighbor's backyard is a dangerous place.

5. Paula and Jeff are a stingy couple.

6. Snakes do not deserve their bad reputation.

7. Pollution causes many problems in American cities.

8. New fathers should receive at least two weeks of "paternity leave." .

9. People with low self-esteem often need to criticize others.

10. Learning to write effectively is largely a matter of practice.

Identifying Topics, Topic Sentences, and Support

The following activity will sharpen your sense of the differences between topics, topic sentences, and supporting sentences.

Breaking Down the Parts of a Paragraph	**ACTIVITY 3**

Each group of items below includes one topic, one main idea (expressed in a topic sentence), and two supporting details for that idea. In the space provided, label each item with one of the following:

> **T**   topic
> **MI** main idea
> **SD** supporting details

1. _____ a. The weather in the summer is often hot and sticky.

   _____ b. Summer can be an unpleasant time of year.

   _____ c. Summer.

   _____ d. Bug bites, poison ivy, and allergies are a big part of summertime.

2. _____ a. The new Ultimate sports car is bound to be very popular.

   _____ b. The company has promised to provide any repairs needed during the first three years at no charge.

   _____ c. Because it gets thirty miles per gallon of gas, it offers real savings on fuel costs.

   _____ d. The new Ultimate sports car.

3. _____ a. Decorating an apartment doesn't need to be expensive.

   _____ b. A few plants add a touch of color without costing a lot of money.

   _____ c. Inexpensive braided rugs can be bought to match nearly any furniture.

   _____ d. Decorating an apartment.

4. _____ a. Long practice sessions and busy game schedules take too much time away from schoolwork.

_____ b. High school sports.

_____ c. The competition between schools may become so intense that, depending on the outcome of one game, athletes are either adored or scorned.

_____ d. High school sports put too much pressure on young athletes.

5. _____ a. After mapping out the best route to your destination, phone ahead for motel reservations.

_____ b. A long car trip.

_____ c. Following a few guidelines before a long car trip can help you avoid potential problems.

_____ d. Have your car's engine tuned as well, and have the tires, brakes, and exhaust system inspected.

Step 2: Back Up Your Point

To support your point, you need to provide specific reasons, examples, and other details that explain and develop it. The more precise and particular your supporting details are, the better your readers can "see," "hear," and "feel" them.

Understanding General versus Specific Ideas

A paragraph is made up of a main idea, which is general, and the specific ideas that support it. So to write well, you must understand the difference between general and specific ideas.

It is helpful to realize that you use general and specific ideas all the time in your everyday life. For example, in choosing a film to rent, you may think, "Which should I rent, an action movie, a comedy, or a romance?" In such a case, *film* is the general idea, and *action movie, comedy,* and *romance* are the specific ideas.

Or you may decide to begin an exercise program. In that case, you might consider walking, pilates, or lifting weights. In this case, *exercise* is the general idea, and *walking, pilates,* and *lifting weights* are the specific ideas.

Or if you are talking to a friend about a date that didn't work out well, you may say, "The dinner was terrible, the car broke down, and we had little to say to each other." In this case, the general idea is *the date didn't work out well,* and the specific ideas are the three reasons you named.

The following activities will give you experience in recognizing the relationship between general and specific. They will also provide a helpful background for the information and additional activities that follow.

Identifying General Ideas

Each group of words consists of one general idea and four specific ideas. The general idea includes all the specific ideas. Underline the general idea in each group.

EXAMPLE

subway   bus   train   <u>public transportation</u>   railway

1. raspy   high-pitched   voice   deep   screechy

2. breakfast food   scrambled eggs   Belgian waffles   smoked bacon   orange juice

3. Mars   Venus   planet   Saturn   Earth

4. pill   syrup   caplet   tablet   pain reliever

5. zoology   botany   chemistry   science   biology

6. surfing   kayaking   water sports   rafting   waterskiing

7. peony   flower   rose   daisy   tulip

8. Indian   Pacific   Atlantic   ocean   Mediterranean

9. ceremony   wedding   funeral   graduation   baptism

10. yup   yeah   yes   yep   yesh

Developing Specific Ideas

In each item below, one idea is general and the others are specific. The general idea includes the specific ones. In the spaces provided, write in two more specific ideas that are covered by the general idea.

EXAMPLE

General: exercises

Specific: chin-ups, jumping jacks,   <u>sit-ups</u>,   <u>push-ups</u>

> **HINT**   Refer to the images in the margins when answering item 5.

1. *General:* pizza toppings

   Specific: sausage, mushrooms,   _____,   _____

2. *General:* furniture

   Specific: rocking chair, coffee table,   _____,   _____

3. *General:* magazines

   Specific: Reader's Digest, Newsweek,   _____,   _____

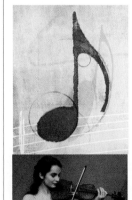

4. *General:* birds

   Specific: eagle, pigeon, _____ , _____

5. *General:* music

   Specific: jazz, classical, _____ , _____

6. *General:* cold symptoms

   Specific: aching muscles, watery eyes, _____ , _____

7. *General:* children's games

   Specific: hopscotch, dodgeball, _____ , _____

8. *General:* transportation

   Specific: plane, motorcycle, _____ , _____

9. *General:* city problems

   Specific: overcrowding, pollution, _____ , _____

10. *General:* types of TV shows

    Specific: cartoons, reality shows, _____ , _____

ACTIVITY 6	**What Ideas Have in Common**

Read each group of specific ideas below. Then circle the letter of the general idea that tells what the specific ideas have in common. Note that the general idea should not be too broad or too narrow. Begin by trying the example item, and then read the explanation that follows.

EXAMPLE

Specific ideas: peeling potatoes, washing dishes, cracking eggs, cleaning out refrigerator

The general idea is

a. household jobs.

b. kitchen tasks.

c. steps in making dinner.

> EXPLANATION: It is true that the specific ideas are all household jobs, but they have in common something even more specific—they are all tasks done in the kitchen. Therefore, answer *a* is too broad, and the correct answer is *b.* Answer *c* is too narrow because it doesn't cover all the specific ideas. Although two of them could be steps in making a dinner ("peeling potatoes" and "cracking eggs"), two have nothing to do with making dinner.

1. *Specific ideas:* crowded office, rude coworkers, demanding boss, unreasonable deadlines

   The general idea is

   a. problems.

   b. work problems.

   c. problems with work schedules.

2. *Specific ideas:* cactus, rosebush, fern, daisy

   The general idea is

   a. plants.

   b. plants that have thorns.

   c. plants that grow in the desert.

3. *Specific ideas:* Band-Aids, gauze, antiseptic, aspirin

   The general idea is

   a. supplies.

   b. first-aid supplies.

   c. supplies for treating a headache.

4. *Specific ideas:* trout, whales, salmon, frogs

   The general idea is

   a. animals.

   b. fish.

   c. animals living in water.

5. *Specific ideas:* Hershey bar, lollipop, mints, fudge

   The general idea is

   a. food.

   b. candy.

   c. chocolate.

6. *Specific ideas:* "Go to bed," "Pick up that trash," "Run twenty laps," "Type this letter."

   The general idea is

   a. remarks.

   b. orders.

   c. the boss's orders.

7. *Specific ideas:* "I had no time to study," "The questions were unfair," "I had a headache," "The instructor didn't give us enough time."

   The general idea is

   a. statements.

   b. excuses for being late.

   c. excuses for not doing well on a test.

8. *Specific ideas:* candle, sun, headlight, flashlight

   The general idea is

   a. things that are very hot.

   b. light sources for a home.

   c. sources of light.

9. *Specific ideas:* driving with expired license plates, driving over the speed limit, parking without putting money in the meter, driving without a license

   The general idea is:

   a. ways to cause a traffic accident.

   b. traffic problems.

   c. ways to get a ticket.

10. *Specific ideas:* "Are we there yet?" "Where do people come from?" "Can I have that toy?" "Do I have to go to bed now?"

    The general idea is

    a. Things adults say to one another.

    b. Things children ask adults.

    c. Things children ask at school.

ACTIVITY 7 | What Is the General Idea?

In the following items, the specific ideas are given but the general ideas are unstated. Fill in the blanks with the general ideas.

EXAMPLE

General idea: _____ car problems _____

Specific ideas: flat tire   dented bumper
                   cracked windshield   dirty oil filter

1. *General idea:* _____

   Specific ideas: nephew   grandmother
                      aunt   cousin

2. *General idea:* _____

   Specific ideas: boots   sneakers
                      sandals   slippers

3. *General idea:* _____

   Specific ideas: camping   hiking
                      fishing   hunting

4. *General idea:* _____

   Specific ideas: broom   sponge
                      mop   glass cleaner

5. *General idea:* _____

   Specific ideas: cloudy   sunny

                     snowy   rainy

6. *General idea:* _____

   Specific ideas: Spread mustard on slice of bread

                     Add turkey and cheese

                     Put lettuce on top of cheese

                     Cover with another slice of bread

7. *General idea:* _____

   Specific ideas: thermos of lemonade   insect repellent

                     basket of food   blanket

8. *General idea:* _____

   Specific ideas: fleas in carpeting   loud barking

                     tangled fur   veterinary bills

9. *General idea:* _____

   Specific ideas: diabetes   cancer

                     appendicitis   broken leg

10. *General idea:* _____

   Specific ideas: flooded basements   wet streets

                     rainbow   overflowing rivers

Recognizing Specific Details

Specific details are examples, reasons, particulars, and facts. Such details are needed to support and explain a topic sentence effectively. They provide the evidence needed for us to understand, as well as to feel and experience, a writer's point.

Below is a topic sentence followed by two sets of supporting sentences. Write a check mark next to the set that provides sharp, specific details.

Topic sentence: **Ticket sales for a recent Rolling Stones concert proved that the classic rock band is still very popular.**

_____ a.   Fans came from everywhere to buy tickets to the concert. People wanted good seats and were willing to endure a great deal of various kinds of discomfort as they waited in line for many hours. Some people actually waited for days, sleeping at night in uncomfortable circumstances. Good tickets were sold out extremely quickly.

_____ b.   The first person in the long ticket line spent three days standing in the hot sun and three nights sleeping on the concrete without even a pillow. The man behind her waited equally long in his wheelchair. The ticket window opened at 10:00 A.M., and the tickets for the good seats— those in front of the stage—were sold out an hour later.

> **EXPLANATION:** The second set (*b*) provides specific details. Instead of a vague statement about fans who were "willing to endure a great deal of various kinds of discomfort," we get vivid details we can see and picture clearly: "three days standing in the hot sun," "three nights sleeping on the concrete without even a pillow," and "The man behind her waited equally long in his wheelchair."
>
> Instead of a vague statement that tickets were "sold out extremely quickly," we get exact and vivid details: "The ticket window opened at 10:00 A.M., and the tickets for the good seats—those in front of the stage—were sold out an hour later."

Specific details are often like a movie script. They provide us with such clear pictures that we could make a film of them if we wanted to. You would know just how to film the information given in the second set of sentences. You would show the fans in line under a hot sun and, later, sleeping on the concrete. The first person in line would be shown sleeping without a pillow under her head. You would show tickets finally going on sale, and after an hour you could show the ticket seller explaining that all of the seats in front of the stage were sold out.

In contrast, the writer of the first set of sentences (*a*) fails to provide the specific information needed. If you were asked to make a film based on set *a*, you would have to figure out on your own just what particulars to show.

When you are working to provide specific supporting information in a paper, it might help to ask yourself, "Could someone easily film this information?" If the answer is yes, your supporting details are specific enough for your readers to visualize.

ACTIVITY 8 | Specific vs. General Support

Each topic sentence in this activity is followed by two sets of supporting details. Write *S* (for *specific*) in the space next to the set that provides specific support for the point. Write *G* (for *general*) next to the set that offers only vague general support.

1. *Topic sentence:* Alonzo was relieved when he received the results from his physical exam.

   _____ a.   Alonzo's blood pressure was 120/80, which is within the normal range for men. His cholesterol ratio was below 4, which is good for men of his age.

   _____ b.   Alonzo's doctor told him that his blood pressure was normal. He also learned that his cholesterol levels were normal.

2. *Topic sentence:* When preparing meals on a budget, canned meats and beans provide cost-effective alternatives.

    _____ a. Canned meat can be used rather than fresh meat to prepare meals. Canned fish can also be used. Canned beans are another alternative when preparing economical meals.

    _____ b. Spam can be used instead of sirloin beef to prepare stews and stir-fry dishes. Canned tuna can be used to make baked casseroles and pasta meals. Canned kidney, pinto, and black beans can be used instead of ground beef to make chili and grilled burgers.

3. *Topic sentence:* My college campus provides students with valuable resources.

    _____ a. The writing tutors at the Learning Center help students find topics and assist them with revision and editing. The reference librarians at the library help students locate appropriate books and online journals for their research papers. The academic advisers at the Counseling Office notify students about required and elective courses during registration.

    _____ b. Tutors on campus help students with the different stages of their writing. Librarians help students with their research by locating different sources in the library and online. Counselors on campus provide students with useful information on course registration.

4. *Topic sentence:* RateMyProfessor.com provides students with a reliable source of information for finding out information about their professors.

    _____ a. On RateMyProfessor.com, students evaluate their professors. Professors are scored on their quality of teaching. They are also rated in other areas. The most helpful section of a rating is the user comments.

    _____ b. On RateMyProfessor.com, students give their professors a "scorecard." Professors are scored on their quality of teaching under the categories "good," "average," and "poor." They are also rated in terms of "easiness," "clarity," and "helpfulness." Some teachers are even awarded a "hot" chili pepper rating. The user comments—the most helpful section of the Web site—allows students to write honestly about what they liked and disliked about their professors.

5. *Topic sentence:* Employers are providing different work options to help employees reduce the cost of commuting to and from work.

    _____ a. Some employers are allowing their employees to work from home one day a week. Some employers are providing a condensed work week. Some employers are encouraging transportation alternatives and providing public transit incentives.

_____ b. Some employers are allowing employees to telecommute one day a week by using their home computer, the Internet, and phone and video conferencing. Some employers are condensing the work week from five eight-hour days to four ten-hour days. Some employers are encouraging employees to car pool, and they are paying for monthly bus and rail passes.

ACTIVITY 9 | Specific vs. General Support in a Paragraph

At several points in each of the following paragraphs, you are given a choice of two sets of supporting details. Write S (for _specific_) in the space next to the set that provides specific support for the point. Write G (for _general_) next to the set that offers only vague, general support.

Paragraph 1

My daughter is as shy as I am, and it breaks my heart to see her dealing with the same problems I had to deal with in my childhood because of my shyness. I feel very sad for her when I see the problems she has making friends.

_____ a. It takes her a long time to begin to do the things other children do to make friends, and her feelings get hurt very easily over one thing or another. She is not at all comfortable about making connections with her classmates at school.

_____ b. She usually spends Christmas vacation alone because by that time of year she doesn't have friends yet. Only when her birthday comes in the summer is she confident enough to invite school friends to her party. Once she sends out the invitations, she almost sleeps by the telephone, waiting for the children to respond. If they say they can't come, her eyes fill with tears.

I recognize very well her signs of shyness, which make her look smaller and more fragile than she really is.

_____ c. When she has to talk to someone she doesn't know well, she speaks in a whisper and stares sideways. Pressing her hands together, she lifts her shoulders as though she wished she could hide her head between them.

_____ d. When she is forced to talk to anyone other than her family and her closest friends, the sound of her voice and the position of her head change. Even her posture changes in a way that makes it look as if she's trying to make her body disappear.

It is hard for me to watch her passing unnoticed at school.

———— e. She never gets chosen for a special job or privilege, even though she tries her best, practicing in privacy at home. She just doesn't measure up. Worst of all, even her teacher seems to forget her existence much of the time.

———— f. Although she rehearses in our basement, she never gets chosen for a good part in a play. Her voice is never loud or clear enough. Worst of all, her teacher doesn't call on her in class for days at a time.

Paragraph 2

It is said that the dog is man's best friend, but I strongly believe that the honor belongs to my computer. A computer won't fetch a stick for me, but it can help me entertain myself in many ways.

———— a. If I am bored, tired, or out of ideas, the computer allows me to explore things that interest me, such as anything relating to the world of professional sports.

———— b. The other day, I used my computer to visit the National Football League's Web site. I was then able to get injury updates for players on my favorite team, the Philadelphia Eagles.

While the dog is a faithful friend, it does not allow me to be a more responsible person the way my computer does.

———— c. I use my computer to pay all my bills online. I also use it to balance my checkbook and keep track of my expenses. Now I always know how much money is in my account at the end of the month.

———— d. The computer helps me be responsible with financial matters because it records my transactions. With the computer, I have access to more information, which allows me to make good decisions with my money.

A dog might help me meet strangers I see in the park, but the computer helps me meet people who share my interests.

———— e. With my computer, I can go online and find people with every type of hobby or interest. Thousands of blogs and discussion groups are available featuring people from all over the country—and the world. The computer can even allow me to develop meaningful personal relationships with others.

———— f. Two months ago, I discovered a Web site for people in my community who enjoy hiking. I'm planning to meet a group next Saturday for a day hike. And earlier this year, I met my wonderful fiancée, Shelly, through an online dating service.

Providing Specific Details

| ACTIVITY 10 | **Getting Specific** |

Each of the following sentences contains a general word or words, set off in *italic* type. Substitute sharp, specific words in each case.

EXAMPLE

After the parade, the city street was littered with *garbage*.

After the parade, the city street was littered with multicolored confetti, dirty

popcorn, and lifeless balloons.

1. If I had enough money, I'd visit *several places*.

   _____

   _____

2. It took her *a long time* to get home.

   _____

   _____

3. Ron is often stared at because of his *unusual hair color and hairstyle*.

   _____

   _____

4. After you pass *two buildings*, you'll see my house on the left.

   _____

   _____

5. Nia's purse is crammed with *lots of stuff*.

   _____

   _____

6. I bought *some junk food* for the long car trip.

   _____

   _____

7. The floor in the front of my car is covered with *things*.

   _____

   _____

8. When his mother said no to his request for a toy, the child *reacted strongly*.

   _____

   _____

9. Devan gave his girlfriend a *surprise present* for Valentine's Day.

_____

_____

10. My cat can *do a wonderful trick.*

_____

_____

Selecting Details That Fit

The details in your paper must all clearly relate to and support your opening point. If a detail does not support your point, leave it out. Otherwise, your paper will lack unity. For example, see if you can circle the letter of the two sentences that do *not* support the following topic sentence.

Topic sentence: **Tom is a very talented person.**

a. Tom is always courteous to his professors.

b. He has created beautiful paintings in his art course.

c. Tom is the lead singer in a local band.

d. He won an award in a photography contest.

e. He is hoping to become a professional photographer.

EXPLANATION: Being courteous may be a virtue, but it is not a talent, so sentence *a* does not support the topic sentence. Also, Tom's desire to become a professional photographer tells us nothing about his talent; thus, sentence *e* does not support the topic sentence either. The other three statements all clearly back up the topic sentence. Each in some way supports the idea that Tom is talented—in art, as a singer, or as a photographer.

Details That Don't Fit   ACTIVITY 11

In each group below, circle the two items that do *not* support the topic sentence.

1. *Topic sentence:* Carla seems attracted only to men who are unavailable.

a. She once fell in love with a man serving a life sentence in prison.

b. Her parents worry about her inability to connect with a nice single man.

c. She wants to get married and have kids before she is thirty.

d. Her current boyfriend is married.

e. Recently she had a huge crush on a Catholic priest.

2. *Topic sentence:* Some dog owners have little consideration for other people.

   a. Obedience lessons can be a good experience for both the dog and the owner.

   b. Some dog owners let their dogs leave droppings on the sidewalk or in other people's yards.

   c. They leave the dog home alone for hours, and it barks and howls and wakes the neighbors.

   d. Some people keep very large dogs in small apartments.

   e. Even when small children are playing nearby, owners let their bad-tempered dogs run loose.

3. *Topic sentence:* Dr. Eliot is a very poor teacher.

   a. He cancels class frequently with no explanation.

   b. When a student asks a question that he can't answer, he becomes irritated with the student.

   c. He got his PhD at a university in another country.

   d. He's taught at the college for many years and is on a number of faculty committees.

   e. He puts off grading papers until the end of the semester, and then returns them all at once.

4. *Topic sentence:* Some doctors seem to think it is all right to keep patients waiting.

   a. Pharmaceutical sales representatives sometimes must wait hours to see a doctor.

   b. The doctors stand in the hallway chatting with nurses and secretaries even when they have a waiting room full of patients.

   c. Patients sometimes travel long distances to consult with a particular doctor.

   d. When a patient calls before an appointment to see if the doctor is on time, the answer is often yes even when the doctor is two hours behind schedule.

   e. Some doctors schedule appointments in a way that ensures long lines, to make it appear that they are especially skillful.

5. *Topic sentence:* Several factors were responsible for the staggering loss of lives when the *Titanic* sank.

   a. More than 1,500 people died in the *Titanic* disaster; only 711 survived.

   b. Despite warnings about the presence of icebergs, the captain allowed the *Titanic* to continue at high speed.

   c. If the ship had hit the iceberg head-on, its watertight compartments might have kept it from sinking; however, it hit on the side, resulting in a long, jagged gash through which water poured in.

   d. The *Titanic*, equipped with the very best communication systems available in 1912, sent out SOS messages.

   e. When the captain gave orders to abandon the *Titanic*, many passengers refused because they believed the ship was unsinkable, so many lifeboats were only partly filled.

Providing Details That Fit

Writing Specific Details   ACTIVITY 12

Each topic sentence in this activity is followed by one supporting detail. See if you can add a second detail in each case. Make sure your detail supports the topic sentence.

1. *Topic sentence:* There are valid reasons why students miss deadlines.

   a. Students may have more than one paper to write on any given day.

   b. _____

2. *Topic sentence:* Those who serve in the military make many sacrifices.

   a. They leave their families to serve on tours of duty.

   b. _____

3. *Topic sentence:* Sabrina has such a positive outlook on life.

   a. When she lost her job, she contacted an employment agency right away.

   b. _____

4. *Topic sentence:* There are many advantages to group work.

   a. Everyone has talents to contribute.

   b. _____

5. *Topic sentence:* Everyone should take measures to prevent identity theft.

   a. Passwords should be changed regularly.

   b. _____

Providing Support   ACTIVITY 13

Working in pairs, see if you can add *two* supporting details for each of the following topic sentences.

1. *Topic sentence:* The managers of this apartment building don't care about their renters.

   a. Mrs. Harris has been asking them to fix her leaky faucet for two months.

   b. _____

   c. _____

2. *Topic sentence:* None of the shirts for sale were satisfactory.

   a. Some were attractive but too expensive.

   b. _____

   c. _____

3. *Topic sentence:* After being married for forty years, Mr. and Mrs. Lambert have grown similar in odd ways.

   a. They both love to have a cup of warm apple juice just before bed.

   b. _____

   c. _____

4. *Topic sentence:* It is a special time for me when my brother is in town.

   a. We always catch the latest sci-fi thriller and then stop for pizza.

   b. _____

   c. _____

5. *Topic sentence:* Our neighbor's daughter is very spoiled.

   a. When anyone else in the family has a birthday, she gets several presents too.

   b. _____

   c. _____

Providing Details in a Paragraph

ACTIVITY 14	Adding Details to a Paragraph

The following paragraph needs specific details to back up its three supporting points. In the spaces provided, write two or three sentences of convincing details for each supporting point.

A Disappointing Concert

Although I had looked forward to seeing my favorite band in concert, the experience was disappointing. For one thing, our seats were terrible, in two ways. _____

_____

_____

_____

In addition, the crowd made it hard to enjoy the music. _____

_____

_____

_____

_____

continued

And finally, the band members acted as if they didn't want to be there. _____

_____

_____

_____

Omitting and Grouping Details in Planning a Paragraph

One common way to develop material for a paper involves three steps: (1) Make a list of details about your point, (2) omit details that don't truly support your point, and (3) group remaining details together in logical ways. Omitting details that don't fit and grouping related details together are part of learning how to write effectively.

Grouping Details	**ACTIVITY 15**

See if you can figure out a way to put the following details into three groups. Write *A* in front of the details that go with one group, *B* in front of the details that go with a second group, and *C* in front of the details that make up a third group. Cross out the four details that do not relate to the topic sentence.

Topic sentence: My brother Sean caused our parents lots of headaches when he was a teenager.

_____ In constant trouble at school

_____ While playing a joke on his lab partner, nearly blew up the chemistry lab

_____ Girlfriend was eight years older than he and had been married twice

_____ Girlfriend had a very sweet four-year-old son

_____ Parents worried about people Sean spent his time with

_____ Several signs that he was using drugs

_____ Failed so many courses that he had to go to summer school in order to graduate

_____ Was suspended twice for getting into fights between classes

_____ Our father taught math at the high school we attended

_____ His money just disappeared, and he never had anything to show for it

_____ His best pal had been arrested for armed robbery

Mike's paragraph about working at the diner and truck stop (Chapter 1, p. 8) uses listing order: It lists three reasons why it was the worst job he ever had, and each of those three reasons is introduced by one of the preceding transitions. In the following spaces, write in the three transitions:

First of all _____   Second _____   Finally _____

The first reason in the paragraph about working at the plant is introduced with *first of all*, the second reason by *second*, and the third reason by *finally*.

| ACTIVITY 17 | Using Listing Order |

Use *listing order* to arrange the scrambled list of sentences below. Number each supporting sentence 1, 2, 3, . . . so that you go from the least important item to what is presented as the most important item.

Note that transitions will help by making clear the relationships between some of the sentences.

Topic sentence: I am no longer a big fan of professional sports, for a number of reasons.

_____ Basketball and hockey continue well into the baseball season, and football doesn't have its Super Bowl until the middle of winter, when basketball should be at center stage.

_____ In addition, I detest the high fives, taunting, and trash talk that so many professional athletes now indulge in during games.

_____ Second, I am bothered by the length of professional sports seasons.

_____ Also, professional athletes have no loyalty to a team or city, as they greedily sell their abilities to the highest bidder.

_____ For one thing, greed is the engine running professional sports.

_____ There are numerous news stories of professional athletes in trouble with the law because of drugs, guns, fights, traffic accidents, or domestic violence.

_____ After a good year, athletes making millions become unhappy if they aren't rewarded with a new contract calling for even more millions.

_____ But the main reason I've become disenchanted with professional sports is the disgusting behavior of so many of its athletes.

Time Order

When a writer uses time order, supporting details are presented in the order in which they occurred. *First* this happened; *next* this; *after* that, this; and so on. Many paragraphs, especially paragraphs that tell a story or give a series of directions, are organized in a time order.

Transition words that show time relationships include the following:

first	before	after	when	then
next	during	now	while	until
as	soon	later	often	finally

Read the following paragraph, which is organized in time order. See if you can underline the six transition words that show the time relationships.

> Della had a sad experience while driving home last night. She traveled along the dark, winding road that led toward her home. She was only two miles from her house when she noticed a glimmer of light in the road. The next thing she knew, she heard a sickening thud and realized she had struck an animal. The light, she realized, had been its eyes reflected in her car's headlights. Della stopped the car and ran back to see what she had hit. It was a handsome cocker spaniel, with blond fur and long ears. As she bent over the still form, she realized there was nothing to be done. The dog was dead. Della searched the dog for a collar and tags. There was nothing. Before leaving, she walked to several nearby houses, asking if anyone knew who owned the dog. No one did. Finally Della gave up and drove on. She was sad to leave someone's pet lying there alone.

The main point of the paragraph is stated in its first sentence: "Della had a sad experience while driving home last night." The support for this point is all the details of Della's experience. Those details are presented in the order in which they occurred. The time relationships are highlighted by these transitions: *while, when, next, as, before,* and *finally.*

Using Time Order   ACTIVITY 18

Use *time order* to arrange the scrambled sentences below. Number the supporting sentences in the order in which they occur in time (1, 2, 3, . . .).

Note that transitions will help by making clear the relationships between sentences.

Topic sentence: If you have difficulty sleeping, the following steps should help you sleep better.

_____ Also avoid taking naps during the daytime.

_____ A good night's sleep starts by getting up early each morning.

_____ During the evening, avoid drinking caffeine, which is a stimulant.

_____ Finally, go to bed at a reasonable and regular time each evening.

_____ During the daytime, fit regular exercise into your schedule.

_____ Before you go to bed, avoid reading.

_____ First, check with your doctor to rule out medical problems such as sleep apnea.

_____ In addition, avoid watching TV before you go to bed.

More about Using Transitions

As already stated, transitions are signal words that help readers follow the direction of the writer's thoughts. To see the value of transitions, look at the two versions of the short paragraph below. Check the version that is easier to read and understand.

_____ a.   There are several sources that you can use for your writing assignments. Your own experience is a major resource. For an assignment about communication skills, for instance, you can draw on your own experiences in college, at work, and in everyday life. Other people's experiences are extremely useful. You may have heard people you know or even people on TV talking about communication skills. You can also interview people. Books, magazines, and the Internet are good sources of material for assignments. Many experts, for example, have written about various aspects of communication skills.

_____ b.   There are several sources that you can use for your writing assignments. First of all, your own experience is a major resource. For an assignment about communication skills, for instance, you can draw on your own experiences in college, at work, and in everyday life. In addition, other people's experiences are extremely useful. You may have heard people you know or even people on TV talking about communication skills. You can also interview people. Finally, books, magazines, and the Internet are good sources of material for assignments. Many experts, for example, have written about various aspects of communication skills.

> **EXPLANATION:** You no doubt chose the second version, *b.* The listing transitions—*first of all, in addition,* and *finally*—make it clear when the author is introducing a new supporting point. The reader of paragraph *b* is better able to follow the author's line of thinking and to note that three main sources of material for assignments are being listed: your own experience, other people's experiences, and books, magazines, and the Internet.

Using Transitions   ACTIVITY 19

The following paragraphs use listing order or time order. In each case, fill in the blanks with appropriate transitions from the box above the paragraph. Use each transition once.

1.

after	now	first	soon	while

My husband has developed an involving hobby, in which I, unfortunately, am unable to share. He _____ enrolled in ground flight instruction classes at the local community college. The lessons were all about air safety regulations and procedures. _____ passing a difficult exam, he decided to take flying lessons at the city airport. Every Monday he would wake at six o'clock in the morning and drive happily to the airport, eager to see his instructor. _____ he was taking lessons, he started to buy airplane magazines and talk about them constantly. "Look at that Cessna 150," he would say. "Isn't she a beauty?" _____, after many lessons, he is flying by himself. _____ he will be able to carry passengers. That is my biggest nightmare. I know he will want me to fly with him, but I am not a lover of heights. I can't understand why someone would leave the safety of the ground to be in the sky, defenseless as a kite.

2.

finally	for one thing	second

The karate class I took last week convinced me that martial arts may never be my strong point. _____, there is the issue of balance. The instructor asked everyone in class to stand on one foot to practice kicking. Each time I tried, I wobbled and had to spread my arms out wide to avoid falling. I even stumbled into Mr. Kim, my instructor, who glared at me. _____, there was the issue of flexibility. Mr. Kim asked us to stretch and touch our toes. Everyone did this without a problem—except me. I could barely reach my knees before pain raced up and down my back. _____, there was my lack of coordination. When everyone started practicing blocks, I got confused. I couldn't figure out where to move my arms and legs. By the time I got the first move right, the whole group had finished three more. By the end of my first lesson, I was completely lost.

3.
| later | soon | when | then |

At the age of thirty-one I finally had the opportunity to see snow for the first time in my life. It was in New York City on a cloudy afternoon in November. My daughter and I had gone to the American Museum of Natural History. _____ we left the museum, snow was falling gently. I thought that it was so beautiful! It made me remember movies I had seen countless times in my native Brazil. We decided to find a taxi. _____ we were crossing Central Park, snuggled in the cozy cab, watching the snow cover trees, bushes, branches, and grass. We were amazed to see the landscape quickly change from fall to winter. _____ we arrived in front of our hotel, and I still remember stepping on the crisp snow and laughing like a child who is touched by magic. _____ that day, I heard on the radio that another snowstorm was coming. I was naive enough to wait for thunder and the other sounds of a rainstorm. I did not know yet that snow, even a snowstorm, is silent and soft.

4.
| last of all | another | first of all | in addition |

Public school students who expect to attend school from September to June, and then have a long summer vacation, may be in for a big surprise before long. For a number of reasons, many schools are switching to a year-round calendar. _____, many educators point out that the traditional school calendar was established years ago when young people had to be available during the summer months to work on farms, but this necessity has long since passed. _____ reason is that a longer school year accommodates individual learning rates more effectively—that is, fast learners can go into more depth about a subject that interests them, while those who learn at a slower pace have more time to master the essential material. _____, many communities have gone to year-round school to relieve overcrowding, since students can be put on different schedules throughout the year. _____, and perhaps most important, educators feel that year-round schools eliminate the loss of learning that many students experience over a long summer break.

Step 4: Write Clear, Error-Free Sentences

If you use correct spelling and follow the rules of grammar, punctuation, and usage, your sentences will be clear and well written. But by no means must you have all that information in your head. Even the best writers need to use reference materials to be sure their writing is correct. So when you write your papers, keep a good dictionary and grammar handbook nearby.

In general, however, save them for after you've gotten your ideas firmly down in writing. You'll find as you write paragraphs that you will make a number of sentence errors. Simply ignore them until you get to a later draft of your paper, when there will be time enough to make the needed corrections. Part 3 of this text focuses on sentence skills.

Four Bases for Revising Writing

In this chapter, you've learned four essential steps in writing an effective paragraph. The following box shows how these steps lead to four standards, or bases, you can use in evaluating and revising paragraphs.

Four Steps ➡	Four Bases
1. If you make one point and stick to that point,	➡ your writing will have *unity*.
2. If you back up the point with specific evidence,	➡ your writing will have *support*.
3. If you organize and connect the specific evidence,	➡ your writing will have *coherence*.
4. If you write clear, error-free sentences,	➡ your writing will demonstrate effective *sentence skills*.

my mother perform certain household chores that I've really come to hate. ¹⁴My father expects me to live at home until I am married to a Vietnamese man. ¹⁵When that happens, he assumes I will obey my husband just as I obey him. ¹⁶I do not want to be a bad daughter, but I want to live like my American female friends.

Fill in the blanks: The first spot where supporting details are needed occurs after sentence number _____. The second spot occurs after sentence number _____. The third spot occurs after sentence number _____.

Base 3: Coherence

Understanding Coherence

Once you have determined that a paragraph is unified and supported, check to see if the writer has a clear and consistent way of organizing the material.

The third base of effective writing is *coherence*. The supporting ideas and sentences in a composition must be organized in a consistent way so that they cohere, or "stick together." Key techniques for tying material together are choosing a clear method of organization (such as time order or emphatic order) and using transitions and other connecting words as signposts.

> **TIP**   To check a paragraph for coherence, ask yourself these questions:
> 1. Does the paragraph have a clear method of organization?
> 2. Are transitions and other connecting words used to tie the material together?

Evaluating Paragraphs for Coherence

ACTIVITY 22	**Looking for Organization and Coherence**

Answer the questions about coherence that follow the paragraph below.

Why I Bought a Handgun

¹I bought a handgun to keep in my house for several reasons. ²Most important, I have had a frightening experience with an obscene phone caller. ³For several weeks, a man has called me once or twice a day, sometimes as late as three in the morning. ⁴As soon as I pick up the phone, he whispers something obscene or threatens me by saying, "I'll get you." ⁵I decided to buy a gun because crime is increasing in my neighborhood. ⁶One neighbor's house was burglarized while she was at work; the thieves not only stole her appliances but also threw

continued

paint around her living room and slashed her furniture. [7]Not long after this incident, an elderly woman from the apartment house on the corner was mugged on her way to the supermarket. [8]The man grabbed her purse and threw her to the ground, breaking her hip. [9]Buying a gun was my response to listening to the nightly news. [10]It seemed that every news story involved violence of some kind—rapes, murders, muggings, and robberies. [11]I wondered if some of the victims in the stories would still be alive if they had been able to frighten the criminal off with a gun. [12]As time passed, I became more convinced that I should keep a gun in the house.

a. The paragraph should use emphatic order. Write *1* before the reason that seems slightly less important than the other two, *2* before the second-most-important reason, and *3* before the most important reason.

_____ Obscene phone caller

_____ Crime increase in neighborhood

_____ News stories about crime

b. Before which of the three reasons should the transitional words *first of all* be added? _____

c. Before which of the three reasons could the transition *in addition* be added? _____

d. Which words show emphasis in sentence 2? _____

e. In sentence 8, to whom does the pronoun *her* refer? _____

_____

f. How often does the key word *gun* appear in the paragraph? _____

_____

g. What is a synonym for *burglarized* in sentence 6? _____

Base 4: Sentence Skills

Understanding Sentence Skills

Errors in grammar, punctuation, sentence structure, mechanics, and even formatting can detract greatly from your writing; the fourth base, **sentence skills**, requires that you identify, fix, and avoid these types of mistakes. Error-free sentences allow readers to focus on the content of a paragraph as a whole. Poor grammar and sentence skills can be merely distracting, or they can change the meaning of a sentence entirely; they also lessen a writer's credibility. For instance, a potential employer might think, "If he can't spell the word *political,* does he really have an interest in working on my campaign?"

Part 3 of this book focuses on a wide range of sentence skills. You should review all the skills carefully. Doing so will ensure that you know the most important rules of grammar, punctuation, and usage—rules needed to write clear, error-free sentences.

Checking for Sentence Skills

Sentence skills and the other bases of effective writing are summarized in the following chart and on the inside back cover of the book.

A Summary of the Four Bases of Effective Writing

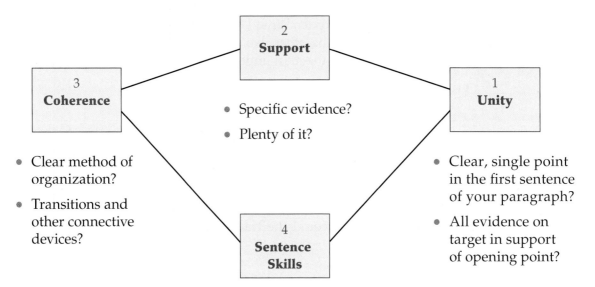

- Fragments eliminated? (162–178)
- Run-ons eliminated? (179–194)
- Correct verb forms? (210–230, 241–251)
- Subject and verb agreement? (231–240)
- Faulty modifiers and faulty parallelism eliminated? (283–288, 295–303)
- Faulty pronouns eliminated? (252–262, 263–274)
- Capital letters used correctly? (324–333)
- Punctuation marks where needed?

    (a) Apostrophe (342–353)   (d) Semicolon; colon (379–381)

    (b) Quotation marks (354–364)   (e) Hyphen; dash (381–382)

    (c) Comma (365–378)   (f) Parentheses (382–383)

- Correct paper format? (319–323)
- Needless words eliminated? (423–434)

Evaluating Paragraphs for Sentence Skills

Identifying Sentence Errors

Working with a partner, identify the sentence-skills mistakes at the under-lined spots in the paragraph that follows. From the box below, choose the letter that describes each mistake and write it in the space provided. The same mistake may appear more than once. Use Part 3: Sentence Skills (pp. 150–435) as a reference.

a. fragment (162–178)	d. apostrophe mistake (342–353)
b. run-on (179–194)	e. faulty parallelism (295–303)
c. mistake in subject-verb agreement (231–240)	

Looking Out for Yourself

It's sad but true: "If you don't look out for yourself, no one else will." For example, some people have a false idea about the power of a college degree, they think that once they possesses the degree, the world will be waiting on their doorstep. In fact, nobody is likely to be on their doorstep unless, through advance planning, they has prepared themselves for a career. The kind in which good job opportunities exist. Even after a person has landed a job, however, a healthy amount of self-interest is needed. People who hide in corners or with hesitation to let others know about their skills doesn't get promotions or raises. Its important to take credit for a job well done, whether the job involves writing a report, organized the office filing system, or calming down an angry customer. Also, people should feel free to ask the boss for a raise. If they work hard and really deserve it. Those who look out for themselves get the rewards, people who depend on others to help them along get left behind.

1. _____ 2. _____ 3. _____ 4. _____ 5. _____

6. _____ 7. _____ 8. _____ 9. _____ 10. _____

ACTIVITY 24	Evaluating Paragraphs for All Four Bases: Unity, Support, Coherence, and Sentence Skills

In this activity, you will evaluate paragraphs in terms of all four bases: unity, support, coherence, and sentence skills. Evaluative comments follow each paragraph below. Circle the letter of the statement that best applies in each case.

1.

Looks Shouldn't Matter, But They Do

Often, job applicants are discriminated against based on physical appearance. First of all, some employers will not hire a man who wears an earring even though a woman who wears earrings is not singled out. In addition, someone with a facial piercing on the lip, nose, or eyebrow is often treated unfairly in the job market. Finally, some employers will not hire a person who has a visible tattoo yet they hire people whose tattoos are hidden.

    a.   The paragraph is not unified.
    b.   The paragraph is not adequately supported.
    c.   The paragraph is not well organized.
    d.   The paragraph does not show a command of sentence skills.
    e.   The paragraph is well written in terms of the four bases.

2.

Getting Better Gas Mileage

There is several ways to get better gas mileage from your car. First of all, properly maintain your car. Regularly check the air pressure in the tires owing to the fact that under-inflated tires can use up more gas. A dirty air filter will also cause your car to consume more fuel. Next, driving efficiently. When on the roadway, drive at no more than sixty miles per our. The faster you drive the more gas will be guzzled by your car. At stop signs and traffic lights, avoid sudden starts and stops. Lastly, lighten your car load. Clean out the trunk of your car and avoid hauling items unnecessarily. Added weight decrease fuel economy. Even though someone cannot control the price at the gas pump; we can control how we use the gas in our fuel tank.

    a.   The paragraph is not unified.
    b.   The paragraph is not adequately supported.
    c.   The paragraph is not well organized.
    d.   The paragraph does not show a command of sentence skills.
    e.   The paragraph is well written in terms of the four bases.

3.

Tips on Bringing Up Children

In some ways, children should be treated as mature people. Adults should not use baby talk with children. Using real words with children helps them develop language skills more quickly. Baby talk makes children feel patronized, frustrated, and confused, for they want to understand and communicate with adults by learning their speech. So animals should be called cows and dogs, not "moo-moos" and "bow-wows." Parents should be consistent when disciplining children. If a parent tells a child, "You cannot have dessert unless you put away your toys," it is important that the parent follow through on the warning. By being consistent, parents will teach children responsibility and give them a stable center around which to grow. Children should be allowed and encouraged to make simple decisions. At a restaurant, children should be allowed to decide what to order. Regarding finances, they should be able to choose if and how they want to spend their money. Parents will thus be helping their children prepare for the complex decisions that they will have to deal with later in life.

---

a.   The paragraph is not unified.

b.   The paragraph is not adequately supported.

c.   The paragraph is not well organized.

d.   The paragraph does not show a command of sentence skills.

e.   The paragraph is well written in terms of the four bases.

4.

Gambling My Life Away

I see now that my compulsive gambling hurt my family life. First of all, I argued constantly with my wife. When we first married, she did not seem to mind that I would bet on football and basketball games, but she began to mind when bookies started calling our home. In addition, we were always short of money for bills. I am not proud to say that my wife had to get a second job just to pay for daily expenses, such as gas and groceries. Most regrettably, I ignored my children. I spent most nights at sports bars watching the games I had placed bets on. When I was home, I preferred to play online poker rather than help my children with their homework or play with them at the park. In hindsight, I see that I gambled away not only my money but my family.

---

a.   The paragraph is not unified.

b.   The paragraph is not adequately supported.

c.   The paragraph is not well organized.

d.   The paragraph does not show a command of sentence skills.

e.   The paragraph is well written in terms of the four bases.

5.

Children Are Expensive

The cost of raising a child keeps increasing. Many families know this fact all too well. For one thing, child care costs are getting higher every year. Parents pay more today for a babysitter or for day care. Teachers' salaries, however, are not going up. For another thing, children's clothing costs more. A pair of children's athletic shoes can easily cost over fifty dollars. Budget-conscious parents should shop at discount and outlet garment stores. In addition, food also costs more. Providing nutritious food is more costly because of rising grocery prices. Sadly, a Happy Meal at McDonald's is often cheaper, but not as nutritious, as a freshly prepared sandwich at home. Health care costs are also getting higher. If a parent is fortunate to have health insurance, that parent may find more of his or her paycheck going toward the monthly premium. Other health-care expenses, such as prescription and over-the-counter drugs, are getting more expensive too.

---

a. The paragraph is not unified.

b. The paragraph is not adequately supported.

c. The paragraph is not well organized.

d. The paragraph does not show a command of sentence skills.

e. The paragraph is well written in terms of the four bases.

WRITING ASSIGNMENT

Write a paragraph about a valued material possession. Here are some suggestions:

Car	Appliance
Computer	Cell phone
TV	Photo album
iPod	Piece of clothing
Piece of furniture	Stereo system
Piece of jewelry	Piece of hobby equipment
Camera	Video game console

Your topic sentence should center on the idea that there are several reasons this possession is so important to you. Provide specific examples and details to develop each reason.

Use the following checklist as a guide while you are working on your paragraph:

Yes	No	
_____	_____	Do you begin with a point?
_____	_____	Do you provide relevant, specific details that support the point?
_____	_____	Do you use the words *first of all, second,* and *finally* to introduce your three supporting details?
_____	_____	Do you have a closing sentence?
_____	_____	Are your sentences clear and free of obvious errors?

EXPLORING WRITING ONLINE

Visit a favorite Web site of yours and evaluate it for unity, support, coherence, and sentence skills. Then write a paragraph in which you present your evaluation. Use the following questions to help you:

Unity: *Can you easily identify what the Web site's goals are?*

Support: *Does the site contain valuable information, and is that information presented in an effective way?*

Coherence: *Is the site organized and easy to navigate?*

Sentence Skills: *Can you find typos, spelling mistakes, or awkward sentences?*

RESPONDING TO IMAGES

Focusing on the third base, *coherence,* describe the organizing principles of this site, as introduced on its home page, shown here.

For additional materials on Chapter 3, visit www.mhhe.com/langan.

Nine Patterns of Paragraph Development

CHAPTER PREVIEW

Important Considerations in Paragraph Development

Patterns of Development

Exemplification

Description

Narration

Process

Cause and Effect

Comparison or Contrast

Definition

Division-Classification

Argument

RESPONDING TO IMAGES

These photographs capture life before and after Hurricane Katrina hit the Gulf Coast. Compare or contrast these photographs, paying attention to which specific details changed or stayed constant after the hurricane struck.

Important Considerations in Paragraph Development

Before you begin work on particular types of paragraphs, there are several general considerations about writing to keep in mind.

Knowing Your Subject

Whenever possible, write on a subject that interests you. You will then find it easier to put more time into your work. Even more important, try to write on a subject that you already know something about. If you do not have direct experience with the subject, you should at least have indirect experience—knowledge gained through thinking, prewriting, reading, or talking about the subject.

If you are asked to write on a topic about which you have no experience or knowledge, you should do whatever research is required to gain the information you need. Without direct or indirect experience, or the information you gain through research, you may not be able to provide the specific evidence needed to develop whatever point you are trying to make. Your writing will be starved for specifics.

Knowing Your Purpose and Audience

The three most common purposes of writing are to inform, to persuade, and to entertain. Each is described briefly below.

- To **inform**—to give information about a subject. Authors who are writing to inform want to provide facts that will explain or teach something to readers. For example, an informative paragraph about sandwiches might begin, "Eating food between two slices of bread—a sandwich—is a practice that has its origins in eighteenth-century England."

- To **persuade**—to convince the reader to agree with the author's point of view on a subject. Authors who are writing to persuade may give facts, but their main goal is to argue or prove a point to readers. A persuasive paragraph about sandwiches might begin, "There are good reasons why every sandwich should be made with whole-grain bread."

- To **entertain**—to amuse and delight; to appeal to the reader's senses and imagination. Authors write to entertain in various ways, through fiction and nonfiction. An entertaining paragraph about sandwiches might begin, "What I wanted was a midnight snack, but what I got was better—the biggest, most magical sandwich in the entire world."

Your audience will be primarily your instructor and sometimes other students. Your instructor is really a symbol of the larger audience you should see yourself writing for—an audience of educated adults who expect you to present your ideas in a clear, direct, organized way. If you can learn to write to persuade or inform such a general audience, you will have accomplished a great deal.

A Note on Tone

It will also be helpful for you to write some paragraphs for a more specific audience. By so doing, you will develop an ability to choose words and adopt a tone of voice that is just right for a given purpose and a given group of people. *Tone* reveals the attitude that a writer has toward a subject. It is expressed through the words and details the writer selects. Just as a speaker's voice can project a range of feelings, a writer's voice can project one or more tones, or feelings: anger, sympathy, hopefulness, sadness, respect, dislike, and so on.

Patterns of Development

Traditionally, writing has been divided into the following patterns of development:

- Exposition
   Exemplification
   Process
   Cause and effect
   Comparison or contrast
   Definition
   Division-Classification

- Description

- Narration

- Argumentation

In *exposition*, the writer provides information about and explains a particular subject. Patterns of development within exposition include giving examples (*exemplification*), detailing a *process* of doing or making something, analyzing *causes and effects*, *comparing* or *contrasting*, *defining* a term or concept, and *dividing* something into parts or *classifying* it into categories.

In addition to exposition, three other patterns of development are common: description, narration, and argumentation. A *description* is a verbal picture of a person, place, or thing. In *narration*, a writer tells the story of something that happened. Finally, in *argumentation*, a writer attempts to support a controversial point or defend a position on which there is a difference of opinion.

Each pattern has its own internal logic and provides its own special strategies for imposing order on your ideas.

> ### TIP   As you practice each pattern, you should remember the following:
>
> - Although each paragraph that you write will involve one predominant pattern, very often one or more additional patterns may be involved as well. For instance, the paragraph "My Job at the Crescent Falls Diner and Truck Stop" that you have already read (page 8) presents a series of examples showing why Mike disliked his job. There is also an element of narration, as the writer recounts his experience as a story.
>
> - Additionally, the paragraph shows how conditions caused this negative effect. No matter which pattern or patterns you use, each paragraph will probably involve some form of argumentation. You will advance a point and then go on to support your point. To convince the reader that your point is valid, you may use a series of examples, or narration, or description, or some other pattern of organization. For instance, a writer could advance the opinion that good horror movies can be easily distinguished from bad horror movies and then supply comparative information about both to support her claim. Much of your writing, in short, will have the purpose of persuading your reader that the idea you have advanced is valid.

1. Exemplification

In our daily conversations, we often provide *examples*—that is, details, particulars, and specific instances—to explain statements that we make. Consider the several statements and supporting examples in the following box:

Statement	Examples
Wal-Mart was crowded today.	There were at least four carts waiting at each of the checkout counters, and it took me forty-five minutes to get through a line.
The corduroy shirt I bought is poorly made.	When I washed it, the colors began to fade, one button cracked and another fell off, a shoulder seam opened, and the sleeves shrank almost two inches.
My son Peter is unreliable.	If I depend on him to turn off a pot of beans in ten minutes, the family is likely to eat burned beans. If I ask him to turn down the thermostat before he goes to bed, the heat is likely to stay on all night.

In each case, the examples help us *see for ourselves* the truth of the statement that has been made. In paragraphs, too, explanatory examples help the audience fully understand a point. Lively, specific examples also add interest to a piece of writing.

A Paragraph to Consider

Walking Billboards

[1]Many I Americans have turned into driving, walking billboards. [2]As much as we all claim to hate commercials on television, we don't seem to have any qualms about turning ourselves into commercials. [3]Our car bumpers, for example, advertise lake resorts, underground caverns, and amusement parks. [4]Also, we wear clothes marked with other people's initials and slogans. [5]Our fascination with the names of designers shows up on the backs of our sneakers and the pockets of our shirts and blue jeans. [6]Furthermore, we wear T-shirts filled with all kinds of advertising messages. [7]For instance, people are willing to wear shirts that read "Dillon Construction," "Nike," or even "I Got Crabs at Ed's Seafood Palace." [8]These messages belong on highway billboards. [9]In conclusion, we say we hate commercials, but we actually pay people for the right to advertise their products.

QUESTIONS

About Unity

1. Which sentence in "Walking Billboards" is irrelevant to the point that Americans are walking billboards? (*Write the sentence number here.*)

    _____

About Support

2. How many specific examples are given that show that Americans are walking billboards?

    _____ two _____ three _____ four _____ five _____ six

About Coherence

3. What transition words and phrases are used in "Walking Billboards"?

    _____   _____   _____   _____   _____

Writing an Exemplification Paragraph

WRITING ASSIGNMENT

Complete this unfinished paragraph (in the following box), which has as its topic sentence, "My husband Roger is a selfish person." Provide the supporting details needed to develop the examples of Roger's selfishness. The first example has been done for you.

A Selfish Person

My husband Roger is a selfish person. For one thing, he refuses to move out of the city, even though it is a bad place to raise the children. *We inherited some money when my parents died, and it might be enough for a down payment on a small house in a nearby town. But Roger says he would miss his buddies in the neighborhood.*

Also, when we go on vacation, we always go where Roger wants to go. _____

_____

_____

_____

Another example of Roger's selfishness is that he always spends any budget money that is left over. _____

_____

_____

_____

Finally, Roger leaves all the work of caring for the children to me.

_____

_____

_____

_____

PREWRITING

a. On a separate piece of paper, jot down a couple of answers for each of the following questions:

- What specific vacations did the family go on because Roger wanted to go? Write down particular places, length of stay, time of year. What vacations has the family never gone on (for example, to visit the wife's relatives), even though the wife wanted to?

- What specific items has Roger bought for himself (rather than for the whole family's use) with leftover budget money?

- What chores and duties involved in the everyday caring for the children has Roger never done?

Your instructor may ask you to work with one or two other students in generating the details needed to develop the three examples in the paragraph. The groups may then be asked to read their details aloud, with the class deciding which details are the most effective for each example.

Here, and in general in your writing, try to generate *more* supporting material than you need. You are then in a position to choose the most convincing details for your paper.

b. Read over the details you have generated and decide which sound most effective. Jot down additional details as they occur to you.

c. Take your best details, reshape them as needed, and use them to complete the paragraph about Roger.

REVISING: PEER REVIEW

Read the paragraph to a classmate or friend with these questions in mind to make sure you have covered the four bases of effective writing:

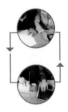

CHECKLIST FOR EXEMPLIFICATION: THE FOUR BASES

ABOUT *UNITY*

✔ Do all of the examples I provide support the central idea that Roger is selfish?

ABOUT *SUPPORT*

✔ Are there enough examples to make my point about Roger and convince others to agree with me?

✔ Do I appeal to my readers' senses with vivid, specific examples?

ABOUT *COHERENCE*

✔ Have I presented the examples in my paragraph in the most effective order?

ABOUT *SENTENCE SKILLS*

✔ Have I used specific rather than general words?

✔ Are my sentences varied in length and structure?

✔ Have I checked for spelling and other sentence skills, as listed on the inside back cover of the book?

Continue revising your work until you and your reader can answer *yes* to all these questions.

BEYOND THE CLASSROOM

Exemplification

Imagine that you are a restaurant manager who needs to write a paragraph-long article for the training manual about high-quality customer service. Explain this concept by providing specific examples so that your employees understand how important customer service is in the competitive food service industry.

2. Description

When you describe something or someone, you give your readers a picture in words. To make this "word picture" as vivid and real as possible, you must observe and record specific details that appeal to your readers' senses (sight, hearing, taste, smell, and touch). More than any other type of writing, a descriptive paragraph needs sharp, colorful details.

Here is a description in which only the sense of sight is used:

A rug covers the living-room floor.

In contrast, here is a description rich in sense impressions:

A thick, reddish-brown shag rug is laid wall to wall across the living-room floor. The long, curled fibers of the shag seem to whisper as you walk through them in your bare feet, and when you squeeze your toes into the deep covering, the soft fibers push back at you with a spongy resilience.

Sense impressions include sight (*thick, reddish-brown shag rug; laid wall to wall; walk through them in your bare feet; squeeze your toes into the deep covering; push back*), hearing (*whisper*), and touch (*bare feet, soft fibers, spongy resilience*). The sharp, vivid images provided by the sensory details give us a clear picture of the rug and enable us to share the writer's experience.

A Paragraph to Consider

My Teenage Son's Room

[1]I push open the door with difficulty. [2]The doorknob is loose and has to be jiggled just right before the catch releases from the doorjamb. [3]Furthermore, as I push at the door, it runs into a basketball shoe lying on the floor. [4]I manage to squeeze in through the narrow opening. [5]I am immediately aware of a pungent odor in the room, most of which is coming from the closet, to my right. [6]That's the location of a white wicker clothes hamper, heaped with grass-stained jeans, sweat-stained T-shirts, and smelly socks. [7]But the half-eaten burrito, lying dried and unappetizing on the bedside table across the room, contributes a bit of aroma, as does the glass

continued

of curdled, sour milk sitting on the sunny windowsill. [8]To my left, the small wire cage on Greg's desk is also fragrant, but pleasantly. [9]From its nest of sweet-smelling cedar chips, the gerbil peers out at me with its bright eyes, its tiny claws scratching against the cage wall. [10]The floor around the wastebasket that is next to the desk is surrounded by what appears to be a sprinkling of snowballs. [11]They're actually old wadded-up school papers, and I can picture Greg sitting on his bed, crushing them into balls and aiming them at the "basket"—the trash can. [12]I glance at the bed across from the desk and chuckle because pillows stuffed under the tangled nest of blankets make it look as if someone is still sleeping there, though I know Greg is in history class right now. [13]I step carefully through the room, trying to walk through the obstacle course of science-fiction paperbacks, a wristwatch, sports magazines, and a dust-covered computer on which my son stacks empty soda cans. [14]I leave everything as I find it, but tape a note to Greg's door saying, "Isn't it about time to clean up?"

QUESTIONS

About Unity

1. Does this paragraph have a topic sentence?

   _____

About Support

2. Label as *sight, touch, hearing,* or *smell* all the sensory details in the following sentences.

   That's the location of a white wicker clothes hamper, heaped with

   grass-stained jeans, sweat-stained T-shirts, and smelly socks.

About Coherence

3. Spatial signals (*above, next to, to the right,* and so on) are often used to help organize details in a descriptive paragraph. List four space signals that appear in "My Teenage Son's Room":

   _____

Writing a Descriptive Paragraph

Write a paragraph describing a certain person's room. Use as your topic sentence "I could tell by looking at the room that a _____ lived there." There are many kinds of people who could be the focus for such a

WRITING ASSIGNMENT

paragraph. You can select any one of the following, or think of another type of person.

Photographer	Music lover	Carpenter
Cook	TV addict	Baby
Student	Camper	Cat or dog lover
Musician	Hacker	World traveler
Hunter	Cheerleader	Drug addict
Slob	Football player	Little boy or girl
Outdoors person	Actor	Alcoholic
Doctor	Dancer	Swimmer

PREWRITING

a. After choosing a topic, spend a few minutes making sure it will work. Prepare a list of all the details you can think of that support the topic. For example, a student who planned to describe a soccer player's room made this list:

soccer balls

shin guards

posters of professional soccer teams

soccer trophies

shirt printed with team name and number

autographed soccer ball

medals and ribbons

photos of player's own team

sports clippings

radio that looks like soccer ball

soccer socks

soccer shorts

If you don't have enough details, choose another type of person. Check your new choice by listing details before committing yourself to the topic.

b. You may want to use other prewriting techniques, such as freewriting or questioning, to develop more details for your topic. As you continue prewriting, keep the following in mind:

  • Everything in the paragraph should support your point. For example, if you are writing about a soccer player's room, every detail should serve to show that the person who lives in that room plays and loves soccer. Other details—for example, the person's computer, tropical fish tank, or daily "to-do" list—should be omitted.

- Description depends on the use of specific rather than general descriptive words. For example:

General	Specific
Mess on the floor	The obstacle course of science-fiction paperbacks, a wristwatch, sports magazines, and a dust-covered computer on which my son stacks empty soda cans
Ugly turtle tub	Large plastic tub of dirty, stagnant-looking water containing a few motionless turtles
Bad smell	Unpleasant mixture of strong chemical deodorizers, urine-soaked newspapers, and musty sawdust
Nice skin	Soft, velvety brown skin

Remember that you want your readers to experience the room vividly. Your words should be as detailed as a clear photograph, giving readers a real feel for the room. Appeal to as many senses as possible. Most of your description will involve the sense of sight, but you may be able to include details about touch, hearing, and smell as well.

- Spatial order is a good way to organize a descriptive paragraph. Move as a visitor's eye might move around the room, from right to left or from larger items to smaller ones. Here are a few transition words of the sort that show spatial relationships.

to the left	across from	on the opposite side
to the right	above	nearby
next to	below	

Such transitions will help prevent you—and your reader—from getting lost as the description proceeds.

c. Before you write, see if you can make a scratch outline based on your list. Here is one possible outline of the paragraph about the soccer player's room. Note that the details are organized according to spatial order—from the edges of the room in toward the center.

Topic sentence: I could tell by looking at the room that a soccer player lived there.

1. Walls

2. Bookcase

3. Desk

4. Chair

5. Floor

d. Then proceed to write a first draft of your paragraph.

REVISING: PEER REVIEW

Read your descriptive paragraph slowly out loud to a friend or classmate. Ask the friend to close his or her eyes and try to picture the room as you read. Read it out loud a second time. To ensure you have covered the four bases of effective writing, ask your friend to answer these questions:

CHECKLIST FOR DESCRIPTION: THE FOUR BASES

ABOUT *UNITY*

✔ Does every detail in the paragraph support the topic sentence? Here's one way to find out: Ask your friend to imagine omitting the key word or words (in the case of our example, *soccer player*) in your topic sentence. Would readers know what word should fit in that empty space?

ABOUT *SUPPORT*

✔ Are the details specific and vivid rather than general?

✔ Has the writer included details that appeal to as many senses as possible?

ABOUT *COHERENCE*

✔ Does the paragraph follow a logical spatial order?

✔ Has the writer used transitions (such as *on top of, beside,* and *to the left of*) to help the reader follow that order?

ABOUT *SENTENCE SKILLS*

✔ Has the writer carefully proofread his or her paragraph, using the list on the inside back cover of the book, and corrected all sentence-skills mistakes, including spelling?

Continue revising your work until you and your reader can answer *yes* to all these questions.

BEYOND THE CLASSROOM

Description

Imagine that you are an interior designer. Write a paragraph describing a design for one of the following: a child's bedroom, a kitchen, a small restaurant, a porch, or a bakery. In your prewriting, you might list all the relevant needs of the people who live or work in the space you are designing. Consider issues such as storage space, appropriate lighting and colors, and the first thing people should or would notice when they walk in. Then put all the parts together so that they work well as a whole. Use a spatial order in your paragraph to help readers "see" your room.

CHAPTER 4   Nine Patterns of Paragraph Development   97

3. Narration

At times we make a statement clear by relating in detail something that has happened. In the story we tell, we present the details in the order in which they happened. A person might say, for example, "I was embarrassed yesterday," and then go on to illustrate the statement with the following narrative:

> I was hurrying across campus to get to a class. It had rained heavily all morning, so I was hopscotching my way around puddles in the pathway. I called to two friends ahead to wait for me, and right before I caught up to them, I came to a large puddle that covered the entire path. I had to make a quick choice of either stepping into the puddle or trying to jump over it. I jumped, wanting to seem cool, since my friends were watching, but didn't clear the puddle. Water splashed everywhere, drenching my shoe, sock, and pants cuff, and spraying the pants of my friends as well. "Well done, Dave!" they said. My embarrassment was all the greater because I had tried to look so casual.

The speaker's details have made his moment of embarrassment vivid and real for us, and we can see and understand just why he felt as he did.

A Paragraph to Consider

Deceptive Appearance

[1]Outward appearance can be deceptive. [2]Eric, a friendly and good-humored college student, is a prime example. [3]On the days when Eric is absent from classes, his professors seem to miss his lively personality. [4]One day after psychology class, Eric asked his classmate Mona if she wanted to have lunch with him, and she felt happy that Eric wanted to be her friend. [5]Later, while they were sitting at a booth together eating double cheeseburgers and home fries, Eric took out a small brown envelope with several kinds of colorful pills inside. [6]"Which one?" he asked. [7]"They're great because you'll be so amped up that you won't need to sleep for a week." [8]Mona must have looked surprised because Eric said, "Don't worry." [9]He went on to say, "They're not very expensive, and I'll even cut you a break this time." [10]Mona told him that she didn't want any pills. [11]Finally, Eric said, "Your loss," and then got up and walked away without even saying good-bye or paying for his portion of the lunch bill. [12]Mona felt very disappointed. [13]Eric didn't want to be her friend. [14]He only wanted to find more people to buy his drugs.

Copyright © 2010 The McGraw-Hill Companies, Inc. All rights reserved.

QUESTIONS

About Unity

1. Which sentence in this paragraph should be omitted in the interest of unity? (*Write the sentence number here.*)

_____

About Support

2. What do you think is the best (most real and vivid) detail or image in the paragraph "Deceptive Appearance"?

_____

About Coherence

3. Does the paragraph use time order or emphatic order to organize details?

_____

4. What are at least three transitions words used in this paragraph?

_____

Writing a Narrative Paragraph

WRITING ASSIGNMENT

Write a paragraph about an experience in which a certain emotion was predominant. The emotion might be fear, pride, satisfaction, embarrassment, or any of these:

Frustration	Sympathy	Shyness
Love	Bitterness	Disappointment
Sadness	Violence	Happiness
Terror	Surprise	Jealousy
Shock	Nostalgia	Anger
Relief	Loss	Hate
Envy	Silliness	Nervousness

The experience you write about should be limited in time. Note that the paragraph presented in this chapter details an experience that occurred within a relatively short period of time: one frustrating night of babysitting.

A good way to bring an event to life for your readers is to include some dialogue, as the writers of two of the three paragraphs in this chapter have done. Words that you said, or that someone else said, help make a situation come alive. First, though, be sure to check the section on quotation marks on pages 354–364.

PREWRITING

a. Begin by freewriting. Think of an experience or event that caused you to feel a certain emotion strongly. Then spend ten minutes writing freely about the experience. Do not worry at this point about spelling or grammar or putting things in the right order. Instead, just try to get down all the details you can think of that seem related to the experience.

b. This preliminary writing will help you decide whether your topic is promising enough to develop further. If it is not, choose another emotion and repeat step *a*. If it does seem promising, do two things:

- First, write your topic sentence, underlining the emotion you will focus on. For example, "My first day in kindergarten was one of the *scariest* days of my life."

- Second, make up a list of all the details involved in the experience. Then number these details according to the order in which they occurred.

c. Referring to your list of details, write a rough draft of your paragraph. Use time signals such as *first, then, after, next, while, during,* and *finally* to help connect details as you move from the beginning to the middle to the end of your narrative. Be sure to include not only what happened but also how you felt about what was going on.

REVISING: PEER REVIEW

Put your first draft away for a day or so. When you return to your paragraph, share it with a friend or classmate whose judgment you trust. Go over the following questions with your reader to make sure you have covered the four bases of effective writing:

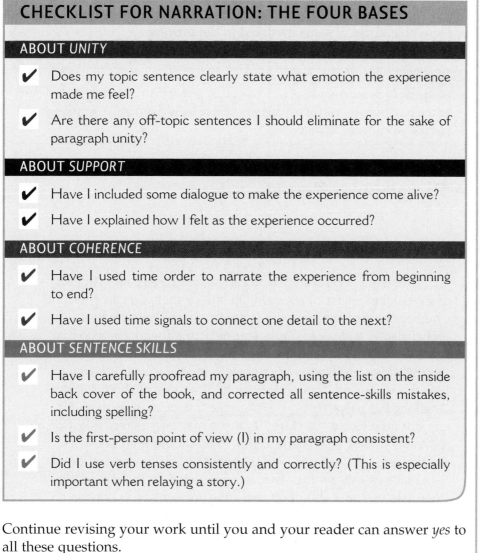

CHECKLIST FOR NARRATION: THE FOUR BASES

ABOUT *UNITY*

✔ Does my topic sentence clearly state what emotion the experience made me feel?

✔ Are there any off-topic sentences I should eliminate for the sake of paragraph unity?

ABOUT *SUPPORT*

✔ Have I included some dialogue to make the experience come alive?

✔ Have I explained how I felt as the experience occurred?

ABOUT *COHERENCE*

✔ Have I used time order to narrate the experience from beginning to end?

✔ Have I used time signals to connect one detail to the next?

ABOUT *SENTENCE SKILLS*

✔ Have I carefully proofread my paragraph, using the list on the inside back cover of the book, and corrected all sentence-skills mistakes, including spelling?

✔ Is the first-person point of view (I) in my paragraph consistent?

✔ Did I use verb tenses consistently and correctly? (This is especially important when relaying a story.)

Continue revising your work until you and your reader can answer *yes* to all these questions.

BEYOND THE CLASSROOM

Narration

Imagine that one of your oldest friends has to make a difficult decision of some kind. Narrate a relevant story from your own experience (or the experience of someone you know) that will help your friend carefully weigh the decision he or she must make. In your paragraph, include a comment or two about how your story relates to your friend's situation. Throughout, try to be helpful without being condescending. You can also be entertaining, as long as you are careful to stay sensitive to the problem at hand.

4. Process

Every day we perform many activities that are *processes*—that is, series of steps carried out in a definite order. Many of these processes are familiar and automatic: for example, tying shoelaces, changing bed linen, using a vending machine, and starting a car. We are thus seldom aware of the sequence of steps making up each activity. In other cases, such as when we are asked for directions to a particular place, or when we try to read and follow the directions for a new table game, we may be painfully conscious of the whole series of steps involved in the process.

> **TIP**   In process writing, you are often giving instruction to the reader, so the pronoun *you* can appropriately be used. As a general rule, though, do not use *you* in your writing.

A Paragraph to Consider

How to Harass an Instructor

¹There are several steps you can take to harass an instructor during a class. ²First of all, show up late so that you can interrupt the beginning of the instructor's presentation. ³Saunter in nonchalantly and try to find a seat next to a friend. ⁴In a normal tone of voice, speak some words of greeting to your friends as you sit down, and scrape your chair as loudly as possible while you make yourself comfortable in it. ⁵Then just sit there and do anything but pay attention. ⁶When the instructor sees that you are not involved in the class, he or she may pop a quick question, probably hoping to embarrass you. ⁷You should then say, in a loud voice, "I DON'T KNOW THE ANSWER." ⁸This declaration of ignorance will throw the instructor off guard. ⁹If the instructor then asks you why you don't know the answer, say, "I don't even know what page we're on" or "I thought the assignment was boring,

continued

so I didn't do it." [10]After the instructor calls on someone else, get up loudly from your seat, walk to the front of the classroom, and demand to be excused for an emergency visit to the washroom. [11]Stay there at least fifteen minutes and take your time coming back. [12]On your way back, find a vending machine and buy yourself a snack; this class is boring, so you deserve a pick-me-up. [13]If the instructor asks you where you've been when you reenter the room, simply ignore the question and go to your seat. [14]Flop into your chair, slouching back and extending your legs as far out as possible. [15]When the instructor informs you of the assignment that the class is working on, heave an exaggerated sigh and very slowly open up your book and start turning the pages. [16]About a half hour before class is over, begin to look at the clock every few minutes. [17]Ten minutes before dismissal time, start noisily packing up your books and papers. [18]Then get up and begin walking to the door a couple of minutes before the class is supposed to end. [19]The instructor will look at you and wonder whether it wouldn't have been better to go into business instead of education.

About Unity

1. Which sentence should be eliminated in the interest of paragraph unity? (*Write the sentence number here.*)

   _____

About Support

2. After which sentence in "How to Harass an Instructor" are supporting details (examples) needed?

   _____

About Coherence

3. Does this paragraph use time order or emphatic order?

   _____

QUESTIONS

Writing a Process Paragraph

Choose one of the following topics to write about in a process paragraph.

   How to feed a family on a budget

   How to break up with a boyfriend or girlfriend

   How to balance a checkbook

   How to change a car or bike tire

WRITING ASSIGNMENT

How to get rid of house or garden pests, such as mice, roaches, or wasps

How to play a simple game, such as checkers

How to parallel park

How to shorten a skirt or pants

How to meet new people, for either dating or friendship

How to plant a garden

How to get started on Facebook

How to fix a leaky faucet, a clogged drain, or the like

How to build a campfire or start a fire in a fireplace

How to study for an important exam

How to conduct a yard or garage sale

How to wash dishes efficiently, clean a bathroom, or do laundry

How to create the perfect online dating profile

PREWRITING

a. Begin by freewriting on your topic for ten minutes. Do not worry about spelling, grammar, organization, or other matters of form. Just write whatever comes into your head regarding the topic. Keep writing for more than ten minutes if ideas keep coming to you. This freewriting will give you a base of raw material to draw from during the next phase of your work on the paragraph. After freewriting, you should have a sense of whether there is enough material available for you to write a process paragraph about the topic. If so, continue as explained below. If there is not enough material, choose another topic and freewrite about *it* for ten minutes.

b. Write a clear, direct topic sentence stating the process you are going to describe. For instance, if you are going to describe a way to study for major exams, your topic sentence might be "My study-skills instructor has suggested a good way to study for major exams." Or you can state in your topic sentence the process and the number of steps involved: "My technique for building a campfire involves four main steps."

c. List all the steps you can think of that may be included in the process. At this point, don't worry about how each step fits or whether two steps overlap. Here, for example, is the list prepared by a student who is writing about how to sneak into the house at night.

Quiet on stairs

Come in after Dad's asleep

House is freezing at night

Bring key

Know which steps to avoid

Lift up front door

Late parties on Saturday night

Don't turn on bathroom light

Avoid squeaky spots on floor

Get into bed quietly

Undress quietly

d. Number your items in the order in which they occur; strike out items that do not fit in the list; add others that come to mind. The student writer did this step as follows:

~~Quiet on stairs~~

2   Come in after Dad's asleep

~~House is freezing at night~~

1   Bring key

5   Know which steps to avoid

3   Lift up front door

~~Late parties on Saturday night~~

6   Don't turn on bathroom light

4   Avoid squeaky spots on floor

8   Get into bed quietly

7   Undress quietly

e. Use your list as a guide to write the first draft of your paragraph. As you write, try to think of additional details that will support your opening sentence. Do not expect to finish your paragraph in one draft. After you complete your first rough draft, in fact, you should be ready to write a series of drafts as you work toward the goals of unity, support, and coherence.

REVISING: PEER REVIEW

After you have written the first draft of your paragraph, set it aside for a while if you can. Then read it out loud, either to yourself or (better yet) to a friend or classmate who will be honest with you about how it sounds. Reexamine your paragraph with these questions in mind to make sure you have covered the four bases of effective writing:

CHECKLIST FOR PROCESS: THE FOUR BASES

ABOUT *UNITY*

✔   An effective process composition describes a series of events in a way that is clear and easy to follow. Are the steps in your paragraph described in a clear, logical way?

ABOUT *SUPPORT*

✔   Does your paragraph explain every necessary step so that a reader could perform the task described?

ABOUT *COHERENCE*

✔   Have you used transitions such as *first, next, also, then, after, now, during,* and *finally* to make the paper move smoothly from one step to another?

ABOUT *SENTENCE SKILLS*

✔   Is the point of view consistent? For example, if you begin by writing "This is how I got rid of mice" (first person), do not switch to "You must buy the right traps" (second person). Write this paragraph either from the first-person point of view (using *I* and *we*) or from the second-person point of view (*you*)—do not jump back and forth between the two.

✔   Have you corrected any sentence-skills mistakes that you noticed while reading the paragraph out loud? Have you checked the composition for sentence skills, including spelling, as listed on the inside back cover of this book?

Continue revising your work until you and your reader can answer *yes* to all these questions.

Imagine that you have to train someone to take your place in any job you've held (or currently hold); if you have never held a job, you can train this person to take your place as a student. Write a process paragraph that describes what a day on the job entails. Break the day's activities down into steps, making sure to include what advance preparation your replacement might need.

BEYOND THE CLASSROOM

Process

5. Cause and Effect

What caused Pat to drop out of school? Why are soap operas so popular? Why does our football team do so poorly each year? How has retirement affected Dad? What effects does divorce have on children? Every day we ask such questions and look for answers. We realize that situations have causes and effects—good or bad. By examining causes and effects, we seek to understand and explain things.

A Paragraph to Consider

New Puppy in the House

[1]Buying a new puppy can have significant effects on a household. [2]For one thing, the puppy keeps the entire family awake for at least two solid weeks. [3]Every night when the puppy is placed in its box, it begins to howl, yip, and whine. [4]Even after the lights go out and the house quiets down, the puppy continues to moan. [5]A second effect is that the puppy tortures the family by destroying material possessions. [6]Every day something different is damaged. [7]Family members find chewed belts and shoes, gnawed table legs, and ripped sofa cushions leaking stuffing. [8]In addition, the puppy often misses the paper during the paper-training stage of life, thus making the house smell like the public restroom at a city bus station. [9]Maybe the most serious problem, though, is that the puppy causes family arguments. [10]Parents argue with children about who is supposed to feed and walk the dog. [11]Children argue about who gets to play with the puppy first. [12]Puppies are adorable, and no child can resist their charm. [13]Everyone argues about who left socks and shoes around for the puppy to find. [14]These continual arguments, along with the effects of sleeplessness and the loss of valued possessions, can really disrupt a household. [15]Only when the puppy gets a bit older does the household settle back to normal.

QUESTIONS

About Unity

1. Which sentence does not support the opening idea and should be omitted? (*Write the sentence number here.*)

    _____

About Support

2. How many effects of bringing a new puppy into the house are given in this paragraph?

    _____ one   _____ two   _____ three   _____ four

About Coherence

3. What words signal the effect that the author feels may be the most important?

    _____

Writing a Cause-and-Effect Paragraph

WRITING ASSIGNMENT

Choose one of the following three topic sentences and brief outlines. Each is made up of three supporting points (causes or effects). Your task is to turn the topic sentence and outline into a cause-and-effect paragraph.

Option 1
Topic sentence: There are several reasons why parenthood makes people more responsible.
(1) Ensure that children's needs are met (*cause*)
(2) Cannot think only of themselves (*cause*)
(3) Provide children with a better life (*cause*)

Option 2
Topic sentence: My divorce has changed my life in positive ways.
(1) Enrolled in college (*effect*)
(2) More quality time with children (*effect*)
(3) Began exercising regularly (*effect*)

Option 3
Topic sentence: Lack of sleep makes daily life more difficult.
(1) Difficulty focusing on homework (*cause*)
(2) Irritable all the time (*cause*)
(3) More prone to colds and the flu (*cause*)

PREWRITING

a. After you've chosen the option that appeals to you most, jot down all the details you can think of that might go under each of the supporting points. Use separate paper for your lists. Don't worry yet about whether you can use all the items—your goal is to generate more material than you need. Here, for example, are some of the details generated by the author of "New Puppy in the House" to back up her supporting points.

Topic sentence: Having a new puppy disrupts a household.

1. Keeps family awake
   a. Whines at night
   b. Howls
   c. Loss of sleep
2. Destroys possessions
   a. Chews belts and shoes
   b. Chews furniture
   c. Tears up toys it's supposed to fetch
3. Has accidents in house
   a. Misses paper
   b. Disgusting cleanup
   c. Makes house smell bad
4. Causes arguments
   a. Arguments about walking dog
   b. Arguments about feeding dog
   c. Arguments about who gets to play with dog
   d. Arguments about vet bills

b. Now go through the details you have generated and decide which are most effective. Strike out the ones you decide are not worth using. Do other details occur to you? If so, jot them down as well.

c. Now you are ready to write your paragraph. Begin the paragraph with the topic sentence you chose. Make sure to develop each of the supporting points from the outline into a complete sentence, and then back it up with the best of the details you have generated.

REVISING: PEER REVIEW

Review your paragraph with a friend or classmate. The two of you should keep these questions in mind to make sure you have covered the four bases of effective writing:

CHECKLIST FOR CAUSE AND EFFECT: THE FOUR BASES

ABOUT *UNITY*

✔ Have you begun the paragraph with the topic sentence provided?

✔ Are any sentences in your paragraph not directly relevant to this topic sentence?

ABOUT *SUPPORT*

✔ Is each supporting point stated in a complete sentence?

✔ Have you provided effective details to back up each supporting point?

ABOUT *COHERENCE*

✔ Have you used transitions such as *in addition*, *another thing*, and *also* to make the relationships between the sentences clear?

ABOUT *SENTENCE SKILLS*

✔ Have you avoided wordiness?

✔ Have you proofread the paragraph for sentence-skills errors, including spelling, as listed on the inside back cover of the book?

Continue revising your work until you and your reader can answer *yes* to all these questions.

BEYOND THE CLASSROOM

Cause and Effect

Imagine that you are a retail store manager and must write a letter to one of your employees. Not only is this person a poor salesperson but also he or she has a negative attitude and lacks leadership qualities. Write a paragraph that explains three ways in which this person has negatively impacted the company, and then write another paragraph in which you ask this person to help you understand the causes of his or her behavior and attitude.

6. Comparison or Contrast

Comparison and contrast are two everyday thought processes. When we *compare* two things, we show how they are similar; when we *contrast* two things, we show how they are different. We might compare or contrast two brand-name products (for example, Nike versus Adidas running shoes), two television shows, two instructors, two jobs, two friends, or two courses of action we could take in a given situation. The purpose of comparing and contrasting is to understand each of the two things more clearly and, at times, to make judgments about them.

There are two common methods, or formats, of development in a comparison or contrast paper. One format presents the details *one side at a time*. The other presents the details *point by point*.

Two Paragraphs to Consider

Read these sample paragraphs of comparison or contrast and then answer the questions that follow.

Two Views on Toys

¹Children and adults have very different preferences. ²First, there is the matter of taste. ³Adults pride themselves on taste, while children ignore the matter of taste in favor of things that are fun. ⁴Adults, especially grandparents, pick out tasteful toys that go unused, while children love the cheap playthings advertised on television. ⁵Second, of course, there is the matter of money. ⁶The new games on the market today are a case in point. ⁷Have you ever tried to lure a child away from some expensive game in order to get him or her to play with an old-fashioned game or toy? ⁸Finally, there is a difference between an adult's and a child's idea of what is educational. ⁹Adults, filled with memories of their own childhood, tend to be fond of the written word. ¹⁰Today's children, on the other hand, concentrate on anything electronic. ¹¹These things mean much more to them than to adults. ¹²Next holiday season, examine the toys that adults choose for children. ¹³Then look at the toys the children prefer. ¹⁴You will see the difference.

Mike and Helen

¹Mike and Helen, a married couple we know, look very much alike. ²They are both short, dark-haired, and slightly pudgy. ³Like his wife, Mike has a good sense of humor. ⁴Both Mike and Helen can be charming when they want to be, and they seem to handle small crises in a calm, cool way. ⁵A problem such as an overflowing washer, a stalled car, or a sick child is not a cause for panic; they seem to take such events in stride. ⁶In contrast to Helen, though, Mike tends to be disorganized. ⁷He is late for appointments and unable to keep important documents—bank records, receipts, and insurance papers—where he can find them. ⁸Also unlike Helen, Mike tends to hold a grudge. ⁹He is slow to forget a cruel remark, a careless joke, or an unfriendly slight. ¹⁰Another difference between these two is how they like to spend their free time; while Mike enjoys swimming, camping, and fishing, Helen prefers to stay inside and read or play chess.

QUESTIONS

About Unity

1. Which paragraph lacks a topic sentence?

_____

2. Which paragraph has a topic sentence that is too broad?

_____

About Support

3. Which paragraph contains almost no specific details?

_____

4. Which paragraph provides more complete support?

_____

About Coherence

5. What method of development (one side at a time or point by point) is used in "Mike and Helen"?

_____

6. What method of development is used in "Two Views in Toys"?

_____

RESPONDING TO IMAGES

Compare or contrast these two photographs of men cooking:

Writing a Comparison or Contrast Paragraph

Write a comparison or contrast paragraph on one of the following topics:

WRITING ASSIGNMENT

Two holidays

Two instructors

Two children

Two kinds of eaters

Two drivers

Two coworkers

Two members of a team (or two teams)

Two singers or groups

Two pets

Two parties

Two jobs

Two characters in the same movie or TV show

Two homes

Two neighborhoods

Two cartoon strips

Two cars

Two friends

Two crises

Two bosses or supervisors

Two magazines

PREWRITING

a. Choose your topic, the two subjects you will write about.

b. Decide whether your paragraph will *compare* the two subjects (discuss their similarities), *contrast* them (discuss their differences), or do both. If you choose to write about differences, you might write about how a musical group you enjoy differs from a musical group you dislike. You might discuss important differences between two employers you have had or between two neighborhoods you've lived in. You might contrast a job you've had in a car factory with a job you've had as a receptionist.

c. Write a direct topic sentence for your paragraph. Here's an example: "My job in a car-parts factory was very different from my job as a receptionist."

d. Come up with at least three strong points to support your topic sentence. If you are contrasting two jobs, for example, your points might be that they differed greatly (1) in their physical setting, (2) in the skills they required, and (3) in the people they brought you into contact with.

e. Use your topic sentence and supporting points to create a scratch outline for your paragraph. For the paragraph about jobs, the outline would look like this:

Topic sentence: My job in a car-parts factory was very different from my job as a receptionist.

1. The jobs differed in physical setting.

2. The jobs differed in the skills they required.

3. The jobs differed in the people they brought me into contact with.

f. Under each of your supporting points, jot down as many details as occur to you. Don't worry yet about whether the details all fit perfectly or whether you will be able to use them all. Your goal is to generate a wealth of material to draw on. An example:

Topic sentence: My job in a car-parts factory was very different from my job as a receptionist.

1. The jobs differed in physical setting.
    Factory loud and dirty
    Office clean and quiet
    Factory full of machines, hunks of metal, tools
    Office full of desks, files, computers
    Factory smelled of motor oil
    Office smelled of new carpet
    Windows in factory too high and grimy to look out of
    Office had clean windows onto street

2. The jobs differed in the skills and behavior they required.
    Factory required physical strength
    Office required mental activity
    Didn't need to be polite in factory
    Had to be polite in office
    Didn't need to think much for self in factory
    Constantly had to make decisions in office

3. The jobs differed in the people they brought me into contact with.
    In factory, worked with same crew every day
    In office, saw constant stream of new customers
    Most coworkers in factory had high school education or less
    Many coworkers and clients in office well educated
    Coworkers in factory spoke variety of languages
    Rarely heard anything but English in office

g. Decide which format you will use to develop your paragraph: one side at a time or point by point. Either is acceptable; it is up to you to decide which you prefer. The important thing is to be consistent: Whichever format you choose, be sure to use it throughout the entire paragraph.

h. Write the first draft of your paragraph.

REVISING: PEER REVIEW

Put your composition away for a day or so. You will return to it with a fresh perspective and a better ability to critique what you have written. Share your paragraph with a friend or fellow classmate. Together, read your paragraph with these questions in mind to make sure you have covered the four bases of effective writing:

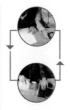

CHECKLIST FOR COMPARISON OR CONTRAST: THE FOUR BASES

ABOUT *UNITY*

✔ Does your topic sentence make it clear what two things you are comparing or contrasting?

✔ Do all sentences in the paragraph stay on topic?

ABOUT *SUPPORT*

✔ Have you compared or contrasted the subjects in at least three important ways?

✔ Have you provided specific details that effectively back up your supporting points?

ABOUT *COHERENCE*

✔ If you have chosen the point-by-point format, have you consistently discussed a point about one subject, then immediately discussed the same point about the other subject before moving on to the next point?

✔ If you have chosen the one-side-at-a-time format, have you discussed every point about one of your subjects, then discussed the same points *in the same order* about the second subjects?

✔ Have you used appropriate transitions, such as *first, in addition, also,* and *another way,* to help readers follow your train of thought?

ABOUT *SENTENCE SKILLS*

✔ Have you carefully proofread your paragraph, using the guidelines on the inside back cover of the book, and corrected all sentence-skills mistakes, including spelling?

Continue revising your work until you and your reader can answer *yes* to all these questions.

Imagine that a new club has opened in the building next to your house/
apartment/dorm. At first, you were thrilled—but then loud music and
screaming patrons started making it nearly impossible for you to study
or sleep. Seven days a week, the club stays open until 2:00 A.M.

1. Write a paragraph-long letter of complaint to the club owners,
    contrasting life before and after the club opened.

2. Write an e-mail on the same topic to one of your friends.

3. How do the two pieces of writing (for two different purposes/
    audiences) differ from each other? How are they similar?

7. Definition

In talking with other people, we sometimes offer informal definitions to
explain just what we mean by a particular term. Suppose, for example, we
say to a friend, "Karen can be so clingy." We might then expand on our
idea of "clingy" by saying, "You know, a clingy person needs to be with
someone every single minute. If Karen's best friend makes plans that don't
include her, she becomes hurt. And when she dates someone, she calls him
several times a day and gets upset if he even goes to the grocery store without her. She hangs on to people too tightly." In a written definition, we
make clear in a more complete and formal way our own personal understanding of a term. Such a definition typically starts with one meaning of a
term. The meaning is then illustrated with a series of examples or a story.

A Paragraph to Consider

Absent-Minded Professor

¹My English teacher is an absent-minded professor. ²For example,
when she lectures on a given subject one day, she forgets where
she left off and asks us to tell her the next day. ³Then there are our
papers. ⁴She gives us topics to write about and gives us a due date,
but when the due date comes around, we have to remind her that
they're due. ⁵Furthermore, it sometimes takes weeks before we get
our papers back. ⁶One time, I worked really hard on an assignment
on dolphins. ⁷These animals have always fascinated me. ⁸After I
turned it in, it took her a month to return it, and then the grade was
only a B. ⁹She had made no corrections, just a couple of check marks
on the margins. ¹⁰I felt so frustrated and powerless. ¹¹Some students
like having absent-minded professors because they do not have to
work as hard and feel that they're getting away with something. ¹²But
they're getting the short end of their education. ¹³Absent-minded
professors do not know how much harm they're doing to their
students, and it's just plain not fair to us.

About Unity

1. Which sentence in the "Absent-Minded Professor" is irrelevant to the unity of the paragraph and should be eliminated? (*Write the sentence number here.*)

   _____

About Support

2. Which four sentences provide extended examples for one of the supporting points in "Absent-Minded Professor"? (*Write the sentence numbers here.*)

   _____

About Coherence

3. What are the four transitions used within the "Absent-Minded Professor" paragraph?

   _____   _____   _____   _____

QUESTIONS

Writing a Definition Paragraph

Write a paragraph that defines the term *TV addict*. Base your paragraph on the topic sentence and three supporting points provided below.

> *Topic sentence:* Television addicts are people who will watch all the programs they can, for as long as they can, without doing anything else.
>
> (1) TV addicts, first of all, will watch anything on the tube, no matter how bad it is. . . .
>
> (2) In addition, addicts watch more hours of TV than normal people do. . . .
>
> (3) Finally, addicts feel that TV is more important than other people or any other activities that might be going on. . . .

WRITING ASSIGNMENT

PREWRITING

a. Generate as many examples as you can for each of the three qualities of a TV addict. You can do this by asking yourself the following questions:

   - What are some truly awful shows that I (or TV addicts I know) watch just because the television is turned on?

   - What are some examples of the large amounts of time that I (or TV addicts I know) watch television?

   - What are some examples of ways that I (or TV addicts I know) neglect people or give up activities in order to watch TV?

   Write down every answer you can think of for each question. At this point, don't worry about writing full sentences or even about grammar or spelling. Just get your thoughts down on paper.

DEFINE "GOOD."

RESPONDING TO IMAGES

Explain to someone who doesn't know what "good" means why this cartoon is funny.

b. Look over the list of examples you have generated. Select the strongest examples you have thought of. You should have at least two or three for each quality. If not, ask yourself the questions in step *a* again.

c. Write out the examples you will use, this time expressing them in full, grammatically correct sentences.

d. Start with the topic sentence and three points provided in the assignment. Fill in the examples you've generated to support each point and write a first draft of your paragraph.

REVISING: PEER REVIEW

Put your first draft away for a day or so. When you come back to it, reread it critically and ask a friend or classmate to read it as well. The two of you should keep these questions in mind to make sure you have covered the four bases of effective writing:

CHECKLIST FOR DEFINITION: THE FOUR BASES

ABOUT *UNITY*

✔ Have you used the topic sentence and the three supporting points that were provided?

✔ Does every sentence in the paragraph help define the term *TV addict?*

ABOUT *SUPPORT*

✔ Have you backed up each supporting point with at least two examples?

✔ Does each of your examples effectively illustrate the point that it backs up?

ABOUT *COHERENCE*

✔ Have you used appropriate transitional language (*another, in addition, for example*) to tie your thoughts together?

✔ Are all transitional words correctly used?

ABOUT *SENTENCE SKILLS*

✔ Have you carefully proofread your paragraph, using the guidelines on the inside back cover of the book, and corrected all sentence-skills mistakes, including spelling?

✔ Have you used a consistent point of view throughout the paragraph?

Continue revising your work until you and your reader can answer *yes* to all these questions.

Imagine that you are applying for a grant from your town or city government to build a community garden in an urban area or a community theater in a rural/suburban one. To make such an appeal effective, you will need to define *community;* such a definition will help you to show that the garden or theater will enhance the lives of everyone in this particular community. Use examples or one extended example to illustrate each of your general points.

BEYOND THE CLASSROOM

Definition

8. Division-Classification

If you were doing the laundry, you might begin by separating the clothing into piles. You would then put all the whites in one pile and all the colors in another. Or you might classify the laundry, not according to color, but according to fabric—putting all cottons in one pile, polyesters in another, and so on. *Classifying* is the process of taking many things and separating them into categories. We generally classify to better manage or understand many things. Librarians classify books into groups (novels, travel, health, etc.) to make them easier to find. A scientist sheds light on the world by classifying all living things into two main groups: animals and plants.

Dividing, in contrast, is taking one thing and breaking it down into parts. We often divide, or analyze, to better understand, teach, or evaluate something. For instance, a tinkerer might take apart a clock to see how it works; a science text might divide a tree into its parts to explain their functions. A music reviewer may analyze the elements of a band's performance—for example, the skill of the various players, rapport with the audience, selections, and so on.

In short, if you are classifying, you are sorting *numbers of things* into categories. If you are dividing, you are breaking *one thing* into parts. It all depends on your purpose—you might classify flowers into various types or divide a single flower into its parts.

Two Paragraphs to Consider

Types of E-Mail

[1]As more and more people take advantage of e-mailing, three categories of e-mail have emerged. [2]One category of e-mail is junk mail. [3]When most people sign on to their computers, they are greeted with a flood of get-rich-quick schemes, invitations to pornographic Web sites, and ads for a variety of unwanted products. [4]E-mail users quickly become good at hitting the "delete" button to get rid of this garbage. [5]The second category that clogs most people's electronic mailbox is forwarded mail, most of which also gets deleted without being read. [6]The third and best category of e-mail is genuine personal e-mail from genuine personal friends. [7]Getting such real, thoughtful e-mail can almost make up for the irritation of the other two categories.

Planning a Trip

[1]Designating a destination where the political and societal conditions are healthy and secure is the first and most important step in planning a trip. [2]Unstable governments very often lead to social unrest and violence. [3]Once settling on a general location, devising a budget is the next step. [4]The cost of living in some countries can be drastically higher than others. [5]When the destination is settled on, becoming familiar with the religious and cultural customs of the country is highly recommended. [6]What is accepted in the United States may be considered illegal or insulting in a foreign country. [7]For example, in Islamic countries, women are expected to cover their entire body and head. [8]In many instances, women wear veils across the face with a small slit positioned in front of the eyes. [9]Showing up in a tank top and shorts will very likely jeopardize one's sense of security and safety. [10]Now it is time to purchase an airline ticket and again, research is strongly advised in order to obtain the best possible deal. [11]Depending on one's idea of fun, planning an itinerary can be exceedingly complicated or relatively simple. [12]If lying on a lounge chair and sipping a cocktail by the water's edge is the desired activity, then planning the itinerary will be quite effortless. [13]But if a traveler is interested in involving himself or herself in some rigorous activities such as mountain climbing, scuba diving, or kayaking, planning the itinerary will probably require a lot more time. [14]Many people do not realize that there is in fact a lot of research involved in planning a trip. [15]These people should not be so careless, as they could expose themselves to extremely dangerous situations. [16]It is frustrating that so few people take research seriously.

QUESTIONS

About Unity

1. Which paragraph lacks a topic sentence?

   _____

2. Which sentence(s) in "Planning a Trip" should be eliminated in the interest of paragraph unity? (*Write the sentence number[s] here.*)

   _____

About Support

3. Which aspect of "Planning a Trip" lacks specific details?

   _____

4. After which sentence in "Types of E-Mail" are supporting details needed? (*Write the sentence number here.*)

   _____

About Coherence

5. Which paragraph uses emphatic order to organize its details?

_____

6. Which words in "Types of E-mail" signal the most important detail?

_____

Writing a Division-Classification Paragraph

Below are four options to develop into a classification paragraph. Each one presents a topic to classify into three categories. Choose one option to develop into a paragraph.

WRITING ASSIGNMENT

Option 1
Casino gambling
(1) Blackjack
(2) Poker
(3) Slot machine

Option 3
Home gym equipment
(1) Treadmill
(2) Elliptical machine
(3) Stationary bicycle

Option 2
Movies
(1) Action
(2) Comedy
(3) Horror

Option 4
House pets
(1) Dogs
(2) Cats
(3) Birds

PREWRITING

a. Begin by doing some freewriting on the topic you have chosen. For five or ten minutes, simply write down everything that comes into your head when you think about "casino gambling," "house pets," or whichever option you choose. Don't worry about grammar, spelling, or organization—just write.

b. Now that you've "loosened up your brain" a little, try asking yourself questions about the topic and writing down your answers. If you are writing about house pets, for instance, you might ask questions like these:

- What are some unique qualities for each kind of house pet?

- How do these house pets differ? How are they similar?

- What would dog owners say about their dogs? What would cat owners say about their cats? What would bird owners say about their birds?

Write down whatever answers occur to you for these and other questions. Again, do not worry at this stage about writing correctly. Instead, concentrate on getting down all the information you can think of that supports your three points.

c. Reread the material you have accumulated. If some of the details you have written make you think of even better ones, add them. Select the details that best support your three points. Number them in the order you will present them.

d. Restate your topic as a grammatically complete topic sentence. For example, if you're writing about home gym equipment, your topic sentence might be "Home gym equipment can be divided into three categories." Turn each of your three supporting points into a full sentence as well.

e. Using your topic sentence and three supporting sentences and adding the details you have generated, write the first draft of your paragraph.

REVISING: PEER REVIEW

Put your work away for a couple of days. Then reread it with a critical eye and have a friend or classmate read it as well. Ask your reader to give you honest feedback as the two of you answer the following questions.

CHECKLIST FOR DIVISION-CLASSIFICATION: THE FOUR BASES

ABOUT *UNITY*

✔ Does the paragraph include a complete topic sentence and three supporting points?

ABOUT *SUPPORT*

✔ Have you backed up each supporting point with strong, specific details?

ABOUT *COHERENCE*

✔ Does the paragraph successfully classify types of casino gambling, movies, home gym equipment, or house pets?

ABOUT *SENTENCE SKILLS*

✔ Have you carefully proofread the paragraph, using the list on the inside back cover of the book, and corrected all sentence-skills mistakes, including spelling?

✔ Have you used specific rather than general words?

Continue revising your work until you and your reader can answer *yes* to all these questions.

BEYOND THE CLASSROOM

Division-Classification

Imagine that you are a real estate agent and someone new to the area has asked you for suggestions about where to look for a home. Write a paragraph classifying local neighborhoods into three or more types. For each type, include an explanation with one or more examples.

9. Argument

Most of us know someone who enjoys a good argument. Such a person usually challenges any sweeping statement we might make. "Why do you say that?" he or she will ask. "Give your reasons." Our questioner then listens carefully as we cite our reasons, waiting to see if we really do have solid evidence to support our point of view. In an argument, the two parties each present their supporting evidence. The goal is to determine who has the more solid evidence to support his or her point of view. A questioner may make us feel a bit nervous, but we may also appreciate the way he or she makes us think through our opinions.

The ability to advance sound, compelling arguments is an important skill in everyday life. We can use argument to get an extension on a term paper, obtain a favor from a friend, or convince an employer that we are the right person for a job. Understanding persuasion based on clear, logical reasoning can also help us see through the sometimes faulty arguments advanced by advertisers, editors, politicians, and others who try to bring us over to their side.

A Paragraph to Consider

Living Alone

[1]Living alone is quite an experience. [2]People who live alone, for one thing, have to learn to do all kinds of tasks by themselves. [3]They must learn—even if they have had no experience—to change fuses, put up curtains and shades, temporarily dam an overflowing toilet, cook a meal, and defrost a refrigerator. [4]When there is no father, husband, mother, or wife to depend on, a person can't fall back on the excuse, "I don't know how to do that." [5]Those who live alone also need the strength to deal with people. [6]Alone, singles must face noisy neighbors, unresponsive landlords, dishonest repair people, and aggressive bill collectors. [7]Because there are no buffers between themselves and the outside world, people living alone have to handle every visitor—friendly or unfriendly—alone. [8]Finally, singles need a large dose of courage to cope with occasional panic and unavoidable loneliness. [9]That weird thump in the night is even more terrifying when there is no one in the next bed or the next room. [10]Frightening weather or unexpected bad news is doubly bad when the worry can't be shared. [11]Even when life is going well, little moments of sudden loneliness can send shivers through the heart. [12]Struggling through such bad times taps into reserves of courage that people may not have known they possessed. [13]Facing everyday tasks, confronting all types of people, and handling panic and loneliness can shape singles into brave, resourceful, and more independent people.

QUESTIONS

About Unity

1. The topic sentence in "Living Alone" is too broad. Circle the topic sentence that states accurately what the paragraph is about.

    a. Living alone can make one a better person.

    b. Living alone can create feelings of loneliness.

    c. Living alone should be avoided.

2. How many reasons are given to support the topic sentence in this paragraph?

    _____ one _____ two _____ three _____ four

About Coherence

3. What are the three main transition words in this paragraph?

    _____ _____ _____

Writing an Argument Paragraph

WRITING ASSIGNMENT

Develop an argument paragraph based on one of these statements:

Condoms should (*or* should not) be made available in schools.

_____ (*name a specific athlete*) is the athlete most worthy of admiration in his *or* her sport.

Television is one of the best (*or* worst) inventions of this century.

_____ make the best (*or* worst) pets.

Cigarette and alcohol advertising should (*or* should not) be banned.

Teenagers make poor parents.

_____ is one public figure today who can be considered a hero.

This college needs a better _____ (cafeteria *or* library *or* student center *or* grading policy *or* attendance policy).

PREWRITING

a. Make up brief outlines for any three of the preceding statements. Make sure you have three separate and distinct reasons for each statement. Below is an example of a brief outline for a paragraph making another point.

Large cities should outlaw passenger cars.
1. Cut down on smog and pollution
2. Cut down on noise
3. Make more room for pedestrians

b. Decide, perhaps through discussion with your instructor or classmates, which of your outlines is the most promising for development into a paragraph. Make sure your supporting points are logical by asking yourself in each case, "Does this item truly support my topic sentence?"

c. Do some prewriting. Prepare a list of all the details you can think of that might actually support your point. Don't limit yourself; include more details than you can actually use. Here, for example, are details generated by the writer of "Living Alone":

Deal with power failures	Noisy neighbors
Nasty landlords	Develop courage
Scary noises at night	Do all the cooking
Spiders	Home repairs
Bill collectors	Obscene phone calls
Frightening storms	Loneliness

d. Decide which details you will use to develop your paragraph. Number the details in the order in which you will present them. Because presenting the strongest reason last (emphatic order) is the most effective way to organize an argument paragraph, be sure to save your most powerful reason for last. Here is how the author of "Living Alone" made decisions about details:

1   Deal with power failures
4   Nasty landlords
7   Scary noises at night
    ~~Spiders~~
6   Bill collectors
8   Frightening storms
5   Noisy neighbors
10 Develop courage
2   Do all the cooking
3   Home repairs
    ~~Obscene phone calls~~
9   Loneliness

e. Write the first draft of your paragraph. As you write, develop each reason with specific details. For example, in "Living Alone," notice how the writer makes the experience of living alone come alive with phrases like "That weird thump in the night" or "little moments of sudden loneliness can send shivers through the heart."

REVISING: PEER REVIEW

Put your paragraph away for a day or so. Then, share your paragraph with a partner and refer to the following questions to make sure you have covered the four bases of effective writing:

CHECKLIST FOR ARGUMENT: THE FOUR BASES

ABOUT *UNITY*

✔ Imagine that your audience is a jury who will ultimately render a verdict on your argument. Have you presented a convincing case? If you were on the jury, would you both understand and be favorably impressed by this argument?

✔ Does every one of your supporting points help prove the argument stated in your topic sentence?

ABOUT *SUPPORT*

✔ Have you backed up your points of support with specific details?

✔ Have you appealed to your readers' senses with these details?

ABOUT *COHERENCE*

✔ Have you used emphatic order in your paragraph, saving the most important, strongest detail for last?

ABOUT *SENTENCE SKILLS*

✔ Have you used strong verbs (rather than *is* and *to be*) throughout?

✔ Have you written your argument in the active, rather than passive, voice? (see pages 249–250)

✔ Have you checked your paper for sentence-skills mistakes, including spelling?

Continue revising your work until you and your partner can answer *yes* to all these questions.

BEYOND THE CLASSROOM

Argument

Imagine that you have implemented a new procedure at work, one that will make your workplace more efficient. For example, if you work at a retail store, you may have reorganized the customer files by zip code rather than by last name. Write a one-paragraph memo to your supervisor explaining in detail why you chose to implement this procedure and why he or she would approve or endorse this change. Do your best to convince your supervisor that your idea brings more efficiency.

REFLECTIVE ACTIVITY

1. Reread two or three paragraphs you have written in response to the writing assignments in this chapter. Are these paragraphs unified? Do any contain off-target sentences?

2. Are the paragraphs coherent, or do you need to add transitions? Which ones?

3. Does each paragraph contain enough support?

EXPLORING WRITING ONLINE

Examine your college's home page and consider what patterns of development it uses—and for what purposes. In your response, consider some of the following questions: How does the home page describe and/or define your school, and does it serve to narrate your college's story? As a prospective student, what kind of first impression does this page (not the site as a whole) offer? How is it an *argument* or advertisement for you school? How does it use *classification* and/or *division* as organizing principles? Does the site seem easy to navigate? What might you, as a current student, use the site for?

RESPONDING TO IMAGES

The following images address the topic of same-sex marriage. Why do you think the photographs were taken? Consider issues of purpose and audience. What patterns of development are at work in each image? How might the reason a photograph is taken differ from how it is used in a textbook?

For additional materials on Chapter 4, visit www.mhhe.com/langan.

5

Moving from Paragraph to Essay

CHAPTER PREVIEW

What Is an Essay?

- Differences between an Essay and a Paragraph
- The Form of an Essay

Important Points about the Essay

- Introductory Paragraph
- Supporting Paragraphs
- Transitional Sentences
- Concluding Paragraph

Essays to Consider

Planning the Essay

- Outlining the Essay
- Form for Planning the Essay

Practice in Writing the Essay

- Understanding the Two Parts of a Thesis Statement
- Supporting the Thesis with Specific Evidence
- Identifying Introductions
- Revising an Essay for All Four Bases: Unity, Support, Coherence, and Sentence Skills

Essay Assignments

RESPONDING TO IMAGES

Italian artist Leonardo da Vinci focused on different aspects of the human form in Mona Lisa (pictured here). What can an artist learn about drawing the human form by focusing on one particular aspect of it, such as a hand?

What Is an Essay?

Differences between an Essay and a Paragraph

An essay is simply a paper composed of several paragraphs, rather than one paragraph. In an essay, subjects can and should be treated more fully than they would be in a single-paragraph paper.

The main idea or point developed in an essay is called the *thesis statement* or *thesis sentence* (rather than, as in a paragraph, the *topic sentence*). The thesis statement appears in the introductory paragraph, and it is then developed in the supporting paragraphs that follow. A short concluding paragraph closes the essay.

The Form of an Essay

The following diagram shows the form of an essay.

Introductory Paragraph

> Introduction
> Thesis statement
> Plan of development:
> Points 1, 2, 3

The *introduction* attracts the reader's interest.

The *thesis statement* (or *thesis sentence*) states the main idea advanced in the paper.

The *plan of development* is a list of points that support the thesis. The points are presented in the order in which they will be developed in the paper.

First Supporting Paragraph

> Topic sentence (point 1)
> Specific evidence

The *topic sentence* advances the first supporting point for the thesis, and the *specific evidence* in the rest of the paragraph develops that first point.

Second Supporting Paragraph

> Topic sentence (point 2)
> Specific evidence

The *topic sentence* advances the second supporting point for the thesis, and the *specific evidence* in the rest of the paragraph develops that second point.

Third Supporting Paragraph

> Topic sentence (point 3)
> Specific evidence

The *topic sentence* advances the third supporting point for the thesis, and the *specific evidence* in the rest of the paragraph develops that third point.

Concluding Paragraph

> Summary, Conclusion, or both

A *summary* is a brief restatement of the thesis and its main points. A *conclusion* is a final thought or two stemming from the subject of the paper.

A Model Essay

Mike, the writer of the paragraph on working in a diner and truck stop (page 8), later decided to develop his subject more fully. Here is the essay that resulted.

Introductory paragraph

First supporting paragraph

Second supporting paragraph

Third supporting paragraph

Concluding paragraph

My Job at the Crescent Falls Diner and Truck Stop

[1]In the course of working my way through school, I have taken many jobs I would rather forget. [2]I have spent nine hours a day lifting heavy automobile and truck batteries off the end of an assembly belt. [3]I have risked the loss of eyes and fingers working a punch press in a textile factory. [4]I have served as a ward aide in a mental hospital, helping care for brain-damaged men who would break into violent fits at unexpected moments. [5]But none of these jobs was as dreadful as my job at the Crescent Falls Diner and Truck Stop. [6]The work was physically hard; the pay was poor; and, most of all, the working conditions were dismal.

[7]First, the job made enormous demands on my strength and energy. [8]For ten hours, I waited on tables, carried heavy trays of food and dirty dishes, cleaned bathrooms, and unloaded heavy cartons from delivery trucks. [9]The trays weighed from twenty to fifty pounds. [10]The cartons of food and restaurant supplies could weigh as much as 75 pounds, and I sometimes unloaded full truck trailers by myself.

[11]I would not have minded the difficulty of the work so much if the pay had not been so poor. [12]I was paid minimum wage, plus tips. [13]At first, I thought this would be fine, but then I learned that I would have to share my tips with the kitchen staff and cashiers. [14]The first night, I made over $50 in tips, but I brought home less than $8. [15]To make enough money for the following semester's college tuition, I had to work about sixty hours per week. [16]If I worked overtime, I was paid my regular hourly salary. [17]There was no overtime bonus.

[18]But even more than the low pay, what upset me about my job was the working conditions. [19]Sometimes, I had to wash dishes in a corner of the kitchen that was extremely hot and steamy. [20]Once, when unloading a large delivery truck, I strained my back and was laid up for about a week—without pay, of course! [21]Finally, the manager was a tyrant. [22]I never seemed to get my orders out quickly enough for him, nor could I ever clean the tables to his satisfaction. [23]He disliked and envied college students, and he went out of his way to favor other employees over me. [24]For example, while some of my co-workers got off for holidays, I was expected to work. [25]When I asked for two days off to attend a wedding in Georgia, he threatened to fire me. [26]He made negative comments about the way I combed my hair and the clothes I wore. [27]Once he even made a slur about my race.

[28]I stayed on the job for five months, all the while hating the difficulty of the work, the low pay, and the conditions under which I worked. [29]By the time I quit, I was determined never to do such degrading work again.

Important Points about the Essay

Introductory Paragraph

An introductory paragraph has certain purposes or functions and can be constructed using various methods.

Purposes of the Introduction

An introductory paragraph should do three things:

1. Attract the reader's *interest.* Using one of the suggested methods of introduction described under "Common Methods of Introduction" can help draw the reader into your paper.

2. Present a *thesis sentence*—a clear, direct statement of the central idea that you will develop in your paper. The thesis statement, like a topic sentence, should have a keyword or keywords reflecting your attitude about the subject. For example, in the essay on the Crescent Diner and Truck Stop job, the keyword is *dreadful.*

3. Indicate a *plan of development*—a preview of the major points that will support your thesis statement, listed in the order in which they will be presented. In some cases, the thesis statement and plan of development may appear in the same sentence. In other cases, the plan of development may be omitted.

Introductory Paragraphs ACTIVITY 1

1. In "My Job at the Crescent Falls Diner and Truck Stop," which sentences are used to attract the reader's interest?

   _____ sentences 1 to 3 _____ 1 to 4 _____ 1 to 5

2. The thesis in "My Job at the Crescent Falls Diner and Truck Stop" is presented in

   _____ sentence 4 _____ sentence 5 _____ sentence 6

3. Is the thesis followed by a plan of development?

   _____ Yes _____ No

4. Which words in the plan of development announce the three major supporting points in the essay? Write them below.

   a. _____

   b. _____

   c. _____

Common Methods of Introduction

Four common methods of introducing an essay are as follows:

a. Begin with a broad statement and narrow it down to your thesis statement.

b. Present an idea or situation that is the opposite of the one you will develop.

c. Tell a brief story.

d. Ask one or more questions.

| **ACTIVITY 2** | **Identifying Methods of Introduction** |

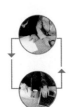

Following are four introductions. In the space provided, write the letter of the method of introduction used in each case. You may work with a partner to complete this activity.

_____ 1. Last week I was in the kitchen preparing dinner when I heard my nine-year-old daughter shriek from behind the computer. I was so startled that I dropped the knife onto the floor. As I ran to where she was doing her homework, she looked up, obviously stunned, and uttered, "That's *too* gross, Mom!" When I looked at the screen, I too was shocked to find an image that was clearly pornographic. Even though I thought I carefully monitored how my children used the computer, I did not realize that one wrong click could bring them to one of the million "adult" sites on the Internet. As a concerned parent, I urge all parents to install software on their home computers that blocks access to porno-graphic Web sites.

_____ 2. We Americans love our fast food. Instead of picking up groceries on the way home, we pick up a bucket of crispy fried chicken and a side of mashed potatoes and gravy. Instead of making a sandwich on whole-grain bread, we order a three-topping pizza with extra cheese. If fast food were nutritious, there would not be a problem, but most of the fast food we love is loaded with too much fat, sodium, and sugar. The sad reality is that at least a third of all Americans are battling obesity, and fast food is a leading culprit. If we prepare our meals at home, we can control the food we eat. We Americans, therefore, should say no to fast food and yes to home-cooked meals.

_____ 3. Most college students are hard working. They regu-larly attend classes and labs, they diligently take notes and ask questions, and they do their homework and study for exams. Even if a class is boring or an instructor is annoying, they still make an effort to learn. After all, these students are paying for their education. Some students, however, think that they are still in high school and carry over the mentality that "getting by" is good enough. Instructors should be able to dis-enroll slacker students—those who skip classes, borrow lecture notes, use paper mills, and cheat on exams—because they are taking up valuable seats that could be occupied by those students who truly want to learn.

_____ 4. What are your vices? Do you need your cigarettes even though you know that smoking causes lung cancer? Do you have one too many "cold ones" after a long day of work even though you know that you shouldn't? Do you find yourself lying even though you know that "honesty is the best policy"? Do you gamble? Do you do drugs? Have you cheated on someone? Most of us have bad habits that we know we should stop doing but don't until something terrible happens.

Supporting Paragraphs

Most essays have three supporting points, developed in three separate paragraphs. (Some essays will have two supporting points; others will have four or more.) Each of the supporting paragraphs should begin with a topic sentence that states the point to be detailed in that paragraph. Just as the thesis provides a focus for the entire essay, topic sentences provide a focus for each supporting paragraph.

Supporting Paragraphs	ACTIVITY 3

1. What is the topic sentence for the first supporting paragraph of "My Job at the Crescent Falls Diner and Truck Stop"? (*Write the sentence number here.*) _____

2. What is the topic sentence for the second supporting paragraph? _____

3. What is the topic sentence for the third supporting paragraph? _____

Transitional Sentences

In paragraphs, transitions and other connective devices (pages 67–73) are used to help link sentences. Similarly, in an essay, *transitional sentences* are used to help tie the supporting paragraphs together. Such transitional sentences usually occur near the end of one paragraph or the beginning of the next.

In "My Job at the Crescent Falls Diner and Truck Stop," the first transitional sentence is

> I would not have minded the difficulty of the work so much if the pay had not been so poor.

In this sentence, the keyword *difficulty* reminds us of the point of the first supporting paragraph, while *pay* tells us the point to be developed in the second supporting paragraph.

ACTIVITY 4	**Transitional Sentences**

Here is the other transitional sentence in "My Job at the Crescent Falls Diner and Truck Stop":

> But even more than the low pay, what upset me about my job was the working conditions.

> *Complete the following statement:* In the preceding sentence, the key-words _____ echo the point of the second supporting paragraph, and the keywords _____ announce the topic of the third supporting paragraph.

Concluding Paragraph

The concluding paragraph often summarizes the essay by briefly restating the thesis and, at times, the main supporting points. Also, the conclusion brings the paper to a natural and graceful end, sometimes leaving the reader with a final thought on the subject.

ACTIVITY 5	**The Concluding Paragraph**

1. Which sentence in the concluding paragraph of "My Job at the Crescent Falls Diner and Truck Stop" restates the thesis and supporting points of the essay? _____

2. Which sentence contains the concluding thought of the essay? _____

Essays to Consider

Read the following two student essays and then answer the questions that follow.

Definition of a Football Fan

[1]What is a football fan? [2]The word "fan" is an abbreviation of "fanatic," meaning "an insane or crazy person." [3]In the case of football fans, the term is appropriate. [4]They behave insanely, they are insane about the past, and they are insanely loyal.

[5]First of all, football fans just plain behave insanely. [6]They wear their official team T-shirts and warm-up jackets to the mall, the supermarket, the classroom, and even—if they can get away with it—to work. [7]If the team offers a giveaway item, the fans rush to the stadium to claim the hat or sports bag or water bottle that is being handed out that day. [8]Even the fact that fans spend the coldest months of

---

continued

pauses "because of the enormity of the knife descending and cutting into living flesh, because of the unbearable blood," and the pig escapes. ⁹Three chapters later, however, Jack leads some boys on a successful hunt. ¹⁰He returns triumphantly with a freshly killed pig and reports excitedly to the others, "I cut the pig's throat." ¹¹Yet Jack twitches as he says this, and he wipes his bloody hands on his shorts as if eager to remove the stains. ¹²There is still some civilization left in him.

¹³After the initial act of killing the pig, Jack's refusal to cooperate with Ralph shows us that this civilized part is rapidly disappearing. ¹⁴With no adults around, Ralph has made some rules. ¹⁵One is that a signal fire must be kept burning. ¹⁶But Jack tempts the boys watching the fire to go hunting, and the fire goes out. ¹⁷Another rule is that at a meeting, only the person holding a special seashell has the right to speak. ¹⁸In Chapter 5, another boy is speaking when Jack rudely tells him to shut up. ¹⁹Ralph accuses Jack of breaking the rules. ²⁰Jack shouts: "Bollocks to the rules! We're strong—we hunt! If there's a beast, we'll hunt it down! We'll close in and beat and beat and beat—!" ²¹He gives a "wild whoop" and leaps off the platform, throwing the meeting into chaos. ²²Jack is now much more savage than civilized.

²³The most obvious proof of Jack's corruption comes in Chapter 8, when he establishes his own murderous society. ²⁴Insisting that Ralph is not a "proper chief" because he does not hunt, Jack asks for a new election. ²⁵After he again loses, Jack announces, "I'm going off by myself. . . . Anyone who wants to hunt when I do can come too." ²⁶Eventually, nearly all the boys join Jack's "tribe." ²⁷Following his example, they paint their faces like savages, sacrifice to "the beast," brutally murder two of their schoolmates, and nearly succeed in killing Ralph as well. ²⁸Jack has now become completely savage—and so have the others.

²⁹Through Jack Merridew, then, Golding shows how easily moral laws can be forgotten. ³⁰Freed from grown-ups and their rules, Jack learns to kill living things, defy authority, and lead a tribe of murdering savages. ³¹Jack's example is a frightening reminder of humanity's potential for evil. ³²The "beast" the boys try to hunt and kill is actually within every human being.

QUESTIONS

1. In which essay does the thesis statement appear in the last sentence of the introductory paragraph?

_____

2. In the essay on <u>Lord of the Flies</u>, which sentence of the introductory

   paragraph contains the plan of development? _____

3. Which method of introduction is used in "Definition of a Football Fan"?

   a. General to narrow   c. Incident or story

   b. Stating importance of topic   d. One or more questions

the year huddled on icy metal benches in places like Chicago proves that fans behave insanely. [9]When they go to a game, which they do as often as possible, they also decorate their bodies. [10]True football fans not only put on their team jackets and grab their pennants, but they also paint their heads to look like helmets. [11]At the game, these fans devote enormous energy to trying to get a "wave" going.

[12]In addition, football fans are insanely fascinated by the past. [13]They talk about William "Refrigerator" Perry's 1985 Super Bowl touchdown as though it had happened last week. [14]They describe the "Fog Bowl" as if dense fog blanketed yesterday's game, not 1988's playoff match between the Philadelphia Eagles and the Chicago Bears. [15]They excitedly discuss John Elway's final game before retiring—when he won the 1999 Super Bowl and received MVP honors—as if it were current news. [16]If you can't manage to get excited about such ancient history, they look at you as though you were the insane one.

[17]Most of all, football fans are insanely loyal to the team of their choice, often dangerously so. [18]Should their beloved team lose three in a row, fans may begin to react negatively as a way to hide their broken hearts. [19]They still obsessively watch each game and spend the entire day afterward listening to the postgame commentary on TV. [20]Furthermore, this intense loyalty makes fans dangerous. [21]To anyone who dares to say to a loyal fan that another team has better players or coaches, or God forbid, to anyone wandering near the home cheering section wearing the jacket of the opposing team, physical injuries such as bloody noses, black eyes, and broken bones are real possibilities.

[22]From February through August, football fans act like any other human beings. [23]They pay their taxes, take out the garbage, and complain about the high cost of living. [24]However, when September rolls around, the team's colors are displayed, the sports record books come off the shelves, and the devotion returns. [25]For the true football fan, another season of insanity has begun.

An Interpretation of Lord of the Flies

[1]Modern history has shown us the evil that exists in human beings. [2]Assassinations are common, governments use torture to discourage dissent, and six million Jews were exterminated during World War II. [3]In Lord of the Flies, William Golding describes a group of schoolboys shipwrecked on an island with no authority figures to control their behavior. [4]One of the boys soon yields to dark forces within himself, and his corruption symbolizes the evil in all of us. [5]First, Jack Merridew kills a living creature; then, he rebels against the group leader; and finally, he seizes power and sets up his own murderous society.

[6]The first stage in Jack's downfall is his killing of a living creature. [7]In Chapter 1, Jack aims at a pig but is unable to kill. [8]His upraised arm

continued

Important Points about the Essay

Introductory Paragraph

An introductory paragraph has certain purposes or functions and can be constructed using various methods.

Purposes of the Introduction

An introductory paragraph should do three things:

1. Attract the reader's *interest.* Using one of the suggested methods of introduction described under "Common Methods of Introduction" can help draw the reader into your paper.

2. Present a *thesis sentence*—a clear, direct statement of the central idea that you will develop in your paper. The thesis statement, like a topic sentence, should have a keyword or keywords reflecting your attitude about the subject. For example, in the essay on the Crescent Diner and Truck Stop job, the keyword is *dreadful.*

3. Indicate a *plan of development*—a preview of the major points that will support your thesis statement, listed in the order in which they will be presented. In some cases, the thesis statement and plan of development may appear in the same sentence. In other cases, the plan of development may be omitted.

Introductory Paragraphs	ACTIVITY 1

1. In "My Job at the Crescent Falls Diner and Truck Stop," which sentences are used to attract the reader's interest?

   _____ sentences 1 to 3   _____ 1 to 4   _____ 1 to 5

2. The thesis in "My Job at the Crescent Falls Diner and Truck Stop" is presented in

   _____ sentence 4   _____ sentence 5   _____ sentence 6

3. Is the thesis followed by a plan of development?

   _____ Yes   _____ No

4. Which words in the plan of development announce the three major supporting points in the essay? Write them below.

   a. _____

   b. _____

   c. _____

Common Methods of Introduction

Four common methods of introducing an essay are as follows:

a. Begin with a broad statement and narrow it down to your thesis statement.

4. Complete the following outline of "Definition of a Football Fan":

    a. _____

    b. _____

    c. _____

5. How does the essay "An Interpretation of <u>Lord of the Flies</u>" connect the first supporting paragraph with the second one?

    _____

6. *Complete the following statement:* Emphatic order is shown in the last supporting paragraph of "Definition of a Football Fan" with the words *most of all;* and in the last supporting paragraph of "An Interpretation of <u>Lord of the Flies</u>" with the words _____

7. Which essay uses time order as well as emphatic order to organize its three supporting paragraphs? _____

8. List four major transitions used in the supporting paragraphs of "An Interpretation of <u>Lord of the Flies</u>."

    a. _____   c. _____

    b. _____   d. _____

Planning the Essay
Outlining the Essay

When you write an essay, planning is crucial for success. You should plan your essay by outlining in two ways:

1. Prepare a scratch outline. This should consist of a short statement of the thesis followed by the main supporting points for the thesis. Here is Mike's scratch outline for his essay on the diner and truck stop:

> *Working at the Crescent Falls Diner and Truck Stop was my worst job.*
> 1. *Hard work*
> 2. *Poor pay*
> 3. *Bad working conditions*

Do not underestimate the value of this initial outline—or the work involved in achieving it. Be prepared to do a good deal of plain hard thinking at this first and most important stage of your paper.

2. Prepare a more detailed outline. The outline form that follows will serve as a guide. Your instructor may ask you to submit a copy of this form either before you actually write an essay or along with your finished essay.

Form for Planning the Essay

To write an effective essay, use a form such as the one that follows.

Opening remarks

Thesis statement _____ _____ _____

_____

Plan of development

Topic sentence 1 _____

_____

Specific supporting evidence

Topic sentence 2 _____

_____

Specific supporting evidence

Topic sentence 3 _____

_____

Specific supporting evidence

Summary, closing remarks, or both

Practice in Writing the Essay

In this section, you will expand and strengthen your understanding of the essay form as you work through the following activities.

Understanding the Two Parts of a Thesis Statement

In this chapter, you have learned that effective essays center on a thesis, or main point, that a writer wishes to express. This central idea is usually presented as a *thesis statement* in an essay's introductory paragraph.

A good thesis statement does two things. First, it tells readers an essay's *topic*. Second, it presents the *writer's attitude, opinion, idea,* or *point* about that topic. For example, look at the following thesis statement:

Celebrities are often poor role models.

In this thesis statement, the topic is *celebrities;* the writer's main point is that *celebrities are often poor role models.*

Topics and Main Points	**ACTIVITY 6**

For each thesis statement, single-underline the topic and double-underline the main point that the writer wishes to express about it.

1. My roommate Chang-Yoon helped me overcome prejudice.

2. Raising a family as a single parent can actually have certain benefits.

3. Being the eldest child has its own rewards.

4. Those who want to quit smoking should pledge to do so, throw away all their cigarettes, and ask their friends and family to support their brave efforts.

5. Internet advertisers use several media-savvy techniques to interact directly with online customers.

6. Jealousy often results from lack of self-confidence, lack of self-fulfillment, and lack of trust.

7. Parents should teach their children at an early age how to protect themselves from online predators.

8. My sales techniques benefitted greatly from a weekend seminar on customer needs, customer relationships, and customer negotiation.

9. Adults should feel free to engage in fun activities that they enjoyed as children.

10. Teachers should take certain steps to communicate more openly with their students.

Supporting the Thesis with Specific Evidence

The first essential step in writing a successful essay is to form a clearly stated thesis. The second basic step is to support the thesis with specific reasons or details.

To ensure that your essay will have adequate support, you may find an informal outline very helpful. Write down a brief version of your thesis idea, and then work out and jot down the three points that will support your thesis.

Here is the scratch outline that was prepared for one essay:

> The college cafeteria is poorly managed.
>
> The checkout lines are always long.
>
> The floor and tables are often dirty.
>
> Food choices are often limited.

A scratch outline like the previous one looks simple, but developing it often requires a good deal of careful thinking. The time spent on developing a logical outline is invaluable, though. Once you have planned the steps that logically support your thesis, you will be in an excellent position to go on to write an effective essay.

| ACTIVITY 7 | **Using Specific Evidence** |

Following are five informal outlines in which two points (*a* and *b*) are already provided. Complete each outline by adding a third logical supporting point (*c*).

1. Success in college can be attributed to several reasons.
   a. Regularly attend classes
   b. Devote enough time to studying
   c. _____

2. *MySpace.com* is an important part of my life.
   a. Keep in touch with friends and family
   b. Share life's ups and downs
   c. _____

3. My "significant other" has three qualities I admire.
   a. Sense of humor
   b. Charming personality
   c. _____

4. A break-up is always filled with mixed feelings.
   a. Anger
   b. Sadness
   c. _____

5. Being promoted to shift manager was a mistake.
   a. Difficult to supervise employees who still see you as their equal
   b. Difficult to monitor employees who steal from the company
   c. _____

Identifying Introductions

The following box lists the six common methods for introducing an essay that are discussed in this chapter.

1. Broad statement	4. Incident or story
2. Contrast	5. Question
3. Relevance	6. Quotation

Methods of Introduction	ACTIVITY 8

Review the methods of introduction on pages 129–131 with a partner. Next, refer to the box preceding and read the following six introductory paragraphs. Together, in the space provided, write the number of the kind of introduction used in each paragraph. Each kind of introduction is used once.

Paragraph A _____

Is bullying a natural, unavoidable part of growing up? Is it something that everyone has to endure as a victim, practice as a bully, or tolerate as a bystander? Does bullying leave deep scars on its victims, or is it fairly harmless? Does being a bully indicate some deep-rooted problems, or is it not a big deal? These and other questions need to be looked at as we consider the three forms of bullying: physical, verbal, and social.

Paragraph B _____

In a perfect school, students would treat each other with affection and respect. Differences would be tolerated, and even welcomed. Kids would become more popular by being kind and supportive. Students would go out of their way to make sure one another felt happy and comfortable. But most schools are not perfect. Instead of being places of respect and tolerance, they are places where the hateful act of bullying is widespread.

Paragraph C _____

Students have to deal with all kinds of problems in schools. There are the problems created by difficult classes, by too much homework, or by personality conflicts with teachers. There are problems with scheduling the classes you need and still getting some of the ones you want. There are problems with bad cafeteria food, grouchy principals, or overcrowded classrooms. But one of the most difficult problems of all has to do with a terrible situation that exists in most schools: bullying.

Paragraph D _____

Eric, a new boy at school, was shy and physically small. He quickly became a victim of bullies. Kids would wait after school, pull out his shirt, and punch and shove him around. He was called such names as "Mouse Boy" and "Jerk Boy." When he sat down during lunch hour, others would leave his table. In gym games he was never thrown the ball, as if he didn't exist. Then one day he came to school with a gun. When the police were called, he told them he just couldn't take it anymore. Bullying had hurt him badly, just as it hurts many other students. Every member of a school community should be aware of bullying and the three hateful forms that it takes: physical, verbal, and social bullying.

Paragraph E _____

A British prime minister once said, "Courage is fire, and bullying is smoke." If that is true, there is a lot of "smoke" present in most schools today. Bullying in schools is a huge problem that hurts both its victims and the people who practice it. Physical, verbal, and social bullying are all harmful in their own ways.

Paragraph F _____

A pair of students bring guns and homemade bombs to school, killing a number of their fellow students and teachers before taking their own lives. A young man hangs himself on Sunday evening rather than attend school the following morning. A junior high school girl is admitted to the emergency room after cutting her wrists. What do all these horrible reports have to do with each other? All were reportedly caused by a terrible practice that is common in schools: bullying.

Revising an Essay for All Four Bases: Unity, Support, Coherence, and Sentence Skills

You know from your work on paragraphs that there are four bases a paper must cover to be effective. In the following activity, you will evaluate and revise an essay in terms of all four bases: *unity, support, coherence,* and *sentence skills.*

ACTIVITY 9	**Revising an Essay**

Comments follow each supporting paragraph and the concluding paragraph. Circle the letter of the *one* statement that applies in each case.

Paragraph 1: Introduction

A Group of People Who Should Be Helped

One day walking to class, I ran into a homeless man. He was dirty and disheveled. It looked and smelled like he hadn't bathed in days. My college is located downtown near a homeless shelter, and I guess the homeless like to stay close to the facility. He asked me for some change. At first I thought about how much pocket money I had, then quickly I thought about a comment I had heard on the news or in some magazine. It was about how some homeless ask for money so they can purchase drugs. So I offered to buy him a breakfast combo at the nearby fast-food place. I still remember what he told me: "Man, I just want some money. You gonna give me some or not?" I realized then he did not want my money for food, but for alcohol or drugs. That incident made me think about how much help these people need. A group of people that I believe should be helped is the homeless.

Paragraph 2: First Supporting Paragraph

> Many homeless men are veterans of the United States. If we help them get back on their feet by providing them shelters and veterans' assistance, they would be able to become productive citizens once again. Many require medical attention that they can receive free through the local VA hospital. They can receive their monthly stipends from the government, so they can take care of their daily needs, like food and transportation. The VA hospitals and clinics can provide them with the necessary drug rehabilitation program that would allow them to take back their lives and no longer live on the streets begging for money to support their habits.

   a. Paragraph 2 contains an irrelevant sentence.
   b. Paragraph 2 lacks transition words.
   c. Paragraph 2 lacks supporting details at one key spot.
   d. Paragraph 2 contains a fragment and a run-on.

Paragraph 3: Second Supporting Paragraph

> Another reason the homeless should be helped is that many homeless women are mothers too. These homeless mothers with children should be able to live in a safe and clean shelter while their children attend school. They should be provided with job training courses and also get any social service resource available from the local government. Often, these women can qualify for housing assistance, food stamps, and other free services. The only thing they need is to be steered in the right direction. This is important, for they are the role models for their children, and providing a stable environment for them is part of the American dream.

   a. Paragraph 3 contains an irrelevant sentence.
   b. Paragraph 3 lacks transition words.
   c. Paragraph 3 lacks supporting details at one key spot.
   d. Paragraph 3 contains a fragment and a run-on.

Paragraph 4: Third Supporting Paragraph

> Finally, the most important reason why we should help the homeless is that they are living in the United States of America. We are the richest country in the world, and we should be able to provide for individuals when they can't provide for themselves. We spend countless dollars on objects like cars, houses, pets, and clothing. The communities in which they live should have volunteer efforts like food and clothing drives to aid those in need.

a. Paragraph 4 contains an irrelevant sentence.

b. Paragraph 4 lacks transition words.

c. Paragraph 4 lacks supporting details at one key spot.

d. Paragraph 4 contains a fragment and a run-on.

Paragraph 5: Concluding Paragraph

> Therefore, there are many reasons why a group of people I believe should be helped is the homeless. If we all make an effort to care for one another as a community. Help each other the best way we can, we can eliminate or ease some of the social ills in our communities.

a. Paragraph 5 contains an irrelevant sentence.

b. Paragraph 5 lacks transition words.

c. Paragraph 5 lacks supporting details at one key spot.

d. Paragraph 5 contains a fragment and a run-on.

Essay Assignments

WRITING ASSIGNMENT 1

Balancing School, Work, and Family Demands

Many college students struggle to balance school, work, and family. Write an essay about how you are able to balance the many demands in your life. In your introduction, you might begin with a brief story about a particular incident that illustrates your roles as a student, an employee, a spouse, a parent, a mentor, and/or a community member. End your introductory paragraph with your thesis statement and plan of development.

Here are some thesis statements that may help you think about and develop your own essay.

Thesis statement: Time management is the key to balancing my life as a college student, a single mom, and a full-time pharmacy technician.

(A *supporting* paragraph on managing your time as a college student, for example, might focus on the fact that you use a personal organizer and Post-it notes to keep track of your due dates.)

Thesis statement: The only way that I can juggle school, a girlfriend, and coaching is by taking good care of my health.

(A *supporting* paragraph on taking care of your health might explain how you and your girlfriend work out together at the gym and then cook a healthy—and romantic—meal together at home afterward.)

Thesis statement: I learned the hard way that I need at least seven hours of sleep each night if want to be a student on the dean's list, a loving parent to my three-year-old son, and a caregiver for my aging dad.

(A *supporting* paragraph on the need for adequate sleep could begin with this topic sentence: "If I get adequate sleep, I'm able to pay attention in class." Such a sentence might then be followed with some specific examples to support the main point of your paragraph.)

> **HINT**   Listing transitions such as *first of all, second, another, also, in addition, finally,* and so on may help you introduce your supporting paragraphs as well as set off different supporting details within those paragraphs.

WRITING ASSIGNMENT 2

Life Improvement

If you were given the time and resources to improve your life, what would you do and how would this change make your life better? Write an essay in which you describe what you would do, and then explain how this change would improve your life in three specific ways. Here are some examples:

> If I could pay off all my outstanding debts, I would improve my credit score, rent a larger apartment, and ask my girlfriend to marry me.

> If I had the time to go to school full-time, I would finish my college degree, apply for a full-time accountant job, and study for the CPA exam.

> If I didn't have to work the night shift, I would pick up my kids right after school, help them with their homework, and take them to the neighborhood park to play basketball before dinner.

To develop support for this essay, make a list of all the possible changes that you would like to make in your life. Don't worry about the practical details, such as cost. Then go back to your list and brainstorm all the benefits that each of these changes would bring to you. Alternatively, you could do some freewriting about the changes that you would like to see in your life. Use the ideas you generated to select one change and three positive effects. These prewriting techniques—listing and freewriting—are both helpful ways of getting started with an essay and thinking about it on paper.

WRITING ASSIGNMENT 3

Something Special

Imagine that your apartment or house is burning down. Of course, the best strategy would be to get yourself and others out of the building as quickly as possible. But suppose you knew for sure that you had time to rescue three of your possessions. Which three would you choose? Write an essay in which you discuss the three things in your home that you would most want to save from a fire.

Begin by doing some prewriting to find the items you want to write about. You could, for instance, try making a list and then choosing several of the most likely candidates. Then you could freewrite about each of those candidates. In this way, you are likely to find three possessions that will make strong subjects for this essay. Each will be the basis of a supporting paragraph. Each supporting paragraph will focus on why the object being discussed is so important to you. Make your support as specific and colorful as possible, perhaps using detailed descriptions, anecdotes, or quotations to reveal the importance of each object.

In planning your introduction, consider beginning with a broad, general idea and then narrowing it down to your thesis statement. Here, for example, is one such introduction for this paper:

> I have many possessions that I would be sad to lose. Because I love to cook, I would miss various kitchen appliances that provide me with

so many happy cooking adventures. I would also miss the wonderful electronic equipment that entertains me every day, including my large flat-screen TV and my Nintendo Wii. I would miss the various telephones on which I have spent many interesting hours chatting in every part of my apartment, including the bathtub. But if my apartment were burning down, I would most want to rescue three things that are irreplaceable and hold great meaning for me—the silverware set that belonged to my grandmother, my mother's wedding gown, and my giant photo album.

WRITING ASSIGNMENT 4

Teaching the Basics

What are you experienced in? Fixing cars? Growing flowers? Baking? Waiting on customers? Solving math problems? Write an essay teaching readers the basics of an activity in which you have some experience. If you're not sure about which activity to choose, use prewriting to help you find a topic you can support strongly. Once you've chosen your topic, continue to prewrite as a way to find your key points and organize them into three supporting paragraphs. The key details of waiting on customers in a diner, for instance, might be divided according to time order, as seen in the following topic sentences:

Topic sentence for supporting paragraph 1: Greeting customers and taking their orders should not be done carelessly.

Topic sentence for supporting paragraph 2: There are right and wrong ways to bring customers their food and to keep track of them during their meal.

Topic sentence for supporting paragraph 3: The final interaction with customers may be brief, but it is important.

> **HINT**   To make your points clear, be sure to use detailed descriptions and concrete examples throughout your essay. Also, you may want to use transitional words such as *first, then, also, another, when, after, while,* and *finally* to help organize your details.

WRITING ASSIGNMENT 5

Advantages or Disadvantages of Single Life

More and more people are remaining single longer, and almost half of the people who marry eventually divorce and become single again. Write an essay on the advantages or disadvantages of single life. Each of your three supporting paragraphs will focus on one advantage or one disadvantage. To decide which approach to take, begin by making two lists. A list of advantages might include:

More freedom of choice

Lower expenses

Fewer responsibilities

Dating opportunities

A list of disadvantages could include:

Loneliness

Depression on holidays

Lack of support in everyday decisions

Disapproval of parents and family

Go on to list as many specific details as you can think of to support your advantages and disadvantages. Those details will help you decide whether you want your thesis to focus on benefits or drawbacks. Then create a scratch outline made up of your thesis statement and each of your main supporting points. Put the most important or most dramatic supporting point last.

In your introduction, you might gain your reader's interest by asking several questions or by telling a brief, revealing story about single life. As you develop your supporting paragraphs, make sure that each paragraph begins with a topic sentence and focuses on one advantage or disadvantage of single life. While writing the essay, continue developing details that vividly support each of your points.

In a concluding paragraph, provide a summary of the points in your paper as well as a final thought to round off your discussion. Your final thought might be in the form of a prediction or a recommendation.

Detailed writing assignments follow each of the twenty readings in Part 4. As you work on those assignments, you will find it helpful to turn back to the writing activities in this chapter.

REFLECTIVE ACTIVITY

1. Reread one of the essays you wrote for an assignment in this chapter. Does your essay have a thesis that states both a topic and a main point? If not, does that affect the effectiveness of the essay? In what way(s)? How might you rewrite this thesis to make it stronger?

2. Is the evidence you provided to support the thesis specific or is it vague and general? How can you make this detail more specific? What other detail might you add to improve the paragraph?

3. Is each of the essay's paragraphs unified and coherent? If not, what ways have you learned so far to correct the problem?

EXPLORING WRITING ONLINE

Visit a favorite Web site of yours and think about how its home page is like an introductory paragraph. Specifically, examine how the home page attracts readers' interest, presents a central idea, and provides an overview of the entire site. Then write an essay in which you present your analysis.

RESPONDING TO IMAGES

These three photographs of the Sistine Chapel's ceiling zoom in closer and closer to focus on Michelangelo's famous depiction of God's finger touching Adam's. Write a paragraph describing any one of these images. Then make an outline for a larger essay that compares and contrasts the three photographs.

For additional materials on Chapter 5, visit www.mhhe.com/langan.

In college, you may want to ask your classmates to give you feedback on your writing, and you may want to help them with their writing. As you are reading the following paragraph written by Deepak for a geology class, think about what advice you would offer him as he prepares to write his final draft by using the questions that follow.

The Sun's Effect

[1]The sun has an effect on the weather. [2]First, the sun warms the surface of the earth. [3]Some parts of land warm faster than others. [4]A parking lot, for instance, absorbs the sun's heat more quickly than a forest. [5]All land, however, absorbs the sun's heat faster than a body of water. [6]A forest, therefore, warms more quickly than a large lake or ocean. [7]The warmed land and water give off heat to the air above them. [8]The hot air rises, and it goes up, cooler air moves in to replace it. [9]In addition to the sun, clouds affect the weather.

---

1. The topic sentence (see above) states the paragraph's main point, which is a little broad. How could Deepak narrow and focus his topic sentence?

   _____

2. Does any sentence stray from the main point? If so, indicate the sentence.

   _____

3. What are some transitional words and phrases that Deepak uses in his paragraph?

   _____   _____   _____   _____   _____

4. Write a revision of this paragraph, using the checklist that follows as a guide.

5. How might this paragraph be turned into an essay? Make an outline that shows how Deepak might expand and develop his point.

A CHECKLIST: Four Bases

Unity

✔ Every sentence in my paragraph is relevant to my main point or topic sentence, which is _____
_____ .

✔ A sentence, detail, or word that I have omitted for the sake of unity is _____
_____ .

✔ The pattern or patterns of development I'm using serve my topic and point well because _____
_____ .

Support

✔ My main idea is supported by several supporting points or by one extended example, which are/is _____ .

✔ Several examples of specific evidence for this point/these points are:
_____
_____ .

✔ I appeal to my readers' five senses with vivid descriptions, such as _____
and _____ .

Coherence

✔ I use one or more patterns of development, which is/are _____
_____, to organize my paragraph.

✔ I use the following transition words or signals to make my paragraph easy for readers to follow:
_____ .

Sentence Skills

Grammar

✔ I use parallelism to balance my words and ideas. (pp. 295–303)

✔ I use pronouns and their antecedents correctly. (pp. 252–274)

✔ My paragraph includes no misplaced or dangling modifiers. (pp. 283–294)

✔ I read my paragraph out loud to help catch typos and awkward or grammatically incorrect sentences.

Style

✓ I use active verbs, rather than "is" and "to be." Some examples of active verbs I use are
_____ and _____ . (pp. 249–250)

✓ I use a consistent point of view throughout the paragraph. It is written in the _____
person. (pp. 258–262)

✓ I use specific, concrete language throughout, avoiding vague or abstract words.

Notes

_____

_____

_____

_____

_____

_____

_____

_____

_____

_____

_____

_____

_____

_____

_____

_____

_____

_____

_____

_____

_____

_____

3

Sentence Skills

SECTION I
Sentences

SECTION II
Verbs, Pronouns, and Agreement

SECTION III
Modifiers and Parallelism

SECTION IV
Punctuation and Mechanics

SECTION V
Word Use

PART 3 WILL

- explain the basic skills needed to write clear, error-free sentences

- provide numerous activities so that you can practice these skills enough to make them habits

- In addition, each chapter in Part 3 concludes with one or more review tests, allowing you to immediately test your understanding of each skill

EXPLORING WRITING PROMPT:

We see short bits of writing on traffic signs, in restaurant menus, on flyers posted in hallways, on highway billboards, or in captions rolling along the bottom of our television screens. Sometimes, such writing is done quickly with little attention paid to editing for

correctness. During the next week, be particularly alert to such items. In a notebook or journal, keep a record of examples containing errors in spelling, punctuation, word choice, and other sentence skills—the areas covered in Part 3. You can start with the sign pictured above.

SECTION PREVIEW

6 **Subjects and Verbs**

7 **Fragments**

8 **Run-Ons**

9 **Sentence Variety I**

RESPONDING TO IMAGES

1. *Why is the writing in the child's drawing a fragment? How might you make it a complete sentence? For more on fragments, see pp. 162–178.*

2. *This sign features a comma splice, which is a type of run-on sentence. What are two ways in which you could fix this error? For more on comma splices, see p. 180.*

3. *Would you pay less attention to a sign that was confusing or grammatically incorrect? Why or why not?*

CHAPTER 6

Subjects and Verbs

INTRODUCTORY ACTIVITY

Understanding subjects and verbs is a major step toward mastering many sentence skills. As a speaker of English, you already have an instinctive feel for these basic building blocks of English sentences. See if you can insert an appropriate word in each space that follows. The answer will be a subject.

1. _____ is one of my favorite Web sites.

2. _____ told me a secret.

3. A _____ is all I need to make me happy.

4. _____ appeared in my dreams.

Now insert an appropriate word in the following spaces. Each answer will be a verb.

5. The student _____ for the exam.

6. My children _____ much faster than I do.

7. Every night, I _____ my friends.

8. Kalani _____ home right after class.

Finally, insert appropriate words in the following spaces. Each answer will be a subject in the first space and a verb in the second.

9. A _____ slowly _____ into the room.

10. Many _____ today _____ the Internet.

11. The _____ never _____ me.

12. The _____ nervously _____ you for help.

CHAPTER PREVIEW

A Simple Way to Find a Subject

A Simple Way to Find a Verb

More about Subjects and Verbs

- Distinguishing Subjects from Prepositional Phrases
- Verbs of More than One Word
- Compound Subjects and Verbs

The basic building blocks of English sentences are subjects and verbs. Understanding them is an important first step toward mastering a number of sentence skills.

Every sentence has a subject and a verb. Who or what the sentence speaks about is called the *subject;* what the sentence says about the subject is called the *verb*. In the following sentences, the subject is underlined once and the verb twice:

People gossip.

The truck belched fumes.

He waved at me.

Alaska contains the largest wilderness area in the United States.

That woman is a millionaire.

The pants feel itchy.

A Simple Way to Find a Subject

To find a subject, ask *who* or *what* the sentence is about. As shown below, your answer is the subject.

Who is the first sentence about? People

What is the second sentence about? The truck

Who is the third sentence about? He

What is the fourth sentence about? Alaska

Who is the fifth sentence about? That woman

What is the sixth sentence about? The pants

It helps to remember that the subject of a sentence is always a *noun* (any person, place, or thing) or a pronoun. A *pronoun* is simply a word like *he, she, it, you,* or *they* used in place of a noun. In the preceding sentences, the subjects are persons (*People, He, woman*), a place (*Alaska*), and things (*truck, pants*). And note that one pronoun (*He*) is used as a subject.

A Simple Way to Find a Verb

To find a verb, ask what the sentence *says about* the subject. As shown below, your answer is the verb.

What does the first sentence *say about* people? They gossip.

What does the second sentence *say about* the truck? It belched (fumes).

What does the third sentence *say about* him? He waved (at me).

What does the fourth sentence *say about* Alaska? It contains (the largest wilderness area in the United States).

What does the fifth sentence *say about* that woman? She is (a millionaire).

What does the sixth sentence *say about* the pants? They feel (itchy).

A second way to find the verb is to put *I, you, he, she, it,* or *they* in front of the word you think is a verb. If the result makes sense, you have a verb. For example, you could put *they* in front of *gossip* in the first sentence in the preceding list, with the result, *they gossip,* making sense. Therefore, you know that *gossip* is a verb. You could use the same test with the other verbs as well.

Finally, it helps to remember that most verbs show action. In "People gossip," the action is *gossiping.* In "The truck belched fumes," the action is *belching.* In "He waved at me," the action is *waving.* In "Alaska contains the largest wilderness area in the United States," the action is *containing.*

Certain other verbs, known as *linking verbs,* do not show action. They do, however, give information about the subject of the sentence. In "That woman is a millionaire," the linking verb *is* tells us that the woman is a millionaire. In "The pants feel itchy," the linking verb *feel* gives us the information that the pants are itchy.

Finding Subjects and Verbs

ACTIVITY 1

In each of the following sentences, draw one line under the subject and two lines under the verb.

> **HINT** To find the subject, ask *who* or *what* the sentence is about. Then to find the verb, ask what the sentence *says about* the subject.

1. Rachel poured extra-virgin olive oil into the skillet.

2. The company offered a fifty-dollar rebate on every energy-efficient refrigerator bought during the month of June.

3. The talk show host introduced ten-year-old Drake as a future *American Idol* star.

4. Taryn adjusted the volume on her iPod as she entered the library.

5. The discarded cigarette butt burned a hole in the upholstery.

6. The bathroom upstairs is infested with cockroaches.

7. Royden tripped over the tangled cables behind my office desk.

8. The sports drink quenched my thirst.

9. The lawn trimmer tossed small rocks and other debris into the air.

10. Volunteers collected canned meats, beans, and peanut butter for the food bank.

| ACTIVITY 2 | **Subjects and Linking Verbs** |

Follow the directions given for Activity 1. Note that all the verbs here are linking verbs.

> **HINT**   Who is item 1 about? What linking verb gives us information about them?

1. My parents are not very sociable.
2. I am always nervous on the first day of classes.
3. Tri Lee was the first person to finish the exam.
4. Our dog becomes friendly after a few minutes of growling.
5. Liz seems ready for a nervous breakdown.
6. That plastic hot dog looks good enough to eat.
7. Most people appear slimmer in clothes with vertical stripes.
8. Many students felt exhausted after finishing the placement exam.
9. A cheeseburger has more than seven times as much sodium as French fries.
10. Yesterday, my phone seemed to be ringing constantly.

| ACTIVITY 3 | **Subjects and Verbs** |

Follow the directions given for Activity 1.

> **HINT**   What is item 1 about? What did they do?

1. The rabbits ate more than their share of my garden.
2. My father prefers his well-worn jeans to new ones.
3. A local restaurant donated food for the homeless.
4. Stanley always looks ready for a fight.
5. An elderly couple relaxed on a bench in the shopping mall.
6. Lightning brightened the dark sky for a few seconds.
7. Our town council voted for a curfew on Halloween.
8. Lynn's sore throat kept her home from work today.
9. Surprisingly, Charlotte's little sister decided not to go to the circus.
10. As usual, I chose the slowest checkout line in the supermarket.

More about Subjects and Verbs

Distinguishing Subjects from Prepositional Phrases

The subject of a sentence never appears within a prepositional phrase. A *prepositional phrase* is simply a group of words beginning with a preposition and ending with the answer to the question *what, when,* or *where.* Here is a list of common prepositions.

Common Prepositions				
about	before	by	inside	over
above	behind	during	into	through
across	below	except	of	to
among	beneath	for	off	toward
around	beside	from	on	under
at	between	in	onto	with

When you are looking for the subject of a sentence, it is helpful to cross out prepositional phrases.

~~In the middle of the night~~, we heard footsteps ~~on the roof~~.

The magazines ~~on the table~~ belong ~~in the garage~~.

~~Before the opening kickoff~~, a brass band marched ~~onto the field~~.

The hardware store ~~across the street~~ went ~~out of business~~.

~~In spite of our advice~~, Sally quit her job ~~at Burger King~~.

Subjects and Prepositional Phrases

ACTIVITY 4

Cross out prepositional phrases. Then draw a single line under subjects and a double line under verbs.

> **HINT**   What are the two prepositional phrases in item 1? What is the subject? What does the sentence say about her?

1. By accident, my girlfriend dropped her set of keys into the toilet at the public restroom.

2. Before the trial, the defense attorney quickly read through her trial notes.

3. My two-year-old daughter Olivia sleeps in my bed on stormy nights.

4. I applied for a pre-approved credit card from my bank.

5. On Friday nights, my family watches movies on our newly purchased LCD TV.

6. Over the weekend, Patrice wrote a five-page research paper on indigenous rights for her political science class.

7. The wireless connection from my neighbor's apartment allows me access to the Internet for free.

8. On Thursday, several foreign-born soldiers received U.S. citizenship during the naturalization ceremony at the Federal Building.

9. All my friends, except Nino, play the video game *Grand Theft Auto* on their home computers.

10. The spicy horseradish beneath the raw tuna in my *nigiri* sushi roll burned the back of my tongue.

Verbs of More Than One Word

Many verbs consist of more than one word. Here, for example, are some of the many forms of the verb *help:*

Some Forms of the Verb *Help*		
helps	should have been helping	will have helped
helping	can help	would have been helped
is helping	would have been helping	has been helped
was helping	will be helping	had been helped
may help	had been helping	must have helped
should help	helped	having helped
will help	have helped	should have been helped
does help	has helped	had helped

The following are sentences that contain verbs of more than one word:

Yolanda is working overtime this week.

Another book has been written about the Kennedy family.

We should have stopped for gas at the last station.

The game has just been canceled.

Words such as *not, just, never, only,* and *always* are not part of the verb, although they may appear within the verb.

Yolanda is not working overtime next week.

The boys should just not have stayed out so late.

The game has always been played regardless of the weather.

No verb preceded by *to* is ever the verb of a sentence.

Sue <u>wants</u> to go with us.

The newly married couple <u>decided</u> to rent a house for a year.

The store <u>needs</u> extra people to help out at Christmas.

No *-ing* word by itself is ever the verb of a sentence. (It may be part of the verb, but it must have a helping verb in front of it.)

We planning the trip for months. (This is not a sentence because the verb is not complete.)

We <u>were planning</u> the trip for months. (This is a complete sentence.)

Verbs of More than One Word	**ACTIVITY 5**

Draw a single line under subjects and a double line under verbs. Be sure to include all parts of the verb.

> **HINT** Who or what is item 1 about? What does it say about him, her, or them? What two words make up the verb?

1. Ellen has chosen blue dresses for her bridesmaids.

2. You should plan your weekly budget more carefully.

3. Felix has been waiting in line for tickets all morning.

4. We should have invited Terri to the party.

5. I would have preferred a movie with a happy ending.

6. Classes were interrupted three times today by a faulty fire alarm.

7. Sam can touch his nose with his tongue.

8. I have been encouraging my mother to quit smoking.

9. Joe has just agreed to feed his neighbor's fish over the holiday.

10. Many students have not been giving much thought to selecting a major.

Compound Subjects and Verbs

A sentence may have more than one verb:

The <u>dancer</u> <u>stumbled</u> and <u>fell</u>.

<u>Eva</u> <u>washed</u> her hair, <u>blew</u> it dry, and <u>parted</u> it in the middle.

A sentence may have more than one subject:

<u>Cats</u> and <u>dogs</u> <u>are</u> sometimes the best of friends.

The striking <u>workers</u> and their <u>bosses</u> <u>could</u> not <u>come</u> to an agreement.

A sentence may have several subjects and several verbs:

Holly and I read the book and reported on it to the class.

Pete, Nick, and Fran caught the fish in the morning, cleaned them in the afternoon, and ate them that night.

| ACTIVITY 6 | **Compound Subjects and Verbs** |

Draw a single line under subjects and a double line under verbs. Be sure to mark *all* the subjects and verbs.

>   What two things is item 1 about? What does it say about them?

1. Boards and bricks make a nice bookcase.
2. We bought a big bag of peanuts and finished it by the movie's end.
3. A fly and a bee hung lifelessly in the spider's web.
4. The twins look alike but think, act, and dress quite differently.
5. Canned salmon and tuna contain significant amounts of calcium.
6. I waited for the bubble bath to foam and then slipped into the warm tub.
7. The little girl in the next car waved and smiled at me.
8. The bird actually dived under the water and reappeared with a fish.
9. Singers, dancers, and actors performed at the heart-association benefit.
10. The magician and his assistant bowed and disappeared in a cloud of smoke.

REVIEW TEST 1

Draw one line under the subjects and two lines under the verbs. To help find subjects, cross out prepositional phrases as necessary. Underline all the parts of a verb.

>   You may find more than one subject and verb in a sentence.

1. Most noodle soups at the Vietnamese restaurant contain beef broth, flat rice noodles, and fresh basil leaves.
2. The security guard on duty at my workplace noticed a suspicious person lurking behind the warehouse.
3. The credit counseling center may be able to help me with my late payments.

4. After several minutes, the Chihuahua yelped loudly and scratched on the screen door.

5. Wireless carriers should not charge an early termination fee to cell phone users.

6. The project manager looked at the blueprints before visiting the job site.

7. Before the end of the day, Royce needs to call his son's teacher at school.

8. Between you and me, none of the children should have been running in the hall.

9. Thunderstorms and hurricanes swept through the northern part of the state.

10. Alberto used his employee discount to purchase a washing machine for his mom.

REVIEW TEST 2

Follow the directions given for Review Test 1.

1. Gasoline from the broken fuel line dripped onto the floor of the garage.

2. All the carrot tops in the garden had been eaten by rabbits.

3. An old man with a plastic trash bag collected aluminum cans along the road.

4. The majority of people wait until April 15 to file their income tax.

5. My brother became a college freshman at the age of forty-two.

6. At the delicatessen, Linda and Paul ate corned beef sandwiches and drank root beer.

7. The window fan made a clanking sound during the night and kept us from sleeping.

8. An umbrella tumbled across the street in the gusty wind and landed between two cars.

9. Telephones in the mayor's office rang continuously with calls from angry citizens about the city tax increase.

10. A teenager pushed a woman, grabbed her purse, and ran off through the crowd.

For additional material on Chapter 6, visit www.mhhe.com/langan.

7

Fragments

CHAPTER PREVIEW

What Fragments Are

Dependent-Word
Fragments

-ing and *to* Fragments

Added-Detail Fragments

Missing-Subject
Fragments

INTRODUCTORY ACTIVITY

Every sentence must have a subject and a verb and must express a complete thought. A word group that lacks a subject or a verb and does not express a complete thought is a *fragment*.

What follows are a number of fragments and sentences. See if you can complete the statement that explains each fragment.

1. Telephones. *Fragment*

   Telephones ring. *Sentence*

   "Telephones" is a fragment because, although it has a subject (*Telephones*), it lacks a _____ (*ring*) and so does not express a complete thought.

2. Explains. *Fragment*

   Darrell explains. *Sentence*

   "Explains" is a fragment because, although it has a verb (*Explains*), it lacks a _____ (*Darrell*) and does not express a complete thought.

3. Scribbling notes in class. *Fragment*

   Jayne was scribbling notes in class. *Sentence*

   "Scribbling notes in class" is a fragment because it lacks a _____ (*Jayne*) and also part of the _____ (*was*). As a result, it does not express a complete thought.

4. When the dentist began drilling. *Fragment*

   When the dentist began drilling, I closed my eyes. *Sentence*

   "When the dentist began drilling" is a fragment because we want to know *what happened when* the dentist began drilling. The word group does not follow through and _____.

Answers are on page 620.

What Fragments Are

Every sentence must have a subject and a verb and must express a complete thought. A word group that lacks a subject or a verb and does not express a complete thought is a *fragment*. Following are the most common types of fragments that people write:

- Dependent-word fragments
- *-ing* and *to* fragments
- Added-detail fragments
- Missing-subject fragments

Once you understand the specific kind or kinds of fragments that you might write, you should be able to eliminate them from your writing. The following pages explain all four types of fragments.

Dependent-Word Fragments

Some word groups that begin with a dependent word are fragments. Here is a list of common dependent words:

Common Dependent Words	
after	unless
although, though	until
as	what, whatever
because	when, whenever
before	where, wherever
even though	whether
how	which, whichever
if, even if	while
in order that	who
since	whose
that, so that	

Whenever you start a sentence with one of these dependent words, you must be careful that a dependent-word fragment does not result. The word group beginning with the dependent word *After* in the following selection is a fragment.

<u>After I stopped drinking coffee.</u> I began sleeping better at night.

A *dependent statement*—one starting with a dependent word such as *After*—cannot stand alone. It depends on another statement to complete the thought. "After I stopped drinking coffee" is a dependent statement. It leaves us hanging. We expect in the same sentence to find out *what happened after* the writer stopped drinking coffee. When a writer does not follow through and complete a thought, a fragment results.

To correct the fragment, simply follow through and complete the thought:

After I stopped drinking coffee, I began sleeping better at night.

Remember, then, that *dependent statements by themselves* are fragments. They must be attached to a statement that makes sense standing alone.

Here are two other examples of dependent-word fragments that need to be corrected.

Brian sat nervously in the dental clinic. <u>While waiting to have his wisdom tooth pulled.</u>

Maria decided to throw away the boxes. <u>That had accumulated for years in the basement.</u>

> **EXPLANATION:** "While waiting to have his wisdom tooth pulled" is a fragment; it does not make sense standing by itself. We want to know in the same statement *what Brian did* while waiting to have his tooth pulled. The writer must complete the thought. Likewise, "That had accumulated for years in the basement" is not in itself a complete thought. We want to know in the same statement what *that* refers to.

How to Correct Dependent-Word Fragments

In most cases, you can correct a dependent-word fragment by attaching it to the sentence that comes after it or to the sentence that comes before it:

After I stopped drinking coffee, I began sleeping better at night.
(The fragment has been attached to the sentence that comes after it.)

Brian sat nervously in the dental clinic while waiting to have his wisdom tooth pulled.
(The fragment has been attached to the sentence that comes before it.)

Maria decided to throw away the boxes that had accumulated for years in the basement.
(The fragment has been attached to the sentence that comes before it.)

Another way of correcting a dependent-word fragment is to eliminate the dependent word and make a new sentence:

I stopped drinking coffee.

He was waiting to have his wisdom tooth pulled.

They had accumulated for years in the basement.

Do not use this second method of correction too frequently, however, because it may cut down on interest and variety in your writing style.

Use a comma if a dependent-word group comes at the *beginning* of a sentence:

After I stopped drinking coffee, I began sleeping better at night.

However, do not generally use a comma if the dependent-word group comes at the end of a sentence:

> Brian sat nervously in the dental clinic while waiting to have his wisdom tooth pulled.

> Maria decided to throw away the boxes that had accumulated for years in the basement.

Sometimes the dependent words *who, that, which,* or *where* appear not at the very start but *near* the start of a word group. A fragment often results.

> Today I visited Melissa Cooper. <u>A friend who is in the hospital.</u>

"A friend who is in the hospital" is not in itself a complete thought. We want to know in the same statement *who* the friend is. The fragment can be corrected by attaching it to the sentence that comes before it:

> Today I visited Melissa Cooper, a friend who is in the hospital.

EXPLANATION: Here a comma is used to set off "a friend who is in the hospital," which is extra material placed at the end of the sentence.

TIP Some instructors refer to a dependent-word fragment as a dependent clause. A clause is simply a group of words having a subject and a verb. A clause may be independent (expressing a complete thought and able to stand alone) or dependent (not expressing a complete thought and not able to stand alone). A dependent clause by itself is a fragment. It can be corrected simply by adding an independent clause.

Correcting Dependent-Word Fragments — ACTIVITY 1

Turn each of the dependent-word groups into a sentence by adding a complete thought. Put a comma after the dependent-word group if a dependent word starts the sentence.

EXAMPLES

Before I begin college

Before I begin college, I want to brush up on my math and English skills.

The horoscope forecast that I read

The horoscope forecast that I read predicted new love, but I am happily

married.

HINT For item 1, describe something you do before you log off from the computer.

1. Before I log off from the computer

   _____

   _____

2. Even though I cheated

   _____

   _____

3. Although my parents never went to college

   _____

   _____

4. The pills that the doctor prescribed

   _____

   _____

5. If I remember correctly

   _____

   _____

ACTIVITY 2   **Combining Sentences to Correct Dependent-Word Fragments**

Underline the dependent-word fragment (or fragments) in each selection. Then correct each fragment by attaching it to the sentence that comes before or the sentence that comes after—whichever sounds more natural. Put a comma after the dependent-word group if it starts the sentence.

> **HINT**   In item 1, which word group begins with a dependent word?

1. When the waitress coughed in his food. Frank lost his appetite. He didn't even take home a doggy bag.

   _____

   _____

2. Our power went out. During a thunderstorm. I lost the paper I was writing on the computer.

   _____

   _____

3. Tony doesn't like going to the ballpark. If he misses an exciting play. There's no instant replay.

   _____

   _____

4. After the mail carrier comes. I run to our mailbox. I love to get mail. Even if it is only junk mail.

    _____

    _____

5. Even though she can't read. My little daughter likes to go to the library. She chooses books with pretty covers. While I look at the latest magazines.

    _____

    _____

-ing and *to* Fragments

When a word ending in *-ing* or the word *to* appears at or near the start of a word group, a fragment may result. Such fragments often lack a subject and part of the verb.

Underline the word groups in the following examples that contain *-ing* words. Each of these is an *-ing* fragment.

EXAMPLE 1

I spent all day in the employment office. <u>Trying to find a job that suited me</u>. The prospects looked bleak.

EXAMPLE 2

Danielle surprised Brian on the nature hike. <u>Picking blobs of resin off pine trees</u>. Then she chewed them like bubble gum.

EXAMPLE 3

Eric took an aisle seat on the bus. <u>His reason being that he had more legroom</u>.

> **TIP** People sometimes write *-ing* fragments because they think the subject in one sentence will work for the next word group as well. In Example 1, they might think the subject *I* in the opening sentence will also serve as the subject for "Trying to find a job that suited me." But the subject must actually be *in* the sentence.

How to Correct *-ing* Fragments

1. Attach the fragment to the sentence that comes before it or the sentence that comes after it, whichever makes sense. Example 1 could read, "I spent all day in the employment office, trying to find a job that suited me." (Note that here a comma is used to set off "trying to find a job that suited me," which is extra material placed at the end of the sentence.)

» OR «

2. Add a subject and change the *-ing* verb part to the correct form of the verb. Example 2 could read, "She picked blobs of resin off pine trees."

» OR «

3. Change *being* to the correct form of the verb *be* (*am, are, is, was, were*). Example 3 could read, "His reason was that he had more legroom."

How to Correct *to* Fragments

As previously noted, when *to* appears at or near the start of a word group, a fragment sometimes results.

> Fragment: To remind people of their selfishness. Otis leaves handwritten notes on cars that take up two parking spaces.

The first word group in the preceding example is a *to* fragment. It can be corrected by adding it to the sentence that comes after it.

> Correct: To remind people of their selfishness, Otis leaves handwritten notes on cars that take up two parking spaces.

> EXPLANATION: Here a comma is used to set off "To remind people of their selfishness," which is introductory material in the sentence.

ACTIVITY 3	Correcting *-ing* Fragments

Underline the *-ing* fragment in each of the three items that follow. Then make the fragment a sentence by rewriting it, using the method described in parentheses.

EXAMPLE

Everyone at the meeting heard Tina's stomach growl. <u>Not having eaten breakfast</u>. She tried to satiate her hunger with a breath mint.

(Add the fragment to the sentence that comes after it.)

Not having eaten breakfast, she tried to satiate her hunger with a breath mint.

_____

1. Desmond looked anxiously at his cell phone. Waiting for his supervisor to return his call. He needed to call in sick to work.

   (Add the *-ing* fragment to the preceding sentence.)

   _____

   _____

2. Using one of the computers at the library. Hari could not access several Web sites, which he later learned were blocked.

   (Add the fragment to the sentence that comes after it.)

   _____

   _____

3. A virus infected my computer. As a result, destroying data.

    (Add the subject *it* and change the verb *destroying* to the correct form, *destroyed.*)

    _____

    _____

Correcting *-ing* or *to* Fragments

ACTIVITY 4

Underline the *-ing* or *to* fragment in each selection. Then rewrite each selection correctly, using one of the methods of correction described on pages 167–168.

 In item 1, add the *-ing* fragment to the preceding sentence.

1. Some workers dug up the street near our house. Causing frequent vibrations inside. By evening, all the pictures on our walls were crooked.

    _____

    _____

2. I had heard about the surprise party for me. I therefore walked slowly into the darkened living room. Preparing to look shocked.

    _____

    _____

3. Dribbling skillfully up the court. Luis looked for a teammate who was open. Then he passed the ball.

    _____

    _____

4. As I was dreaming of a sunny day at the beach, the alarm clock rang. Wanting to finish the dream. I pushed the Snooze button.

    _____

    _____

5. To get back my term paper. I went to see my English instructor from last semester. I also wanted some career advice.

    _____

    _____

Added-Detail Fragments

Added-detail fragments lack a subject and a verb. They often begin with one of the following words or phrases.

also	except	including
especially	for example	such as

See if you can underline the one added-detail fragment in each of these examples:

EXAMPLE 1

Tony has trouble accepting criticism. <u>Except from Lola.</u> She has a knack for tact.

EXAMPLE 2

My apartment has its drawbacks. <u>For example, no hot water in the morning.</u>

EXAMPLE 3

I had many jobs while in school. <u>Among them, busboy, painter, and security guard.</u>

> **TIP**   People often write added-detail fragments for much the same reason they write *-ing* fragments. They think the subject and verb in one sentence will serve for the next word group as well. But the subject and verb must be in *each* word group.

How to Correct Added-Detail Fragments

1. Attach the fragment to the complete thought that precedes it. Example 1 could read: "Tony has trouble accepting criticism, except from Lola." (Note that here a comma is used to set off "except from Lola," which is extra material placed at the end of the sentence.)

» OR «

2. Add a subject and a verb to the fragment to make it a complete sentence. Example 2 could read: "My apartment has its drawbacks. For example, there is no hot water in the morning."

» OR «

3. Change words as necessary to make the fragment part of the preceding sentence. Example 3 could read: "Among the many jobs I had while in school have been busboy, painter, and security guard."

Identifying and Correcting Fragments

Underline the fragment in each selection that follows. Then make it a sentence by rewriting it, using the method described in parentheses.

EXAMPLE

My husband and I share the household chores. <u>Including meals.</u> I do the cooking and he does the eating.

(Add the fragment to the preceding sentence.)

My husband and I share the household chores, including meals.

1. Denise puts things off until the last minute. For example, waiting until the night before a test to begin studying.

   (Add the subject *she* and change *waiting* to the proper form of the verb, *waits*.)

   _____

   _____

2. My eleventh-grade English teacher picked on everybody. Except the athletes. They could do no wrong.

   (Add the fragment to the preceding sentence.)

   _____

   _____

3. Bernardo always buys things out of season. For example, an air conditioner in December. He saves a lot of money this way.

   (Add the subject and verb *he bought.*)

   _____

   _____

Identifying and Correcting Added-Detail Fragments

Underline the added-detail fragment in each selection. Then rewrite that part of the selection needed to correct the fragment. Use one of the three methods of correction described on page 170.

HINT   In item 1, attach the added-detail fragment to the preceding sentence.

1. My daughter faithfully watches the programs on the Disney Channel. Including *Hannah Montana, Wizards of Waverly Place,* and *The Suite Life of Zack and Cody.* She has never missed a single episode.

   _____

   _____

   _____

2. There are certain snacks I love to eat when I watch TV. Especially micro-wave popcorn. So I always try to keep several bags in the cupboard.

_____

_____

3. Some of the printers in the computer lab are unreliable. The ink-jet one, for instance. It often needs a new printer cartridge.

_____

_____

4. By noon, the stadium parking lot was packed with tailgaters. With some of them grilling barbeque ribs and drinking ice-cold beer.

_____

_____

5. Some Web sites contain annoying pop-up advertisements. For example, free online game Web sites. These sites are filled with distracting mar-keting messages.

_____

_____

Missing-Subject Fragments

In each example, underline the word group in which the subject is missing.

EXAMPLE 1

One example of my grandfather's generosity is that he visits sick friends in the hospital. <u>And takes along get-well cards with a few dollars folded in them.</u>

EXAMPLE 2

The weight lifter grunted as he heaved the barbells into the air. <u>Then, with a loud groan, dropped them.</u>

> **TIP** People write missing-subject fragments because they think the subject in one sentence will apply to the next word group as well. But the subject, as well as the verb, must be in *each* word group to make a sentence.

How to Correct Missing-Subject Fragments

1. Attach the fragment to the preceding sentence. Example 1 could read: "One example of my grandfather's generosity is that he visits sick friends in the hospital and takes along get-well cards with a few dollars folded in them."

» OR «

2. Add a subject (which can often be a pronoun standing for the subject in the preceding sentence). Example 2 could read: "Then, with a loud groan, he dropped them."

Correcting Missing-Subject Fragments

Underline the missing-subject fragment in each selection. Then rewrite that part of the selection needed to correct the fragment. Use one of the two methods of correction previously described.

 In item 1, the missing subject is *he*.

1. Jack tripped on his shoelace. Then looked around to see if anyone had noticed.

   _____

   _____

2. I started the car. And quickly turned down the blaring radio.

   _____

   _____

3. The fire in the fireplace crackled merrily. Its orange-red flames shot high in the air. And made strange shadows all around the dark room.

   _____

   _____

4. The receptionist at that office is not very well trained. She was chewing gum and talking with a coworker at the same time she took my call. And forgot to take my name.

   _____

   _____

5. My elderly aunt never stands for long on a bus ride. She places herself in front of a seated young man. And stands on his feet until he gets up.

   _____

   _____

TIP   How to Check for Fragments

1. Read your paper aloud from the *last* sentence to the *first*. You will be better able to see and hear whether each word group you read is a complete thought.
2. If you think any word group is a fragment, ask yourself: Does this contain a subject and a verb and express a complete thought?
3. More specifically, be on the lookout for the most common fragments.
   - Dependent-word fragments (starting with words such as *after, because, since, when,* and *before*)
   - *-ing* and *to* fragments (*-ing* or *to* at or near the start of a word group)
   - Added-detail fragments (starting with words such as *for example, such as, also,* and *especially*)
   - Missing-subject fragments (a verb is present but not the subject)

| ACTIVITY 8 | **Editing and Rewriting** |

Working with a partner, read the following short paragraph and underline the five fragments. Then use the space provided to correct the fragments. Feel free to discuss the rewrite quietly with your partner and refer back to the chapter when necessary.

> [1]Did you know that one in every five children is overweight? [2]If you think that these kids will simply outgrow their "baby fat." [3]You're wrong. [4]The number of overweight children in this country has doubled in the past twenty years. [5]Creating a health epidemic. [6]Too many children spend hours watching television. [7]And playing video games when they should be outside playing. [8]They consume sugary, high-calorie snacks. [9]When they should be eating fresh fruits and low-fat yogurt. [10]These children are at a higher risk for high cholesterol, high blood pressure, and type 2 diabetes. [11]They are also more likely to be teased at school, miss school, and develop low self-esteem. [12]These problems often follow them through adolescence and into adulthood. [13]Sadly, overweight kids have a 70 percent greater chance of becoming overweight adults. [14]Everyone, however, can make a difference. [15]For example, being a positive role model. [16]So, live a healthy life. [17]Turn off your television and take a twenty-minute walk.

1. _____

_____

2. _____

_____

3. _____

_____

4. _____

_____

5. _____

| ACTIVITY 9 | **Creating Sentences** |

Working with a partner, make up your own short fragments test as directed.

1. Write a dependent-word fragment in the space below. Then correct the fragment by making it into a complete sentence. You may want to begin your fragment with the word *before, after, when, because,* or *if.*

   Fragment _____

   Sentence _____

2. In the space below, write a fragment that begins with a word that has an *-ing* ending. Then correct the fragment by making it into a complete sentence. You may want to begin your fragment with the word *laughing, walking, shopping,* or *talking.*

Fragment _____

Sentence _____

3. Write an added-detail fragment in the space below. Then correct the fragment by making it into a complete sentence. You may want to begin your fragment with the word *also, especially, except,* or *including.*

Fragment _____

Sentence _____

REFLECTIVE ACTIVITY

1. Look at the paragraph that you revised in Activity 8. How has correcting fragments improved the paragraph? Is it clearer? Easier to read? Explain.

2. Explain what it is about fragments that you find most difficult to remember and apply. Use an example to make your point clear. Feel free to refer to anything in this chapter.

REVIEW TEST 1

Turn each of the following word groups into a complete sentence. Use the space provided.

EXAMPLES

Wanting to impress everyone
Wanting to impress everyone, I told a white lie.

Until the semester begins
Until the semester begins, I plan to work forty hours a week.

1 After we left the classroom

_____

2. Whenever the weather is bad

_____

3. Behind the TV stand

_____

4. If I am late for my class

_____

5. Tyler, who is extremely successful

_____

6. To get to trust each other better

_____

7. Which was surprising

_____

8. Will see me tomorrow

_____

9. Texting a message on my phone

_____

10. Guessing the answer

_____

_____

REVIEW TEST 2

Underline the fragment in each item that follows. Then correct the fragment in the space provided.

EXAMPLE

Sam received all kinds of junk mail. <u>Then complained to the post office.</u> Eventually, some of the mail stopped coming.
Then he complained to the post office.

1. Fascinated, Nina stared at the stranger. Who was standing in the doorway. She wondered if she could convince him they had met before.

_____

_____

2. Trees can survive on a steep mountain slope if they obey two rules. They must grow low to the ground. And bend with the wind.

_____

_____

3. While waiting in line at the supermarket. I look in people's baskets. Their food choices give hints about their personalities.

_____

_____

4. I saw spectacular twin rainbows through the kitchen window. So I rushed to get my camera. To take a picture before they vanished.

_____

_____

5. Whenever you buy cotton clothes, get them one size too large. By allowing for shrinkage. You will get a longer life out of them.

_____

_____

6. My nutty cousin cuts the address labels off his magazines. Then pastes them on envelopes. This way, he doesn't have to write his return address.

_____

_____

7. Marian never has to buy ketchup or mustard. Because she saves the extra packets that come with fast-food orders.

_____

_____

8. The soccer players were amazing. Using their feet as well as most people use their hands.

_____

_____

9. My husband climbed his first mountain yesterday. Now he's calling all our friends. To tell them about his peak experience.

_____

_____

10. The trivia book listed some interesting facts about Babe Ruth. For instance, he spoke German fluently. Also, kept cool on hot days by putting wet cabbage leaves under his cap.

_____

_____

REVIEW TEST 3

In the space provided, write C if a word group is a complete sentence; write *frag* if it is a fragment. The first two are done for you.

__*frag*__ 1. When the bus drivers went on strike.

___C___ 2. I saw many people giving rides to strangers.

_____ 3. Some even drove out of their way for others.

_____ 4. Especially when the weather was bad.

_____ 5. One rainy day, I saw an elderly woman pull her cab over to the curb.

_____ 6. Yelling and waving for five shivering students to get into her car.

_____ 7. Until the strike finally ended.

_____ 8. Scenes like that were not uncommon.

_____ 9. It seems that community problems bring people together.

_____ 10. By weakening the feeling that we live very separate lives.

Now correct the *fragments* you have found. Attach each fragment to the sentence that comes before or after it, or make whatever other change is needed to turn the fragment into a sentence. Use the space provided. The first one is corrected for you.

1. *When the bus drivers went on strike, I saw many people giving rides to strangers.*

2. _____

   _____

3. _____

   _____

4. _____

5. _____

   _____

REVIEW TEST 4

On separate paper, write quickly for five minutes about the town or city where you live. Don't worry about spelling, punctuation, finding exact words, or organizing your thoughts. Just focus on writing as many words as you can without stopping.

After you have finished, go back and make whatever changes are needed to correct any fragments in your writing.

For additional materials on Chapter 7, visit **www.mhhe.com/langan**.

Run-Ons

CHAPTER 8

CHAPTER PREVIEW

What Are Run-Ons?

Correcting Run-Ons

Method 1: Period and a Capital Letter

Method 2: Comma and a Joining Word

Method 3: Semicolon

Method 4: Subordination

INTRODUCTORY ACTIVITY

A run-on occurs when two sentences are run together with no adequate sign given to mark the break between them. Shown below are four run-on sentences, each followed by a correct sentence. See if you can complete the statement that explains how each run-on is corrected.

1. A man coughed in the movie theater the result was a chain reaction of copycat coughing.

    A man coughed in the movie theater. The result was a chain reaction of copycat coughing.

The run-on has been corrected by using a _____ and a capital letter to separate the two complete thoughts.

2. I heard laughter inside the house, no one answered the bell.

    I heard laughter inside the house, but no one answered the bell.

The run-on has been corrected by using a joining word, _____ , to connect the two complete thoughts.

3. A car sped around the corner, it sprayed slush all over the pedestrians.

    A car sped around the corner; it sprayed slush all over the pedestrians.

The run-on has been corrected by using a _____ to connect the two closely related thoughts.

4. I had a campus map, I still could not find my classroom building.

    Although I had a campus map, I still could not find my classroom building.

The run-on has been corrected by using the subordinating word _____ to connect the two closely related thoughts.

Answers are on page 620.

What Are Run-Ons?

A *run-on* is two complete thoughts that are run together with no adequate sign given to mark the break between them. As a result of the run-on, the reader is confused, unsure of where one thought ends and the next one begins. Two types of run-ons are fused sentences and comma splices.

Some run-ons have no punctuation at all to mark the break between two or more thoughts. Such run-ons are known as *fused sentences:* They are fused or joined together as if they were only one thought.

> *Fused Sentence*
>
> Rita decided to stop smoking she didn't want to die of lung cancer.

> *Fused Sentence*
>
> The exam was postponed the class was canceled as well.

In other run-ons, known as *comma splices,* a comma is used to connect or "splice" together the two complete thoughts. However, a comma alone is *not enough* to connect two complete thoughts. Some connection stronger than a comma alone is needed.

> *Comma Splice*
>
> Rita decided to stop smoking, she didn't want to die of lung cancer.

> *Comma Splice*
>
> The exam was postponed, the class was canceled as well.

Comma splices are the most common kind of run-on. Students sense that some kind of connection is needed between thoughts, so they put a comma at the dividing point. But the comma alone is *not sufficient.* A stronger, clearer mark is needed between the two thoughts.

> **TIP**   Some instructors refer to each complete thought in a run-on as an *independent clause*. A *clause* is simply a group of words having a subject and a verb. A clause may be *independent* (expressing a complete thought and able to stand alone) or *dependent* (not expressing a complete thought and not able to stand alone). A run-on is two independent clauses that are run together with no adequate sign given to mark the break between them.
>
> Some instructors believe that the term *run-ons* should be applied only to fused sentences, not to comma splices. But for many other instructors, and for our purposes in this book, the term *run-on* applies equally to fused sentences and comma splices. The bottom line is that you do not want either fused sentences or comma splices in your writing.

A Warning: Words That Can Lead to Run-Ons

People often write run-ons when the second complete thought begins with one of the following words. Be on the alert for run-ons whenever you use these words:

I	we	there	now
you	they	this	then
he, she, it		that	next

Correcting Run-Ons

Here are four common methods of correcting a run-on:

1. Use a period and a capital letter to separate the two complete thoughts. (In other words, make two separate sentences of the two complete thoughts.)

   Rita decided to stop smoking. She didn't want to die of lung cancer.

   The exam was postponed. The class was canceled as well.

   » OR «

2. Use a comma plus a joining word (*and, but, for, or, nor, so, yet*) to connect the two complete thoughts.

   Rita decided to stop smoking, for she didn't want to die of lung cancer.

   The exam was postponed, and the class was canceled as well.

   » OR «

3. Use a semicolon to connect the two complete thoughts.

   Rita decided to stop smoking; she didn't want to die of lung cancer.

   The exam was postponed; the class was canceled as well.

4. Use subordination.

   Because Rita didn't want to die of lung cancer, she decided to stop smoking.

   When the exam was postponed, the class was canceled as well.

The following pages will give you practice in all four methods of correcting run-ons. The use of subordination will be explained further on page 202, in a chapter that deals with sentence variety.

Method 1: Period and a Capital Letter

One way of correcting a run-on is to use a period and a capital letter at the break between the two complete thoughts. Use this method especially if the thoughts are not closely related or if another method would make the sentence too long.

Correcting Fused Sentences	ACTIVITY 1

Locate the split in each of the following run-ons. Each is a *fused sentence*—that is, each consists of two sentences fused or joined together with no punctuation at all between them. Reading each sentence aloud will help you "hear" where a major break or split in the thought occurs. At such a point, your voice will probably drop and pause.

> **HINT**   Correct the run-on by putting a period at the end of the first thought and a capital letter at the start of the second thought. In item 1, *The fern hadn't been watered in a month* is a complete thought. *Its leaves looked like frayed brown shoelaces* is also a complete thought.

EXAMPLE

Gary was not a success at his job ⟨. H⟩his mouth moved faster than his hands.

1. The fern hadn't been watered in a month its leaves looked like frayed brown shoelaces.

2. Newspapers are piled up on the neighbors' porch they must be out of town.

3. Joyce's recipe for chocolate fudge is very easy to make it is also very expensive.

4. Watching television gave the old man something to do he didn't have many visitors anymore.

5. Jon accidentally ruined his favorite black shirt a few drops of bleach spilled onto it in the laundry room.

6. The first Olympic Games were held in 776 BC. the only event was a footrace.

7. Gloria decorated her apartment creatively and cheaply she papered her bedroom walls with magazine covers.

8. There were papers scattered all over Lena's desk she spent twenty minutes looking for a missing receipt.

9. Spring rain dripped into the fireplace the room smelled like last winter's fires.

10. The car swerved dangerously through traffic its rear bumper sticker read, "School's Out—Drive Carefully."

ACTIVITY 2   Correcting Run-Ons—Fused Sentences and Comma Splices

Locate the split in each of the following run-ons. Some of the run-ons are fused sentences, and some of them are *comma splices*—run-ons spliced or joined together only with a comma. Correct each run-on by putting a period at the end of the first thought and a capital letter at the start of the next thought.

> **HINT**   In item 1, *My father* is the subject of the first complete thought. *He* is the subject of the second one.

1. My father is a very sentimental man he still has my kindergarten drawings.

2. Sue dropped the letter into the mailbox then she regretted mailing it.

3. Certain street names are very common the most common is "Park."

4. Bacteria are incredibly tiny a drop of liquid may contain fifty million of them.

5. The fastest dog in the world is the greyhound it can run over forty-one miles an hour.

6. Mandy's parents speak only Chinese she speaks Chinese, English, and French.

7. My iPod stopped working its battery needs to be charged.

8. A shadow on the kitchen wall was lovely it had the shape of a plant on the windowsill.

9. The little girl hated seeing her father drink one day, she poured all his liquor down the kitchen drain.

10. Children have been born at odd times for instance, James was born on February 29 during leap year.

Writing the Next Sentence ACTIVITY 3

Write a second sentence to go with each sentence below. Start the second sentence with the word given in the margin.

EXAMPLE

My wireless all-in-one printer is so convenient. <u>It allows me to print,</u> It
<u>scan, copy, and fax documents.</u>

1. The oysters were placed on the grill until their shells popped open. ____ Then
_____

2. I need to update the antivirus software on my computer. _____ It
_____

3. Ashlee sent me several urgent text messages last night. _____ She
_____

4. Students who take studio art classes spend hours on their projects. ____ They
_____

5. After the recent sewage spill, people were afraid to swim in the There
ocean. _____
_____

Method 2: Comma and a Joining Word

Another way of correcting a run-on is to use a comma plus a joining word to connect the two complete thoughts. Joining words (also called *coordinating conjunctions*) include *and, but, for, or, nor, so,* and *yet.* Here is what the four most common joining words mean:

and   in addition, along with

Lynn was watching *Monday Night Football,* and she was doing her homework.

 And means *in addition:* Lynn was watching *Monday Night Football; in addition,* she was doing her homework.

but   however, except, on the other hand, just the opposite

I voted for the president two years ago, but I would not vote for him today.

 But means *however:* I voted for the president two years ago; *however,* I would not vote for him today.

for   because, the reason why, the cause for something

Saturday is the worst day to shop, for people jam the stores.

 For means *because:* Saturday is the worst day to shop *because* people jam the stores. If you are not comfortable using *for,* you may want to use *because* instead of *for* in the activities that follow. If you do use *because,* omit the comma before it.

so   as a result, therefore

Our son misbehaved again, so he was sent upstairs without dessert.

 So means *as a result:* Our son misbehaved again; *as a result,* he was sent upstairs without dessert.

| ACTIVITY 4 | **Connecting Two Thoughts** |

Insert the comma and the joining word (*and, but, for, so*) that logically connects the two thoughts in each sentence.

EXAMPLE

A trip to the zoo always depresses me. I hate to see animals in cages.
                                                        ⸝, for

1. I want to stop smoking I don't want to gain weight.

2. Packages are flown to distant cities during the night vans deliver them the next morning.

3. The grass turned brown in the summer's heat the grapes shriveled and died on the vine.

4. Craig wanted to buy his girlfriend a ring he began saving ten dollars a week.

5. I enjoy watching television I feel guilty about spending so much time in front of the tube.

6. It was too hot indoors to study I decided to go down to the shopping center for ice cream.

7. I don't like to go to the doctor's office I'm afraid one of the other patients will make me really sick.

8. This world map was published only three years ago the names of some countries are already out of date.

9. Nate is color-blind his wife lays out his clothes every morning.

10. We knew there had been a power failure all our digital clocks were blinking "12:00."

Using Commas and Joining Words

ACTIVITY 5

Add a complete, closely related thought to each of the following statements. When you write the second thought, use a comma plus the joining word shown at the left.

EXAMPLE

I was sick with the flu, but I still had to study for the test.   but

1. We have the same taste in clothes   but

   _____

   _____

2. Keisha needed a little break from studying   so

   _____

   _____

3. I hammered two nails into the wall   and

   _____

   _____

4. The house was unusually quiet   for

   _____

   _____

5. Harry meant to stick to his diet   but

   _____

   _____

Method 3: Semicolon

A third method of correcting a run-on is to use a semicolon to mark the break between two thoughts. A *semicolon* (;) is made up of a period above a comma and is sometimes called a *strong comma.* The semicolon signals more of a pause than a comma alone but not quite the full pause of a period.

Occasional use of semicolons can add variety to sentences. For some people, however, the semicolon is a confusing mark of punctuation. Keep in mind that if you are not comfortable using it, you can and should use one of the first two methods of correcting a run-on sentence.

Semicolon Alone

Here are some earlier sentences that were connected with a comma plus a joining word. Now they are connected with a semicolon. Notice that a semicolon, unlike a comma, can be used alone to connect the two complete thoughts in each sentence.

> Lynn was watching *Monday Night Football;* she was doing her homework as well.

> I voted for the president two years ago; I would not vote for him today.

> Saturday is the worst day to shop; people jam the stores.

ACTIVITY 6	**Using Semicolons**

Insert a semicolon where the break occurs between the two complete thoughts in each of the following sentences.

EXAMPLE

He had hair implants; it looked very natural.

1. I ordered a Grand Slam Breakfast at Denny's the bacon and over-easy eggs were cooked perfectly.

2. Sabina invited me to her wedding it was held in Maui on a beautiful private beach.

3. Professor Williams scowled at the class her facial expression told the story.

4. Remarkably, the crime rates in our neighborhood have decreased auto thefts and burglaries are on the decline.

5. The Grand Canyon is ancient it is millions of years old.

Semicolon with a Transition

A semicolon is sometimes used with a transitional word and a comma to join two complete thoughts:

> I figured that the ball game would cost me about fifty dollars; however, I didn't consider the high price of food and drinks.

Fred and Denise have a low-interest mortgage on their house; otherwise, they would move to another neighborhood.

Sharon didn't understand the instructor's point; therefore, she asked him to repeat it.

> **TIP** Sometimes transitional words do not join complete thoughts but are merely interrupters in a sentence:
>
> My parents, moreover, plan to go on the trip.
> I believe, however, that they'll change their minds.

Transitional Words

Here is a list of common transitional words and phrases (also known as *adverbial conjunctions*).

Common Transitional Words		
however	moreover	therefore
on the other hand	in addition	as a result
nevertheless	also	consequently
instead	furthermore	otherwise

Using Logical Transitions

ACTIVITY 7

For each item, choose a logical transitional word from the box above and write it in the space provided. In addition, put a semicolon *before* the transition and a comma *after* it.

EXAMPLE

It was raining harder than ever _; however,_ Bobby was determined to go to the amusement park.

> **HINT** In item 1, "car" and "payments" are the subjects of the two complete thoughts.

1. A new car is always fun to drive _____ the payments are never fun to make.

2. The fork that fell into our garbage disposal looks like a piece of modern art _____ it is useless.

3. Auto races no longer use gasoline _____ spectators have nothing to fear from exhaust fumes.

4. We got to the stadium two hours before the game started _____ all the parking spaces were already taken.

5. Mice use their sensitive whiskers as feelers _____ they scurry along close to walls.

ACTIVITY 8 | **Using Semicolons and Commas**

Punctuate each sentence by using a semicolon and a comma.

EXAMPLE

Our tap water has a funny taste; consequently,we buy bottled water to drink.

> **HINT** To correctly punctuate item 1, first locate the transitional word that joins the two complete thoughts.

1. Nora lives two blocks from the grocery store nevertheless she always drives there.

2. The little boy ate too much Halloween candy as a result he got a stomachache.

3. Our dog protects us by barking at strangers however he also barks at our friends.

4. Jeff cut back a few hours on his work schedule otherwise he would have had very little time for studying.

5. My sister invited her ex-husband over to celebrate the holiday with the children furthermore she bought a gift for him from the children.

Method 4: Subordination

A fourth method of joining related thoughts is to use subordination. *Subordination* is a way of showing that one thought in a sentence is not as important as another thought. Here are three sentences where one idea is subordinated to (made less emphatic than) the other idea:

Because Rita didn't want to die of lung cancer, she decided to stop smoking.

The wedding reception began to get out of hand when the guests started to throw food at each other.

Although my brothers wanted to watch a *Lost* rerun, the rest of the family insisted on turning to the network news.

Dependent Words

Notice that when we subordinate, we use dependent words such as *because, when,* and *although.* Following is a brief list of common dependent words (see also the list on page 197). Subordination is explained in full on page 202.

Common Dependent Words

after	before	unless
although	even though	until
as	if	when
because	since	while

Using Dependent Words

ACTIVITY 9

Choose a logical dependent word from the preceding box and write it in the space provided.

EXAMPLE

_____Until_____ I was six, I thought chocolate milk came from brown cows.

HINT   In item 1, which dependent word best signals that something extends from the past (July 4, 2008) to the present?

1. Will hasn't had a cigarette _____ July 4, 2008.

2. _____ you're willing to work hard, don't sign up for Professor Dunn's class.

3. The lines at that supermarket are so long _____ there are too few cashiers.

4. _____ reading the scary novel, my sister had nightmares for days.

5. My boss gave me smoked salmon for my birthday _____ he knows I'm a vegetarian.

Using Subordination

ACTIVITY 10

Rewrite the five sentences that follow (all taken from this chapter) so that one idea is subordinate to the other. Use one of the dependent words from the box "Common Dependent Words."

EXAMPLE

Auto races no longer use gasoline; spectators have nothing to fear from exhaust fumes.

Since auto races no longer use gasoline, spectators have nothing to fear from

exhaust fumes.

HINT   For item 1, select a dependent word that logically connects the two ideas (a wish to stop smoking and a wish not to gain weight).

1. I want to stop smoking; I don't want to gain weight.

   _____

   _____

2. It was too hot indoors to study; I decided to go down to the shopping center for ice cream.

   _____

   _____

3. He had hair implants; it looked very natural.

   _____

   _____

4. Professor Williams scowled at the class; her facial expression told the story.

   _____

   _____

5. This world map was published only three years ago; the names of some countries are already out of date.

   _____

   _____

ACTIVITY 11   Editing and Rewriting

Working with a partner, read carefully the short paragraph that follows and underline the five run-ons. Then use the space provided to correct the five run-ons. Feel free to discuss the rewrite quietly with your partner and refer back to the chapter when necessary.

[1]When Mark began his first full-time job, he immediately got a credit card, a used sports car was his first purchase. [2]Then he began to buy expensive clothes that he could not afford he also bought impressive gifts for his parents and his girlfriend. [3]Several months passed before Mark realized that he owed an enormous amount of money. [4]To make matters worse, his car broke down, a stack of bills suddenly seemed to be due at once. [5]Mark tried to cut back on his purchases, he soon realized he had to cut up his credit card to prevent himself from using it. [6]He also began keeping a careful record of his spending he had no idea where his money had gone till then. [7]He hated to admit to his family and friends that he had to get his budget under control. [8]However, his girlfriend said she did not mind inexpensive dates, and his parents were proud of his growing maturity.

_____

_____

_____

_____

_____

_____

_____

_____

Creating Sentences

Working with a partner, make up your own short run-ons test as directed.

1. Write a run-on sentence. Then rewrite it, using a period and a capital letter to separate the thoughts into two sentences.

   Run-on

   _____

   Rewrite

   _____

2. Write a sentence that has two complete thoughts. Then rewrite it, using a comma and a joining word to correctly join the complete thoughts.

   Two complete thoughts

   _____

   Rewrite

   _____

3. Write a sentence that has two complete thoughts. Then rewrite it, using a semicolon to correctly join the complete thoughts.

   Two complete thoughts

   _____

   Rewrite

   _____

REFLECTIVE ACTIVITY

1. Look at the paragraph that you revised in Activity 11. Explain how run-ons affect the paragraph.

2. In your own written work, which type of run-on are you most likely to write: comma splices or fused sentences? Why do you tend to make this kind of mistake?

3. Which method for correcting run-ons are you most likely to use in your own writing? Which are you least likely to use? Why?

REVIEW TEST 1

In the space provided, write *R-O* beside run-on sentences. Write *C* beside the one sentence that is punctuated correctly. Some of the run-ons have no punctuation between the two complete thoughts; others have only a comma.

Correct each run-on by using (1) a period and a capital letter; (2) a comma and a joining word *and, but, for, so*; or (3) a semicolon. Do not use the same method of correction for every sentence.

EXAMPLE

_____R-O_____ Sam never saved his work,^{so} he lost his paper when his computer crashed.

_____ 1. Americans spend millions of dollars each year on bottled water critics argue that tap water is equally safe to drink.

_____ 2. Isaiah is confident that the trucking company will hire him he has a valid CDL license and a clean traffic abstract.

_____ 3. The mechanic said that many hybrid cars have transmission problems I am glad that I purchased a gasoline-powered subcompact car, which is equally fuel efficient.

_____ 4. This summer brought record-breaking drought conditions many farmers are being forced to plant fewer crops or irrigate water into their fields.

_____ 5. Sydney decided to use recycled plastic to build an outdoor deck her children asked her to build a doghouse with the extra lumber.

_____ 6. Mark worried that the canned chili sauce he ate while on his camping trip was recalled for botulism he did not experience any symptoms of food poisoning.

_____ 7. Parents who sign up their children for mixed martial arts hope that the sport will provide physical exercise, self-confidence, and personal discipline their children, however, say that they are simply having fun.

_____ 8. The Ladies Professional Golf Association (LPGA) was founded in 1950, making it the oldest female professional sports organization in the United States.

_____ 9. Witnesses reported that the bank robber was a woman security cameras revealed that the thief was a man carrying a handbag and wearing a wig and lipstick.

_____ 10. Today, the average American teenager works 16 hours per week parents and educators are concerned that these part-time jobs leave little time for homework or sleep.

REVIEW TEST 2

Correct each run-on by using subordination. Choose from among the following dependent words.

after	before	unless
although	even though	until
as	if	when
because	since	while

EXAMPLE

Tony hated going to a new barber, he was afraid of butchered hair.

Because Tony was afraid of butchered hair, he hated going to a new barber.

1. Mom was frying potatoes, the heat set off the smoke alarm.

_____

_____

2. I love animals I'm not ready to take on the responsibility of a pet.

_____

_____

3. Lani leaves a lecture class, she reviews and clarifies her notes.

_____

_____

4. Matthew jogs, he thinks over his day's activities.

_____

_____

5. My mother puts apples in the fruit bowl she first washes the wax off them.

_____

_____

6. I began to shake on the examining table the nurse reached out and held my hand.

_____

_____

7. Some pets are easy to care for, others require patience and lots of hard work.

_____

_____

8. Molly forgot to turn the oven off her homemade bread looked like burned toast.

_____

_____

9. A wheel hit a crack in the sidewalk the skateboard shot out from under Dan.

_____

_____

10. John Grisham and Stephen King make huge fortunes with their novels most writers barely make a living.

_____

_____

REVIEW TEST 3

On a separate piece of paper, write six sentences, each of which has two complete thoughts. In two of the sentences, use a period and a capital letter between the thoughts. In another two sentences, use a comma and a joining word (*and, but, or, nor, for, so, yet*) to join the thoughts. In the final two sentences, use a semicolon to join the thoughts.

REVIEW TEST 4

Write for five minutes about something that makes you angry. Don't worry about spelling, punctuation, finding exact words, or organizing your thoughts. Just focus on writing as many words as you can without stopping.

After you have finished, go back and make whatever changes are needed to correct any run-on sentences in your writing.

For additional materials on Chapter 8, visit **www.mhhe.com/langan**.

Sentence Variety I

Four Traditional Sentence Patterns

Sentences in English are traditionally described as *simple, compound, complex,* or *compound-complex.*

The Simple Sentence

A simple sentence has a single subject-verb combination.

Children play.

The game ended early.

My car stalled three times last week.

The lake has been polluted by several neighboring streams.

A simple sentence may have more than one subject:

Lola and Tony drove home.

The wind and heat dried my hair.

or more than one verb:

The children smiled and waved at us.

The lawn mower smoked and sputtered.

or several subjects and verbs:

Manny, Kira, and Jack lubricated my car, replaced the oil filter, and cleaned the spark plugs.

CHAPTER PREVIEW

Four Traditional Sentence Patterns

- The Simple Sentence

- The Compound Sentence

- The Complex Sentence

- The Compound-Complex Sentence

Review of Subordination and Coordination

The Simple Sentence	**ACTIVITY 1**

On separate paper, write:

Three sentences, each with a single subject and verb

Three sentences, each with a single subject and a double verb

Three sentences, each with a double subject and a single verb

In each case, underline the subject once and the verb twice. (See pages 150–161 if necessary for more information on subjects and verbs.)

The Compound Sentence

A compound, or "double," sentence is made up of two (or more) simple sentences. The two complete statements in a compound sentence are usually connected by a comma plus a joining word (*and, but, for, or, nor, so, yet*).

A compound sentence is used when you want to give equal weight to two closely related ideas. The technique of showing that ideas have equal importance is called *coordination*.

Following are some compound sentences. Each sentence contains two ideas that the writer considers equal in importance.

The rain increased, so the officials canceled the game.

Denise wanted to go shopping, but Fred refused to drive her.

Hollis was watching television in the family room, and April was upstairs on the phone.

I had to give up wood carving, for my arthritis had become very painful.

ACTIVITY 2	**The Compound Sentence**

Combine the following pairs of simple sentences into compound sentences. Use a comma and a logical joining word (*and, but, for, so*) to connect each pair.

 If you are not sure what *and, but, for,* and *so* mean, review page 184.

EXAMPLE

- The children wanted to eat pizza.
- I picked up fried chicken on the way home.

  The children wanted to eat pizza, but I picked up fried chicken on the way home.

1. • I am majoring in digital media arts.
   • I hope to find a job doing video-game animation.

   _____

   _____

2. • My children were spending too much time in front of the TV and computer.
   • I signed up my entire family for a one-year gym membership.

   _____

   _____

3. • Nicole's skin was blemished and sun damaged.

   • She consulted with a plastic surgeon about a chemical face peel.

   _____

   _____

4. • Riley insists on buying certified-organic fruits and vegetables.

   • I cannot distinguish organic from conventionally grown produce.

   _____

   _____

5. • I was recently promoted to shift manager at work.

   • I need to drop down to part-time status at school next semester.

   _____

   _____

Writing Compound Sentences   ACTIVITY 3

On a separate piece of paper, write five compound sentences of your own. Use a different joining word (*and, but, for, or, nor, so, yet*) to connect the two complete ideas in each sentence.

The Complex Sentence

A complex sentence is made up of a simple sentence (a complete statement) and a statement that begins with a dependent word. Here is a list of common dependent words:

Dependent Words		
after	if, even if	when, whenever
although, though	in order that	where, wherever
as	since	whether
because	that, so that	which, whichever
before	unless	while
even though	until	who
how	what, whatever	whose

> **TIP**   The two parts of a complex sentence are sometimes called an *independent clause* and a *dependent clause*. A *clause* is simply a word group that contains a subject and a verb. An *independent clause* expresses a complete thought and can stand alone. A *dependent clause* does not express a complete thought in itself and "depends on" the independent clause to complete its meaning. Dependent clauses always begin with a dependent or subordinating word.

A complex sentence is used when you want to emphasize one idea over another in a sentence. Look at the following complex sentence:

Because I forgot the time, I missed the final exam.

The idea that the writer wants to emphasize here—*I missed the final exam*—is expressed as a complete thought. The less important idea—*Because I forgot the time*—is subordinated to the complete thought. The technique of giving one idea less emphasis than another is called *subordination.*

Following are other examples of complex sentences. In each case, the part starting with the dependent word is the less emphasized part of the sentence.

While Aisha was eating breakfast, she began to feel sick.

I checked my money *before* I invited Pedro for lunch.

When Jerry lost his temper, he also lost his job.

Although I practiced for three months, I failed my driving test.

ACTIVITY 4	Creating Complex Sentences

Use logical dependent words to combine the following pairs of simple sentences into complex sentences. Place a comma after a dependent statement when it starts the sentence.

EXAMPLE

- I applied for a low-interest student loan.
- I spoke to a financial aid counselor about my options.

  After I spoke to a financial aid counselor about my options, I applied for a

  low-interest student loan.

> **HINT** In item 1, use the dependent word *while*.

1. • Lydia read the quarterly reports.
   • Her assistant drove them to a regional sales meeting.

   _____

   _____

2. • Keiko laughed hysterically.
   • She heard the punch line to the joke.

   _____

   _____

3. • I wanted to order the chef's seafood special.

    • The kitchen ran out of fresh prawns.

    _____

    _____

4. • Raymond refuses to drink from a public water fountain.

    • He is afraid that he will catch an infectious disease.

    _____

    _____

5. • I want to register for a calculus class.

    • I need to take the math placement exam.

    _____

    _____

Using Subordination

ACTIVITY 5

Rewrite the following sentences, using subordination rather than coordination. Include a comma when a dependent statement starts a sentence.

EXAMPLE

The hair dryer was not working right, so I returned it to the store.

Because the hair dryer was not working right, I returned it to the store.

_____

HINT   In item 1, use the dependent word *as*.

1. Carlo set the table, and his wife finished cooking dinner.

    _____

    _____

2. Maggie could have gotten good grades, but she did not study enough.

    _____

    _____

3. I watered my drooping African violets, and they perked right up.

    _____

    _____

CONNECT WRITING

Meet Emilio. He and his family just returned home from a trip where they received incredibly poor service at their hotel. He is writing a letter to the hotel manager about the experience. He has all the facts listed, but his ideas don't seem to connect in any clear way. Help Emilio connect his ideas by creating complex sentences using subordination.

mhconnectwriting.com

4. The little boy kept pushing the "down" button, but the elevator didn't come any more quickly.

    _____

    _____

5. I never really knew what pain was, and then I had four impacted wisdom teeth pulled at once.

    _____

    _____

| ACTIVITY 6 | **Using *Who*, *Which*, or *That*** |

Combine the following simple sentences into complex sentences. Omit repeated words. Use the dependent words *who*, *which*, or *that*.

> ## HINT
> • The word *who* refers to persons.
> • The word *which* refers to things.
> • The word *that* refers to persons or things.

Use commas around the dependent statement only if it seems to interrupt the flow of thought in the sentence. (See pages 365–378 for more about commas.)

EXAMPLES

- Clyde picked up a hitchhiker.
- The hitchhiker was traveling around the world.

  Clyde picked up a hitchhiker who was traveling around the world.

  _____

- Larry is a sleepwalker.
- Larry is my brother.

  Larry, who is my brother, is a sleepwalker.

  _____

1. • Karen just gave birth to twins.

    • Karen is an old friend of mine.

    _____

    _____

2. • The tea burned the roof of my mouth.

    • The tea was hotter than I expected.

    _____

    _____

3. • I dropped the camera.

    • My sister had just bought the camera.

    _____

    _____

4. • Ashaki brought us some enormous oranges.

    • Ashaki is visiting from California.

    _____

    _____

5. • Liz used a steam cleaner to shampoo her rugs.

    • The rugs were dirtier than she had expected.

    _____

    _____

Writing Complex Sentences   ACTIVITY 7

On a separate piece of paper, write eight complex sentences, using, in turn, the dependent words *unless, if, after, because, when, who, which,* and *that.*

The Compound-Complex Sentence

A compound-complex sentence is made up of two (or more) simple sentences and one or more dependent statements. In the following examples, there is a solid line under the simple sentences and a dotted line under the dependent statements.

> When the power line snapped, Jack was listening to the stereo, and Linda was reading in bed.

> After I returned to school following a long illness, the math teacher gave me makeup work, but the history teacher made me drop her course.

Using Joining Words and Dependent Words   ACTIVITY 8

Read through each sentence to get a sense of its overall meaning. Then insert a logical joining word (*and, or, but, for,* or *so*) and a logical dependent word (*because, since, when,* or *although*).

  In item 1, use *after* and *for.*

1. _____ you listen to our professor's lecture, read the assigned pages in the textbook, _____ the information will be much more relevant.

2. _____ I ride the bus to work, I always intend to read the newspaper, _____ I usually end up listening to new songs on my iPod.

3. My daughter told the truth _____ I asked her about skipping classes, _____ she also explained why she hates junior high school.

4. _____ I am on a strict budget now, I am trying to resist buying lattes at Starbucks, _____ I brew myself coffee before leaving the house.

5. Daniel wanted to attend the event, _____ he had to work a double shift _____ several of his coworkers called in sick.

ACTIVITY 9 | **Writing Compound-Complex Sentences**

On a separate piece of paper, write five compound-complex sentences.

Review of Subordination and Coordination

Subordination and coordination are ways of showing the exact relationship of ideas within a sentence. Through **subordination,** we show that one idea is less important than another. When we subordinate, we use dependent words such as *when, although, while, because,* and *after.* (See the list of common dependent words on page 197.) Through **coordination,** we show that ideas are of equal importance. When we coordinate, we use the words *and, but, for, or, nor, so,* and *yet.*

ACTIVITY 10 | **Using Subordination or Coordination**

Working with a fellow classmate, use subordination or coordination to combine the following groups of simple sentences into one or more longer sentences. Be sure to omit repeated words. Since various combinations are possible, you might want to jot down several combinations on a separate piece of paper. Then read them aloud to find the combination that sounds best.

Keep in mind that, very often, the relationship among ideas in a sentence will be clearer when subordination rather than coordination is used.

EXAMPLE

- My car does not start on cold mornings.
- I think the battery needs to be replaced.

- I already had it recharged once.
- I don't think charging it again would help.

  Because my car does not start on cold mornings, I think the battery needs

  to be replaced. I already had it recharged once, so I don't think charging it

  again would help.

> **HINT** Use a comma at the end of a word group that starts with a dependent word (as in "Because my car does not start on cold mornings, . . .").

> **HINT** Use a comma between independent word groups connected by *and, but, for, or, nor, so,* and *yet* (as in "I already had it recharged once, so . . ."). In item 1, use *although,* two commas, and the joining word *so.*

1.
- Jaylen likes loud music.
- His parents can't stand it.
- He wears earphones.

  _____

  _____

  _____

  _____

2.
- The volcano erupted.
- The sky turned black with smoke.
- Nearby villagers were frightened.
- They clogged the roads leading to safety.

  _____

  _____

  _____

3.
- Min-Yeng had a haircut today.
- She came home and looked in the mirror.
- She decided to wear a hat for a few days.
- She thought she looked like a bald eagle.

  _____

  _____

  _____

  _____

4. • I ran out of gas on the way to work.

   • I discovered how helpful strangers can be.

   • A passing driver saw I was stuck.

   • He drove me to the gas station and back to my car.

   _____

   _____

   _____

   _____

5. • Our dog often rests on the floor in the sunshine.

   • He waits for the children to get home from school.

   • The sunlight moves along the floor.

   • He moves with it.

   _____

   _____

   _____

   _____

6. • My father was going to be late from work.

   • We planned to have a late dinner.

   • I was hungry before dinner.

   • I ate a salami and cheese sandwich.

   • I did this secretly.

   _____

   _____

   _____

   _____

7. • A baseball game was scheduled for early afternoon.

   • It looked like rain.

   • A crew rolled huge tarps to cover the field.

   • Then the sun reappeared.

   _____

   _____

   _____

   _____

8. • Cassy worries about the pesticides used on fruit.

   • She washes apples, pears, and plums in soap and water.

   • She doesn't rinse them well.

   • They have a soapy flavor.

   _____

   _____

   _____

9. • Charlene needed to buy stamps.

   • She went to the post office during her lunch hour.

   • The line was long.

   • She waited there for half an hour.

   • She had to go back to work without stamps.

   _____

   _____

   _____

10. • The weather suddenly became frigid.

   • Almost everyone at work caught a cold.

   • Someone brought a big batch of chicken soup.

   • She poured it into one of the office coffeepots.

   • The pot was empty by noon.

   _____

   _____

   _____

REVIEW TEST 1

Combine each group of short sentences into one sentence. Various combinations are possible. Choose the combination that reads most smoothly and clearly and that sounds most appropriate in the context of surrounding sentences. Use a separate piece of paper.

Here is an example of a group of sentences and some possible combinations:

EXAMPLE

- Carly moved in the desk chair.
- Her moving was uneasy.
- The chair was hard.
- She worked at the assignment.
- The assignment was for her English class.

Carly moved uneasily in the hard desk chair, working at the assignment for her English class.

Moving uneasily in the hard desk chair, Carly worked at the assignment for her English class.

Carly moved uneasily in the hard desk chair as she worked at the assignment for her English class.

While she worked at the assignment for her English class, Carly moved uneasily in the hard desk chair.

HINT   In combining short sentences into one sentence, omit repeated words where necessary.

Doctor's Waiting Room

- People visit the doctor.
- Their ordeal begins.

- A patient has an appointment for 2:00.
- He is told he will have to wait.
- The wait will be at least one hour.

- Other people arrive.
- Everyone takes a seat.
- Soon the room becomes crowded.

- Some people read old magazines.
- Others count the stripes.
- The stripes are in the wallpaper.

- Some people look at each other.
- Some people may smile.
- No one talks to anyone else.

- Some people are very sick.
- They cough a lot.
- They hold tissues to their noses.

- The people around them turn away.
- They hold their breath.
- They are afraid of becoming infected.

- Time passes.
- It passes slowly.
- All the people count.
- They count the number of people ahead of them.

- The long-awaited moment finally arrives.
- The receptionist comes into the waiting area.

- She looks at the patient.
- She says the magic words.
- "The doctor will see you now."

REVIEW TEST 2

Combine each group of short sentences into one sentence. Various combinations are possible. Choose the combination that reads most smoothly and clearly and that sounds most appropriate in the context of surrounding sentences. Use a separate piece of paper.

> **HINT** In combining short sentences into one sentence, omit repeated words where necessary.

A Remedy for Shyness

- Linda Nelson was shy.
- She seldom met new people.
- She spent a lot of time alone.

- Too often Linda avoided speaking.
- She did not want to take a risk.
- The risk was embarrassing herself.

- Luckily, Linda got some advice.
- The advice was good.
- She got the advice from her cousin Rose.
- Linda decided to try to change.
- She would change her behavior.

- Rose told Linda not to blame herself for being shy.
- She told her the shyness made her seem attractive.
- She told her the shyness made her seem modest.

- Rose encouraged her to talk to others.
- Linda began to join conversations at school.
- Linda began to join conversations at work.

- Gradually, Linda learned something.
- She could start conversations.
- She could start them herself.
- She could do this even though her heart pounded.
- She could do this even though her stomach churned.

- Linda still feels uncomfortable sometimes.
- She is doing things that once seemed impossible.

- Linda joined a bowling league.
- She did this recently.
- Some of her new friends invited her to join.
- The friends were from work.

- She is not the best bowler on the team.
- She is winning a victory over shyness.
- She is winning, thanks to her cousin's help.
- She is winning, thanks to her own determination.

- Linda is a happier person today.
- She has taken charge of her life.
- She has made herself a more interesting person.

REFLECTIVE ACTIVITY

1. Read your answers to Activity 10 in this chapter. When did you use subordination? When did you use coordination? Which of the two methods do you find easier to use?

2. Read what you wrote for Review Tests 1 and 2 in this chapter. What methods for creating variety did you use when combining sentences? Why do you think your sentences are better than the originals?

For additional materials on Chapter 9, visit www.mhhe.com/langan.

Verbs, Pronouns, and Agreement

SECTION PREVIEW

10 Standard English Verbs

11 Irregular Verbs

12 Subject-Verb Agreement

13 Consistent Verb Tense

14 Additional Information about Verbs

15 Pronoun Reference, Agreement, and Point of View

16 Pronoun Types

LOVER'S LEAP

1827 — · — 1973

The poetic lines inscribed on the boulder below is a replica of those carved in 1827 by Thomas W. Farrar.
Thomas W. Farrar was the Founder and first Grand Master of the Masonic Lodge in Alabama 1821~22~24.
This historical site donated to the public by Jonas W. Schwab in 1935.
The work was done and fence provided by Thomas W. Martin and George B. Ward.

ERECTED BY SHADES CREST GARDEN CLUB, JEFFERSON COUNTY, BIRMINGHAM, ALABAMA
APRIL 18, 1973

RESPONDING TO IMAGES

How could you change this sign's wording to make it grammatically correct?
What specific errors have been made?

10 Standard English Verbs

CHAPTER PREVIEW

Regular Verbs: Dialect and Standard Forms

• Present Tense Endings

• Past Tense Endings

Three Common Irregular Verbs: Dialect and Standard Forms

INTRODUCTORY ACTIVITY

Underline what you think is the correct form of the verb in each pair of sentences that follows.

That radio station once (play, played) top-forty hits.

It now (play, plays) classical music.

When Jean was a little girl, she (hope, hoped) to become a movie star.

Now she (hope, hopes) to be accepted at business school.

At first, my father (juggle, juggled) with balls of yarn.

Now that he is an expert, he (juggle, juggles) raw eggs.

On the basis of the previous examples, see if you can complete the following statements.

1. The first sentence in each pair refers to an action in the (past time, present time), and the regular verb has an _____ ending.

2. The second sentence in each pair refers to an action in the (past time, present time), and the regular verb has an _____ ending.

Answers are on page 622.

Many people have grown up in communities where nonstandard verb forms are used in everyday life. Such nonstandard forms include *they be, it done, we has, you was, she don't,* and *it ain't.* Community dialects have richness and power, but in college and the world at large, Standard English verb forms must be used. Standard English helps ensure clear communication among English-speaking people everywhere, and it is especially important in the world of work.

This chapter compares the community dialect and the Standard English forms of a regular verb and three common irregular verbs.

Regular Verbs: Dialect and Standard Forms

The following chart compares community dialect (nonstandard) and Standard English forms of the regular verb *talk*.

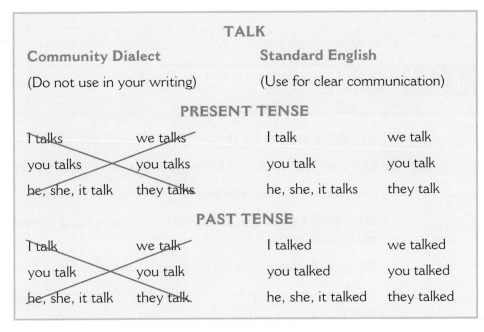

TALK			
Community Dialect		**Standard English**	
(Do not use in your writing)		(Use for clear communication)	
PRESENT TENSE			
I talks	we talks	I talk	we talk
you talks	you talks	you talk	you talk
he, she, it talk	they talks	he, she, it talks	they talk
PAST TENSE			
I talk	we talk	I talked	we talked
you talk	you talk	you talked	you talked
he, she, it talk	they talk	he, she, it talked	they talked

One of the most common nonstandard forms results from dropping the endings of regular verbs. For example, people might say "Rose work until ten o'clock tonight" instead of "Rose works until ten o'clock tonight." Or they'll say "I work overtime yesterday" instead of "I worked overtime yesterday." To avoid such nonstandard usage, memorize the forms shown above for the regular verb *talk*. Then do the activities that follow. These activities will help you make it a habit to include correct verb endings in your writing.

Present Tense Endings

The verb ending -*s* or -*es* is needed with a regular verb in the present tense when the subject is *he, she, it,* or any one person or thing.

He	He lifts weights.
She	She runs.
It	It amazes me.
One person	Their son Ted swims.
One person	Their daughter Terri dances.
One thing	Their house jumps at night with all the exercise.

Using Standard Verb Forms ACTIVITY 1

All but one of the ten sentences that follow need -*s* or -*es* endings. Cross out the nonstandard verb forms and write the standard forms in the spaces provided. Mark with a *C* the one sentence that needs no change.

EXAMPLE

__ends__   The sale ~~end~~ tomorrow.

> ## HINT
>
> Add *s* to *drive* in item 1.

_____   1. Tim drive too fast for me.

_____   2. Our washing machine always get stuck at the rinse cycle.

_____   3. Roberto practice his saxophone two hours each day.

_____   4. Whenever I serve meat loaf, my daughter make a peanut butter sandwich.

_____   5. My grandfather brush his teeth with baking soda.

_____   6. While watching television in the evening, Sara usually fall asleep.

_____   7. Mom always wakes me by saying, "Get up, the day is growing older."

_____   8. On my old car radio, a static sound come from every station but one.

_____   9. My little sister watch fireworks with her hands over her ears.

_____   10. The broken cell phone buzz like an angry wasp.

| ACTIVITY 2 | **Using Present Tense -s Verb Endings** |

Rewrite the short selection that follows, adding present tense -*s* verb endings in the ten places where they are needed.

> My little sister want to be a singer when she grow up. She constantly hum and sing around the house. Sometimes she make quite a racket. When she listen to music on the radio, for example, she sing very loudly in order to hear herself over the radio. And when she take a shower, her voice ring through the whole house because she think nobody can hear her from there.

_____

_____

_____

_____

_____

Past Tense Endings

The verb ending -d or -ed is needed with a regular verb in the past tense.

Yesterday we finished painting the apartment.

I completed the paper an hour before class.

Ty's car stalled on his way to work this morning.

Using Standard Verb Forms: -d and -ed Endings	ACTIVITY 3

All but one of the ten sentences that follow need -d or -ed endings. Cross out the nonstandard verb forms and write the standard forms in the spaces provided. Mark with a C the one sentence that needs no change.

EXAMPLE

___jumped___   The cat ~~jump~~ onto my lap when I sat down.

┌───┐
| **HINT**   In item 1, add ed to spill. |
└───┘

_____ 1. A waiter at the new restaurant accidentally spill ice water into Phil's lap.

_____ 2. In a prim Indiana town, a couple was actually jail for kissing in public.

_____ 3. While ironing my new shirt this morning, I burn a hole right through it.

_____ 4. Fran wrapped the gag gift in waxed paper and tie it with dental floss.

_____ 5. Pencil marks dotted Matt's bedroom wall where he measure his height each month.

_____ 6. My brother was eating too fast and almost choked on a piece of bread.

_____ 7. Last summer, a burglar smash my car window and stole my jacket.

_____ 8. The kids construct an obstacle course in the basement out of boxes and toys.

_____ 9. The rain came down so hard it level the young cornstalks in our garden.

_____ 10. As Alfonso pulled up to the red light, he suddenly realize his brakes were not working.

ACTIVITY 4	**Using Past Tense Verb Endings**

Rewrite this selection, adding past tense -*d* or -*ed* verb endings where needed.

> Brad hate working long hours, but he need money to support his growing family and to pay for school. He start working at the auto body shop when he graduate from high school because he like cars, but now the job bore him. He wish that he could spend more time at home with his wife and new baby girl. He also want to dedicate more time to his homework. Brad knew that he had made his own choices, so he decide to appreciate his job, his family, and his chance to move ahead in life.

_____

_____

_____

_____

_____

Three Common Irregular Verbs: Dialect and Standard Forms

The following charts compare the community dialect (nonstandard) and Standard English forms of the common irregular verbs *be*, *have*, and *do*.

> **TIP**   For more on irregular verbs, see Chapter 11, beginning on page 220.

BE			
Community Dialect		**Standard English**	
(Do not use in your writing)		(Use for clear communication)	
PRESENT TENSE			
I be (*or* is)	we be	I am	we are
you be	you be	you are	you are
he, she, it be	they be	he, she, it is	they are
PAST TENSE			
I were	we was	I was	we were
you was	you was	you were	you were
he, she, it were	they was	he, she, it was	they were

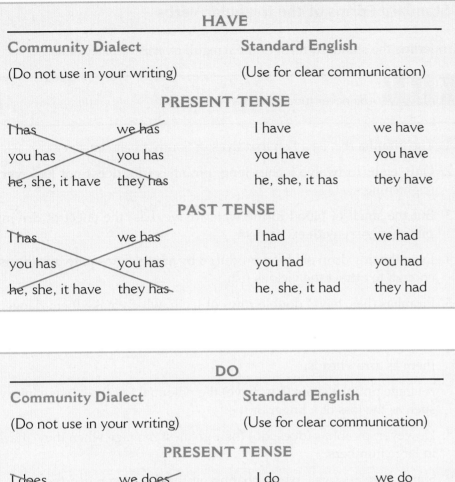

HAVE

Community Dialect		Standard English	
(Do not use in your writing)		(Use for clear communication)	

PRESENT TENSE

Community Dialect		Standard English	
~~I has~~	~~we has~~	I have	we have
~~you has~~	~~you has~~	you have	you have
~~he, she, it have~~	~~they has~~	he, she, it has	they have

PAST TENSE

Community Dialect		Standard English	
~~I has~~	~~we has~~	I had	we had
~~you has~~	~~you has~~	you had	you had
~~he, she, it have~~	~~they has~~	he, she, it had	they had

DO

Community Dialect		Standard English	
(Do not use in your writing)		(Use for clear communication)	

PRESENT TENSE

Community Dialect		Standard English	
~~I does~~	~~we does~~	I do	we do
~~you does~~	~~you does~~	you do	you do
~~he, she, it do~~	~~they does~~	he, she, it does	they do

PAST TENSE

Community Dialect		Standard English	
~~I done~~	~~we done~~	I did	we did
~~you done~~	~~you done~~	you did	you did
~~he, she, it done~~	~~they done~~	he, she, it did	they did

CONNECT WRITING

Meet Sergey. He's writing a Wiki posting for his culinary arts class. They're putting together a Wiki cookbook and he wants to explain how to cook perfectly steamed white rice. He's unsure how to use all the different verb forms and is worried that his cooking instructions are unclear. Help Sergey recognize all the different verb forms for regular and irregular verbs in his writing.

mhconnectwriting.com

TIP Many people have trouble with one negative form of *do*. They will say, for example, "She don't listen" instead of "She doesn't listen," or they will say "This pen don't work" instead of "This pen doesn't work." Be careful to avoid the common mistake of using *don't* instead of *doesn't*.

ACTIVITY 5	Standard Forms of the Irregular Verbs

Underline the standard form of the irregular verbs *be, have,* or *do.*

> **HINT**   *Be* never functions as a verb by itself.

1. The piranha (be, is) a fish that lives in South American rivers.
2. Only eight to twelve inches long, piranhas (do, does) not look very frightening.
3. But the smell of blood in the water (have, has) the effect of driving piranhas crazy with excitement.
4. Even the tiny drop of blood produced by a single mosquito bite (be, is) enough to attract the vicious fish.
5. Piranhas (has, have) double rows of teeth, which make them dangerous hunters.
6. Those teeth (be, are) so sharp that some Native American tribes use them as arrowheads.
7. A single piranha's bite (has, have) the potential to cause severe injury, such as the loss of a finger or toe.
8. However, piranhas (does, do) their greatest damage when they attack in large numbers.
9. Some travelers (was, were) boating on the Amazon when they saw a school of piranhas strip a four-hundred-pound hog to a skeleton in minutes.
10. "What the piranha (does, do) is believable only if you see it," reported one witness.

ACTIVITY 6	Identifying and Correcting Nonstandard Verbs

Cross out the nonstandard verb form in each sentence. Then write the standard form of *be, have,* or *do* in the space provided.

> **HINT**   *You does* is never a correct form.

_____   1. If you does your assignments on time, you may not understand my friend Albert.

_____   2. Albert be the world's worst procrastinator.

_____ 3. Procrastinators be people who always put things off.

_____ 4. They has problems with deadlines of all kinds.

_____ 5. Albert were a procrastinator at the age of six.

_____ 6. The boy next door have a few friends over for lunch one day.

_____ 7. Albert's parents was upset when they learned Albert got there three hours late.

_____ 8. They done the neighbors a favor by taking Albert home at once.

_____ 9. Today, Albert still do everything at the last minute or even later.

_____ 10. He have plans to join Procrastinators Anonymous—when he gets around to it.

Using Standard Forms of _be, have,_ and _do_ ACTIVITY 7

Fill in each blank with the standard form of _be, have,_ or _do._

My cousin Rita _____ decided to lose thirty pounds, so she _____ put herself on a rigid diet that _____ not allow her to eat anything that she enjoys. Last weekend, while the family _____ at Aunt Jenny's house for dinner, all Rita _____ to eat _____ a can of Diet Delight peaches. We _____ convinced that Rita meant business when she joined an exercise club whose members _____ to work out on enormous machines and _____ twenty sit-ups just to get started. If Rita _____ reach her goal, we _____ all going to be very proud of her. But I would not be surprised if she _____ not succeed, because this _____ her fourth diet this year.

REVIEW TEST 1

Underline the standard verb form.

1. A double-shot espresso (help, helps) me start the day.

2. Jordan carefully (choose, chooses) his classes according to his major.

3. My current supervisor (don't, doesn't) know that I was fired from my last job.

4. After I left work, I (remember, remembered) that I forgot to shut down my computer.

5. The receptionist at the counter will probably (ask, asked) me to make an appointment first.

6. If we (was, were) quicker, we could have bought tickets to the concert, which is sold out now.

7. Leanne's sister (is, are) adopting a child from Kazakhstan.

8. A police officer (stop, stopped) me on the highway for driving five miles over the speed limit.

9. When the applicant (answer, answered) the interview questions, she impressed everyone.

10. *Newsweek* (did, done) a cover story on childhood obesity.

REVIEW TEST 2

Cross out the nonstandard verb form in each of the sentences that follow. Then write the Standard English verb form in the space at the left, as shown.

EXAMPLE

played Yesterday morning, the children play quietly in the sandbox.

_____ 1. Making promises be easier than keeping them.

_____ 2. Baked potatoes doesn't have as many calories as I thought.

_____ 3. The game were lost when the other team scored a fourth-quarter touchdown.

_____ 4. Our psychology professor ride a motorcycle to school.

_____ 5. The mayor cover his face from photographers as he was escorted to jail.

_____ 6. The large dog growl fiercely when I approached my neighbor's house.

_____ 7. Lightning struck a nearby building last night and cause a major fire.

_____ 8. Many childhood diseases, such as scarlet fever and whooping cough, has almost vanished in the United States.

_____ 9. Natalie turned the television on during the day because the house sound too quiet without it.

_____ 10. That restaurant offers free nonalcoholic drinks to the person who be the driver for a group.

For additional materials on Chapter 10, visit **www.mhhe.com/langan**.

Irregular Verbs

CHAPTER PREVIEW

A Brief Review of Regular Verbs

List of Irregular Verbs

Troublesome Irregular Verbs

INTRODUCTORY ACTIVITY

You may already have a sense of which common English verbs are regular and which are not. To test yourself, fill in the past tense and past participle of each verb below. Five are regular verbs and so take *-d* or *-ed* in the past tense and past participle. For these verbs, write *R* under *Verb Type* and then write their past tense and past participle verb forms. Five are irregular verbs and will probably not sound right when you try to add *-d* or *-ed*. For these verbs, write *I* under *Verb Type*. Also, see if you can write in their irregular verb forms.

Present	Verb Type	Past	Past Participle
hide	*I*	*hid*	*hidden*
1. talk			
2. read			
3. sing			
4. taste			
5. pick			
6. make			
7. feel			
8. type			
9. become			
10. mail			

Answers are on page 623.

A Brief Review of Regular Verbs

Every verb has four principal forms: present, past, past participle, and present participle. These forms can be used to build all the verb tenses (the times shown by a verb).

Most verbs in English are regular. The past and past participle of a regular verb are formed by adding *-d* or *-ed* to the present. The *past participle* is the form of the verb used with the helping verbs *have, has,* or *had* (or some form of *be* with passive verbs, which are explained on page 249). The *present participle* is formed by adding *-ing* to the present.

Here are the principal forms of some regular verbs:

Present	Past	Past Participle	Present Participle
laugh	laughed	laughed	laughing
ask	asked	asked	asking
touch	touched	touched	touching
decide	decided	decided	deciding
explode	exploded	exploded	exploding

List of Irregular Verbs

Irregular verbs have irregular forms in the past tense and past participle. For example, the past tense of the irregular verb *grow* is *grew*; the past participle is *grown*.

Almost everyone has some degree of trouble with irregular verbs. When you are unsure about the form of a verb, you can check the following list of irregular verbs. (The present participle is not shown on this list because it is formed simply by adding *-ing* to the base form of the verb.) Or you can check a dictionary, which gives the principal forms of irregular verbs.

Present	Past	Past Participle
arise	arose	arisen
awake	awoke *or* awaked	awoke *or* awaked
be (am, are, is)	was (were)	been
become	became	become
begin	began	begun
bend	bent	bent
bite	bit	bitten
blow	blew	blown
break	broke	broken
bring	brought	brought
build	built	built
burst	burst	burst
buy	bought	bought

Present	Past	Past Participle
catch	caught	caught
choose	chose	chosen
come	came	come
cost	cost	cost
cut	cut	cut
do (does)	did	done
draw	drew	drawn
drink	drank	drunk
drive	drove	driven
eat	ate	eaten
fall	fell	fallen
feed	fed	fed
feel	felt	felt
fight	fought	fought
find	found	found
fly	flew	flown
freeze	froze	frozen
get	got	got *or* gotten
give	gave	given
go (goes)	went	gone
grow	grew	grown
have (has)	had	had
hear	heard	heard
hide	hid	hidden
hold	held	held
hurt	hurt	hurt
keep	kept	kept
know	knew	known
lay	laid	laid
lead	led	led
leave	left	left
lend	lent	lent
let	let	let
lie	lay	lain
light	lit	lit

Present	Past	Past Participle
lose	lost	lost
make	made	made
meet	met	met
pay	paid	paid
ride	rode	ridden
ring	rang	rung
rise	rose	risen
run	ran	run
say	said	said
see	saw	seen
sell	sold	sold
send	sent	sent
shake	shook	shaken
shrink	shrank	shrunk
shut	shut	shut
sing	sang	sung
sit	sat	sat
sleep	slept	slept
speak	spoke	spoken
spend	spent	spent
stand	stood	stood
steal	stole	stolen
stick	stuck	stuck
sting	stung	stung
swear	swore	sworn
swim	swam	swum
take	took	taken
teach	taught	taught
tear	tore	torn
tell	told	told
think	thought	thought
wake	woke *or* waked	woken *or* waked
wear	wore	worn
win	won	won
write	wrote	written

ACTIVITY 1 — Identifying Incorrect Verb Forms

Cross out the incorrect verb form in the following sentences. Then write the correct form of the verb in the space provided.

EXAMPLE

___began___   When the mud slide started, the whole neighborhood ~~begun~~ going downhill.

> **HINT** In item 1, use the past tense of *come*.

_____ 1. The coach caught Otto when he come in two hours after curfew.

_____ 2. We standed out in the rain all night to buy tickets to the concert.

_____ 3. The Romans had builded a network of roads so the army could travel more quickly from place to place.

_____ 4. Our championship team has swam in every important meet this year.

_____ 5. The nervous mother holded her child's hand tightly as they crossed the busy street.

_____ 6. Hakeem drived in circles for an hour before he admitted that he was lost.

_____ 7. He had wrote the answers to all the questions before anyone else had finished the first page.

_____ 8. The tornado blowed the sign from the top of the bank, and it landed five blocks away in the motel swimming pool.

_____ 9. Kathy buyed school clothes with the money she earned from her summer job.

_____ 10. The poker players knowed they were in trouble when the stranger shuffled the cards with one hand.

ACTIVITY 2 — Using Present Tense, Past Tense, and Past Participle Verbs

For each of the italicized verbs in the following sentences, fill in the three missing forms in the order shown in the box:

> a. Present tense, which takes an -s ending when the subject is *he, she, it*, or any *one person or thing* (see page 211)
>
> b. Past tense
>
> c. Past participle—the form that goes with the helping verb *have, has*, or *had*

EXAMPLE

My nephew loves to *break* things. Every Christmas he (a) ___breaks___ his new toys the minute they're unwrapped. Last year he (b) ___broke___ five toys in seven minutes and then went on to smash his family's new china platter. His mother says he won't be happy until he has (c) ___broken___ their hearts.

HINT   In item 1, add an *s* to *sleep* in choice a. Use the past tense of *sleep* for b and c.

1. Did you ever go to *sleep* on a water bed? My cousin Ysabel (a) _____ on one. Last year I spent the weekend at Ysabel's apartment, and I (b) _____ on it. Since then I have (c) _____ on it several more times, without once getting seasick.

2. A dreadful little boy in my neighborhood loves to *ring* my doorbell and run away. Sometimes he (a) _____ it several times a day. The last time it (b) _____ over and over, I finally refused to answer the door. Then I found out that the mail carrier had (c) _____ the doorbell to deliver a gift from my boyfriend.

3. Why does every teacher ask us to *write* about our summer vacations? Most students (a) _____ about what really happened, but that is usually too dull. I (b) _____ an essay about being taken aboard an alien spacecraft. I bet it was the most interesting essay anybody has ever (c) _____ for my teacher's English class.

4. My sister never has to *stand* in line for a movie very long. She always (a) _____ for a few minutes and then walks straight to the entrance. "I (b) _____ in line as long as I could," she tells the ticket taker. "In fact," she continues in a weak voice, "I have (c) _____ in line too long already. I feel faint." She is always ushered inside immediately.

5. As usual, Ron planned to *swim* at least a hundred laps before breakfast. He knew that an Olympic hopeful (a) _____ while others sleep. That morning he (b) _____ with a deliberate stroke, counting the rhythm silently. He had (c) _____ this way daily for the last two years. It was a price he was willing to pay to be one of the best.

6. I know a woman who likes to *buy* things and return them after she uses them. For example, she always (a) _____ new shoes to wear for special occasions. Then she wears them for the event and returns them the next day. Once she (b) _____ a complete outfit, wore it twice, and returned it a week later. Whenever I shop, I worry that I have (c) _____ something that she has used and returned.

7. Craig sat in his car at the rural crossroads and wondered which direction to *choose*. Should he (a) _____ left or right? He sighed and turned right, knowing that if he (b) _____ the wrong way, he would run out of gas before finding his way back to the highway. After several anxious minutes, he spotted an Exxon sign. He pulled into the service station, grateful that he had (c) _____ the right direction after all.

8. My friend Alice loves to *eat*. But no matter how much she (a) _____, she stays thin. Her husband, on the other hand, is fat. "Why?" he jokingly complains. "I (b) _____ very little today. In fact," he adds with a grin, "all my life I have (c) _____ just one meal a day. Of course, it usually lasts from morning till night."

9. All the kids in the neighborhood waited each winter for Mahoney's pond to *freeze*. They knew that a sudden cold snap (a) _____ only the surface. It took at least a week of low temperatures before the pond (b) _____ more than a few inches deep. Mr. Mahoney checked the ice each day. When it had finally (c) _____ to a depth of six inches, he gave his permission for the children to skate on it.

10. It is important for people to *give* blood. A healthy person can (a) _____ a pint of blood in less than fifteen minutes with little or no discomfort. The first time I (b) _____ blood, I was afraid the needle would hurt, but all I felt was a slight pinch. I have (c) _____ blood many times since then. Each time I do, I feel good, knowing that my gift will help other people.

Troublesome Irregular Verbs

Three common irregular verbs that often give people trouble are *be*, *have*, and *do*. See pages 214–215 for a discussion of these verbs. Three sets of other irregular verbs that can lead to difficulties are *lie-lay*, *sit-set*, and *rise-raise*.

Lie-Lay

The principal forms of *lie* and *lay* are as follows:

Present	Past	Past Participle
lie	lay	lain
lay	laid	laid

> **TIP** *To lie* means *to rest* or *recline*. *To lay* means *to put something down*.

To Lie	**To Lay**
Anthony *lies* on the couch.	I *lay* the mail on the table.
This morning he *lay* in the tub.	Yesterday I *laid* the mail on the counter.
He has *lain* in bed all week with the flu.	I have *laid* the mail where everyone will see it.

Using *lie* and *lay*

ACTIVITY 3

Underline the correct verb.

> **HINT** Use a form of *lie* if you can substitute *recline*. Use a form of *lay* if you can substitute *place*.

> **HINT** Since the kitten is resting, what is the correct answer?

1. On warm sunny days, Serena's kitten often (lies, lays) on the bedroom windowsill.

2. (Lying, Laying) too long in bed in the morning can give me a headache.

3. The Magna Carta (lay, laid) the foundation for the establishment of the English Parliament.

4. He was certain he had (lain, laid) the tiles in a straight line until he stepped back to look.

5. I (lay, laid) down on the couch and pressed my face into the pillow.

Sit-Set

The principal forms of *sit* and *set* are as follows:

Present	Past	Past Participle
sit	sat	sat
set	set	set

To *sit* means *to take a seat* or *to rest*. To *set* means *to put* or *to place*.

To Sit	To Set
I *sit* down during work breaks.	Antonio *sets* out the knives, forks, and spoons.
I *sat* in the doctor's office for three hours.	His sister already *set* out the dishes.
I have always *sat* in the last desk.	They have just *set* out the dinner ware.

ACTIVITY 4   Using *set* and *sit*

Underline the correct form of the verb.

> **HINT**   Use a form of *sit* if you can substitute *rest*. Use a form of *set* if you can substitute *place*. Since Dillon placed the Shuffle, what is the correct verb?

1. Dillon had (sat, set) his iPod Shuffle on the counter for only a few seconds before someone walked off with it.

2. Zena (sat, set) her heavy backpack down on the floor, and then she proceeded to take out her calculus textbook, graphing calculator, and class notes.

3. The cardiologist told me to (sit, set) down before she went over my x-ray results.

4. I (sat, set) a candle on the mantel in the living room to remember my younger sister, who died of leukemia last month.

5. Jackson was (sitting, setting) the box down on the floor when he heard his spine crack.

Rise-Raise

The principal forms of *rise* and *raise* are as follows:

Present	Past	Past Participle
rise	rose	risen
raise	raised	raised

To *rise* means *to get up* or *to move up*. To *raise* (which is a regular verb with simple *-ed* endings) means *to lift up* or *to increase in amount*.

To Rise	To Raise
The soldiers *rise* at dawn.	I'm going to *raise* the stakes in the card game.
The crowd *rose* to applaud the batter.	I *raised* the shades to let in the sun.
Dracula has *risen* from the grave.	I would have quit if the company had not *raised* my salary.

Using *rise* and *raise*

ACTIVITY 5

Underline the correct verb.

> **HINT** Use a form of *rise* if you can substitute *get up* or *move up*. Use a form of *raise* if you can substitute *lift up* or *increase*. Since heat moves upward, what is the correct verb?

1. It is usually warmer upstairs because heat (rises, raises).

2. The new owner (rose, raised) the rent, so now I will have to look for another apartment.

3. We (rose, raised) at three o'clock in the morning to watch the meteor shower.

4. After four days of rain, the river had (risen, raised) over its banks and threatened to flood the highway.

5. A single sailboat made them (rise, raise) the drawbridge, stopping traffic in both directions for fifteen minutes.

REFLECTIVE ACTIVITY

1. Reread some paragraphs or essays you have written in this course (see Chapters 4 and 5 for writing assignments). Underline all of the verbs you used in this work.

2. Check that the present and past tense endings of all regular verbs are correct, as explained in Chapter 10. Pay special attention to forms of *be*, *have*, and *do*.

3. Check that the present and past tense endings of all irregular verbs are correct, as explained in this chapter. If not, correct them.

REVIEW TEST 1

Cross out the incorrect verb form in each sentence. Then write the correct form of the verb in the space provided.

_____   1. The sound of the lawnmower in the front yard waked up my baby from her late morning nap.

_____ 2. Your two pairs of cotton cargo pants may have shrinked because I accidentally ran them through the dryer on the high setting.

_____ 3. No one thought to ask the woman at the bus stop if she was waiting for the express route, which was delayed at the bus terminal.

_____ 4. Rob sold his Honda motorcycle for a good price on Craigslist.

_____ 5. This morning's earthquake might have shook the picture frames and figurines on the shelf.

_____ 6. The invitation indicated that casual attire should be wore to the event, but most of the guests came in formal wear.

_____ 7. During final exam week, I sleeped under three hours a night.

_____ 8. Few people spoken up at the neighborhood board meeting about the proposed legislation.

_____ 9. The breakfast meeting at the hotel costed the company over five hundred dollars.

_____ 10. I flown on standby to save on the cost of airfare.

REVIEW TEST 2

Write short sentences using the form noted for the following irregular verbs.

EXAMPLE

Past of *ride* _The Lone Ranger rode into the sunset._

1. Present of *shake* _____

2. Past participle of *write* _____

3. Past participle of *begin* _____

4. Past of *go* _____

5. Past participle of *grow* _____

6. Present of *speak* _____

7. Past of *bring* _____

8. Present of *do* _____

9. Past participle of *give* _____

10. Past of *drink* _____

For additional materials on Chapter 11, visit **www.mhhe.com/langan**.

Subject-Verb Agreement

INTRODUCTORY ACTIVITY

As you read each pair of sentences, write an *X* beside the sentence that you think uses the underlined word correctly.

The postings on the college gossip site <u>is</u> very cruel. _____

The postings on the college gossip site <u>are</u> very cruel. _____

There <u>was</u> many résumés for the supervisor to read. _____

There <u>were</u> many résumés for the supervisor to read. _____

Everybody <u>want</u> wireless Internet access on campus. _____

Everybody <u>wants</u> wireless Internet access on campus. _____

On the basis of the above examples, see if you can complete the following statements.

1. In the first two pairs of sentences, the subjects are _____ and _____. Since both these subjects are plural, the verb must be plural.

2. In the last pair of sentences, the subject, *Everybody*, is a word that is always (singular, plural), so its accompanying verb must be (singular, plural).

Answers are on page 624.

CHAPTER PREVIEW

Words between the Subject and the Verb

Verb before the Subject

Indefinite Pronouns

Compound Subjects

Who, Which,* and *That

A verb must agree with its subject in number. A *singular subject* (one person or thing) takes a singular verb. A *plural subject* (more than one person or thing) takes a plural verb. Mistakes in subject-verb agreement are sometimes made in the following situations:

- When words come between the subject and the verb
- When a verb comes before the subject
- With indefinite pronouns
- With compound subjects
- With *who, which*, and *that*

Each situation is explained in depth on the following pages.

Words between the Subject and the Verb

Words that come between the subject and the verb do not change subject-verb agreement. In the following sentence

The breakfast cereals in the pantry are made mostly of sugar.

the subject (*cereals*) is plural, so the verb (*are*) is plural. The words *in the pantry* that come between the subject and the verb do not affect subject-verb agreement. To help find the subject of certain sentences, cross out prepositional phrases (explained on page 157):

One of the crooked politicians was jailed for a month.

The boxes in my grandmother's attic contained old family photos and long-forgotten toys.

Following is a list of common prepositions.

COMMON PREPOSITIONS				
about	before	by	inside	over
above	behind	during	into	through
across	below	except	of	to
among	beneath	for	off	toward
around	beside	from	on	under
at	between	in	onto	with

ACTIVITY 1	Words between Subjects and Verbs

Draw one line under the subject. Then lightly cross out any words that come between the subject and the verb. Finally, draw two lines under the correct verb in parentheses.

EXAMPLE

The <u>price</u> ~~of the stereo speakers~~ (is, are) too high for my wallet.

 In item 1, cross out the preposition between the subject and verb.

1. A trail of bloodstains (leads, lead) to the spot where the murder was committed.

2. The winter clothes in the hall closet (takes, take) up too much room.

3. A basket of fancy fruit and nuts (was, were) delivered to my house.

4. The garbled instructions for assembling the bicycle (was, were) almost impossible to follow.

5. Smoke from the distant forest fires (is, are) visible from many miles away.

6. Workers at that automobile plant (begins, begin) each day with a period of exercise.

7. The earliest date on any of the cemetery gravestones (appears, appear) to be 1804.

8. The line of cars in the traffic jam (seems, seem) to extend for miles.

9. Several boxes in the corner of the attic (contains, contain) old family pictures.

10. Sleeping bags with the new insulation material (protects, protect) campers even in subzero temperatures.

Verb before the Subject

A verb agrees with its subject even when the verb comes *before* the subject. Words that may precede the subject include *there, here,* and, in questions, *who, which, what,* and *where.*

> Inside the storage shed are the garden tools.
>
> At the street corner were two panhandlers.
>
> There are times when I'm ready to quit my job.
>
> Where are the instructions for assembling the bed?

> **TIP**   If you are unsure about the subject, ask *who* or *what* of the verb. With the first sentence above, you might ask, "What is inside the storage shed?" The answer, garden *tools,* is the subject.

Verbs That Precede Subjects	ACTIVITY 2

Draw one line under the subject. Then draw two lines under the correct verb in parentheses.

> **HINT**   To find the subject in item 1, ask "What is coming from behind the wall?"

1. There (is, are) a scratching noise coming from behind this wall.

2. On the bottom of the jar of preserves (is, are) the berries.

3. Floating near the base of the dock (was, were) several discarded aluminum cans.

4. In the middle of the woods behind our home (sits, sit) an abandoned cabin.

5. There (was, were) so many students talking at once that the instructor shouted for quiet.

6. Outside the novelty shop at the mall (stands, stand) a life-size cutout of W. C. Fields.

7. Coming out of the fog toward the frightened boys (was, were) the menacing shape of a large dog.

8. In the rear of the closet (was, were) the basketball sneakers that I thought I had lost.

9. On the table in the doctor's office (is, are) some magazines that are five years old.

10. Lining one wall of the gym (was, were) a row of lockers for the team members.

Indefinite Pronouns

The following words, known as *indefinite pronouns,* always take singular verbs.

INDEFINITE PRONOUNS			
(-*one* words)	(-*body* words)	(-*thing* words)	
one	nobody	nothing	each
anyone	anybody	anything	either
everyone	everybody	everything	neither
someone	somebody	something	

TIP   *Both* always takes a plural verb.

ACTIVITY 3   **Using Verbs with Indefinite Pronouns**

Write the correct form of the verb in the space provided.

HINT   The indefinite pronoun *something* requires a singular verb.

keeps, keep

1. Something always _____ me from getting to bed on time.

works, work

2. Nobody that I know _____ as hard as Manuel.

pays, pay

3. Neither of the jobs offered to me _____ more than eight dollars an hour.

has, have

4. Both of the speakers _____ told us more than we care to know about the dangers of water pollution.

slip   5. Someone in Inez's apartment house _____ an unsigned valentine under her door every year.

lean   6. Anything sitting on the old wooden floor _____ to one side.

cts,   7. Each of my friends _____ to be invited to my new in-ground
ct   pool.

were   8. Not one of the three smoke detectors in the house _____ working
         properly.

stop   9. Only one of all the brands of waxes _____ the rust on my car
         from spreading.

ave   10. Just about everybody who hates getting up early for work _____
          jumped out of bed at 6:00 a.m. to go on vacation.

Compound Subjects

Subjects joined by *and* generally take a plural verb.

> Yoga and biking are Lola's ways of staying in shape.

> Ambition and good luck are the keys to his success.

When subjects are joined by *either . . . or, neither . . . nor,* or *not only . . . but also,* the verb agrees with the subject closer to the verb.

> Either the restaurant manager or his assistants deserve to be fired for
> the spoiled meat used in the stew.

> **EXPLANATION:** The nearer subject, *assistants*, is plural, and so the
> verb is plural.

Using Verbs with Compound Subjects   ACTIVITY 4

Write the correct form of the verb in the space provided.

1. The pilates and spinning classes _____ to help me stay in shape,
   but the key to fitness is a sensible diet.

2. Either the tongue ring or dragon tattoo _____ responsible for Zack's
   appeal.

3. A double shot of espresso and two pumps of hazelnut syrup _____
   all I need to start my morning.

4. The lecture podcasts and study guides _____ me prepare for
   exams.

ess,   5. Neither Mick Jagger nor my favorite rock band, The Rolling
esses   Stones, _____ my ten-year old daughter, who prefers
          Disney's Hannah Montana.

Who, Which, and *That*

When *who, which,* and *that* are used as subjects of verbs, they take singular verbs if the word they stand for is singular, and they take plural verbs if the word they stand for is plural. For example, in the sentence

Gary is one of those people <u>who</u> <u>are</u> very private.

the verb is plural because *who* stands for *people,* which is plural. On the other hand, in the sentence

Gary is a person <u>who</u> <u>is</u> very private.

the verb is singular because *who* stands for *person,* which is singular.

ACTIVITY 5	**Using *who, which,* or *that* with Verbs**

Write the correct form of the verb in the space provided.

> **H I N T**   *Who* stands for a singular subject and requires a singular verb.

has, have

goes, go

becomes, become

tastes, taste

is, are

1. The young man who _____ mowed my grass for years just left for college.

2. The jacket that _____ with those pants is at the cleaners.

3. Women who _____ police officers often have to prove themselves more capable than do their male coworkers.

4. The restaurant serves hamburgers that _____ like dry cereal.

5. The ceiling in Kevin's bedroom is covered with stars, which _____. arranged in the shape of the constellations.

ACTIVITY 6	**Editing and Rewriting**

Working with a partner, read the short paragraph below and see if you can underline the five mistakes in subject-verb agreement. Then use the space provided to correct these five errors. Feel free to discuss the rewrite quietly with your partner and refer back to the chapter when necessary.

> When most people think about cities, they do not thinks about wild animals. But in my city apartment, there is enough creatures to fill a small forest. In the daytime, I must contend with the pigeons.

continued

These unwanted guests at my apartment makes a loud feathery mess on my bedroom windowsill. In the evening, my apartment is visited by roaches. These large insects creep onto my kitchen floor and walls after dark and frighten me with their shiny glistening bodies. Later at night, my apartment is invaded by mice. Waking from sleep, I can hear their little feet tapping as they scurry behind walls and above my ceiling. Everybody I know think I should move into a new apartment. What I really need is to go somewhere that have fewer wild creatures—maybe a forest!

CONNECT WRITING

Meet Devon. He has created a family Web site with his wife and two children. They have each written an entry for the Web site and Devon has noticed that each one contains errors in subject-verb agreement. Help Devon locate and correct all the subject-verb agreement mistakes before posting his family's entries.

mhconnectwriting.com

Creating Sentences

ACTIVITY 7

Working with a partner, write sentences as directed. Use a separate piece of paper. For each item, pay special attention to subject-verb agreement.

1. Write a sentence in which the words *in the cafeteria* or *on the table* come between the subject and verb. Underline the subject of your sentence and circle the verb.

2. Write a sentence that begins with the words *There is* or *There are*. Underline the subject of your sentence and circle the verb.

3. Write a sentence in which the indefinite pronoun *nobody* or *anything* is the subject.

4. Write a sentence with the compound subject *manager and employees*. Underline the subject of your sentence and circle the verb.

REFLECTIVE ACTIVITY

1. Look at the paragraph about the apartment that you revised in Activity 6. Which rule involving subject-verb agreement gave you the most trouble? How did you figure out the correct answer?

2. Five situations involving subject-verb agreement have been discussed in this chapter. Explain which one is most likely to cause you problems.

REVIEW TEST 1

Complete each of the following sentences using *is, are, was, were, have,* or *has.*
Underline the subject of each of these verbs. In some cases you will need to
provide that subject.

EXAMPLE

The <u>hot dogs</u> in that luncheonette _____ *are hazardous to your health.* _____

1. In my glove compartment _____

2. The cat and her three kittens _____

3. I frequently see people who _____

4. Neither of the wrestlers _____

5. Scattered across the parking lot _____

6. The dust under my bed _____

7. There are _____

8. My friend and his brother _____

9. The newspapers that accumulate in my garage _____

_____

10. It was one of those movies that _____

_____

REVIEW TEST 2

Underline the correct verb in the parentheses. Note that you will first have
to determine the subject of each sentence. To find subjects in certain sentences, you may find it helpful to cross out prepositional phrases.

1. Sadly, none of the food at weddings (is, are) particularly good.

2. One of my roommates in college (wants, want) to become a software
   engineer so that she can create cutting-edge video and computer
   games.

3. The cost of all my utilities, which include electricity, water, cable, and
   phone, (is, are) ridiculous.

4. High-speed chases and grisly car accidents (seems, seem) to be the
   focus on many reality television shows.

5. Not one of the red-tag specials advertised in yesterday's newspaper
   (was, were) on the shelf when I arrived at the discount department
   store this morning.

6. Once a year, Jackie and her girlfriends (takes, take) a weekend trip to
   Las Vegas for shopping, dining, and gambling.

7. The online articles that the librarian located for the student (was, were) originally published in print.

8. Squeaking from underneath the refrigerator (was, were) a tiny mouse caught in a forgotten spring-based trap.

9. The nurses on strike at the metropolitan hospital (wants, want) safe staffing ratios and retirement security.

10. Neither Dad nor my brother Miguel (wants, want) to talk about their experiences as combat soldiers in the Iraq War.

11. There (was, were) a laptop computer left in one of the carrels at the library.

12. A kleptomaniac will steal anything that (is, are) not nailed down.

13. A few girls at my daughter's high school (plans, plan) to try out for the football team.

14. There is rarely a person among the political candidates who (is, are) humble yet confident.

15. Not only the air ducts but also the plumbing in the abandoned building (is, are) infested with rats.

16. Everyone in my history class (believes, believe) that the professor grades unfairly, but nobody is willing to approach her.

17. Homebuyers should be warned that "fixer-upper" houses on the market often (requires, require) costly repairs.

18. The private e-mail message that I sent in confidence to a few coworkers (was, were) forwarded to my supervisor.

19. Economics (is, are) a subject that requires strong analytic skills.

20. The most popular car colors in the United States (is, are) silver and pearl white.

REVIEW TEST 3

There are ten mistakes in subject-verb agreement in the following passage. Cross out each incorrect verb and write the correct form above it. In addition, underline the subject of each of the verbs that must be changed.

> After almost forty years on television, there is few honors that
>
> *Sesame Street* has not won. The awards are deserved, for *Sesame*
>
> *Street* is a show that treat children with respect. Most children's
>
> programs consists of cheaply made cartoons that is based on the
>
> adventures of a superhero or a video-game character. Unfortunately,
>
> *continued*

children's TV programs are generally so poor because quality kids' shows does not make the profits that the networks demand. Both the superhero story and the video-game story is easy to slap together. By contrast, the producers of *Sesame Street* spends enormous amounts of time and money researching how children learn. Another reason for the low profits are the nature of the audience. Because children have little money to spend on sponsors' products, each of the networks charge bottom rates for advertising during children's programs. *Sesame Street,* a nonprofit show, does not even accept ads. And income from the sale of *Sesame Street* products are used to do an even better job of producing the show.

For additional materials on Chapter 12, visit **www.mhhe.com/langan**.

Consistent Verb Tense

INTRODUCTORY ACTIVITY

See if you can find and underline the two mistakes in verb tense in the following selection.

> When Computer Warehouse had a sale, Alex decided to buy a new computer. He planned to set up the machine himself and hoped to connect to the Internet right away. When he arrived home, however, Alex discovers that setting up a wireless hub could be complicated and confusing. The directions sounded as if they had been written for engineers. After two hours of frustration, Alex gave up and calls a technician for help.

Now try to complete the following statement:

Verb tenses should be consistent. In the selection above, two verbs have to be changed because they are mistakenly in the (*present, past*) _____ tense while all the other verbs in the selection are in the (*present, past*) _____ tense.

Answers are on page 624.

Answers are on page 624.

CHAPTER PREVIEW

Keeping Tenses Consistent

Keeping Tenses Consistent

Do not shift tenses unnecessarily. If you begin writing a paper in the present tense, don't shift suddenly to the past. If you begin in the past, don't shift without reason to the present. Notice the inconsistent verb tenses in the following example:

Incorrect   Smoke <u>spilled</u> from the front of the overheated car. The driver <u>opens</u> up the hood, then <u>jumped</u> back as steam <u>billows</u> out.

The verbs must be consistently in the present tense:

Correct   Smoke <u>spills</u> from the front of the overheated car. The driver <u>opens</u> up the hood, then <u>jumps</u> back as steam <u>billows</u> out.

Or the verbs must be consistently in the past tense:

Correct   Smoke <u>spilled</u> from the front of the overheated car. The driver <u>opened</u> up the hood, then <u>jumped</u> back as steam <u>billowed</u> out.

| **ACTIVITY 1** | **Avoiding Unnecessary Tense Shifts** |

In each item, one verb must be changed so that it agrees in tense with the other verbs. Cross out the incorrect verb and write the correct form in the space at the left.

EXAMPLE

<u>confused</u>   I rewrote my essay after the tutor told me that my introduction ~~confuse~~ him.

 HINT   Change *answer* to past tense to agree with the rest of the sentence.

CONNECT WRITING

Meet Teena. She's working on her advice column, *Teena Talks.* She really likes the advice she's giving her readers, but her writing is hard to follow because she keeps shifting verb tense. Help Teena locate and correct all the confusing shifts in verb tense so that she can respond to her readers with clarity.

mhconnectwriting.com

_____   1. The salesperson at the electronics store showed me several home theater systems and answer all my questions.

_____   2. On Tuesday, I skipped lunch so that I could study for an exam, and later I grab a bag of chips from the vending machine.

_____   3. The judges thanked the contestants and then announce the winner of the contest.

_____   4. Before I began college, I work full-time as a data entry clerk for a supply company.

_____   5. When Serena was late for dinner, I call her workplace and her home.

_____   6. The apartment I rented in the city was ideal. The landlord allow me to make minor improvements, which included painting the kitchen and installing new window blinds.

_____   7. The dental hygienist show my children how to brush their teeth properly.

_____   8. Last night, Todd impulsively stop at the convenience store to buy a pack of cigarettes.

_____   9. While in Las Vegas, my neighbor place twelve quarters into a Megabucks slot machine and won an impressive jackpot.

_____   10. The campus seemed busy on the first day of school; the parking lot was packed with cars, the bookstore was crammed with students buying textbooks, and the cafeteria was crowd with students buying coffee before their first class.

Change the verbs where needed in the following selection so that they are consistently in the past tense. Cross out each incorrect verb and write the correct form above it, as shown in the example. You will need to make ten corrections.

Years ago, I live in an old apartment building where I got little peace and quiet. For one thing, I often heard the constant fights that went on in the adjoining apartment. The husband yells about killing his wife, and she screamed right back about leaving him or having him arrested. In addition, the people in the apartment above me have four noisy kids. Sometimes it seem as if football games were going on upstairs. The noise reach a high point when I got home from work, which also happened to be the time the kids return from school. If the kids and neighbors were not disturbing me, I always had one other person to depend on—the superintendent, who visits my apartment whenever he felt like it. He always had an excuse, such as checking the water pipes or caulking the windows. But each time he came, I suspect he just wants to get away from his noisy family, which occupied the basement apartment. I move out of that apartment as soon as I was able to.

Change verbs as necessary in the following selection so that they are consistently in the past tense. Cross out each incorrect verb and write the correct form above it. You will need to make ten corrections in all.

As a kid, I never really enjoyed the public swimming pool. First, there were all sorts of rules that prevent me from having much fun in the water. One was that children under the age of fourteen had to be accompanied by an adult. I didn't like having to beg a parent or a

continued

neighbor to take me swimming every time I want to go. Another rule was that girls are not allowed in the water without bathing caps. The required bathing cap was so tight that it cause a heavy pressure mark on my forehead. Also, it often gives me a headache. Second, I wasn't a very good swimmer then. Most of the time I find myself hanging on to the side of the pool. And whenever I attempted a graceful dive, I end up doing a belly flop. Finally, many of the kids tease me. Some of them liked splashing water into my face, which force me to swallow chlorine and a dead bug or two. Even worse was the boy who sneaks up behind me all summer long to dump ice cubes down the back of my swimsuit.

For additional materials on Chapter 13, visit www.mhhe.com/langan.

CHAPTER 14

Additional Information about Verbs

Verb Tense

Verbs tell us the time of an action. The time that a verb shows is usually called *tense*. The most common tenses are the simple present, past, and future. In addition, there are nine other tenses that enable us to express more specific ideas about time than we could with the simple tenses alone. Following are the twelve verb tenses, with examples. Read them to increase your sense of the many different ways of expressing time in English.

CHAPTER PREVIEW

Verb Tense
- Present Perfect
- Past Perfect
- Present Progressive
- Past Progressive

Verbals
- Infinitive
- Participle
- Gerund

Active and Passive Verbs

Tenses	Examples
Present	I *work*. Jill *works*.
Past	Henry *worked* on the lawn.
Future	You *will work* overtime this week.
Present perfect	Gail *has worked* hard on the puzzle. They *have worked* well together.
Past perfect	They *had worked* eight hours before their shift ended.
Future perfect	The volunteers *will have worked* many unpaid hours.
Present progressive	I *am* not *working* today. You *are working* the second shift. The dryer *is* not *working* properly.
Past progressive	She *was working* outside. The plumbers *were working* here this morning.
Future progressive	The sound system *will be working* by tonight.
Present perfect progressive	Married life *has* not *been working* out for that couple.
Past perfect progressive	I *had been working* overtime until recently.
Future perfect progressive	My sister *will have been working* at that store for eleven straight months by the time she takes a vacation next week.

The perfect tenses are formed by adding *have, has,* or *had* to the past participle (the form of the verb that ends, usually, in *-ed*). The progressive tenses are formed by adding *am, is, are, was,* or *were* to the present participle (the form of the verb that ends in *-ing*). The perfect progressive tenses are formed by adding *have been, has been,* or *had been* to the present participle.

Certain tenses are explained in more detail on the following pages.

Present Perfect
(*have* or *has* + past participle)

The present perfect tense expresses an action that began in the past and has recently been completed or is continuing in the present.

The city *has* just *agreed* on a contract with the sanitation workers.

Anthony's parents *have lived* in that house for twenty years.

Jen *has enjoyed* mystery novels since she was a little girl.

Past Perfect
(*had* + past participle)

The past perfect tense expresses a past action that was completed before another past action.

Grace *had learned* to dance by the time she was five.

The class *had* just *started* when the fire bell rang.

Bad weather *had* never *been* a problem on our vacations until last year.

Present Progressive
(*am, is,* or *are* + the *-ing* form)

The present progressive tense expresses an action still in progress.

I *am taking* an early train into the city every day this week.

Alexys *is playing* softball over at the field.

The vegetables *are growing* rapidly.

Past Progressive
(*was* or *were* + the *-ing* form)

The past progressive expresses an action that was in progress in the past.

I *was spending* eighty dollars a week on cigarettes before I quit.

Last week, the store *was selling* many items at half price.

My friends *were driving* over to pick me up when the accident occurred.

Using the Correct Verb Tense

For the sentences that follow, fill in the present or past perfect or the present or past progressive of the verb shown. Use the tense that seems to express the meaning of each sentence best. You may work in pairs for this activity.

EXAMPLE

This summer, Mike ___is parking___ cars at a French restaurant.   park

1. In the past few years, several shark attacks _____ off the shores of Maui.   occur

2. Miho _____ taking her English and math placement tests before she received a call from the hospital about her father.   finish

3. Millions of children _____ reading *Harry Potter* books.   grow up

4. I _____ insulin to control my diabetes, but my endocrinologist says that I can control the disease through exercise and diet.   take

5. After two months, I _____ only three pages of my term paper.   write

6. The students in Mr. Pascual's sixth-grade class _____ money for their trip to Washington, DC, by recycling aluminum cans and glass bottles.   raise

7. Gayle _____ several Take Back the Night events at the Women's Center in March.   organize

8. The mayor _____ a speech at the neighborhood board meeting when the civil defense siren sounded.   present

9. Thousands of people _____ in support of children's health care legislation.   testify

10. Until last year, my daughter _____ with Bratz dolls, but now all she wants to do is play computer and video games.   play

Verbals

Verbals are words formed from verbs. Verbals, like verbs, often express action. They can add variety to your sentences and vigor to your writing style. The three kinds of verbals are *infinitives, participles,* and *gerunds.*

Infinitive

An infinitive is *to* plus the base form of the verb.

> I started *to practice.*

> Don't try *to lift* that table.

> I asked Russ *to drive* me home.

Participle

A participle is a verb form used as an adjective (a descriptive word). The present participle ends in *-ing*. The past participle ends in *-ed* or has an irregular ending.

> *Favoring* his *cramped* leg, the *screaming* boy waded out of the pool.

> The *laughing* child held up her *locked* piggy bank.

> *Using* a shovel and a bucket, I scooped water out of the *flooded* basement.

Gerund

A gerund is the *-ing* form of a verb used as a noun.

> *Studying* wears me out.

> *Playing* basketball is my main pleasure during the week.

> Through *jogging,* you can get yourself in shape.

| ACTIVITY 2 | **Using Infinitives, Participles, and Gerunds** |

In the space beside each sentence, identify the italicized word as a participle (*P*), an infinitive (*I*), or a gerund (*G*).

_____ 1. The aroma of *baking* sourdough bread lured diners into the restaurant.

_____ 2. My professor told us that *reusing* our old papers is plagiarism.

_____ 3. Caitlin wants *to enlist* in the U.S. Army once she graduates from high school.

_____ 4. Online *investing* requires skill and knowledge, but novice investors are often overly eager to play the stock market.

_____ 5. Community volunteers tried *to paint* over the graffiti left by vandals.

_____ 6. Some marine scientists suggest that the *decaying* flesh of another shark is an effective shark repellent.

_____ 7. *Whispering* softly, my coworker cautioned me that our manager was in a foul mood.

_____ 8. I forced myself to read the *boring* textbook, but I remembered very little of what I had read.

_____ 9. *Copying* my classmate's notes is a poor substitute for attending class on my own.

_____ 10. *To quit* smoking, Blaise stopped going to places where he would usually smoke, such as nightclubs and bars.

Active and Passive Verbs

When the subject of a sentence performs the action of a verb, the verb is in the *active voice*. When the subject of a sentence receives the action of a verb, the verb is in the *passive voice*.

The passive form of a verb consists of a form of the verb *be* plus the past participle of the main verb. Look at the active and passive forms of the verbs below.

Active	**Passive**
Tyra *ate* the vanilla pudding. (The subject, *Tyra*, is the doer of the action.)	The vanilla pudding *was eaten* by Tyra. (The subject, *pudding*, does not act. Instead, something happens to it.)
The plumber *replaced* the hot water heater. (The subject, *plumber*, is the doer of the action.)	The hot water heater *was replaced* by the plumber. (The subject, *heater*, does not act. Instead, something happens to it.)

In general, active verbs are more effective than passive verbs. Active verbs give your writing a simpler and more vigorous style. The passive form of verbs is appropriate, however, when the performer of an action is unknown or is less important than the receiver of the action. For example:

My house was vandalized last night.
(The performer of the action is unknown.)

Mark was seriously injured as a result of your negligence.
(The receiver of the action, *Mark,* is being emphasized.)

Making Sentences Active	**ACTIVITY 3**

Change the following sentences from passive voice to active voice. Note that in some cases you may have to add a subject.

EXAMPLES

The motorcycle was ridden by John.

John rode the motorcycle.

The basketball team was given a standing ovation.

The crowd gave the basketball team a standing ovation.

> **EXPLANATION:** In the second example, a subject had to be added.

 HINT Who clamored to photograph the celebrities? Make them the subject of item 1.

1. The celebrities on the red carpet were photographed by the clamoring paparazzi.

   _____

   _____

2. The stained-glass window was broken by a large falling branch.

   _____

   _____

3. A five-day extension on the research project was given to students by the professor.

   _____

   _____

4. The hotel was destroyed by a fire that started with a cigarette.

   _____

   _____

5. The pressures of dealing with life and death must be faced by doctors.

   _____

   _____

6. Blood was drawn by the phlebotomist to randomly test employees for illegal drug use.

   _____

   _____

7. The kitchen shelves were covered by a thick layer of yellowish grease.

   _____

   _____

8. Trash in the neighborhood park was removed by a group of volunteers.

   _____

   _____

9. Thousands of dollars have been gambled away by Keith playing online video poker.

   _____

   _____

10. "Gently used" prom and bridal dresses were donated by women of all ages to high school girls in need of gowns.

   _____

   _____

REFLECTIVE ACTIVITY

Reread any paragraphs or essays that you have written thus far for this class, and underline all of the verbs.

1. Have you used verb tenses consistently? If not, correct them.

2. Circle verbs that are in the present perfect, past perfect, present progressive, or past progressive tense. Have you used the correct forms? If not, revise your work.

3. Have you used the passive voice? Would the active voice have been better in these sentences? If so, rewrite the sentences using the active voice.

REVIEW TEST

On a separate piece of paper, write three sentences for each of the following forms:

1. Present perfect tense

2. Past perfect tense

3. Present progressive tense

4. Past progressive tense

5. Infinitive

6. Participle

7. Gerund

8. Passive voice (when the performer of the action is unknown or is less important than the receiver of an action—see page 249)

For additional materials on Chapter 14, visit **www.mhhe.com/langan**.

Pronoun Reference, Agreement, and Point of View

CHAPTER PREVIEW

Pronoun Reference

Pronoun Agreement

• Indefinite Pronouns

Pronoun Point of View

INTRODUCTORY ACTIVITY

Read each pair of sentences below, noting the underlined pronouns. Then see if you can circle the correct letter in each of the statements that follow.

1. a. None of my daughters gave <u>their</u> teacher a difficult time in kindergarten.
   b. None of my daughters gave <u>her</u> teacher a difficult time in kindergarten.

2. a. At the library, <u>they</u> helped me find online journal articles.
   b. At the library, <u>the librarians</u> helped me find online journal articles.

3. a. I want to apply for that job because <u>you</u> will have the opportunity to seek promotions.
   b. I want to apply for that job because <u>I</u> will have the opportunity to seek promotions.

In the first pair, (a, b) uses the underlined pronoun correctly because the pronoun refers to *None,* which is a singular word.
In the second pair, (a, b) is correct because otherwise the pronoun reference would be unclear.
In the third pair, (a, b) is correct because the pronoun point of view should not be shifted unnecessarily.

Answers are on page 625.

Pronouns are words that take the place of nouns (persons, places, or things). In fact, the word *pronoun* means *for a noun.* Pronouns are shortcuts that keep you from unnecessarily repeating words in writing. Here are some examples of pronouns:

Melinda shampooed *her* dog. (*Her* is a pronoun that takes the place of *Melinda.*)

As the door swung open, *it* creaked. (*It* replaces *door.*)

When the motorcyclists arrived at McDonald's, *they* removed *their* helmets. (*They* and *their* replace *motorcyclists.*)

This section presents rules that will help you avoid three common mistakes people make with pronouns. The rules are as follows:

1. A pronoun must refer clearly to the word it replaces.

2. A pronoun must agree in number with the word or words it replaces.

3. Pronouns should not shift unnecessarily in point of view.

Pronoun Reference

A sentence may be confusing and unclear if a pronoun appears to refer to more than one word, as in this sentence:

I locked my suitcase in my car, and then it was stolen.

(*What* was stolen? It is unclear whether the suitcase or the car was stolen.)

I locked my suitcase in my car, and then my car was stolen.

A sentence may also be confusing if the pronoun does not refer to any specific word. Look at this sentence:

We never buy fresh vegetables at that store because they charge too much.

(*Who* charges too much? There is no specific word that *they* refers to. Be clear.)

We never buy fresh vegetables at that store because the owners charge too much.

Here are additional sentences with unclear pronoun reference. Read the explanations of why they are unclear and look carefully at the ways they are corrected.

CONNECT WRITING

Meet Asher. He's writing an email to his mom, but thinks some of his pronouns are unclear. He wants to show his mom he's learning something in college, but is afraid she won't think so from his writing. Help Asher locate and correct his pronoun reference mistakes.

mhconnectwriting.com

Unclear	**Clear**
Amy told Gina that she had gained weight.	Amy told Gina, "You've gained weight."
(*Who* had gained weight: Amy or Gina? Be clear.)	(Quotation marks, which can sometimes be used to correct an unclear reference, are explained in Chapter 27.)
My older brother is an electrician, but I'm not interested in it. (There is no specific word that *it* refers to. It does not make sense to say, "I'm not interested in electrician.")	My older brother is an electrician, but I'm not interested in becoming one.
Our instructor did not explain the assignment, which made me angry. (Does *which* mean that the instructor's failure to explain the assignment made you angry, or that the assignment itself made you angry? Be clear.)	I was angry that our instructor did not explain the assignment.

| ACTIVITY 1 | **Pronoun Reference** |

Rewrite each of the following sentences to make clear the vague pronoun reference. Add, change, or omit words as necessary.

EXAMPLE

Lana thanked Maggie for the gift, which was very thoughtful of her.

Lana thanked Maggie for the thoughtful gift.

> **HINT**   In item 1, what does *it* stand for?

1. Sienna removed the blanket from the sofa bed and folded it up.

   _____

   _____

2. The defendant told the judge he was mentally ill.

   _____

3. Before the demonstration, they passed out signs for us to carry.

   _____

   _____

4. Kristy complained to Rachel that her boyfriend was being dishonest.

   _____

   _____

5. Because I didn't rinse last night's dishes, it smells like a garbage can.

   _____

   _____

6. The students watched a film on endangered species, which really depressed them.

   _____

   _____

7. The veterinarian said that if I find a tick on my dog, I should get rid of it immediately.

   _____

   _____

8. My sister removed the curtains from the windows so that she could wash them.

   _____

   _____

9. Richard said his acupuncture therapist could help my sprained shoulder, but I don't believe in it.

_____

_____

10. I discovered when I went to sell my old textbooks that they've put out new editions, and nobody wants to buy them.

_____

_____

Pronoun Agreement

A pronoun must agree in number with the word or words it replaces. If the word a pronoun refers to is singular, the pronoun must be singular; if the word is plural, the pronoun must be plural. (The word a pronoun refers to is known as the *antecedent*.)

Emma agreed to lend me her Coldplay CDs.

The gravediggers sipped coffee during their break.

In the first example, the pronoun *her* refers to the singular word *Emma;* in the second example, the pronoun *their* refers to the plural word *gravediggers.*

Pronoun Agreement	ACTIVITY 2

Write the appropriate pronoun (*they, their, them, it*) in the blank space in each of the following sentences.

EXAMPLE

My credit cards got me into debt, so I shredded ____them____.

> **HINT** In item 1, which word best takes the place of *disposable contact lenses?*

1. Even though I should replace my disposable contact lenses every week, I often forget to change _____ out.

2. Several legislators proposed a bill to establish a registry of convicted murderers, but these lawmakers still need to determine the cost of _____ proposal.

3. Many educators have had to change the way that _____ teach in order to comply with the No Child Left Behind Act of 2001.

4. After I promised my children that I would take them to the movies on Friday, I had to tell _____ that the hospital needed me to work an additional shift.

5. Less than a week after I placed a backorder for my textbook, the bookstore called to say that _____ had arrived.

Indefinite Pronouns

The following words, known as *indefinite pronouns,* are always singular.

INDEFINITE PRONOUNS		
(*-one* words)	(*-body* words)	
one	nobody	each
anyone	anybody	either
everyone	everybody	neither
someone	somebody	

Either of the apartments has its drawbacks

One of the girls lost her skateboard

Everyone in the class must hand in his paper tomorrow.

In each example, the pronoun is singular because it refers to one of the indefinite pronouns. There are two important points to remember about indefinite pronouns.

1: Using Gender-Appropriate Pronouns

The previous example suggests that everyone in the class is male. If the students were all female, the pronoun would be *her.* If the students were a mixed group of males and females, the pronoun form would be *his or her.*

Everyone in the class must hand in *his or her* paper tomorrow.

Some writers still follow the traditional practice of using *his* to refer to both men and women. Many now use *his or her* to avoid an implied sexual bias. Perhaps the best practice, though, is to avoid using either *his* or the somewhat awkward *his or her.* This can often be done by rewriting a sentence in the plural:

All students in the class must hand in *their* papers tomorrow.

Here are some examples of sentences that can be rewritten in the plural.

Singular: A young child is seldom willing to share her toys with others.

Plural:	Young children are seldom willing to share their toys with others.
Singular:	Anyone who does not wear his seat belt will be fined.
Plural:	People who do not wear their seat belts will be fined.
Singular:	A newly elected politician should not forget his or her campaign promises.
Plural:	Newly elected politicians should not forget their campaign promises.

2: Using Plural Pronouns with Indefinite Pronouns

In informal spoken English, *plural* pronouns are often used with indefinite pronouns. Instead of saying

Everybody has *his or her* own idea of an ideal vacation.

we are likely to say

Everybody has *their* own idea of an ideal vacation.

Here are other examples:

Everyone in the class must pass in *their* papers.

Everybody in our club has *their* own idea about how to raise money.

No one in our family skips *their* chores.

In such cases, the indefinite pronouns are clearly plural in meaning. Also, the use of such plurals helps people avoid the awkward *his or her*. In time, the plural pronoun may be accepted in formal speech or writing. Until that happens, however, you should use the grammatically correct singular form in your writing. Note: some instructors *do* accept plural pronouns with indefinite pronouns; check with yours.

Using Pronouns Correctly ACTIVITY 3

Underline the correct pronoun.

EXAMPLE

Neither of those houses has (<u>its</u>, their) own garage.

> **EXPLANATION:** *Neither* is a singular subject and requires a singular pronoun.

 In item 1, *neither* requires a singular pronoun.

1.   Neither of the men was aware that (his, their) voice was being taped.

2.   One of the waiters was fired for failing to report all (his, their) tips.

3.   We have three dogs, and each of them has (its, their) own bowl.

4.   During the intermission, everyone had to wait a while for (her, their) turn to get into the ladies' room.

5.   All of the presents on the table had tiny gold bows on (it, them).

6.   Mr. Alvarez refuses to let anyone ride in his car without using (his or her, their) seat belt.

7.   It seems that neither of the mothers is comfortable answering (her, their) teenager's questions about sex.

8.   If anybody in the men's club objects to the new rules, (he, they) should speak up now.

9.   Nobody on the women's basketball team had enough nerve to voice (her, their) complaints to the coach.

10. Before being allowed to go on the class trip, each student had to have (his or her, their) parents sign a permission form.

CONNECT WRITING

Meet Nigel. He is writing horoscopes for the school newspaper and is having trouble with his Pisces forecast. After reading over the forecast again, he realizes that his writing shifts between first person, second person, and third person rather than sticking to one point of view. Help Nigel locate and correct the confusing shifts in his forecast.

mhconnectwriting.com

Pronoun Point of View

Pronouns should not shift their point of view unnecessarily. When writing a paper, be consistent in your use of first-, second-, or third-person pronouns.

Type of Pronoun	Singular	Plural
First-person pronouns	I (my, mine, me)	we (our, us)
Second-person pronouns	you (your)	you (your)
Third-person pronouns	he (his, him)	they (their, them)
	she (her)	
	it (its)	

> **TIP**   Any person, place, or thing, as well as any indefinite pronoun such as *one, anyone, someone,* and so on (see page 256), is a third-person word.

For instance, if you start writing in the first-person *I*, don't jump suddenly to the second-person *you*. Or if you are writing in the third-person *they*, don't shift unexpectedly to *you*. Look at the following examples.

Inconsistent	Consistent
One reason that *I* like living in the city is that *you* always have a wide choice of sports events to attend. (The most common mistake people make is to let a *you* slip into their writing after they start with another pronoun.)	One reason that *I* like living in the city is that *I* always have a wide choice of sports events to attend.
Someone who is dieting should have the support of friends; *you* should also have plenty of willpower.	*Someone* who is dieting should have the support of friends; *he* or *she* should also have plenty of willpower.
Students who work while *they* are going to school face special challenges. For one thing, *you* seldom have enough study time.	Students who work while *they* are going to school face special challenges. For one thing, *they* seldom have enough study time.

Correcting Inconsistent Pronouns   ACTIVITY 4

Cross out inconsistent pronouns in the following sentences and write the correction above the error.

EXAMPLE

I work much better when the boss doesn't hover over ~~you~~ me with instructions on what to do.

> **H I N T**   Since the sentence in item 1 begins in first person, change *your* to a first-person pronoun.

1. A good horror movie makes my bones feel like ice and gets your blood running cold.

2. People buy groceries from that supermarket because you know it has the best prices in the area.

3. One experience that almost everyone fears is when you have to speak in front of a crowd of people.

4. If students attend class regularly and study hard, you should receive good grades.

5. I drive on back roads instead of major highways because you can avoid traffic.

6. The spread of many illnesses, such as the flu and common cold, could be reduced if people just washed your hands.

7. Faith enjoys watching soap operas because then you can worry about someone else's problems instead of your own.

8. Our street was so slippery after the ice storm that you could barely take a step without falling down.

9. Mrs. Almac prefers working the three-to-eleven shift because that way you can still have a large part of your day free.

10. All of us at work voted to join the union because we felt it would protect your rights.

REFLECTIVE ACTIVITY

1. Reread a paragraph or essay you have written for this course or any other course you are taking this semester. Underline each pronoun. Then, ask whether the pronoun agrees with its antecedent (the word it refers to). If not, correct the problem.

2. Reread your paragraph or essay again. Have you maintained pronoun consistency? Pay special attention to sentences that use the pronoun *you*. Correct any inconsistencies. Why do you think pronoun consistency is important? In what way has correcting for consistency improved the essay?

REVIEW TEST 1

Underline the correct word in the parentheses.

1. Jamon set the package on the table before (it, the package) broke.

2. During the lecture, students listened attentively from (his or her, their) seats.

3. I enjoy listening to music on my iPod because (you, I) can download individual songs.

4. Almost all the Thai curry dishes I enjoy have (its, their) own unique flavor.

5. My mom talks on the phone to my sister every day because (she, my sister) is homesick.

6. I like going to school because (they, the teachers) are committed to helping me learn.

7. Neither one of the injured basketball players on the girls' team wanted to give up (her, their) spot on the team.

8. When Trevor visited the hospital, (they, the nurses) told him that his brother was discharged that morning.

9. Even if you want to socialize with your friends on the weekend, (you, I) need to finish your homework first.

10. Not one of the students in the class knew what (his or her, their) mid-term grade was.

Cross out the pronoun error in each sentence and write the correction in the space provided. Then circle the letter that correctly describes the type of error that was made.

EXAMPLES

~~Anyone~~ turning in their papers late will be penalized.

_____Students_____

Mistake in: a. pronoun reference   (b.) pronoun agreement

When Clyde takes his son Paul to the park, ~~he~~ enjoys himself.

_____Paul (or Clyde)_____

Mistake in: (a.) pronoun reference   b. pronoun point of view

From where we stood, ~~you~~ could see three states.

_____we_____

Mistake in: a. pronoun agreement   (b.) pronoun point of view

1. A good salesperson knows that you should be courteous to customers.

_____

Mistake in: a. pronoun agreement   b. pronoun point of view

2. Neither of the girls who flunked bothered to bring their grades home.

_____

Mistake in: a. pronoun reference   b. pronoun agreement

3. When the shabbily dressed woman walked into the fancy hotel, they weren't very polite to her.

_____

Mistake in: a. pronoun agreement   b. pronoun reference

4. Nobody seems to add or subtract without their calculator anymore.

_____

Mistake in: a. pronoun agreement   b. pronoun point of view

5. Denise went everywhere with Nina until she moved to Texas last year.

   _____

   Mistake in: a. pronoun agreement   b. pronoun reference

6. Everyone on my street believes they saw a strange glow in the sky last night.

   _____

   Mistake in: a. pronoun agreement   b. pronoun point view

7. In baking desserts, people should follow the directions carefully or you are likely to end up with something unexpected.

   _____

   Mistake in: a. pronoun reference   b. pronoun point of view

8. When Jerry added another card to the delicate structure, it fell down.

   _____

   Mistake in: a. pronoun reference   b. pronoun point of view

9. Anyone who wants to join the car pool should leave their name with me.

   _____

   Mistake in: a. pronoun agreement   b. pronoun reference

10. Any working mother knows that you need at least a twenty-five-hour day.

    _____

    Mistake in: a. pronoun agreement   b. pronoun point of view

 HINT   In item 10, you will also need to correct a verb form.

For additional materials on Chapter 15, visit **www.mhhe.com/langan**.

INTRODUCTORY ACTIVITY

In each pair, write a check beside the sentence that you think uses pronouns correctly.

Andy and *I* enrolled in a Web design course. _____

Andy and *me* enrolled in a Web design course. _____

The police officer pointed to my sister and *me*. _____

The police officer pointed to my sister and *I*. _____

Meg prefers men *whom* take pride in their bodies. _____

Meg prefers men *who* take pride in their bodies. _____

The players are confident that the league championship is *theirs'*. _____

The players are confident that the league championship is *theirs*. _____

Them concert tickets are too expensive. _____

Those concert tickets are too expensive. _____

Our parents should spend some money on *themself* for a change.

Our parents should spend some money on *themselves* for a change. _____

Answers are on page 625.

CHAPTER PREVIEW

Subject and Object Pronouns

- Subject Pronouns
- Object Pronouns

Relative Pronouns

- Points to Remember about Relative Pronouns

Possessive Pronouns

Demonstrative Pronouns

Reflexive Pronouns

- Points to Remember about Reflexive Pronouns

Subject and Object Pronouns

Pronouns change their form depending on the place they occupy in a sentence. What follows is a list of subject and object pronouns:

Subject Pronouns	Object Pronouns
I	me
you	you (no change)
he	him
she	her
it	it (no change)
we	us
they	them

Subject Pronouns

Subject pronouns are subjects of verbs.

They are getting tired. (*They* is the subject of the verb *are getting*.)

She will decide tomorrow. (*She* is the subject of the verb *will decide*.)

We organized the game. (*We* is the subject of the verb *organized*.)

Several rules for using subject pronouns and some common mistakes people make in using them are explained below.

Rule 1

Use a subject pronoun in a sentence with a compound (more than one) subject.

Incorrect	**Correct**
Nate and *me* went shopping yesterday.	Nate and *I* went shopping yesterday.
Him and *me* spent lots of money.	*He* and *I* spent lots of money.

If you are not sure which pronoun to use, try each pronoun by itself in the sentence. The correct pronoun will be the one that sounds right. For example, "*Me* went shopping yesterday" does not sound right; "I went shopping yesterday" does.

Rule 2

Use a subject pronoun after forms of the verb *be*. Forms of *be* include *am, are, is, was, were, has been, have been,* and others.

It was *I* who telephoned.

It may be *they* at the door.

It is *she.*

These sentences may sound strange and stilted to you, since this rule is seldom actually followed in conversation. When we speak with one another, forms such as "It was me," "It may be them," and "It is her" are widely accepted. In formal writing, however, the grammatically correct forms are still preferred. You can avoid having to use a subject pronoun after *be* simply by rewording a sentence. Here is how the preceding examples could be reworded:

I was the one who telephoned.

They may be at the door.

She is here.

Rule 3

Use subject pronouns after *than* or *as* when a verb is understood after the pronoun.

You read faster than I (read). (The verb *read* is understood after *I*.)

Tom is as stubborn as I (am). (The verb *am* is understood after *I*.)

We don't go out as much as they (do). (The verb *do* is understood after *they*.)

> **TIP** Avoid mistakes by mentally adding the "missing" verb to the end of the sentence.

> **TIP** Use object pronouns after *as* or *than* when a verb is not understood after the pronoun.
>
> The law applies to you as well as me.
>
> Our boss paid Monica more than me.

CONNECT WRITING

Meet Sunil. He's helping a classmate write an email to their professor about an upcoming absence. He thinks the first draft of the letter is sincere, but believes there are errors with subject and object pronouns in some of the sentences. Help Sunil locate and correct the pronoun case mistakes before his classmate sends the email to their professor.

mhconnectwriting.com

Object Pronouns

Object pronouns (*me, him, her, us, them*) are objects of verbs or prepositions. (Prepositions are connecting words such as *for, at, about, to, before, by, with,* and *of.* See also page 157.)

Raisa chose *me.* (*Me* is the object of the verb *chose.*)

We met *them* at the ballpark. (*Them* is the object of the verb *met.*)

Don't mention UFOs to *us.* (*Us* is the object of the preposition *to.*)

I live near *her.* (*Her* is the object of the preposition *near.*)

People are sometimes uncertain about what pronoun to use when two objects follow the verb.

Incorrect	**Correct**
I spoke to George and *he.*	I spoke to George and *him.*
She pointed at Linda and *I.*	She pointed at Linda and *me.*

If you are not sure which pronoun to use, try each pronoun by itself in the sentence. The correct pronoun will be the one that sounds right. For example, "I spoke to he" doesn't sound right; "I spoke to him" does.

ACTIVITY 1   Identifying Subject and Object Pronouns

Underline the correct subject or object pronoun in each of the following sentences. Then show whether your answer is a subject or an object pronoun by circling the *S* or *O* in the margin.

 In item 1, the correct pronoun is the object of the preposition *to.*

S   O   1. I left the decision to (her, she).

S   O   2. (She, Her) and Louise look enough alike to be sisters.

S   O   3. Just between you and (I, me), these rolls taste like sawdust.

S   O   4. The certified letter was addressed to both (she, her) and (I, me).

S   O   5. If (he, him) and Vic are serious about school, why are they absent so much?

S   O   6. Practically everyone is better at crossword puzzles than (I, me).

S   O   7. It was (they, them) who left the patio furniture outside during the rainstorm.

S   O   8. The creature who climbed out of the coffin scared Chris and (I, me) half to death.

S   O   9. (We, Us) tenants are organizing a protest against the dishonest landlord.

S   O 10. When we were little, my sister and (I, me) invented a secret language.

ACTIVITY 2   Using Subject or Object Pronouns

For each sentence, write an appropriate subject or object pronoun in the space provided. Try to use as many different pronouns as possible.

 Along with *Gerald,* this pronoun is part of the sentence's subject in item 1.

1. Gerald and _____ forgot to lock the door the night our restaurant was robbed.

2. The referee disqualified Tyray and _____ for fighting.

3. I have seldom met two people as boring as _____.

4. If you and _____ don't lose patience, we'll finish sanding this floor by tonight.

5. Our professor told _____ students that our final exam would be a take-home test.

6. Chase and _____ drove on the interstate highway for ten hours with only one stop.

7. I don't follow sports as much as _____.

8. You know better than _____ how to remove lipstick stains.

9. Maggie and _____ spent several hours yesterday looking for the lost puppy.

10. The store manager praised _____ for being the best cashiers in the department.

Relative Pronouns

Relative pronouns do two things at once. First, they refer to someone or something already mentioned in the sentence. Second, they start a short word group that gives additional information about this someone or something. Here is a list of relative pronouns:

RELATIVE PRONOUNS	
who	which
whose	that
whom	

Here are some sample sentences:

The only friend *who* really understands me is moving away.

The child *whom* Ben and Arlene adopted is from Korea.

Chocolate, *which* is my favorite food, upsets my stomach.

I guessed at half the questions *that* were on the test.

In the example sentences, *who* refers to *friend, whom* refers to *child, which* refers to *chocolate,* and *that* refers to *questions.* In addition, each of the relative pronouns begins a group of words that describes the person or thing being referred to. For example, the words *whom Ben and Arlene adopted* tell which child the sentence is about, and the words *which is my favorite food* give added information about chocolate.

> **TIP** Phrases using the relative pronoun *which* are set off by commas, whereas phrases using *that* are not.

Points to Remember about Relative Pronouns

- *Whose* means *belonging to whom.* Be careful not to confuse *whose* with *who's,* which means *who is.*

- *Who, whose,* and *whom* all refer to people. *Which* refers to things. *That* can refer to either people or things.

    I don't know *whose* book this is.

    Don't sit on the chair, *which* is broken.

    Let's elect a captain *who* cares about winning.

- *Who, whose, whom,* and *which* can also be used to ask questions. When they are used in this way, they are called *interrogative pronouns:*

    Who murdered the secret agent?

    Whose fingerprints were on the bloodstained knife?

    To *whom* have the detectives been talking?

    Which suspect is going to confess?

> **TIP** In informal usage, *who* is generally used instead of *whom* as an interrogative pronoun. Informally, we can say or write, "*Who* are you rooting for in the game?" or "*Who* did the instructor fail?" More formal usage would call for *whom:* "*Whom* are you rooting for in the game?" "*Whom* did the instructor fail?"

- *Who* and *whom* are used differently. *Who* is a subject pronoun. Use *who* as the subject of a verb:

    Let's see *who* will be teaching the course.

Whom is an object pronoun. Use *whom* as the object of a verb or a preposition:

    Dr. Kelsey is the instructor *whom* I like best.

    I haven't decided for *whom* I will vote.

You may want to review the material on subject and object pronouns on pages 263–267.

Here is an easy way to decide whether to use *who* or *whom*. Find the first verb after the place where the *who* or *whom* will go. See if it already has a subject. If it does have a subject, use the object pronoun *whom*. If there is no subject, give it one by using the subject pronoun *who*. Notice how *who* and *whom* are used in the sentences that follow:

> I don't know *who* sideswiped my car.

> The suspect *whom* the police arrested finally confessed.

In the first sentence, *who* is used to give the verb *sideswiped* a subject. In the second sentence, the verb *arrested* already has a subject, *police*. Therefore, *whom* is the correct pronoun.

Identifying Correct Relative Pronouns   ACTIVITY 3

Underline the correct pronoun in each of the following sentences.

> **HINT**   *Who* refers only to people; it cannot refer to the word *books* in item 1.

1. Some of the books (who, that) I borrowed from the public library are overdue now.

2. One TV show (that, who) I enjoy is *NCIS*.

3. My dad, (who, whom) enjoys sports, taught me how to play football, soccer, and basketball.

4. My computer, (who, which) I purchased three years ago, is now outdated.

5. The store manager (who, whom) I spoke to on the phone said that I could return the unopened merchandise.

Using Relative Pronouns   ACTIVITY 4

On a separate piece of paper, write five sentences using *who, whose, whom, which,* and *that.*

Possessive Pronouns

Possessive pronouns show ownership or possession.

> Brad shut off the engine of *his* motorcycle.

> The keys are *mine.*

Following is a list of possessive pronouns:

POSSESSIVE PRONOUNS

my, mine	our, ours
your, yours	your, yours
his	their, theirs
her, hers	
its	

> **TIP**   A possessive pronoun *never* uses an apostrophe. (See also page 344).
>
> | **Incorrect** | **Correct** |
> |---|---|
> | That coat is *hers'*. | That coat is *hers*. |
> | The card table is *theirs'*. | The card table is *theirs*. |

ACTIVITY 5   **Correcting Possessive Pronouns**

Cross out the incorrect pronoun form in each of the sentences that follow. Write the correct form in the space at the left.

EXAMPLE

___My___   ~~Me~~ stomach is hungry, so I will have a light snack before dinner.

_____   1. Is this BlackBerry hers'?

_____   2. The sushi without horseradish is mines.

_____   3. My husband came home and told me that the new Chevrolet Suburban SUV in the driveway is ours'.

_____   4. Even after I had charged it's battery, my cell phone still wasn't working.

_____   5. Marisa and Jo often remind they children that they need to budget their money if they want to go to Disney World next summer.

Demonstrative Pronouns

Demonstrative pronouns point to or single out a person or thing. There are four demonstrative pronouns:

DEMONSTRATIVE PRONOUNS

this	these
that	those

Generally speaking, *this* and *these* refer to things close at hand; *that* and *those* refer to things farther away.

Is anyone using *this* spoon?

I am going to throw away *these* magazines.

I just bought *that* old white pickup at the curb.

Pick up *those* toys in the corner.

Do not use *them, this here, that there, these here,* or *those there* to point something out. Use only *this, that, these,* or *those.*

Incorrect	Correct
Them tires are badly worn.	*Those* tires are badly worn.
This here book looks hard to read.	*This* book looks hard to read.
That there candy is delicious.	*That* candy is delicious.
Those there squirrels are pests.	*Those* squirrels are pests.

Correcting Demonstrative Pronouns

ACTIVITY 6

Cross out the incorrect form of the demonstrative pronoun and write the correct form in the space provided.

EXAMPLE

___Those___   ~~Them~~ clothes need washing.

_____   1. This here town isn't big enough for both of us, Tex.

_____   2. Let's hurry and get them seats before someone else does.

_____   3. That there dress looked better on the hanger than it does on you.

_____   4. Let me try one of those there chocolates before they're all gone.

_____   5. Watch out for them potholes the next time you drive my car.

Using Demonstrative Pronouns

ACTIVITY 7

Write four sentences using *this, that, these,* and *those.*

_____

_____

_____

_____

Reflexive Pronouns

Reflexive pronouns are pronouns that refer to the subject of a sentence. Here is a list of reflexive pronouns:

REFLEXIVE PRONOUNS	
myself	ourselves
yourself	yourselves
himself	themselves
herself	
itself	

Sometimes a reflexive pronoun is used for emphasis:

You will have to wash the dishes *yourself.*

We *ourselves* are willing to forget the matter.

The manager *himself* stole merchandise from the store.

Points to Remember about Reflexive Pronouns

- In the plural, *-self* becomes *-selves.*

    Lola covered *herself* with insect repellent.

    They treated *themselves* to a Bermuda vacation.

- Be careful that you do not use any of the following incorrect forms as reflexive pronouns.

Incorrect	Correct
He believes in *hisself.*	He believes in *himself.*
We drove the children *ourself.*	We drove the children *ourselves.*
They saw *themself* in the fun house mirror.	They saw *themselves* in the fun house mirror.
I'll do it *meself.*	I'll do it *myself.*

ACTIVITY 8 | **Using Reflexive Prounouns**

Cross out the incorrect form of the reflexive pronoun and write the correct form in the space at the left.

EXAMPLE

themselves   She believes that God helps those who help ~~themself~~.

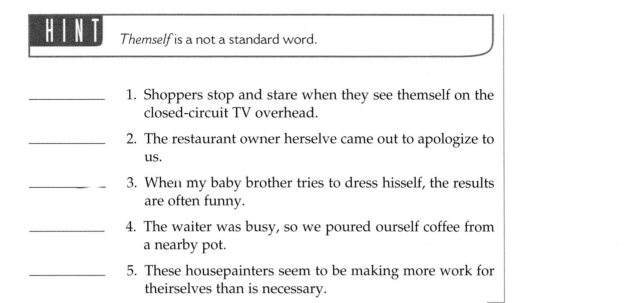

> ## HINT
>
> *Themself* is a not a standard word.
>
> _____ 1. Shoppers stop and stare when they see themself on the closed-circuit TV overhead.
>
> _____ 2. The restaurant owner herselve came out to apologize to us.
>
> _____ 3. When my baby brother tries to dress hisself, the results are often funny.
>
> _____ 4. The waiter was busy, so we poured ourself coffee from a nearby pot.
>
> _____ 5. These housepainters seem to be making more work for theirselves than is necessary.

REFLECTIVE ACTIVITY

1. Review your answers to Activity 3 in this chapter. Explain why you think the word you chose is correct.

2. Read the sentences you wrote for Activity 4 in this chapter. Explain why the pronoun you chose in each case (*who, whom, whose, which,* or *that*) is correct. For example, why might you have chosen *who* and not *whom*?

REVIEW TEST 1

Underline the correct pronoun in the parentheses.

1. The waitress finally brought Danielle and (I, me) our order.

2. I hope my son behaves (hisself, himself) at preschool.

3. Hand me (that, that there) fiddle and I'll play you a tune.

4. If it were up to (she, her), men wouldn't have the right to vote.

5. Jack, (who, whom) has worked here for almost thirty years, is ready to retire.

6. Vera dressed much more casually than (I, me) for the party.

7. You won't get very far on the bike unless you add more air to (its, it's) tires.

8. We'll be reading (this, this here) stack of books during the semester.

9. The apartment of (his, him) is next to a chemical processing plant.

10. The ducks circled the lake until they were sure that no one was around but (theirselves, themselves).

REVIEW TEST 2

Cross out the pronoun error in each sentence and write the correct form in the space at the left.

EXAMPLE

_____I_____   Terry and ~~me~~ have already seen the movie.

_____   1. The chili that Manny prepared was too spicy for we to eat.

_____   2. I checked them wires, but I couldn't find any faulty connections.

_____   3. The old Chevy, who has 110,000 miles on it, is still running well.

_____   4. When him and his partner asked me to step out of my car, I knew I was in trouble.

_____   5. Omar realized that he would have to change the tire hisself.

_____   6. My husband is much more sentimental than me.

_____   7. I hope you'll come visit us in July while the garden is looking its' best.

_____   8. The CDs are mines, but you can listen to them whenever you wish.

_____   9. This here dog is friendly as long as you move slowly.

_____   10. Vicky and me are going to the concert at the fairgrounds.

REVIEW TEST 3

On a separate piece of paper, write sentences that use each of the following words or phrases.

EXAMPLE

Kim and her   *I forgot to tell Kim and her about the pop quiz.*

1. ourselves

2. Sabrina and me

3. Those

4. The Pavarti family and us

5. Lee and he

6. smarter than I

7. its

8. whom

9. you and me

10. Marco and them

For additional materials on Chapter 16, visit **www.mhhe.com/langan**.

Modifiers and Parallelism

SECTION PREVIEW

17 Adjectives and Adverbs

18 Misplaced Modifiers

19 Dangling Modifiers

20 Faulty Parallelism

21 Sentence Variety II

© Luc Cromheecke. Used by permission.

RESPONDING TO IMAGES

If you had to diagnose this real-life error in grammatical language, what might you call it? (Hint: It's one of the chapter titles in this section.)

Adjectives and Adverbs

CHAPTER PREVIEW

Adjectives

- What Are Adjectives?
- Using Adjectives to Compare
- Points to Remember about Adjectives

Adverbs

- What Are Adverbs?
- A Common Mistake with Adjectives and Adverbs
- *Well* and *Good*

INTRODUCTORY ACTIVITY

Write in an appropriate word or words to complete each of the sentences below.

1. The teenage years were a _____ time for me.

2. The mechanic listened _____ while I described my car problem.

3. Basketball is a _____ game than football.

4. My brother is the _____ person in our family.

Now see if you can complete the following sentences.

The word inserted in the first sentence is an (adjective, adverb); it describes the word *time*.

The word inserted in the second sentence is an (adjective, adverb);

it probably ends in the two letters _____ and describes the word *listened*.

The word inserted in the third sentence is a comparative adjective; it may be preceded by *more* or end in the two

letters _____.

The word inserted in the fourth sentence is a superlative adjective; it may be preceded by *most* or end in the three

letters _____.

Answers are on page 626.

Adjectives and adverbs are descriptive words. Their purpose is to make the meaning of the words they describe more specific.

Adjectives

What Are Adjectives?

Adjectives describe nouns (names of persons, places, or things) or pronouns.

Charlotte is a *kind* woman. (The adjective *kind* describes the noun *woman*.)

He is *tired*. (The adjective *tired* describes the pronoun *he*.)

An adjective usually comes before the word it describes (as in *kind woman*). But it can also come after forms of the verb *be* (*is, are, was, were*, and so on). Less often, an adjective follows verbs such as *feel, look, smell, sound, taste, appear, become*, and *seem*.

The bureau is *heavy*. (The adjective *heavy* describes the bureau.)

These pants are *itchy*. (The adjective *itchy* describes the pants.)

The children seem *restless*. (The adjective *restless* describes the children.)

Using Adjectives to Compare

For most short adjectives, add *-er* when comparing two things and add *-est* when comparing three or more things.

I am *taller* than my brother, but my father is the *tallest* person in the house.

The farm market sells *fresher* vegetables than the corner store, but the *freshest* vegetables are the ones grown in my own garden.

For most *longer* adjectives (two or more syllables), add *more* when comparing two things and *most* when comparing three or more things.

Backgammon is *more enjoyable* to me than checkers, but chess is the *most enjoyable* game of all.

My mother is *more talkative* than my father, but my grandfather is the *most talkative* person in the house.

> **T I P** If an adjective ends in *y*, such as *happy* or *witty*, it must have three or more syllables to use *more* or *most* instead of *-er* or *-est* endings.

Points to Remember about Adjectives

- Be careful not to use both an *-er* ending and *more*, or both an *-est* ending and *most*.

Incorrect	Correct
Football is a *more livelier* game baseball.	Football is a *livelier* game than baseball.
Tod Traynor was voted the *most likeliest* to succeed in our high school class.	Tod Traynor was voted the *most likely* to succeed in our high school class.

- Pay special attention to the following words, each of which has irregular forms.

	Comparative (Two)	Superlative (Three or More)
bad	worse	worst
good, well	better	best
little	less	least
much, many	more	most

ACTIVITY 1 Using Comparatives and Superlatives

Fill in the comparative or superlative forms for the following adjectives. Two are done for you as examples.

	Comparative (Two)	Superlative (Three or More)
firm	firmer	firmest
organized	more organized	most organized
tough	_____	_____
practical	_____	_____
quiet	_____	_____
aggressive	_____	_____
clear	_____	_____

ACTIVITY 2 Using the Correct Superlative or Comparative Forms

Add to each sentence the correct form of the adjective in the margin.

EXAMPLE

bad

The _____worst_____ day of my life was the one when my house caught fire.

> **HINT** In item 1, consider: what is the superlative form of good?

good

1. I hope the _____ days of my life are still to come.

dirty

2. The water in Mudville is _____ than the name of the town.

considerate

3. If Tyrone were _____, he would have more friends.

bad

4. The announcement of a surprise quiz gave me a _____ headache than this morning's traffic did.

5. The _____ scene in the horror movie was when dead people began crawling out of their graves.   scary

6. As hard as it is to believe, he is an even _____ dependable worker than his brother.   little

7. In an effort to look _____, Bob replaced his thick glasses with wire-rimmed ones.   stylish

8. June is even _____ than her sister; she once burst out laughing at a wedding and had to run out of the church.   silly

9. The computers in the library must be the _____ machines on Earth.   slow

10. Estella ordered a tossed salad as her main course, so she could have the _____ dessert on the menu.   fattening

Adverbs

What Are Adverbs?

Adverbs describe verbs, adjectives, other adverbs, or whole phrases. An adverb usually ends in -*ly*.

> Charlotte spoke *kindly* to the confused man. (The adverb *kindly* describes the verb *spoke*.)

> The man said he was *completely* alone in the world. (The adverb *completely* describes the adjective *alone*.)

> Charlotte listened *very* sympathetically to his story. (The adverb *very* describes the adverb *sympathetically*.)

A Common Mistake with Adjectives and Adverbs

Perhaps the most common mistake that people make with adjectives and adverbs is to use an adjective instead of an adverb after a verb.

Incorrect	**Correct**
Tim breathed *heavy*.	Tim breathed *heavily*.
I rest *comfortable* in that chair.	I rest *comfortably* in that chair.
She learned *quick*.	She learned *quickly*.

Using Adjectives or Adverbs	**ACTIVITY 3**

Underline the adjective or adverb needed in each sentence.

> In item 1, an adverb is required to describe the verb *need*.

CONNECT WRITING

Meet Zach. He is trying to write a description of one of his skateboards for an online classified ad. He's added adjectives and adverbs to his writing to make his ad more detailed, but he isn't sure if he's used them correctly. Help Zach locate and correct his adjective and adverb mistakes before posting his ad.

mhconnectwriting.com

1. I need a vacation (bad, badly).

2. The police reacted (harsh, harshly) to the noisy demonstrators.

3. The truck groaned as it crept up the (steep, steeply) grade.

4. My boss tells me (frequent, frequently) that I do a good job.

5. Did you answer every question in the interview (truthful, truthfully)?

6. If you think your decision was right, you'll sleep (peaceful, peacefully).

7. Walter the werewolf smiled at the (bright, brightly) moonlight shining through his bedroom window.

8. Nate was playing the stereo so (loud, loudly) that both the dog and the cat were cowering in the basement.

9. The surgeon stitched the wound very (careful, carefully) so that the scar would not be noticeable.

10. Eli dressed (nice, nicely) for his first meeting with his girlfriend's parents.

Well and *Good*

Two words often confused are *well* and *good*. *Good* is an adjective; it describes nouns. *Well* is usually an adverb; it describes verbs. *Well* (rather than *good*) is also used when referring to a person's health.

Here are some examples:

I became a *good* swimmer. (*Good* is an adjective describing the noun *swimmer*.)

For a change, two-year-old Rodney was *good* during the church service. (*Good* is an adjective describing Rodney and comes after *was*, a form of the verb *be*.)

Maryann did *well* on that exam. (*Well* is an adverb describing the verb *did*.)

I explained that I wasn't feeling *well*. (*Well* is used in reference to health.)

| ACTIVITY 4 | **Using *well* or *good*** |

Write *well* or *good* in the sentences that follow.

> **HINT**   In item 1, an adverb is needed to describe the verb *was doing*.

1. I suspected that I was doing _____ in my world civilization class, but I never thought that I would score a 98 percent on the final exam.

2. As a manager, I am always looking for _____, reliable employees who work hard and get along well with others.

3. My friends assure me that George, my blind date this Saturday night,

   is a _____ man.

4. The Army buddy who gave my uncle's eulogy knew him _____.

5. Horacio told the therapist that he was feeling _____, but he was still having nightmares and anxiety attacks.

REVIEW TEST 1

Underline the correct word (adjective or adverb) in the parentheses.

1. When I found out that the landlord intended to increase my rent, I moved back in with my parents (immediate, immediately).

2. During the massage, the therapist pressed (deep, deeply) into the muscles of my neck and shoulders.

3. For as long as I can remember, my teachers have tried to get me to write more (neat, neatly).

4. Judy's parents were deeply disturbed that her grades were (worse, more worse) than ever.

5. My grandfather says that teenagers acted just as (unpredictable, unpredictably) when he was a boy as they do today.

6. The plane taxied (rapid, rapidly) down the runway but then came to a complete stop.

7. The crowd booed (loud, loudly) when the referee ejected the player from the game.

8. Although Al thought his accounting exam was the (difficultest, most difficult) test he had ever taken, he got an A on it.

9. Holding the purple felt-tipped pen (loose, loosely), Gina drew graceful spirals in her notebook.

10. Phil played so (good, well) in the soccer game that the coach asked him to join the team.

REVIEW TEST 2

Write sentences that use each of the following adjectives and adverbs correctly.

1. confident _____

   _____

2. nervously _____

   _____

3. well _____

   _____

4. more impulsive _____

_____

5. better _____

_____

6. cleverly _____

_____

7. worst _____

_____

8. rough _____

_____

9. most annoying _____

_____

10. sweeter _____

_____

REFLECTIVE ACTIVITY

1. Review your answers to Activity 3 and Activity 4 in this chapter. Explain why you think the word you chose is correct.

2. Read the sentences you wrote for Review Test 2 in this chapter. Is the word that you were asked to use an adjective or an adverb? If an adjective, what noun or pronoun in the sentence does it describe? If an adverb, what verb, adjective, or other adverb does it describe?

For additional materials on Chapter 17, visit www.mhhe.com/langan.

Misplaced Modifiers

CHAPTER PREVIEW

What Misplaced
Modifiers Are and How
to Correct Them

INTRODUCTORY ACTIVITY

Because of misplaced words, each of the sentences below has more than one possible meaning. In each case, see if you can explain both the intended meaning and the unintended meaning.

1. The grocery clerk won the Mega Millions lottery working at the supermarket.

    Intended meaning: _____

    Unintended meaning: _____

    _____

2. The social worker met with the terminally ill patient's family who works for the hospital.

    Intended meaning:_____

    Unintended meaning: _____

    _____

Answers are on page 626.

What Misplaced Modifiers Are and How to Correct Them

Misplaced modifiers are words that, because of awkward placement, do not describe the words the writer intended them to describe. Misplaced modifiers often confuse the meaning of a sentence. To avoid them, place words as close as possible to what they describe.

Misplaced Words	Correctly Placed Words
They could see the Goodyear blimp *sitting on the front lawn.* (The *Goodyear blimp* was sitting on the front lawn?)	Sitting on the front lawn, they could see the Goodyear blimp. (The intended meaning—that the Goodyear blimp was visible from the front lawn—is now clear.)
We had a hamburger after the movie, *which was too greasy for my taste.* (The *movie* was too greasy for my taste?)	After the movie, we had a hamburger, which was too greasy for my taste. (The intended meaning—that the hamburger was greasy—is now clear.)

Our phone *almost rang* fifteen times last night.
(The phone *almost rang* fifteen times, but in fact did not ring at all?)

Our phone rang almost fifteen times last night.
(The intended meaning—that the phone rang a little under fifteen times—is now clear.)

Other single-word modifiers to watch out for include *only, even, hardly, nearly,* and *often.* Such words should be placed immediately before the word they modify.

| ACTIVITY 1 | Fixing Misplaced Modifiers |

Underline the misplaced word or words in each sentence. Then rewrite the sentence, placing related words together to make the meaning clear.

EXAMPLE

Anita returned the hamburger to the supermarket <u>that was spoiled</u>.

Anita returned the hamburger that was spoiled to the supermarket.

HINT   Who is *at the back of the cage* in item 1?

1. The tiger growled at a passerby at the back of his cage.

   _____

   _____

2. Lee hung colorful scarves over her windows made of green and blue silk.

   _____

   _____

3. We watched the fireworks standing on our front porch.

   _____

   _____

4. Jason almost has two hundred friends on Facebook.

   _____

   _____

5. The salesclerk exchanged the blue sweater for a yellow one with a smile.

   _____

   _____

6. We all stared at the man in the front row of the theater with curly purple hair.

_____

_____

7. I love the cookies from the bakery with the chocolate frosting.

_____

_____

8. The faculty decided to strike during their last meeting.

_____

_____

9. Larry looked on as his car burned with disbelief.

_____

_____

10. My cousin sent me instructions on how to get to her house in a letter.

_____

_____

Placing Modifiers Correctly　　　　　　　　　ACTIVITY 2

Rewrite each sentence, adding the _italicized_ words. Make sure that the intended meaning is clear and that two different interpretations are not possible.

EXAMPLE

I use a flash drive to store my computer files. (Insert _that I keep on my key chain._)

I use a flash drive that I keep on my key chain to store my computer files.

> **H I N T**　　Who is _using caution_ in item 1?

1. I rolled down my car window only a few inches for the police officer. (Insert _using caution._)

_____

_____

2. Tabloids publish unflattering photos of celebrities who are arrested for drunk driving or possession of illicit drugs. (Insert _all over the world._)

_____

_____

3. The mongoose was brought to Hawaii to kill rats but has since destroyed much of the native plant life. (Insert *which resembles the ferret.*)

_____

_____

4. Led Zeppelin's fourth album has sold 22 million copies. (Insert *almost.*)

_____

_____

5. Elisa decided to undergo laser eye surgery to correct her astigmatism. (Insert *at the university medical center*).

_____

_____

REFLECTIVE ACTIVITY

Review your answers to Activity 1 in this chapter. Explain why your corrections make the sentences clearer and more logical.

REVIEW TEST 1

Write *M* for *misplaced* or *C* for *correct* in front of each sentence.

_____ 1. I keep a twenty-dollar bill under the car seat for emergencies.

_____ 2. I keep a twenty-dollar bill for emergencies under the car seat.

_____ 3. This morning, I planned my day in the shower.

_____ 4. In the shower this morning, I planned my day.

_____ 5. While skating, Ben ran over a dog's tail.

_____ 6. Ben ran over a dog's tail skating.

_____ 7. I could hear my neighbors screaming at each other through the apartment wall.

_____ 8. Through the apartment wall, I could hear my neighbors screaming at each other.

_____ 9. For the family reunion, we cooked hamburgers and hot dogs on an outdoor grill.

_____ 10. For the family reunion on an outdoor grill we cooked hamburgers and hot dogs.

_____ 11. Virgil visited the old house, still weak with the flu.

_____ 12. Virgil, still weak with the flu, visited the old house.

_____ 13. While still weak with the flu, Virgil visited the old house.

_____ 14. My teenage son nearly grew three inches last year.

_____ 15. My teenage son grew nearly three inches last year.

_____ 16. The instructor explained how to study for the final exam at the end of her lecture.

_____ 17. The instructor explained how to study at the end of her lecture for the final exam.

_____ 18. At the end of her lecture, the instructor explained how to study for the final exam.

_____ 19. In the library, I read that a deadly virus was spread through an air-conditioning system.

_____ 20. I read that a deadly virus was spread through an air-conditioning system in the library.

REVIEW TEST 2

Underline the five misplaced modifiers in the following passage. Then, in the spaces that follow, show how you would correct them.

[1]The young teenagers who almost hang out in our town library every night are becoming a major nuisance. [2]They show up on weeknights and infuriate the otherwise mild librarians throwing spitballs and paper airplanes. [3]Some of the kids hide out behind stacks of bookcases; others indulge in continual adolescent flirting games. [4]The noise many of these teenagers make is especially offensive to some of the older library patrons, who often give looks to the clusters of young people that are disapproving. [5]One time there was so much noise that a librarian lost her temper and yelled at some boys to be quiet or leave the library at the top of her lungs. [6]The worst recent offense took place when a soaking-wet dog was led into the middle of the library by a junior high school boy with a stubby tail and the meanest-looking face one could ever imagine.

Sentence number: _____

Correction:

_____

Sentence number: _____

Correction:

_____

Sentence number: _____

Correction:

_____

Sentence number: _____

Correction:

_____

Sentence number: _____

Correction:

_____

_____

For additional materials on Chapter 18, visit **www.mhhe.com/langan**.

Dangling Modifiers

INTRODUCTORY ACTIVITY

Because of dangling modifiers, each of the sentences below has more than one possible meaning. In each case, see if you can explain both the intended meaning and the unintended meaning.

1. Sizzling, the customer at the restaurant enjoyed her grilled T-bone steak.

    Intended meaning: _____

    _____

    Unintended meaning: _____

    _____

2. Arriving home from college, Eric's parents threw a huge barbeque party for him.

    Intended meaning: _____

    _____

    Unintended meaning: _____

Answers are on page 627.

What Dangling Modifiers
Are and How to Correct Them

A modifier that opens a sentence must be followed immediately by the word it is meant to describe. Otherwise, the modifier is said to be *dangling,* and the sentence takes on an unintended meaning. For example, look at this sentence:

> While sleeping in his backyard, a Frisbee hit Bill on the head.

The unintended meaning is that the *Frisbee* was sleeping in his backyard. What the writer meant, of course, was that *Bill* was sleeping in his backyard. The writer should have placed *Bill* right after the modifier, revising the rest of the sentence as necessary:

> While sleeping in his backyard, *Bill* was hit on the head by a Frisbee.

The sentence could also be corrected by adding the missing subject and verb to the opening word group:

> While *Bill* was sleeping in his backyard, a Frisbee hit him on the head.

Other sentences with dangling modifiers follow. Read the explanations of why they are dangling and look carefully at how they are corrected.

Dangling	**Correct**
Having almost no money, my survival depended on my parents. (*Who* has almost no money? The answer is not *survival* but *I*. The subject *I* must be added.)	Having almost no money, *I* depended on my parents for survival. *Or:* Since I had almost no money, I depended on my parents for survival.
Riding his bike, a German shepherd bit Tony on the ankle. (*Who* is riding the bike? The answer is not *German shepherd,* as it unintentionally seems to be, but *Tony*. The subject *Tony* must be added.)	Riding his bike, *Tony* was bitten on the ankle by a German shepherd. *Or:* While *Tony* was riding his bike, a German shepherd bit him on the ankle.
When trying to lose weight, all snacks are best avoided. (*Who* is trying to lose weight? The answer is not *snacks* but *you*. The subject *you* must be added.)	When trying to lose weight, *you* should avoid all snacks. *Or:* When *you* are trying to lose weight, avoid all snacks.

CONNECT WRITING

Meet Ajay. He's having trouble writing a letter to his daughter's principal about her food allergies. He's worried that some of his ideas are unclear because of where he's placed them in his sentences. Help Ajay locate and correct the misplaced and dangling modifiers in his letter to make it more readable.

mhconnectwriting.com

These examples make clear two ways of correcting a dangling modifier. Decide on a logical subject and do one of the following:

1. Place the subject *within* the opening word group:

   > Since *I* had almost no money, I depended on my parents for survival.

TIP   In some cases an appropriate subordinating word such as *since* must be added, and the verb may have to be changed slightly as well.

2. Place the subject right *after* the opening word group:

   > Having almost no money, *I* depended on my parents for survival.

Sometimes even more rewriting is necessary to correct a dangling modifier. What is important to remember is that a modifier must be placed as close as possible to the word that it modifies.

Correcting Dangling Modifiers

Rewrite each sentence to correct the dangling modifier. Mark the one sentence that is correct with a *C*.

> **HINT**   What is *hanging safely on a wall* in item 1?

1. Hanging safely on a wall, a security guard pointed to the priceless painting.

   _____

   _____

2. At the age of five, my mother bought me a chemistry set.

   _____

   _____

3. While it was raining, shoppers ran into the stores.

   _____

   _____

4. Having turned sour, I would not drink the milk.

   _____

   _____

5. Updating my Facebook profile, my hot tea turned cold.

   _____

   _____

6. Piled high with dirty dishes, Pete hated to look at the kitchen sink.

   _____

   _____

7. Having locked my keys in the car, the police had to open it for me.

   _____

   _____

8. Drooping and looking all dried out, the children watered the plants.

   _____

   _____

9. After sitting through a long lecture, my foot was asleep.

_____

_____

10. Being late, stopping at Starbucks was out of the question.

_____

_____

| ACTIVITY 2 | **Placing Modifiers Correctly** |

Complete the following sentences. In each case, a logical subject should follow the opening words.

EXAMPLE

Checking my monthly credit card statement, <u>I discovered that the</u> <u>restaurant had charged me twice for my meal.</u>

1. Since starting college, _____.

2. After finishing the first semester, _____.

3. While listening to music downloads, _____.

4. Before starting a family, _____.

5. At the age of sixteen, _____.

REFLECTIVE ACTIVITY

Review your answers to Activity 1. Explain why your corrections make the sentences clearer and more logical.

REVIEW TEST 1

Write *D* for *dangling* or *C* for *correct* in front of each sentence. Remember that the opening words are a dangling modifier if they are not followed immediately by a logical subject.

_____ 1. Burning quickly, the firefighters turned several hoses on the house.

_____ 2. Because the house was burning quickly, firefighters turned several hoses on it.

_____ 3. While focusing the camera, several people wandered out of view.

_____ 4. While I focused the camera, several people wandered out of view.

_____ 5. When I peered down from the thirtieth floor, the cars looked like toys.

_____ 6. Peering down from the thirtieth floor, the cars looked like toys.

_____ 7. The cars looked like toys peering down from the thirtieth floor.

_____ 8. Riding in the rear of the bus, the sudden starts and stops were sickening.

_____ 9. For passengers riding in the rear of the bus, the sudden starts and stops were sickening.

_____ 10. Speaking excitedly, the phone seemed glued to Sara's ear.

_____ 11. The phone seemed glued to Sara's ear as she spoke excitedly.

_____ 12. In a sentimental frame of mind, the music brought tears to Beth's eyes.

_____ 13. As Beth was in a sentimental frame of mind, the music brought tears to her eyes.

_____ 14. When Helen suddenly became sick, I drove her to the doctor's office.

_____ 15. Suddenly sick, I drove Helen to the doctor's office.

_____ 16. The pancake was browned on one side, so Mark flipped it over.

_____ 17. Browned on one side, Mark flipped the pancake over.

_____ 18. Hanging by her teeth, the acrobat's body swung back and forth.

_____ 19. Hanging by her teeth, the acrobat swung back and forth.

_____ 20. While hanging by her teeth, the acrobat's body swung back and forth.

REVIEW TEST 2

Underline the five dangling modifiers in this passage. Then correct them in the spaces provided.

[1]Have you ever thought about what life was like for the first generation of your family to come to America? [2]Or have you wondered what your grandparents did for fun when they were your age?

continued

³Family stories tend to be told for two or three generations and then disappear because no one ever records them. ⁴Using a camcorder, these stories can be saved for the future. ⁵Here are some hints for conducting interviews with older members of your family. ⁶Thinking hard about what you really want to know, good questions can be prepared in advance. ⁷Try to put the people you interview at ease by reassuring them that you value what they have to say. ⁸Nervous about the camera, stories might not come so easily to them otherwise. ⁹Remember that most people have never been interviewed before. ¹⁰Listening carefully to everything the person says, your interview will be more successful. ¹¹By respecting their feelings, your older relatives will be delighted to share their stories. ¹²The videos you record will be valued by your family for many years to come.

Sentence number: _____

Correction:

_____

_____

Sentence number: _____

Correction:

_____

_____

Sentence number: _____

Correction:

_____

_____

Sentence number: _____

Correction:

_____

Sentence number: _____

Correction:

_____

_____

For additional materials on Chapter 19, visit **www.mhhe.com/langan**.

Faulty Parallelism

CHAPTER PREVIEW
Parallelism Explained

INTRODUCTORY ACTIVITY

Read aloud each pair of sentences below. Write a check mark beside the sentence that reads more smoothly and clearly and sounds more natural.

Pair 1

_____ I use my TV remote control to change channels, to adjust the volume, and for turning the set on and off.

_____ I use my TV remote control to change channels, to adjust the volume, and to turn the set on and off.

Pair 2

_____ One option the employees had was to take a cut in pay; the other was longer hours of work.

_____ One option the employees had was to take a cut in pay; the other was to work longer hours.

Pair 3

_____ The refrigerator has a cracked vegetable drawer, one of the shelves is missing, and a strange freezer smell.

_____ The refrigerator has a cracked vegetable drawer, a missing shelf, and a strange freezer smell.

Answers are on page 627.

Parallelism Explained

Words in a pair or series should have parallel structure. By balancing the items in a pair or series so that they have the same kind of structure, you will make the sentence clearer and easier to read. Notice how the parallel sentences that follow read more smoothly than the nonparallel ones.

Nonparallel (Not Balanced)

Brit spends her free time reading, listening to music, and she works in the garden.

Parallel (Balanced)

Brit spends her free time reading, listening to music, and working in the garden.
(A balanced series of -ing words: *reading, listening, working.*)

Nonparallel (Not Balanced)	**Parallel (Balanced)**
After the camping trip I was exhausted, irritable, and wanted to eat.	After the camping trip I was exhausted, irritable, and hungry. (A balanced series of descriptive words: *exhausted, irritable, hungry.*)
My hope for retirement is to be healthy, to live in a comfortable house, and having plenty of money.	My hope for retirement is to be healthy, to live in a comfortable house, and to have plenty of money. (A balanced series of *to* verbs: *to be, to live, to have.*)
Nightly, Fred puts out the trash, checks the locks on the doors, and the burglar alarm is turned on.	Nightly, Fred puts out the trash, checks the locks on the doors, and turns on the burglar alarm. (Balanced verbs and word order: *puts out the trash, checks the locks, turns on the burglar alarm.*)

Balanced sentences are not a skill you need to worry about when you are writing first drafts. But when you rewrite, you should try to put matching words and ideas into matching structures. Such parallelism will improve your writing style.

ACTIVITY 1	**Using Parallelism**

The one item in each list that is not parallel in form to the other items is crossed out. In the space provided, rewrite that item in parallel form. The first one has been done for you as an example.

1. fresh food

   attractive setting

   ~~service that is fast~~

   fast service
   _____

2. screaming children

   dogs that howl

   blaring music

   _____

3. slow

   speaks rudely

   careless

   _____

4. to hike

   swimming

   boating

   _____

5. noisy neighbors

   high rent

   security that is poor

   _____

6. cleaning of the apartment

   paid the bills

   did the laundry

   _____

7. looking good
   to have fun
   feeling fine

   _____

8. healthy soups
   tasty sandwiches
   desserts that are inexpensive

   _____

9. under the desk drawers
   the floor of the closet
   behind the bedroom curtains

   _____

10. works at the supermarket
    singer in the church choir
    coaches the Little League team

    _____

Correcting Nonparallel Sentences

The unbalanced part of each sentence is *italicized*. Rewrite this part so that it matches the rest of the sentence.

EXAMPLE

In the afternoon, I changed two diapers, ironed several shirts, and *was studying* for two exams. studied_____

1. Taiyaba dropped a coin into the slot machine, pulled the lever, and *was waiting* to strike it rich.

   _____

2. Studying a little each day is more effective than *to cram.*

   _____

3. Many old people fear loneliness, *becoming ill,* and poverty.

   _____

4. My pet peeves are screeching chalk, *buses that are late,* and dripping sinks.

   _____

5. The magazine cover promised stories on losing weight quickly, *how to attract* a rich spouse, and finding the perfect haircut.

   _____

6. As smoke billowed around her, Paula knew her only choices were to jump or *suffocation.*

   _____

7. The principal often pestered students, yelled at teachers, and *was interrupting* classes.

   _____

8. People immigrate to America with hopes of finding freedom, happiness, and *in order to become financially secure.*

   _____

ACTIVITY 2

CONNECT WRITING

Meet Yelina. She's very impressed with the slides her classmate put together for his class presentation, but thinks a few of his ideas could be presented more clearly. Some of the words paired together in his sentences do not have a parallel structure. Help Yelina and her classmate locate and correct the parallelism mistakes in the class presentation.

mhconnectwriting.com

9. Once inside the zoo gates, Julio could hear lions roaring, *the chirping of birds,* and elephants trumpeting.

_____

10. As a child, I had nightmares about a huge monster that came out of a cave, *was breathing fire,* and wanted to barbecue me.

_____

REFLECTIVE ACTIVITY

Review your answers to Activity 2. Explain why your corrections make the sentences clearer and more logical.

ACTIVITY 3 | Writing Parallel Sentences

Complete the following statements. The first two parts of each statement are parallel in form; the part that you add should be parallel in form as well.

EXAMPLE

Three things I could not live without are my cell phone, my laptop, and my morning coffee.

1. The new reality TV show is disappointing: The premise is absurd, the cast members are uninteresting, and _____

_____ .

2. As a parent, I promise to love my child unconditionally, to provide for my child's needs, and _____

_____ .

3. As the students waited for the professor to arrive for class, they rummaged through their backpacks, silenced their phones, and _____

_____ .

4. During my first year in my own apartment, I learned how to fix leaky toilets and torn screens, how to survive on instant ramen and frozen pizzas, and _____

_____ .

5. Online dating is popular, unpredictable, and _____

_____ .

Editing and Rewriting

Working with a partner, read carefully the short paragraph below and cross out the five instances of faulty parallelism. Then use the space provided to correct the instances of faulty parallelism. Feel free to discuss the rewrite quietly with your partner and refer back to the chapter when necessary.

> Running is an exercise that can be good for you mentally, physically, and also be helpful for your emotions. A beginning runner should keep three things in mind: the warm-up session, the actual time that you are running, and the cool-down period. Never start a run without first having warmed up through stretching exercises. Stretching reduces muscle stiffness, decreases the possibility of injury, and it's a good method to gradually increase the heart rate. During the run itself, move at a comfortable pace. Your breathing should be steady and with depth. Finally, remember to cool down after a run. An adequate cool-down period allows time for the body to relax and the normalizing of the heart rate.

_____

_____

_____

_____

_____

_____

_____

_____

_____

_____

1. Look at the paragraph that you revised in Activity 4. How does parallel form improve the paragraph?

2. How would you evaluate your own use of parallel form? When you write, do you use it almost never, at times, or often? How would you benefit from using it more?

| ACTIVITY 5 | **Creating Sentences** |

Working with a partner, make up your own short test on faulty parallelism, as directed.

1. Write a sentence that includes three things you want to do tomorrow. One of those things should not be in parallel form. Then correct the faulty parallelism.

   Nonparallel _____

   _____

   Parallel _____

   _____

2. Write a sentence that names three positive qualities of a person you like or three negative qualities that you don't like.

   Nonparallel _____

   _____

   Parallel _____

   _____

3. Write a sentence that includes three everyday things that annoy you.

   Nonparallel _____

   _____

   Parallel _____

   _____

REVIEW TEST 1

Cross out the unbalanced part of each sentence. Then rewrite the unbalanced part so that it matches the other item or items in the sentence.

EXAMPLE

I enjoy texting my friends and ~~to chat~~ online.

chatting _____

1. Andreas is known to skip classes, make excuses, and then he borrows his classmates' notes.

   _____

2. Before my blind date, I bought a new outfit, got a haircut, and to work out at the gym.

_____

3. The children at the preschool had fingerpaint-stained hands, jelly-smudged lips, and their faces were smiling.

_____

4. Zach listened to his iPod, was text messaging his friends, and surfed online all at the same time.

_____

5. My homemade pesto recipe calls for extra-virgin olive oil, several sprigs of fresh basil, and pine nuts that were roasted.

_____

6. When I want to relax, I grab a cold soda, open a bag of chips, turn on the TV, and I like to watch whatever sports game is on.

_____

7. The mail brought utility bills, monthly statements from the bank, and credit card applications.

_____

8. Samantha goes to Las Vegas every year with her friends to gamble, to eat at the buffets, and she sees at least one show.

_____

9. This summer, Kalani will travel to Samoa, Tahiti, and he is going to Guam.

_____

10. My baby enjoys her mechanical swing, her gym mat, and her bouncer that plays music.

_____

REVIEW TEST 2

Each group of sentences contains two errors in parallelism. Underline these errors. Then, on the lines below, rewrite each item that doesn't match to make it parallel with the other item or items in the sentence.

1. When Phil left for work, he felt bright and cheerful. But by midafternoon he was coughing, wheezing, and shivers ran throughout his body. He left work, drove home, and was crawling into bed, where he stayed for the next four days.

a. _____

b. _____

2. I never spend money on fancy wrapping paper. When people get a present, they generally want to rip off the paper and be looking at what's inside. So I wrap my gifts in either plain brown grocery bags or Sunday comics that are colorful.

    a. _____

    b. _____

3. Failing students can be kinder than to pass them. There is little benefit to passing a student to a level of work he or she can't do. In addition, it is cruel to graduate a student from high school who has neither the communication skills nor the skills at math needed to get along in the world.

    a. _____

    b. _____

4. The little boy drew back from his new babysitter. Her long red nails, black eye makeup, and jewelry that jangled all frightened him. He was sure she was either a bad witch or a queen who was evil.

    a. _____

    b. _____

5. An actress stopped in the middle of a Broadway show and scolded flash photographers in the audience. She said they can either have a photo session or they can be enjoying the show, but they can't do both. The photographers sank down in their seats, their cameras were put away, and quietly watched the show.

    a. _____

    b. _____

REVIEW TEST 3

Cross out the five nonparallel parts in the following passage. Correct them in the spaces between the lines.

> When a few people in one community decided to form a
> homeowners' association, many of their neighbors were skeptical.
> Some objected to stirring things up, and others were feeling the dues
> were too high. But many neighbors joined, and their first big success
> was a garage sale. They scheduled a day for everybody in the
> neighborhood to bring unwanted items to a community center. Big
> appliances and other items that are heavy were picked up by

continued

volunteers with trucks. The association promoted the sale by placing ads in newspapers and with the distribution of fliers at local shopping centers. Dozens of families took part. After that, the association helped plant trees, start a Crime Watch Program, and in repairing cracked sidewalks. Members now receive discounts from local merchants and theater owners. This association's success has inspired many more neighbors to join and people in other neighborhoods, who are starting their own organizations.

For additional materials on Chapter 20, visit www.mhhe.com/langan.

Sentence Variety II

CHAPTER PREVIEW

-ing Word Groups

-ed Word Groups

-ly Openers

To Openers

Prepositional Phrase Openers

Series of Items

• Adjectives in Series

• Verbs in Series

Like Chapter 9, this chapter will show you a variety of ways to write effective and varied sentences. You will learn more about the many ways you can express your ideas. The practices here will also reinforce much of what you have learned in this section about modifiers and the use of parallelism.

-ing Word Groups

Use an *-ing* word group at some point in a sentence. Here are examples:

> The doctor, *hoping* for the best, examined the X-rays.

> *Jogging* every day, I soon raised my energy level.

> **TIP** More information about *-ing* words, also known as *present participles*, appears on page 248.

ACTIVITY 1 | **Combining Sentences with *-ing* Words**

Combine each pair of sentences below into one sentence by using an *-ing* word and omitting repeated words. Use a comma or commas to set off the *-ing* word group from the rest of the sentence.

EXAMPLE

- The city bus is fuel efficient.

- It runs on solar energy.

  The city bus, running on solar energy, is fuel efficient.

1. • The students began leaving the lecture hall.

   • They gathered up their books and backpacks.

   _____

   _____

2. • Susan was involved in a hit-and-run accident.

   • She was crossing the street with her daughter.

   _____

   _____

3. • Arnold parked his motorcycle on the school lawn.

   • He was rushing to class.

   _____

   _____

4. • The nurse brought the patient his pain medication.

   • The nurse acted quickly.

   _____

   _____

5. • The football coach buried his face in his hands.

   • He knew that his team would lose the game.

   _____

   _____

Using -ing Word Groups

ACTIVITY 2

On a separate piece of paper, write five sentences of your own that contain *-ing* word groups.

-ed Word Groups

Use an *-ed* word group at some point in a sentence. Here are examples:

Tired of studying, I took a short break.

Mary, *amused* by the joke, told it to a friend.

I opened my eyes wide, *shocked* by the red "F" on my paper.

> **TIP**   More information about *-ed* words, also known as *past participles*, appears on page 248.

Combining Sentences with -ed Words

ACTIVITY 3

Combine each of the following pairs of sentences into one sentence by using an *-ed* word and omitting repeated words. Use a comma or commas to set off the *-ed* word group from the rest of the sentence.

EXAMPLE

   • Tim woke up with a start.

   • He was troubled by a dream.

   Troubled by a dream, Tim woke up with a start.

   or   Tim, troubled by a dream, woke up with a start.

1. • Mary sat up suddenly in bed.
   • She was startled by thunder.

   _____

   _____

2. • My parents decided to have a second wedding.
   • They have been married for fifty years.

   _____

   _____

3. • Erica wouldn't leave her car.
   • She was frightened by the large dog near the curb.

   _____

   _____

4. • The old orange felt like a marshmallow.
   • It was dotted with mold.

   _____

   _____

5. • Scott made a huge sandwich and popped popcorn.
   • He was determined to have plenty to eat during the movie.

   _____

   _____

| ACTIVITY 4 | **Using -ed Word Groups** |

On a separate piece of paper, write five sentences of your own that contain -ed word groups.

-ly Openers

Use an -ly word to open a sentence. Here are examples:

Gently, he mixed the chemicals together.

Anxiously, the contestant looked at the game clock.

Skillfully, the quarterback rifled a pass to his receiver.

> **TIP** More information about -ly words, which are also known as *adverbs*, appears on page 279.

Combining Sentences with -*ly* Words

Combine each of the following pairs of sentences into one sentence by starting with an -*ly* word and omitting repeated words. Place a comma after the opening -*ly* word.

EXAMPLE

- I asked my supervisor for the weekend off.

- I was nervous.

Nervously, I asked my supervisor for the weekend off.

> **HINT** Begin your revised sentence in item 1 with *Hungrily*.

CONNECT WRITING

Meet Rika. She's trying to write a blog entry about the newest restaurant in town, *Grillin's Good*, but some of her ideas seem repetitive. Help Rika use different opening words or phrases to vary her sentences.

mhconnectwriting.com

1. • We ordered extra-large pepperoni pizzas and buffalo wings.
   • We were hungry.

   _____

   _____

2. • Nino left the party.
   • He left all of a sudden.

   _____

   _____

3. • I watched TV all afternoon.
   • I was lazy.

   _____

   _____

4. • David returned the customer's phone call.
   • He was eager.

   _____

   _____

5. • The visiting team won the game in double overtime.
   • The win was a surprise.

   _____

   _____

| ACTIVITY 6 | Using *-ly* Words |

On a separate piece of paper, write five sentences of your own that begin with *-ly* words.

To Openers

Use a *to* word group to open a sentence. Here are examples:

> *To* succeed in that course, you must attend every class.
>
> *To* help me sleep better, I learned to quiet my mind through meditation.
>
> *To* get good seats, we went to the game early.

 TIP The combination of *to* and a verb, also known as an *infinitive*, is explained on page 247.

| ACTIVITY 7 | Combining Sentences with *to* Word Groups |

Combine each of the following pairs of sentences into one sentence by starting with a *to* word group and omitting repeated words. Use a comma after the opening *to* word group.

EXAMPLE

- I fertilize the grass every spring.
- I want to make it greener.

To make the grass greener, I fertilize it every spring.

 HINT In item 1, your combined sentence should omit these words: *she did this*.

1. • Lily put a thick towel on the bottom of the tub.
   • She did this to make the tub less slippery.

   _____

   _____

2. • We now keep our garbage in the garage.
   • We do this to keep raccoons away.

   _____

   _____

3. • Bill pressed two fingers against the large vein in his neck.

   • He did this to count his pulse.

   _____

   _____

4. • My aunt opens her dishwasher when it begins drying.

   • She does this to steam her face.

   _____

   _____

5. • We looked through our closets for unused clothing.

   • We did this to help out the homeless.

   _____

   _____

| **Using to** | ACTIVITY 8 |

On a separate piece of paper, write five sentences of your own that begin with _to_ word groups.

Prepositional Phrase Openers

Use prepositional phrase openers. Here are examples:

From the beginning, I disliked my boss.

In spite of her work, she failed the course.

After the game, we went to a movie.

> **TIP** Prepositional phrases include words such as _in, from, of, at, by,_ and _with_. A list of common prepositions appears on page 157.

| **Combining Sentences by Opening with Prepositional Phrases** | ACTIVITY 9 |

Combine each of the following groups of sentences into one sentence by omitting repeated words. Start each sentence with a suitable prepositional phrase and put the other prepositional phrases in places that sound right. Generally, you should use a comma after the opening prepositional phrase.

EXAMPLE

   • A fire started.

   • It did this at 5:00 A.M.

   • It did this inside the garage.

   At 5:00 A.M., a fire started inside the garage.

> ## HINT
> Begin item 1's sentence with *About once a week*.

1. • We have dinner with my parents.
   • We do this about once a week.
   • We do this at a restaurant.

   _____

   _____

2. • I put the dirty cups away.
   • I did this before company came.
   • I put them in the cupboard.

   _____

   _____

3. • My eyes roamed.
   • They did this during my English exam.
   • They did this around the room.
   • They did this until they met the instructor's eye.

   _____

   _____

4. • The little boy drew intently.
   • He did this in a comic book.
   • He did this for twenty minutes.
   • He did this without stopping once.

   _____

   _____

5. • A playful young orangutan wriggled.
   • He did this at the zoo.
   • He did this in a corner.
   • He did this under a paper sack.

   _____

   _____

| **Using Prepositional Phrases** | **ACTIVITY 10** |

On a separate piece of paper, write five sentences of your own, each beginning with a prepositional phrase and containing at least one other prepositional phrase.

Series of Items

Use a series of items. Following are two of the many items that can be used in a series: adjectives and verbs.

Adjectives in Series

Adjectives are descriptive words. Here are examples:

> The *husky young* man sanded the *chipped, weather-worn* paint off the fence.

Husky and *young* are adjectives that describe *man; chipped* and *weather-worn* are adjectives that describe *paint.* More information about adjectives appears in Appendix B.

| **Using Adjectives in a Series** | **ACTIVITY 11** |

Combine each of the following groups of sentences into one sentence by using adjectives in a series and omitting repeated words. Use a comma between adjectives only when *and* inserted between them sounds natural.

EXAMPLE

- I sewed a set of buttons onto my coat.
- The buttons were shiny.
- The buttons were black.
- The coat was old.
- The coat was green.

    I sewed a set of shiny black buttons onto my old green coat.

> **H I N T**   Begin the sentence in item 1 with *The old, peeling shingles.*

1. - The shingles blew off the roof during the storm.
   - The shingles were old.
   - The shingles were peeling.
   - The storm was blustery.

   _____

   _____

2. • The dancer whirled across the stage with his partner.
   • The dancer was lean.
   • The dancer was powerful.
   • The partner was graceful.
   • The partner was elegant.

   _____

   _____

3. • A rat scurried into the kitchen of the restaurant.
   • The rat was large.
   • The rat was furry.
   • The kitchen was crowded.

   _____

   _____

4. • The moon lit up the sky like a streetlamp.
   • The moon was full.
   • The moon was golden.
   • The sky was cloudy.
   • The streetlamp was huge.
   • The streetlamp was floating.

   _____

   _____

5. • The doorbell of the house played a tune.
   • The doorbell was oval.
   • The doorbell was plastic.
   • The house was large.
   • The house was ornate.
   • The tune was loud.
   • The tune was rock.

   _____

   _____

| **Writing with Adjectives in Series** | **ACTIVITY 12** |

Look at the accompanying photograph and write five sentences about it that contain a series of adjectives.

Verbs in Series

Verbs are words that express action. Here are examples:

> In my job as a cook's helper, I *prepared* salads, *sliced* meat and cheese, and *made* all kinds of sandwiches.

Basic information about verbs appears in Appendix A.

| **Combining Sentences with Verbs in a Series** | **ACTIVITY 13** |

Working with a fellow classmate, combine each group of sentences into one sentence by using verbs in a series and omitting repeated words. Use a comma between verbs in a series.

EXAMPLE

- At the gym, Dirk asked his friend to spot him on the free weights.
- He did several lateral pull-downs.
- He jumped on the elliptical machine for twenty minutes.

At the gym, Dirk asked his friend to spot him on the bench press, did several lateral pull-downs, and jumped on the elliptical machine for twenty minutes.

HINT   What three things did the robber do in item 1?

1. • The robber scanned the liquor store for a surveillance camera.

   • He fidgeted with his dark sunglasses and baseball cap.

   • He signaled to the clerk behind the counter that he had a handgun.

   _____

   _____

   _____

2. • In the sports bar, Tanner placed a bet on his favorite basketball team.

   • He took a swig from his bottle of Budweiser.

   • He sat back to watch the NBA playoff semifinals.

   _____

   _____

   _____

3. • The phlebotomist pressed down on Logan's forearm.

   • She slid the needle into his arm.

   • She let out a heavy sigh as the needle missed his vein.

   _____

   _____

4. • The comedy hypnotist invited a volunteer to the stage.

   • He quickly brought her into a trance.

   • He offered her a clove of garlic, which she thought was a cashew nut.

   _____

   _____

5. • The paparazzo stalked the Hollywood actor on vacation.

   • He adjusted his telephoto lens.

   • He snapped hundreds of candid photos.

   _____

   _____

| ACTIVITY 14 | **Using Verbs in Series** |

On a separate piece of paper, write five sentences of your own that use verbs in a series.

> **TIP** The chapter on parallelism (pages 295–303) gives you practice in some of the other kinds of items that can be used in a series.

Combine each group of short sentences into one sentence. Various combinations are possible. Choose the combination that reads most smoothly and clearly and that sounds most appropriate in the context of the surrounding sentences.

> **HINT** In combining short sentences into one sentence, omit repeated words where necessary. Use separate paper. The story continues in the next review test.

Dracula's Revenge

- Mike Raines had a dislike.
- The dislike was of horror movies.
- His friends were different.
- They loved to see such movies.

- They would always invite Mike to go with them.
- He would always refuse.

- He thought horror films were stupid.
- The actors were covered with fake blood.
- They were pretending to writhe in agony.

- Mike thought their behavior was disgusting.
- He did not think their behavior was frightening.

- Once his friends persuaded him to come with them.
- They went to see a movie.
- The movie was called *Halloween 14—The Horror Continues*.

- Mike found it ridiculous.
- He laughed aloud through parts of the movie.
- They were the scariest parts.

- His friends were embarrassed.
- They were so embarrassed they moved.
- They moved away from him.
- They moved to another part of the theater.

- Then one night Mike was alone.
- He was alone in his house.
- His mother was out for the evening.
- He turned on the television.

- A movie was playing.
- It was called *Nosferatu*.

- It was the original film version of the Dracula story.
- The film version was silent.
- It was made in Germany.
- It was made in 1922.

REVIEW TEST 2

Combine each group of short sentences into one sentence. Various combinations are possible. Choose the combination that reads most smoothly and clearly and that sounds most appropriate in the context of the surrounding sentences.

> In combining short sentences into one sentence, omit repeated words where necessary. Use a separate piece of paper. The story continues from the previous review test.

- The movie was not gory at all.
- There were no teenage girls in it getting chased.
- There were no teenage girls in it getting murdered.

- The villain was a vampire.
- He was hideous.
- He was shriveled.
- He was terrifying.

- His victims did not die.
- His victims grew weaker.
- They grew weaker after every attack.

- The vampire reminded Mike of a parasite.
- The parasite was terrible.
- It was a dead thing.
- It was feeding off the living.

- Mike trembled.
- He was trembling at the thought of such a creature.
- It could be lurking just out of sight.
- It could be lurking in the darkness.

- Then he heard a scraping noise.
- The noise was at the front door.
- He almost cried out in terror.

- The door opened quickly.
- Cold air rushed in.
- His mother appeared.
- She was back from her date.

- His mother smiled at him.
- She called out, "Hello."
- She paused in the foyer to take off her coat.

- Mike was relieved to see her.
- His relief was enormous.
- He rushed up to greet her.

- The spell of the movie was broken.
- Mike locked the door on the night.

REFLECTIVE ACTIVITY

1. Review your answers to Review Tests 1 and 2. What method did you use to combine sentences in each group?

2. In what ways are your answers more interesting and effective than the originals?

For additional materials on Chapter 21, visit www.mhhe.com/langan.

IV Punctuation and Mechanics

SECTION PREVIEW

22 Paper Format

23 Capital Letters

24 Numbers and Abbreviations

25 End Marks

26 Apostrophes

27 Quotation Marks

28 Commas

29 Other Punctuation Marks

RESPONDING TO IMAGES

How does each of the signs above misuse punctuation, capitalization, and/or mechanics—and how is the direction or information in each sign changed or confused because of this error or errors? Have you seen similar mistakes in signs posted on campus? On the road? In a restaurant? In a newspaper or book?

Paper Format

CHAPTER 22

INTRODUCTORY ACTIVITY

CHAPTER PREVIEW

Guidelines for Preparing a Paper

Check the paper opening below that seems clearer and easier to read.

_____ A

	Dangers of Prescription Drugs
	Careless consumers can harm themselves with
	prescription drugs. To begin with, consumers should always
	be aware of the possible side effects of a prescription drug.

_____ B

	"dangers of prescription drugs"
	Careless consumers can harm themselves with prescription drugs.
	To begin with, consumers should always be aware of the possible
	side effects of a prescription drug. They should take the time.

What are four reasons for your choice?

_____

_____

_____

_____

Answers are on page 628.

Guidelines for Preparing a Paper

Here are guidelines to follow in preparing a paper for an instructor.

1. Use standard letter-sized 8½ by 11 paper.

2. Leave wide margins (1 to 1½ inches) all around the paper. In particular, do not crowd the right-hand or bottom margin. This white space makes your paper more readable and leaves the instructor room for comments.

3. Always use black as your font color, and choose a font style that is easy to read, such as Times New Roman. Avoid fancy or distracting colors and fonts. Make sure the type is large enough to be readable but not overwhelming. Most instructors prefer fonts in the 10–12 point range.

4. If you write by hand (check whether your instructor permits it):

   • Use a pen with blue or black ink (*not* a pencil).

   • Be careful not to overlap letters and not to make decorative loops on letters.

   • On narrow-ruled paper, write on every other line.

   • Make all your letters distinct. Pay special attention to *a, e, i, o,* and *u*—five letters that people sometimes write illegibly.

5. Center the title of your paper on the first line of the first page. Do not put quotation marks around the title. Do not underline the title. Capitalize all the major words in a title, including the first word. Short connecting words within a title, such as *of, for, the, in, to,* and all prepositions, are not capitalized.

6. Skip a line between the title and the first line of your text. Indent the first line of each paragraph about five spaces (half an inch) from the left-hand margin.

7. Make commas, periods, and other punctuation marks firm and clear. Leave a slight space after each period.

8. If you break a word at the end of a line, break only between syllables. Do not break words of one syllable.

9. Put your name, date, and course number where your instructor asks for them.

Remember these points about the title and the first sentence of your paper.

10. The title should be one or several words that tell what the paper is about. It should usually *not* be a complete sentence. For example, if you are writing a paper about your jealous sister, the title could simply be "My Jealous Sister."

11. Do not rely on the title to help explain the first sentence of your paper. The first sentence must be independent of the title. For instance, if the title of your paper is "My Jealous Sister," the first sentence should *not* be, "She has been this way as long as I can remember." Rather, the first sentence might be, "My sister has always been a jealous person."

Correcting Formatting Errors

Identify the mistakes in format in the following lines from a student composition. Explain the mistakes in the spaces provided. One mistake is described for you as an example.

	"Being a younger sister"
	When I was young, I would gladly have donated my older sister to ano-
	ther family. First of all, most of my clothes were hand-me-downs. I ra-
	rely got to buy anything new to wear. My sister took very good care
	of her clothes, which only made the problem worse. Also, she was always
	very critical of everything.

1. Break words at correct syllable divisions (an-other). _____

2. _____

3. _____

4. _____

5. _____

6. _____

Writing Titles

As already stated, a title should tell in several words what a paper is about. Often a title can be based on the sentence that expresses the main idea of a paper.

Following are five main-idea sentences from student papers. Write a suitable specific title for each paper, basing the title on the main idea.

EXAMPLE

Title: Aging Americans as Outcasts

Our society treats aging Americans as outcasts in many ways.

HINT What is a three-word subject for the paper in item 1?

1. Title: _____

Pets offer a number of benefits to their owners.

2. Title: _____

Since I have learned to budget carefully, I no longer run out of money at the end of the week.

3.   Title: _____

Studying regularly with a study group has helped me raise my grades.

4.   Title: _____

Grandparents have a special relationship with their grandchildren.

5.   Title: _____

My decision to eliminate junk food from my diet has been good for my health and my budget.

ACTIVITY 3	Rewriting Dependent Sentences

In four of the five following sentences, the writer has mistakenly used the title to help explain the first sentence. But as previously noted, you must *not* rely on the title to explain your first sentence. Rewrite the sentences so that they are independent of the title. Write *Correct* under the one sentence that is independent.

EXAMPLE

Title: Flunking an Exam

First sentence: I managed to do this because of several bad habits.

Rewritten: I managed to flunk an exam because of several bad habits.

> **HINT**   Indicate the words that *this* stands for in item 1.

EXAMPLE

Title: Finishing a Marathon

First sentence: I managed to do this because I followed a strict training schedule.

Rewritten: I managed to finish a marathon because I followed a strict training schedule.

1.   Title: Effective Communication

First sentence: This is often the key to a healthy relationship.

Rewritten: _____

_____

2.   Title: Reality TV Shows

First sentence: They are popular for several reasons.

Rewritten: _____

_____

3.   Title: My First Day of College

First sentence: My first day of college was the most nervous day of my adult life.

Rewritten: _____

4. Title: The Best Vacation I Ever Had

   First sentence: It began when my friends from high school booked a one-week trip to Cancun, Mexico.

   Rewritten: _____

   _____

5. Title: Professional Athletes on Steroids

   First sentence: Most of them say that they don't use it to enhance athletic performance.

   Rewritten: _____

   _____

REVIEW TEST

Use the space below to rewrite the following sentences from a student paper, correcting the mistakes in format.

	teachers should encourage cheating
	Teachers warn students about the dangers of it, but they should encourage the-
	ir students to cheat at least once. When I was a senior in high school, I cheated on a
	take-home history test. Although I studied, I was not able to answer all the questions,
	so I looked online and copied down information from a few Web sites. I was so worried
	that I would be caught that I could not look directly at my teacher when I turned in my
	test. All week, I thought that he would confront me about my cheating. Instead, my
	teacher gave me an "A" on the test. I felt so guilty that I vowed never to cheat again,
	and I have never cheated since.

For additional materials on Chapter 22, visit www.mhhe.com/langan.

23 CHAPTER

Capital Letters

CHAPTER PREVIEW

Main Uses of Capital Letters

Other Uses of Capital Letters

Unnecessary Use of Capitals

INTRODUCTORY ACTIVITY

You probably know a good deal about the uses of capital letters. Answering the questions below will help you check your knowledge.

1. Write the full name of a person you know: _____

2. In what city and state were you born? _____

3. What is your present street address? _____

4. Name a country where you would like to travel: _____

5. Name a school that you attended: _____

6. Give the name of a store where you buy food: _____

7. Name a company where you or anyone you know

   works: _____

8. Which day of the week is the busiest for you? _____

9. What holiday is your favorite? _____

10. Which brand of toothpaste do you use? _____

11. Give the brand name of a candy you like: _____

12. Name a song or a television show you enjoy: _____

13. Write the title of a magazine or newspaper you

    read: _____

Items 14–16

Three capital letters are needed in the example below. Underline the words you think should be capitalized. Then write them, capitalized, in the spaces provided.

> on Super Bowl Sunday, my roommate said, "let's buy some snacks and invite a few friends over to watch the game." i knew my plans to write a term paper would have to be changed.

14. _____   15. _____   16. _____

Answers are on page 629.

Main Uses of Capital Letters

Capital letters are used with:

1. First word in a sentence or direct quotation

2. Names of persons and the word *I*

3. Names of particular places

4. Names of days of the week, months, and holidays

5. Names of commercial products

6. Titles of books, magazines, articles, films, television shows, songs, poems, stories, papers that you write, and the like

7. Names of companies, associations, unions, clubs, religious and political groups, and other organizations

Each use is illustrated on the pages that follow.

First Word in a Sentence or Direct Quotation

Our company has begun laying people off.

The doctor said, "This may hurt a bit."

"My husband," said Martha, "is a light eater. When it's light, he starts to eat."

> **EXPLANATION:** In the third example above, *My* and *When* are capitalized because they start new sentences. But is is not capitalized because it is part of the first sentence.

Names of Persons and the Word *I*

At the picnic, I met Tony Curry and Lola Morrison.

Names of Particular Places

After graduating from Gibbs High School in Houston, I worked for a summer at a nearby Holiday Inn on Clairmont Boulevard.

But   Use small letters if the specific name of a place is not given.

After graduating from high school in my hometown, I worked for a summer at a nearby hotel on one of the main shopping streets.

Names of Days of the Week, Months, and Holidays

This year, Memorial Day falls on the last Thursday in May.

But   Use small letters for the seasons—summer, fall, winter, and spring.

In the early summer and fall, my hay fever bothers me.

Names of Commercial Products

The consumer magazine gave high ratings to Cheerios breakfast cereal, Breyer's ice cream, and Progresso chicken noodle soup.

But   Use small letters for the *type* of product (breakfast cereal, ice cream, chicken noodle soup, and the like).

Titles of Books, Magazines, Articles, Films, Television Shows, Songs, Poems, Stories, Papers That You Write, and the Like

My oral report was on *The Diary of a Young Girl,* by Anne Frank.

While watching *All My Children* on television, I thumbed through *Cosmopolitan* magazine and the *New York Times.*

Names of Companies, Associations, Unions, Clubs, Religious and Political Groups, and Other Organizations

A new bill before Congress is opposed by the National Rifle Association.

My wife is Jewish; I am Roman Catholic. We are both members of the Democratic Party.

My parents have life insurance with Prudential, auto insurance with Allstate, and medical insurance with United Healthcare.

ACTIVITY 1	**Capitalizing Names and Titles**

In the sentences that follow, cross out the words that need capitals. Then write the capitalized forms of the words in the space provided. The number of spaces tells you how many corrections to make in each case.

EXAMPLE

Rhoda said, "~~why~~ should I bother to *eat* this ~~hershey~~ bar? I should just apply it directly to my hips."_____Why_____   _____Hershey_____

> **HINT**   The word *I* and names of organizations are capitalized.

1. Sometimes i still regret not joining the boy scouts when I was in grade school.

   _____   _____   _____

2. On the friday after thanksgiving, Carole went to target to buy gifts for her family.

   _____   _____   _____

3. In the box office of the regal cinema is a sign saying, "if you plan to see an R-rated movie, be ready to show your ID."

   _____   _____   _____

4. In many new england towns, republicans outnumber democrats five to one.

   _____   _____   _____   _____

5. Nelson was surprised to learn that both state farm and nationwide have insurance offices in the prudential building.

   _____   _____   _____   _____   _____

6. Magazines such as *time* and *newsweek* featured articles about the fires that devastated part of southern california.

   _____   _____   _____

7. The rose grower whom Steve works for said that the biggest rose-selling holidays are valentine's day and mother's day.

   _____   _____   _____   _____

8. With some pepsis and fritos nearby, the kids settled down to play a game on the macintosh computer.

   _____   _____   _____

9. Bob's ford taurus was badly damaged when he struck a deer last saturday.

   _____   _____   _____

10. Though Julie Andrews excelled in the broadway version of *my fair lady,* Audrey Hepburn was cast as the female lead in the movie version.

   _____   _____   _____   _____

Other Uses of Capital Letters

Capital letters are also used with:

- Names that show family relationships
- Titles of persons when used with their names
- Specific school courses
- Languages
- Geographic locations
- Historic periods and events
- Races, nations, and nationalities
- Opening and closing of a letter

Each use is illustrated on the pages that follow.

Names That Show Family Relationships

Aunt Sally and Uncle Jack are selling their house.

I asked Grandfather to start the fire.

Is Mother feeling better?

But   Do not capitalize words such as *mother, father, grandmother, grandfather, uncle, aunt,* and so on when they are preceded by *my* or another possessive word.

My aunt and uncle are selling their house.

I asked my grandfather to start the fire.

Is my mother feeling better?

Titles of Persons When Used with Their Names

I wrote an angry letter to Senator Blutt.

Can you drive to Dr. Stein's office?

We asked Professor Bushkin about his attendance policy.

But   Use small letters when titles appear by themselves, without specific names.

I wrote an angry letter to my senator.

Can you drive to the doctor's office?

We asked our professor about his attendance policy.

Specific School Courses

My courses this semester include Accounting I, Introduction to Computer Science, Business Law, General Psychology, and Basic Math.

But   Use small letters for general subject areas.

This semester I'm taking mostly business courses, but I have a psychology course and a math course as well.

Languages

Lydia speaks English and Spanish equally well.

Geographic Locations

I lived in the South for many years and then moved to the West Coast.

But   Use small letters in giving directions.

Go south for about five miles and then bear west.

Historic Periods and Events

One essay question dealt with the Battle of the Bulge in World War II.

Races, Nations, and Nationalities

The census form asked whether I was African American, Native American, Hispanic, or Asian.

Last summer I hitchhiked through Italy, France, and Germany.

The city is a melting pot for Koreans, Vietnamese, and Mexican Americans.

But Use small letters when referring to *whites* or *blacks*.

Both whites and blacks supported our mayor in the election.

Opening and Closing of a Letter

Dear Sir: Sincerely yours,

Dear Madam: Truly yours,

Capitalize only the first word in a closing.

Where Is Capitalization Needed?	**ACTIVITY 2**

Cross out the words that need capitals in the following sentences. Then write the capitalized forms of the words in the spaces provided. The number of spaces tells you how many corrections to make in each case.

1. My uncle david, who has cirrhosis of the liver, added his name to the national waiting list for organ transplants.

   _____   _____

2. My daughter asked me to buy her a magenta pink motorola razr phone and bluetooth headset for her sixteenth birthday.

   _____   _____   _____

3. Former united states president jimmy carter received the nobel peace prize in 2002.

   _____   _____   _____   _____   _____

   _____   _____   _____

4. Terisa spoke to the class about her experience as a pacific islander from samoa who is now living on the east coast.

   _____   _____   _____   _____

   _____

5. Next semester, I want to register for principles of marketing and two other business courses.

   _____   _____

Unnecessary Use of Capitals

| ACTIVITY 3 | Where Is Capitalization Unnecessary? |

Many errors in capitalization are caused by adding capitals where they are not needed. Cross out the incorrectly capitalized letters in the following sentences and write the correct forms in the spaces provided. The number of spaces tells you how many corrections to make in each sentence.

1. Everyone waits for Mariko's Husband, who is from Texas, to make his famous Barbeque Ribs.

   _____ _____ _____

2. One of Stuart's English professors at his Community College worked for Google as a Technical Writer.

   _____ _____ _____ _____

3. The Electronics Store at Meadowland Mall is having a sale on Televisions and DVD Players.

   _____ _____ _____ _____

4. Several Community Organizations are sponsoring a Food Drive at the neighborhood homeless shelter.

   _____ _____ _____ _____

5. Bridget spoke to her daughter's Science Teacher about the upcoming field trip to the Tidal Pools at Sunset Grove Beach.

   _____ _____ _____ _____

| ACTIVITY 4 | Editing and Rewriting |

Working with a partner, read the short paragraph below and mark off the fifteen spots where capital letters are missing. Then use the space provided to rewrite the passage, adding capital letters where needed. Feel free to discuss the passage quietly with your partner and refer back to the chapter when necessary.

> The morning that I visited the lincoln memorial, it was raining. It was a quiet thursday in late october, and the air was cold. I was with uncle walt, and we had spent the morning visiting the smithsonian institution together. After lunch, my uncle said to me, "now we're going to go someplace that you'll never forget." When we arrived, I was overwhelmed by lincoln's massive statue, which dwarfed everything around it—just as the man had done in life. To my left I was aware of the silently flowing potomac river. Engraved

continued

on one of the marble walls was the gettysburg address. I read those familiar words and remained there for a time in silence, touched by the simple eloquence of that speech. I then snapped just one picture with my kodak camera and walked down the stone steps quietly.   The photograph still sits on my desk today as a reminder of that special visit.

_____

_____

_____

_____

_____

_____

_____

_____

_____

Creating Sentences

Working with a partner, write a sentence (or two) as directed. Pay special attention to capital letters.

1. Write about a place you like (or want) to visit. Be sure to give the name of the place, including the city, state, or country where it is located.

2. Write a sentence (or two) in which you state the name of your elementary school, your favorite teacher or subject, and your least favorite teacher or subject.

3. Write a sentence (or two) that includes the names of three brand-name products that you often use. You may begin the sentence with the words, "Three brand-name products I use every day are . . ."

4. Think of the name of your favorite musical artist or performer. Then write a sentence in which you include the musician's name and the title of one of his or her songs.

5. Write a sentence in which you describe something you plan to do two days from now. Be sure to include the date and day of the week.

REFLECTIVE ACTIVITY

1. What would writing be like without capital letters? Use an example or two to help show how capital letters are important to writing.

2. What three uses of capital letters are most difficult for you to remember? Explain, giving examples.

REVIEW TEST 1

Cross out the words that need capitals in the following sentences. Then write the capitalized forms of the words in the spaces provided. The number of spaces tells you how many corrections to make in each sentence.

EXAMPLE

During halftime of the ~~saturday~~ afternoon football game, my sister said, "~~let's~~ get some hamburgers from ~~wendy~~'s or put a pizza in the oven."

   Saturday   *Let's*   *Wendy's*

1. When he saw the commercial that said "just do it," Lance put on his nike running shoes and went to the store to get some ice cream.

  _____   _____

2. Millions of years ago, america's midwest was covered by a great inland sea.

  _____   _____

3. One of our thanksgiving traditions is sending a check to an organization such as greenpeace, which helps protect the environment.

  _____   _____

4. If you drive onto route 10 in tallahassee, florida, and stay on that road, you'll eventually end up in california.

  _____   _____   _____   _____

5. Just before english class this morning, Arlene titled her final paper "my argument for an A."

  _____   _____   _____

6. I read in the book *royal lives* that when an ancient egyptian king died, his servants were often killed and buried with him.

  _____   _____   _____

7. dear mr. Bradford:
This is the third and final time I will write to complain about the leak in my bathroom.
sincerely,
Anne Morrison

_____ _____ _____

8. "After age eighty," grandma ida would say, "time passes very quickly. it seems as though it's time for breakfast every fifteen minutes."

_____ _____ _____

9. Dr. Green, who teaches a course called cultural anthropology, spent last summer on an archaeological dig in israel.

_____ _____ _____

10. During the singing of "the star-spangled banner," many fans at yankee stadium drank sodas, read their programs, or chatted with each other.

_____ _____ _____

_____ _____ _____

REVIEW TEST 2

On a separate piece of paper, write:

- seven sentences demonstrating the seven main uses of capital letters.

- eight sentences demonstrating the eight other uses of capital letters.

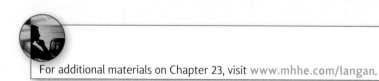

For additional materials on Chapter 23, visit www.mhhe.com/langan.

24

Numbers and Abbreviations

CHAPTER PREVIEW

Numbers
Abbreviations

INTRODUCTORY ACTIVITY

Write a check mark beside the item in each pair that you think uses numbers correctly.

I left the gym at 7:30, but I only completed 75 percent of my workout routine. _____

I left the gym at seven-thirty, but I only completed seventy-five percent of my workout routine. _____

85 people applied for the government job, but there are only 15 permanent positions. _____

Eighty-five people applied for the government job, but there are only fifteen permanent positions. _____

Write a check mark beside the item in each pair that you think uses abbreviations correctly.

My daughter's preschool teacher, Mrs. Landry, likes to start class at 9 am sharp. _____

My daughter's preschool teacher, Mrs. Landry, likes to start class at 9 a.m. sharp. _____

I waited one hr. to see Dr. Lee, but my exam only took five mins. _____

I waited one hour to see Dr. Lee, but my exam only took five minutes. _____

Answers are on page 629.

Numbers

Keep the following three rules in mind when using numbers.

Rule 1

Spell out numbers that take no more than two words. Otherwise, use numerals—the numbers themselves.

Last year Tina bought nine new CDs.

Ray struck out fifteen batters in Sunday's softball game.

But

Tina now has 114 CDs in her collection.

Already this season Ray has recorded 168 strikeouts.

You should also spell out a number that begins a sentence.

One hundred fifty first-graders throughout the city showed flu symptoms today.

Rule 2

Be consistent when you use a series of numbers. If some numbers in a sentence or paragraph require more than two words, then use numbers themselves throughout the selection.

That executive who tried to cut 250 employees' salaries owns 8 cars, 4 homes, 3 boats, and 1 jet.

Rule 3

Use numbers to show dates, times, addresses, percentages, exact sums of money, and parts of a book.

John F. Kennedy was killed on November 22, 1963.

My job interview was set for 10:15. (*But:* Spell out numbers before *o'clock.* For example: The time was then changed to eleven o'clock.)

Janet's new address is 118 North 35 Street.

Almost 40 percent of my meals are eaten at fast-food restaurants.

The cashier rang up a total of $18.35. (*But:* Round amounts may be expressed as words. For example: The movie has an eight-dollar admission charge.)

Read Chapter 6 in your math textbook and answer questions 1 to 5 on page 250.

CONNECT WRITING

Meet Ronit. She's very excited to be adopting a baby girl from Kazakhstan and is throwing a party to celebrate the adoption. She's almost finished writing out the invitations, but keeps stumbling over how to write numbers correctly. Help Ronit locate and correct all the number mistakes in her adoption party invitation.

mhconnectwriting.com

Using Numbers

ACTIVITY 1

Working with a partner, use the three rules to make the corrections needed in these sentences.

HINT   In item 1, use numerals to show time.

1. During the summer, I like to stay up until two thirty a.m. playing video games and chatting online with my gamer friends.

2. This semester, Mohammed is taking 5 classes and two labs.

3. My dog Missy, an adorable Maltese, is 11 years old—that's 77 in people years.

4. Every day Mike gets up at 5 o'clock to run 4 miles.

5. Americans waste over fifteen percent of the food that they purchase from supermarkets and restaurants.

6. An adult human body has two hundred and six bones.

7. Dr. Martin Luther King Jr. was born on January fifteenth.

8. Someone ate over 200 pickled jalapeño peppers at the State Fair of Texas.

9. My cousin went to Las Vegas to get married on July seventh, two thousand and seven, supposedly the luckiest day of the year.

10. Akira Kurosawa's film The 7 *Samurai* was nominated for an Academy Award in 1954.

Abbreviations

While abbreviations are a helpful time-saver in note-taking, you should avoid most abbreviations in formal writing. Listed below are some of the few abbreviations that are acceptable in compositions. Note that a period is used after most abbreviations.

- Mr., Mrs., Ms., Jr., Sr., Dr., when used with proper names:

  Mr. Rollin   Ms. Peters   Dr. Coleman

- Time references:

  A.M. or AM or a.m.   P.M. or PM or p.m.   BC/AD or B.C./A.D.

- First or middle initial in a name:

  T. Alan Parker   Linda M. Evans

- Organizations, technical words, and trade names known primarily by initials:

  ABC   CIA   UNESCO   GM   AIDS   DNA

 ACTIVITY 2   ## Using Abbreviations

Cross out the words that should not be abbreviated and correct them in the spaces provided.

> **H I N T**   No words should be abbreviated in item 1.

1. After I placed the "bike for sale" ad in the newsp., the tele. rang nonstop for a week.

   _____   _____

2. Sharon bought two bush. of ripe tomatoes at the farm mkt. on Rt. 73.

   _____   _____   _____

3. On Mon., NASA will announce its plans for a Sept. flight to Mars.

   _____   _____

4. The psych class was taught by Dr. Aronson, a noted psychiatrist from Eng.

   _____   _____

5. The best things on the menu are the chick. pot pie and the mac. and cheese.

   _____   _____

6. Several baby opossums (each of which weighs less than an oz.) can fit into a tbsp.

   _____   _____

7. I didn't have time to study for my chem. test on Sun., but I studied for four hrs. yesterday.

   _____   _____   _____

8. Every Jan., our co. gives awards for the best employee suggestions of the previous yr.

   _____   _____   _____

9. Lawrence T. Johnson lost his lic. to practice medicine when the state board discovered he never went to med. school.

   _____   _____

10. Mick, a vet. who served in Iraq, started his own photography bus. after graduating from a community coll.

   _____   _____   _____

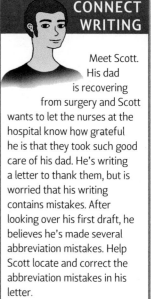

REVIEW TEST

Cross out the mistake or mistakes in numbers and abbreviations and correct them in the spaces provided.

1. Best Buy's 4-day sale starts this coming Thurs.

   _____   _____

2. One suspect had blue eyes and brn. hair and was over 6 ft. tall.

   _____   _____   _____

3. Answers to the chpt. questions start on p. two hundred and ninety-three.

   _____   _____   _____

4. With Dec. twenty-fifth only hrs. away, little Abby couldn't eat or sleep.

   _____   _____   _____

5. Over 200 children helped in the collection of seven hundred and thirty-two dollars for UNICEF.

   _____   _____

6. My growing 15-year-old son wears sz. 11 shoes that look like boats.

   _____   _____

7. My 3 years of Spanish in h.s. helped me to get a job in the city health clinic.

   _____   _____   _____

8. The robber was sentenced to 10 yrs. in prison for holding up a bank on Pacific Blvd.

   _____   _____   _____

9. I canceled my appt. when I got an emerg. call that my mother had been taken to the hosp.

   _____   _____   _____

10. When city employees staged a strike on Mon., more than 70 pct. of them didn't show up for work.

    _____   _____

For additional materials on Chapter 24, visit www.mhhe.com/langan.

End Marks

INTRODUCTORY ACTIVITY

Add the end mark needed in each of the following sentences.

1. All week I have been feeling depressed_____

2. What is the deadline for handing in the paper_____

3. The man at the door wants to know whose car is double-parked_____

4. That truck ahead of us is out of control_____

Answers are on page 630.

Answers are on page 630.

A sentence always begins with a capital letter. It always ends with a period, a question mark, or an exclamation point.

CHAPTER PREVIEW

Period (.)
Question Mark (?)
Exclamation Point (!)

Period (.)

Use a period after a sentence that makes a statement.

More single parents are adopting children.

It has rained for most of the week.

Use a period after most abbreviations.

Mr. Brady	B.A.	Dr. Ballard
Ms. Peters	a.m.	Tom Ricci, Jr.

Question Mark (?)

Use a question mark after a *direct* question.

When is your paper due?

How is your cold?

Tom asked, "When are you leaving?"

"Why can't we all stop arguing?" Rosa asked.

Do *not* use a question mark after an *indirect* question (a question not in the speaker's exact words).

She asked when the paper was due.

He asked how my cold was.

Tom asked when I was leaving.

Rosa asked why we couldn't all stop arguing.

CONNECT WRITING

Meet Sita. She's writing a feature story that focuses on her interview with the lead vocalist in the rock band *Dom Boys*. She got a lot of great information from her interview, but her writing seems confusing. Help Sita locate and correct the confusing shifts between indirect and direct questions in her article.

mhconnectwriting.com

Exclamation Point (!)

Use an exclamation point after a word or sentence that expresses strong feeling.

Come here!

Ouch! This pizza is hot!

That truck just missed us!

 TIP   Be careful not to overuse exclamation points.

ACTIVITY 1

Using End Punctuation

Add a period, question mark, or exclamation point as needed to each of the following sentences.

 HINT   Item 1 is a *direct* question.

CONNECT WRITING

Meet Andrew. His Vietnamese parents have recently learned English and have asked him to proofread the personal messages they've written in several greeting cards. Andrew has found his parents have either used the wrong end mark at times or have forgotten to put an end mark. Help Andrew locate and correct all the end mark mistakes in his parents' messages.

mhconnectwriting.com

1. Why can't I find my car keys when I'm rushing out the door _____

2. My husband asked me if I wanted a back rub or a foot massage _____

3. The pedestrian yelled to the speeding motorist, "Watch out, jerk _____"

4. When Chandra told me that she had been raped, I was shocked _____

5. Dr. Klein is not a medical doctor; he earned his doctorate in psychology _____

6. Fred, who loved practical jokes and silly pranks, would often say, "Gotcha _____"

7. Famous actors, musicians, and athletes have posed with milk moustaches in popular "Got milk _____" ads.

8. Ratsami asked me if I knew of anyone who could repair the roof that had been damaged in the storm _____

9. Jordan answered my question by asking me, "What do *you* think _____"

10. Ms. Caraway will replace Mr. Lee as the chief financial officer _____

Add a period, question mark, or exclamation point as needed to each of the following sentences.

1. My birthday present was wrapped in old newspapers and yellowed Scotch tape _____

2. Did you know that washing in very hot water can dry out your skin _____

3. The bride stunned everyone when she appeared in a purple lace gown _____

4. Don't eat that poisonous mushroom _____

5. How did you get a wad of gum in your hair _____

6. That boy is waving a loaded gun _____

7. All through the interview, my stomach grumbled and my hands shook _____

8. If you won the lottery, what would you do with the prize money _____

9. I wonder if we should have a New Year's Eve party this year _____

10. Look out for that swerving car _____

REFLECTIVE ACTIVITY

1. Review your answers to the Review Test at the end of Chapter 24 (pages 337–338). In each case, explain why the change you made is correct.

2. Review your answers to the Review Test at the end of this chapter. In each case, explain why the change you made is correct.

3. How do the answers in these two review tests help to make the sentences stronger and clearer?

For additional materials on Chapter 25, visit www.mhhe.com/langan.

Apostrophes

CHAPTER PREVIEW

Apostrophes in Contractions

- Four Contractions to Note Carefully

Apostrophes to Show Ownership or Possession

- Points to Remember

- Apostrophes versus Possessive Pronouns

- Apostrophes versus Simple Plurals

- Apostrophes with Plural Words Ending in -s

INTRODUCTORY ACTIVITY

Look carefully at the three items below. Then see if you can answer the questions that follow each item.

1. the desk of the manager = the manager's desk

   the car of Hakim = Hakim's car

   the teeth of my dog = my dog's teeth

   the smile of the woman = the woman's smile

   the briefcase of my mother = my mother's briefcase

   What is the purpose of the apostrophe in each example above?

   _____

2. He is my best friend. = He's my best friend.

   I am afraid of spiders. = I'm afraid of spiders.

   Do not watch too much TV. = Don't watch too much TV.

   They are an odd couple. = They're an odd couple.

   It is a wonderful movie. = It's a wonderful movie.

   What is the purpose of the apostrophe in each example above?

   _____

3. Several buildings were damaged by the severe storm. One building's roof was blown off and dropped in a nearby field.

   Why does the apostrophe belong in the second sentence but not the first?

   _____

   _____

Answers are on page 630.

The two main uses of the apostrophe are:

- To show the omission of one or more letters in a contraction
- To show ownership or possession

Each use is explained on the pages that follow.

Apostrophes in Contractions

A contraction is formed when two words are combined to make one word. An apostrophe is used to show where letters are omitted in forming the contraction. Here are two contractions:

have + not　　= haven't (the *o* in *not* has been omitted)

I　　+ will　= I'll (the *wi* in *will* has been omitted)

The following are some other common contractions:

I	+ am	= I'm	it	+ is	= it's
I	+ have	= I've	it	+ has	= it's
I	+ had	= I'd	is	+ not	= isn't
who	+ is	= who's	could	+ not	= couldn't
do	+ not	= don't	I	+ would	= I'd
did	+ not	= didn't	they	+ are	= they're
let	+ us	= let's	there	+ is	= there's

> **TIP**   The combination *will* + *not* has an unusual contraction: *won't*.

Combining Words
ACTIVITY 1

Combine the following words into contractions. One is done for you.

she　+ is　　= ___she's___　　you　+ will　　= _____

you　+ have　= _____　　we　+ would　= _____

have + not　　= _____　　could + not　　= _____

he　　+ has　= _____　　they + will　　= _____

we　　+ are　= _____　　does + not　　= _____

Forming Contractions
ACTIVITY 2

Write the contraction for the words in parentheses.

EXAMPLE

He (could not) ___couldn't___ come.

HINT   An apostrophe replaces the letter *o* in both answers in item 1.

1. I (did not) _____ like the movie, but the popcorn (was not) _____ bad.

2. Tara (does not) _____ hide her feelings well, so if (she is) _____ angry, you will know it.

3. (You are) _____ taking the wrong approach with Len, as he (cannot) _____ stand being lectured.

4. This (is not) _____ the first time (you have) _____ embarrassed me in public.

5. (We would) _____ love to have you stay for dinner if you (do not) _____ mind eating leftovers.

TIP   Even though contractions are common in everyday speech and in written dialogue, usually it is best to avoid them in formal writing.

ACTIVITY 3   **Using the Apostrophe**

Write five sentences using the apostrophe in different contractions.

1. _____

2. _____

3. _____

4. _____

5. _____

Four Contractions to Note Carefully

Four contractions that deserve special attention are *they're, it's, you're,* and *who's.* Sometimes these contractions are confused with the possessive words *their, its, your,* and *whose.* The following list shows the difference in meaning between the contractions and the possessive words.

Contractions	**Possessive Words**
they're (means *they are*)	their (means *belonging to them*)
it's (means *it is* or *it has*)	its (means *belonging to it*)
you're (means *you are*)	your (means *belonging to you*)
who's (means *who is*)	whose (means *belonging to whom*)

Possessive words are explained further below.

Using Apostrophes Correctly

ACTIVITY 4

Underline the correct form (the contraction or the possessive word) in each of the following sentences. Use the contraction whenever the two words of the contraction (*they are, it is, you are, who is*) would also fit.

 The sentence in item 1 contains one contraction and one possessive word.

1. (Your, You're) hunger for knowledge means that (you're, your) a good student.

2. I listened to (you're, your) advice and bought a Toyota Prius because (it's, its) hybrid engine should save me money at the gas pump.

3. At the Super Bowl party, Ron wondered (who's, whose) Coke he accidentally drank, so he asked his friends, "(Who's, Whose) without a drink?"

4. (They're, There) are a few pieces of leftover pizza in the refrigerator, but I would ask your roommates if (they're, there) planning to eat any first.

5. (It's, Its) unfortunate that (they're, there) closing the only mom-and-pop grocery store in the neighborhood.

Apostrophes to Show Ownership or Possession

To show ownership or possession, we can use such words as *belongs to, owned by,* or (most commonly) *of.*

the computer *that belongs to* Uwem

the grades *possessed by* Travis

the house *owned by* my mother

the sore arm *of* the pitcher

But the apostrophe plus *s* (if the word is singular or does not end in *-s*) is often the quickest and easiest way to show possession. Thus we can say:

Uwem's computer

Travis's grades

my mother's house

the pitcher's sore arm

Points to Remember

1. The 's goes with the owner or possessor (in the examples given, *Uwem, Travis, mother,* and *pitcher*). What follows is the person or thing possessed (in the examples given, *computer, grades, house,* and *sore arm*). An easy way to determine the owner or possessor is to ask the question "Who owns it?" In the first example, the answer to the question "Who owns the computer?" is *Uwem.* Therefore, the 's goes with *Uwem.*

2. In handwriting, there should always be a break between the word and the 's.

$$\text{Uwem's} \qquad not \qquad \text{Uwem's}$$

Yes   No

3. A singular word ending in *-s* (such as *Travis* in the earlier example) also shows possession by adding an apostrophe plus *s* (Travis's).

ACTIVITY 5	**Using 's to Show Possession**

Working with a partner, rewrite the italicized part of each sentence below, using 's to show possession. Remember that the 's goes with the owner or possessor.

EXAMPLES

The motorcycle owned by Jordan is a frightening machine.

Jordan's motorcycle

The roommate of my brother is a sweet and friendly person.

My brother's roommate

> **HINT**   In item 1, who owns the *voice*?

1. The *voice of the singer* had a relaxing effect on the crowd.

    _____

2. *The garage of Dawn* has so much furniture stored in it that there's no room for her car.

    _____

3. *The law of Murphy* states, "Anything that can go wrong will go wrong."

    _____

4. All the financial-planning information has been stored in the *memory of the computer.*

    _____

5. Because *the mother of my wife* is in jail for forgery, I call her my motheroutlaw.

_____

6. Where is the rest of *the meat loaf of yesterday,* which I was planning to eat for lunch?

_____

7. *The promotion of my sister* to vice president of the company was well earned.

_____

8. *The bratty little brother of Alexis* has grown up to become a charming young man.

_____

9. The judges reversed *the call of the referee* after they viewed the replay.

_____

10. Thousands of gallons of crude oil spilled into the ocean when *the hull of the tanker* ruptured in the storm.

_____

Indentifying Possessive Nouns   ACTIVITY 6

Underline the word in each sentence that needs *'s*. Then write the word correctly in the space at the left.

HINT In item 1, the hoof belongs to the horse.

_____ 1. The trainer removed a nail from the horse hoof.

_____ 2. My brother appetite is like a bottomless pit.

_____ 3. Jamal pulled his young son hand away from the kerosene heater.

_____ 4. The comedian trademarks were long cigars and red socks.

_____ 5. No matter when you dial the landlord number, nobody answers the phone.

_____ 6. The assistant manager always takes credit for Ted ideas.

_____ 7. We all froze when the bank teller wig fell off.

_____ 8. Some people never feel other people problems are their concern.

_____ 9. Nita hires an accountant to prepare her dance studio tax returns each year.

_____ 10. The screen door slammed on the little girl fingers.

| ACTIVITY 7 | **Making Words Possessive** |

Add *'s* to each of the following words to make it the possessor or owner of something. Then write sentences using the words. Your sentences can be serious or playful. One is done for you as an example.

1. Aaron _____Aaron's_____

   Aaron's girlfriend sends him over forty text messages a day. _____

2. bus _____

   _____

3. computer _____

   _____

4. Ross _____

   _____

5. pizza _____

   _____

Apostrophes versus Possessive Pronouns

Do not use an apostrophe with possessive pronouns. They already show ownership. Possessive pronouns include *his, hers, its, yours, ours,* and *theirs.*

Incorrect	**Correct**
The bookstore lost its' lease.	The bookstore lost its lease.
The racing bikes were theirs'.	The racing bikes were theirs.
The change is yours'.	The change is yours.
His' problems are ours', too.	His problems are ours, too.
Her' cold is worse than his'.	Her cold is worse than his.

Apostrophes versus Simple Plurals

When you want to make a word plural, just add *s* at the end of the word. Do *not* add an apostrophe. For example, the plural of the word *movie* is *movies*, not *movie's* or *movies'*.

Look at this sentence:

When Sally's cat began catching birds, the neighbors called the police.

The words *birds* and *neighbors* are simple plurals, meaning more than one bird, more than one neighbor. The plural is shown by adding *-s* only. (More information about plurals starts on page 397.) On the other hand, the *'s* after *Sally* shows possession—that Sally owns the cat.

Apostrophes vs. Simple Plurals

In the spaces provided under each sentence, add the one apostrophe needed and explain why the other words ending in *s* are simple plurals.

EXAMPLE

Originally, the cuffs of mens pants were meant for cigar ashes.

cuffs: _simple plural meaning more than one cuff_

mens: _men's, meaning "belonging to men"_

ashes: _simple plural meaning more than one ash_

HINT	In item 1, what possesses the *aromas?*

1. The pizza parlors aromas seeped through the vents to our second-floor apartment.

   parlors: _____

   aromas: _____

   vents: _____

2. A police cars siren echoed through the streets and buildings of the city.

   cars: _____

   streets: _____

   buildings: _____

3. Karens tomato plants are taller than the six-foot stakes she used to support them.

   Karens: _____

   plants: _____

   stakes: _____

4. Because of the lakes high bacteria level, officials prohibited boating, swimming, and fishing there.

   lakes: _____

   officials: _____

5. I have considered applying for many positions, but an exterminators job is not one of them.

   positions: _____

   exterminators: _____

6. The candlelights glow fell gently on the pale white plates and ruby-red goblets.

candlelights: _____

plates: _____

goblets: _____

7. Crackers layered with cheese and apple slices are my fathers favorite snack.

Crackers: _____

slices: _____

fathers: _____

8. Within a day, that insects eggs will turn into glistening white worms.

insects: _____

eggs: _____

worms: _____

9. Seabirds skidding along the oceans edge at midnight looked like miniature moonlight surfers.

Seabirds: _____

oceans: _____

surfers: _____

10. My daughters prayers were answered when the heavy snow caused all the schools in the area to close for the rest of the week.

daughters: _____

prayers: _____

schools: _____

Apostrophes with Plural Words Ending in -s

Plurals that end in -s show possession simply by adding the apostrophe, rather than an apostrophe plus s.

Both of my *neighbors'* homes have been burglarized recently.

The many *workers'* complaints were ignored by the company.

All the *campers'* tents were damaged by the hailstorm.

ACTIVITY 9	**Missing Apostrophes**

Add an apostrophe where needed in each sentence that follows.

HINT   In item 1, whose *union* is it?

1. The nurses union protested my layoff.

2. My two sisters feet are the same size, so they share their shoes.

3. The lions keeper has worked with those lions since birth.

4. The Tylers new flat screen TV was mistakenly delivered to our house.

5. The photo album that was lost contained my parents wedding pictures.

Editing and Rewriting

ACTIVITY 10

Working with a partner, read the short paragraph below. Underline ten places where you could rewrite, using apostrophes to indicate contractions and possessives. Then rewrite those parts in the spaces that follow. Feel free to discuss the rewrite quietly with your partner and refer back to the chapter when necessary.

> The dog of my neighbor is evil. For one thing, it barks constantly, even when there is nothing to bark at. Because of the constant barking of the dog, I cannot sleep at night. The dog also growls menacingly whenever it sees me. One time, it tried to charge at me through the fence of my landlord. Luckily for me, the fence was strong enough to restrain the dog. I have tried to talk to my neighbor about the problem, but he refuses to listen. He thinks there is nothing wrong with the behavior of the dog. But that is because the dog does not show its fangs to him.

_____

_____

_____

_____

_____

Creating Sentences

ACTIVITY 11

Working with a partner, write sentences that use apostrophes as directed.

1. Write a sentence describing something a friend owns. For instance, you might mention a pet or a material possession.

_____

2. Using an apostrophe to show a contraction, write a sentence about something at school or work that you feel is wrong and needs to be changed. The image in the accompanying photo might provide you with some ideas.

   _____

   _____

3. Write a sentence that correctly uses the word *teachers*. Then write a second sentence that correctly uses the word *teacher's*.

   _____

   _____

REFLECTIVE ACTIVITY

1. Look at the paragraph about the dog that you just revised. How has adding apostrophes affected the paragraph?

2. Explain what it is about apostrophes that you find most difficult to remember and apply. Use an example to make your point clear.

REVIEW TEST 1

In each sentence, cross out the two words that need apostrophes. Then write the words correctly in the spaces provided.

1. That authors latest horror novel isnt so horrifying.

   _____   _____

2. "I dont get it," I confessed after hearing Pams long, complicated joke.

   _____   _____

3. Luckily the motorcycles gas tank handnt been scratched in the collision.

   _____   _____

4. Whos been stealing the Sunday papers from my doorsteps before Im awake?

   _____   _____

5. Nadias aunts never start the day without asking an astrologers advice.

   _____   _____

6. I, too, would like to take a shower, if theres any water left by the time youre finished.

   _____   _____

7. Olivia watched sadly as the highway departments bulldozer demolished the house shed grown up in.

   _____   _____

8. Sylvia wasnt on time for her first day of work because her mothers car broke down on the highway.

   _____   _____

9. The coach said theres no room on the team for players who dont want to win.

   _____   _____

10. The authorities guess is that a radical protest group put the toxic chemical in the towns water supply.

    _____   _____

Rewrite the following sentences, changing each underlined phrase into either a contraction or a possessive.

1. Joe was not happy to hear the high-pitched sound of the drill of the dentist.

   _____

   _____

2. The weather forecast of today assured us that it is definitely going to be sunny, cloudy, or rainy.

   _____

   _____

3. The enthusiasm of my brother Manny for baseball is so great that he will even wear his glove and cap when he watches a game on TV.

   _____

   _____

4. Many parents think the influence of television is to blame for the poor performance of their children in school.

   _____

   _____

For additional materials on Chapter 26, visit www.mhhe.com/langan.

Quotation Marks

CHAPTER PREVIEW

Quotation Marks to Set Off the Words of a Speaker or Writer

• Indirect Quotations

Quotation Marks to Set Off the Titles of Short Works

Other Uses of Quotation Marks

INTRODUCTORY ACTIVITY

Read the following scene and underline all the words enclosed within quotation marks. Your instructor may also have you dramatize the scene with one person reading the narration and three persons acting the speaking parts—Clyde, Charlotte, and Sam. The speakers should imagine the scene as part of a stage play and try to make their words seem as real and true-to-life as possible.

At a party that Clyde and his wife, Charlotte, recently hosted, Clyde got angry at a guy named Sam who kept bothering Charlotte. "Listen, man," Clyde said, "what's this thing you have for my wife? There are lots of other women at this party."

"Relax," Sam replied. "Charlotte is very attractive, and I enjoy talking with her."

"Listen, Sam," Charlotte said, "I've already told you three times that I don't want to talk to you anymore. Please leave me alone."

"Look, there's no law that says I can't talk to you if I want to," Sam challenged.

"Sam, I'm only going to say this once," Clyde warned. "Lay off my wife, or leave this party *now*."

Sam grinned at Clyde smugly. "You've got good liquor here. Why should I leave? Besides, I'm not done talking with Charlotte."

Clyde went to his basement and was back a minute later holding a two-by-four. "I'm giving you a choice," Clyde said. "Leave by the door or I'll slam you out the window."

Sam left by the door.

1. On the basis of the above selection, what is the purpose of quotation marks?

   _____

2. Do commas and periods that come after a quotation go inside or outside the quotation marks?

   _____

Answers are on page 631.

The two main uses of quotation marks are as follows. Each use is explained here.

1. To set off the exact words of a speaker or writer
2. To set off the titles of short works

Quotation Marks to Set Off the Words of a Speaker or Writer

Use quotation marks when you want to show the exact words of a speaker or writer.

"Who left the cap off the toothpaste?" Lisa demanded.

(Quotation marks set off the exact words that Lisa spoke.)

Ben Franklin wrote, "Keep your eyes wide open before marriage, half shut afterward."

(Quotation marks set off the exact words that Ben Franklin wrote.)

"You're never too young," Aunt Fern told me, "to have a heart attack."

(Two pairs of quotation marks are used to enclose the aunt's exact words.)

Maria complained, "I look so old some days. Even makeup doesn't help. I feel as though I'm painting a corpse!"

(Note that the end quotes do not come until the end of Maria's speech. Place quotation marks before the first quoted word of a speech and after the last quoted word. As long as no interruption occurs in the speech, do not use quotation marks for each new sentence.)

> **EXPLANATION:** In the four preceding examples, notice that a comma sets off the quoted part from the rest of the sentence. Also observe that commas and periods at the end of a quotation always go inside the quotation marks.

Complete the following statements, which explain how capital letters, commas, and periods are used in quotations. Refer to the four examples as guides.

• Every quotation begins with a _____ letter.

• When a quotation is split (as in the sentence about Aunt Fern), the second part does not begin with a capital letter unless it is a

_____ sentence.

• _____ are typically used to separate the quoted part of a sentence from the rest of the sentence.

• Commas and periods that come at the end of a quotation

go _____ quotation marks.

The answers are *capital*, *new*, *Commas*, and *inside*.

| ACTIVITY 1 | **Using Quotation Marks** |

Insert quotation marks where needed in the sentences that follow.

 In item 1, put quotes around the words on the sticker.

1. The chilling bumper sticker read, You can't hug children with nuclear arms.

2. One day we'll look back on this argument, and it will seem funny, Bruce assured Rosa.

3. Hey, lady, this is an express line! shouted the cashier to the woman with a full basket.

4. My grandfather was fond of saying, Happiness is found along the way, not at the end of the road.

5. When will I be old enough to pay the adult fare? the child asked.

6. On his deathbed, Oscar Wilde is supposed to have said, Either this wallpaper goes or I do.

7. The sign on my neighbor's front door reads, Never mind the dog. Beware of owner.

8. I'm not afraid to die, said Woody Allen. I just don't want to be there when it happens.

9. My son once told me, Sometimes I wish I were little again. Then I wouldn't have to make so many decisions.

10. I don't feel like cooking tonight, Eve said to Adam. Let's just have fruit.

| ACTIVITY 2 | **Formatting Quotations** |

Rewrite the following sentences, adding quotation marks where needed. Use a capital letter to begin a quotation and use a comma to set off a quoted part from the rest of the sentence.

EXAMPLE

I can't eat another bite Jeremy told his grandmother.

"I can't eat another bite," Jeremy told his grandmother.

HINT In item 1, add a comma and put quotes around the firefighter's words.

1. The firefighter asked the neighbors is there anyone else still in the building?

_____

_____

2. You'll have to remove your sunglasses the security guard reminded the customers at the bank.

_____

_____

3. Upon eating a few drops of Horacio's homemade habanero sauce, Trudy yelped, that's hot!

_____

_____

4. Good things come to those who wait Zhao told himself as he waited in line for hours to buy an iPhone.

_____

_____

5. If at first you don't succeed, my wife joked, you should read the directions.

_____

_____

Writing with Quotation Marks   ACTIVITY 3

1. Write three quotations that appear in the first part of a sentence.

EXAMPLE "Let's go shopping," I suggested.

a. _____

b. _____

c. _____

2. Write three quotations that appear at the end of a sentence.

EXAMPLE Bob asked, "Have you had lunch yet?"

a. _____

b. _____

c. _____

3. Write three quotations that appear at the beginning and end of a sentence.

EXAMPLE "If the bus doesn't come soon," Mary said, "we'll freeze."

a. _____

b. _____

c. _____

Indirect Quotations

An indirect quotation is a rewording of someone else's comments rather than a word-for-word direct quotation. The word *that* often signals an indirect quotation.

Direct Quotation	**Indirect Quotation**
George said, "My son is a daredevil." (George's exact spoken words are given, so quotation marks are used.)	George said that his son is a daredevil. (We learn George's words indirectly, so no quotation marks are used.)
Carol's note to Nate read, "I'm at the neighbors'. Give me a call." (The exact words that Carol wrote in the note are given, so quotation marks are used.)	Carol left a note for Nate saying that she would be at the neighbors' and he should give her a call. (We learn Carol's words indirectly, so no quotation marks are used.)

ACTIVITY 4	**Using Dialogue**

Rewrite the following sentences, changing words as necessary to convert the sentences into direct quotations. The first one is done for you as an example.

1. Agnes told me as we left work that Henry got a raise.

   Agnes said to me as we left work, "Henry got a raise."

2. I said that it was hard to believe, since Henry is a do-nothing.

   _____

   _____

3. Agnes replied that even so, he's gone up in the world.

   _____

   _____

4. I told her that she must be kidding.

   _____

   _____

5. Agnes laughed and said that Henry was moved from the first to the fourth floor today.

   _____

   _____

Converting Quotations into Indirect Statements

Rewrite the following sentences, converting each direct quotation into an indirect statement. In each case, you will have to add the word *that* or *if* and change other words as well.

EXAMPLE

The receptionist asked Kathryn, "Did you make an appointment?"

The receptionist asked Kathryn if she had made an appointment.

 HINT   Begin the sentence in item 1 with *Josh muttered that.*

1. Josh muttered, "I'm so tired of studying for finals."

2. The dental hygienist asked me, "Do you brush and floss regularly?"

3. Leona asked Matt, "Would you mind if I copied your lecture notes?"

4. The security guard asked me, "Have you seen any suspicious activity in the building?"

5. The delivery driver asked, "Would you mind signing for the package?"

CONNECT WRITING

Meet Kwan. He's written the first draft of an article for the school newspaper in which he reviews a popular restaurant near campus. Although his facts are correct, he's confused indirect and direct quotations, making the article difficult to read. Help Kwan locate and correct the confusing shifts between indirect and direct quotations in his restaurant review.

mhconnectwriting.com

Quotation Marks to Set Off the Titles of Short Works

Titles of short works are usually set off by quotation marks, whereas titles of long works are underlined or italicized. Use quotation marks to set off the titles of short works such as articles in books, newspapers, or magazines; chapters in a book; and short stories, poems, and songs. On the other hand, you should underline or italicize the titles of books, newspapers, magazines, plays, movies, music albums, and television shows. See the following examples.

Quotation Marks	Underlines
the article "The Toxic Tragedy"	in the book <u>Who's Poisoning America</u>
the article "New Cures for Headaches"	in the newspaper the <u>New York Times</u>
the article "When the Patient Plays Doctor"	in the magazine <u>Family Health</u>
the chapter "Connecting with Kids"	in the book <u>Straight Talk</u>
the story "The Dead"	in the book <u>Dubliners</u>
the poem "Birches"	in the book <u>The Complete Poems of Robert Frost</u>
the song "Some Enchanted Evening"	in the album <u>South Pacific</u>
	the television show <u>Grey's Anatomy</u>
	the movie <u>Rear Window</u>

> **TIP**   In printed form, the titles of long works are usually set off by italics—slanted type that looks *like this*.

ACTIVITY 6   **Using Quotations in Titles**

Use quotation marks or underlines as needed.

> **HINT**   Underline the name of the TV show in item 1.

1. My sister programmed her TiVo so she won't have to miss any more episodes of General Hospital.

2. Rhianna grabbed the National Enquirer and eagerly began to read the article I Had a Space Alien's Baby.

3. Our exam will cover two chapters, The Study of Heredity and The Origin of Diversity, in our biology textbook, Life.

4. The last song on the bluegrass program was called I Ain't Broke but I'm Badly Bent.

5. The classic 1980s movie Stand by Me was actually based on The Body, a short story written by Stephen King.

6. At last night's performance of Annie Get Your Gun, the audience joined the cast in singing There's No Business Like Show Business.

7. A typical article in Cosmopolitan has a title like How to Hook a Man without Letting Him Know You're Fishing.

8. One way Joanne deals with depression is to get out her Man of La Mancha album and play the song The Impossible Dream.

9. I read the article How Good Is Your Breakfast? in Consumer Reports while munching a doughnut this morning.

10. According to a Psychology Today article titled Home on the Street, there are 36,000 people living on New York City's sidewalks.

Other Uses of Quotation Marks

Here are two more uses of quotation marks.

1. To set off special words or phrases from the rest of a sentence (italics can also be used for this purpose):

   Many people spell the words "all right" as one word, "alright," instead of correctly spelling them as two words.

   I have trouble telling the difference between "principal" and "principle."

2. To mark off a quotation within a quotation. For this purpose, single quotation marks (' ') are used:

   Ben Franklin said, "The noblest question in the world is, 'What good may I do in it?'"

   "If you want to have a scary experience," Nick told Fran, "read Stephen King's story 'The Mangler' in his book *Night Shift*."

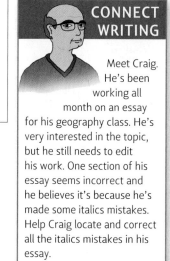

CONNECT WRITING

Meet Craig. He's been working all month on an essay for his geography class. He's very interested in the topic, but he still needs to edit his work. One section of his essay seems incorrect and he believes it's because he's made some italics mistakes. Help Craig locate and correct all the italics mistakes in his essay.

mhconnectwriting.com

Editing and Rewriting

ACTIVITY 7

Working with a partner, read the short paragraph below and circle the places where quotation marks are needed. Then use the space provided to rewrite the paragraph, adding quotation marks where necessary. Feel free to discuss the rewrite quietly with your partner and refer back to the chapter if you have questions.

Harry and his friend Susan got stuck in an elevator. Another man was stuck with them. Harry turned to Susan and asked, Has this ever happened to you before?

Once, she said, About ten years ago in a department store. We weren't stuck long.

Harry took a deep breath. We're lucky only three of us are here. I don't like being closed up in small places, especially crowded ones.

Then the other man asked, Is there a phone or something here so we can talk to somebody?

Susan looked around and noticed a small panel in the corner of the elevator. A sign just over the panel read Open in Case of Emergency.

I think it might be in there, she said, pointing to the sign.

The man opened the panel, found a telephone, and dialed the security number written nearby. Can anyone hear me? he asked.

continued

A voice on the phone said, Yes, and we know you're stuck.   Just wait a few minutes.

When Harry heard that people knew about their problem, he let out a sigh.   I sure hope they can fix this quickly, he said softly, wringing his hands.

Susan put her arm around him and smiled.   Don't worry.   We'll be out of here in no time.

_____

_____

_____

_____

_____

_____

_____

_____

_____

_____

_____

ACTIVITY 8   Creating Sentences

Working with a partner, write sentences that use quotation marks as directed.

1. Write a sentence in which you quote a favorite expression of someone you know. Identify the person's relationship to you.

    EXAMPLE

    My brother Sam often says after a meal, "That wasn't bad at all."

    _____

    _____

2. Write a quotation that contains the words *Ron asked Rose.* Write a second quotation that includes the words *Rose replied.*

    _____

    _____

3. Write a sentence that interests or amuses you from a book, magazine, or newspaper. Identify the title and author of the book, magazine article, or newspaper article.

EXAMPLE

In her book <u>At Wit's End</u>, Erma Bombeck advises, "Never go to a doctor whose office plants have died."

_____

_____

REFLECTIVE ACTIVITY

1. Look at the paragraph about the elevator that you previously revised. Explain how adding quotation marks has affected the paragraph.

2. What would writing be like without quotation marks? Explain, using an example, how quotation marks are important to understanding writing.

3. Explain what it is about quotation marks that is most difficult for you to remember and apply. Use an example to make your point clear. Feel free to refer back to anything in this chapter.

REVIEW TEST 1

Place quotation marks around the exact words of a speaker or writer in the sentences that follow.

1. Give me a break! Charlie shouted to no one in particular.

2. My mother always says, Some are wise, and some are otherwise.

3. Why do men continue to wear ties when they serve no purpose? asked Paul.

4. Take all you want, but eat all you take, read the sign in the cafeteria.

5. One of Mark Twain's famous lines is, Man is the only animal that blushes—or needs to.

6. My friend the radio announcer loses his voice every time we drive under a bridge, said the comedian.

7. The first time my daughter had a headache, she told me, Mommy, I have a pain in my brain.

8. If your parachute doesn't open, the skydiving instructor joked, bring it back, and we'll give you a new one.

9. The novelist ended a letter to his brother by saying, I'm sorry for writing such a long letter. I didn't have time for a shorter one.

10. Work fascinates me, said the comedian. I could sit and watch it for hours.

REVIEW TEST 2

Place quotation marks around the exact words of a speaker in the sentences that follow. Three of the sentences contain indirect quotations and do not require quotation marks.

EXAMPLE

Soon after moving into their new house, Mike said to Marian, "Why don't we have a party? It'd be a good way to meet all our neighbors."

1. Nice idea, said Marian, but way too much work.

2. It won't be that bad. We'll grill hamburgers and ask everybody to bring a side dish, Mike answered.

3. Marian said that she would agree to the idea if Mike called all the guests.

4. Hi, this is Mike Josephs, your new neighbor in 44B, Mike said each time he called someone.

5. Afterward, he told Marian that everything was under control.

6. I told them we'd provide burgers and plenty of drinks, Mike explained, and they'll bring everything else.

7. When the party started, the first guests arrived saying, We brought potato salad—we hope that's all right!

8. Then guests number two, three, and four arrived, also announcing that they had brought potato salad.

9. As the sixth bowl of potato salad arrived, Mike mumbled to Marian Maybe I should have made some more suggestions about what people should bring.

10. Oh, well, I really love potato salad, Marian said.

REVIEW TEST 3

Go through the comics section of a newspaper to find a comic strip that amuses you. Be sure to choose a strip where two or more characters are speaking to each other. Write a full description that will enable people who have not read the comic strip to visualize it clearly and appreciate its humor. Describe the setting and action in each panel and enclose the words of the speakers in quotation marks.

For additional materials on Chapter 27, visit www.mhhe.com/langan.

Commas

INTRODUCTORY ACTIVITY

Commas often (though not always) signal a minor break or pause in a sentence. Each of the six pairs of sentences below illustrates one of six main uses of the comma. Read each pair of sentences aloud and place a comma wherever you feel a slight pause occurs. Then choose the rule that applies from the box at the bottom of the page, and write its letter on the line provided.

_____ 1. You can use a credit card write out a check or provide cash.

   The old house was infested with red ants roaches and mice.

_____ 2. To start the car depress the accelerator and turn the ignition key.

   Before you go hiking buy a comfortable pair of shoes.

_____ 3. Leeches creatures that suck human blood are valuable to medical science.

   George Derek who was just arrested was a classmate of mine.

_____ 4. Our professor said the exam would be easy but I thought it was difficult.

   Wind howled through the trees and rain pounded against the window.

_____ 5. Emily asked "Why is it so hard to remember your dreams the next day?"

   "I am so tired after work" Lily said "that I fall asleep right away."

_____ 6. Bert has driven 1500000 accident-free miles in his job as a trucker.

   The Gates Trucking Company of Newark New Jersey gave Bert an award on August 26 2009 for his superior safety record.

   a. separate items in a list
   b. separate introductory material from the sentence
   c. separate words that interrupt the sentence
   d. separate complete thoughts in a sentence
   e. separate direct quotations from the rest of the sentence
   f. separate numbers, addresses, and dates in everyday writing

Answers are on page 632.

CHAPTER PREVIEW

Six Main Uses of the Comma

- Commas between Items in a Series
- Commas after Introductory Material
- Commas around Words Interrupting the Flow of Thought
- Commas between Complete Thoughts Connected by Joining Words
- Commas with Direct Quotations
- Commas with Everyday Material

Unnecessary Use of Commas

Six Main Uses of the Comma

Commas are used mainly as follows:

- To separate items in a series

- To set off introductory material

- On both sides of words that interrupt the flow of thought in a sentence

- Between two complete thoughts connected by *and, but, for, or, nor, so, yet*

- To set off a direct quotation from the rest of a sentence

- To set off certain everyday material

You may find it helpful to remember that the comma often marks a slight pause, or break, in a sentence. These pauses or breaks occur at the points where the six main comma rules apply. Sentence examples for each of the comma rules are given on the following pages; read these sentences aloud and listen for the minor pauses or breaks that are signaled by commas.

However, you should keep in mind that commas are far more often overused than underused. As a general rule, you should *not* use a comma unless a given comma rule applies or unless a comma is otherwise needed to help a sentence read clearly. A good rule of thumb is that "when in doubt" about whether to use a comma, it is often best to "leave it out."

After reviewing each of the comma rules that follow, you will practice adding commas that are needed and omitting commas that are not needed.

Commas between Items in a Series

Use a comma to separate items in a series.

Magazines, paperback novels, and textbooks crowded the shelves.

Hard-luck Sam needs a loan, a good-paying job, and a close friend.

Pat sat in the doctor's office, checked her watch, and flipped nervously through a magazine.

Mira bit into the ripe, juicy apple.

More and more people entered the crowded, noisy stadium.

> **TIP** A comma is used between two descriptive words in a series only if the word *and* inserted between the words sounds natural. You could say:
>
> Mira bit into the ripe *and* juicy apple.
>
> More and more people entered the crowded *and* noisy stadium.
>
> But notice in the following sentences that the descriptive words do not sound natural when *and* is inserted between them. In such cases, no comma is used.
>
> The model wore a classy black dress. ("A classy *and* black dress" doesn't sound right, so no comma is used.)
>
> Dr. Van Helsing noticed two tiny puncture marks on the patient's neck. ("Two *and* tiny puncture marks" doesn't sound right, so no comma is used.)

Commas between Items in a Series — ACTIVITY 1

Place commas between items in each series.

1. Mae-Lin tossed her sunglasses a bottle of water and a recent issue of *Every Day with Rachel Ray* into her tote bag.

2. Steve uses the computer to check email play games surf the Internet download music and send instant messages.

3. In the Williams' backyard are an igloo-shaped doghouse several plastic toys trampled flowers and a cracked ceramic gnome.

Necessary and Unnecessary Commas — ACTIVITY 2

For each item, cross out the one comma that is not needed. Add the one comma that is needed between items in a series.

1. I discovered gum wrappers, pennies and a sock hidden, under the seats when I vacuumed my car.

2. Squirrels Canada geese, two white swans, and clouds of mosquitoes, populate Farwell Park.

3. Lewis dribbled twice, spun to his left and lofted his patented hook shot over the outstretched arms, of the Panthers' center.

Commas after Introductory Material

Use a comma to set off introductory material.

Fearlessly, Jessie picked up the slimy slug.

Just to annoy Steve, she let it crawl along her arm.

Although I have a black belt in karate, I decided to go easy on the demented bully who had kicked sand in my face.

Mumbling under her breath, the woman picked over the tomatoes.

If the introductory material is brief, the comma is sometimes omitted. In the activities here, you should include the comma.

| ACTIVITY 3 | **Commas after Introductory Clauses** |

Place commas after introductory material.

HINT   In item 1, the last introductory word is *airport*.

1. Before I left for the airport I turned off my water heater and unplugged my appliances.
2. If you left your backpack at the library you should call Campus Security.
3. Wanting to help others Brian volunteers at the Meals on Wheels program.

| ACTIVITY 4 | **More Neccessary and Unnecessary Commas** |

For each item, cross out the one comma that is not needed. Add the one comma that is needed after introductory material.

HINT   In item 1, add a comma to the first sentence and omit the comma in the second.

1. Using metallic cords from her Christmas presents young Ali made several bracelets for herself. After that, she took a long ribbon, and tied a bow around her dog's head.
2. As the bride smiled and strolled past me down the aisle I saw a bead of sweat roll, from her forehead down her cheek. Remembering my own wedding, I knew she wasn't sweating from the heat.
3. When my children were young, I wrote interesting anecdotes about them in a notebook. For example I wrote a note to remind me, that my son once wanted to be a yo-yo maker.

Commas around Words Interrupting the Flow of Thought

Use a comma before and after words that interrupt the flow of thought in a sentence.

The car, cleaned and repaired, is ready to be sold.

Martha, our new neighbor, used to work as a bartender at Rexy's Tavern.

Taking long walks, especially after dark, helps me sort out my thoughts.

Usually you can "hear" words that interrupt the flow of thought in a sentence. However, when you are not sure if certain words are interrupters, remove them from the sentence. If it still makes sense without the words, you know that the words are interrupters and that the information they give is nonessential. Such nonessential information is set off with commas. In the following sentence

Susie Hall, who is my best friend, won a new car in the *Reader's Digest* sweepstakes.

the words *who is my best friend* are extra information, not needed to identify the subject of the sentence, *Susie Hall.* Put commas around such nonessential information. On the other hand, in the sentence

The woman who is my best friend won a new car in the *Reader's Digest* sweepstakes.

The words *who is my best friend* supply essential information that we need to identify the woman. If the words were removed from the sentence, we would no longer know which woman won the sweepstakes. Commas are not used around such essential information.

Here is another example:

The Shining, a novel by Stephen King, is the scariest book I've ever read.

Here the words *a novel by Stephen King* are extra information, not needed to identify the subject of the sentence, *The Shining.* Commas go around such nonessential information. On the other hand, in the sentence

Stephen King's novel *The Shining* is the scariest book I've ever read.

the words *The Shining* are needed to identify the novel because he has written more than one. Commas are not used around such essential information.

Most of the time you will be able to "hear" words that interrupt the flow of thought in a sentence and will not have to think about whether the words are essential or nonessential.

CONNECT WRITING

Meet Amy. She has been keeping track of current events in a journal for her Political Science class. She's written some very detailed notes, but is struggling with how to use commas correctly. Help Amy find and correct the comma mistakes in her notes.

mhconnectwriting.com

| T I P | Some instructors refer to nonessential or extra information that is set off by commas as a *nonrestrictive clause*. Essential information that interrupts the flow of thought is called a *restrictive clause*. No commas are used to set off a restrictive clause. |

| ACTIVITY 5 | Commas That Set Off Interrupters |

Add commas to set off interrupting words.

> **HINT**   In item 1, the interrupting words are *assisted by no one.*

1. The supply control clerk assisted by no one conducted a quarterly inventory on Tuesday.
2. Jo Ann and Craig who were engaged for a year married last July at a winery in Sonoma.
3. The lawn furniture rusted beyond repair needs to be thrown out.

| ACTIVITY 6 | More Necessary and Unnecessary Commas |

For each item, cross out the one comma that is not needed. Add the comma that is needed to completely set off the interrupting words.

> **HINT**   In item 1, the interrupting words are *even the most gigantic.*

1. All trees, even the most gigantic are only 1 percent living tissue; the rest, is deadwood.
2. The city council in a rare fit, of wisdom, established a series of bicycle paths around town.
3. John Adams and Thomas Jefferson, the second and third presidents, of the United States died on the same day in 1826.
4. My aunt, a talkative, woman married a patient man who is a wonderful listener.

Commas between Complete Thoughts Connected by Joining Words

Use a comma between two complete thoughts connected by *and, but, for, or, nor, so,* or *yet* (joining words).

> My parents threatened to throw me out of the house, so I had to stop playing the drums.
>
> The polyester bedsheets had a gorgeous design, but they didn't feel as comfortable as plain cotton sheets.
>
> The teenage girls walked along the hot summer streets, and the teenage boys drove by in their shiny cars.

> **TIP**   The comma is optional when the complete thoughts are short:
> Hunter relaxed but Bob kept working.
> The soda was flat so I poured it away.
> We left school early for the furnace had broken down.

Be careful not to use a comma in sentences having *one* subject and a *double* verb. The comma is used only in sentences made up of two complete thoughts (two subjects and two verbs). In the sentence

> Mary lay awake that stormy night and listened to the thunder crashing.

there is only one subject (*Mary*) and a double verb (*lay* and *listened*). No comma is needed. Likewise, the sentence

> The quarterback kept the ball and plunged across the goal line for a touchdown.

has only one subject (*quarterback*) and a double verb (*kept* and *plunged*); therefore, no comma is needed.

Commas That Connect Complete Thoughts

ACTIVITY 7

Place a comma before a joining word that connects two complete thoughts (two subjects and two verbs). Remember, do *not* place a comma within sentences that have only one subject and a double verb. Mark sentences that are correct with a C.

> **HINT**   In item 1, *but* connects two complete thoughts.

1. The apartment Kate looked at was clean and spacious but the rent was too expensive for her budget.

2. Our power went out during the thunderstorm so we decided to eat dinner by candlelight.

3. Eddie is building a kayak in his garage and plans to take it down the Columbia River next year.

4. I desperately need more storage space for I can't seem to throw anything away.

5. The helicopter hovered overhead and lowered a rescue line to the downed pilot.

6. Travis was going to quit his job at the supermarket but he changed his mind after getting a raise.

7. One of the men got ready to leave work at four but put his coat away upon seeing his boss.

8. The family expected Valerie to go to college but she went to work after eloping with her boyfriend.

9. Bobby pleaded with his parents to buy him a computer for his schoolwork but he spends most of his time playing games on it.

10. The doctor examined me for less than ten minutes and then presented me with a bill for two hundred dollars.

Commas with Direct Quotations

Use a comma or commas to set off a direct quotation from the rest of a sentence.

"Please take a number," said the deli clerk.

Chris told Sophia, "I've just signed up for a course on Web-page design."

"Those who sling mud," a famous politician once said, "usually lose ground."

"Reading this book," complained Stan, "is about as interesting as watching paint dry."

> **TIP** Commas and periods at the end of a quotation go inside quotation marks. See also page 355.

ACTIVITY 8

Setting Off Quotations with Commas

In each sentence, add the one or more commas needed to set off the quoted material.

> **HINT** In item 1, add a comma after the quoted material.

1. "Think before you speak" said my dad.
2. "A child miseducated" said John F. Kennedy "is a child lost."
3. "Before you leave the building" muttered the night patrol officer "be sure to sign out."

ACTIVITY 9

More Necessary and Unnecessary Commas

In each item, cross out the one comma that is not needed to set off a quotation. Add the comma(s) needed to set off a quotation from the rest of the sentence.

> **HINT** In item 1, add a comma before the quoted material.

1. "If you're looking for a career change," read the poster, in the subway station "consider the US Armed Forces."
2. "Your arms look fine" said the swimming instructor, "but you keep forgetting, to kick."
3. "Did you really think" the judge asked, the defendant, "you could kill both your parents and then ask for mercy because you're an orphan?"

Commas with Everyday Material

Use commas to set off certain everyday material, as shown in the following sections.

Persons Spoken to

I think, Bella, that you should go to bed.

Please turn down the stereo, Mark.

Please, sir, can you spare a dollar?

Dates

Our house was burglarized on June 28, 2009, and two weeks later on July 11, 2009.

Addresses

Robyn's sister lives at 342 Red Oak Drive, Los Angeles, California 90057. She is moving to Manchester, Vermont, after her divorce.

> **TIP** No comma is used before a zip code.

Openings and Closings of Letters

Dear Marilyn,	Sincerely,
Dear John,	Truly yours,

In formal letters, a colon is used after the opening:

Dear Sir:

Dear Madam:

Numbers

Government officials estimate that Americans spend about 785,000,000 hours a year filling out federal forms.

Adding Commas

ACTIVITY 10

Place commas where needed.

> **HINT** Two commas are needed in item 1.

1. Excuse me madam but your scarf is in my soup.
2. Before age eighteen, the average child spends 6000 hours in school and 15000 hours watching television.

3. The famous ocean liner *Titanic* sank in the Atlantic Ocean on April 151912.

4. Teresa

   What do you think of this psychology lecture? Will you meet me for lunch after class? I'll treat. Text me your answer right away.

   Love
Jeff

5. The zoo in Washington D.C. purchases 50000 pounds of meat; 6 500 loaves of bread; 114000 live crickets; and other foods for its animals each year.

Unnecessary Use of Commas

Remember that if no clear rule applies for using a comma, it is usually better not to use one. As stated previously, "When in doubt, leave it out." Following are some typical examples of unnecessary commas.

Incorrect

Sharon told me, that my socks were different colors.

(A comma is not used before *that* unless the flow of thought is interrupted.)

The union negotiations, dragged on for three days.

(Do not use a comma between a simple subject and verb.)

I waxed all the furniture, and cleaned the windows.

(Use a comma before *and* only with more than two items in a series or when *and* joins two complete thoughts.)

Liz carried, the baby into the house.

(Do not use a comma between a verb and its object.)

I had a clear view, of the entire robbery.

(Do not use a comma before a prepositional phrase.)

| ACTIVITY 11 | **Eliminating Unnecessary Commas** |

Cross out commas that do not belong. Some commas are correct. Do not add any commas.

1. We grew a pumpkin last year, that weighed over one hundred pounds.

2. Anyone with a failing grade, must meet with the instructor during office hours.

3. Last weekend a grizzly bear attacked a hiker, who got too close to its cubs.

4. After watching my form, on the high-diving board, Mr. Riley, my instructor, asked me if I had insurance.

5. Rosa flew first to Los Angeles, and then she went to visit her parents, in Mexico City.

6. The tall muscular man wearing the dark sunglasses, is a professional wrestler.

7. Onions, radishes, and potatoes, seem to grow better in cooler climates.

8. Whenever Vincent is in Las Vegas, you can find him at the blackjack table, or the roulette wheel.

9. While I watched in disbelief, my car rolled down the hill, and through the front window of a Chinese restaurant.

10. The question, sir, is not, whether you committed the crime, but, when you committed the crime.

Editing and Rewriting

Working with a partner, read carefully the short paragraph below and cross out the five misplaced commas. Then insert the ten additional commas needed. Feel free to discuss the rewrite quietly with your partner and refer back to the chapter when necessary.

Dear Olivia,

On Tuesday, May 5 2009 my husband, and I were unable to sleep because of the loud music coming from your apartment. When I first heard the music I didn't say anything to you because it was still early. But the music, along with loud, laughter and talking, continued until around four o'clock in the morning. At midnight, my husband went into the hallway to see what was happening and he ran into one of your guests. The man who seemed very drunk stared at him, and said "Go back to bed, old man." The next morning, we found beer cans pizza boxes, and cigarette butts, piled outside our door. This is unacceptable. We have written this letter to you as a warning. The next time something like this happens we will call the police, and the building manager. We don't want to cause trouble with you but we will not tolerate another incident like what happened that night.

Sincerely,

Rose Connelly

| ACTIVITY 13 | **Creating Sentences** |

Working with a partner, write sentences that use commas as directed.

1. Write a sentence mentioning three items you want to get the next time you go to the store.

    _____

    _____

2. Write two sentences describing how you relax after getting home from school or work. Start the first sentence with *After* or *When*. Start the second sentence with *Next*.

    _____

    _____

3. Write a sentence that tells something about your favorite movie, book, television show, or song. Use the words *which is my favorite movie* (or *book, television show,* or *song*) after the name of the movie book, television show, or song.

    _____

    _____

4. Write two complete thoughts about a person you know. The first thought should mention something that you like about the person. The second thought should mention something you don't like. Join the two thoughts with *but.* Do not use the name of a classmate.

    _____

    _____

5. Invent a line that Lola might say to Tony. Use the words *Lola said* in the sentence. Then include Tony's reply, using the words *Tony responded.*

    _____

    _____

6. Write a sentence about an important event in your life. Include the day, month, and year of the event.

    _____

    _____

REFLECTIVE ACTIVITY

1. Look at the letter that you revised on page 375. Explain how adding commas has affected the paragraph.

2. What would writing be like without the comma? How do commas help writing?

3. What is the most difficult comma rule for you to remember and apply? Explain, giving an example.

REVIEW TEST 1

Do three things: (1) Cross out the one comma that is not needed; (2) add the one comma that is needed; and (3) in the space provided, write the letter of the rule that applies for each comma you added.

a. Between items in a series
b. After introductory material
c. Around interrupters

d. Between complete thoughts
e. With direct quotations

_____ 1. *Harry Potter and the Deathly Hallows*, the seventh and final book in the *Harry Potter* series sold over eight million copies, on the first day of its release.

_____ 2. Pretending to be a babysitter the shoplifter slipped several CDs, into her baby stroller.

_____ 3. Emmett, who recently adopted a baby girl, rushed to the supermarket, to buy infant formula, baby wipes and disposable diapers.

_____ 4. "Before I leave on my business trip" Emily told her two children, "I want both of you to promise me, that you will *not* torment the dog or Dad."

_____ 5. Brandie, a breast cancer survivor religiously wears her pink, "awareness bracelet" to remember her victory over the disease.

_____ 6. Recognizing the deadly effects of cigarette smoking the Walt Disney Company has banned depictions of smoking, in its films.

_____ 7. Kurt rehearsed the exact moment for months but he still stumbled over his own words, when he asked Keisha to marry him.

_____ 8. Everyone at the barbeque party enjoyed the mustard-coated oil-drizzled Alaskan, Copper River sockeye salmon fillets roasted on cedar planks.

＿＿＿ 9. Mahatma Gandhi, was wise when he said "We must be the change we wish to see."

＿＿＿ 10. The substitute teacher tried to enforce the class rules yet students misbehaved by sending text messages, and playing games on their cell phones.

REVIEW TEST 2

Insert commas where needed. One sentence does not need commas. Mark it with a C.

1. Some people believe that television can be addictive but I think they're wrong.

2. While there are people who turn on their TVs upon waking up in the morning I don't do that.

3. I turn on my TV only upon sitting down for breakfast and then I watch the *Today Show*.

4. I don't need to watch game shows soap operas and situation comedies to get through the day.

5. Instead I watch all these programs simply because I enjoy them.

6. I also keep the TV turned on all evening because thanks to cable and On Demand there is always something decent to watch.

7. If I did not have good viewing choices I would flick off the TV without hesitation.

8. Lots of people switch channels rapidly to preview what is on.

9. I on the other hand turn immediately to the channel I know I want.

10. In other words I am not addicted; I am a selective viewer who just happens to select a lot of shows.

REVIEW TEST 3

On a separate piece of paper, write six sentences, with each sentence demonstrating one of the six main comma rules.

For additional materials on Chapter 28, visit www.mhhe.com/langan.

Other Punctuation Marks

CHAPTER PREVIEW

Colons (:)

Semicolons (;)

Dashes (—)

Hyphens (-)

Parentheses ( )

INTRODUCTORY ACTIVITY

Each sentence below needs one of the following punctuation marks.

See if you can insert the correct mark(s) in each case.

1. The following items were on my son's Christmas list an iPod, a PlayStation, and a skateboard.

2. An admirer gave me chocolate dipped strawberries for Valentine's Day.

3. Everyone in the household misses Indy, our pet cat who lived for fourteen years 1994–2008 .

4. As students, we need to take college seriously we are now responsible for our own learning.

5. The stray dog was malnourished, dirty, abused   but happy to have been rescued.

Answers are on page 633.

Colons (:)

The colon is a mark of introduction. Use the colon at the end of a complete statement to do the following:

- Introduce a list:

  My little brother has three hobbies: playing video games, racing his Hot Wheels cars all over the floor, and driving me crazy.

- Introduce a long quotation:

  Janet's paper was based on a passage from George Eliot's novel *Middlemarch*: "If we had a keen vision and feeling of all ordinary human life, it would be like hearing the grass grow and the squirrel's heart beat, and we should die of that roar which lies on the other side of silence. As it is, the quickest of us walk about well wadded with stupidity."

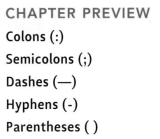

CONNECT WRITING

Meet Sofia. She's working on two letters for a non-profit organization that sponsors women's shelters. She feels pretty good about her writing skills, but is not sure if she's using colons and semicolons correctly. Help Sofia locate and correct all the colon and semicolon mistakes in her two letters.

mhconnectwriting.com

> **TIP** In formal writing, indent long quotations, and do not set them off with quotation marks; a "long quotation" is generally four lines or longer.

- Introduce an explanation:

> There are two ways to do this job: the easy way and the right way.

Two minor uses of the colon are after the opening in a formal letter (*Dear Sir or Madam:*) and between the hour and the minute in writing the time (*The bus will leave for the game at 11:45*).

ACTIVITY 1	**Using Colons**

Place colons where needed.

> **HINT**   Add a colon before the explanation in item 1.

1. Roger is on a "see-food" diet if he sees food, he eats it.

2. Brenda had some terrible problems last summer her mother suffered a heart attack, her husband lost his job, and one of her children was arrested for shoplifting.

3. Andy Rooney wrote in one of his columns "Doctors should never talk to ordinary people about anything but medicine. When doctors talk politics, economics, or sports, they reveal themselves to be ordinary mortals, idiots just like the rest of us. That isn't what any of us wants our doctors to be."

Semicolons (;)

The semicolon signals more of a pause than the comma alone but not quite the full pause of a period. Use a semicolon to do the following:

- Join two complete thoughts that are not already connected by a joining word such as *and, but, for,* or *so*:

> The chemistry lab blew up; Professor Thomas was fired.

> I once stabbed myself with a pencil; a black mark has been under my skin ever since.

- Join two complete thoughts that include a transitional word such as *however, otherwise, moreover, furthermore, therefore,* or *consequently*:

> I changed and made the bed; moreover, I cleaned the entire bedroom.

> Tara finished typing the paper; however, she forgot to bring it to class.

> **TIP**   The first two uses of the semicolon are treated in more detail on pages 186–188.

- Separate items in a series when the items themselves contain commas:

> This fall I won't have to work on Labor Day, September 7; Veterans Day, November 11; or Thanksgiving Day, November 26.

> At the final Weight Watchers' meeting, prizes were awarded to Sally Johnson, for losing 20 pounds; Irving Ross, for losing 26 pounds; and Betty Mills, the champion loser, who lost 102 pounds.

Using Semicolons

Place semicolons where needed.

 Add a semicolon before the transitional word in item 1.

1. Christina returned the wallet that she had found at the library consequently, she felt proud of herself for being honest.

2. My friends could tell that I had been crying my eyes were puffy and bloodshot.

3. I invited Vida, who's my roommate Rami, who's Vida's boyfriend and Rachel, who's my best friend.

CONNECT WRITING

Meet Li Mei. She has purchased postcards from the college bookstore, which she plans to send to family and friends back home in China. She's glad she's written out her messages on Post-it notes first when she realizes she's made several dash mistakes in her writing. Help Li Mei locate and correct all the dash mistakes in her messages before she adds them to the postcards.

mhconnectwriting.com

Dashes (—)

A dash signals a degree of pause longer than a comma but not as complete as a period. Use the dash to set off words for dramatic effect.

> I suggest—no, I insist—that you stay for dinner.

> The prisoner walked toward the electric chair—grinning.

> A meaningful job, a loving wife, and a car that wouldn't break down all the time—these are the things he wanted in life.

Using the Dash

Place dashes where needed.

 One dash is needed in item 1.

1. The members of the Polar Bear Club marched into the icy sea shivering.

2. The actress's wedding her third in three years included a dozen bridesmaids and a flock of white doves.

3. My sociology class meets at the worst possible time eight o'clock on Monday morning.

CONNECT WRITING

Meet Angela. She's written a stir fry recipe that she plans to submit to her college's cookbook. The dish has to be simple and easy and she hopes that what she wrote is clear. However, after reading her recipe aloud, she thinks there may be hyphen mistakes. Help Angela locate and correct all the hyphen mistakes in her recipe so that no one misunderstands the directions.

mhconnectwriting.com

Hyphens (-)

Use a hyphen in the following ways:

- With two or more words that act as a single unit describing a noun:

  The society ladies nibbled at the deep-fried grasshoppers.

  A white-gloved waiter then put some snails on their table.

  Your dictionary will often help when you are unsure about whether to use a hyphen between words.

- To divide a word at the end of a line of writing or typing:

  Although it was raining, the teams decided to play the championship game that day.

> **TIPS**
> 1. Divide a word only between syllables. Use your dictionary (see page 387) to be sure of correct syllable divisions.
> 2. Do not divide words of one syllable.
> 3. Do not divide a word if you can avoid dividing it.

ACTIVITY 4   **Using Hyphens**

Working with a partner, place hyphens where needed.

> **HINT**   Two hyphens are needed in item 1.

1. Grandpa needs to throw out his console TV and rabbit ear antenna and buy a new high definition TV.

2. Sideway Inn, a hole in the wall diner located downtown, serves both comfort food and upscale, hoity toity dishes.

3. The people in my hometown are honest, hard working folks, but they aren't very friendly to out of towners.

Parentheses ( )

Use parentheses to do the following:

- Set off extra or incidental information from the rest of a sentence:

  The chapter on drugs in our textbook (pages 234–271) contains some frightening statistics.

  The normal body temperature of a cat (101° to 102°) is 3° higher than the temperature of its owner.

- Enclose letters or numbers that signal items in a series:

  Three steps to follow in previewing a textbook are to (1) study the title, (2) read the first and last paragraphs, and (3) study the headings and subheadings.

> T I P   Do not use parentheses too often in your writing.

Using Parentheses

Working in pairs, add parentheses where needed.

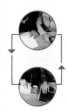

> H I N T   Put the extra information in item 1 in parentheses.

1. According to the 2000 Census, a majority of Americans 80 percent had earned a high school diploma.

2. That instructor's office hours 3:00 to 4:00 p.m. are impossible for any student with an afternoon job.

3. Since I am forgetful, I often 1 make a list and then 2 check off items I have done. Now, where did I put my list?

REVIEW TEST 1

At the appropriate spot or spots, insert the punctuation mark shown in the margin.

EXAMPLE

The speed dating event was a success; I met several people I wanted to see again.   ;

1. That catalog lists some unusual items a sausage stuffer, an electric foot warmer, and a remote-control car starter.   :

2. My brother's jokes none of which I can repeat are unfunny and tasteless.   —

3. These days, many two career couples have decided not to have children.   -

4. The section on space travel in my daughter's science book Chapters 10–11 is sadly out of date.   ()

5. Anne Frank wrote in her diary "It's a wonder I haven't abandoned all my ideals; they seem so absurd and impractical. Yet I cling to them because I still believe, in spite of everything, that people are truly good at heart."   :

6. The frightened hamster darted from room to room finally, it crawled under a dresser.   ;

7. Credit card bills, the mortgage payment, and car repairs no wonder my paycheck doesn't last till the end of the month.   —

8. Someone once defined a self confident person as one who does crossword puzzles in pen instead of pencil.   -

( )   9. Three ways to save money on home repairs are 1 get several estimates, 2 avoid costly designer products, and 3 do it yourself.

;   10. I ordered several items online from Macy's: two suitcases, one maroon and one blue; an extra-large, machine-washable sweater and a canvas gym bag.

REVIEW TEST 2

CONNECT WRITING

Meet Tyler. He's trying to write instructions for the pet sitter who will be watching his two dogs, Goldie and Locks, while he is out of town. He's included a lot of information in the list, but his instructions aren't clear. He thinks it could be that he's used parentheses incorrectly. Help Tyler locate and correct all the parentheses mistakes in his instructions.

mhconnectwriting.com

On a separate piece of paper, write two sentences using each of the following punctuation marks: colon, semicolon, dash, hyphen, parentheses.

For additional materials on Chapter 29, visit www.mhhe.com/langan.

Word Use

SECTION PREVIEW

30 **Dictionary Use**

31 **Spelling Improvement**

32 **Omitted Words and Letters**

33 **Commonly Confused Words**

34 **Effective Word Choice**

RESPONDING TO IMAGES

What's wrong with the candy heart's message? How would you fix it? Looking at the Section Preview, in which chapter do you think this type of error will be discussed?

30 CHAPTER

Dictionary Use

CHAPTER PREVIEW

Spelling

Syllabication

Pronunciation

• Vowel Sounds

The Schwa

Accent Marks

Full Pronunciation

Other Information about Words

• Parts of Speech

• Principal Parts of Irregular Verbs

• Plural Forms of Irregular Nouns

• Meanings

• Etymology

• Usage Labels

• Synonyms

INTRODUCTORY ACTIVITY

The dictionary is an indispensable tool, as will be apparent if you try to answer the following questions *without* using one.

1. Which one of the following words is spelled incorrectly?

   fortutious   macrobiotics   stratagem

2. If you wanted to hyphenate the following word correctly, at which points would you place the syllable divisions?

   h i e r o g l y p h i c s

3. What common word has the sound of the first *e* in the word *chameleon?* _____

4. Where is the primary accent in the following word?

   o c t o g e n a r i a n

5. What are the two separate meanings of the word *earmark?*

   _____

   _____

Your dictionary is a quick and sure authority on all these matters: spelling, syllabication, pronunciation, and word meanings. And as this chapter will show, it is also a source for many other kinds of information.

Answers are on page 633.

The dictionary is a valuable tool. To take advantage of it, you need to understand the main kinds of information that a dictionary gives about a word. Look at the information provided for the word *dictate* in the following entry from the *American Heritage Dictionary*, fourth paperback edition.*

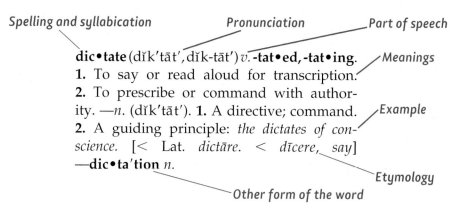

Spelling and syllabication   *Pronunciation*   *Part of speech*

dic•tate (dĭk′tāt′, dĭk-tāt′) *v.* **-tat•ed, -tat•ing**.   *Meanings*
1. To say or read aloud for transcription.
2. To prescribe or command with author-
ity. —*n.* (dĭk′tāt′). **1.** A directive; command.   *Example*
2. A guiding principle: *the dictates of con-*
science. [< Lat. *dictāre.* < *dīcere,* say]
—**dic•ta′tion** *n.*

Etymology

Other form of the word

Spelling

The first bit of information, in the **boldface** (heavy type) entry itself, is the spelling of *dictate.* You probably already know the spelling of *dictate,* but if you didn't, you could find it by pronouncing the syllables in the word carefully and then looking it up in the dictionary.

Using a Dictionary   ACTIVITY 1

Use your dictionary to correct the spelling of the following words:

argueing _____	appearence _____
freind _____	representative _____
mortage _____	yestarday _____
referance _____	unanamous _____
beautaful _____	visator _____
marrage _____	unnusual _____
acheive _____	hammar _____
tournement _____	commited _____
ninty _____	vegtable _____

Syllabication

The second bit of information that the dictionary gives, also within the boldface entry, is the syllabication of *dic•tate.* Note that a dot separates each syllable (or part) of the word.

Marking Syllable Divisions   ACTIVITY 2

Use your dictionary to mark the syllable divisions in the following words. Also indicate how many syllables are in each word.

ven ture	(_____ syllables)
ob ses sion	(_____ syllables)
en er get ic	(_____ syllables)
in spi ra tion al	(_____ syllables)

Noting syllable divisions will enable you to *hyphenate* a word: divide it at the end of one line of writing and complete it at the beginning of the next line. You can correctly hyphenate a word only at a syllable division, and you may have to check your dictionary to make sure of the syllable divisions for a particular word.

Pronunciation

The third bit of information in the sample dictionary entry is the pronunciation of *dictate*: (dǐk′tāt′) or (dǐk-tāt′). You already know how to pronounce *dictate*, but if you did not, the information within the parentheses would serve as your guide.

Vowel Sounds

You will probably use the pronunciation key in your dictionary mainly as a guide to pronouncing different vowel sounds (*vowels* are the letters *a, e, i, o,* and *u*). Here is the pronunciation key that appears in the paperback *American Heritage Dictionary:*

ă pat   ā pay   â care   ä father   ě pet   ē be   ǐ pit   ī tie   î pier
ŏ pot   ō toe   ô paw, for   oi noise   o͝o took   o͞o boot   ou out
th thin   *th* this   ŭ cut   û urge   yo͞o abuse   zh vision
ə about, item, edible, gallop, circus

This key tells you, for example, that the short *a* is pronounced like the *a* in *pat*, the long *a* is like the *a* in *pay*, and the short *i* is like the *i* in *pit*.

> **TIP**   A long vowel always has the sound of its own name.

ACTIVITY 3   **Understanding Vowel Sounds**

Look at the pronunciation key in your own dictionary. The key is probably located in the front of the dictionary or at the bottom of every page. What common word in the key tells you how to pronounce each of the following sounds?

ě _____   ō _____

ī _____   ŭ _____

ŏ _____   o͞o _____

The Schwa (ə)

The symbol ə looks like an upside-down *e.* It is called a *schwa,* and it stands for the unaccented sound in such words as *about, item, edible, gallop,* and *circus.* More approximately, it stands for the sound *uh*—like the *uh* that speakers sometimes make when they hesitate. Perhaps it would help to remember that *uh,* as well as ə, could be used to represent the schwa sound.

Here are three of the many words in which the schwa sound appears: *socialize* (sō′shə līz or sō′shuh līz); *legitimate* (lə jĭt′ ə mĭt or luh jĭt′ uh mĭt); *oblivious* (ə blĭv′ē əs or uh blĭv′ē uhs).

| **Using the Schwa** | **ACTIVITY 4** |

Open your dictionary to any page, and you will almost surely be able to find three words that make use of the schwa in the pronunciation in parentheses after the main entry. Write three such words and their pronunciations in the following spaces:

1. _____

2. _____

3. _____

Accent Marks

Some words contain both a primary accent, shown by a heavy stroke (′), and a secondary accent, shown by a lighter stroke (′). For example, in the word *vicissitude* (vĭ sĭs′ ĭ tōōd′), the stress, or accent, goes chiefly on the second syllable (sĭs′), and, to a lesser extent, on the last syllable (tōōd′).

Use your dictionary to add stress marks to the following words:

notorious (nō tôr ē əs)   enterprise (ĕn tər prīz)

instigate (ĭn stĭ gāt)   irresistible (ĭr ĭ zĭs tə bəl)

equivocate (ĭ kwĭv ə kāt)   probability (prŏb ə bĭl ĭ tē)

millennium (mə lĕn ē əm)   representative (rĕp rĭ zen tə tĭv)

Full Pronunciation

Use your dictionary to write out the full pronunciation (the information given in parentheses) for each of the following words:

1. magnate _____

2. semblance _____

3. satiate _____

4. bastion _____

5. celestial _____

6. extraneous _____

7. edifice _____

8. incipient _____

9. fallacious _____

10. ostracize _____

11. phlegmatic _____

12. proximity _____

13. anachronism _____

14. felicitous _____

15. extemporaneous _____

Now practice pronouncing each word. Use the pronunciation key in your dictionary as an aid to sounding out each syllable. Do *not* try to pronounce a word all at once; instead, work on mastering *one syllable at a time.* When you can pronounce each of the syllables in a word successfully, then say them in sequence, add the accent, and pronounce the entire word.

Other Information about Words

Parts of Speech

The dictionary entry for *dictate* includes the abbreviation *v.* This indicates that the meanings of *dictate* as a verb will follow. The abbreviation *n.* is then followed by the meanings of *dictate* as a noun.

| ACTIVITY 5 | **Using a Dictionary's Abbreviations Key** |

At the front of your dictionary, you will probably find a key that will explain the meanings of abbreviations used in the dictionary. Use the key to fill in the meanings of the following abbreviations:

pl. = _____

sing. = _____

adj. = _____

adv. = _____

Principal Parts of Irregular Verbs

Dictate is a regular verb and forms its principal parts by adding *-d, -d,* and *-ing* to the stem of the verb. When a verb is irregular, the dictionary lists its principal parts. For example, with *begin* the present tense comes first (the entry itself, *begin*). Next comes the past tense (*began*), and then the past participle (*begun*)—the form of the verb used with such helping words as *have, had,* and *was.* Then comes the present participle (*beginning*)—the *-ing* form of the word.

Principal Parts

ACTIVITY 6

Look up the principal parts of the following irregular verbs and write them in the spaces provided. The first one has been done for you.

Present	Past	Past Participle	Present Participle
see	saw	seen	seeing
choose			
know			
speak			

Plural Forms of Irregular Nouns

The dictionary supplies the plural forms of all irregular nouns. (Regular nouns form the plural by adding -s or -es.)

TIP   See pages 397–399 for more information about plurals.

Writing Plural Forms

ACTIVITY 7

Write the plurals of the following nouns:

country _____

volcano _____

curriculum _____

woman _____

Meanings

When a word has more than one meaning, its meanings are numbered in the dictionary, as with the sample verb *dictate*. In many dictionaries, the most common meanings are presented first. The introductory pages of your dictionary will explain the order in which meanings are presented.

Using Sentence Context

ACTIVITY 8

Use the sentence context to try to explain the meaning of the underlined word in each of the following sentences. Write your definition in the space provided. Then look up and record the dictionary meaning of the word. Be sure to select the meaning that best fits the word as it is used in the sentence.

1.   Honesty is a cardinal rule in my family.

Your definition:

_____

Dictionary definition: _____

_____

2. The union strike put management in a ticklish situation.

Your definition: _____

Dictionary definition: _____

3. Ben lacks confidence, probably because his parents constantly railed at him.

Your definition: _____

_____

Dictionary definition: _____

_____

Etymology

Etymology refers to the history of a word. Many words have origins in foreign languages, such as Greek (abbreviated Gk in the dictionary) or Latin (L). Such information is usually enclosed in brackets and is more likely to be present in an online or hardbound desk dictionary than in a paperback one. A good desk dictionary will tell you, for example, that the word *cannibal* derives from the name of the man-eating tribe, the Caribs, that Christopher Columbus discovered on Cuba and Haiti.

The following are some good desk dictionaries:

The American Heritage Dictionary

Random House College Dictionary

Webster's New Collegiate Dictionary

Webster's New World Dictionary

| ACTIVITY 9 | **Etymology** |

See if your dictionary says anything about the origins of the following words.

magazine _____

anatomy _____

frankfurter _____

Usage Labels

As a general rule, use only Standard English words in your writing. If a word is not Standard English, your dictionary will probably give it a usage label such as *informal, nonstandard, slang, vulgar, obsolete, archaic,* or *rare.*

Usage

Look up the following words and record how your dictionary labels them. Remember that a recent hardbound desk dictionary or the online *Oxford English Dictionary* will always be the best source of information about usage.

sharp (meaning *attractive*)

_____

hard-nosed

_____

sass (meaning *to talk impudently*)

_____

ain't

_____

put-down

_____

Synonyms

A *synonym* is a word that is close in meaning to another word. Using synonyms helps you avoid unnecessary repetition of the same word in a paper. A paperback dictionary is not likely to give you synonyms for words, but a good desk dictionary will. (You might also want to own a *thesaurus*, a book that lists synonyms and antonyms. An *antonym* is a word approximately opposite in meaning to another word.)

Synonyms

Consult a desk dictionary that gives synonyms for the following words, and write some of the synonyms in the spaces provided.

desire _____

ask _____

cry _____

Items 1–5

Use your dictionary to answer the following questions.

1. How many syllables are in the word *antonym*? _____

2. Where is the primary accent in the word *hierarchy*? _____

3. In the word *table*, the *a* is pronounced like

   a. short *o*

   b. short *a*

   c. schwa

   d. long *a*

4. In the word *mobility*, the *y* is pronounced like

   a. schwa

   b. short *a*

   c. long *e*

   d. short *e*

5. In the word *adept*, the *a* is pronounced like

   a. short *a*

   b. schwa

   c. short *i*

   d. long *e*

Items 6–10

There are five misspelled words in the following sentence. Cross out each misspelled word and write the correct spelling in the spaces provided.

I went to the pharmucy after work to pick up several perscriptions, including pills that were recomended to me by my physican for allargies.

6. _____

7. _____

8. _____

9. _____

10. _____

 For additional materials on Chapter 30, visit www.mhhe.com/langan.

Spelling Improvement

CHAPTER PREVIEW

Step 1: Using the Dictionary

Step 2: Keeping a Personal Spelling List

Step 3: Mastering Commonly Confused Words

Step 4: Using a Computer's Spell-Checker

Step 5: Understanding Basic Spelling Rules

Step 6: Understanding Plurals

Step 7: Mastering a Basic Word List

INTRODUCTORY ACTIVITY

See if you can circle the word that is misspelled in each of the following pairs:

akward	*or*	awkward
exercise	*or*	exercize
business	*or*	buisness
worried	*or*	worryed
shamful	*or*	shameful
begining	*or*	beginning
partys	*or*	parties
sandwichs	*or*	sandwiches
heroes	*or*	heros

Answers are on page 634.

Poor spelling often results from bad habits developed in early grade-school years. With work, such habits can be corrected. If you can write your name without misspelling it, there is no reason why you can't do the same with almost any word in the English language. Following are seven steps you can take to improve your spelling.

Step 1: Using the Dictionary

Get into the habit of using the dictionary. When you write a paper, allow yourself time to look up the spelling of all the words you are unsure about. Do not underestimate the value of this step just because it is such a simple one. By using the dictionary, you can probably make yourself a 95 percent better speller.

Step 2: Keeping a Personal Spelling List

Keep a list of words you misspell, and study those words regularly.

> **TIP**   When you have trouble spelling long words, try to break each word into syllables and see whether you can spell the syllables. For example, *misdemeanor* can be spelled easily if you can hear and spell in turn its four syllables: *mis-de-mean-or*. The word *formidable* can be spelled more easily if you hear and spell in turn its four syllables: *for-mi-da-ble*. Remember: Try to see, hear, and spell long words in terms of their syllables.

Step 3: Mastering Commonly Confused Words

Master the meanings and spellings of the commonly confused words on pages 407–422. Your instructor may assign twenty words for you to study at a time and give you a series of quizzes until you have mastered all the words.

Step 4: Using a Computer's Spell-Checker

Most word-processing programs feature a *spell-checker* that will identify incorrect words and suggest correct spellings. If you are unsure how to use yours, consult the program's "help" function. Spell-checkers are not foolproof; they will fail to catch misused homonyms like the words *your* and *you're*.

Step 5: Understanding Basic Spelling Rules

Explained briefly here are three rules that may improve your spelling. While exceptions sometimes occur, these rules hold true most of the time.

1. ***Change y to i.***   When a word ends in a consonant plus *y,* change *y* to *i* when you add an ending.

try + ed = tried	marry + es = marries
worry + es = worries	lazy + ness = laziness
lucky + ly = luckily	silly + est = silliest

2. ***Final silent e.***   Drop a final *e* before an ending that starts with a vowel (the vowels are *a, e, i, o,* and *u*).

hope + ing = hoping	sense + ible = sensible
fine + est = finest	hide + ing = hiding

Keep the final *e* before an ending that starts with a consonant.

use + ful = useful   care + less   = careless

life + like = lifelike   settle + ment = settlement

3. ***Doubling a final consonant.***   Double the final consonant of a word when all the following are true:

   a.   The word is one syllable or is accented on the last syllable.

   b.   The word ends in a single consonant preceded by a single vowel.

   c.   The ending you are adding starts with a vowel.

sob   + ing = sobbing   big   + est = biggest

drop   + ed   = dropped   omit   + ed   = omitted

admit + ing = admitting   begin + ing = beginning

Using Correct Endings   ACTIVITY 1

Combine the following words and endings by applying the previous three rules.

HINT   Change *y* to *i* in item 1.

1. hurry   + ed   = _____   6. commit + ed   = _____

2. admire   + ing = _____   7. dive   + ing = _____

3. deny   + es   = _____   8. hasty   + ly   = _____

4. jab   + ing = _____   9. propel   + ing = _____

5. magnify + ed   = _____   10. nudge   + es   = _____

Step 6: Understanding Plurals

Most words form their plurals by adding *-s* to the singular.

Singular	Plural
blanket	blankets
pencil	pencils
street	streets

Some words, however, form their plurals in special ways, as shown in the rules that follow.

- Words ending in *-s, -ss, -z, -x, -sh,* or *-ch* usually form the plural by adding *-es*.

kiss	kisses	inch	inches
box	boxes	dish	dishes

- Words ending in a consonant plus *y* form the plural by changing *y* to *i* and adding *-es.*

party	parties	county	counties
baby	babies	city	cities

- Some words ending in *f* change the *f* to *v* and add *-es* in the plural.

leaf	leaves	life	lives
wife	wives	yourself	yourselves

- Some words ending in *o* form their plurals by adding *-es.*

potato	potatoes	mosquito	mosquitoes
hero	heroes	tomato	tomatoes

- Some words of foreign origin have irregular plurals. When in doubt, check your dictionary.

antenna	antennae	crisis	crises
criterion	criteria	medium	media

- Some words form their plurals by changing letters within the word.

man	men	foot	feet
tooth	teeth	goose	geese

- Combined words (words made up of two or more words) form their plurals by adding *-s* to the main word.

brother-in-law	brothers-in-law
passerby	passersby

ACTIVITY 2	**Using Plural Endings or Forms**

Complete these sentences by filling in the plural of the word at the right.

> **HINT** A word ending in *s* forms the plural by adding *-es.*

1. Nathan told his boss that the metro _____ were running late this morning, which is why he missed the sales meeting.   bus

2. Jorge collects military insignia _____ from World War II.   patc

3. The endocrinologist told Elisa about several new _____ for people with diabetes.   ther.

4. I baked three _____ of chocolate chip cookies for my son's sixth-grade graduation ceremony.   batc

5. The scuba divers explored the coral _____ on the island.   reef

6. Tyler mashed three ripe _____ for the guacamole.   avoc

7. Jarik stopped at the ATM to withdraw two _____ but later wondered if he should have taken out an additional twenty. | fifty

8. The security guard uses a handheld metal detector to find concealed _____ and other weapons. | knife

9. Lynette wishes that at least one of her _____ will get pregnant so that she can become a grandmother. | daughter-in-law

10. I wrote several tentative _____ for my argument essay. | thesis

Step 7: Mastering a Basic Word List

Make sure you can spell all the words in the following list. They are some of the words used most often in English. Again, your instructor may assign twenty words for you to study at a time and give you a series of quizzes until you have mastered the words.

ability	beautiful	daughter
absent	because	death
accident	become	decide
across	before	deposit
address	begin	describe
advertise	being	different
advice	believe	direction
after	between	distance
again	bottom 40	doubt
against	breathe	dozen
all right	building	during
almost	business	each
a lot	careful	early
although	careless	earth
always	cereal	education
among	certain	either
angry	change	English
animal	cheap	enough 80
another	chief	entrance
answer 20	children	everything
anxious	church	examine
apply	cigarette	exercise
approve	clothing	expect
argue	collect	family
around	color	flower
attempt	comfortable	foreign
attention	company	friend
awful	condition	garden
awkward	conversation 60	general
balance	daily	grocery
bargain	danger	guess

happy	ocean	sleep
heard	offer	smoke
heavy	often	something
height	omit	soul
himself	only	started
holiday	operate	state
house 100	opportunity	straight
however	original	street
hundred	ought	strong 200
hungry	pain	student
important	paper	studying
instead	pencil	success
intelligence	people	suffer
interest	perfect	surprise
interfere	period	teach
kitchen	personal	telephone
knowledge	picture	theory
labor	place 160	thought
language	pocket	thousand
laugh	possible	through
leave	potato	ticket
length	president	tired
lesson	pretty	today
letter	problem	together
listen	promise	tomorrow
loneliness	property	tongue
making 120	psychology	tonight
marry	public	touch
match	question	travel 220
matter	quick	truly
measure	raise	understand
medicine	ready	unity
middle	really	until
might	reason	upon
million	receive	usual
minute	recognize	value
mistake	remember	vegetable
money	repeat 180	view
month	restaurant	visitor
morning	ridiculous	voice
mountain	said	warning
much	same	watch
needle	sandwich	welcome
neglect	send	window
newspaper	sentence	would
noise	several	writing
none 140	shoes	written
nothing	should	year
number	since	yesterday 240

CONNECT WRITING

Meet Roberto. He's applying for a part-time construction job. He made a photocopy of the application form and just finished filling it in. He wants to check his answers for spelling mistakes, correct them, and then fill out the actual form. Help Roberto locate and correct all the spelling mistakes in his application.

mhconnectwriting.com

Items 1–10

Use the three basic spelling rules to spell the following words.

1. admire   + able   = _____

2. drop   + ing   = _____

3. big   + est   = _____

4. gamble   + ing   = _____

5. luxury   + es   = _____

6. immediate + ly   = _____

7. imply   + es   = _____

8. plan   + ed   = _____

9. involve   + ment = _____

10. refer   + ed   = _____

Items 11–14

Circle the correctly spelled plural in each pair.

11. daisies   daisys

12. bookshelfs   bookshelves

13. mosquitos   mosquitoes

14. crisis   crises

Items 15–20

Circle the correctly spelled word (from the basic word list) in each pair.

15. tommorrow   tomorrow

16. height   hieght

17. needel   needle

18. visiter   visitor

19. hungry   hungery

20. writting   writing

For additional materials on Chapter 31, visit www.mhhe.com/langan.

Omitted Words and Letters

CHAPTER PREVIEW

Finding Omitted Words and Letters

- Omitted Words
- Omitted –s Endings

INTRODUCTORY ACTIVITY

Some people drop small connecting words such as *of, and,* or *in* when they write. They may also drop the *-s* endings of plural nouns. See if you can find the six places in the passage below where letters or words have been dropped. Supply whatever is missing.

> Two glass bottle of apple juice lie broken the supermarket aisle. Suddenly, a toddler who has gotten away from his parents appears at the head of the aisle. He spots the broken bottles and begins to run toward them. His chubby body lurches along like wind-up toy, and his arm move excitedly up and down. Luckily, alert shopper quickly reacts to the impending disaster and blocks the toddler's path. Then the shopper waits with crying, frustrated little boy until his parents show up.

Answers are on page 634.

Be careful not to leave out words or letters when you write. The omission of words such as *a, an, of, to,* or *the* or the *-s* ending needed on nouns or verbs may confuse and irritate your readers. They may not want to read what they regard as careless work.

Finding Omitted Words and Letters

Finding omitted words and letters, like finding many other sentence-skills mistakes, is a matter of careful proofreading. You must develop your ability to look carefully at a page to find places where mistakes may exist.

The exercises here will give you practice in finding omitted words and omitted *-s* endings on nouns. Another section of this book (pages 211–212) gives you practice in finding omitted *-s* endings on verbs.

Omitted Words

| **Adding Missing Words** | **ACTIVITY 1** |

Add the omitted word (*a, an, the, of,* or *to*) as needed.

EXAMPLE

> Some people regard television as ^atranquilizer that provides temporary relief from ^{the}pain and anxiety ^{of}modern life.

 Four changes are needed in item 1.

1. I grabbed metal bar on roof of subway car as the train lurched into station.

2. For most our country's history, gold was basis the monetary system.

3. Maggie made about a quart French-toast batter—enough soak few dozen slices.

4. Several pairs sneakers tumbled around in dryer and banged against glass door.

5. To err is human and to forgive is divine, but never make a mistake in the first place takes lot of luck.

6. Raccoons like wash their food in stream with their nimble, glovelike hands before eating.

7. When I got the grocery store, I realized I had left my shopping list in glove compartment my car.

8. Reality shows are inexpensive way for networks make high profit.

9. Soap operas, on other hand, are very expensive to produce because the high salaries of many cast members.

10. One memorable Friday the thirteenth, a friend mine bought black cat and broken mirror and walked under ladder. He had a wonderful day!

Omitted -s Endings

The plural form of regular nouns usually ends in *-s*. One common mistake that some people make with plurals is to omit this *-s* ending. People who drop the ending from plurals when speaking also tend to do it when writing. This tendency is especially noticeable when the meaning of the sentence shows that a word is plural.

Ed and Mary pay seven hundred dollar a month for an apartment that has only two room.

The -*s* ending has been omitted from *dollars* and *rooms*.

The activities that follow will help you correct the habit of omitting the -*s* endings from plurals.

| ACTIVITY 2 | Using -*s* Endings |

Add -*s* endings where needed.

EXAMPLE

Bill beat me at several game^s of darts.

> # HINT   Two -*s* endings are needed in item 1.

CONNECT WRITING

Meet Roberto. He's applying for a part-time construction job and needs to submit a cover letter with his application form. After looking at the first draft of his letter he knows he's omitted words. Help Roberto locate all the omitted words in his cover letter and make the necessary corrections.

mhconnectwriting.com

1. Many sightseer flocked around the disaster area like ghoul.

2. Martha has two set of twins, and all of their name rhyme.

3. Dozen of beetle are eating away at the rosebush in our yard.

4. Since a convention of dentist was in town, all the restaurant had waiting line.

5. Until the first of the year, worker in all department will not be permitted any overtime.

6. Blinking light, such as those on video game or police car, can trigger seizures in person with epilepsy.

7. Ray and his friends invented several game using an old rubber radiator hose and two plastic ball.

8. My thirteen-year-old has grown so much lately that she doesn't fit into the shoe and jean I bought for her a couple of month ago.

9. While cleaning out her desk drawers, Ann found a page of postage stamp stuck together and a couple of dried-up pen.

10. Worker fed large log and chunk of wood into the huge machine, which spit out chip and sawdust from its other end.

Writing with Plural Forms

Write sentences that use plural forms of the following pairs of words.

EXAMPLE

file, folder <u>I save my computer files in folders on the desktop.</u>

1. gambler, casino

   _____

   _____

2. recycling bin, bottle

   _____

   _____

3. diver, shark

   _____

   _____

4. sports fan, game

   _____

   _____

5. cherry, grape

   _____

   _____

> **T I P** People who drop the -s ending on nouns also tend to omit endings on verbs. Pages 211–212 will help you correct the habit of dropping verb endings.

Insert the two small connecting words needed in each sentence.

1. When I opened freezer door, box of ice cream fell out.

2. Hiking along trail next to the lake, we came to very muddy stretch.

3. The newlyweds rented apartment with two rooms and bath.

4. I had walk all the way up to our fifth-floor office because elevator was broken.

5. Unfortunately, the road leading wealth is a lot longer than one leading to poverty.

REVIEW TEST 2

Insert the two -s endings needed in each sentence.

1. The animal shelter finds people who are willing to adopt abandoned dog and cat.

2. Teacher who are strict help student learn how to be responsible.

3. I brought home dozen of brochure from the job fair.

4. Now that I am forty, I can see fine wrinkle line at the corners of my eye.

5. I failed to read the direction carefully, so I missed several answer.

For additional materials on Chapter 32, visit **www.mhhe.com/langan**.

Commonly Confused Words

CHAPTER 33

INTRODUCTORY ACTIVITY

Circle the five words that are misspelled in the following passage. Then write their correct spellings in the spaces provided.

If your a resident of a temperate climate, you may suffer from feelings of depression in the winter and early spring. Scientists are now studying people who's moods seem to worsen in winter, and there findings show that the amount of daylight a person receives is an important factor in "seasonal depression." When a person gets to little sunlight, his or her mood darkens. Its fairly easy to treat severe cases of seasonal depression; the cure involves spending a few hours a day in front of full-spectrum fluorescent lights that contain all the components of natural light.

1. _____
2. _____
3. _____
4. _____
5. _____

Answers are on page 634.

CHAPTER PREVIEW

Homonyms

Other Words Frequently Confused

Incorrect Word Forms

Homonyms

The following commonly confused words are known as *homonyms;* they have the same sounds but different meanings and spellings. Complete the activities for each set of words, and check off and study any words that give you trouble.

COMMON HOMONYMS

all ready	knew	principal	to
already	new	principle	too
			two
brake	know	right	
break	no	write	wear
			where
coarse	pair	than	
course	pear	then	weather
			whether
hear	passed	their	
here	past	there	whose
		they're	who's
hole	peace		
whole	piece	threw	your
		through	you're
its	plain		
it's	plane		

ACTIVITY 1	**Homonyms**

all ready　　completely prepared

already　　previously, before

　　We were *all ready* to go, for we had eaten and packed *already* that morning.

Fill in the blanks: Phil was _____ for his driver's test, since he

had _____ memorized the questions and regulations.

Write sentences using *all ready* and *already.*

_____

_____

brake　　stop

break　　come apart

　　Dot slams the *brake* pedal so hard that I'm afraid I'll *break* my neck in her car.

Fill in the blanks: While attempting to _____ a speed record, the

racecar driver had to _____ for a spectator who had wandered

onto the track.

Write sentences using *brake* and *break.*

_____

_____

coarse   rough

course   part of a meal; a school subject; direction; certainly (with *of*)

Micah muttered in a *coarse* tone, "Of *course* you know it all."

Fill in the blanks: The first _____, fresh oysters, included several

_____ grains of sand.

Write sentences using *coarse* and *course*.

_____

_____

hear   perceive with the ear

here   in this place

If I *hear* another insulting ethnic joke *here,* I'll leave.

Fill in the blanks: Unless you sit right _____ in one of the front rows, you

won't be able to _____ a single thing the soft-spoken lecturer says.

Write sentences using *hear* and *here*.

_____

_____

hole   empty spot

whole   entire

If there is a *hole* in the tailpipe, I'm afraid we will have to replace the
whole exhaust assembly.

Fill in the blanks: If you eat the _____ portion of chili, it will prob-

ably burn a _____ in your stomach.

Write sentences using *hole* and *whole*.

_____

_____

its   belonging to it

it's   contraction of *it is* or *it has*

The kitchen floor has lost *its* shine because *it's* been used as a roller-
skating rink by the children.

Fill in the blanks: Our living-room carpet has lost _____ vivid color

since _____ been exposed to so much sunlight.

Write sentences using *its* and *it's*.

_____

_____

knew   past tense of *know*

new   not old

I *knew* that the *new* resident manager would work out fine.

Fill in the blanks: As soon as I put on my _____ white shoes, I _____ that my puppy would soil them.

Write sentences using *knew* and *new.*

_____

_____

know   to understand

no   a negative

I never *know* who might drop in even though *no* one is expected.

Fill in the blanks: I _____ there are _____ openings in your company at present, but please keep my résumé in case anything turns up.

Write sentences using *know* and *no.*

_____

_____

pair   set of two

pear   fruit

The dessert consisted of a *pair* of thin biscuits topped with vanilla ice cream and poached *pear* halves.

Fill in the blanks: We spotted a _____ of bluejays on our dwarf _____ tree.

Write sentences using *pair* and *pear.*

_____

_____

passed   went by; succeeded in; handed to

past   time before the present; by, as in "I drove past the house."

After Edna *passed* the driver's test, she drove *past* all her friends' houses and honked the horn.

Fill in the blanks: Norman couldn't understand why he'd been _____ over for the promotion, because his _____ work had been very good.

Write sentences using *passed* and *past*.

_____

_____

peace   calm

piece   part

    The *peace* of the little town was shattered when a *piece* of a human body was found in the town dump.

Fill in the blanks: We ate in _____ until my two brothers started

fighting over who would get the last _____ of blueberry pie.

Write sentences using *peace* and *piece*.

_____

_____

plain   simple

plane   aircraft

    The *plain* truth is that I'm afraid to fly in a *plane*.

Fill in the blanks: The officials were surprised to find the stolen government

_____ parked in _____ view.

Write sentences using *plain* and *plane*.

_____

_____

principal   main; a person in charge of a school; amount of money
                 borrowed

principle   law or standard

    My *principal* goal in child rearing is to give my daughter strong *principles* to live by.

Fill in the blanks: My _____ reason for turning down the part-

time job is that it's against my _____s to work on weekends.

Write sentences using *principal* and *principle*.

_____

_____

HINT It might help to remember that the *e* in *principle* is also in *rule*— the meaning of *principle*.

right   correct; opposite of *left;* something to which one is entitled

write   to put words on paper

It is my *right* to refuse to *write* my name on your petition.

Fill in the blanks: The instructor said if the students' outlines were not

_____, they would have to _____ them again.

Write sentences using *right* and *write.*

_____

_____

than   used in comparisons

then   at that time

I glared angrily at my boss, and *then* I told him our problems were more serious *than* he suspected.

Fill in the blanks: Felix hiked seven miles and _____ chopped fire-

wood; he was soon more tired _____ he'd been in years.

Write sentences using *than* and *then.*

_____

_____

 It might help to remember that *then* (the word spelled with an *e*) is a time signal (*time* also has an *e*).

their   belonging to them

there   at that place; a neutral word used with verbs such as *is, are, was, were, have,* and *had*

they're   contraction of *they are*

The customers *there* are satisfied because *they're* being given a discount on *their* purchases.

Fill in the blanks: I told the owner of the video store that I'm going _____

right after work so that I can return _____ DVDs, and fortunately

_____ not going to charge me a late fee.

Write sentences using *their, there,* and *they're.*

_____

_____

threw   past tense of *throw*

through   from one side to the other; finished

When a character in a movie *threw* a cat *through* the window, I had to close my eyes.

Fill in the blanks: When Lee was finally _____ studying for her

psychology final, she _____ her textbook and notes into her closet.

Write sentences using *threw* and *through.*

_____

_____

to	verb part, as in *to smile;* toward, as in "I'm going to school."
too	overly, as in "The pizza was *too* hot"; also, as in "The coffee was hot, *too.*"
two	the number 2

Bryce went *to* college *to* earn a degree in computer science. (The first *to* means *toward;* the second *to* is a verb part that goes with *earn.*)

Movie tickets are *too expensive;* popcorn and drinks are expensive, *too.* (The first *too* means *overly;* the second *too* means *also.*)

The *two* couples went on a double date. (the number 2)

Fill in the blanks: My _____ coworkers are _____ polite _____ tell me the

truth.

Write sentences using *to, too,* and *two.*

_____

_____

CONNECT WRITING

Meet Roberto. He's working on his résumé to apply for a part-time construction job, but he thinks he may have used some words incorrectly. Help Roberto locate and correct all the commonly confused words in his résumé.

mhconnectwriting.com

wear	to have on
where	in what place

I work at a nuclear reactor, *where* one must *wear* a radiation-detection badge at all times.

Fill in the blanks: At the college _____ Ann goes, almost all the

students _____ very casual clothes to class.

Write sentences using *wear* and *where.*

_____

_____

weather	atmospheric conditions
whether	if it happens that; in case; if

Because of the threatening *weather,* it's not certain *whether* the game will be played.

Fill in the blanks: After I hear the _____ report, I'll decide

_____ I'll drive or take the train to my sister's house.

Write sentences using *weather* and *whether*.

_____

_____

whose   belonging to whom

who's   contraction of *who is* and *who has*

The man *who's* the author of the latest diet book is a man *whose* ability to cash in on the latest craze is well known.

Fill in the blanks: The cousin _____ visiting us is the one _____ car was just demolished by a tractor trailer.

Write sentences using *whose* and *who's*.

_____

_____

your   belonging to you

you're   contraction of *you are*

Since *your* family has a history of heart disease, *you're* the kind of person who should take extra health precautions.

Fill in the blanks: If _____ not going to eat any more, could I have what's left on _____ plate?

Write sentences using *your* and *you're*.

_____

_____

Other Words Frequently Confused

Following is a list of other words that people frequently confuse. Complete the activities for each set of words, and check off and study the ones that give you trouble.

COMMONLY CONFUSED WORDS			
a	among	desert	learn
an	between	dessert	teach
accept	beside	does	loose
except	besides	dose	lose
advice	can	fewer	quiet
advise	may	less	quite
affect	clothes	former	though
effect	cloths	latter	thought

Commonly Confused Words

a, an Both *a* and *an* are used before other words to mean, approximately, *one.*

Generally you should use *an* before words starting with a vowel (*a, e, i, o, u*):

an absence   an exhibit   an idol   an offer   an upgrade

Generally you should use *a* before words starting with a consonant (all other letters):

a pen   a ride   a digital clock   a movie   a neighbor

Fill in the blanks: When it comes to eating, I am lucky; I can eat like

_____ elephant and stay as thin as _____ snake.

Write sentences using *a* and *an.*

_____

_____

accept receive; agree to

except exclude; but

If I *accept* your advice, I'll lose all my friends *except* you.

Fill in the blanks: Everyone _____ my parents was delighted when

I decided to _____ the out-of-town job offer.

Write sentences using *accept* and *except.*

_____

_____

advice noun meaning *an opinion*

advise verb meaning *to counsel, to give advice*

Jake never listened to his parents' *advice,* and he ended up listening to a cop *advise* him of his rights.

Fill in the blanks: My father once gave me some good _____:

never _____ people on anything unless they ask you to.

Write sentences using *advice* and *advise.*

_____

_____

affect verb meaning *to influence*

effect verb meaning *to bring about something;* noun meaning *result*

My sister Sarah cries for *effect*, but her act no longer *affects* my parents.

Fill in the blanks: Some school officials think suspension will _____ students positively, but many students think its main _____ is time off from school.

Write sentences using affect *and* effect.

_____

_____

among   implies three or more

between   implies only two

At the end of the meal, my sister and I split the cost *between* the two of us rather than *among* all the people in our party.

Fill in the blanks: I told my assistant to look _____ my files for the report that I placed _____ two folders.

Write sentences using among *and* between.

_____

_____

beside   along the side of

besides   in addition to

Jared sat *beside* Jen. *Besides* them, there were ten other people at the Tupperware party.

Fill in the blanks: Elena refused to sit _____ Carlos in class because he always fidgeted, and, _____, he couldn't keep his mouth shut.

Write sentences using beside *and* besides.

_____

_____

can   refers to the ability to do something

may   refers to permission or possibility

If you *can* work overtime on Saturday, you *may* take Monday off.

Fill in the blanks: Joanne certainly _____ handle the project, but she _____ not have time to complete it by the deadline.

Write sentences using can *and* may.

_____

_____

clothes   articles of dress

cloths   pieces of fabric

I tore up some old *clothes* to use as polishing *cloths.*

Fill in the blanks: I keep a bag of dust _____ in the corner of

my _____ closet.

Write sentences using *clothes* and *cloths.*

_____

_____

desert   a stretch of dry land; to abandon one's post or duty

dessert   last part of a meal

Don't *desert* us now; order a sinful *dessert* along with us.

Fill in the blanks: I know my willpower will _____ me whenever

there are brownies for _____.

Write sentences using *desert* and *dessert.*

_____

_____

does   form of the verb *do*

dose   amount of medicine

Eve *does* not realize that a *dose* of brandy is not the best medicine for
the flu.

Fill in the blanks: A _____ of aspirin _____ wonders for Sue's

arthritis.

Write sentences using *does* and *dose.*

_____

_____

fewer   used with things that can be counted

less   refers to amount, value, or degree

I missed *fewer* writing classes than Rafael, but I wrote *less* effectively
than he did.

Fill in the blanks: Francesca is taking _____ courses this semester

because she has _____ free time than she did last year.

Write sentences using *fewer* and *less.*

_____

_____

former	refers to the first of two items named
latter	refers to the second of two items named

I applied for two jobs at the employment office; the *former* involves working with preschool children, and the *latter* involves working in sales.

Fill in the blanks: My toddler enjoys eating both fruits and vegetables; the _____ includes bananas and pears, and the _____ includes beans and squash.

Write sentences using *former* and *latter*.

_____

_____

 HINT   Be sure to distinguish *latter* from *later* (meaning *after some time*).

learn	to gain knowledge
teach	to give knowledge

After Roz *learns* the new dance, she is going to *teach* it to me.

Fill in the blanks: My dog is very smart; she can _____ any new trick I _____ her in just minutes.

Write sentences using *learn* and *teach*.

_____

_____

loose	not fastened; not tight-fitting
lose	misplace; fail to win

I am afraid I'll *lose* my ring; it's too *loose* on my finger.

Fill in the blanks: Those slippers are so _____ that every time I take a step, I _____ one.

Write sentences using *loose* and *lose*.

_____

_____

quiet	peaceful
quite	entirely; really; rather

After a busy day, the children were not *quiet,* and their parents were *quite* tired.

Fill in the blanks: After moving furniture all day, Vince was _____

exhausted, so he found a _____ place and lay down for a nap.

Write sentences using *quiet* and *quite.*

_____

_____

though   despite the fact that

thought   past tense of *think*

     Though I enjoyed the band, I *thought* the cover charge of forty dollars
was too high.

Fill in the blanks: Even _____ my paper was two weeks late,

I _____ the instructor would accept it.

Write sentences using *though* and *thought.*

_____

_____

Incorrect Word Forms

Following is a list of incorrect word forms that people sometimes use in
their writing. Complete the activities for each word, and check off and
study any words that give you trouble.

INCORRECT WORD FORMS		
being that	could of	should of
can't hardly	irregardless	would of
couldn't hardly	must of	

Incorrect Word Forms	**ACTIVITY 3**

being that   Incorrect! Use *because* or *since.*
     I'm going to bed now ~~being that~~ I must get up early tomorrow. *(because)*

Correct the following sentences.

1. Being that our stove doesn't work, we'll have tuna salad for dinner.

2. I never invite both of my aunts over together, being that they don't
   speak to each other.

3. I'm taking a day off tomorrow being that it's my birthday.

can't hardly   Incorrect! Use *can hardly* or *could hardly*.

couldn't hardly

Small store owners ~~can't~~ ^{can} hardly afford to offer large discounts.

Correct the following sentences.

1. I couldn't hardly enjoy myself at the theater because my brother gave me a play-by-play account of the entire movie, which he had seen three times.

2. I can't hardly believe that I spent over fifty dollars on gasoline to fill up my SUV.

3. By one o'clock in the afternoon, everyone can't hardly keep from falling asleep in class.

could of   Incorrect! Use *could have*.

I could ~~of~~ ^{have} done better on that test.

Correct the following sentences.

1. The sidewalk was so hot you could of toasted bread on it.

2. The moon was so bright you could of read by it.

3. The peach pie was so good that I could of eaten it all.

irregardless   Incorrect! Use *regardless*.

~~Irregardless~~ <u>Regardless</u> of what anyone says, he will not change his mind.

Correct the following sentences.

1. Irregardless of your feelings about customers, you must treat them with courtesy.

2. Jay jogs every day irregardless of the weather.

3. Anyone can learn to read irregardless of age.

must of   Incorrect! Use *must have, should have, would have*.

should of

would of

I should ~~of~~ ^{have} applied for a loan when my credit was good.

Correct the following sentences.

1. I must of dozed off during the movie.

2. If Marty hadn't missed class yesterday, he would of known about today's test.

3. You should of told me to stop at the supermarket.

REVIEW TEST 1

These sentences check your understanding of *its, it's; there, their, they're; to, too, two;* and *your, you're.* Underline the correct word in the parentheses. Rather than guess, look back at the explanations of the words when necessary.

1. It seems whenever (your, you're) at the doctor's office, (your, you're) symptoms disappear.

2. The boss asked his assistant (to, too, two) rearrange the insurance files, placing each in (its, it's) proper sequence.

3. You'll get (your, you're) share of the pizza when (its, it's) cool enough (to, too, two) eat.

4. (Its, It's) a terrible feeling when (your, you're) (to, too, two) late (to, too, two) help someone.

5. (To, Too, Two) eat insects, most spiders use their (to, too, two) fangs to inject a special poison that turns (there, their, they're) victim's flesh into a soupy liquid they can drink.

6. (Its, It's) a fact that (there, their, they're) are (to, too, two) many violent shows on TV.

7. (There, Their, They're) is no valid reason for the (to, too, two) of you (to, too, two) have forgotten about turning in (your, you're) assignments.

8. If you (to, too, two) continue (to, too, two) drive so fast, (its, it's) likely you'll get ticketed by the police.

9. "My philosophy on guys is that (there, their, they're) just like buses," said Regina. "If you miss one, (there, their, they're) is always another one coming by in a little while."

10. "(Its, It's) about time you (to, too, two) showed up," the manager huffed. "(There, Their, They're) is already a line of customers waiting outside."

REVIEW TEST 2

The following sentences check your understanding of a variety of commonly confused words. Underline the correct word in the parentheses. Rather than guess, look back at the explanations of the words when necessary.

1. When (your, you're) (plain, plane) arrives, call us (weather, whether) (its, it's) late or not.

2. You (should have, should of) first found out (whose, who's) really (to, too, two) blame before coming in (hear, here) and making false accusations.

3. When Jack drove (threw, through) his old neighborhood, he (could hardly, couldn't hardly) recognize some of the places he (knew, new) as a child.

4. The (affect, effect) of having drunk (to, too, two) much alcohol last night was something like having (a, an) jackhammer drilling (among, between) my ears.

5. I was (quiet, quite) surprised to learn that in the (passed, past), (our, are) town was the site of (a, an) Revolutionary War battle.

6. Of (coarse, course) (its, it's) important to get good grades while (your, you're) in school, but it (does, dose) not hurt to (know, now, no) the (right, write) people when (your, you're) looking for a job.

7. If (your, you're) interested in listening to a great album, take my (advice, advise) and pick up a copy of *Sgt. Pepper's Lonely Hearts Club Band*; (its, it's) been voted the most popular rock album in history.

8. (Being that, Since) Barry has failed all five quizzes and one major exam and didn't hand in the midterm paper, he (though, thought) it would be a good idea (to, too, two) drop the (coarse, course).

9. (Their, There, They're) is (know, no) greater feeling (than, then) that of walking (threw, through) a forest in the spring.

10. I spent the (hole, whole) day looking (threw, through) my history notes, but when it came time to take the exam, I still (could hardly, couldn't hardly) understand the similarities (among, between) the Korean War, World War I, and World War II.

REVIEW TEST 3

On a separate piece of paper, write short sentences using the ten words shown below.

their	effect
your	passed
it's	here
then	brake
too (meaning *also*)	whose

For additional materials on Chapter 33, visit **www.mhhe.com/langan**.

INTRODUCTORY ACTIVITY

Put a check beside the sentence in each pair that makes more effective and appropriate use of words.

1. After shooting hoops with my bros, I downed a soda. _____

   After playing basketball with my friends, I quickly drank a soda. _____

2. Even though my essay was short and sweet, I gave 110 percent. _____

   Even though my essay was concise, I tried my best. _____

3. I will endeavor to finalize the report subsequent to lunch. _____

   I will try to finish the report after lunch. _____

4. In the event that my daughter calls during the time that I am in a meeting, please tell her that I am unavailable at the present time. _____

   If my daughter calls while I am in a meeting, please tell her that I am unavailable. _____

Now see if you can circle the correct number in each case:

Pair (1, 2, 3, 4) contains a sentence with slang; pair (1, 2, 3, 4) contains a sentence with a cliché; pair (1, 2, 3, 4) contains a sentence with inflated words; and pair (1, 2, 3, 4) contains a wordy sentence.

Answers are on page 635.

CHAPTER PREVIEW

Slang

Clichés

Inflated Words

Wordiness

Choose your words carefully when you write. Always take the time to think about your word choices, rather than simply using the first word that comes to mind. You want to develop the habit of selecting words that are appropriate and exact for your purposes. One way you can show sensitivity to language is by avoiding slang, clichés, inflated words, and wordiness.

Slang

We often use slang expressions when we talk because they are so vivid and colorful. However, slang is usually out of place in formal writing. Here are some examples of slang expressions:

I heard that Dominique's date was just *arm candy*.

House music is *sick*.

Josh is too *web shy*.

My boss hates it when I *reverse telecommute*.

The Red Bull I drank to *pull an all-nighter* was *fierce*.

Sadly, some of the designs on <u>Project Runway</u> don't have the *wow factor*.

I heard that Sam's *DJing* was *über cool*.

The photos you uploaded are *facebookable*.

Slang expressions have a number of drawbacks. They go out of date quickly, they become tiresome if used excessively in writing, and they may communicate clearly to some readers but not to others. Also, the use of slang can be an evasion of the specific details that are often needed to make one's meaning clear in writing. For example, in "Dominique's date was just arm candy," the writer has not provided specific details about Dominique's date necessary for us to understand the statement clearly. What was it about her date's appearance—physique, height, hair style, clothing, smile— that made this person so attractive? In general, then, you should avoid slang in your writing. If you are in doubt about whether an expression is slang, it may help to check a recently published hardbound dictionary.

| ACTIVITY 1 | **Avoiding Slang** |

Rewrite the following sentences, replacing the italicized slang words with more formal ones.

EXAMPLE

I was so *bummed* when my teacher *got on my case*.

I was so discouraged when my teacher scolded me.

 In item 1, consider: what do "two-timing" and "My bad" mean?

1. When I confronted my ex-boyfriend about *two-timing* me, he simply shrugged and said, "*My bad*."

   _____

   _____

2. My friend thinks that Chantel is *phat*, but I think she's too *emo*.

   _____

   _____

3. Rayna is on her cell phone *24-7*, but *it's all good.*

   _____

   _____

4. Joe wanted to *blow* the family dinner so that he could *hook up* with his friends.

   _____

   _____

5. Everyone at the gym thinks that Gavin is *juicing*, but he swears that he doesn't use *roids* to get his *six-pack*.

   _____

   _____

CONNECT WRITING

Meet Antonio. He works as a student intern at the career counseling center on his college campus. A former student has asked him to make sense of a meeting agenda from her new job. The agenda contains so many slang terms that she can't figure out what's going to be discussed at the upcoming meeting. Help Antonio locate and correct the slang used in the agenda.

mhconnectwriting.com

Clichés

Clichés are expressions that have been worn out through constant use. Some typical clichés are listed below.

COMMON CLICHÉS	
all work and no play	sad but true
at a loss for words	saw the light
better late than never	short and sweet
drop in the bucket	sigh of relief
easier said than done	singing the blues
had a hard time of it	taking a big chance
in the nick of time	time and time again
in this day and age	too close for comfort
it dawned on me	too little, too late
it goes without saying	took a turn for the worse
last but not least	under the weather
make ends meet	where he (*or* she) is coming from
needless to say	word to the wise
on top of the world	work like a dog

Clichés are common in speech but make your writing seem tired and stale. Also, they are often an evasion of the specific details that you must work to provide in your writing. You should, then, avoid clichés and try to express your meaning in fresh, original ways.

ACTIVITY 2   Avoiding Clichés

CONNECT WRITING

Meet Antonio. He works as a student intern at the career counseling center on his college campus. A former student has asked him to make sense of a memo he received from one of his supervisors. The memo is confusing because the supervisor used clichés instead of being direct and to the point. Help Antonio locate and correct the clichés in the memo.

mhconnectwriting.com

Underline the cliché in each of the following sentences. Then substitute specific, fresh words for the trite expression.

EXAMPLE

My parents supported me through some <u>trying times.</u>

rough years

> **HINT**   In item 1, *to make a long story short* is a cliché.

1. To make a long story short, my sister decided to file for divorce.

    _____

2. As quick as a wink, the baby tipped over the open box of oatmeal.

    _____

3. Any advice my friends give me goes in one ear and out the other.

    _____

4. I felt like a million dollars when I got my first A on a college test.

    _____

5. These days, well-paying jobs for high school graduates are few and far between.

    _____

WRITING ASSIGNMENT

Write a short paragraph describing the kind of day you had yesterday. Try to put as many clichés as possible into your writing. For example, "I had a long hard day. I had a lot to get done, and I kept my nose to the grindstone." By making yourself aware of clichés in this way, you should lessen the chance that they will appear in your writing.

Inflated Words

Some people feel that they can improve their writing by using fancy, elevated words rather than simpler, more natural words. But artificial and stilted language more often obscures their meaning than communicates it clearly.

Here are some unnatural-sounding sentences:

The football combatants left the gridiron.

His instructional technique is a very positive one.

At the counter, we inquired about the arrival time of the aircraft.

I observed the perpetrator of the robbery depart from the retail establishment.

The same thoughts can be expressed more clearly and effectively by using plain, natural language:

The football players left the field.

His teaching style energizes students.

At the counter, we asked when the plane would arrive.

I saw the robber leave the store.

Following is a list of some other inflated words and the simple words that could replace them.

Inflated Words	Simpler Words
component	part
delineate	describe
facilitate	help
finalize	finish
initiate	begin
manifested	shown
subsequent to	after
to endeavor	to try
transmit	send

Avoiding Inflated Words

ACTIVITY 3

Cross out the two inflated words in each sentence. Then substitute clear, simple language for the inflated words.

EXAMPLE

Sally was ~~terminated~~ from her ~~employment~~.

Sally was fired from her job.

> **HINT** In item 1, replace *query* and *associates* with simpler words.

1. Please query one of our sales associates.

   _____

   _____

2. The meteorological conditions are terrible today.

   _____

   _____

3. My parents desire me to obtain a college degree.

    _____

    _____

4. Do not protrude your arm out of the car, or an accident might ensue.

    _____

    _____

5. Many conflagrations are caused by the careless utilization of portable heaters.

    _____

    _____

Wordiness

Wordiness—using more words than necessary to express a meaning—is often a sign of lazy or careless writing. Your readers may resent the extra time and energy they must spend when you have not done the work needed to make your writing direct and concise.

Here is a list of some wordy expressions that could be reduced to single words.

Wordy Form	Short Form
a large number of	many
a period of a week	a week
arrive at an agreement	agree
at an earlier point in time	before
at the present time	now
big in size	big
due to the fact that	because
during the time that	while
five in number	five
for the reason that	because
good benefit	benefit
in every instance	always
in my opinion	I think
in the event that	if
in the near future	soon
in this day and age	today
is able to	can
large in size	large

plan ahead for the future	plan
postponed until later	postponed
red in color	red
return back	return

Here are examples of wordy sentences:

At this point in time in our country, the amount of violence seems to be increasing every day.

I called to the children repeatedly to get their attention, but my shouts did not get any response from them.

Omitting needless words improves these sentences:

Violence is increasing in our country.

I called to the children repeatedly, but they didn't respond.

Omitting Unnecessary Words

ACTIVITY 4

Rewrite the following sentences, cutting unnecessary words.

EXAMPLE

Starting as of the month of June, I will be working at the store on a full-time basis.

As of June, I will be working at the store full-time.

 In item 1, the first part of the sentence and *as of yet* are wordy.

1. It is a well-known and proven fact that there is no cure as of yet for the common cold.

   _____

2. The main point that I will try to make in this paper is that our state should legalize and permit gambling.

   _____

3. Due to the fact that Chen's car refused to start up, he had to take public transportation by bus to his place of work.

   _____

4. When I was just a little boy, I already knew in my mind that my goal was to be a stockbroker in the future of my life.

   _____

5. The exercises that Susan does every day of the week give her more energy with which to deal with the happenings of everyday life.

   _____

CONNECT WRITING

Meet Eva. She works as an intern at the career counseling center on her college campus. She's helping a student revise an email message to his new supervisor. The email is unclear because the student has written too many wordy phrases. Help Eva locate all the wordy phrases and revise the message using clear and concise wording.

mhconnectwriting.com

REVIEW TEST 1

Certain words are italicized in the following sentences. In the space provided, identify whether the words are slang (*S*), clichés (*C*), or inflated words (*IW*). Then replace them with more effective words.

_____   1.   Donna *came out of her shell* after she joined a singing group at school.

_____

_____   2.   The receptionist *penciled me in* for next Friday.

_____

_____   3.   I'm *suffering from a temporary depletion of all cash reserves.*

_____

_____   4.   That was *totally random* of me.

_____

_____   5.   I got angry at the park visitors who did not put their *waste materials* in the *trash receptacle.*

_____

_____   6.   Hearing I had passed the accounting final really *took a load off my mind.*

_____

_____   7.   We all thought it was *too good to be true* when the instructor said that most of us would get A's in the course.

_____

_____   8.   Fred *asserted to* the collection agency that he had sent the *remuneration.*

_____

_____   9.   Even though Brad's married, he still enjoys *eye candy.*

_____

_____   10.   This book was written by a millionaire who *didn't have a dime to his name* as a boy.

_____

Rewrite the following sentences, omitting unnecessary words.

1. At 6:00 early this morning, I suddenly heard a loud and noisy banging by someone at the front door of my apartment.

    _____

    _____

2. The fact of the matter is that I did not remember until, of course, just now that I had an appointment to meet you.

    _____

    _____

3. We are very pleased to have the opportunity to inform you that your line of credit on your credit card with us has just been increased.

    _____

    _____

4. At this point in time, the company has no plan of adding to anyone's salary by giving a raise in pay in the near or distant future.

    _____

    _____

5. If you are out on the job market seeking a job, you just might benefit from professional help to assist you in your search for employment.

    _____

    _____

For additional materials on Chapter 34, visit www.mhhe.com/langan.

A WRITER'S TEMPLATE

See if you can locate and correct the eight sentence-skills mistakes in the following passage written by Quang for a geography class. The mistakes are listed in the box below. As you locate each mistake, write the number of the sentence containing that mistake. Use the spaces provided. Then, on a separate sheet of paper, correct the mistakes.

Where in the World?

¹Lines of latitude and longitude is the imaginary grid geographers use to locate places on the earth. ²Latitude is the position of a point on the earths surface in relation to the equator. ³The distance is measured in degrees beginning at the equator and going toward one of the earth's poles. ⁴Any point on the equator has a latitude of zero degrees. ⁵This is written 0°. ⁶The north pole has a latitude of 90° north, and the South Pole has a latitude of 90° south. ⁷As a result a point halfway between the North Pole and the equator would be located at 45° north. ⁸Lines of longitude are imaginary lines running north and south, they divide the globe into 360 equal slices. ⁹The main lines of longitude are called meridians. ¹⁰All meridians pass through the North and South Poles. ¹¹The prime meridian or first meridian is the imaginary line that runs from the North Pole to the South Pole and passes through Greenwich, England, just outside London. ¹²This line is 0° longitude. ¹³So, now can you find your global address?

---

1 run-on _____	1 apostrophe mistake _____
1 mistake in subject-verb agreement _____	2 capitalization mistakes _____
1 missing comma after introductory words _____	2 missing commas around an interrupter _____

A WRITER'S CHECKLIST: Sentence Skills

Clear and Correct Sentences

✔ My paragraph/essay is free of fragments.

✔ My paragraph/essay contains no comma splices or fused sentences.

✔ Throughout, my sentence structure is varied.

Verbs, Pronouns, and Agreement

✔ In every sentence, my subjects agree with my verbs.

✔ I use verb tenses consistently.

✔ When I use pronouns, it is clear what (or which) noun they refer to.

Modifiers and Parallelism

✔ I use adjectives and adverbs correctly.

✔ My sentences contain no misplaced or dangling modifiers; it is clear what each modifier refers to.

✔ I have avoided faulty parallelism in my paragraph/essay.

Punctuation and Mechanics

✔ I use capitalization in appropriate places.

✔ I use end punctuation, apostrophes, quotation marks, commas, and other forms of punctuation correctly.

✔ I formatted my paper according to my instructor's guidelines or the instructions in Chapter 22.

Word Use

✔ I looked up any words whose meanings or spellings I was unsure of in a dictionary. I also used a spell-checker.

✔ I did not misuse any of the commonly confused words listed in Chapter 33.

✔ Throughout, I was careful to choose my words effectively, according to the guidelines in Chapter 34. I have avoided slang, clichés, inflated words, and wordiness.

CORRECTION SYMBOLS

Here is a list of symbols your instructor may use when marking papers. The numbers in parentheses refer to the pages that explain the skill involved.

agr	Correct the mistake in agreement of subject and verb (231–240) or pronoun and the word the pronoun refers to (252–262).
apos	Correct the apostrophe mistake (342–353).
bal	Balance the parts of the sentence so they have the same (parallel) form (295–303).
cap	Correct the mistake in capital letters (324–333).
coh	Revise to improve coherence (67–73; 76–77).
comma	Add a comma (365–378).
CS	Correct the comma splice (179–194).
DM	Correct the dangling modifier (289–294).
det	Support or develop the topic more fully by adding details (50–67; 75–76).
frag	Attach the fragment to a sentence or make it a sentence (162–178).
lc	Use a lowercase (small) letter rather than a capital (324–333).
MM	Correct the misplaced modifier (283–288).
¶	Indent for a new paragraph.
no ¶	Do not indent for a new paragraph.
pro	Correct the pronoun mistake (252–274).
quot	Correct the mistake in quotation marks (354–364).
R-O	Correct the run-on (179–194).
sp	Correct the spelling error (385–422).
trans	Supply or improve a transition (67–73).
und	Underline (359–360).
verb	Correct the verb or verb form (209–230; 241–251).
wordy	Omit needless words (428–431).

WC	Replace the word marked with a more accurate one (word choice).
?	Write the illegible word clearly.
/	Eliminate the word, letter, or punctuation mark so slashed.
^	Add the omitted word or words.
;/:/-/—	Add semicolon (380), colon (379); hyphen (382), or dash (381).
✓	You have something fine or good here: an expression, a detail, an idea.

PART

Readings for Writers

GOALS AND VALUES

Sister Helen Mrosla, "All the Good Things," p. 442

Paul Logan, "Rowing the Bus," p. 448

Rick Bragg, "All She Has—$150,000—Is Going to a University," p. 455

Mee Her, "Bowling to Find a Lost Father," p. 462

Rose Del Castillo Guilbault, "The Conveyor-Belt Ladies," p. 468

Firoozeh Dumas, "The 'F Word,'" p. 475

EDUCATION AND SELF-IMPROVEMENT

Ben Carson, "Do It Better," p. 483

Janny Scott, "How They Get You to Do That," p. 492

Grant Berry, "A Change of Attitude," p. 501

Beth Johnson, "Let's Get Specific," p. 511

B. J. Penn, "Stance," p. 521

EXPLORING WRITING PROMPT

In what ways do you think reading can help you become a better writer? Make a list of your ideas and keep it handy throughout the course. Be sure to add to your list as you work through the selections in Part 4 and uncover new ways reading has helped you become a better writer.

Natalie Goldberg, "Baking a Cake," p. 525

Robert S. Feldman, "Why Go to College?" p. 531

HUMAN GROUPS
AND SOCIETY

Katherine Barrett, "Old before Her Time," p. 537

Amy Tan, "The Most Hateful Words," p. 546

Bill Wine, "Rudeness at the Movies," p. 551

Luis J. Rodriguez, "Turning Youth Gangs Around," p. 558

Maya Angelou, "Reclaiming Our Home Place," p. 566

Al Gore, "Consume Less, Conserve More," p. 572

Paul Boutin, "A Grand Unified Theory of YouTube and MySpace," p. 579

Introduction to the Readings

The reading selections in Part 4 will help you find topics for writing. Some of the selections provide helpful practical information. For example, you'll learn how you can conserve energy and reduce carbon emissions to help the planet and how to avoid being manipulated by clever ads. Other selections deal with thought-provoking aspects of contemporary life, exploring the popularity of YouTube and MySpace or why people behave in certain ways at the movies. Still other selections are devoted to a celebration of human goals and values; one essay, for example, examines the often difficult, yet rewarding relationship between father and child. The varied subjects should inspire lively class discussions as well as serious individual thought. The selections should provide a continuing source of high-interest material for a wide range of writing assignments.

They will also help develop reading skills, which offer direct benefits to you as a writer. First, through close reading, you will learn how to recognize the main idea or point of a selection and how to identify and evaluate the supporting material that develops that main idea. In your writing, you will aim to achieve the same essential structure: an overall point followed by detailed, valid support for that point. Second, close reading will help you explore a selection and its possibilities thoroughly. The more you understand about what is said in a piece, the more ideas and feelings you may have about writing on an assigned topic or a related topic of your own. A third benefit of close reading is becoming more aware of authors' stylistic devices—for example, their introductions and conclusions, their ways of presenting and developing a point, their use of transitions, and their choice of language to achieve a particular tone. Recognizing these devices in other people's writing will help you expand your own range of writing techniques.

The Format of Each Selection

Each selection begins with a short **Preview** that gives helpful background information about the author and the work. This is followed by **Words to Watch,** a list of difficult words in the selection, with their paragraph numbers. You may find it helpful to look up the definitions of these words in a dictionary to remind yourself of meanings or to learn new ones. Within the reading itself, each listed word is marked with a small colored bullet (•). When you're reading, if you are not sure of the definition of a word marked with this bullet, don't hesitate to look it up. The selection is then followed by several sets of questions.

- First, there are **Vocabulary in Context** questions to help you expand your knowledge of selected words.

- **Reading Comprehension Questions** foster several important reading skills: recognizing a subject or topic, determining the thesis or main idea, identifying key supporting points, and making inferences. Answering the questions will enable you and your instructor to check quickly your basic understanding of a selection.

More significantly, as you move from one selection to the next, you will sharpen your reading skills as well as strengthen your thinking skills—two key factors in becoming a better writer.

- Following the comprehension questions are several **Discussion Questions.** In addition to dealing with content, these questions focus on **Structure, Style,** and **Tone.**

Finally, several **Writing Assignments** accompany each selection. Many of the assignments provide suggestions for prewriting and appropriate methods of development. Some readings also feature related images and **Responding to Images** writing prompts. When writing your responses to the readings, you will have opportunities to apply all the methods of development presented in Chapter 4 of this book.

How to Read Well: Four General Steps

Skillful reading is an important part of becoming a skillful writer. Following are four steps that will help make you a better reader—both of the selections here and in your reading at large.

1 Concentrate as You Read

To improve your concentration, follow these tips. First, read in a place where you can be quiet and alone. Don't choose a spot where a TV or stereo is on or where friends or family are talking nearby. Next, sit in an upright position when you read. If your body is in a completely relaxed position, sprawled across a bed or nestled in an easy chair, your mind is also going to be completely relaxed. The light muscular tension that comes from sitting upright in a chair promotes concentration and keeps your mind ready to work. Finally, consider using your index finger (or a pen) as a pacer while you read. Lightly underline each line of print with your index finger as you read down a page. Hold your hand slightly above the page and move your finger at a speed that is a little too fast for comfort. This pacing with your index finger, like sitting upright on a chair, creates a slight physical tension that will keep your body and mind focused and alert.

2 Skim Material before You Read It

In skimming, you spend about two minutes rapidly surveying a selection, looking for important points and skipping secondary material. Follow this sequence when skimming:

- Begin by reading the overview that precedes the selection.

- Then study the title of the selection for a few moments. A good title is the shortest possible summary of a selection; it often tells you in several words what a selection is about.

- Next, form a basic question (or questions) based on the title. Forming questions out of the title is often a key to locating a writer's main idea—your next concern in skimming.

- Read the first two or three paragraphs and the last two or three paragraphs in the selection. Very often a writer's main idea, if it is directly stated, will appear in one of these paragraphs and will relate to the title.

- Finally, look quickly at the rest of the selection for other clues to important points. Are there any subheads you can relate in some way to the title? Are there any words the author has decided to emphasize by setting them off in *italic* or **boldface** type? Are there any major lists of items signaled by words such as *first, second, also, another*, and so on?

3 Read the Selection Straight through with a Pen Nearby

Don't slow down or turn back; just aim to understand as much as you can the first time through. Place a check or star beside answers to basic questions you formed from the title and beside other ideas that seem important; you can also mark the passage or page with a tab or bookmark. Number lists of important points *1, 2, 3. . . .* Circle words you don't understand. Put question marks in the margin next to passages that are unclear and that you will want to reread.

4 Work with the Material

Go back and reread passages that were not clear the first time through. Look up words that block your understanding of ideas and write their meanings in the margin. Also, carefully reread the areas you identified as most important; doing so will deepen your understanding of the material. Now that you have a sense of the whole, prepare a short outline of the selection by answering the following questions on a sheet of paper:

- What is the main idea?

- What key points support the main idea?

- What seem to be other important points in the selection?

By working with the material in this way, you will significantly increase your understanding of a selection. Effective reading, just like effective writing, does not happen all at once. Rather, it is a process. Often you begin with a general impression of what something means, and then, by working at it, you move to a deeper level of understanding of the material.

How to Answer the **Vocabulary in Context** Questions

To decide on the meaning of an unfamiliar word, consider its context. Ask yourself, "Are there any clues in the sentence that suggest what this word means?"

How to Answer the **Reading Comprehension Questions**

Several important reading skills are involved in the reading comprehension questions that follow each selection. The skills are:

- Summarizing the selection by providing a title for it
- Determining the main idea
- Recognizing key supporting details
- Making inferences

The following hints will help you apply each of these reading skills:

- *Subject or title.* Remember that the title should accurately describe the *entire* selection. It should be neither too broad nor too narrow for the material in the selection. It should answer the question "What is this about?" as specifically as possible. Note that you may at times find it easier to do the "title" question *after* the "main idea" question.

- *Main idea.* Choose the statement that you think best expresses the main idea or thesis of the entire selection. Remember that the title will often help you focus on the main idea. Then ask yourself, "Does most of the material in the selection support this statement?" If you can answer *yes* to this question, you have found the thesis.

- *Key details.* If you were asked to give a two-minute summary of a selection, the major details are the ones you would include in that summary. To determine the key details, ask yourself, "What are the major supporting points for the thesis?"

- *Inferences.* Answer these questions by drawing on the evidence presented in the selection and on your own common sense. Ask yourself, "What reasonable judgments can I make on the basis of the information in the selection?"

*   *   *

The readings begin on the next page. Enjoy!

All the Good Things

Sister Helen Mrosla

PREVIEW

Sometimes the smallest things we do have the biggest impact. A teacher's impulsive idea, designed to brighten a dull Friday afternoon class, affected her students more than she ever dreamed. Sister Helen Mrosla's moment of classroom inspiration took on a life of its own, returning to visit her at a most unexpected time. Her account of the experience reminds us of the human heart's endless hunger for recognition and appreciation.

WORDS TO WATCH

mischievousness (1)
incessantly (2)
accustomed (2)
novice (3)
edgy (8)
pallbearer (17)

He was in the first third-grade class I taught at Saint Mary's School 1 in Morris, Minnesota. All thirty-four of my students were dear to me, but Mark Eklund was one in a million. He was very neat in appearance but had that happy-to-be-alive attitude that made even his occasional mischievousness• delightful.

Mark talked incessantly.• I had to remind him again and again that talking 2 without permission was not acceptable. What impressed me so much, though, was his sincere response every time I had to correct him for misbehaving— "Thank you for correcting me, Sister!" I didn't know what to make of it at first, but before long I became accustomed• to hearing it many times a day.

One morning my patience was growing thin when Mark talked once 3 too often, and then I made a novice• teacher's mistake. I looked at him and said, "If you say one more word, I am going to tape your mouth shut!"

It wasn't ten seconds later when Chuck blurted out, "Mark is talking 4 again." I hadn't asked any of the students to help me watch Mark, but since I had stated the punishment in front of the class, I had to act on it.

I remember the scene as if it had occurred this morning. I walked to my 5 desk, very deliberately opened my drawer, and took out a roll of masking tape. Without saying a word, I proceeded to Mark's desk, tore off two pieces of tape and made a big X with them over his mouth. I then returned to the front of the room. As I glanced at Mark to see how he was doing, he winked at me.

That did it! I started laughing. The class cheered as I walked back to 6 Mark's desk, removed the tape, and shrugged my shoulders. His first words were, "Thank you for correcting me, Sister."

At the end of the year I was asked to teach junior-high math. The years 7 flew by, and before I knew it Mark was in my classroom again. He was more handsome than ever and just as polite. Since he had to listen carefully to my instruction in the "new math," he did not talk as much in ninth grade as he had talked in the third.

One Friday, things just didn't feel right. We had worked hard on a new 8 concept all week, and I sensed that the students were frowning, frustrated

with themselves—and edgy• with one another. I had to stop this crankiness before it got out of hand. So I asked them to list the names of the other
students in the room on two sheets of paper, leaving a space after each
name. Then I told them to think of the nicest thing they could say about
each of their classmates and write it down.

It took the remainder of the class period to finish the assignment, and as 9
the students left the room, each one handed me the papers. Charlie smiled.
Mark said, "Thank you for teaching me, Sister. Have a good weekend."

That Saturday, I wrote down the name of each student on a separate sheet 10
of paper, and I listed what everyone else had said about that individual.

On Monday I gave each student his or her list. Before long, the entire 11
class was smiling. "Really?" I heard whispered. "I never knew that meant
anything to anyone!" "I didn't know others liked me so much!"

No one ever mentioned those papers in class again. I never knew if the 12
students discussed them after class or with their parents, but it didn't matter. The exercise had accomplished its purpose. The students were happy
with themselves and one another again.

That group of students moved on. Several years later, after I returned 13
from a vacation, my parents met me at the airport. As we were driving
home, Mother asked me the usual questions about the trip—the weather,
my experiences in general. There was a slight lull in the conversation.
Mother gave Dad a sideways glance and simply said, "Dad?" My father
cleared his throat as he usually did before something important. "The
Eklunds called last night," he began. "Really?" I said. "I haven't heard
from them in years. I wonder how Mark is."

Dad responded quietly. "Mark was killed in Vietnam," he said. "The funeral 14
is tomorrow, and his parents would like it if you could attend." To this day
I can still point to the exact spot on I-494 where Dad told me about Mark.

I had never seen a serviceman in a military coffin before. Mark looked so 15
handsome, so mature. All I could think at that moment was, Mark, I would
give all the masking tape in the world if only you would talk to me.

The church was packed with Mark's friends. Chuck's sister sang "The 16
Battle Hymn of the Republic." Why did it have to rain on the day of the
funeral? It was difficult enough at the graveside. The pastor said the usual
prayers, and the bugler played "Taps." One by one, those who loved Mark
took a last walk by the coffin and sprinkled it with holy water.

I was the last one to bless the coffin. As I stood there, one of the soldiers 17
who had acted as pallbearer• came up to me. "Were you Mark's math
teacher?" he asked. I nodded as I continued to stare at the coffin. "Mark
talked about you a lot," he said.

After the funeral, most of Mark's former classmates headed to Chuck's 18
farmhouse for lunch. Mark's mother and father were there, obviously
waiting for me. "We want to show you something," his father said, taking
a wallet out of his pocket. "They found this on Mark when he was killed.
We thought you might recognize it."

Opening the billfold, he carefully removed two worn pieces of note- 19
book paper that had obviously been taped, folded and refolded many
times. I knew without looking that the papers were the ones on which I
had listed all the good things each of Mark's classmates had said about
him. "Thank you so much for doing that," Mark's mother said. "As you
can see, Mark treasured it."

Mark's classmates started to gather around us. Charlie smiled rather 20 sheepishly and said, "I still have my list. It's in the top drawer of my desk at home." Chuck's wife said, "Chuck asked me to put his list in our wedding album." "I have mine too," Marilyn said. "It's in my diary." Then Vicki, another classmate, reached into her pocketbook, took out her wallet, and showed her worn and frazzled list to the group. "I carry this with me at all times," Vicki said without batting an eyelash. "I think we all saved our lists."

That's when I finally sat down and cried. I cried for Mark and for all 21 his friends who would never see him again.

VOCABULARY IN CONTEXT

1. The word *incessantly* in "Mark talked incessantly. I had to remind him again and again that talking without permission was not acceptable" (paragraph 2) means

   a. slowly.

   b. quietly.

   c. constantly.

   d. pleasantly.

2. The word *edgy* in "We had worked hard on a new concept all week, and I sensed that the students were frowning, frustrated with themselves— and edgy with one another. I had to stop this crankiness before it got out of hand" (paragraph 8) means

   a. funny.

   b. calm.

   c. easily annoyed.

   d. dangerous.

READING COMPREHENSION QUESTIONS

1. Which of the following would be the best alternative title for this selection?

   a. Talkative Mark

   b. My Life as a Teacher

   c. More Important Than I Knew

   d. A Tragic Death

2. Which sentence best expresses the main idea of the selection?

   a. Although Sister Helen sometimes scolded Mark Eklund, he appreciated her devotion to teaching.

   b. When a former student of hers died, Sister Helen discovered how important one of her assignments had been to him and his classmates.

   c. When her students were cranky one day, Sister Helen had them write down something nice about each of their classmates.

   d. A pupil whom Sister Helen was especially fond of was tragically killed while serving in Vietnam.

3. Upon reading their lists for the first time, Sister Helen's students
   a. were silent and embarrassed.
   b. were disappointed.
   c. pretended to think the lists were stupid, although they really liked them.
   d. smiled and seemed pleased.

4. In the days after the assignment to write down something nice about one another,
   a. students didn't mention the assignment again.
   b. students often brought their lists to school.
   c. Sister Helen received calls from several parents complaining about the assignment.
   d. Sister Helen decided to repeat the assignment in every one of her classes.

5. According to Vicki,
   a. Mark was the only student to have saved his list.
   b. Vicki and Mark were the only students to have saved their lists.
   c. Vicki, Mark, Charlie, Chuck, and Marilyn were the only students to have saved their lists.
   d. all the students had saved their lists.

6. The author implies that
   a. she was surprised to learn how much the lists had meant to her students.
   b. Mark's parents were jealous of his affection for Sister Helen.
   c. Mark's death shattered her faith in God.
   d. Mark's classmates had not stayed in touch with one another over the years.

7. *True or false?* _____ The author implies that Mark had gotten married.

8. We can conclude that when Sister Helen was a third-grade teacher, she
   a. was usually short-tempered and irritable.
   b. wasn't always sure how to discipline her students.
   c. didn't expect Mark to do well in school.
   d. had no sense of humor.

DISCUSSION QUESTIONS

About Content

1. What did Sister Helen hope to accomplish by asking her students to list nice things about one another?

2. At least some students were surprised by the good things others wrote about them. What does this tell us about how we see ourselves and how we communicate our views of others?

3. "All the Good Things" has literally traveled around the world. Not only has it been reprinted in numerous publications, but many readers have sent it out over the Internet for others to read. Why do you think so many people love this story? Why do they want to share it with others?

About Structure

4. This selection is organized according to time. What three separate time periods does it cover? What paragraphs are included in the first time period? The second? The third?

5. Paragraph 8 includes a cause-and-effect structure. What part of the paragraph is devoted to the cause? What part is devoted to the effect? What transition word signals the break between the cause and the effect?

6. What does the title "All the Good Things" mean? Is this a good title for the essay? Why or why not?

About Style and Tone

7. Sister Helen is willing to let her readers see her weaknesses as well as her strengths. Find a place in the selection in which the author shows herself as less than perfect.

8. What does Sister Helen accomplish by beginning her essay with the word "he"? What does that unusual beginning tell the reader?

9. How does Sister Helen feel about her students? Find evidence that backs up your opinion.

10. Sister Helen comments on Mark's "happy-to-be-alive" attitude. What support does she provide that makes us understand what Mark was like?

RESPONDING TO IMAGES

From looking at the photograph below, what can you tell about the relationship between the students and their instructor? What specific visual clues help you draw these conclusions?

WRITING ASSIGNMENTS

Assignment 1: Writing a Paragraph

Early in her story, Sister Helen refers to a "teacher's mistake" that forced her to punish a student in front of the class. Write a paragraph about a time you gave in to pressure to do something because others around you expected it. Explain what the situation was, just what happened, and how you felt afterward. Here are two sample topic sentences:

> Even though I knew it was wrong, I went along with some friends who shoplifted at the mall.

> Just because my friends did, I made fun of a kid in my study hall who was a slow learner.

Assignment 2: Writing a Paragraph

Sister Helen's students kept their lists for many years. What souvenir of the past have you kept for a long time? Why? Write a paragraph describing the souvenir, how you got it, and what it means to you. Begin with a topic sentence such as this:

> I've kept a green ribbon in one of my dresser drawers for over ten years because it reminds me of an experience I treasure.

Assignment 3: Writing an Essay

It's easy to forget to let others know how much they have helped us. Only after one of the students died did Sister Helen learn how important the list of positive comments had been to her class. Write an essay about someone to whom you are grateful and explain what that person has done for you. In your thesis statement, introduce the person and describe his or her relationship to you. Also include a general statement of what that person has done for you. Your thesis statement can be similar to any of these:

> My brother Roy has been an important part of my life.

> My best friend Meg helped me through a major crisis.

> Mrs. Morrison, my seventh-grade English teacher, taught me a lesson for which I will always be grateful.

Use freewriting to help you find interesting details to support your thesis statement. You may find two or three separate incidents to write about, each in a paragraph of its own. Or you may find it best to use several paragraphs to give a detailed narrative of one incident or two or three related events. (Note how Sister Helen uses several separate "scenes" to tell her story.) Whatever your approach, use some dialogue to enliven key parts of your essay. (Review the reading to see how Sister Helen uses dialogue throughout her essay.)

Alternatively, write an essay about three people to whom you are grateful. In that case, each paragraph of the body of your essay would deal with one of those people. The thesis statement in such an essay might be similar to this:

> There are three people who have made a big difference in my life.

Rowing the Bus

Paul Logan

PREVIEW	WORDS TO WATCH
There is a well-known saying that goes something like this: All that is necessary in order for evil to triumph is for good people to do nothing. Even young people are forced to face cruel behavior and to decide how they will respond to it. In this essay, Paul Logan looks back at a period of schoolyard cruelty in which he was both a victim and a participant. With unflinching honesty, he describes his behavior then and how it helped to shape the person he has become.	simulate (1) feigning (5) taunted (6) belittled (6) gait (7) rift (9) stoic (13)

When I was in elementary school, some older kids made me row the 1
bus. Rowing meant that on the way to school I had to sit in the dirty bus
aisle littered with paper, gum wads, and spitballs. Then I had to simulate●
the motion of rowing while the kids around me laughed and chanted,
"Row, row, row the bus." I was forced to do this by a group of bullies who
spent most of their time picking on me.

I was the perfect target for them. I was small. I had no father. And 2
my mother, though she worked hard to support me, was unable to afford
clothes and sneakers that were "cool." Instead she dressed me in outfits
that we got from "the bags"—hand-me-downs given as donations to a
local church.

Each Wednesday, she'd bring several bags of clothes to the house and 3
pull out musty, wrinkled shirts and worn bell-bottom pants that other
families no longer wanted. I knew that people were kind to give things to
us, but I hated wearing clothes that might have been donated by my classmates. Each time I wore something from the bags, I feared that the other
kids might recognize something that was once theirs.

Besides my outdated clothes, I wore thick glasses, had crossed eyes, 4
and spoke with a persistent lisp. For whatever reason, I had never learned
to say the "s" sound properly, and I pronounced words that began with
"th" as if they began with a "d." In addition, because of my severely
crossed eyes, I lacked the hand and eye coordination necessary to hit or
catch flying objects.

As a result, footballs, baseballs, soccer balls and basketballs became my 5
enemies. I knew, before I stepped onto the field or court, that I would do
something clumsy or foolish and that everyone would laugh at me. I feared
humiliation so much that I became skillful at feigning● illnesses to get out
of gym class. Eventually I learned how to give myself low-grade fevers so
the nurse would write me an excuse. It worked for a while, until the gym
teachers caught on. When I did have to play, I was always the last one chosen to be on any team. In fact, team captains did everything in their power
to make their opponents get stuck with me. When the unlucky team captain
was forced to call my name, I would trudge over to the team, knowing that

no one there liked or wanted me. For four years, from second through fifth grade, I prayed nightly for God to give me school days in which I would not be insulted, embarrassed, or made to feel ashamed.

I thought my prayers were answered when my mother decided to 6 move during the summer before sixth grade. The move meant that I got to start sixth grade in a different school, a place where I had no reputation. Although the older kids laughed and snorted at me as soon as I got on my new bus—they couldn't miss my thick glasses and strange clothes—I soon discovered that there was another kid who received the brunt of their insults. His name was George, and everyone made fun of him. The kids taunted • him because he was skinny; they belittled • him because he had acne that pocked and blotched his face; and they teased him because his voice was squeaky. During my first gym class at my new school, I wasn't the last one chosen for kickball; George was.

George tried hard to be friends with me, coming up to me in the cafete- 7 ria on the first day of school. "Hi. My name's George. Can I sit with you?" he asked with a peculiar squeakiness that made each word high-pitched and raspy. As I nodded for him to sit down, I noticed an uncomfortable silence in the cafeteria as many of the students who had mocked George's clumsy gait • during gym class began watching the two of us and whispering among themselves. By letting him sit with me, I had violated an unspoken law of school, a sinister code of childhood that demands there must always be someone to pick on. I began to realize two things. If I befriended George, I would soon receive the same treatment that I had gotten at my old school. If I stayed away from him, I might actually have a chance to escape being at the bottom.

Within days, the kids started taunting us whenever we were together. 8 "Who's your new little buddy, Georgie?" In the hallways, groups of students began mumbling about me just loud enough for me to hear, "Look, it's George's ugly boyfriend." On the bus rides to and from school, wads of paper and wet chewing gum were tossed at me by the bigger, older kids in the back of the bus.

It became clear that my friendship with George was going to cause me 9 several more years of misery at my new school. I decided to stop being friends with George. In class and at lunch, I spent less and less time with him. Sometimes I told him I was too busy to talk; other times I acted distracted and gave one-word responses to whatever he said. Our classmates, sensing that they had created a rift • between George and me, intensified their attacks on him. Each day, George grew more desperate as he realized that the one person who could prevent him from being completely isolated was closing him off. I knew that I shouldn't avoid him, that he was feeling the same way I felt for so long, but I was so afraid that my life would become the hell it had been in my old school that I continued to ignore him.

Then, at recess one day, the meanest kid in the school, Chris, decided 10 he had had enough of George. He vowed that he was going to beat up George and anyone else who claimed to be his friend. A mob of kids formed and came after me. Chris led the way and cornered me near our school's swing sets. He grabbed me by my shirt and raised his fist over my head. A huge gathering of kids surrounded us, urging him to beat me up, chanting "Go, Chris, go!"

"You're Georgie's new little boyfriend, aren't you?" he yelled. The 11 hot blast of his breath carried droplets of his spit into my face. In a complete betrayal of the only kid who was nice to me, I denied George's friendship.

"No, I'm not George's friend. I don't like him. He's stupid," I blurted 12 out. Several kids snickered and mumbled under their breath. Chris stared at me for a few seconds and then threw me to the ground.

"Wimp. Where's George?" he demanded, standing over me. Someone 13 pointed to George sitting alone on top of the monkey bars about thirty yards from where we were. He was watching me. Chris and his followers sprinted over to George and yanked him off the bars to the ground. Although the mob quickly encircled them, I could still see the two of them at the center of the crowd, looking at each other. George seemed stoic,* staring straight through Chris. I heard the familiar chant of "Go, Chris, go!" and watched as his fists began slamming into George's head and body. His face bloodied and his nose broken, George crumpled to the ground and sobbed without even throwing a punch. The mob cheered with pleasure and darted off into the playground to avoid an approaching teacher.

Chris was suspended, and after a few days, George came back to 14 school. I wanted to talk to him, to ask him how he was, to apologize for leaving him alone and for not trying to stop him from getting hurt. But I couldn't go near him. Filled with shame for denying George and angered by my own cowardice, I never spoke to him again.

Several months later, without telling any students, George transferred 15 to another school. Once in a while, in those last weeks before he left, I caught him watching me as I sat with the rest of the kids in the cafeteria. He never yelled at me or expressed anger, disappointment, or even sadness. Instead he just looked at me.

In the years that followed, George's silent stare remained with me. It 16 was there in eighth grade when I saw a gang of popular kids beat up a sixth-grader because, they said, he was "ugly and stupid." It was there my first year in high school, when I saw a group of older kids steal another freshman's clothes and throw them into the showers. It was there a year later, when I watched several seniors press a wad of chewing gum into the hair of a new girl on the bus. Each time that I witnessed another awkward, uncomfortable, scared kid being tormented, I thought of George, and gradually his haunting stare began to speak to me. No longer silent, it told me that every child who is picked on and taunted deserves better, that no one—no matter how big, strong, attractive, or popular—has the right to abuse another person.

Finally, in my junior year when a loudmouthed, pink-skinned bully 17 named Donald began picking on two freshmen on the bus, I could no longer deny George. Donald was crumpling a large wad of paper and preparing to bounce it off the back of the head of one of the young students when I interrupted him.

"Leave them alone, Don," I said. By then I was six inches taller and, 18 after two years of high-school wrestling, thirty pounds heavier than I had been in my freshman year. Though Donald was still two years older than me, he wasn't much bigger. He stopped what he was doing, squinted, and stared at me.

"What's your problem, Paul?" 19

I felt the way I had many years earlier on the playground when I 20 watched the mob of kids begin to surround George.

"Just leave them alone. They aren't bothering you," I responded quietly. 21

"What's it to you?" he challenged. A glimpse of my own past, of row- 22 ing the bus, of being mocked for my clothes, my lisp, my glasses, and my absent father flashed in my mind.

"Just don't mess with them. That's all I am saying, Don." My fingertips 23 were tingling. The bus was silent. He got up from his seat and leaned over me, and I rose from my seat to face him. For a minute, both of us just stood there, without a word, staring.

"I'm just playing with them, Paul," he said, chuckling. "You don't 24 have to go psycho on me or anything." Then he shook his head, slapped me firmly on the chest with the back of his hand, and sat down. But he never threw that wad of paper. For the rest of the year, whenever I was on the bus, Don and the other troublemakers were noticeably quiet.

Although it has been years since my days on the playground and the 25 school bus, George's look still haunts me. Today, I see it on the faces of a few scared kids at my sister's school—she is in fifth grade. Or once in a while I'll catch a glimpse of someone like George on the evening news, in a story about a child who brought a gun to school to stop the kids from picking on him, or in a feature about a teenager who killed herself because everyone teased her. In each school, in almost every classroom, there is a George with a stricken face, hoping that someone nearby will be strong enough to be kind—despite what the crowd says—and brave enough to stand up against people who attack, tease, or hurt those who are vulnerable.

If asked about their behavior, I'm sure the bullies would say, "What's 26 it to you? It's just a joke. It's nothing." But to George and me, and everyone else who has been humiliated or laughed at or spat on, it is everything. No one should have to row the bus.

VOCABULARY IN CONTEXT

1. The word *simulate* in "Then I had to simulate the motion of rowing while the kids around me laughed and chanted, 'Row, row, row the bus'" (paragraph 1) means

   a. sing.

   b. ignore.

   c. imitate.

   d. release.

2. The word *rift* in "I decided to stop being friends with George. . . . Our classmates, sensing that they had created a rift between George and me, intensified their attacks on him" (paragraph 9) means

   a. friendship.

   b. agreement.

   c. break.

   d. joke.

READING COMPREHENSION QUESTIONS

1. Which of the following would be the best alternative title for this selection?

   a. A Sixth-Grade Adventure

   b. Children's Fears

   c. Dealing with Cruelty

   d. The Trouble with Busing

2. Which sentence best expresses the main idea of the selection?

   a. Although Paul Logan was the target of other students' abuse when he was a young boy, their attacks stopped as he grew taller and stronger.

   b. When Logan moved to a different school, he discovered that another student, George, was the target of more bullying than he was.

   c. Logan's experience of being bullied and his shame at how he treated George eventually made him speak up for someone else who was teased.

   d. Logan is ashamed that he did not stand up for George when George was being attacked by a bully on the playground.

3. When Chris attacked George, George reacted by

   a. fighting back hard.

   b. shouting for Logan to help him.

   c. running away.

   d. accepting the beating.

4. Logan finally found the courage to stand up for abused students when he saw

   a. Donald about to throw paper at a younger student.

   b. older kids throwing a freshman's clothes into the shower.

   c. seniors putting bubble gum in a new student's hair.

   d. a gang beating up a sixth-grader whom they disliked.

5. *True or false?* _____ After Logan confronted Donald on the bus, Donald began picking on Logan as well.

6. *True or false?* _____ The author suggests that his mother did not care very much about him.

7. The author implies that, when he started sixth grade at a new school,

   a. he became fairly popular.

   b. he decided to try out for athletic teams.

   c. he was relieved to find a kid who was more unpopular than he.

   d. he was frequently beaten up.

8. We can conclude that

   a. the kids who picked on George later regretted what they had done.

   b. George and the author eventually talked together about their experience in sixth grade.

c. the author thinks kids today are kinder than they were when he was in sixth grade.

d. the author is a more compassionate person now because of his experience with George.

DISCUSSION QUESTIONS

About Content

1. Logan describes a number of incidents involving students' cruelty to other students. Find at least three such incidents. What do they seem to have in common? Judging from such incidents, what purpose does cruel teasing seem to serve?

2. Throughout the essay, Paul Logan talks about cruel but ordinary school behavior. But in paragraph 25, he briefly mentions two extreme and tragic consequences of such cruelty. What are those consequences, and why do you think he introduces them? What is he implying?

About Structure

3. Overall, the author uses narration to develop his points. Below, write three time transitions he uses to advance his narration.

    _____   _____   _____

4. Logan describes the gradual change within him that finally results in his standing up for two students who are being abused. Where in the narrative does Logan show how internal changes may be taking place within him? Where in the narrative does he show that his reaction to witnessing bullying has changed?

5. Paul Logan titled his selection "Rowing the Bus." Yet very little of the essay actually deals with the incident the title describes. Why do you think Logan chose that title?

About Style and Tone

6. Good descriptive writing involves the reader's senses. Give examples of how Logan appeals to our senses in paragraphs 1–4 of "Rowing the Bus."

    Sight _____

    Smell _____

    Hearing _____

7. What is Logan's attitude toward himself regarding his treatment of George? Find three phrases that reveal his attitude and write them here.

WRITING ASSIGNMENTS

Assignment 1: Writing a Paragraph

Logan writes, "In each school, in almost every classroom, there is a George with a stricken face." Think of a person who filled the role of George in one of your classes. Then write a descriptive paragraph about that person, explaining why he or she was a target and what form the teasing took. Be sure to include a description of your own thoughts and actions regarding the student who was teased. Your topic sentence might be something like one of these:

> A girl in my fifth-grade class was a lot like George in "Rowing the Bus."
>
> Like Paul Logan, I suffered greatly in elementary school from being bullied.

Try to include details that appeal to two or three of the senses.

Assignment 2: Writing a Paragraph

Paul Logan feared that his life at his new school would be made miserable if he continued being friends with George. So he ended the friendship, even though he felt ashamed of doing so. Think of a time when you have wanted to do the right thing but felt that the price would be too high. Maybe you knew a friend was doing something dishonest and wanted him to stop but were afraid of losing his friendship. Or perhaps you pretended to forget a promise you had made because you decided it was too difficult to keep. Write a paragraph describing the choice you made and how you felt about yourself afterward.

Assignment 3: Writing an Essay

Logan provides many vivid descriptions of incidents in which bullies attack other students. Reread these descriptions, and consider what they teach you about the nature of bullies and bullying. Then write an essay that supports the following main idea:

> Bullies seem to share certain qualities.

Identify two or three qualities; then discuss each in a separate paragraph. You may use two or three of the following as the topic sentences for your supporting paragraphs, or come up with your own supporting points:

> Bullies are cowardly.
>
> Bullies make themselves feel big by making other people feel small.
>
> Bullies cannot feel very good about themselves.
>
> Bullies are feared but not respected.
>
> Bullies act cruelly in order to get attention.

Develop each supporting point with one or more anecdotes or ideas from any of the following: your own experience, your understanding of human nature, and "Rowing the Bus."

All She Has—$150,000—Is Going to a University

Rick Bragg

<table>
<tr><td>

PREVIEW

When we think of philanthropists—people who give a lot of money to charity—we usually think of very wealthy people like Bill and Melinda Gates or the Walton family. These are people who can afford to give away millions of dollars and still live luxuriously. In this article from the *New York Times*, however, we learn of an amazing woman who worked hard all of her life and, although very poor, managed to save $150,000 by denying herself even the most simple comforts and necessities. What's even more amazing is that she has given it all away to help young people go to college!

</td><td>

WORDS TO WATCH

anticipation (6)
piqued (9)
obscurity (9)
predominantly (12)
affluent (15)
indefinite (17)
stipulation (17)
beneficiaries (17)

</td></tr>
</table>

Oseola McCarty spent a lifetime making other people look nice. Day after day, for most of her 87 years, she took in bundles of dirty clothes and made them clean and neat for parties she never attended, weddings to which she was never invited, graduations she never saw. 1

She had quit school in the sixth grade to go to work, never married, never had children, and never learned to drive because there was never any place in particular she wanted to go. All she ever had was the work, which she saw as a blessing. Too many other black people in rural Mississippi did not have even that. 2

She spent almost nothing, living in her old family home, cutting the toes out of shoes if they did not fit right and binding her ragged Bible with Scotch tape to keep Corinthians from falling out. Over the decades, her pay—mostly dollar bills and change—grew to more than $150,000. 3

"More than I could ever use," Miss McCarty said the other day without a trace of self-pity. So she is giving her money away, to finance scholarships for black students at the University of Southern Mississippi here in her hometown, where tuition is $2,400 a year. 4

"I wanted to share my wealth with the children," said Miss McCarty, whose only real regret is that she never went back to school. "I never minded work, but I was always so busy, busy. Maybe I can make it so the children don't have to work like I did." 5

People in Hattiesburg call her donation the Gift. She made it, in part, in anticipation● of her death. 6

As she sat in her warm, dark living room, she talked of that death matter-of-factly, the same way she talked about the possibility of an afternoon thundershower. To her, the Gift was a preparation, like closing the bedroom windows to keep the rain from blowing in on the bedspread. 7

"I know it won't be too many years before I pass on," she said, "and I just 8
figured the money would do them a lot more good than it would me."

Her donation has piqued• interest around the nation. In a few short 9
days, Oseola McCarty, the washerwoman, has risen from obscurity• to
a notice she does not understand. She sits in her little frame house, just
blocks from the university, and patiently greets the reporters, business
leaders and others who line up outside her door.

"I live where I want to live, and I live the way I want to live," she said. 10
"I couldn't drive a car if I had one. I'm too old to go to college. So I planned
to do this. I planned it myself."

It has been only three decades since the university integrated. "My 11
race used to not get to go to that college," she said. "But now they can."

When asked why she had picked this university instead of a predomi- 12
nantly• black institution, she said, "Because it's here; it's close."

While Miss McCarty does not want a building named for her or a 13
statue in her honor, she would like one thing in return: to attend the
graduation of a student who made it through college because of her gift.
"I'd like to see it," she said.

Business leaders in Hattiesburg, 110 miles northeast of New Orleans, 14
plan to match her $150,000, said Bill Pace, the executive director of the
University of Southern Mississippi Foundation, which administers donations to the school.

"I've been in the business 24 years now, in private fund raising," 15
Mr. Pace said. "And this is the first time I've experienced anything like
this from an individual who simply was not affluent,• did not have the
resources and yet gave substantially. In fact, she gave almost everything
she has.

"No one approached her from the university; she approached us. 16
She's seen the poverty, the young people who have struggled, who need
an education. She is the most unselfish individual I have ever met."

Although some details are still being worked out, the $300,000—Miss 17
McCarty's money and the matching sum—will finance scholarships into
the indefinite• future. The only stipulation• is that the beneficiaries• be
black and live in southern Mississippi.

The college has already awarded a $1,000 scholarship in Miss 18
McCarty's name to an 18-year-old honors student from Hattiesburg,
Stephanie Bullock.

Miss Bullock's grandmother, Ledrester Hayes, sat in Miss McCarty's 19
tiny living room the other day and thanked her. Later, when Miss McCarty
left the room, Mrs. Hayes shook her head in wonder.

"I thought she would be some little old rich lady with a fine car and a 20
fine house and clothes," she said. "I was a seamstress myself, worked two
jobs. I know what it's like to work like she did, and she gave it away."

The Oseola McCarty Scholarship Fund bears the name of a woman 21
who bought her first air-conditioner just three years ago and even now
turns it on only when company comes. Miss McCarty also does not
mind that her tiny black-and-white television set gets only one channel,
because she never watches anyway. She complains that her electricity bill
is too high and says she never subscribed to a newspaper because it cost
too much.

The pace of Miss McCarty's walks about the neighborhood is slowed 22 now, and she misses more Sundays than she would like at Friendship Baptist Church. Arthritis has left her hands stiff and numb. For the first time in almost 80 years, her independence is threatened.

"Since I was a child, I've been working," washing the clothes of doc- 23 tors, lawyers, teachers, police officers, she said. "But I can't do it no more. I can't work like I used to."

She is 5 feet tall and would weigh 100 pounds with rocks in her pock- 24 ets. Her voice is so soft that it disappears in the squeak of the screen door and the hum of the air-conditioner.

She comes from a wide place in the road called Shubuta, Miss., a 25 farming town outside Meridian, not far from the Alabama line. She quit school, she said, when the grandmother who reared her became ill and needed care.

"I would have gone back," she said, "but the people in my class had 26 done gone on, and I was too big. I wanted to be with my class."

So she worked, and almost every dollar went into the bank. In time, all 27 her immediate family died. "And I didn't have nobody," she said. "But I stayed busy."

She took a short vacation once, as a young woman, to Niagara Falls. 28 The roar of the water scared her. "Seemed like the world was coming to an end," she said.

She stayed home, mostly, after that. She has lived alone since 1967.   29

Earlier this year her banker asked what she wanted done with her 30 money when she passed on. She told him that she wanted to give it to the university, now rather than later; she set aside just enough to live on.

She says she does not want to depend on anyone after all these years, 31 but she may have little choice. She has been informally adopted by the first young person whose life was changed by her gift.

As a young woman, Stephanie Bullock's mother wanted to go to the 32 University of Southern Mississippi. But that was during the height of the integration battles, and if she had tried her father might have lost his job with the city.

It looked as if Stephanie's own dream of going to the university would 33 also be snuffed out, for lack of money. Although she was president of her senior class in high school and had grades that were among the best there, she fell just short of getting an academic scholarship. Miss Bullock said her family earned too much money to qualify for most Federal grants but not enough to send her to the university.

Then, last week, she learned that the university was giving her $1,000, in 34 Miss McCarty's name. "It was a total miracle," she said, "and an honor."

She visited Miss McCarty to thank her personally and told her that she 35 planned to "adopt" her. Now she visits regularly, offering to drive Miss McCarty around and filling a space in the tiny woman's home that has been empty for decades.

She feels a little pressure, she concedes, not to fail the woman who helped 36 her. "I was thinking how amazing it was that she made all that money doing laundry," said Miss Bullock, who plans to major in business.

She counts on Miss McCarty's being there four years from now, when 37 she graduates.

VOCABULARY IN CONTEXT

1. The phrase *in anticipation of* in "She made it, in part, in anticipation of her death" (paragraph 6) means
    a. in preparation for.
    b. in spite of.
    c. because of.
    d. in regard to.

2. The word *piqued* in "Her donation has piqued interest around the nation" (paragraph 9) means
    a. decreased.
    b. aroused.
    c. experienced.
    d. accelerated.

3. The word *affluent* in "And this is the first time I've experienced anything like this from an individual who simply was not affluent. . . ." (paragraph 15) means
    a. poor.
    b. generous.
    c. wealthy.
    d. middle class.

READING COMPREHENSION QUESTIONS

1. Which sentence best expresses the selection's main point?
    a. "People in Hattiesburg call her donation the Gift."
    b. "She is the most unselfish individual I have ever met."
    c. "So she worked, and almost every dollar went into the bank."
    d. "She's seen the poverty, the young people who have struggled, who need an education."

2. Which of the following is the main idea of paragraph 2?
    a. Oseola McCarty quit school in the sixth grade.
    b. Oseola McCarty never married and never had children.
    c. Oseola McCarty was happy to have work.
    d. Too many black people in Mississippi didn't have work.

3. Oseola McCarty's only regret is that
    a. she didn't travel more.
    b. she quit school at sixteen.
    c. she couldn't go to college.
    d. she never went back to school.

4. In return for her generosity, Miss McCarty would like to

   a. have a building named after her.

   b. have her portrait hung in one of the university's buildings.

   c. have a statue erected in her honor.

   d. see one of the scholarship students graduate.

5. Miss McCarty earned all of the money she saved by

   a. cleaning other people's homes.

   b. working in a factory.

   c. waiting on tables in a restaurant.

   d. doing people's laundry.

6. Which of the following did Miss McCarty *not* do in order to save money?

   a. Pack her own lunch each day.

   b. Cut holes in her shoes to make them fit better.

   c. Refuse to subscribe to a newspaper.

   d. Repair her Bible with tape.

7. *True or false?* _____. Miss McCarty quit school in the sixth grade because she had to care for her younger brothers and sisters.

8. Miss McCarty occasionally misses church these days because

   a. the minister's sermons are boring.

   b. she sometimes doesn't know what day it is.

   c. her car won't start.

   d. her arthritis makes it hard for her to walk there.

DISCUSSION QUESTIONS

About Content

1. List a few of the ways that Miss McCarty was able to save so much money during her lifetime. Then, examine your lifestyle and make a list of the things you might do without in order to save money.

2. The author tells us that Miss McCarty is making her donation "in part, in anticipation of her death." How does this 87-year-old woman feel about the fact that she may soon die? What does this tell us about her character?

3. Why has Miss McCarty decided to create a scholarship fund? What does this reason tell us about her?

4. Why was Stephanie Bullock's grandmother so amazed after meeting Miss McCarty?

About Structure

5. Bragg's essay contains several examples (illustrations) of Miss McCarty's thriftiness as a way to explain her personality or character. In what paragraphs does he use description to do this?

6. Bragg includes evidence to show that people in the community and throughout the nation are impressed with and supportive of Miss McCarty. Find two or three places where the author includes such evidence.

About Style and Tone

7. Where does Bragg use direct quotations to show how extraordinary Miss McCarty is?

8. The essay ends with Stephanie Bullock's looking forward to Miss McCarty's attending her graduation. How does this relate to the way the essay begins?

WRITING ASSIGNMENTS

Assignment 1: Writing a Paragraph

Oseola McCarty is an example for all of us. Do you know people who are generous with their money, time, or affection? Do they volunteer at community food pantries, at hospitals, or at pet shelters? Do they simply offer their neighbors help when it is needed? Write a paragraph explaining why you think someone you know might be called "generous."

The topic sentence of your paragraph should identify the person (either by name or relationship to you) and briefly state what shows that he or she is generous. Here are some examples of a topic sentence that might work for such a paragraph:

> My Aunt Jesse spends nearly all of her free time working at a local homeless shelter.

> The word *generous* defines my grandfather; last summer he spent his entire vacation helping to rebuild a neighbor's home that had been destroyed by fire.

Assignment 2: Writing a Paragraph

Miss McCarty used a variety of clever methods to save a lot of money. Write a paragraph in which you explain one way you might save money each week. Your topic sentence might look like one of these.

> Packing my lunch rather than buying it in the college cafeteria will save me enough to pay for my books next semester.

> Renting an old movie and watching it with friends on Friday nights will save me about $20 per week in entertainment costs.

> Taking public transportation rather than driving to work will save about $50 per week.

After stating your main idea, provide details to prove or develop it. For example, if you are arguing that taking public transportation is cheaper than driving to work, you should let your reader know how much a round-trip bus ticket in your area costs and then compare it to the amount of money you spend on gasoline each day. You can also figure in the costs of maintaining your car (tires, tune-ups, oil changes, etc.) and of purchasing auto insurance.

Assignment 3: Writing an Essay

Near the end of this selection, we learn that Stephanie Bullock may not have been able to attend the university had it not been for the Oseola McCarty scholarship. Stephanie's "family earned too much money to qualify for most Federal grants but not enough to send her to the university."

All students face obstacles while trying to earn their college degrees. Think about some of the obstacles you have faced in getting admitted to college and/or that you face right now as you pursue your studies. Try making a list of such obstacles as a way to collect details that you might put into an essay explaining what stands in the way of attaining your dream. At first, don't worry about organizing your details—just keep adding to your list. It might turn out to look something like this:

- Work 60 hours per week during summer/holidays
- Work part-time during the school year
- No social life
- No personal life/depressing
- Boss won't cut me slack
- Study 40 hours a week, maybe more
- Student loans worry me
- Have to travel 15 miles to work every afternoon—cost of gas/travel killing me
- Math course especially hard
- My major may be too difficult for me
- Have trouble making my 8 am class
- Need to learn how to study—college and high school very different

Eventually you will have enough information to organize your essay. Here's a scratch outline of what your essay might look like:

1. Difficult major and schedule
   a. Must take 2 prerequisite math courses before I start calculus
   b. Required to take foreign language, which is hard for me
   c. Only open English comp. course was at 8 am this semester

continued

2. Working too many hours outside school—having trouble meeting expenses

   a. 60 hours during summers/holidays

   b. 20 hours during school year

   c. Still need to take out loans

   d. Work schedule sometimes interferes with classes—boss not understanding

3. No social/personal life

   a. See my girlfriend once a week, sometimes less frequently

   b. Lost contact with many high school friends

   c. Tired all the time—never get more than 5 hours of sleep

   d. Get depressed over bad grades

Use your scratch outline as the blueprint or guide for your rough draft. However, remember that, as you draft, other ideas and bits of information will begin to pop into your head. If so, try to include them in the draft if appropriate. Finally, revise your draft at least once—several times, if necessary—and then edit for grammar, punctuation, and mechanics.

Bowling to Find a Lost Father

Mee Her

PREVIEW	WORDS TO WATCH
Mee Her, who was a refugee from Laos, came to the United States in 1976 and settled in California with her family. She earned a BA from Fresno State University and an MA from the California School of Professional Psychology. This essay mentions her father's "Hmong orientation." The Hmong are an ethnic group living in Laos, Thailand, Myanmar, and Vietnam.	orientation (2) productivity (2) ideal (3) sophisticated (3) dutiful (4)

We all held our breath as the ball slowly rolled down the alley. Then, 1 just as it was about to hit the pins, it dropped into the gutter. Ahhh... We sighed in disappointment. My father slowly turned toward us. His eyes sparkled like those of a little boy, and a big smile was printed on his face. Then he joyfully chuckled as he walked to his seat. I never thought my father would enjoy playing with us. In fact, I never thought he'd enjoy fun.

But on that evening when I taught him how to bowl, I did more than teach him how to hit pins. I had taken the first step toward bridging a gap which had been created between him and his children.

My father had never played with us. I guess that came with his Hmong orientation• in valuing hard work. He told us that play was a waste of meaningful time which could be better used for productivity.• **2**

If we were still living in Laos where children don't have to go to school, and all they do is work in the field with parents, my father's orientation would be the ideal.• There, children would work hard on the farms, then, during break times, they would listen to parents tell stories of their own childhood. Parents also either would teach "music" lessons to their children with instruments that they created out of bamboo sticks or they would teach them how to blow and make music out of leaves. This kept the relationship between children and their parents close. But in this country, where everything is so sophisticated,• parents don't know how to be close to their children. **3**

I remembered my relationship with my father as a child. We went everywhere together. He took me to the hospital where he worked, to the fields, or to feed the stock on the farm. I remember the times my father took me to the hospital with him. My father would teach me how his medical instruments were used, or he would show me to his patients. I felt so close to him. However, since we came to this country my relationship with my father has changed. He no longer knows how to be the father he used to be for us. He began to build walls around us by becoming so overly protective. He did not let us play outside or go out with our friends, using concepts of hard work to keep us at home like dutiful• Hmong children. I felt emotionally distant from him. Somehow the gap seemed so great that neither he nor his children knew how to bridge it. As it turned out, I ignored our relationship altogether. **4**

It wasn't until my third year in college that I decided to make my first move to re-create the relationship between my father and me. I had moved away from home when I started college. The time and distance made me miss the closeness that I used to have with him. I was beginning to see the need for closeness between my parents and the other children too. My father must have tried to keep the gap from getting larger when he became overly protective of us. It must have been frightening to live with children who did not live in the same world that he did. He couldn't play video games with them or couldn't understand ear-busting rock 'n' roll. He didn't even know how to play soccer or volleyball! And those were the things that his children did for enjoyment in this country. **5**

Poor Dad. It was not his fault that he did not know how to be included in our lives. It was just that he didn't know how to get involved with his children. That was why my brothers and sisters and I decided to introduce my father to bowling. **6**

I remember that day well when my brother, sisters, dad, and I went bowling. Dad was a little hesitant to come with us, but we all persuaded him. When we got to the bowling alley, we showed him how to hold the ball. Then we taught him how to throw the ball. It was a little bit foreign for me to be the one teaching my father, and I sensed that Father felt odd, too. But once he got the hang of it, he did well. He even made a couple of strikes! **7**

I think it was much more than bowling that father enjoyed. It was the 8 emotional closeness that he felt with us which made him come back to bowl again. The next time we went bowling, he was teaching the younger children to bowl. As I watched him beam so happily with the kids, it occurred to me that this was the beginning of building a bridge across a long-created gap between Dad and his children. Another thought came to my mind too. I wonder why it had taken me so long to show my father how to bowl. Was I waiting for him to make the first move? Was I waiting for him to teach me instead? But how could he have done that when he didn't know how?

VOCABULARY IN CONTEXT

1. The phrase *orientation* in "I guess that came with his Hmong orientation in valuing hard work" (paragraph 2) means
   a. difficulty.
   b. understanding of.
   c. attitude.
   d. fear of.

2. In paragraph 3, the word *ideal* in "In Laos . . . my father's orientation would be ideal" means
   a. perfect.
   b. possible.
   c. inappropriate.
   d. understandable.

READING COMPREHENSION QUESTIONS

1. Which of the following would be the best alternative title for this selection?
   a. A Laotian Father in America
   b. Bowling: A Family Sport
   c. Reconnecting with My Father
   d. Waiting for My Father

2. Which sentence best expresses the main idea of this selection?
   a. Bowling is a sport for the entire family.
   b. Coming to America caused the ties between my father and his children to weaken.
   c. Playing together helped my father and his children reconnect.
   d. Laotian immigrants face problems similar to those faced by other immigrants.

3. In the past, Her's father never played with his children because
   a. he believed play was a waste of valuable time.
   b. he didn't have time.
   c. he was cold and unloving.
   d. the children were afraid of him.

4. The relationship between parents and children in Laos was
   a. distant.
   b. very formal.
   c. warm and loving.
   d. based on strict rules.

5. *True or false?* _____ The relationship between Her and her father changed drastically after they came to America.

6. *True or false?* _____ Once in America, Her's father wanted his children to be independent.

7. From what we read in paragraph 4, we can infer that in Laos, Her's father was
   a. an attorney.
   b. a government official.
   c. a doctor.
   d. an army officer.

8. Why, according to Her, don't Americans "know how to be close to their children"?
   a. American society is more complex than Laotian society.
   b. American parents aren't emotionally attached to their children.
   c. American society does not value parents.
   d. Americans value material things too much.

DISCUSSION QUESTIONS

About Content

1. What was it that caused Her's father to go bowling a second time?

2. Do you agree with Her that it must have been "frightening" for her father to live with children who had adopted American culture and an American lifestyle (paragraph 5)? In a sentence or two, explain how he must have felt.

   _____

   _____

   _____

3. Why does the author feel "odd" teaching her father to bowl (paragraph 7)? Have you ever taught a parent or grandparent something new—perhaps how to use a cell phone, send an e-mail, or conduct an Internet search? Explain the feelings you experienced as you did this. Were you proud? Excited? Embarrassed?

   _____

   _____

   _____

About Structure

4. Parts of this essay rely on narrative details. Explain how the author reveals the passage of time in paragraphs 4, 5, and 6.

5. Her begins by describing her father at the bowling alley. Should she have started with their lives in Laos?

About Style and Tone

6. In paragraph 2, the author describes her father negatively. Does her attitude change later in the essay? Explain how.

7. Most of the essay is about the author's father. However, in her conclusion, Her shows that it is about her as well. What is she saying about herself in paragraph 8?

RESPONDING TO IMAGES

People who believe in the value of families know that the group is often more important than the individual. They also know that to be a family means to share. What does this photograph tell you about sharing? About being a family?

WRITING ASSIGNMENTS

Assignment 1: Writing a Paragraph

In paragraph 1, Her says that she never thought her father would enjoy playing with his children. Write a paragraph in which you discuss an incident in which a person you know did something you didn't expect of him or her. The purpose of this paragraph is to show that, in fact, you might not have known your subject as well as you first thought. Try to focus on someone with whom you have a close relationship and whom you might write about in concrete detail.

Assignment 2: Writing a Paragraph

Recall an incident in which you and one or both of your parents, grandparents, or other close relative achieved the same kind of emotional connection as the one we read about in Her's essay. Narrate this incident in as much detail as possible, remembering to include, of course, what occurred, what was said, and how each of you felt about it.

Assignment 3: Writing an Essay

In her conclusion, Her expresses some regret over not having reached out to her father sooner—"Was I waiting for him to make the first move?"

Regret over not having tried hard enough to connect with others is all too common in a world in which we too often forget the value of other people. Is there someone with whom you would like to establish a stronger friendship, repair a broken relationship, or bridge an emotional gap like the one Her experienced? This individual could be a relative, a classmate, a friend, a neighbor, a former teacher, or an old sweetheart. Then again, it could be someone you have only just met and with whom you would like to establish a closer relationship.

Write an essay in which you offer yourself advice about how to do this. Start by discussing the person and explaining the relationship you have had with him or her. In addition, explain why you want to strengthen or repair that relationship. Then, discuss some ways in which you might establish a better, stronger, or closer relationship with this person. Her took her father bowling, but you might suggest other methods to do this. For example, you might

- invite the individual to dinner at your home.

- offer to help him or her with an important task.

- write him or her a letter apologizing for or explaining a past problem or difficult situation.

- invite the person to a picnic, party, sporting event, or some other type of entertainment.

If the person is a student, ask him or her to study with you. If you have drifted apart from a sibling or other relative, contact him or her via letter, e-mail, or telephone, and explain that you want to become close again for the sake of family harmony.

Close your essay by explaining the rewards you and the other person might get from this improved or strengthened relationship.

The Conveyor-Belt Ladies

Rose Del Castillo Guilbault

PREVIEW	WORDS TO WATCH
This essay first appeared in the *San Francisco Chronicle's* section "This World" in 1990. In it, Del Castillo Guilbault tells the story of what she learned about migrant workers, about manual labor, and about herself—knowledge that made a significant change in her life.	grueling (4) tedious (4) strenuous (4) gregarious (12) bawdy (12) dyspeptic (12) impending (17) fatalism (19) impressionable (21) crescendo (29) anticlimactic (30)

1   The conveyor-belt ladies were the migrant women, mostly from Texas, I worked with during the summers of my teenage years. I call them conveyor-belt ladies because our entire relationship took place while sorting tomatoes on a conveyor belt.

2   We were like a cast in a play where all the action occurs on one set. We'd return day after day to perform the same roles, only this stage was a vegetable-packing shed, and at the end of the season there was no applause. The players could look forward only to the same uninspiring parts on a string of grim real-life stages.

3   The women and their families arrived in May for the carrot season, spent the summer in the tomato sheds, and stayed through October for the bean harvest. After that, they emptied the town, some returning to their homes in Texas (cities like McAllen, Douglas, Brownsville), while others continued on the migrant trail, picking cotton in the San Joaquin Valley or grapefruits and oranges in the Imperial Valley.

4   Most of these women had started in the fields. The vegetable-packing sheds were a step up, easier than the back-breaking, grueling• work the field demanded. The work was more tedious• than strenuous,• paid better, provided fairly steady hours and clean bathrooms. Best of all, you weren't subjected to the elements.

5   The summer I was 16, my mother got jobs for both of us as tomato sorters. That's how I came to be included in the seasonal sorority of the conveyor belt.

6   The work consisted of standing and picking flawed tomatoes off the conveyor belt before they rolled off into the shipping boxes at the end of the line. These boxes were immediately loaded onto waiting delivery trucks, so it was crucial not to let imperfect tomatoes through.

7   The work could be slow or intense, depending on the quality of the tomatoes and how many there were. Work increased when the company's deliveries got backlogged or after rainy weather had delayed picking.

8   During those times, it was not unusual to work from 7 A.M. to midnight, playing catch-up. I never heard anyone complain about the overtime. Overtime meant desperately needed extra money.

I was not happy to be part of the agricultural workforce. I would have 9 preferred working in a dress shop or babysitting, like my friends. But I had a dream that would cost a lot of money—college. And the fact was, this was the highest-paying work I could do.

But it wasn't so much the work that bothered me. I was embarrassed 10 because only Mexicans worked at packing sheds. I had heard my schoolmates joke about the "ugly, fat Mexican women" at the sheds. They ridiculed the way they dressed and laughed at the "funny way" they talked. I feared working with them would irrevocably stigmatize me, setting me further apart from my Anglo classmates.

At 16 I was more American than Mexican and, with adolescent arro- 11 gance, felt superior to these "uneducated" women. I might be one of them, I reasoned, but I was not like them.

But it was difficult not to like the women. They were a gregarious,• 12 entertaining group, easing the long, monotonous hours with bawdy• humor, spicy gossip, and inventive laments. They poked fun at all the male workers and did hysterical impersonations of a dyspeptic• Anglo supervisor. Although he didn't speak Spanish (other than "*Mujeres, trabajo, trabajo!*" Women, work, work!), he seemed to sense he was being laughed at. That would account for the sudden rages when he would stamp his foot and forbid us to talk until break time.

"I bet he understands Spanish and just pretends so he can hear what 13 we say," I whispered to Rosa.

"*Ay, no, hija*, it's all the buzzing in his ears that alerts him that these 14 *viejas* [old women] are bad-mouthing him!" Rosa giggled.

But it would have been easier to tie the women's tongues in a knot than 15 to keep them quiet. Eventually the ladies had their way and their fun, and the men learned to ignore them.

We were often shifted around, another strategy to keep us quiet. This 16 gave me ample opportunity to get to know everyone, listen to their life stories, and absorb the gossip.

Pretty Rosa described her romances and her impending• wedding to 17 a handsome field worker. Bertha, a heavy-set, dark-skinned woman, told me that Rosa's marriage would cause nothing but headaches because the man was younger and too handsome. Maria, large, moon-faced and placid, described the births of each of her nine children, warning me about the horrors of childbirth. Pragmatic Minnie, a tiny woman who always wore printed cotton dresses, scoffed at Maria's stupidity, telling me she wouldn't have so many kids if she had ignored that good-for-nothing priest and gotten her tubes tied!

In unexpected moments, they could turn melancholic: recounting the 18 babies who died because their mothers couldn't afford medical care; the alcoholic, abusive husbands who were their "cross to bear"; the racism they experienced in Texas, where they were branded "dirty Mexicans" or "Mexican dogs" and not allowed in certain restaurants.

They spoke with the detached fatalism• of people with limited choices 19 and alternatives. Their lives were as raw and brutal as ghetto streets— something they accepted with an odd grace and resignation.

I was appalled and deeply affected by these confidences. The injustices 20 they endured enraged me; their personal struggles overwhelmed me. I knew I could do little but sympathize.

My mother, no stranger to suffering, suggested I was too impression- 21
able• when I emotionally told her the women's stories. "That's nothing,"
she'd say lightly. "If they were in Mexico, life would be even harder. At
least there's opportunities here, you can work."

My icy arrogance quickly thawed, that first summer, as my respect for 22
the conveyor-belt ladies grew.

I worked in the packing sheds for several summers. The last season 23
also turned out to be the last time I lived at home. It was the end of a
chapter in my life, but I didn't know it then. I had just finished junior college and was transferring to the university. I was already overeducated for
seasonal work, but if you counted the overtime, no other jobs came close
to paying so well, so I went back one last time.

The ladies treated me with warmth and respect. I was a college stu- 24
dent, deserving of special treatment.

Aguedita, the crew chief, moved me to softer and better-paying jobs 25
within the plant. I went from conveyor belt to shoving boxes down a chute
and finally to weighing boxes of tomatoes on a scale—the highest-paying
position for a woman.

When the union's dues collector showed up, the women hid me in the 26
bathroom. They had decided it was unfair for me to have to join the union
and pay dues, since I worked only during the summer.

"Where's the student?" the union rep would ask, opening the door to 27
a barrage of complaints about the union's unfairness.

Maria (of the nine children) tried to feed me all summer, bringing extra 28
tortillas, which were delicious. I accepted them guiltily, always wondering
if I was taking food away from her children. Others would bring rental
contracts or other documents for me to explain and translate.

The last day of work was splendidly beautiful, warm and sunny. If this 29
had been a movie, these last scenes would have been shot in soft focus,
with a crescendo• of music in the background.

But real life is anticlimactic.• As it was, nothing unusual happened. 30
The conveyor belt's loud humming was turned off, silenced for the season. The women sighed as they removed their aprons. Some of them just
walked off, calling *Hasta la proxima!* Until next time!

But most of the conveyor-belt ladies shook my hand, gave me a bless- 31
ing or a big hug.

"Make us proud!" they said.   32

I hope I have.   33

VOCABULARY IN CONTEXT

1. The word *gregarious* in "they were a gregarious, entertaining group,
   easing the long, monotonous hours with bawdy humor, spicy gossip,
   and inventive laments" (paragraph 12) means

   a. loud.

   b. comical.

   c. friendly.

   d. silly.

2. The word *impending* in "Pretty Rosa described her romances and her impending wedding to a handsome field worker" (paragraph 17) means

   a. upcoming.

   b. past.

   c. fancy.

   d. large.

3. The word *fatalism* in "They spoke with the detached fatalism of people with limited choices and alternatives" (paragraph 19) means

   a. acceptance.

   b. anger.

   c. fear.

   d. sorrow.

READING COMPREHENSION QUESTIONS

1. Which of the following would be the best alternative title for this selection?

   a. Migrant Workers

   b. My Job at the Tomato-Packing Shed

   c. My Summer Job

   d. The End of Adolescent Arrogance

2. Which sentence best expresses the main idea of this selection?

   a. Working with the conveyor-belt ladies changed my mind about the value of labor and of laborers.

   b. Many Mexicans are employed on vegetable farms.

   c. The conveyor-belt ladies were nice to me.

   d. Working in agriculture doesn't pay much.

3. The author admits that when she first started working with the conveyor-belt ladies, she felt

   a. honored to be with these people.

   b. sorry about how hard they had to work.

   c. embarrassed by them.

   d. afraid of them.

4. The author took a job packing tomatoes because

   a. she couldn't find another job.

   b. her parents forced her to.

   c. it was the highest-paying job she could get.

   d. her uncle owned the business.

5. *True or false?* _____ As a teenager, the author was proud of her Mexican heritage.

6. *True or false?* _____ The conveyor-belt ladies did much to make the author become part of their "sorority."

7. We can infer that Del Castillo Guilbault believes that
    a. the conveyor-belt ladies were treated well by their employer.
    b. the conveyor-belt ladies often experienced sorrow and desperation.
    c. the children of the conveyor-belt ladies would one day go to college.
    d. the tomato pickers made more money than the conveyor-belt ladies.

8. The conveyor-belt ladies
    a. distrusted the author.
    b. took the author into their confidence.
    c. thought the author was immature.
    d. envied the author.

DISCUSSION QUESTIONS

About Content

1. Why was the author "not happy to be part of the agricultural workforce"? What would her schoolmates have thought about the conveyor-belt ladies?

2. What about the conveyor-belt ladies made it difficult for the author not to like them?

3. Why did the conveyor-belt ladies hide the author from the union representative? Would they have done this for any other worker in the shed?

4. What does the fact that the conveyor-belt ladies brought the author "rental contracts or other documents . . . to explain and translate" reveal about the author's purpose?

About Structure

5. In paragraph 15, the author tells us that the conveyor-belt ladies had a good time chattering among themselves. How does she develop or prove this idea?

6. Explain why the sentence in paragraph 22 might serve as the essay's thesis.

7. Reread the first two paragraphs and paragraphs 30–33. What do they have in common?

8. Reread paragraphs 22–33, and underline all of the transitional words and phrases you find in them.

About Style and Tone

9. The tone in paragraph 17, which is rather humorous, gives way to a more serious tone in the paragraphs that follow. Find a few words that are used to create that more serious tone.

10. In paragraph 2, the author uses the image of a play "where all the action occurs on one set" to describe her job. Where else does she use effective images? Check paragraphs 10, 12, 17, 28, and 30.

11. The author uses contrast to tell us that the work in the shed was easier than the work in the fields (paragraph 4). Where else does she use contrast?

RESPONDING TO IMAGES

Although it is not always glamorous, financially rewarding, or even respected by others, manual labor can often be a source of great dignity. Write an essay about someone who worked or has worked hard all of his or her life. Do you respect this person for what he or she has accomplished? Why? Write an essay that discusses the kind of worklife this individual has led and explains why you respect him or her so much.

WRITING ASSIGNMENTS

Assignment 1: Writing a Paragraph

"At the end of the season, there was no applause" we learn in paragraph 2. On the surface, this idea is part of the author's comparing her job to a play. However, it also suggests the fact that these women were underappreciated and underpaid.

Write a paragraph about a person or group of people you know well whose efforts are underappreciated. You might consider some of the employees at the discount warehouse where you work or your mother, whose family should recognize her dedication to them more often. Begin by summarizing what your subject or subjects do to merit appreciation. Then, suggest ways in which they might be better rewarded or recognized for their efforts.

Assignment 2: Writing a Paragraph

The author characterizes the boss of the conveyor-belt ladies as "dyspeptic," and she provides a few details to prove her point. Look up the word "dyspeptic" in a dictionary if you are unsure of its meaning. Then, write a paragraph in which you discuss *one* negative or positive characteristic of a boss for whom you have recently worked. The main idea for this paragraph might read like one of these:

> Mary Zito was the kindest employer I have ever had.
>
> Paul Longreen seemed to have eyes in the back of his head.
>
> John Savant expected his employees to work as hard as he did.
>
> Mrs. J., my boss at Hotdog Heaven, could never make up her mind.

Assignment 3: Writing an Essay

The author's purpose in this essay is to show us how her association with the conveyor-belt ladies changed her mind about other members of her culture and about the value of manual labor. Have you ever held a job or had any other kind of experience that caused you to change your mind about a person or a group of people about whom you once thought negatively? What other changes in your attitude or personality did this experience cause?

Write an essay in which you narrate the experience or tell about the job in order to answer questions like the previous ones. Here's a possible outline for your essay:

Thesis: My job at the Acme Cheese Plant opened my eyes to the value of hard work and made me appreciate the people who do it.

Topic Sentence—Paragraph 1: At first I hated the job my dad got me at the Acme Cheese Plant.

 a. The work was strenuous.

 b. I came home smelling like cheese every night.

 c. I had nothing in common with the people I worked with.

Topic Sentence—Paragraph 2: After I got my first paycheck, my attitude began to change.

 a. I knew I would be able to save enough for a year's tuition.

 b. I had enough spending money to take my girlfriend out once a week.

 c. I still stunk when I got home, but a shower took care of that, and then I had the whole night to myself.

Topic Sentence—Paragraph 3: I also gained an appreciation and affection for my coworkers.

 a. They were friendly and open from the start.

 b. They took an interest in my college plans.

continued

> c. *When I nearly cut my finger off, they rushed to me, patched me up, and took me to the hospital in one of their own cars.*
>
> d. *I found that they had hopes and dreams too, that they loved their families, that they worked hard, and that they were well worth knowing.*

Conclude your essay by making reference to your introduction and your thesis. Then, explain how the lesson of this experience has helped you grow and how it might serve you in the future.

The "F Word"

Firoozeh Dumas

PREVIEW	WORDS TO WATCH
Firoozeh Dumas emigrated to Southern California from Iran in 1972. In her book *Funny in Farsi*, from which this essay is taken, Dumas talks about the culture shock she experienced as she grew up in the United States. Farsi is an official language in Iran, Afghanistan, and Tajikistan.	fraught (2) monosyllabic (2) phlegm (2) exotic (3) analogies (3) inquisition (5) affinity (10) postpubescent (10) privy (12) permutation (16)

My cousin's name, Farbod, means "Greatness." When he moved to 1 America, all the kids called him "Farthead." My brother Farshid ("He Who Enlightens") became "Fartshit." The name of my friend Neggar means "Beloved," although it can be more accurately translated as "She Whose Name Almost Incites Riots." Her brother Arash ("Giver") initially couldn't understand why every time he'd say his name, people would laugh and ask him if it itched.

All of us immigrants knew that moving to America would be fraught• 2 with challenges, but none of us thought that our names would be such an obstacle. How could our parents have ever imagined that someday we would end up in a country where monosyllabic• names reign supreme, a land where "William" is shortened to "Bill," where "Susan" becomes "Sue," and "Richard" somehow evolves into "Dick"? America is a great country, but nobody without a mask and a cape has a *z* in his name. And have Americans ever realized the great scope of the guttural sounds they're missing? Okay, so it has to do with linguistic roots, but I do believe this would be a richer country if all Americans could do a little tongue aerobics and learn to pronounce "kh," a sound more commonly associated in this culture with phlegm•, or "gh," the sound usually made by actors in the final moments of a choking

476 PART 4 Readings for Writers

scene. It's like adding a few new spices to the kitchen pantry. Move over, cinnamon and nutmeg, make way for cardamom and sumac.

Exotic° analogies° aside, having a foreign name in this land of Joes 3 and Marys is a pain in the spice cabinet. When I was twelve, I decided to simplify my life by adding an American middle name. This decision serves as proof that sometimes simplifying one's life in the short run only complicates it in the long run.

My name, Firoozeh, chosen by my mother, means "Turquoise" in 4 Persian. In America, it means "Unpronounceable" or "I'm Not Going to Talk to You Because I Cannot Possibly Learn Your Name and I Just Don't Want to Have to Ask You Again and Again Because You'll Think I'm Dumb or You Might Get Upset or Something." My father, incidentally, had wanted to name me Sara. I do wish he had won that argument.

To strengthen my decision to add an American name, I had just fin- 5 ished fifth grade in Whittier, where all the kids incessantly called me "Ferocious." That summer, my family moved to Newport Beach, where I looked forward to starting a new life. I wanted to be a kid with a name that didn't draw so much attention, a name that didn't come with a built-in inquisition° as to when and why I had moved to America and how was it that I spoke English without an accent and was I planning on going back and what did I think of America?

My last name didn't help any. I can't mention my maiden name, 6 because:

"Dad, I'm writing a memoir."   7

"Great! Just don't mention our name."   8

Suffice it to say that, with eight letters, including a z, and four syllables, 9 my last name is as difficult and foreign as my first. My first and last name together generally served the same purpose as a high brick wall. There was one exception to this rule. In Berkeley, and only in Berkeley, my name drew people like flies to baklava. These were usually people named Amaryllis or Chrysanthemum, types who vacationed in Costa Rica and to whom lentils described a type of burger. These folks were probably not the pride of Poughkeepsie, but they were refreshingly nonjudgmental.

When I announced to my family that I wanted to add an American 10 name, they reacted with their usual laughter. Never one to let mockery or good judgment stand in my way, I proceeded to ask for suggestions. My father suggested "Fifi." Had I had a special affinity° for French poodles or been considering a career in prostitution, I would've gone with that one. My mom suggested "Farah," a name easier than "Firoozeh" yet still Iranian. Her reasoning made sense, except that Farrah Fawcett was at the height of her popularity and I didn't want to be associated with somebody whose poster hung in every postpubescent° boy's bedroom. We couldn't think of any American names beginning with *F*, so we moved on to *J*, the first letter of our last name. I don't know why we limited ourselves to names beginning with my initials, but it made sense at that moment, perhaps by the logic employed moments before bungee jumping. I finally chose the name "Julie" mainly for its simplicity. My brothers, Farid and Farshid, thought that adding an American name was totally stupid. They later became Fred and Sean.

That same afternoon, our doorbell rang. It was our new next-door neigh- 11 bor, a friendly girl my age named Julie. She asked me my name and after a moment of hesitation. I introduced myself as Julie. "What a coincidence!" she said. I didn't mention that I had been Julie for only half an hour.

Thus I started sixth grade with my new, easy name and life became 12 infinitely simpler. People actually remembered my name, which was an entirely refreshing new sensation. All was well until the Iranian Revolution, when I found myself with a new set of problems. Because I spoke English without an accent and was known as Julie, people assumed I was American. This meant that I was often privy• to their real feelings about those "damn I-raynians." It was like having those X-ray glasses that let you see people naked, except that what I was seeing was far uglier than people's underwear. It dawned on me that these people would have probably never invited me to their house had they known me as Firoozeh. I felt like a fake.

When I went to college, I eventually went back to using my real name. 13 All was well until I graduated and started looking for a job. Even though I had graduated with honors from UC–Berkeley, I couldn't get a single interview. I was guilty of being a humanities major, but I began to suspect that there was more to my problems. After three months of rejections, I added "Julie" to my résumé. Call it coincidence, but the job offers started coming in. Perhaps it's the same kind of coincidence that keeps African Americans from getting cabs in New York.

Once I got married, my name became Julie Dumas. I went from having 14 an identifiably "ethnic" name to having ancestors who wore clogs. My family and non-American friends continued calling me Firoozeh, while my coworkers and American friends called me Julie. My life became one big knot, especially when friends who knew me as Julie met friends who knew me as Firoozeh. I felt like those characters in soap operas who have an evil twin. The two, of course, can never be in the same room, since they're played by the same person, a struggling actress who wears a wig to play one of the twins and dreams of moving on to bigger and better roles. I couldn't blame my mess on a screenwriter; it was my own doing.

I decided to untangle the knot once and for all by going back to my real 15 name. By then, I was a stay-at-home mom, so I really didn't care whether people remembered my name or gave me job interviews. Besides, most of the people I dealt with were in diapers and were in no position to judge. I was also living in Silicon Valley, an area filled with people named Rajeev, Avishai, and Insook.

Every once in a while, though, somebody comes up with a new per- 16 mutation• and I am once again reminded that I am an immigrant with a foreign name. I recently went to have blood drawn for a physical exam. The waiting room for blood work at our local medical clinic is in the basement of the building, and no matter how early one arrives for an appointment, forty coughing, wheezing people have gotten there first. Apart from reading *Golf Digest* and *Popular Mechanics*, there isn't much to do except guess the number of contagious diseases represented in the windowless room. Every ten minutes, a name is called and everyone looks to see which cough matches that name. As I waited patiently, the receptionist called out, "Fritzy, Fritzy!" Everyone looked around, but no one stood up. Usually, if I'm waiting to be called by someone who doesn't know me, I will respond to just about any name starting with an *F*. Having been called Froozy, Frizzy, Fiorucci, and

Frooz and just plain "Uhhhh . . . ," I am highly accommodating. I did not, however, respond to "Fritzy" because there is, as far as I know, no *t* in my name. The receptionist tried again, "Fritzy, Fritzy DumbAss." As I stood up to this most linguistically original version of my name, I could feel all eyes upon me. The room was momentarily silent as all of these sick people sat united in a moment of gratitude for their own names.

Despite a few exceptions, I have found that Americans are now far more 17 willing to learn new names, just as they're far more willing to try new ethnic foods. Of course, some people just don't like to learn. One mom at my children's school adamantly refused to learn my "impossible" name and instead settled on calling me "F Word." She was recently transferred to New York where, from what I've heard, she might meet an immigrant or two and, who knows, she just might have to make some room in her spice cabinet.

VOCABULARY IN CONTEXT

1. The word *inquisition* in "I wanted to be a kid with a name that didn't draw so much attention, a name that didn't come with a built-in inquisition . . ." (paragraph 5) means
   a. set of questions.
   b. set of associations.
   c. comparison.
   d. torture.

2. The word *permutation* in "Every once in a while, though, somebody comes up with a new permutation and I am once again reminded that I am an immigrant with a foreign name" (paragraph 16) means
   a. nickname.
   b. title.
   c. form of.
   d. slang term.

READING COMPREHENSION QUESTIONS

1. Which of the following would be the best alternative title for this selection?
   a. I Hate My Name
   b. Coming to America
   c. What's in a Name?
   d. Iranian vs. American Culture

2. Which of the following best expresses the main idea of this selection?
   a. Iranian immigrants have had difficulty adjusting to America.
   b. Americans are, on the whole, intolerant of foreigners.
   c. To Americans, Iranian names sound odd.
   d. One should never be ashamed of his or her background or culture.

3. When the author decided to take an American name, her family
    a. encouraged her.
    b. got angry.
    c. thought she was being foolish.
    d. called a psychiatrist.

4. Calling herself "Julie" helped the author to
    a. feel better.
    b. perform better in school.
    c. learn how Americans really felt about Iranians.
    d. see through people's clothing.

5. What resulted from the author's using the name "Julie" in her résumé?
    a. She began to get job offers.
    b. Her parents got angry.
    c. Her brothers laughed.
    d. She decided to look for work in New York.

6. *True or false?* _____ The author went back to her real name after getting married because the people she associated with at the time had no problem with it.

7. We can infer that now, the author
    a. still dislikes her name.
    b. wants to return to Iran.
    c. is proud of her Farsi name.
    d. is still married.

DISCUSSION QUESTIONS

About Content

1. Why in paragraph 2 does Dumas advise Americans to learn new sounds? How will this help them?

2. "Sometimes simplifying one's life in the short run only complicates it in the long run," says Dumas in paragraph 3. What information does she include in the paragraphs that follow to develop or prove this point?

3. Why do you think the author's father tells her not to mention their family name in her memoir?

About Structure

4. One reason Dumas's conclusion is effective is that it recalls something mentioned in paragraph 2. What is that?

5. Much of this essay is organized as a narrative that uses several transitions, making it easy to follow. Pick out the transitional words

and phrases that appear between paragraphs 8 and 14. Write them here:

_____   _____

_____   _____

_____   _____

_____

About Style and Tone

6. The tone of this essay—the writer's attitude toward her subject—is often lighthearted. Find at least three places in which the author uses humor to get her point across.

7. Dumas uses many similes and metaphors to provide both variety and color. Both metaphors and similes make comparisons, but only similes use *like* or *as*. Identify at least three similes and/or metaphors in this essay.

RESPONDING TO IMAGES

This photograph shows immigrants entering the United States through Ellis Island, New York, during the early twentieth century. If you are an immigrant or are the child or grandchild of an immigrant, write an essay in which you explain what difficulties you or your parent or grandparent encountered in trying to adjust to American society. You might also know a recent immigrant. If so, write about her or him. If the subject of your essay is someone other than yourself, try interviewing her or him to gather important information for your essay.

WRITING ASSIGNMENTS

Assignment 1: Writing a Paragraph

Dumas writes "Exotic analogies aside, having a foreign name in this land of Joes and Marys is a pain in the spice cabinet" (paragraph 3). She is telling us, of course, that an Iranian name caused her a great deal of embarrassment and annoyance as she grew up in America.

Is there something about you that people once teased you about or about which you were once sensitive? Your name? Something to do with your appearance? Your culture? Your value system? Your political or religious beliefs?

Write a paragraph in which you explain how you reacted when someone teased or harassed you about this. Limit your paragraph to one event or incident. You might begin with a topic sentence that goes something like this:

> When I first started wearing glasses in sixth grade, my classmates teased me unmercifully.

Assignment 2: Writing a Paragraph

The author of this essay implies that being around people from other cultures is healthy because it broadens us. Think of a person you know from a culture other than your own. What have you learned about this person's culture? Write a paragraph that discusses one way your association with this person has changed you. For example, have you gained an appreciation for her or his religion, values, history, food, or family life? Here's a sentence that might begin such a paragraph:

> Ever since meeting Ravi, I have developed a craving for Indian food.

Assignment 3: Writing an Essay

As a child, Dumas felt embarrassed and uncomfortable with her name. As she grew older, however, her attitude changed, and she became proud of both her name and her heritage. This change is not unusual; it happens to many people. Think of something that embarrassed you or made you feel uncomfortable about yourself, your family, or your culture when you were younger.

Write an essay that, like Dumas's, explains the process by which you dealt with this feeling at various points in your life. End your essay by explaining how you overcame your embarrassment and how you came to be proud of something that once bothered you. The thesis for this essay might read something like this:

> When I was a child, I tried to hide the fact that I excelled at math because I didn't want my classmates and friends to think I was a "nerd."

You might organize your essay using a scratch outline like the following:

1. Ever since first grade, I have been good at math. By seventh grade, I was put into an accelerated math class with, well, a bunch of "nerds."

continued

2. *Some of my fellow basketball-team members poked fun at me, and some of my friends called me "algebra queen."*

3. *I refused to join the math club or to take the advanced placement test for math.*

4. *When I got to college, I realized how foolish I had been.*

5. *I am now majoring in math and even tutoring students like those who had made fun of me in high school.*

Develop each section of your paper with detailed anecdotes about what happened at each stage of the process. As always, provide an effective introduction and conclusion to your essay. For example, the student who was writing the essay described previously might have begun by explaining how embarrassed she got every time her parents bragged about her mathematics skills. She might conclude by explaining that one should never try to hide his or her natural talents or skills, no matter what others may say.

Do It Better!

Ben Carson, M.D., with Cecil Murphey

PREVIEW

If you suspect that you are now as "smart" as you'll ever be, then read the following selection. Taken from the book **Think Big**, it is about Dr. Ben Carson, who was sure he was "the dumbest kid in the class" when he was in fifth grade. Carson tells how he turned his life totally around from what was a path of failure. Today he is a famous neurosurgeon at the Johns Hopkins University Children's Center in Baltimore, Maryland.

WORDS TO WATCH

parochial (20)
trauma (20)
tenement (20)
reluctantly (56)
indifferent (58)
acknowledged (67)
obsidian (74)

"Benjamin, is this your report card?" my mother asked as she picked 1 up the folded white card from the table.

"Uh, yeah," I said, trying to sound casual. Too ashamed to hand it to 2 her, I had dropped it on the table, hoping that she wouldn't notice until after I went to bed.

It was the first report card I had received from Higgins Elementary 3 School since we had moved back from Boston to Detroit, only a few months earlier.

I had been in the fifth grade not even two weeks before everyone con- 4 sidered me the dumbest kid in the class and frequently made jokes about me. Before long I too began to feel as though I really was the most stupid kid in fifth grade. Despite Mother's frequently saying, "You're smart, Bennie. You can do anything you want to do," I did not believe her.

No one else in school thought I was smart, either. 5

Now, as Mother examined my report card, she asked, "What's this 6 grade in reading?" (Her tone of voice told me that I was in trouble.) Although I was embarrassed, I did not think too much about it. Mother knew that I wasn't doing well in math, but she did not know I was doing so poorly in every subject.

While she slowly read my report card, reading everything one word 7 at a time, I hurried into my room and started to get ready for bed. A few minutes later, Mother came into my bedroom.

"Benjamin," she said, "are these your grades?" She held the card in 8 front of me as if I hadn't seen it before.

"Oh, yeah, but you know, it doesn't mean much." 9

"No, that's not true, Bennie. It means a lot." 10

"Just a report card." 11

"But it's more than that." 12

Knowing I was in for it now, I prepared to listen, yet I was not all that 13 interested. I did not like school very much and there was no reason why I should. Inasmuch as I was the dumbest kid in the class, what did I have to look forward to? The others laughed at me and made jokes about me every day.

"Education is the only way you're ever going to escape poverty," she 14 said. "It's the only way you're ever going to get ahead in life and be successful. Do you understand that?"

"Yes, Mother," I mumbled. 15

"If you keep on getting these kinds of grades you're going to spend the 16 rest of your life on skid row, or at best sweeping floors in a factory. That's not the kind of life that I want for you. That's not the kind of life that God wants for you."

I hung my head, genuinely ashamed. My mother had been raising 17 me and my older brother, Curtis, by herself. Having only a third-grade education herself, she knew the value of what she did not have. Daily she drummed into Curtis and me that we had to do our best in school.

"You're just not living up to your potential," she said. "I've got two 18 mighty smart boys and I know they can do better."

I had done my best—at least I had when I first started at Higgins 19 Elementary School. How could I do much when I did not understand anything going on in our class?

In Boston we had attended a parochial• school, but I hadn't learned 20 much because of a teacher who seemed more interested in talking to another female teacher than in teaching us. Possibly, this teacher was not solely to blame—perhaps I wasn't emotionally able to learn much. My parents had separated just before we went to Boston, when I was eight years old. I loved both my mother and father and went through considerable trauma• over their separating. For months afterward, I kept thinking that my parents would get back together, that my daddy would come home again the way he used to, and that we could be the same old family again—but he never came back. Consequently, we moved to Boston and lived with Aunt Jean and Uncle William Avery in a tenement• building for two years until Mother had saved enough money to bring us back to Detroit.

Mother kept shaking the report card at me as she sat on the side of my 21 bed. "You have to work harder. You have to use that good brain that God gave you, Bennie. Do you understand that?"

"Yes, Mother." Each time she paused, I would dutifully say those 22 words.

"I work among rich people, people who are educated," she said. "I 23 watch how they act, and I know they can do anything they want to do. And so can you." She put her arm on my shoulder. "Bennie, you can do anything they can do—only you can do it better!"

Mother had said those words before. Often. At the time, they did 24 not mean much to me. Why should they? I really believed that I was the dumbest kid in fifth grade, but of course, I never told her that.

"I just don't know what to do about you boys," she said. "I'm going 25 to talk to God about you and Curtis." She paused, stared into space, then said (more to herself than to me), "I need the Lord's guidance on what to do. You just can't bring in any more report cards like this."

As far as I was concerned, the report card matter was over. 26

The next day was like the previous ones—just another bad day in 27 school, another day of being laughed at because I did not get a single problem right in arithmetic and couldn't get any words right on the spelling test. As soon as I came home from school, I changed into play clothes and ran outside. Most of the boys my age played softball, or the game I liked best, "Tip the Top."

We played Tip the Top by placing a bottle cap on one of the sidewalk 28 cracks. Then taking a ball—any kind that bounced—we'd stand on a line and take turns throwing the ball at the bottle top, trying to flip it over. Whoever succeeded got two points. If anyone actually moved the cap more than a few inches, he won five points. Ten points came if he flipped it into the air and it landed on the other side.

When it grew dark or we got tired, Curtis and I would finally go inside 29 and watch TV. The set stayed on until we went to bed. Because Mother worked long hours, she was never home until just before we went to bed. Sometimes I would awaken when I heard her unlocking the door.

Two evenings after the incident with the report card, Mother came 30 home about an hour before our bedtime. Curtis and I were sprawled out, watching TV. She walked across the room, snapped off the set, and faced both of us. "Boys," she said, "you're wasting too much of your time in front of that television. You don't get an education from staring at television all the time."

Before either of us could make a protest, she told us that she had been 31 praying for wisdom. "The Lord's told me what to do," she said. "So from now on, you will not watch television, except for two preselected programs each week."

"Just *two* programs?" I could hardly believe she would say such a ter- 32 rible thing. "That's not—"

"And *only* after you've done your homework. Furthermore, you don't 33 play outside after school, either, until you've done all your homework."

"Everybody else plays outside right after school," I said, unable to 34 think of anything except how bad it would be if I couldn't play with my friends. "I won't have any friends if I stay in the house all the time—"

"That may be," Mother said, "but everybody else is not going to be as 35 successful as you are—"

"But, Mother—" 36

"This is what we're going to do. I asked God for wisdom, and this is 37 the answer I got."

I tried to offer several other arguments, but Mother was firm. I glanced 38 at Curtis, expecting him to speak up, but he did not say anything. He lay on the floor, staring at his feet.

"Don't worry about everybody else. The whole world is full of 'every- 39 body else,' you know that? But only a few make a significant achievement."

The loss of TV and play time was bad enough. I got up off the floor, 40 feeling as if everything was against me. Mother wasn't going to let me play with my friends, and there would be no more television—almost none, anyway. She was stopping me from having any fun in life.

"And that isn't all," she said. "Come back, Bennie." 41

I turned around, wondering what else there could be. 42

"In addition," she said, "to doing your homework, you have to read 43 two books from the library each week. Every single week."

"Two books? Two?" Even though I was in fifth grade, I had never read 44 a whole book in my life.

"Yes, two. When you finish reading them, you must write me a book 45 report just like you do at school. You're not living up to your potential, so I'm going to see that you do."

Usually Curtis, who was two years older, was the more rebellious. But 46 this time he seemed to grasp the wisdom of what Mother said. He did not say one word.

She stared at Curtis. "You understand?"   47

He nodded.   48

"Bennie, is it clear?"   49

"Yes, Mother." I agreed to do what Mother told me—it wouldn't have 50 occurred to me not to obey—but I did not like it. Mother was being unfair and demanding more of us than other parents did.

The following day was Thursday. After school, Curtis and I walked 51 to the local branch of the library. I did not like it much, but then I had not spent that much time in any library.

We both wandered around a little in the children's section, not having any 52 idea about how to select books or which books we wanted to check out.

The librarian came over to us and asked if she could help. We explained 53 that both of us wanted to check out two books.

"What kind of books would you like to read?" the librarian asked.   54

"Animals," I said after thinking about it. "Something about animals." 55

"I'm sure we have several that you'd like." She led me over to a sec- 56 tion of books. She left me and guided Curtis to another section of the room. I flipped through the row of books until I found two that looked easy enough for me to read. One of them, *Chip, the Dam Builder*—about a beaver—was the first one I had ever checked out. As soon as I got home, I started to read it. It was the first book I ever read all the way through even though it took me two nights. Reluctantly* I admitted afterward to Mother that I really had liked reading about Chip.

Within a month I could find my way around the children's section like 57 someone who had gone there all his life. By then the library staff knew Curtis and me and the kind of books we chose. They often made sugges- tions. "Here's a delightful book about a squirrel," I remember one of them telling me.

As she told me part of the story, I tried to appear indifferent,* but as 58 soon as she handed it to me, I opened the book and started to read.

Best of all, we became favorites of the librarians. When new books 59 came in that they thought either of us would enjoy, they held them for us. Soon I became fascinated as I realized that the library had so many books—and about so many different subjects.

After the book about the beaver, I chose others about animals—all 60 types of animals. I read every animal story I could get my hands on. I read books about wolves, wild dogs, several about squirrels, and a vari- ety of animals that lived in other countries. Once I had gone through the animal books, I started reading about plants, then minerals, and finally rocks.

My reading books about rocks was the first time the information ever 61 became practical to me. We lived near the railroad tracks, and when Curtis and I took the route to school that crossed by the tracks, I began paying attention to the crushed rock that I noticed between the ties.

As I continued to read more about rocks, I would walk along the 62 tracks, searching for different kinds of stones, and then see if I could identify them.

Often I would take a book with me to make sure that I had labeled each 63 stone correctly.

"Agate," I said as I threw the stone. Curtis got tired of my picking up 64 stones and identifying them, but I did not care because I kept finding new stones all the time. Soon it became my favorite game to walk along the tracks and identify the varieties of stones. Although I did not realize it, within a very short period of time, I was actually becoming an expert on rocks.

Two things happened in the second half of fifth grade that convinced 65 me of the importance of reading books.

First, our teacher, Mrs. Williamson, had a spelling bee every Friday 66 afternoon. We'd go through all the words we'd had so far that year. Sometimes she also called out words that we were supposed to have learned in fourth grade. Without fail, I always went down on the first word.

One Friday, though, Bobby Farmer, whom everyone acknowledged• 67 as the smartest kid in our class, had to spell "agriculture" as his final word. As soon as the teacher pronounced his word, I thought, *I can spell that word.* Just the day before, I had learned it from reading one of my library books. I spelled it under my breath, and it was just the way Bobby spelled it.

If I can spell "agriculture," I'll bet I can learn to spell any other word in the 68 *world. I'll bet I can learn to spell better than Bobby Farmer.*

Just that single word, "agriculture," was enough to give me hope.   69

The following week, a second thing happened that forever changed 70 my life. When Mr. Jaeck, the science teacher, was teaching us about volcanoes, he held up an object that looked like a piece of black, glass-like rock. "Does anybody know what this is? What does it have to do with volcanoes?"

Immediately, because of my reading, I recognized the stone. I waited, 71 but none of my classmates raised their hands. I thought, *This is strange. Not even the smart kids are raising their hands.* I raised my hand.

"Yes, Benjamin," he said.   72

I heard snickers around me. The other kids probably thought it was a 73 joke, or that I was going to say something stupid.

"Obsidian,•" I said.   74

"That's right!" He tried not to look startled, but it was obvious he 75 hadn't expected me to give the correct answer.

"That's obsidian," I said, "and it's formed by the supercooling of lava 76 when it hits the water." Once I had their attention and realized I knew information no other student had learned, I began to tell them everything I knew about the subject of obsidian, lava, lava flow, supercooling, and compacting of the elements.

When I finally paused, a voice behind me whispered, "Is that Bennie 77
Carson?"

"You're absolutely correct," Mr. Jaeck said, and he smiled at me. If he 78
had announced that I'd won a million-dollar lottery, I couldn't have been
more pleased and excited.

"Benjamin, that's absolutely, absolutely right," he repeated with 79
enthusiasm in his voice. He turned to the others and said, "That is wonderful! Class, this is a tremendous piece of information Benjamin has just
given us. I'm very proud to hear him say this."

For a few moments, I tasted the thrill of achievement. I recall thinking, 80
*Wow, look at them. They're all looking at me with admiration. Me, the dummy!
The one everybody thinks is stupid. They're looking at me to see if this is really me
speaking.*

Maybe, though, it was I who was the most astonished one in the 81
class. Although I had been reading two books a week because Mother
told me to, I had not realized how much knowledge I was accumulating.
True, I had learned to enjoy reading, but until then I hadn't realized how
it connected with my schoolwork. That day—for the first time—I realized that Mother had been right. Reading is the way out of ignorance,
and the road to achievement. I did not have to be the class dummy
anymore.

For the next few days, I felt like a hero at school. The jokes about me 82
stopped. The kids started to listen to me. *I'm starting to have fun with this
stuff.*

As my grades improved in every subject, I asked myself, "Ben, is there 83
any reason you can't be the smartest kid in the class? If you can learn about
obsidian, you can learn about social studies and geography and math and
science and everything."

That single moment of triumph pushed me to want to read more. 84
From then on, it was as though I could not read enough books. Whenever
anyone looked for me after school, they could usually find me in my
bedroom—curled up, reading a library book—for a long time, the only
thing I wanted to do. I had stopped caring about the TV programs I was
missing; I no longer cared about playing Tip the Top or baseball anymore.
I just wanted to read.

In a year and a half—by the middle of sixth grade—I had moved to the 85
top of the class.

VOCABULARY IN CONTEXT

1. The word *trauma* in "I loved both my mother and father and went
   through considerable trauma over their separating. For months afterward, I kept thinking that my parents would get back together . . . but
   he never came back" (paragraph 20) means

   a. love.

   b. knowledge.

   c. distance.

   d. suffering.

2. The word *acknowledged* in "One Friday, though, Bobby Farmer, whom everyone acknowledged as the smartest kid in our class, had to spell 'agriculture' as his final word" (paragraph 67) means

   a. denied.

   b. recognized.

   c. forgot.

   d. interrupted.

READING COMPREHENSION QUESTIONS

1. Which of the following would be the best alternative title for this selection?

   a. The Importance of Fifth Grade

   b. The Role of Parents in Education

   c. The Day I Surprised My Science Teacher

   d. Reading Changed My Life

2. Which sentence best expresses the main idea of this selection?

   a. Children who grow up in single-parent homes may spend large amounts of time home alone.

   b. Because of parental guidance that led to a love of reading, the author was able to go from academic failure to success.

   c. Most children do not take school very seriously, and they suffer as a result.

   d. Today's young people watch too much television.

3. Bennie's mother

   a. was not a religious person.

   b. spoke to Bennie's teacher about Bennie's poor report card.

   c. had only a third-grade education.

   d. had little contact with educated people.

4. To get her sons to do better in school, Mrs. Carson insisted that they

   a. stop watching TV.

   b. finish their homework before playing.

   c. read one library book every month.

   d. all of the above.

5. *True or false?* _____ Bennie's first experience with a library book was discouraging.

6. We can conclude that Bennie Carson believed he was dumb because

   a. in Boston he had not learned much.

   b. other students laughed at him.

   c. he had done his best when he first started at Higgins Elementary School, but he still got poor grades.

   d. all of the above.

7. We can conclude that the author's mother believed
    a. education leads to success.
    b. her sons needed to be forced to live up to their potential.
    c. socializing was less important for her sons than a good education.
    d. all of the above.

8. From paragraphs 70–80, we can infer that
    a. Bennie thought his classmates were stupid because they did not know about obsidian.
    b. Mr. Jaeck knew less about rocks than Bennie did.
    c. this was the first time Bennie had answered a difficult question correctly in class.
    d. Mr. Jaeck thought that Bennie had taken too much class time explaining about obsidian.

DISCUSSION QUESTIONS

About Content

1. How do you think considering himself the "dumbest kid in class" affected Bennie's schoolwork?

2. The author recalls his failure in the classroom as an eight-year-old child by writing, "Perhaps I wasn't emotionally able to learn much." Why does he make this statement? What do you think parents and schools can do to help children through difficult times?

3. How did Mrs. Carson encourage Bennie to make school—particularly reading—a priority in his life? What effect did her efforts have on Bennie's academic performance and self-esteem?

4. As a child, Carson began to feel confident about his own abilities when he followed his mother's guidelines. How might Mrs. Carson's methods help adult students build up their own self-confidence and motivation?

About Structure

5. What is the main order in which the details of this selection are organized—time order or listing order? Locate and write below three of the many transitions that are used as part of that time order or listing order.

    _____   _____   _____

6. In paragraph 65, Carson states, "Two things happened in the second half of fifth grade that convinced me of the importance of reading books." What two transitions does Carson use in later paragraphs to help readers recognize those two events? Write those two transitions here:

    _____   _____

About Style and Tone

7. Instead of describing his mother, Carson reveals her character through specific details of her actions and words. Find one paragraph in which

this technique is used, and write its number here: _____. What does this paragraph tell us about Mrs. Carson?

8. Why do you suppose Carson italicizes sentences in paragraphs 67, 68, 71, 80, and 82? What purpose do the italicized sentences serve?

WRITING ASSIGNMENTS

Assignment 1: Writing a Paragraph

The reading tells about some of Carson's most important school experiences, both positive and negative. Write a paragraph about one of your most important experiences in school. To select an event to write about, try asking yourself the following questions:

Which teachers or events in school influenced how I felt about myself?

What specific incidents stand out in my mind as I think back to elementary school?

To get started, you might use freewriting to help you remember and record the details. Then begin your draft with a topic sentence similar to one of the following:

A seemingly small experience in elementary school encouraged me greatly.

If not for my sixth-grade teacher, I would not be where I am today.

My tenth-grade English class was a turning point in my life.

Use concrete details—actions, comments, reactions, and so on—to help your readers see what happened.

Assignment 2: Writing a Paragraph

Reading helped Bennie, and it can do a lot for adults, too. Most of us, however, don't have someone around to make us do a certain amount of personal reading every week. In addition, many of us don't have as much free time as Bennie and Curtis had. How can adults find time to read more? Write a paragraph listing several ways adults can add more reading to their lives.

To get started, simply write down as many ways as you can think of—in any order. Here is an example of a prewriting list for this paper:

Situations in which adults can find extra time to read:

Riding to and from work or school

In bed at night before turning off the light

While eating breakfast or lunch

Instead of watching some TV

In the library

Feel free to use items from the list above, but see if you can add at least one or two of your own ideas as well. Use descriptions and examples to emphasize and dramatize your supporting details.

Assignment 3: Writing an Essay

Mrs. Carson discovered an effective way to boost her children's achievement and self-confidence. There are other ways as well. Write an essay whose thesis statement is "There are several ways parents can help children live up to their potential." Then, in the following paragraphs, explain and illustrate two or three methods parents can use. In choosing material for your supporting paragraphs, you might consider some of these areas, or think of others on your own:

> Assigning regular household "chores" and rewarding a good job
>
> Encouraging kids to join an organization that fosters achievement: Scouts, Little League, religious group, or neighborhood service club
>
> Going to parent-teacher conferences at school and then working more closely with children's teachers—knowing when assignments are due, and so on
>
> Giving a child some responsibility for an enjoyable family activity, such as choosing decorations or food for a birthday party
>
> Setting up a "Wall of Fame" in the home where children's artwork, successful schoolwork, and so on, can be displayed
>
> Setting guidelines (as Mrs. Carson did) for use of leisure time, homework time, and the like

Draw on examples from your own experiences or from someone else's—including those of Bennie Carson, if you like.

How They Get You to Do That

Janny Scott

PREVIEW	WORDS TO WATCH
So you think you're sailing along in life, making decisions based on your own preferences? Not likely! Janny Scott brings together the findings of several researchers to show how advertisers, charitable organizations, politicians, employers, and even your friends get you to say "yes" when you should have said "no"—or, at least, "Let me think about that."	propaganda (2) wielding (3) compliance (4) pervasive (4) proliferates (8) teeming (11) jujitsu (15) peripheral (23) dapper (24) inveterate (24) reciprocity (28) deference (37)

The woman in the supermarket in a white coat tenders a free sample 1
of "lite" cheese. A car salesman suggests that prices won't stay low for long. Even a penny will help, pleads the door-to-door solicitor. Sale ends Sunday! Will work for food.

The average American exists amid a perpetual torrent of propaganda.* 2
Everyone, it sometimes seems, is trying to make up someone else's mind.
If it isn't an athletic shoe company, it's a politician, a panhandler, a pitch-
man, a boss, a billboard company, a spouse.

The weapons of influence they are wielding* are more sophisticated 3
than ever, researchers say. And they are aimed at a vulnerable target—
people with less and less time to consider increasingly complex issues.

As a result, some experts in the field have begun warning the public, 4
tipping people off to precisely how "the art of compliance*" works. Some
critics have taken to arguing for new government controls on one perva-
sive* form of persuasion— political advertising.

The persuasion problem is "the essential dilemma of modern democ- 5
racy," argue social psychologists Anthony Pratkanis and Elliot Aronson,
the authors of *Age of Propaganda: The Everyday Use and Abuse of Persuasion.*

As the two psychologists see it, American society values free speech 6
and public discussion, but people no longer have the time or inclination
to pay attention. Mindless propaganda flourishes, they say; thoughtful
persuasion fades away.

The problem stems from what Pratkanis and Aronson call our "message- 7
dense environment." The average television viewer sees nearly 38,000 commercials a year, they say. "The average home receives . . . [numerous] pieces
of junk mail annually and . . . [countless calls] from telemarketing firms."

Bumper stickers, billboards, and posters litter the public conscious- 8
ness. Athletic events and jazz festivals carry corporate labels. As direct
selling proliferates,* workers patrol their offices during lunch breaks, ped-
dling chocolate and Tupperware to friends.

Meanwhile, information of other sorts multiplies exponentially. 9
Technology serves up ever-increasing quantities of data on every imaginable subject, from home security to health. With more and more information available, people have less and less time to digest it.

"It's becoming harder and harder to think in a considered way about 10
anything," said Robert Cialdini, a persuasion researcher at Arizona State
University in Tempe. "More and more, we are going to be deciding on the
basis of less and less information."

Persuasion is a democratic society's chosen method for decision mak- 11
ing and dispute resolution. But the flood of persuasive messages in recent
years has changed the nature of persuasion. Lengthy arguments have been
supplanted by slogans and logos. In a world teeming* with propaganda,
those in the business of influencing others put a premium on effective
shortcuts.

Most people, psychologists say, are easily seduced by such shortcuts. 12
Humans are "cognitive misers," always looking to conserve attention and
mental energy—leaving themselves at the mercy of anyone who has figured out which shortcuts work.

The task of figuring out shortcuts has been embraced by advertising 13
agencies, market researchers, and millions of salespeople. The public,
meanwhile, remains in the dark, ignorant of even the simplest principles
of social influence.

As a result, laypeople underestimate their susceptibility to persua- 14
sion, psychologists say. They imagine their actions are dictated simply by

personal preferences. Unaware of the techniques being used against them, they are often unwittingly outgunned.

As Cialdini tells it, the most powerful tactics work like jujitsu•: They 15 draw their strength from deep-seated, unconscious psychological rules. The clever "compliance professional" deliberately triggers these "hidden stores of influence" to elicit a predictable response.

One such rule, for example, is that people are more likely to comply 16 with a request if a reason—no matter how silly—is given. To prove that point, one researcher tested different ways of asking people in line at a copying machine to let her cut the line.

When the researcher asked simply, "Excuse me, I have five pages. May 17 I use the Xerox machine?" only 60 percent of those asked complied. But when she added nothing more than, "because I have to make some copies," nearly every one agreed.

The simple addition of "because" unleashed an automatic response, 18 even though "because" was followed by an irrelevant reason, Cialdini said. By asking the favor in that way, the researcher dramatically increased the likelihood of getting what she wanted.

Cialdini and others say much of human behavior is mechanical. 19 Automatic responses are efficient when time and attention are short. For that reason, many techniques of persuasion are designed and tested for their ability to trigger those automatic responses.

"These appeals persuade not through the give-and-take of argument 20 and debate," Pratkanis and Aronson have written, " . . . They often appeal to our deepest fears and most irrational hopes, while they make use of our most simplistic beliefs."

Life insurance agents use fear to sell policies, Pratkanis and Aronson 21 say. Parents use fear to convince their children to come home on time. Political leaders use fear to build support for going to war—for example, comparing a foreign leader to Adolf Hitler.

As many researchers see it, people respond to persuasion in one of two 22 ways: If an issue they care about is involved, they may pay close attention to the arguments; if they don't care, they pay less attention and are more likely to be influenced by simple cues.

Their level of attention depends on motivation and the time available. 23 As David Boninger, a UCLA psychologist, puts it, "If you don't have the time or motivation, or both, you will pay attention to more peripheral• cues, like how nice somebody looks."

Cialdini, a dapper• man with a flat Midwestern accent, describes him- 24 self as an inveterate• sucker. From an early age, he said recently, he had wondered what made him say yes in many cases when the answer, had he thought about it, should have been no.

So in the early 1980s, he became "a spy in the wars of influence." He 25 took a sabbatical and, over a three-year period, enrolled in dozens of sales training programs, learning firsthand the tricks of selling insurance, cars, vacuum cleaners, encyclopedias, and more.

He learned how to sell portrait photography over the telephone. He 26 took a job as a busboy in a restaurant, observing the waiters. He worked in fund-raising, advertising, and public relations. And he interviewed cult recruiters and members of bunco squads.

By the time it was over, Cialdini had witnessed hundreds of tac- 27
tics. But he found that the most effective ones were rooted in six principles. Most are not new, but they are being used today with greater
sophistication on people whose fast-paced lifestyle has lowered their
defenses.

Reciprocity.• People have been trained to believe that a favor must be 28
repaid in kind, even if the original favor was not requested. The cultural
pressure to return a favor is so intense that people go along rather than suffer the feeling of being indebted.

Politicians have learned that favors are repaid with votes. Stores offer 29
free samples—not just to show off a product. Charity organizations ship
personalized address labels to potential contributors. Others accost pedestrians, planting paper flowers in their lapels.

Commitment and Consistency. People tend to feel they should be 30
consistent—even when being consistent no longer makes sense. While consistency is easy, comfortable, and generally advantageous, Cialdini says,
"mindless consistency" can be exploited.

Take the "foot in the door technique." One person gets another to 31
agree to a small commitment, like a down payment or signing a petition.
Studies show that it then becomes much easier to get the person to comply
with a much larger request.

Another example Cialdini cites is the "lowball tactic" in car sales. 32
Offered a low price for a car, the potential customer agrees. Then at the last
minute, the sales manager finds a supposed error. The price is increased.
But customers tend to go along nevertheless.

Social Validation. People often decide what is correct on the basis of what 33
other people think. Studies show that is true for behavior. Hence, sitcom
laugh tracks, tip jars "salted" with a bartender's cash, long lines outside
nightclubs, testimonials, and "man on the street" ads.

Tapping the power of social validation is especially effective under 34
certain conditions: When people are in doubt, they will look to others as a
guide; and when they view those others as similar to themselves, they are
more likely to follow their lead.

Liking. People prefer to comply with requests from people they know and 35
like. Charities recruit people to canvass their friends and neighbors. Colleges get alumni to raise money from classmates. Sales training programs
include grooming tips.

According to Cialdini, liking can be based on any of a number of fac- 36
tors. Good-looking people tend to be credited with traits like talent and
intelligence. People also tend to like people who are similar to themselves
in personality, background, and lifestyle.

Authority. People defer to authority. Society trains them to do so, and in 37
many situations deference• is beneficial. Unfortunately, obedience is often
automatic, leaving people vulnerable to exploitation by compliance professionals, Cialdini says.

As an example, he cites the famous ad campaign that capitalized on 38 actor Robert Young's role as Dr. Marcus Welby, Jr., to tout the alleged health benefits of Sanka decaffeinated coffee.

An authority, according to Cialdini, need not be a true authority. The 39 trappings of authority may suffice. Con artists have long recognized the persuasive power of titles like doctor or judge, fancy business suits, and expensive cars.

Scarcity. Products and opportunities seem more valuable when the sup- 40 ply is limited.

As a result, professional persuaders emphasize that "supplies are lim- 41 ited." Sales end Sunday and movies have limited engagements—diverting attention from whether the item is desirable to the threat of losing the chance to experience it at all.

The use of influence, Cialdini says, is ubiquitous.   42

Take the classic appeal by a child of a parent's sense of consistency: 43 "But you said . . ." And the parent's resort to authority: "Because I said so." In addition, nearly everyone invokes the opinions of like-minded others— for social validation—in vying to win a point.

One area in which persuasive tactics are especially controversial is 44 political advertising—particularly negative advertising. Alarmed that attack ads might be alienating voters, some critics have begun calling for stricter limits on political ads.

In Washington, legislation pending in Congress would, among other 45 things, force candidates to identify themselves at the end of their commercials. In that way, they might be forced to take responsibility for the ads' contents and be unable to hide behind campaign committees.

"In general, people accept the notion that for the sale of products 46 at least, there are socially accepted norms of advertising," said Lloyd Morrisett, president of the Markle Foundation, which supports research in communications and information technology.

"But when those same techniques are applied to the political process— 47 where we are judging not a product but a person, and where there is ample room for distortion of the record or falsification in some cases— there begins to be more concern," he said.

On an individual level, some psychologists offer tips for self-protection. 48

* Pay attention to your emotions, says Pratkanis, an associate   49
  professor of psychology at UC Santa Cruz: "If you start to feel
  guilty or patriotic, try to figure out why." In consumer
  transactions, beware of feelings of inferiority and the sense that
  you don't measure up unless you have a certain product.

* Be on the lookout for automatic responses, Cialdini says. Beware 50
  foolish consistency. Check other people's responses against
  objective facts. Be skeptical of authority, and look out for
  unwarranted liking for any "compliance professionals."

Since the publication of his most recent book, *Influence: The New* 51 *Psychology of Modern Persuasion,* Cialdini has begun researching a new book on ethical uses of influence in business—addressing, among other things, how to instruct salespeople and other "influence agents" to use persuasion in ways that help, rather than hurt, society.

"If influence agents don't police themselves, society will have to step 52 in to regulate . . . the way information is presented in commercial and political settings," Cialdini said. "And that's a can of worms that I don't think anybody wants to get into."

VOCABULARY IN CONTEXT

1. The word *wielding* in "The weapons of influence they are wielding are more sophisticated than ever" (paragraph 3) means
   a. handling effectively.
   b. giving up.
   c. looking for.
   d. demanding.

2. The word *peripheral* in "As David Boninger . . . puts it, 'If you don't have the time or motivation, or both, you will pay attention to more peripheral cues, like how nice someone looks'" (paragraph 23) means
   a. important.
   b. dependable.
   c. minor.
   d. attractive.

READING COMPREHENSION QUESTIONS

1. Which of the following would be the best alternative title for this selection?
   a. Automatic Human Responses
   b. Our Deepest Fears
   c. The Loss of Thoughtful Discussion
   d. Compliance Techniques

2. Which sentence best expresses the selection's main point?
   a. Americans are bombarded by various compliance techniques, the dangers of which can be overcome through understanding and legislation.
   b. Fearful of the effects of political attack ads, critics are calling for strict limits on such ads.
   c. With more and more messages demanding our attention, we find it harder and harder to consider any one subject really thoughtfully.
   d. The persuasion researcher Robert Cialdini spent a three-year sabbatical learning the tricks taught in dozens of sales training programs.

3. *True or false?* _____ According to the article, most laypeople think they are more susceptible to persuasion than they really are.

4. According to the article, parents persuade their children to come home on time by appealing to the children's sense of
    a. fair play.
    b. guilt.
    c. humor.
    d. fear.

5. When a visitor walks out of a hotel and a young man runs up, helps the visitor with his luggage, hails a cab, and then expects a tip, the young man is depending on which principle of persuasion?
    a. reciprocity
    b. commitment and consistency
    c. social validation
    d. liking

6. An inference that can be drawn from paragraph 49 is that
    a. Anthony Pratkanis is not a patriotic person.
    b. one compliance technique involves appealing to the consumer's patriotism.
    c. people using compliance techniques never want consumers to feel inferior.
    d. consumers pay too much attention to their own emotions.

7. One can infer from the selection that
    a. the actor Robert Young was well known for his love of coffee.
    b. Sanka is demonstrably better for one's health than other coffees.
    c. the actor Robert Young was also a physician in real life.
    d. the TV character Marcus Welby, Jr., was trustworthy and authoritative.

8. We can conclude that to resist persuasive tactics, a person must
    a. buy fewer products.
    b. take time to question and analyze.
    c. remain patriotic.
    d. avoid propaganda.

DISCUSSION QUESTIONS

About Content

1. What unusual method did Robert Cialdini apply to learn more about compliance techniques? Were you surprised by any of the ways he used his time during that three-year period? Have you ever been employed in a position in which you used one or more compliance techniques?

2. What are the six principles that Cialdini identifies as being behind many persuasion tactics? Describe an incident in which you were subjected to persuasion based on one or more of these principles.

3. In paragraph 16, we learn that "people are more likely to comply with a request if a reason—no matter how silly—is given." Do you find that to be true? Have you complied with requests that, when you thought about them later, were backed up with silly or weak reasons? Describe such an incident. Why do you think such requests work?

4. In paragraphs 44–47, the author discusses persuasive tactics in political advertising. Why might researchers view the use of such tactics in this area as "especially controversial"?

About Structure

5. What is the effect of Janny Scott's introduction to the essay (paragraphs 1 and 2)? On the basis of that introduction, why is a reader likely to feel that the selection will be worth his or her time?

6. Which of the following best describes the conclusion of the selection?

    a. It just stops.

    b. It restates the main point of the selection.

    c. It focuses on possible future occurrences.

    d. It presents a point of view that is the opposite of views in the body of the selection.

    Is this conclusion effective? Why or why not?

About Style and Tone

7. Why might Robert Cialdini have identified himself to the author as an "inveterate sucker"? How does that self-description affect how you regard Cialdini and what he has to say?

8. The author writes, "People defer to authority. Society trains them to do so, and in many situations deference is beneficial." Where does the author herself use the power of authority to support her own points? In what situations would you consider authority to be beneficial?

RESPONDING TO IMAGES

How does this photograph articulate a cause-and-effect relationship?

WRITING ASSIGNMENTS

Assignment 1: Writing a Paragraph

According to the article, "laypeople underestimate their susceptibility to persuasion. . . . They imagine their actions are dictated simply by personal preferences. Unaware of the techniques being used against them, they are often unwittingly outgunned." After having read the selection, do you believe that statement is true of you? Write a paragraph in which you either agree with or argue against the statement. Provide clear, specific examples of ways in which you are or are not influenced by persuasion.

Your topic sentence might be like either of these:

> After reading "How They Get You to Do That," I recognize that I am more influenced by forms of persuasion than I previously thought.

> Many people may "underestimate their susceptibility to persuasion," but I am not one of those people.

Assignment 2: Writing a Paragraph

Think of an advertisement—on TV, on the Internet, in print, or on a billboard—that you have found especially memorable. Write a paragraph in which you describe it. Provide specific details that make your reader understand why you remember it so vividly. Conclude your paragraph by indicating whether or not the advertisement persuaded you to buy or do what it was promoting.

Assignment 3: Writing an Essay

Robert Cialdini identifies "social validation" as a strong persuasion technique. Social validation involves people's need to do what they hope will get approval from the crowd, rather than thinking for themselves. The essay provides several examples of social validation, such as laughing along with a laugh track and getting in a long line to go to a nightclub.

Choose a person you know for whom the need for social validation is very strong. Write an essay about that person and how the need for social validation has impacted several areas of his or her life. Develop each paragraph with colorful, persuasive examples of the person's behavior. (You may wish to write about an invented person, in which case, feel free to use humorous exaggeration to make your points.)

Here is a possible outline for such an essay:

> *Thesis statement: My cousin Nina has a very strong need for social validation.*
>
> *Topic sentence 1: Instead of choosing friends because of their inner qualities, Nina chooses them on the basis of their popularity.*
>
> *Topic sentence 2: Nina's wardrobe has to be made up of the newest and most popular styles.*
>
> *Topic sentence 3: Instead of having any real opinions of her own, Nina adopts her most popular friend's point of view as her own.*

End your essay with a look into the future of a person whose life is ruled by the need for social validation.

Alternatively, write about the most independent thinker you know, someone who tends to do things his or her way without worrying much about what others say.

A Change of Attitude

Grant Berry

PREVIEW	WORDS TO WATCH

PREVIEW

Every college has them: students the same age as some of their professors, students rushing into class after a full day at work, students carrying photographs—not of their boyfriends or girlfriends, but of the children they too seldom see. In many cases, these students are as surprised as anyone to find themselves in college. In this essay, one such student describes his development from a bored high schooler to a committed college student.

WORDS TO WATCH

decades (3)
striven (3)
suavely (4)
immaculately (4)
cliques (5)
tedious (6)
trudging (6)
nil (6)
smugly (8)
deprivation (16)
scowl (21)
battering (22)

For me to be in college is highly improbable. That I am doing well in 1 school teeters on the illogical. Considering my upbringing, past educational performance, and current responsibilities, one might say, "This guy hasn't got a chance." If I were a racehorse and college were the track, there would be few who would pick me to win, place, or show.

When I told my dad that I was going back to school, the only encour- 2 agement he offered was this: "Send me anywhere, but don't send me back to school." For my father, school was the worst kind of prison, so I was raised believing that school at its best was a drag. My dad thought that the purpose of graduating from high school was so you never had to go back to school again, and I adopted this working stiff's philosophy.

I followed my dad's example the way a man who double-crosses the 3 mob follows a cement block to the bottom of the river. My dad has been a union factory worker for more than two decades,• and he has never striven• to be anything more than average. Nonetheless, he is a good man; I love him very much, and I respect him for being a responsible husband and father. He seldom, if ever, missed a day of work; he never left his paycheck at a bar, and none of our household appliances were ever carted off by a repo-man. He took his family to church each week, didn't light up or lift a glass, and has celebrated his silver anniversary with his first, and only, wife. However, if he ever had a dream of being more than just a shop rat, I never knew about it.

On the other hand, my dreams were big, but my thoughts were small. 4 I was not raised to be a go-getter. I knew I wanted to go to work each day in a suit and tie; unfortunately, I could not define what it was I wanted to do. I told a few people that I wanted to have a job where I could dress suavely• and carry a briefcase, and they laughed in my face. They said, "You'll never be anything," and I believed them. Even now I am envious of an immaculately• dressed businessman. It is not the angry type of jealousy; it is the "wish it were me" variety.

Since I knew I was not going to further my education, and I didn't 5 know what I wanted to do except wear a suit, high school was a disaster. I do not know how my teachers can respect themselves after passing me. In every high school there are cliques* and classifications. I worked just hard enough to stay above the bottom, but I did not want to work hard enough to get into the clique with the honor roll students.

Also, I had always had a problem with reading. When I was a kid, 6 reading for me was slow and tedious.* My eyes walked over words like a snail trudging* through mud. I couldn't focus on what I was reading, and this allowed my young, active mind to wander far from my reading material. I would often finish a page and not remember a single word I had just read. Not only was reading a slow process, but my comprehension was nil.* I wasn't dumb; in fact, I was at a high English level. However, reading rated next to scraping dog poop from the tread of my sneakers. I didn't yet know that reading could be like playing the guitar: The more you do it, the better you get. As far as reading was concerned, I thought I was stuck in the same slow waltz forever.

In junior high and high school, I read only when it was absolutely 7 essential. For example, I had to find out who Spider-Man was going to web, or how many children Superman was going to save each month. I also had to find out which girls were popular on the bathroom walls. I'm ashamed to say that my mother even did a book report for me, first reading the book. In high school, when I would choose my own classes, I took art and electronics rather than English.

Even though I was raised in a good Christian home, the only things I 8 cared about were partying and girls. I spent all of my minimum-wage paycheck on beer, cigarettes, and young ladies. As a senior, I dated a girl who was twenty. She had no restrictions, and I tried to keep pace with her lifestyle. I would stay out drinking until 3:00 A.M. on school nights. The next morning I would sleep through class or just not show up. It became such a problem that the school sent letters to my parents telling them that I would not be joining my classmates for commencement if I didn't show up for class once in a while. This put the fear of the establishment in me because I knew the importance of graduating from high school. Nonetheless, I never once remember doing homework my senior year. Yet in June, they shook my hand and forked over a diploma as I smugly* marched across the stage in a blue gown and square hat.

Since I felt I didn't deserve the piece of paper with the principal's 9 and superintendent's signatures on it, I passed up not only a graduation party but also a class ring and a yearbook. If it were not for my diploma and senior pictures, there would not be enough evidence to convince a jury that I am guilty of attending high school at all. I did, however, celebrate with my friends on graduation night. I got loaded, misjudged a turn, flattened a stop sign, and got my car stuck. When I pushed my car with my girlfriend behind the steering wheel, mud from the spinning tire sprayed all over my nice clothes. It was quite a night, and looking back, it was quite a fitting closure for the end of high school.

After graduation I followed my father's example and went to work, 10 plunging into the lukewarm waters of mediocrity. All I was doing on my job bagging groceries was trading dollars for hours. I worked just hard enough to keep from getting fired, and I was paid just enough to keep from quitting.

Considering the way my father felt about school, college was a subject 11 that seldom came up at our dinner table. I was not discouraged, nor was I encouraged, to go to college; it was my choice. My first attempt at college came when I was nineteen. I had always dreamed of being a disk jockey, so I enrolled in a broadcasting class. However, my experience in college was as forgettable as high school. My habit of not doing homework carried over, and the class was such a yawner that I often forgot to attend. Miraculously, I managed to pull a C, but my dream was weak and quickly died. I did not enroll for the next term. My girlfriend, the one who kept me out late in high school, became pregnant with my child. We were married two days after my final class, and this gave me another excuse not to continue my education.

My first job, and every job since, has involved working with my hands 12 and not my head. I enjoyed my work, but after the money ran out, the month would keep going. One evening my wife's cousin called and said he had a way that we could increase our income. I asked, "How soon can you get here?" He walked us through a six-step plan of selling and recruiting, and when he was finished, my wife and I wanted in. Fumbling around inside his large briefcase, he told us we needed the proper attitude first. Emerging with a small stack of books, he said, "Read these!" Then he flipped the books into my lap. I groaned at the thought of reading all those volumes. If this guy wanted me to develop a good attitude, giving me books was having the opposite effect. However, I wanted to make some extra cash, so I assured him I would try.

I started reading the books each night. They were self-help, positive 13 mental-attitude manuals. Reading those books opened up my world; they put me in touch with a me I didn't know existed. The books told me I had potential, possibly even greatness. I took their message in like an old Chevrolet being pumped full of premium no-lead gasoline. It felt so good I started reading more. Not only did I read at night; I read in the morning before I went to work. I read during my breaks and lunch hour, when waiting for signal lights to turn green, in between bites of food at supper, and while sitting on the toilet. One of the books I read said that there is no limit to the amount of information our brains will hold, so I began filling mine up.

The process of reading was slow at first, just as it had been when I was 14 a kid, but it was just like playing the guitar. If I struck an unclear chord, I would try it again, and if I read something unclear, I would simply read it again. Something happened: The more I read, the better I got at it. It wasn't long before I could focus in and understand without reading things twice. I began feeling good about my reading skills, and because of the types of books I was reading, I started feeling good about myself at the same time.

The income from my day job blossomed while the selling and 15 recruiting business grew demanding, disappointing, and fruitless. We stopped working that soil and our business died, but I was hooked on reading. I now laid aside the self-help books and began reading whatever I wanted. I got my first library card, and I subscribed to *Sports Illustrated.* I found a book of short stories, and I dived into poetry, as well as countless newspaper articles, cereal boxes, and oatmeal packages. Reading, which had been a problem for me, became a pleasure and then a passion.

Reading moved me. As I continued to read in a crowded lunchroom, 16 sometimes I stumbled across an especially moving short story or magazine article. For example, a young Romanian girl was saved from starvation and deprivation° by an adoptive couple from the United States. I quickly jerked the reading material to my face to conceal tears when she entered her new home filled with toys and stuffed animals.

Not only did reading tug at my emotions; it inspired me to make a 17 move. All those positive-mental-attitude books kept jabbing me in the ribs, so last fall, at age twenty-seven, I decided to give college another try. Now I am back in school, but it's a different road I travel from when I was a teenager. Mom and Dad paid the amount in the right-hand column of my tuition bill then, but now I am determined to pay for college myself, even though I must miss the sound of the pizza delivery man's tires on my blacktop driveway. I hope to work my way out of my blue collar by paying for school with blue-collar cash.

As a meat-cutter, I usually spend between 45 and 50 hours a week with 18 a knife in my hand. Some weeks I have spent 72 hours beneath a butcher's cap. In one two-week period I spent 141 hours with a bloody apron on, but in that time I managed to show up for all of my classes and get all of my homework done (except being short a few bibliography cards for my research paper).

Working full-time and raising a family leave me little free time. If I am 19 not in class, I'm studying linking verbs or trying to figure out the difference between compound and complex sentences.

There are other obstacles and challenges staring me in the face. 20 The tallest hurdle is a lack of time for meeting all my obligations. For instance, my wife works two nights a week, leaving me to care for my two daughters. A twelve-hour day at work can lead to an evening coma at home, so when Mom's punching little square buttons on a cash register, I hardly have the energy to pour cornflakes for my kids, let alone outline a research paper.

Going to college means making choices, some of which bring criti- 21 cism. My neighbors, for example, hate my sickly, brown lawn sandwiched between their lush, green, spotless plots of earth, which would be the envy of any football field. Just walking to my mailbox can be an awful reminder of how pitiful my lawn looks when I receive an unforgiving scowl° from one of the groundskeepers who live on either side of me. It is embarrassing to have such a colorless lawn, but it will have to wait because I want more out of life than a half-acre of green turf. Right now my time and money are tied up in college courses instead of fertilizer and weed killer.

But the toughest obstacle is having to take away time from those 22 I love most. I am proud of the relationship I have with my wife and kids, so it tears my guts out when I have to look into my daughter's sad face and explain that I can't go to the Christmas program she's been practicing for weeks because I have a final exam. It's not easy to tell my three-year-old that I can't push her on the swings because I have a cause-and-effect paper to write, or tell my seven-year-old that I can't build a snowman because I have an argument essay to polish. As I tell my family that I can't go sledding with them, my wife lets out a big sigh, and my kids yell, "Puleeze, Daddy, can't you come with us?" At these times I wonder if my dream of a college education can withstand such an emotional battering,• or if it is even worth it. But I keep on keeping on because I must set a good example for the four little eyes that are keeping watch over their daddy's every move. I must succeed and pass on to them the right attitude toward school. This time when I graduate, because of the hurdles I've overcome, there will be a celebration—a proper one.

VOCABULARY IN CONTEXT

1. The word *cliques* in "In every high school there are cliques and classifications. I worked just hard enough to stay above the bottom, but I did not want to work hard enough to get into the clique with the honor roll students" (paragraph 5) means

    a. grades.

    b. schools.

    c. groups.

    d. sports.

2. The word *scowl* in "Just walking to my mailbox can be an awful reminder of how pitiful my lawn looks when I receive an unforgiving scowl from one of the groundskeepers who live on either side of me" (paragraph 21) means

    a. sincere smile.

    b. favor.

    c. angry look.

    d. surprise.

READING COMPREHENSION QUESTIONS

1. Which sentence best expresses the central idea of the selection?

    a. The author was never encouraged to attend college or to challenge himself mentally on the job.

    b. After years of not caring about education, Berry was led by some self-help books to love reading, gain self-esteem, and attend college.

    c. The author's wife and children often do not understand why he is unable to take part in many family activities.

    d. The author was given a high school diploma despite the fact that he did little work and rarely attended class.

2. Which sentence best expresses the main idea of paragraph 13?

    a. Influenced by self-help books, the author developed a hunger for reading.

    b. People who really care about improving themselves will find the time to do it, such as during the early morning, at breaks, and during the lunch hour.

    c. Self-help books send the message that everyone is full of potential and even greatness.

    d. There is no limit to the amount of information the brain can hold.

3. Which sentence best expresses the main idea of paragraph 22?

    a. The author's decision to attend college is hurting his long-term relationship with his wife and daughters.

    b. The author has two children, one age three and the other age seven.

    c. The author enjoys family activities such as attending his children's plays and building snowmen.

    d. Although he misses spending time with his family, the author feels that graduating from college will make him a better role model for his children.

4. The author's reading skills

    a. were strong even when he was a child.

    b. improved as he read more.

    c. were strengthened considerably in high school.

    d. were sharpened by jobs he held after high school graduation.

5. The author's father

    a. was rarely home while the author was growing up.

    b. often missed work and stayed out late at bars.

    c. was a college graduate.

    d. disliked school.

6. In stating that his graduation night "was quite a fitting closure for the end of high school," Berry implies that

    a. he was glad high school was finally over.

    b. car troubles were a common problem for him throughout high school.

    c. his behavior had ruined that night just as it had ruined his high school education.

    d. despite the problems, the evening gave him good memories, just as high school had given him good memories.

7. We can infer from paragraph 21 that the author

    a. does not tend his lawn because he enjoys annoying his neighbors.

    b. receives a lot of mail.

    c. is willing to make sacrifices for his college education.

    d. has neighbors who care little about the appearance of their property.

8. We can infer that the author believes children

    a. should be passed to the next grade when they reach a certain age, regardless of their test scores.

    b. should not require a great deal of time from their parents.

    c. fall into two categories: "born readers" and those who can never learn to read very well.

    d. benefit from having role models who care about education.

DISCUSSION QUESTIONS

About Content

1. The author looks back at this period of reading self-help books as one in which his attitude improved, eventually leading to his enrollment in college. Has a particular occurrence ever sharply changed your outlook on life? Was it something that you read, observed, or directly experienced? How did it happen? How did it change your point of view?

2. Berry writes that his father did not encourage him to go on to college. Nevertheless, he sees many positive things about his father. In what ways was his father a positive role model for him? In other words, is Berry's positive behavior as an adult partly a result of his father's influence? What do you see in your own adult behavior that you can attribute to your parents' influence?

3. Berry discusses some of the difficulties he faces as a result of being in college—struggling to find time to meet his obligations, giving up lawn care, spending less time with his family. What difficulties do you face as a result of fitting college into your life? What obligations must you struggle to fulfill? What activities remain undone?

About Structure

4. In most of his essay, Berry uses time order, but in some places he uses listing order. For example, what does Berry list in paragraphs 20–22?

    _____

5. In closing his essay, Berry writes that at his college graduation, "there will be a celebration—a proper one." With what earlier event is he contrasting this graduation?

    _____

About Style and Tone

6. In explaining that he followed his father's example, the author compares himself to "a man who double-crosses the mob [and] follows a cement block to the bottom of the river." In this comparison, Berry strikingly makes the point that his own actions led him to an undesirable situation. Find two other places where the author uses a

richly revealing comparison. Write those images below, and explain what Berry means by each one.

Image: _____

_____

Meaning: _____

Image: _____

_____

Meaning: _____

7. In the first sentence of Berry's essay, he tells us that it is "highly improbable" for him to be in college. What is his tone in this sentence and in the paragraph that follows?

RESPONDING TO IMAGES

Consider how this photograph of assembly-line workers is structured. Why do you think the photographer chose to take the picture from this particular angle?

WRITING ASSIGNMENTS

Assignment 1: Writing a Paragraph

Children are strongly influenced by the example of their parents (and other significant adults in their lives). For instance, the author of this essay followed his father's example of disliking school and getting a job that did not challenge him mentally.

Think about your growing-up years and about adults who influenced you, both positively and negatively. Then write a paragraph that describes one of these people and his or her influence on you. Supply plenty of vivid examples to help the reader understand how and why this person affected you.

The topic sentence of your paragraph should identify the person (either by name or by relationship to you) and briefly indicate the kind of influence he or she had on you. Here are some examples of topic sentences for this paper:

My aunt's courage in difficult situations helped me to become a stronger person.

My father's frequent trouble with the law made it necessary for me to grow up in a hurry.

The pastor of our church helped me realize that I was a worthwhile, talented person.

Assignment 2: Writing a Paragraph

Write a paragraph about one way that reading has been important in your life, either positively or negatively. To discover the approach you wish to take, think for a moment about the influence of reading throughout your life. When you were a child, was being read to at bedtime a highlight of your day? Did reading out loud in elementary school cause you embarrassment? Do you adore mysteries or true-crime books? Do you avoid reading whenever possible? Find an idea about the role of reading in your life that you can write about in the space of a paragraph. Your topic sentence will be a clear statement of that idea, such as:

> I first learned to read from watching *Sesame Street*.
>
> One key experience in second grade made me hate reading out loud in class.
>
> My parents' attitude toward reading rubbed off on me.
>
> Reading to my child at bedtime is an important time of day for both of us.
>
> Books have taught me some things I never would have learned from friends and family.
>
> There are several reasons why I am not a good reader.
>
> A wonderful self-help book has helped me build my self-esteem.

Develop your main idea with detailed explanations and descriptions. For example, if you decide to write about reading to your child at bedtime, you might describe the positions you and your child take (Is the child in bed? On the floor? On your lap?), one or two of the stories the child and you have loved, some of the child's reactions, and so on.

Assignment 3: Writing an Essay

Berry's graduation-night celebration was a dramatic one and, he states, "a fitting closure for the end of high school." What was your senior prom or high school graduation celebration like? Did you participate in any of the planning and preparation for the events? Were finding a date and shopping for clothing for the prom fun or nerve-racking experiences? Was the event itself wonderful or disappointing? Write an essay telling the story of your graduation celebration from start to finish. Use many sharp descriptive details to help your readers envision events, decorations, clothing, cars, the weather, and so on. In addition, add meaning to your story by telling what you were thinking and feeling throughout the event.

You might try making a list as a way of collecting details for this paper. At first, don't worry about organizing your details. Just keep adding to your list, which might at one point look like this:

> decorations committee
>
> considered asking my cousin to go with me, if necessary
>
> shopping for prom dress with Mom (and arguing)
>
> afraid I'd be asked first by someone I didn't want to go with
>
> talk of being up all night
>
> pressed orchid corsage afterward
>
> florist busy that week
>
> working on centerpieces
>
> feet hurt

Eventually, you will have enough information to begin thinking about the organization of your essay. Here's what the scratch outline for one such essay looks like:

Central idea: My high school prom was a mixture of fun and disappointment.

(1)   *Before the dance*

Work on the decorations com.

Anxiety over getting a date, finally relief

Worn out shopping for a dress

Last-minute preparations (getting flowers, having hair done, decorating ballroom)

(2)   *Night of the dance*

Picture-taking at home

Squeezing gown into car, hem gets stuck in car door and grease rubs on it

Beautiful ballroom

Rotten meal

Great band (even teachers yelling requests)

After two dances had to take off heels

Date kept dancing with others

Danced with my brother, who came with my girlfriend

Early breakfast served at hotel

(3)   *After the dance*

Total exhaustion for two days

Extensive phone analysis of dance with girlfriends

Never went out with that date again

Several years later, prom dress, wrapped in a garbage bag, went to Salvation Army

Perhaps you don't remember your prom or graduation night celebration very well, or don't wish to. Feel free to write about another important social event instead, such as a high school reunion, a family reunion, or your own or someone else's wedding.

Let's Get Specific

Beth Johnson

PREVIEW	WORDS TO WATCH

PREVIEW

Some people are better writers than others. That's obvious to anyone who reads. There are writers whose material you just can't put down—and there are writers whose material you can't put down fast enough. One of the biggest differences between the skillful writer and the poor one is this: The successful writer uses specific, concrete language. Journalist and teacher Beth Johnson explains the power of specific language and demonstrates how any writer can become more skilled in its use.

WORDS TO WATCH

instinctive (2)
prospective (2)
vividly (2)
glaze (3)
blandly (7)
intuitively (8)
swayed (8)
parody (8)
crave (9)
anecdote (12)
compelling (16)
sustain (17)

Imagine that you've offered to fix up your sister with a blind date. "You'll 1 like him," you tell her. "He's really nice." Would that assurance be enough to satisfy her? Would she contentedly wait for Saturday night, happily anticipating meeting this "nice" young man? Not likely! She would probably bombard you with questions: "But what's he like? Is he tall or short? Funny? Serious? Smart? Kind? Shy? Does he work? How do you know him?"

Such questions reveal the instinctive° hunger we all feel for specific 2 detail. Being told that her prospective° date is "nice" does very little to help your sister picture him. She needs concrete details to help her vividly° imagine this stranger.

The same principle applies to writing. Whether you are preparing 3 a research paper, a letter to a friend, or an article for the local newspaper, your writing will be strengthened by the use of detailed, concrete language. Specific language energizes and informs readers. General language, by contrast, makes their eyes glaze° over.

The following examples should prove the point.   4

Dear Sir or Madam:

Please consider my application for a job with your company. I am a college graduate with experience in business. Part-time jobs that I have held during the school year and my work over summer vacations make me well-qualified for employment. My former employers have always considered me a good, reliable worker. Thank you for considering my application.

Sincerely,
Bob Cole

Dear Sir or Madam:

I would like to be considered for an entry-level position in your purchasing department. I graduated in June from Bayside College with a 3.5 GPA and a bachelor's degree in business administration. While at Bayside, I held a part-time job in the college's business office, where I eventually had responsibility for coordinating food purchasing for the school cafeteria. By encouraging competitive bidding among food suppliers, I was able to save the school approximately $2,500 in the school year 1998–1999. During the last three summers (1997–1999), I worked at Bayside Textiles, where I was promoted from a job in the mailroom to the position of assistant purchasing agent, a position that taught me a good deal about controlling costs. Given my background, I'm confident I could make a real contribution to your company. I will telephone you next Tuesday morning to ask if we might arrange an interview.

Sincerely,

Julia Moore

Which of the preceding letters do you think makes a more convincing 5 case for these job seekers? If you're like most people, you would choose the second. Although both letters are polite and grammatically acceptable, the first one suffers badly in comparison with the second for one important reason. It is *general* and *abstract*, while the second is *specific* and *concrete*.

Let's look at the letters again. The differing styles of the two are evi- 6 dent in the first sentence. Bob is looking for "a job with your company." He doesn't specify what kind of job—it's for the employer to figure out if Bob wants to work as a groundskeeper, on an assembly line, or as a salesperson. By contrast, Julia is immediately specific about the kind of job she is seeking—"an entry-level position in your purchasing department." Bob tells only that he is "a college graduate." But Julia tells where she went to college, what her grade point average was, and exactly what she studied.

The contrast continues as the two writers talk about their work experi- 7 ence. Again, Bob talks in vague, general terms. He gives no concrete evidence to show how the general descriptions "well-qualified" and "good, reliable worker" apply to him. But Julia backs up her claims. She tells specifically what positions she's held (buyer for cafeteria, assistant purchasing clerk for textile company), gives solid evidence that she performed her jobs well (saved the school $2,500, was promoted from mailroom), and explains what skills she has acquired (knows about controlling costs). Julia continues to be clear and concrete as she closes the letter. By saying, "I will telephone you next Tuesday morning," she leaves the reader with a helpful, specific piece of information. Chances are, her prospective employer will be glad to take her call. The chances are equally good that Bob will never hear from the company. His letter was so blandly* general that the employer will hardly remember receiving it.

Julia's letter demonstrates the power of specific detail—a power that 8 we all appreciate intuitively.• Indeed, although we may not always be aware of it, our opinions and decisions are frequently swayed• by concrete language. On a restaurant menu, are you more tempted by a "green salad" or "a colorful salad bowl filled with romaine and spinach leaves, red garden-fresh tomatoes, and crisp green pepper rings"? Would being told that a movie is "good" persuade you to see it as much as hearing that it is "a hilarious parody• of a rock documentary featuring a fictional heavy-metal band"? Does knowing that a classmate has "personal problems" help you understand her as well as hearing that "her parents are divorcing, her brother was just arrested for selling drugs, and she is scheduled for surgery to correct a back problem"?

When we read, all of us want—even crave•—this kind of specificity. 9 Concrete language grabs our attention and allows us to witness the writer's world almost firsthand. Abstract language, on the other hand, forces us to try to fill in the blanks left by the writer's lack of specific imagery. Usually we tire of the effort. Our attention wanders. We begin to wonder what's for lunch and whether it's going to rain, as our eyes scan the page, searching for some concrete detail to focus on.

Once you understand the power of concrete details, you will gain 10 considerable power as a writer. You will describe events so vividly that readers will feel they experienced them directly. You will sprinkle your essays with nuggets of detail that, like the salt on a pretzel, add interest and texture.

Consider the following examples and decide for yourself which came 11 from a writer who has mastered the art of the specific detail.

Living at Home

Unlike many college students, I have chosen to live at home with my parents. Naturally, the arrangement has both good and bad points. The most difficult part is that, even though I am an adult, my parents sometimes still think of me as a child. Our worst disagreements occur when they expect me to report to them as though I were still twelve years old. Another drawback to living with my parents is that I don't feel free to have friends over to "my place." It's not that my parents don't welcome my friends in their home, but I can't tell my friends to drop in anytime as I would if I lived alone.

But in other ways, living at home works out well. The most obvious plus is that I am saving a lot of money. I pay room and board, but that doesn't compare to what renting an apartment would cost. There are less measurable advantages as well. Although we do sometimes fall into our old parent-child roles, my parents and I are getting to know each other in new ways. Generally, we relate as adults, and I think we're all gaining a lot of respect for one another.

The Pros and Cons of Living at Home

Most college students live in a dormitory or apartment. They spend their hours surrounded by their own stereos, blaring hip-hop or rock music; their own furnishings, be they leaking beanbag chairs or Salvation Army sofas; and their own choice of foods, from tofu-bean sprout casseroles to a basic diet of Cheetos. My life is different. I occupy the same room that has been mine since babyhood. My school pictures, from gap-toothed first-grader to cocky senior, adorn the walls. The music drifting through my door from the living room ranges from Lawrence Welk to . . . Lawrence Welk. The food runs heavily to Mid-American Traditional: meatloaf, mashed potatoes, frozen peas.

Yes, I live with my parents. And the arrangement is not always ideal. Although I am twenty-four years old, my parents sometimes slip into a time warp and mentally cut my age in half. "Where are you going, Lisa? Who will you be with?" my mother will occasionally ask. I'll answer patiently, "I'm going to have pizza with some people from my psych class." "But where?" she continues. "I'm not sure," I'll say, my voice rising just a hair. If the questioning continues, it will often lead to a blowup. "You don't need to know where I'm going, OK?" I'll say shrilly. "You don't have to yell at me," she'll answer in a hurt voice.

Living at home also makes it harder to entertain. I find myself envying classmates who can tell their friends, "Drop in anytime." If a friend of mine "drops in" unexpectedly, it throws everyone into a tizzy. Mom runs for the dustcloth while Dad ducks into the bedroom, embarrassed to be seen in his comfortable, ratty bathrobe.

On the other hand, I don't regret my decision to live at home for a few years. Naturally, I am saving money. The room and board I pay my parents wouldn't rent the tiniest, most roach-infested apartment in the city. And despite our occasional lapses, my parents and I generally enjoy each other's company. They are getting to know me as an adult, and I am learning to see them as people, not just my parents. I realized how true this was when I saw them getting dressed up to go out recently. Dad was putting on a tie, and Mom one of her best dresses. I opened my mouth to ask where they were going when it occurred to me that maybe they didn't care to be checked up on any more than I did. Swallowing my curiosity, I simply waved good-bye and said, "Have a good time!"

Both passages could have been written by the same person. Both make 12 the same basic points. But the second passage is far more interesting because it backs up the writer's points with concrete details. While the first passage merely *tells* that the writer's parents sometimes treat her like a child, the second passage follows this point up with an anecdote* that *shows* exactly what she means. Likewise with the point about inviting friends over: The first passage only states that there is a problem, but the second one describes in concrete terms what happens if a friend does drop in unexpectedly. The first writer simply says that her room and board costs wouldn't pay for an apartment, but the second is specific about just how inadequate the money would be. And while the first passage uses abstract language to say that the writer and her parents are "getting to know each other in new ways," the second shows what that means by describing a specific incident.

Every kind of writing can be improved by the addition of concrete 13 detail. Let's look at one final example: the love letter.

Dear April,

I can't wait any longer to tell you how I feel. I am crazy about you. You are the most wonderful woman I've ever met. Every time I'm near you I'm overcome with feelings of love. I would do anything in the world for you and am hoping you feel the same way about me.

Love,
Paul

Paul has written a sincere note, but it lacks a certain something. That 14 something is specific detail. Although the letter expresses a lot of positive feelings, it could have been written by practically any love-struck man about any woman. For this letter to be really special to April, it should be unmistakably about her and Paul. And that requires concrete details.

Here is what Paul might write instead.   15

Dear April,

Do you remember last Saturday, as we ate lunch in the park, when I spilled my soda in the grass? You quickly picked up a twig and made a tiny dam to keep the liquid from flooding a busy anthill. You probably didn't think I noticed, but I did. It was at that moment that I realized how totally I am in love with you and your passion for life. Before that I only thought you were the most beautiful woman in the world, with your eyes like sparkling pools of emerald water and your chestnut hair glinting in the sun. But now I recognize what it means when I hear your husky laugh and I feel a tight aching in my chest. It means I could stand on top of the Empire State Building and shout to the world, "I love April Snyder." Should I do it? I'll be waiting for your reply.

Paul

There's no guarantee that April is going to return Paul's feelings, but 16 she certainly has a better idea now just what it is about her that Paul finds so lovable, as well as what kind of guy Paul is. Concrete details have made this letter far more compelling. •

Vague, general language is the written equivalent of baby food. It is 17 adequate; it can sustain° life. But it isn't very interesting. For writing to have satisfying crunch, sizzle, and color, it must be generously supplied with specifics. Whether the piece is a job application, a student essay, or a love letter, it is concrete details that make it interesting, persuasive, and memorable.

VOCABULARY IN CONTEXT

1. The word *swayed* in "our opinions and decisions are frequently swayed by concrete language" (paragraph 8) means
    a. hidden.
    b. repeated.
    c. influenced.
    d. shown to be wrong.

2. The word *compelling* in "she certainly has a better idea now just what it is about her that Paul finds so lovable. . . . Concrete details have made this letter far more compelling" (paragraph 16) means
    a. forceful and interesting.
    b. long and boring.
    c. empty and vague.
    d. silly but amusing.

READING COMPREHENSION QUESTIONS

1. Which sentence best expresses the central idea of the selection?
    a. Communication skills of all types are useful throughout life.
    b. Always be specific when applying for a job.
    c. Specific language will strengthen your writing.
    d. Most people need help with their writing skills.

2. Main ideas may cover more than one paragraph. Which sentence best expresses the main idea of paragraphs 6 and 7?
    a. In letters of application for a job, Bob and Julia have included their background and job goals.
    b. Bob and Julia have written letters of application for a job.
    c. While Bob says only that he's a college graduate, Julia goes into detail about where and what she studied and her grades.
    d. While Bob's job-application letter is probably too vague to be successful, Julia's very specific one is likely to get a positive response.

3. Which sentence best expresses the main idea of paragraph 8?
    a. Julia's letter is a good example of the power of specific details.
    b. Our opinions and decisions are often influenced by specific language.

    c. We want to hear exactly what's in a salad or movie before spending money on it.

    d. When we know just what someone's "personal problems" are, we understand him or her better.

4. Johnson states that abstract language

    a. is rare.

    b. lets us clearly see what the writer's world is like.

    c. tends to lose our attention.

    d. makes us want to read more of the writer's piece.

5. Johnson feels that concrete language

    a. is hard to follow.

    b. makes readers' eyes glaze over.

    c. helps readers picture what the author is writing about.

    d. is not appropriate for a menu or a parody.

6. In paragraphs 6 and 7, the author suggests that Bob Cole

    a. is not qualified to enter the business world.

    b. is lying about his education and work experience.

    c. should have written a less wordy letter.

    d. should have written a more detailed letter.

7. Which of the following sentences can we assume Beth Johnson would most approve of?

    a. Shore City is an amusing but expensive place.

    b. Shore City is an interesting place to spend a bit of time.

    c. Shore City has an amusement park and racetrack, but all the hotel rooms cost over $100 a day.

    d. There is a city near the shore that has some interesting attractions, but its hotels are quite expensive.

8. We can infer from the reading that specific details would be very important in

    a. a novel.

    b. a history textbook.

    c. a biography.

    d. all of the above.

DISCUSSION QUESTIONS

About Content

1. At some earlier point in school, did you learn the importance of writing specifically? If so, do you remember when? If not, when do you think you should have been taught about the power of specific details in writing?

2. Johnson provides three pairs of examples: two job-application letters, two passages about living at home, and two love letters. Which pair most effectively makes her point for you about the value of writing specifically?

3. What kinds of writing will you be doing over the next few weeks, either in or out of school? Will it be papers for other classes, answers to essay questions, reports at work, letters of application for jobs, letters to friends, or other types of writing? Name one kind of writing you will be doing, and give an example of one way you could make that writing more specific.

About Structure

4. Essays often begin with an introduction that prepares readers for the author's central idea. How does Johnson begin her essay? Why do you think she chose this kind of introduction?

_____

_____

_____

5. The authors of the papers on living at home are essentially using listing order. What are they listing?

_____

6. Johnson takes her own advice and uses many concrete details in her essay. Locate two particularly strong examples of specific details in the reading that are not in the three pairs of samples, and write them below:

_____

_____

_____

About Style and Tone

7. Johnson opens her essay in the second-person point of view. As a reader, how do you respond to being addressed directly? Why might Johnson have chosen this approach?

_____

_____

_____

8. In paragraph 10, Johnson writes: "You will sprinkle your essays with nuggets of detail that, like the salt on a pretzel, add interest and texture." What kind of language is she using here?

_____

_____

_____

RESPONDING TO IMAGES

The writer in this illustration plans to use three specific scenes to tell her story. How might the scenes be connected? What story do they tell? Be creative in your response, but make sure your ideas are based on specific visual details in the cartoon.

Copyright © Allen Swerling. Used with permission.

WRITING ASSIGNMENTS

Assignment 1: Writing a Paragraph

Using the same level of detail as Julia's application letter in the reading, write a one-paragraph letter of application for a part-time or a full-time job. Like Julia Moore, be sure to include the following in your paragraph:

> What kind of job you are applying for
> Where you have worked previously
> What positions you have held
> Evidence that you performed your job well
> Which skills you have acquired

Assignment 2: Writing a Paragraph

In this reading, "The Pros and Cons of Living at Home" is a strong example of a "pro and con" analysis—one that details the advantages and disadvantages of something. Think of a topic about which you have conflicting views. It could be a decision you are struggling with, such as changing jobs or moving to a larger (or smaller) house or apartment. Or it could be a situation in which you already find yourself, such as attending school while holding a job or having an elderly parent living with you. Write a paragraph in which you explain in detail what the pros and cons of the issue are.

Once you've chosen a topic, do some prewriting. A good strategy is to make two lists—one of the advantages and the other of the disadvantages. Here is a sample:

Advantages of moving to a smaller apartment

Save money on rent ($325 a month instead of $400 a month)

Save money on utilities (smaller heating bill)

Less space to clean (one bedroom instead of two)

Disadvantages of moving to a smaller apartment

Less space for all my furniture (big chest of drawers, sofa bed)

No spare bedroom (can't have friends sleep over)

Will get more cluttered (little space to display all my trophies, souvenirs, and sports equipment)

If you are not sure about which issue to write about, make lists for two or three topics. Then you'll have a better idea of which one will result in a better paper.

Use the lists of advantages and disadvantages as an outline for your paragraph, adding other ideas as they occur to you. Begin with a topic sentence such as "_____ has both advantages and disadvantages" or "I'm having a hard time deciding whether or not to _____." Next, write the supporting sentences, discussing first one side of the issue and then the other.

Be sure to include plenty of specific details. For inspiration, reread "The Pros and Cons of Living at Home" before writing your essay.

Assignment 3: Writing an Essay

Johnson uses sharp, concrete details to make a point she feels strongly about—that specific language gives writing real power. Write an essay persuading readers of the importance of something you believe in strongly. Be sure to include at least one or two concrete, convincing examples for every point that you make. You might write about the value of something, such as the following:

Regular exercise

Volunteer work

Reading for pleasure

Gardening

Spending time with young (or grown) children

Periodic intense housecleaning

Alternatively, you can write about the negative aspects of something, such as the following:

Excessive television watching

Compulsive shopping

Tabloid journalism

Procrastinating

Smoking

Following is an example of an informal outline for this assignment. As the writer developed this outline into paragraphs, she added, subtracted, and rearranged some of her examples.

Central idea: Cleaning out closets every now and then can be rewarding.

(1) I get rid of things I no longer need, or never needed:

Pair of ten-year-old hiking boots, which I kept because they were expensive but that are thoroughly worn out

continued

Portable TV that no longer works

Yogurt maker given to me by my first husband on our anniversary

(2) I make room for things I do need:

All my shoes and pocketbooks, which can be arranged in neat rows on the shelves instead of crammed into cartons

Christmas presents I buy for my family in July and want to hide

(3) I find things that I thought were lost forever or that I forgot I ever had:

Box of photographs from our first family vacation

My bowling trophy

Presents I bought for last Christmas and forgot about

Stance

B. J. Penn

PREVIEW

"Stance" is the first chapter in B. J. Penn's *Mixed Martial Arts: The Book of Knowledge,* which he wrote with Glen Cordoza and Erich Kraus. Mixed martial arts (MMA) is a sport in which many different boxing and martial arts techniques are used. Penn is a former Ultimate Fighting Championship winner in the welterweight division. This essay contains a number of MMA terms with which you might not be familiar. "Striking" means to attack an opponent with a part of the body. A "sprawl" is a defensive move. "Shooting" involves moving in on the opponent quickly so that the fighter can grapple or wrestle with him.

WORDS TO WATCH

conducive (1)
tailor (1)
imperative (1)
grossly (2)
crucial (3)
topple (3)
erratic (4)
mobility (4)

The foundation of every fighter's stand-up game is his stance. It's good 1 to find a stance that fits your style, but it must be conducive• to both the striking and grappling aspects of the sport. If you can throw excellent strikes from your stance but have a difficult time dropping your level to shoot in or sprawl, you have a serious weakness. If your stance is well suited for shooting and sprawling but not for striking, you also have a serious weakness. It's fine to tailor• your stance to make the most of your strengths, but you can't leave any holes as a result. In MMA, it is imperative• that you cover all bases.

As you work to develop your stance, it is important to keep a few 2
requirements in mind. The most important of these requirements is that
you keep your hands up at all times. It doesn't matter if you grossly•
outclass your opponent in the striking department; the moment you drop
your hands, you give your opponent a puncher's chance. To protect your
face when throwing a punch, you want to keep your opposite hand up,
tuck your chin, and shrug your shoulders slightly to guard your jaw.

Maintaining balance is also crucial.• If your feet are spread too far 3
apart or too close together, your opponent will be able to topple• your
base. And when your base gets toppled, you're pretty much a fish out of
water. The general rule of thumb is to keep your feet spread roughly a
shoulder's width apart. This holds true even as you move about the cage.
If you want to move to the left, step with your left foot and then follow
with your right. If you want to move to your right, step with your right
foot and follow with your left. You never want to cross your feet or get too
spread out.

However, due to the erratic• nature of combat, you won't always be 4
able to maintain a perfect stance. No matter what position you should be
forced into, it is important to always be balanced because that balance is
what allows you to attack and defend. If you only feel comfortable and
have balance when in your traditional stance, every time you are pushed
or knocked out of that stance, your entire offense and defense goes straight
out the window. Acquiring balance and mobility• doesn't always come
easy, but it is worth your time and attention. A dangerous MMA fighter is
one who can attack and defend from any position.

VOCABULARY IN CONTEXT

1. The word *tailor* in "It's fine to tailor your stance to make the most of
   your strengths . . ." (paragraph 1) means
   a. create.
   b. adjust.
   c. reverse.
   d. control.

2. The word *crucial* in "Maintaining balance is also crucial" (paragraph 3)
   means
   a. essential.
   b. unnecessary.
   c. important.
   d. difficult.

3. The word *mobility* in "Acquiring balance and mobility doesn't always
   come easy . . ." (paragraph 4) means
   a. speed.
   b. strength.
   c. ability to move easily.
   d. skill.

READING COMPREHENSION QUESTIONS

1. Which of the following sentences best expresses the main idea of the selection?
   a. It is important to keep your hands up at all times.
   b. A good stance is essential in mixed martial arts.
   c. A perfect stance isn't always possible.
   d. Balance is essential to a good stance.

2. According to Penn, maintaining balance is important because
   a. without balance it is difficult to attack and defend.
   b. you need balance in order to cover all bases.
   c. balance makes you more effective as a fighter.
   d. without balance you cannot grapple your opponent.

3. Keeping your hands up at all times is important
   a. except when you attack.
   b. in order to confuse the opponent.
   c. to defend against punches.
   d. to be ready to strike at any time.

4. *True or false?* _____ If you want to move left, always move your right foot first.

5. We can infer from this essay that learning how to maintain balance and mobility requires
   a. talent.
   b. gymnastic ability.
   c. practice.
   d. poise.

DISCUSSION QUESTIONS

About Content

1. What does Penn mean by "topple your base" in paragraph 3? Explain this in your own words.

   _____

   _____

2. How far apart should a fighter keep his or her feet?

3. Why is it not always possible for a fighter to keep a "perfect stance"?

4. In paragraphs 2, 3, and 4, Penn discusses several requirements for maintaining a good stance. Explain each of those requirements below using your own words.

   Requirement 1: _____

   _____

Requirement 2: _____

_____

Requirement 3: _____

_____

Requirement 4: _____

_____

About Structure

5. What transitions does Penn use at the beginning of each paragraph to maintain coherence between paragraphs?

   Paragraph 2 _____

   Paragraph 3 _____

   Paragraph 4 _____

6. In which paragraph does Penn state his thesis or central idea? Is this the proper place for it?

About Style and Tone

7. In paragraph 4, Penn uses an image (mental picture)—"your entire offense and defense goes straight out the window." Where else does he use an image?

8. Should Penn have defined words such as "shooting" and "sprawling"? What does his not doing so say about his intended audience?

WRITING ASSIGNMENTS

Writing Assignment 1: Writing a Paragraph

Think of a process, activity, sport, art form, or other skill that you are good at—for example, playing basketball, sketching, doing math problems, baking bread, exercising, maintaining a car, fishing, or coordinating your wardrobe. Then, take your lead from Penn, and write a paragraph that discusses the first and most important lesson or requirement that a newcomer to this sport or activity should learn in order to be successful. For example, you might explain the proper way to hold a tennis racket, the best way to bait a hook, or the easiest way to thread a needle.

Writing Assignment 2: Writing a Paragraph

Write a paragraph in which you explain to a fellow student one important requirement for getting good grades in college. Provide as many specific details and examples from your own experience as you can to show why this practical advice is essential to succeeding.

Here are five topic sentences for various paragraphs that might be written in response to this assignment.

Don't take more courses than you have time for, especially if you also have a part-time job.

Attend every class and take careful notes.

Start on assignments early; don't wait until the night before to start a major research paper.

Stick to a rigid study schedule.

Read everything that is assigned to you.

Writing Assignment 3: Writing an Essay

If you responded to Writing Assignment 2, you have probably written a detailed paragraph explaining one of the ways to succeed in college. Put that paragraph into a complete essay that discusses two or three additional ways to earn good grades. You may want to use some of the ideas in the sample topic sentences listed in Writing Assignment 2.

However, remember that your essay will also require an introduction and a conclusion. There are many ways to begin. For example, you might start by explaining how your ideas about studying in college differ from what they were in high school. Another good way to begin is to ask a question such as "Do you want to flunk out of college?" and then list several surefire ways to fail. The last sentence in your introduction might state your thesis, containing at least three major points about how to succeed. It might look something like this: "Succeeding in college requires regular attendance, good note taking, and careful study habits." The body of the essay would develop each of these points.

One interesting way to conclude is by looking to the future and explaining how the advice you have just given might be applied to one's life beyond college.

Baking a Cake
Natalie Goldberg

PREVIEW	WORDS TO WATCH
This selection is from Goldberg's book *Writing Down the Bones: Freeing the Writer Within* (2005). It describes writing as a kind of spiritual exercise, an idea that she got from practicing Zen meditation. This chapter in her book compares writing to baking a cake, the cake being the final product, the ingredients being the details, and the oven heat being the writer's energy and inspiration. Goldberg mentions two authors: Vladimir Nabokov (1899–1977) and Katagiri Roshi (1928–1990). Nabokov was a Russian-American novelist, and Roshi was the founder of the Minnesota Zen Meditation Center.	caress (2) cantankerous (4) censor (4) abstract (5) ecstasy (5) gourmet (5) soufflé (5)

When you bake a cake, you have ingredients: sugar, flour, butter, bak- 1
ing soda, eggs, milk. You put them in a bowl and mix them up, but this
does not make a cake. This makes goop. You have to put them in the oven
and add heat or energy to transform it into cake, and the cake looks nothing like its original ingredients. It's a lot like parents unable to claim their
hippie kids as their own in the sixties. Milk and eggs look at their pound
cake and say, "Not ours." Not egg, not milk, but Ph.D. daughter of refugee
parents—a foreigner in her own home.

In a sense this is what writing is like. You have all these ingredients, 2
the details of your life, but just to list them is not enough. "I was born
in Brooklyn. I have a mother and a father. I am female." You must add
the heat and energy of your heart. This is not just any father; this is your
father. The character who smoked cigars and put too much ketchup on his
steak. The one you loved and hated. You can't just mix the ingredients in
a bowl; they have no life. You must become one with the details in love
or hate; they become an extension of your body. Nabokov says, "Caress•
the divine details." He doesn't say, "Jostle them in place or bang them
around." *Caress* them, touch them tenderly. Care about what is around
you. Let your whole body touch the river you are writing about, so if you
call it yellow or stupid or slow, all of you is feeling it. There should be no
separate you when you are deeply engaged. Katagiri Roshi said: "When
you do zazen [sitting meditation], you should be gone. So zazen does
zazen. Not Steve or Barbara does zazen." This is also how you should be
when you write: Writing does writing. You disappear: You are simply
recording the thoughts that are streaming through you.

The cake is baking in the oven. All that heat goes into the making of 3
that cake. The heat is not distracted, thinking, "Oh, I wanted it to be a chocolate cake, not a pound cake." You don't think as you write, "Oh, I don't
like my life, I should have been born in Illinois." You don't think. You
accept what is and put down its truth. Katagiri Roshi has said: "Literature
will tell you what life is, but it won't tell you how to get out of it."

Ovens can be very cantankerous• sometimes, and you might have 4
to learn ways to turn your heat on. Timing your writing adds pressure
and helps to heat things up and blast through the internal censor.•
Also, keeping your hand moving and not stopping add to the heat, so a
beautiful cake may rise out of the mixture of your daily details. If you
find yourself checking the clock too much as you write, say to yourself
you are going to keep writing until three (or four or five) pages, both
sides, are filled or until the cake is baked, however long that takes. And
you are never sure once the heat begins whether you will get a devil's
food or an angel food cake. There are no guarantees; don't worry. They're
both good to eat.

There are people who try to use heat only, without ingredients, to make 5
a cake. The heat is cozy and feels good, but when you're done, there's not
much there for anyone else to eat. That's usually abstract• writing: We get
a sense there is great warmth there, but we have nothing to bite into. If
you use details, you become better skilled at conveying your ecstasy• or
sorrow. So while you fly around in the heat of the oven, bring in the batter
in the pan so we know exactly what your feelings taste like, so we may
be a gourmet• of them: "Oh, it's a pound cake, a brownie, a light lemon

soufflé."● That is what her feelings feel like. Not "It was great, it was great!" Yes, it was great, but how great? Give us the flavor. In other words, use details. They are the basic unit of writing.

And in using them, you are not only baking cakes and buzzing around 6
the oven. In writing with detail, you are turning to face the world. It is a deeply political act, because you are not just staying in the heat of your own emotions. You are offering up some good solid bread for the hungry.

VOCABULARY IN CONTEXT

1. The word *cantankerous* in "Ovens can be very cantankerous sometimes, and you might have to learn ways to turn your heat on" (paragraph 4) means

   a. uncooperative.

   b. hot.

   c. unpredictable.

   d. dangerous.

2. The word *ecstasy* in "If you use details, you become better skilled at conveying your ecstasy or sorrow" (paragraph 5) means

   a. jealousy.

   b. feelings.

   c. joy.

   d. anger.

READING COMPREHENSION QUESTIONS

1. Which sentence best expresses the central idea of the selection?

   a. Writing and baking are very much alike.

   b. What we put into the baking of a cake can be compared to what we put into a piece of writing.

   c. Writing, like baking a cake, requires a careful mixing of ingredients.

   d. Heat needed to bake a cake is like the energy needed to create a piece of writing.

2. Which of the following best expresses the main idea of paragraph 2?

   a. You must add the heat and energy of your heart.

   b. You must become one with the details in love or hate.

   c. You must care about your subject.

   d. Just including details is not enough.

3. "So zazen does zazen" (paragraph 2) means

   a. in the writing process there should be no separation between the writer and that which is being written.

   b. the writer should meditate before writing.

   c. when writing, you should make sure to put down all your thoughts.

   d. you should always write in a secluded place.

4. *True or false?* _____ Goldberg advises us to check the time as we write and to stop when a certain period of time ends.

5. *True or false?* _____ According to Goldberg, writers never really know how their writing will end up—what kind of product they will produce.

6. The main idea of the last paragraph is that
    a. politicians need to know how to write well.
    b. details are not necessary in good writing as long as there is enough "heat."
    c. writing that contains details always provides the reader with something valuable.
    d. details help you convey your emotions.

DISCUSSION QUESTIONS

About Content

1. Goldberg talks a great deal about the need for detail in good writing. Think about your own writing. Do you provide sufficient details for the reader? Do your details "offer some good solid bread for the hungry" reader?

2. Paragraph 1 tells us that mixing ingredients in a bowl does not make a cake. More is needed. What else is needed, and how does this information apply to the writing process?

3. Goldberg seems to be telling us that we should write about what we know ("details") and that we should write with inspiration, energy, and passion ("heat"). Make a list of topics that you know a lot about and that you might really want to write about—for example, your family, a hobby, a close friend, a social or environmental problem, your job, or your dreams for the future. Then decide which one of these you could write about in the greatest detail and with the greatest passion.

About Structure

4. Does Goldberg's introduction prepare us for the main idea of her essay? In what way?

5. What do the statements of Nabokov and Roshi tell us about the act of writing?

6. This essay is essentially a comparison between steps in two different processes: baking a cake and writing. Find the sentence that introduces these steps and write it here.

About Style and Tone

7. Goldberg sometimes uses language that is familiar, even humorous. For example, in paragraph 1 she says that simply mixing ingredients in a bowl "makes goop." Find other examples of such phrasing.

8. Why does the author address the reader directly by using the second-person pronoun "you"? Why didn't she write something like this: *When someone bakes a cake, he or she has ingredients.*

RESPONDING TO IMAGES

The person in this photograph is both content with what she is doing and intent on doing a good job. Write an essay in which you discuss an activity that you are good at and that you enjoy doing. Make sure to discuss each of the reasons you give.

WRITING ASSIGNMENTS

Assignment 1: Writing a Paragraph

What did you learn about writing from this selection that you did not already know? How can you apply Goldberg's advice to your own writing? Answer these two questions in a paragraph that begins with a topic sentence that goes something like this:

I need to put more details into all of my academic writing.

-OR-

Goldberg has taught me that I need to put more energy into the writing of essays for college classes.

Assignment 2: Writing a Paragraph

Write a paragraph in which you summarize each of the steps that Goldberg uses as she compares the baking of a cake to writing. Make sure to use your own words and sentence structure throughout. Here's a topic sentence like the one you might begin with:

Baking a cake and writing are in a strange way similar.

Assignment 3: Writing an Essay

Write an essay in which you compare what you know about the process of writing with another activity that you are very familiar with. For example, compare writing with

- running a business.
- maintaining a car.
- painting or drawing a picture.
- composing a song.
- playing a musical instrument.

Use clustering, listing, or freewriting to gather information for your essay. Then, make a scratch outline that compares various points that your two subjects have in common. Here's an example of such an outline:

1. Both require knowledge of the basics.
   a. Writers need to know the basics of paragraph/essay structure and grammar.
   b. Musicians should learn to read music.
2. Both require frequent practice.
   a. Writers need to draft and revise their essays; they also need to write often.
   b. Musicians need to play a song over and over to get it right; they also need to learn many different pieces of music.
3. Both require mastery of different styles, techniques, and purposes.
   a. Writers must use a variety of patterns and strategies to develop their ideas.
   b. Musicians must often master a variety of musical styles/ traditions.
4. Both need to learn to take criticism from teachers and audiences/readers.

Follow your outline closely, but don't be slave to it. If new information pops into your head or if you change your mind about a certain point, don't be afraid to include that information or those changes as you draft your paper. As always, remember to write several drafts of your paper and to edit it carefully.

Why Go to College?
Robert S. Feldman

PREVIEW	WORDS TO WATCH
Robert S. Feldman teaches psychology at the University of Massachusetts. This essay first appeared in *P.O.W.E.R Learning: Strategies for Success in College and Life*, a study-skills textbook. Feldman begins the selection by stating the reasons most students give for going to college. He goes on to explain seven other important reasons that many students never consider.	lofty (2) unreflective (2) diversity (9)

Congratulations. You're in college. 1

But *why?* Although it seems as if it should be easy to answer why 2 you're continuing your education, for most students it's not so simple. The reasons that people go to college vary from the practical ("I want to get a good job"), to the lofty• ("I want to learn about people and the world"), to the unreflective• ("Why not?—I don't have anything better to do").

Surveys of first-year college students show that almost three-quarters 3 say they want to learn about things that interest them, get training for a specific career, land a better job, and make more money (see **Figure 1.1**). And, in fact, it's not wrong to expect that a college education helps people find better jobs. On average, college graduates earn about 75 percent more than high school graduates over their working lifetime. That difference adds up: Over the course of their working lifetimes, college graduates earn close to a million dollars more than those with only a high school degree. Furthermore, as jobs become increasingly complex and technologically sophisticated, college will become more and more of a necessity.

But the value of college extends far beyond dollars and cents. Consider 4 these added reasons for pursuing a college education:

- **You'll learn to think critically and communicate better.** Here's 5 what one student said about his college experience after he graduated: "It's not about what you major in or which classes you take. . . . It's really about learning to think and to communicate. Wherever you end up, you'll need to be able to analyze and solve problems—to figure out what needs to be done and do it."

    Education improves your ability to understand the world—to 6 understand it as it now is, and to prepare to understand it as it will be.

- **You'll be able to better deal with advances in knowledge and** 7 **technology that are changing the world.** Genetic engineering . . . drugs to reduce forgetfulness . . . computers that respond to our voices. . . . No one knows what the future will hold, but you can prepare for it through a college education. Education can provide you with the intellectual tools that you can apply regardless of the specific situation in which you find yourself.

FIGURE 1.1
Choosing College
These are the most fre-
quently cited reasons
that first-year college
students gave for why
they enrolled in college
when asked in a national
survey.

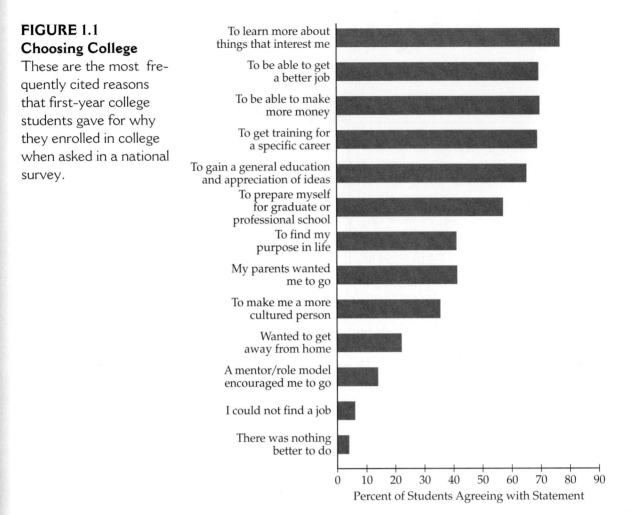

To learn more about things that interest me

To be able to get a better job

To be able to make more money

To get training for a specific career

To gain a general education and appreciation of ideas

To prepare myself for graduate or professional school

To find my purpose in life

My parents wanted me to go

To make me a more cultured person

Wanted to get away from home

A mentor/role model encouraged me to go

I could not find a job

There was nothing better to do

0   10   20   30   40   50   60   70   80   90

Percent of Students Agreeing with Statement

- **You'll learn to adapt to new situations.** College is a different world from high school. It presents new experiences and new challenges. Your adjustment to the college culture will prepare you for future encounters with new situations.   8

- **You'll be better prepared to live in a world of diversity.**° The racial and ethnic composition of the United States is changing rapidly. Whatever your ethnicity, chances are you'll be working and living with people whose backgrounds, lifestyles, and ways of thinking may be entirely different from your own.   9

    You won't be prepared for the future unless you understand others and their cultural backgrounds—as well as how your own cultural background affects you.   10

- **You'll learn to lead a life of community service.** In its broadest sense, community service involves making contributions to the society and community in which you live. College provides you with the opportunity to become involved in community service activities, in some cases even getting course credit for it—a pro- cess called service learning. College also allows you to develop the skills involved in acting toward others with *civility* and respectful, courteous behavior.   11

- **You'll make learning a lifelong habit.** Higher education isn't 12 the end of your education. Education will build upon your natural curiosity about the world, and it will make you aware that learning is a rewarding and never-ending journey.

- **You'll understand the meaning of your own contributions to the** 13 **world.** No matter who you are, you are poised to make your own contributions to society and the world. Higher education provides you with a window to the past, present, and future, and it allows you to understand the significance of your own contributions. Your college education provides you with a compass to discover who you are, where you've been, and where you're going.

VOCABULARY IN CONTEXT

1. The word *lofty* in "The reasons that people go to college vary from the practical . . . to the lofty" (paragraph 2) means
   a. unclear.
   b. high-minded.
   c. selfish.
   d. appealing.

2. The word *diversity* in "You'll be better prepared to live in a world of diversity" (paragraph 9) means
   a. variety.
   b. similarities.
   c. changes.
   d. difficulties.

READING COMPREHENSION QUESTIONS

1. What sentence best expresses the central point of this selection?
   a. Going to college can do more for you than increase your earning power.
   b. A college education helps people understand world events better.
   c. Going to college exposes students to cultures other than their own.
   d. Most students go to college because they are undecided about their future.

2. We can infer from what Feldman says that a few decades from now the majority of Americans will be
   a. Whites.
   b. African Americans.
   c. Latinos.
   d. Latinos and African Americans.

3. A college education will enable you to deal with advances in technology because

   a. most college majors stress science and mathematics.

   b. a college education provides you with learning tools that you can apply to various situations.

   c. a college education can help you predict changes in the future.

   d. a college education will teach you to use current technological tools.

4. According to Feldman, American students need to understand cultures other than their own because

   a. Americans travel a great deal for business.

   b. other cultures will advance faster than American culture.

   c. America is becoming more diverse, and we are in greater contact with other cultures throughout the world.

   d. we need to make our economy more competitive with those of other countries.

5. *True or false?* _____ Feldman believes that after you have gotten a college education, you will have little need to continue learning.

6. *True or false?* _____ The author argues that it is important to understand how your talents and skills can contribute to society.

7. When surveyed, most students responded that they were attending college because they want to

   a. get a good job.

   b. learn more about things that interest them.

   c. learn about other cultures.

   d. make their parents happy.

DISCUSSION QUESTIONS

About Content

1. In paragraph 7, Feldman mentions three technological developments that are changing the world. Give three more examples of such things that have been developed in the past twenty years.

2. The author states that going to college with the idea of getting a better job is not unreasonable. What evidence does he use to back up this idea?

About Structure

3. The essay begins with a summary of reasons that explain why most students want to go to college. Should Feldman have discussed his own seven reasons for going to college before telling us what most students think? Why or why not?

4. Feldman includes a graph that presents "the most frequently cited reasons that first-year college students gave" for going to college. Why does he use a graph to convey this information? Why didn't he just summarize it in a separate paragraph?

About Style and Tone

5. Paragraph 13 includes an image—a mental picture—"Higher education provides you with a window to the past, present, and future, and it allows you to understand the significance of your own contributions." Using your own words, explain what Feldman means. Write your answer in the lines below.

   _____

   _____

   _____

6. Find another image Feldman uses, and explain what it means.

   _____

   _____

   _____

RESPONDING TO IMAGES

College is about more than academics. It can also teach us a great deal about how to work with and get along with others, many of whom come from different cultural backgrounds or have different values from people with whom we are used to associating. Using specific details, write an essay that uses your experiences in college thus far to prove this idea.

WRITING ASSIGNMENTS

Assignment 1: Writing a Paragraph

Feldman says that "Education will build upon your natural curiosity about the world . . ." (paragraph 12). Think about a subject that fascinates you—for example, the process by which mummies were made, the possibility that life exists in outer space, the intelligence of dolphins or other animals, wind power and other alternative methods for generating energy, or ways to stop air pollution. Write a paragraph that explains what it is about this subject that makes you curious about it.

You might start by explaining how important, how exotic, or how strange you think your topic is. Then again, you can begin your paragraph with a question such as:

What makes us want to learn more about global warming?

Does it matter if there is intelligent life in outer space?

Here are a few more sample sentences you might use to start your paragraph.

After seeing the movie *The Mummy*, my interest in how Egyptians prepared their dead for burial became intense.

As a person who appreciates quiet, I have become obsessed with problems caused by inappropriate cell-phone use.

During the recent spike in gasoline prices, I have been learning all I can about alternative automobile fuels.

Assignment 2: Writing a Paragraph

The author claims that going to college will increase your chances of earning more money over your lifetime. However, for some people, college just isn't the right choice. Write a paragraph in which you discuss two or three career paths that you might have taken had you not chosen to go to college. Of course, you can discuss jobs that don't require a college education, but you might want to include those that require training through apprenticeships or the completion of trade school courses as well.

Assignment 3: Writing an Essay

Write an essay in which you explain at least three reasons for going to the college you are now attending.

If you just graduated from high school, you can begin the essay with an introduction that lists reasons—like those in Feldman's essay—that you chose to go to college and not enter the workforce immediately after high school. If you have been out of high school for some time and have just resumed your education, explain what caused you to return to school.

Then, in the body of the essay, develop at least three reasons that you chose to go to the college you are now attending. Here are four sample topic sentences for the body paragraphs for such an essay:

I applied to Wakefield College because it is close to home, making it possible for me to avoid room and board costs.

Firestone Community College has a top-rated hotel-restaurant management curriculum.

I was offered a half-tuition basketball scholarship to attend Townsend College.

I am attending Union Community College in order to improve my grades and eventually transfer to a prestigious university.

Round off your essay with a conclusion that tells the reader how the things you are learning in college will prepare you for a rewarding career and a satisfying life.

Old before Her Time

Katherine Barrett

PREVIEW	WORDS TO WATCH
Most of us wait for our own advanced years to learn what it is like to be old. Patty Moore decided not to wait. At the age of twenty-six, she disguised herself as an eighty-five-year-old woman. What she learned suggests that to be old in our society is both better and worse than is often thought. This selection may give you a different perspective on the older people in your life—on what they are really like inside and on what life is really like for them.	donned (3) gerontology (4) throng (4) nonentity (4) lark (4) anathema (14) jauntily (21) abysmally (24)

This is the story of an extraordinary voyage in time, and of a young 1 woman who devoted three years to a singular experiment. In 1979, Patty Moore—then aged twenty-six—transformed herself for the first of many times into an eighty-five-year-old woman. Her object was to discover firsthand the problems, joys, and frustrations of the elderly. She wanted to know for herself what it's like to live in a culture of youth and beauty when your hair is gray, your skin is wrinkled, and no men turn their heads as you pass.

Her time machine was a makeup kit. Barbara Kelly, a friend and pro- 2 fessional makeup artist, helped Patty pick out a wardrobe and showed her how to use latex to create wrinkles and wrap Ace bandages to give the impression of stiff joints. "It was peculiar," Patty recalls, as she relaxes in her New York City apartment. "Even the first few times I went out, I realized that I wouldn't have to act that much. The more I was perceived as elderly by others, the more 'elderly' I actually became. . . . I imagine that's just what happens to people who really are old."

What motivated Patty to make her strange journey? It was partly 3 her career—as an industrial designer, Patty often focuses on the needs of the elderly. But the roots of her interest are also deeply personal. Extremely close to her own grandparents—particularly her maternal grandfather, now ninety—and raised in a part of Buffalo, New York, where there was a large elderly population, Patty always drew comfort and support from the older people around her. When her own marriage ended in 1979 and her life seemed to be falling apart, she dived into her "project" with all her soul. In all, she donned• her costume more than two hundred times in fourteen states. Here is the remarkable story of what she found.

Columbus, Ohio, May 1979. Leaning heavily on her cane, Pat Moore 4 stood alone in the middle of a crowd of young professionals. They were all attending a gerontology* conference, and the room was filled with animated chatter. But no one was talking to Pat. In a throng* of men and women who devoted their working lives to the elderly, she began to feel like a total nonentity.* "I'll get us all some coffee," a young man told a group of women next to her. "What about me?" thought Pat. "If I were young, they would be offering me coffee, too." It was a bitter thought at the end of a disappointing day—a day that marked Patty's first appearance as "the old woman." She had planned to attend the gerontology conference anyway, and almost as a lark* decided to see how professionals would react to an old person in their midst.

Now, she was angry. All day she had been ignored . . . counted out **5** in a way she had never experienced before. She didn't understand. Why didn't people help her when they saw her struggling to open a heavy door? Why didn't they include her in conversations? Why did the other participants seem almost embarrassed by her presence at the conference— as if it were somehow inappropriate that an old person should be professionally active?

And so, eighty-five-year-old Pat Moore learned her first lesson: The **6** old are often ignored. "I discovered that people really do judge a book by its cover," Patty says today. "Just because I looked different, people either condescended to me or totally dismissed me. Later, in stores, I'd get the same reaction. A clerk would turn to someone younger and wait on her first. It was as if he assumed that I—the older woman—could wait because I didn't have anything better to do."

New York City, October 1979. Bent over her cane, Pat walked slowly **7** toward the edge of the park. She had spent the day sitting on a bench with friends, but now dusk was falling and her friends had all gone home. She looked around nervously at the deserted area and tried to move faster, but her joints were stiff. It was then that she heard the barely audible sound of sneakered feet approaching and the kids' voices. "Grab her, man." "Get her purse." Suddenly an arm was around her throat and she was dragged back, knocked off her feet.

She saw only a blur of sneakers and blue jeans, heard the sounds of **8** mocking laughter, felt fists pummeling her—on her back, her legs, her breasts, her stomach. "Oh, God," she thought, using her arms to protect her head and curling herself into a ball. "They're going to kill me. I'm going to die. . . ."

Then, as suddenly as the boys attacked, they were gone. And Patty **9** was left alone, struggling to rise. The boys' punches had broken the latex makeup on her face, the fall had disarranged her wig, and her whole body ached. (Later she would learn that she had fractured her left wrist, an injury that took two years to heal completely.) Sobbing, she left the park and hailed a cab to return home. Again the thought struck her: What if I really lived in the gray ghetto? . . . What if I couldn't escape to my nice safe home . . . ?

Lesson number two: The fear of crime is paralyzing. "I really under- **10** stand now why the elderly become homebound," the young woman says as she recalls her ordeal today. "When something like this happens, the fear just doesn't go away. I guess it wasn't so bad for me. I could distance myself from what happened . . . and I was strong enough to get up and walk away. But what about someone who is really too weak to run or fight back or protect herself in any way? And the elderly often can't afford to move if the area in which they live deteriorates, becomes unsafe. I met people like this, and they were imprisoned by their fear. That's when the bolts go on the door. That's when people starve themselves because they're afraid to go to the grocery store."

New York City, February 1980. It was a slushy, gray day, and Pat had 11 laboriously descended four flights of stairs from her apartment to go shopping. Once outside, she struggled to hold her threadbare coat closed with one hand and manipulate her cane with the other. Splotches of snow made the street difficult for anyone to navigate, but for someone hunched over, as she was, it was almost impossible. The curb was another obstacle. The slush looked ankle-deep—and what was she to do? Jump over it? Slowly, she worked her way around to a drier spot, but the crowds were impatient to move. A woman with packages jostled her as she rushed past, causing Pat to nearly lose her balance. If I really were old, I would have fallen, she thought. Maybe broken something. On another day, a woman had practically knocked her over by letting go of a heavy door as Pat tried to enter a coffee shop. Then there were the revolving doors. How could you push them without strength? And how could you get up and down stairs, on and off a bus, without risking a terrible fall?

Lesson number three: If small, thoughtless deficiencies in design were 12 corrected, life would be so much easier for older people. It was no surprise to Patty that the "built" environment is often inflexible. But even she didn't realize the extent of the problems, she admits. "It was a terrible feeling. I never realized how difficult it is to get off a curb if your knees don't bend easily. Or the helpless feeling you get if your upper arms aren't strong enough to open a door. You know, I just felt so vulnerable—as if I was at the mercy of every barrier or rude person I encountered."

Fort Lauderdale, Florida, May 1980. Pat met a new friend while shop- 13 ping, and they decided to continue their conversation over a sundae at a nearby coffee shop. The woman was in her late seventies, "younger" than Pat, but she was obviously reaching out for help. Slowly, her story unfolded. "My husband moved out of our bedroom," the woman said softly, fiddling with her coffee cup and fighting back tears. "He won't touch me anymore. And when he gets angry at me for being stupid, he'll even sometimes . . ." The woman looked down, too embarrassed to go on. Pat took her hand. "He hits me; . . . he gets so mean." "Can't you tell anyone?" Pat asked. "Can't you tell your son?" "Oh, no!" the woman almost gasped. "I would never tell the children; they absolutely adore him."

Lesson number four: Even a fifty-year-old marriage isn't necessarily 14 a good one. While Pat met many loving and devoted elderly couples, she was stunned to find others who had stayed together unhappily—because divorce was still an anathema • in their middle years. "I met women who secretly wished their husbands dead, because after so many years they just ended up full of hatred. One woman in Chicago even admitted that she deliberately angered her husband because she knew it would make his blood pressure rise. Of course, that was pretty extreme. . . ."

Patty pauses thoughtfully and continues. "I guess what really made 15 an impression on me, the real eye-opener, was that so many of these older women had the same problems as women twenty, thirty, or forty—problems with men . . . problems with the different roles that are expected of them. As a 'young woman' I, too, had just been through a relationship where I spent a lot of time protecting someone by covering up his problems from family and friends. Then I heard this woman in Florida saying that she wouldn't tell her children their father beat her because she didn't want to disillusion them. These issues aren't age-related. They affect everyone."

Clearwater, Florida, January 1981. She heard the children laughing, 16 but she didn't realize at first that they were laughing at her. On this day, as on several others, Pat had shed the clothes of a middle-income woman for the rags of a bag lady. She wanted to see the extremes of the human condition, what it was like to be old and poor, and outside traditional society as well. Now, tottering down the sidewalk, she was most concerned with the cold, since her layers of ragged clothing did little to ease the chill. She had spent the afternoon rummaging through garbage cans, loading her shopping bags with bits of debris, and she was stiff and tired. Suddenly, she saw that four little boys, five or six years old, were moving up on her. And then she felt the sting of the pebbles they were throwing. She quickened her pace to escape, but another handful of gravel hit her and the laughter continued. They're using me as a target, she thought, horror-stricken. They don't even think of me as a person.

Lesson number five: Social class affects every aspect of an older per- 17 son's existence. "I found out that class is a very important factor when you're old," says Patty. "It was interesting. That same day, I went back to my hotel and got dressed as a wealthy woman, another role that I occasionally took. Outside the hotel, a little boy of about seven asked if I would go shelling with him. We walked along the beach, and he reached out to hold my hand. I knew he must have a grandmother who walked with a cane, because he was so concerned about me and my footing. 'Don't put your cane there; the sand's wet,' he'd say. He really took responsibility for my welfare. The contrast between him and those children was really incredible—the little ones who were throwing pebbles at me because they didn't see me as human, and then the seven-year-old taking care of me. I think he would have responded to me the same way even if I had been dressed as the middle-income woman. There's no question that money does make life easier for older people, not only because it gives them a more comfortable lifestyle, but because it makes others treat them with greater respect."

New York City, May 1981. Pat always enjoyed the time she spent 18 sitting on the benches in Central Park. She'd let the whole day pass by, watching young children play, feeding the pigeons and chatting. One spring day she found herself sitting with three women, all widows, and the conversation turned to the few available men around. "It's been a long time since anyone hugged me," one woman complained. Another agreed. "Isn't that the truth. I need a hug, too." It was a favorite topic, Pat found—the lack of touching left in these women's lives, the lack of hugging, the lack of men.

In the last two years, she found out herself how it felt to walk down 19 Fifth Avenue and know that no men were turning to look after her. Or how it felt to look at models in magazines or store mannequins and know that those gorgeous clothes were just not made for her. She hadn't realized before just how much casual attention was paid to her because she was young and pretty. She hadn't realized it until it stopped.

Lesson number six: You never grow old emotionally. You always need 20 to feel loved. "It's not surprising that everyone needs love and touching and holding," says Patty. "But I think some people feel that you reach a point in your life when you accept that those intimate feelings are in the past. That's wrong. These women were still interested in sex. But more than that, they—like everyone—needed to be hugged and touched. I'd watch two women greeting each other on the street and just holding onto each other's hands, neither wanting to let go. Yet, I also saw that there are people who are afraid to touch an old person; . . . they were afraid to touch me. It's as if they think old age is a disease and it's catching. They think that something might rub off on them."

New York City, September 1981. He was a thin man, rather nattily 21 dressed, with a hat that he graciously tipped at Pat as he approached the bench where she sat. "Might I join you?" he asked jauntily.• Pat told him he would be welcome and he offered her one of the dietetic hard candies that he carried in a crumpled paper bag. As the afternoon passed, they got to talking . . . about the beautiful buds on the trees and the world around them and the past. "Life's for the living, my wife used to tell me," he said. "When she took sick, she made me promise her that I wouldn't waste a moment. But the first year after she died, I just sat in the apartment. I didn't want to see anyone, talk to anyone or go anywhere. I missed her so much." He took a handkerchief from his pocket and wiped his eyes, and they sat in silence. Then he slapped his leg to break the mood and change the subject. He asked Pat about herself, and described his life alone. He belonged to a "senior center" now, and went on trips and had lots of friends. Life did go on. They arranged to meet again the following week on the same park bench. He brought lunch—chicken salad sandwiches and decaffeinated peppermint tea in a thermos—and wore a carnation in his lapel. It was the first date Patty had had since her marriage ended.

Lesson number seven: Life does go on . . . as long as you're flexible 22 and open to change. "That man really meant a lot to me, even though I never saw him again," says Patty, her eyes wandering toward the gray wig that now sits on a wig stand on the top shelf of her bookcase. "He was a real old-fashioned gentleman, yet not afraid to show his feelings— as so many men my age are. It's funny, but at that point I had been through months of self-imposed seclusion. Even though I was in a different role, that encounter kind of broke the ice for getting my life together as a single woman."

In fact, while Patty was living her life as the old woman, some of her 23 young friends had been worried about her. After several years, it seemed as if the lines of identity had begun to blur. Even when she wasn't in makeup, she was wearing unusually conservative clothing, she spent most of her time with older people, and she seemed almost to revel in her role—sometimes finding it easier to be in costume than to be a single New Yorker.

But as Patty continued her experiment, she was also learning a great 24 deal from the older people she observed. Yes, society often did treat the elderly abysmally•; . . . they were sometimes ignored, sometimes victimized, sometimes poor and frightened, but so many of them were survivors. They had lived through two world wars, through the Depression, and into the computer age. "If there was one lesson to learn, one lesson that I'll take with me into my old age, it's that you've got to be flexible," Patty says. "I saw my friend in the park, managing after the loss of his wife, and I met countless other people who picked themselves up after something bad— or even something catastrophic—happened. I'm not worried about them. I'm worried about the others who shut themselves away. It's funny, but seeing these two extremes helped me recover from the trauma in my own life, to pull my life together."

Today, Patty is back to living the life of a single thirty-year-old, and 25 she rarely dons her costumes anymore. "I must admit, though, I do still think a lot about aging," she says. "I look in the mirror and I begin to see wrinkles, and then I realize that I won't be able to wash those wrinkles off." Is she afraid of growing older? "No. In a way, I'm kind of looking forward to it." She smiles. "I know it will be different from my experiment. I know I'll probably even look different. When they aged Orson Welles in *Citizen Kane* he didn't resemble at all the Orson Welles of today."

But Patty also knows that in one way she really did manage to capture 26 the feeling of being old. With her bandages and her stooped posture, she turned her body into a kind of prison. Yet inside she didn't change at all. "It's funny, but that's exactly how older people always say they feel," says Patty. "Their bodies age, but inside they are really no different from when they were young."

VOCABULARY IN CONTEXT

1. The word *nonentity* in "But no one was talking to Pat. In a throng of men and women who devoted their working lives to the elderly, she began to feel like a total nonentity. . . . All day she had been ignored" (paragraphs 4–5) means

   a. expert.

   b. nobody.

   c. experiment.

   d. leader.

2. The word *abysmally* in "society often did treat the elderly abysmally; . . . they were sometimes ignored, sometimes victimized, sometimes poor and frightened" (paragraph 24) means

   a. politely.

   b. absentmindedly.

   c. very badly.

   d. angrily.

READING COMPREHENSION QUESTIONS

1. Which of the following would be the best alternative title for this selection?
   a. How Poverty Affects the Elderly
   b. Similarities between Youth and Old Age
   c. One Woman's Discoveries about the Elderly
   d. Violence against the Elderly

2. Which sentence best expresses the main idea of the selection?
   a. The elderly often have the same problems as young people.
   b. Pat Moore dressed up like an elderly woman over two hundred times.
   c. By making herself appear old, Pat Moore learned what life is like for the elderly in the United States.
   d. Elderly people often feel ignored in a society that glamorizes youth.

3. *True or false?* _____ As they age, people need others less.

4. Pat Moore learned that the elderly often become homebound because of the
   a. fear of crime.
   b. high cost of living.
   c. availability of in-home nursing care.
   d. lack of interesting places for them to visit.

5. One personal lesson Pat Moore learned from her experiment was that
   a. she needs to start saving money for her retirement.
   b. by being flexible she can overcome hardships.
   c. she has few friends her own age.
   d. her marriage could have been saved.

6. From paragraph 2, we can infer that
   a. behaving like an old person was difficult for Moore.
   b. many older people wear Ace bandages.
   c. people sometimes view themselves as others see them.
   d. Barbara Kelly works full-time making people look older than they really are.

7. The article suggests that fifty years ago
   a. young couples tended to communicate better than today's young couples.
   b. divorce was less acceptable than it is today.
   c. verbal and physical abuse was probably extremely rare.
   d. the elderly were treated with great respect.

8. We can conclude that Moore may have disguised herself as an elderly woman over two hundred times in fourteen states because

   a. she and her friend Barbara Kelly continuously worked at perfecting Moore's costumes.

   b. her company made her travel often.

   c. she was having trouble finding locations with large numbers of elderly people.

   d. she wanted to see how the elderly were seen and treated all over the country, rather than in just one area.

DISCUSSION QUESTIONS

About Content

1. Why did Moore decide to conduct her experiment? Which of her discoveries surprised you?

2. Using the information Moore learned from her experiment, list some of the things that could be done to help the elderly. What are some things you personally could do?

3. How do the elderly people Moore met during her experiment compare with the elderly people you know?

4. Lesson number seven in the article is "Life does go on . . . as long as you're flexible and open to change" (paragraph 22). What do you think this really means? How might this lesson apply to situations and people you're familiar with—in which people either were or were not flexible and open to change?

About Structure

5. Most of the selection is made up of a series of Pat Moore's experiences and the seven lessons they taught. Find the sentence used by the author to introduce those experiences and lessons, and write that sentence here:

   _____

6. The details of paragraph 21 are organized in time order, and the author has used a few time transition words to signal time relationships. Find two of those time words, and write them here:

   _____   _____

About Style and Tone

7. What device does the author use to signal that she is beginning a new set of experiences and the lesson they taught? How does she ensure that the reader will recognize what each of the seven lessons is?

8. Do you think Barrett is objective in her treatment of Moore? Or does the author allow whatever her feelings might be for Moore to show in her writing? Find details in the article to support your answer.

RESPONDING TO IMAGES

What is the tone of this photograph, and how is it established? What is the photographer's attitude toward her subject?

WRITING ASSIGNMENT

Assignment 1: Writing a Paragraph

In her experiment, Moore discovered various problems faced by the elderly. Choose one of these areas of difficulty and write a paragraph in which you discuss what could be done in your city to help solve the problem. Following are a few possible topic sentences for this assignment:

> Fear of crime among the elderly could be eased by a program providing young people to accompany them on their errands.

> The courthouse and train station in our town need to be redesigned to allow easier access for the elderly.

> Schools should start adopt-a-grandparent programs, which would enrich the emotional lives of both the young and the old participants.

Assignment 2: Writing a Paragraph

What did you learn from the selection, or what do you already know, about being older in our society that might influence your own future? Write a paragraph in which you list three or four ways you plan to minimize or avoid some of the problems often faced by elderly people. For instance, you may decide to do whatever you can to remain as healthy and strong as possible throughout your life. That might involve quitting smoking and incorporating exercise into your schedule. Your topic sentence might simply be: "There are three important ways in which I hope to avoid some of the problems often faced by the elderly."

Assignment 3: Writing an Essay

Lesson number seven in Barrett's article is "Life does go on . . . as long as you're flexible and open to change" (paragraph 22). Think about one person of any age whom you know well (including yourself). Write an essay in which you show how being (or not being) flexible and open to change has been important in that person's life. Develop your essay with three main examples.

In preparation for writing, think of several key times in your subject's life. Select three times in which being flexible or inflexible had a significant impact on that person. Then narrate and explain each of those times in a paragraph of its own. Here are two possible thesis statements for this essay:

> My grandmother generally made the most of her circumstances by being flexible and open to change.

> When I was a teenager, I could have made life easier for myself by being more flexible and open to change.

Your conclusion for this essay might summarize the value of being flexible or the problems of being inflexible, or both, for the person you are writing about.

Assignment 4: Writing an Essay Using Internet Research

As Moore studied the elderly people around her, she recognized that some were "survivors"—people who adapted successfully to the challenges of aging—and some were not. What can people do, both mentally and physically, to make their later years active and happy? Go online to see what some experts have suggested. Then write an essay on three ways that people can cope well with old age.

Using Google (or another search engine), try one of the following phrases or some related phrase:

growing older and keeping active and happy

happy healthy aging

elderly people and healthy living

You may, of course, use a simple phrase such as "growing older," but that will bring up too many items. As you proceed, you'll develop a sense of how to "track down" and focus a topic by adding more information to your search words and phrases.

The Most Hateful Words

Amy Tan

PREVIEW	WORDS TO WATCH
For years, a painful exchange with her mother lay like a heavy stone on Amy Tan's heart. In the following essay, Tan, author of best-selling novels, including *The Joy Luck Club* and *The Kitchen God's Wife*, tells the story of how that weight was finally lifted. This essay is from her memoir, *The Opposite of Fate*.	stricken (2) tormented (3) forbade (3) impenetrable (3) bequeathed (15)

The most hateful words I have ever said to another human being were 1 to my mother. I was sixteen at the time. They rose from the storm in my chest and I let them fall in a fury of hailstones: "I hate you. I wish I were dead. . . ."

I waited for her to collapse, stricken° by what I had just said. She was 2 still standing upright, her chin tilted, her lips stretched in a crazy smile. "Okay, maybe I die too," she said between huffs. "Then I no longer be your mother!" We had many similar exchanges. Sometimes she actually tried to kill herself by running into the street, holding a knife to her throat. She too had storms in her chest. And what she aimed at me was as fast and deadly as a lightning bolt.

For days after our arguments, she would not speak to me. She 3 tormented° me, acted as if she had no feelings for me whatsoever. I was lost to her. And because of that, I lost, battle after battle, all of them: the times she criticized me, humiliated me in front of others, forbade° me to do this or that without even listening to one good reason why it should be the other way. I swore to myself I would never forget these injustices. I would store them, harden my heart, make myself as impenetrable° as she was.

I remember this now, because I am also remembering another time, 4 just a few years ago. I was forty-seven, had become a different person by then, had become a fiction writer, someone who uses memory and imagination. In fact, I was writing a story about a girl and her mother, when the phone rang.

It was my mother, and this surprised me. Had someone helped her 5 make the call? For a few years now, she had been losing her mind through Alzheimer's disease. Early on, she forgot to lock her door. Then she forgot where she lived. She forgot who many people were and what they had meant to her. Lately, she could no longer remember many of her worries and sorrows.

"Amy-ah," she said, and she began to speak quickly in Chinese. 6 "Something is wrong with my mind. I think I'm going crazy."

I caught my breath. Usually she could barely speak more than two 7 words at a time. "Don't worry," I started to say.

"It's true," she went on. "I feel like I can't remember many things. I 8 can't remember what I did yesterday. I can't remember what happened a long time ago, what I did to you. . . ." She spoke as a drowning person might if she had bobbed to the surface with the force of will to live, only to see how far she had already drifted, how impossibly far she was from the shore.

She spoke frantically: "I know I did something to hurt you."   9

"You didn't," I said. "Don't worry."   10

"I did terrible things. But now I can't remember what. . . . And I just 11 want to tell you . . . I hope you can forget, just as I've forgotten."

I tried to laugh so she would not notice the cracks in my voice. "Really, 12 don't worry."

"Okay, I just wanted you to know."   13

After we hung up, I cried, both happy and sad. I was again that 14 sixteen-year-old, but the storm in my chest was gone.

My mother died six months later. By then she had bequeathed° to me 15 her most healing words, as open and eternal as a clear blue sky. Together we knew in our hearts what we should remember, what we can forget.

VOCABULARY IN CONTEXT

1. The word *stricken* in "I waited for her to collapse, *stricken* by what I had just said" (paragraph 2) means
   a. wounded.
   b. amused.
   c. annoyed.
   d. bored.

2. The word *bequeathed* in "By then she had *bequeathed* to me her most healing words, as open and eternal as a clear blue sky" (paragraph 15) means

   a. denied.

   b. sold.

   c. given.

   d. cursed.

READING COMPREHENSION QUESTIONS

1. Which sentence best expresses the central idea of the selection?

   a. Because of Alzheimer's disease, the author's mother forgot harsh words the two of them had said to each other.

   b. Amy Tan had a difficult relationship with her mother that worsened over the years.

   c. Years after a painful childhood with her mother, Amy Tan was able to realize peace and forgiveness.

   d. Despite her Alzheimer's disease, Amy Tan's mother was able to apologize to her daughter for hurting her.

2. Which sentence best expresses the main idea of paragraphs 1 and 2?

   a. Amy Tan's mother was sometimes suicidal.

   b. Amy Tan wanted to use words to hurt her mother.

   c. It is not unusual for teenagers and their parents to argue.

   d. Amy Tan and her mother had a very hurtful relationship.

3. Which sentence best expresses the main idea of paragraphs 8 and 9?

   a. The author's mother was deeply disturbed by the thought that she had hurt her daughter.

   b. Alzheimer's disease causes people to become confused and unable to remember things clearly.

   c. The author's mother could not even remember what she had done the day before.

   d. The author's mother had changed very little from what she was like when Tan was a child.

4. After arguing with her daughter, the author's mother

   a. would say nice things about her to others.

   b. would immediately forget they had argued.

   c. would refuse to speak to her.

   d. would apologize.

5. When she was a girl, the author swore that she

   a. would never forget her mother's harsh words.

   b. would never be like her mother.

   c. would publicly embarrass her mother by writing about her.

   d. would never have children.

6. The first sign that the author's mother had Alzheimer's disease was

   a. forgetting where she lived.

   b. being able to speak only two or three words at a time.

   c. forgetting people's identities.

   d. forgetting to lock her door.

7. We can infer from paragraph 2 that

   a. the author wished her mother were dead.

   b. the author immediately felt guilty for the way she had spoken to her mother.

   c. the author's mother was emotionally unstable.

   d. the author's mother was physically abusive.

8. The author implies, in paragraphs 9–15, that

   a. she was pleased by her mother's sense of guilt.

   b. her love and pity for her mother were stronger than her anger.

   c. she did not recall what her mother was talking about.

   d. she was annoyed by her mother's confusion.

DISCUSSION QUESTIONS

About Content

1. How would you describe Amy Tan's mother? What kind of mother does she appear to have been?

2. In the discussion at the end of the essay, Tan chooses to keep her emotions hidden from her mother. Why do you think she does this?

3. What does Tan mean by her last line, "Together we knew in our hearts what we should remember, what we can forget."

About Structure

4. Tan makes effective use of parallel structure in writing her story. What are two examples of parallelism that help make her sentences clear and easy to read?

5. Tan begins her essay from the point of view of a sixteen-year-old girl but finishes it from the perspective of a woman in her late forties. Where in the essay does Tan make the transition between those two perspectives? What words does she use to signal the change?

6. Paragraph 5 describes a sequence of events, and the writer uses several transition words to signal time relationships. Locate three of those transitions and write them here:

_____   _____   _____

About Style and Tone

7. What effect does Tan achieve by using so many direct quotations?

8. Tan uses images of the weather throughout her essay. Find three instances in which Tan mentions weather and list them below. What does she accomplish with this technique?

_____   _____   _____

WRITING ASSIGNMENTS

Assignment 1: Writing a Paragraph

Despite being an adult, Tan recalls feeling like a sixteen-year-old girl again when she speaks to her mother. Think about something in your life that has the power to reconnect you to a vivid memory. Write a paragraph in which you describe your memory and the trigger that "takes you back" to it. Begin your paragraph with a topic sentence that makes it clear what you are going to discuss. Then provide specific details so that readers can understand your memory. Here are sample topic sentences.

> Whenever I see swings, I remember the day in second grade when I got into my first fistfight.
>
> The smell of cotton candy takes me back to the day my grandfather took me to my first baseball game.
>
> I can't pass St. Joseph's Hospital without remembering the day, ten years ago, when my brother was shot.

Assignment 2: Writing a Paragraph

In this essay, we see that Tan's relationship with her mother was very complicated. Who is a person with whom you have a complex relationship—maybe a relationship you'd describe as "love-hate" or "difficult"? Write a paragraph about that relationship. Be sure to give examples or details to show readers why you have such difficulties with this person.

Your topic sentence should introduce the person you plan to discuss. For example:

> To me, my mother-in-law is one of the most difficult people in the world. (*Or,* My mother-in-law and I have contrasting points of view on several issues.)
>
> While I respect my boss, he is simply a very difficult person.
>
> Even though I love my sister, I can't stand to be around her.

Be sure to provide specific examples or details to help your reader understand why the relationship is so difficult for you. For example, if you decide to write about your boss, you will want to describe specific behaviors that show just why you consider him or her difficult.

Assignment 3: Writing an Essay

Like Tan's mother, most of us have at some time done something we wish we could undo. If you had a chance to revisit your past and change one of your actions, what would it be? Write an essay describing something you would like to undo.

In your first paragraph, introduce exactly what you did. Here are three thesis statements that students might have written:

> I wish I could undo the night I decided to drive my car while I was drunk.

> If I could undo any moment in my life, it would be the day I decided to drop out of high school.

> One moment from my life I would like to change is the time I picked on an unpopular kid in sixth grade.

Be sure to provide details and, if appropriate, actual words that were spoken so that your readers can "see and hear" what happened. Once you've described the moment that you wish to take back, write three reasons why you feel the way you do. Below is a scratch outline for the first topic.

I wish I could undo the night I decided to drive my car while I was drunk.

1. Caused an accident that hurt others.

2. Lost my license, my car, and my job.

3. Affected the way others treat me.

To write an effective essay, you will need to provide specific details explaining each reason you identify. For instance, to support the third reason above, you might describe new feelings of guilt and anger you have about yourself as well as provide examples of how individual people now treat you differently. To end your essay, you might describe what you would do today if you could replay what happened.

Rudeness at the Movies

Bill Wine

PREVIEW	WORDS TO WATCH
When you're at a movie theater, do loud conversations, the crinkling of candy wrappers, and the wailing of children make you wish you'd gone bowling instead? Do you cringe when your fellow viewers announce plot twists moments before they happen? If so, you'll find a comrade in suffering in the film critic and columnist Bill Wine, who thinks people have come to feel far too at home in theaters. In the following essay, which first appeared as a newspaper feature story, Wine wittily describes what the moviegoing experience all too often is like these days.	ecstatic (2) epidemic (14) galling (14) malodorous (15) superfluous (16) reluctance (18) prescient (20) gregarious (25)

Is this actually happening or am I dreaming? 1

I am at the movies, settling into my seat, eager with anticipation at the 2 prospect of seeing a long-awaited film of obvious quality. The theater is absolutely full for the late show on this weekend evening, as the reviews have been ecstatic• for this cinema masterpiece.

Directly in front of me sits a man an inch or two taller than the Jolly 3 Green Giant. His wife, sitting on his left, sports the very latest in fashionable hairdos, a gathering of her locks into a shape that resembles a drawbridge when it's open.

On his right, a woman spritzes herself liberally with perfume that 4 her popcorn-munching husband got her for Valentine's Day, a scent that should be renamed "Essence of Elk."

The row in which I am sitting quickly fills up with members of Cub 5 Scout Troop 432, on an outing to the movies because rain has canceled their overnight hike. One of the boys, demonstrating the competitive spirit for which Scouts are renowned worldwide, announces to the rest of the troop the rules in the Best Sound Made from an Empty Good-n-Plenty's Box contest, about to begin.

Directly behind me, a man and his wife are ushering three other 6 couples into their seats. I hear the woman say to the couple next to her: "You'll love it. You'll just love it. This is our fourth time and we enjoy it more and more each time. Don't we, Harry? Tell them about the pie-fight scene, Harry. Wait'll you see it. It comes just before you find out that the daughter killed her boyfriend. It's great."

The woman has more to say—much more—but she is drowned out at 7 the moment by the wailing of a six-month-old infant in the row behind her. The baby is crying because his mother, who has brought her twins to the theater to save on babysitting costs, can change only one diaper at a time.

Suddenly, the lights dim. The music starts. The credits roll. And I 8 panic.

I plead with everyone around me to let me enjoy the movie. All I ask, 9 I wail, is to be able to see the images and hear the dialogue and not find out in advance what is about to happen. Is that so much to expect for six bucks, I ask, now engulfed by a cloud of self-pity. I begin weeping unashamedly.

Then, as if on cue, the Jolly Green Giant slumps down in his seat, his 10 wife removes her wig, the Elk lady changes her seat, the Scouts drop their candy boxes on the floor, the play-by-play commentator takes out her teeth, and the young mother takes her two bawling babies home.

Of course I am dreaming, I realize, as I gain a certain but shaky con- 11 sciousness. I notice that I am in a cold sweat. Not because the dream is scary, but from the shock of people being that cooperative.

I realize that I have awakened to protect my system from having to 12 handle a jolt like that. For never—NEVER—would that happen in real life. Not on this planet.

I used to wonder whether I was the only one who feared bad audience 13 behavior more than bad moviemaking. But I know now that I am not. Not by a long shot. The most frequent complaint I have heard in the last few months about the moviegoing experience has had nothing to do with the films themselves.

No. What folks have been complaining about is the audience. Indeed, 14 there seems to be an epidemic• of galling• inconsiderateness and outrageous rudeness.

It is not that difficult to forgive a person's excessive height, or 15 malodorous• perfume, or perhaps even an inadvisable but understandable need to bring very young children to adult movies.

But the talking: that is not easy to forgive. It is inexcusable. Talking— 16 loud, constant, and invariably superfluous•—seems to be standard operating procedure on the part of many movie patrons these days.

It is true, I admit, that after a movie critic has seen several hundred 17 movies in the ideal setting of an almost-empty screening room with no one but other politely silent movie critics around him, it does tend to spoil him for the packed-theater experience.

And something is lost viewing a movie in almost total isolation—a 18 fact that movie distributors acknowledge with their reluctance• to screen certain audience-pleasing movies for small groups of critics. Especially with comedies, the infectiousness of laughter is an important ingredient of movie-watching pleasure.

But it is a decidedly uphill battle to enjoy a movie—no matter how sus- 19 penseful or hilarious or moving—with nonstop gabbers sitting within earshot. And they come in sizes, ages, sexes, colors, and motivations of every kind.

Some chat as if there is no movie playing. Some greet friends as if at a picnic. 20 Some alert those around them to what is going to happen, either because they have seen the film before, or because they are self-proclaimed experts on the predictability of plotting and want to be seen as prescient• geniuses.

Some describe in graphic terms exactly what is happening as if they 21 were doing the commentary for a sporting event on radio. ("Ooh, look, he's sitting down. Now he's looking at that green car. A banana—she's eating a banana.") Some audition for film critic Gene Shalit's job by waxing witty as they critique the movie right before your very ears.

And all act as if it is their constitutional or God-given right. As if their 22 admission price allows them to ruin the experience for anyone and everyone else in the building. But why?

Good question. I wish I knew. Maybe rock concerts and ball games—both 23 environments which condone or even encourage hootin' and hollerin'— have conditioned us to voice our approval and disapproval and just about anything else we can spit out of our mouths at the slightest provocation when we are part of an audience.

But my guess lies elsewhere. The villain, I'm afraid, is the tube. We 24 have seen the enemy and it is television.

We have gotten conditioned over the last few decades to spending most 25 of our screen-viewing time in front of a little box in our living rooms and bedrooms. And when we watch that piece of furniture, regardless of what is on it—be it commercial, Super Bowl, soap opera, funeral procession, prime-time sitcom, Shakespeare play—we chat. Boy, do we chat. Because TV viewing tends to be an informal, gregarious,• friendly, casually interruptible experience, we talk whenever the spirit moves us. Which is often.

All of this is fine. But we have carried behavior that is perfectly 26 acceptable in the living room right to our neighborhood movie theater. And that *isn't* fine. In fact, it is turning lots of people off to what used to be a truly pleasurable experience: sitting in a jammed movie theater and watching a crowd-pleasing movie. And that's a first-class shame.

Nobody wants Fascist-like ushers, yet that may be where we're headed 27 of necessity. Let's hope not. But something's got to give.

Movies during this Age of Television may or may not be better than 28 ever. About audiences, however, there is no question.

They are worse. 29

VOCABULARY IN CONTEXT

1. The word *ecstatic* in "The theater is absolutely full . . . as the reviews have been ecstatic for this cinema masterpiece" (paragraph 2) means
   a. clever.
   b. disappointing.
   c. a little confusing.
   d. very enthusiastic.

2. The word *malodorous* in "It is not that difficult to forgive a person's . . . malodorous perfume" (paragraph 15) means
   a. pleasant.
   b. expensive.
   c. bad-smelling.
   d. hard-to-smell.

READING COMPREHENSION QUESTIONS

1. Which of the following would be the best alternative title for this selection?
   a. Television-Watching Behavior
   b. Today's Movie Audiences
   c. Modern Films
   d. The Life of a Movie Critic

2. Which sentence best expresses the main idea of the selection?
   a. Ushers should now make movie audiences keep quiet.
   b. People talk while they watch television or sports.
   c. Rude audiences are ruining movies for many.
   d. Films have changed in recent years.

3. The author states that in his dream
   a. he had come to the movies with a friend.
   b. he wore a tall hat and sat in front of a person shorter than he is.
   c. the Cub Scouts stopped making noises with empty candy boxes.
   d. the popcorn was too salty.

4. *True or false?* _____ The experience that Wine describes in the first eight paragraphs of this article is typical of what really happens at the movies today.

5. The most frequent complaint the author has heard about movies is that
   a. they are too long.
   b. they are too expensive.
   c. the audiences are too noisy.
   d. the audiences arrive too late.

6. The author suggests that watching television
   a. has affected the behavior of movie audiences.
   b. should be done in silence.
   c. is more fun than seeing movies in a theater.
   d. is a good model for watching movies in theaters.

7. From the selection, we can conclude that the author feels
   a. films aren't as good as they used to be.
   b. teenagers are the rudest members of movie audiences.
   c. talking during a movie is much more common now than it used to be.
   d. tall people should be seated in the back of a theater.

8. In paragraph 27, the author implies that unless audiences become quieter,
   a. movie theaters will be closed.
   b. everyone will watch less television.
   c. movies will get worse.
   d. ushers will have to force talkers to be quiet or leave.

DISCUSSION QUESTIONS

About Content

1. According to Wine, what are some possible causes for people's rude behavior at movies? Of these, which does Wine consider the most likely cause?

2. Do you agree with Wine's theory about why some people are rude at the movies? Why or why not? What might theater operators and other audience members do to control the problem?

3. Have you noticed the problem of noisy audiences in a movie theater? If so, what exactly have you experienced? What, if anything, was done about the problems you encountered?

About Structure

4. Wine writes about a problem. Write here the paragraphs in which Wine presents details that explain and illustrate what that problem is: paragraphs _____ to _____.

5. Wine discusses reasons for the problem he writes about. Write here the paragraphs in which he discusses those reasons: paragraphs _____ to _____.

6. Wine suggests one possible but unwelcome solution for the problem he writes about. Write here the number of the paragraph in which he mentions that solution: _____.

About Style and Tone

7. Wine provides exaggerated descriptions of audience members—for example, he refers to the tall man sitting in front of him as "an inch or two taller than the Jolly Green Giant." Find two other examples of this humorous exaggeration.

   _____

   _____

   Besides making readers smile, why might Wine have described the audience in this way?

   _____

   _____

8. Wine tends to use informal wording and sentence structure. In paragraphs 22–26, for instance, find two examples of his informal wording.

   _____

   _____

   In the same paragraphs, find an example of his informal sentence structure.

   _____

RESPONDING TO IMAGES

How do you know that this photograph was staged? How, specifically, would you suggest that the actors pose more convincingly next time?

WRITING ASSIGNMENTS

Assignment 1: Writing a Paragraph

Which do you prefer—watching a movie on your DVD player or TV at home or seeing it in a movie theater? Drawing on your own experiences, write a paragraph in which you explain why you prefer one viewing location over the other. Provide a strong example or two for each of your reasons. For instance, below is one reason with a specific example to support it.

Reason: One reason I prefer going to a movie theater is that it is definitely more peaceful than watching a film at home.

Supporting example: For instance, when I tried watching *Titanic* at home the other night, I had to check on a crying baby or a fussy toddler every ten minutes. Can you imagine what it is like just as two pairs of lips on the screen are getting close enough to meet, to hear, "Mommy, my tummy hurts." If I go out to the movies, I leave my kids and their diapers in the care of my husband or mother.

Assignment 2: Writing a Paragraph

Using exaggeration and humor, Wine gives his impressions of people's looks and behavior at a movie theater. Write a paragraph describing your impressions of people's looks and behavior at a specific event or place. For instance, you might describe how people look and act at a rock concert, in an elevator, in a singles' hangout, or in a library. Like Wine, use colorful descriptions and quotations. Your topic sentence might be similar to the following:

How people behave on an elevator reveals some key personal qualities.

Try listing ideas to develop your supporting details. For example, below is a list of possible supporting points for the topic sentence above.

Shy people tend to avoid eye contact.

Very friendly people smile and may say something.

Helpful people will keep the elevator from leaving when they see someone rushing toward it.

A romantic couple won't notice anyone else on the elevator.

Impatient people may push the number of their floor more than once.

Assignment 3: Writing an Essay

Rudeness, unfortunately, is not limited to the movie theater. We have all observed rude behavior in various places we often go to. Write an essay on this topic. You might use one of the following thesis statements:

Rude behavior is all too common in several places I often go to.

A common part of life at my neighborhood supermarket is the rude behavior of other shoppers.

In an essay with the first central point, you could write about three places where you have seen rude behavior. Develop each paragraph with one or more vivid examples.

In an essay on the second central point, you would need to come up with two or three general types of rude behavior to write about. Below is one student's outline for an essay with that topic sentence.

Central idea: A common part of life at my neighborhood supermarket is the rude behavior of other shoppers.

(1) Getting in the way of other shoppers

Blocking the aisle with a cart

continued

> Knocking things down and not picking them up
>
> "Parking" in front of all the free samples
>
> (2) Misplacing items
>
> Putting unwanted frozen food on a shelf instead of back in a freezer
>
> Putting unwanted meat on a shelf instead of in a refrigerated section
>
> (3) Unreasonably making others wait at the checkout line
>
> Bringing a bulging cartload to the express line
>
> Keeping a line waiting while running to get "just one more thing" (instead of stepping out of line)
>
> Keeping a line waiting while deciding what not to buy to keep the total price down (instead of keeping track while shopping)

Turning Youth Gangs Around

Luis J. Rodriguez

PREVIEW	WORDS TO WATCH
Luis J. Rodriguez is a writer and social activist who supports causes associated with at-risk youths. He is also one of the founders of the Tia Chuca Press, which publishes on Chicano and minority issues. Rodriguez's most widely read book is *Always Running: La Vida Loca, Gang Days in L.A.* (1993). This essay was first published in *The Nation* magazine in 1994. It argues that we need to do more to prevent at-risk youths from engaging in violent gang activities.	articulate (1) charismatic (1) retaliation (6) initiatory (8) incipient (8) dynamics (10) menial (13) demonize (19) expediency (20) nonexploitative (21) plenary (28) dissuade (30)

Pedro* is a thoughtful, articulate● and charismatic● young man; he 1 listens, absorbs, and responds. His movements are quick, well-developed during his years surviving in the streets of Chicago. Pedro is a 20-year-old gang leader. For most of his life, he has lived off and on between his welfare mother and an uncle. He has been kicked out of schools and has served time in youth detention facilities. He is also a great human being.

*In the interest of privacy, some names in the essay have been changed.

For four months in 1993, the courts designated me as his guardian 2 under a house arrest sentence. He was respectful and polite. He meticulously answered all my messages. He was loved by my 6-year-old son. His best friend happens to be my 19-year-old son Ramiro.

During his stay, I gave Pedro books, including political books to help 3 him become more cognizant of the world. One of these was *Palante*, a photo-text about the Young Lords Party of the 1970s. Pedro, whose family is from Puerto Rico, began to open up to an important slice of history that, until then, he'd never known about. Pedro read *Palante* from cover to cover—as he did other books, for the first time ever.

When Pedro was released from house arrest, he moved out of the 4 neighborhood with his girlfriend and her small boy. He found a job. He remained leader of the gang, but was now talking about struggle, about social change, about going somewhere.

Last November, Pedro was shot three times with a .44. He was hit 5 in his back, leg, and hand. Ramiro and I visited him at the Cook County Hospital. He lived, but he was not the same after that. One day during Pedro's hospital stay, the same gang that had shot him ambushed and killed Angel, a friend of Ramiro and Pedro. Angel, an honor student at one of the best schools in the city, was on his way to school; a news account the next day failed to mention this, reporting only that he was a suspected gang member, as if this fact justified his death.

I tried to persuade Pedro to get his boys to chill. I knew that Ramiro and 6 the others were all sitting ducks. Pedro went through some internal turmoil, but he decided to forbid retaliation.• This was hard for him, but he did it.

Unfortunately, the story doesn't end there. Earlier this year, Pedro 7 allegedly shot and killed one of the guys believed to be behind Angel's murder and his own shooting. Pedro is now a fugitive. I tell you this to convey the complexity of working with youths like Pedro, youths most people would rather write off, but who are also intelligent, creative, and even quite decent. The tragedy is that it is mostly young people like these who are being killed and who are doing the killing. I've seen them in youth prisons, hospitals, and courts throughout the land: young people who in other circumstances might have been college graduates, officeholders, or social activists. Unfortunately, many find themselves in situations they feel unable to pull out of until it's too late.

I've long recognized that most youths like Pedro aren't in gangs to be 8 criminals, killers, or prison inmates. For many, a gang embraces who they are, gives them the initiatory• community they seek and the incipient• authority they need to eventually control their own lives. These are things other institutions, including schools and families, often fail to provide. Yet without the proper guidance, support, and means to contribute positively to society, gang involvement can be disastrous.

This August, a media storm was created when 11-year-old Robert 9 Sandifer of Chicago, known as "Yummy" because he liked to eat cookies, allegedly shot into a crowd and killed a 14-year-old girl. A suspected member of a Southside gang, Yummy disappeared; days later he was found shot in the head. Two teenage members of Yummy's gang are being held in his death. Hours before his murder, a neighbor saw Yummy, who told her, "Say a prayer for me."

This is a tragedy, but without a clear understanding of the social, eco- 10
nomic, and psychological dynamics• that would drive an 11-year-old to
kill, we can only throw up our hands. Yet it isn't hard to figure out the
motive forces behind much of this violence.

Sandifer, for example, was a child of the Reagan years, of substan- 11
tial cuts in community programs, of the worst job loss since the Great
Depression, of more police and prisons, and of fewer options for rec-
reation, education, or work. Here was a boy who had been physically
abused, shuttled from one foster home to another, one juvenile justice
facility after another. At every stage of Robert's young life since birth, he
was blocked from becoming all he could be. But there was nothing to stop
him from getting a gun. From using it. And from dying from one.

No "three strikes, you're out," no trying children as adults, no increased 12
prison spending will address what has created the Pedros and Yummys of
this world. Such proposals deal only with the end results of a process that
will continue to produce its own fuel, like a giant breeder reactor. This is
not a solution.

Gangs are not new in America. The first gangs in the early 1800s were 13
made up of Irish immigrant youths. They lived as second-class citizens.
Their parents worked in the lowest-paid, most menial• jobs. These youths
organized to protect themselves within a society that had no place for them.
Other immigrants followed identical patterns. Today the majority of gang
members are African American and Latino, and they face the same general
predicaments those early immigrants did. But today something deeper is
also happening. Within the present class relations of modern technology-
driven capitalism, many youths, urban and rural, are being denied the chance
to earn a "legitimate" living. An increasing number are white, mostly sons
and daughters of coal miners, factory workers, or farmers.

Los Angeles, which has more gang violence than any other city, expe- 14
rienced the greatest incidence of gang-related acts during the 1980s and
early 1990s, when 300,000 manufacturing jobs were lost in California.
According to the Gang Violence Bridging Project of the Edmund G.
"Pat" Brown Institute of Public Affairs at California State University, Los
Angeles, the areas with the greatest impoverishment and gang growth
were those directly linked to industrial flight.

At the same time, the state of California suffered deep cuts in social 15
programs—most of them coming as a result of the passage in 1978 of
Proposition 13, which decreased state funding for schools after a slash in
property taxes. Since 1980, while California's population has jumped by
35 percent, spending for education has steadily declined. Yet there has
been a 14 percent annual increase in state prison spending during the
past decade; the state legislature has allocated $21 billion over the next
ten years to build twenty new prisons.

Almost all areas in the United States where manufacturing has died 16
or moved away are now reporting ganglike activity. There are seventy-
two large cities and thirty-eight smaller ones that claim to have a "gang
problem," according to a 1992 survey of police departments by the
National Institute of Justice. Chicago, also hard hit by industrial flight,
has many large multigenerational gangs like those in L.A.

What has been the official response? In Chicago "mob action" arrests 17
have been stepped up (when three or more young people gather in certain

proscribed areas, it is considered "mob action"), as have police sweeps of housing projects and "gang-infested" communities. Recently there have been calls to deploy the National Guard against gangs, which is like bringing in a larger gang with more firepower against the local ones. This, too, is not a solution.

I agree that the situation is intolerable. I believe most people—from the 18 Chicago-based Mothers Against Gangs to teachers who are forced to be police officers in their classrooms to people in the community caught in the crossfire—are scared. They are bone-tired of the violence. They are seeking ways out. First we must recognize that our battle is with a society that fails to do all it can for young people—then lays the blame on them.

It's time the voices for viable and lasting solutions be heard. The public 19 debate is now limited to those who demonize• youth, want to put them away, and use repression to curb their natural instincts to re-create the world.

I have other proposals. First, that we realign societal resources in 20 accordance with the following premises: that every child has value and every child can succeed. That schools teach by engaging the intelligence and creativity of all students. That institutions of public maintenance— whether police or social services—respect the basic humanity of all people. That we rapidly and thoroughly integrate young people into the future, into the new technology. And finally, that we root out the basis for the injustice and inequities that engender most of the violence we see today. Sound far-fetched? Too idealistic? Fine. But anything short on imagination will result in "pragmatic," fear-driven, expediency•-oriented measures that won't solve anything but will only play with people's lives.

Actually, the structural/economic foundation for such proposals as 21 I've roughly outlined is already laid. The computer chip has brought about revolutionary shifts in the social order. The only thing that isn't in place is the nonexploitative,• nonoppressive relations between people required to complete this transition.

I know what some people are thinking. What about being tough on 22 crime? Let me be clear: I hate crime. I hate drugs. I hate children murdering children. But I know from experience that it doesn't take guts to put money into inhumane, punishment-driven institutions. In fact, such policies make our communities even less safe. It's tougher to walk these streets, to listen to young people, to respect them and help fight for their well-being. It's tougher to care.

For the past two years, I've talked to young people, parents, teach- 23 ers, and concerned officials in cities as far-flung as Hartford, Brooklyn, Phoenix, Seattle, Lansing, Denver, Boston, El Paso, Washington, Oakland, San Antonio, and Compton. I've seen them grope with similar crises, similar pains, similar confusions.

Sometimes I feel the immensity of what we're facing—talking to Teens 24 on Target in Los Angeles, a group made up of youths who have been shot, some in wheelchairs; or to teenage mothers in Tucson, one child caring for another; or to incarcerated young men at the maximum security Illinois Youth Center at Joliet. I felt it when a couple of young women cried in Holyoke, Massachusetts, after I read a poem about a friend who had been murdered by the police, and when I addressed a gym full of students at Jefferson High School in Fort Worth and several young people lined up to hug me, as if they had never been hugged before.

Because I have to deal with people like Yummy and Pedro every day, 25 I decided this summer to do something more than just talk. With the help of Patricia Zamora from the Casa Aztlan Community Center in Chicago's Mexican community of Pilsen, I worked with a core of young people, gang and nongang, toward finding their own solutions, their own organizations, their own empowerment. In the backyard of my Chicago home, some thirty people, mostly from the predominantly Puerto Rican area of Humboldt Park (my son's friends and Pedro's homeys) and Pilsen, were present. They agreed to reach out to other youths and hold retreats, weekly meetings, and a major conference. All summer they worked, without money, without resources, but with a lot of enthusiasm and energy. They hooked up with the National Organizing Committee, founded in 1993 by revolutionary fighters including gang members, welfare recipients, trade unionists, teachers, and parents from throughout the United States. The N.O.C. offered them technical and educational assistance.

The young people's efforts culminated in the Youth '94 Struggling for 26 Survival Conference, held in August at the University of Illinois, Chicago. More than a hundred young people from the city and surrounding communities attended. They held workshops on police brutality, jobs and education, and peace in the neighborhoods. A few gang members set aside deadly rivalries to attend this gathering.

Although there were a number of mishaps, including a power failure, 27 the youths voted to keep meeting. They held their workshops in the dark, raising issues, voicing concerns, coming up with ideas. I was the only adult they let address their meeting. The others, including parents, teachers, counselors, resource people, and a video crew from the Center for New Television, were there to help with what the young people had organized.

Then the building personnel told us we had to leave because it was 28 unsafe to be in a building without power. We got Casa Aztlan to agree to let us move to several of their rooms to continue the workshops; I felt we would probably lose about half the young people in the fifteen-minute ride between sites. Not only did we hang on to most of the youths, we picked up a few more along the way. In a flooded basement with crumbling walls in Casa Aztlan we held the final plenary• session. The youths set up a roundtable, at which it was agreed that only proposed solutions would be entertained. A few read poetry. It was a success, but then the young people wouldn't let it be anything else.

Youth Struggling for Survival is but one example of young people 29 tackling the issues head-on. There are hundreds more across America. In the weeks before the November 8 elections in California, thousands of junior high and high school students, mostly Latino, walked out of schools in the Los Angeles area. Their target: Proposition 187, intended to deny undocumented immigrants access to education, social services, and non-emergency health care.

These young people need guidance and support; they don't need 30 adults to tell them what to do and how to do it; to corral, crush, or dissuade• their efforts. We must reverse their sense of helplessness. The first step is to invest them with more authority to run their own lives, their communities, even their schools. The aim is to help them stop being instruments of their own death and to choose a revolutionary service to life.

We don't need a country in which the National Guard walks our children to school, or pizza-delivery people carry sidearms, or prisons outnumber colleges. We can be more enlightened. More inclusive. More imaginative. And, I'm convinced, this is how we can be more safe. 31

VOCABULARY IN CONTEXT

1. The word *articulate* in "Pedro is a thoughtful, articulate and charismatic young man" (paragraph 1) means
   a. well-spoken.
   b. intelligent.
   c. handsome.
   d. powerful.

2. The word *dynamics* in "This is a tragedy, but without a clear understanding of the social, economic, and psychological dynamics that would drive an 11-year-old to kill, we can only throw up our hands" (paragraph 10) means
   a. problems.
   b. reasons.
   c. rewards.
   d. appeals.

3. The word *menial* in "Their parents worked in the lowest-paid, most menial jobs" (paragraph 13) means
   a. skilled.
   b. unskilled.
   c. illegal.
   d. useless.

READING COMPREHENSION QUESTIONS

1. Which of the following would be the best alternative title for this selection?
   a. The Complex Issues of Working with Youth Gangs
   b. Solving Our Gang Problem
   c. Youth Gangs: A Menace That Can Be Stopped
   d. Causes of Youth Violence

2. Which sentence best expresses the main idea of this selection?
   a. "Gangs are not new in America."
   b. "I hate crime."
   c. "These young people need guidance and support; they don't need adults to tell them what to do and how to do it; to corral, crush, or dissuade their efforts."
   d. "It doesn't take guts to put money into inhumane, punishment-driven institutions."

3. According to Rodriguez, why do young people join gangs?
   a. To get out of poverty.
   b. To feel powerful.
   c. To get a sense of belonging and direction.
   d. To seek safety.

4. What is the relationship between unemployment and youth gangs?
   a. As unemployment increases, gang membership increases.
   b. When gang membership increases, unemployment increases.
   c. When unemployment increases, gang membership decreases.
   d. When unemployment increases, gang membership stays the same.

5. *True or false?* _____ Ethnic groups other than Latinos and African Americans have never formed gangs.

6. *True or false?* _____ According to Rodriguez, the number of white gang members is increasing.

7. Rodriguez objects to California's Proposition 13 (1978) because it
   a. took police off the streets.
   b. required the National Guard to patrol large cities.
   c. decreased state funding for education.
   d. decreased funding for prisons.

8. We can infer from paragraph 17 that Rodriguez
   a. believes the National Guard can help solve the problem.
   b. is a member of the National Guard.
   c. does not think that using the National Guard will help.
   d. believes people don't want the National Guard to interfere.

9. By contacting the National Organizing Committee, the youths who met at the author's house were able to
   a. book a speaker for their meeting.
   b. obtain some literature that would tell them how to organize.
   c. apply for a grant.
   d. obtain educational and technical assistance.

DISCUSSION QUESTIONS

About Content

1. Summarize the five proposals that the author makes to solve the gang problem (paragraph 20). Use your own words.

   a. _____

   b. _____

c. _____

d. _____

e. _____

2. How does Rodriguez argue against the objection that his ideas might be too "far-fetched"?

3. Why did junior high and high school students walk out of the L.A. schools before the elections of 1994? Why did they "target" Proposition 187?

About Structure

4. Why do you think some of the names in this article have been changed?

5. Why does the author introduce this essay with the story of Pedro? How does it help him support what he says in the rest of the essay?

About Style and Tone

6. In paragraph 12, the author says that continuing to imprison gang members deals "only with the end results of a process that will continue to produce its own fuel, like a giant breeder reactor." How does the image at the end of this sentence help Rodriguez make his point?

7. How would you describe Rodriguez's tone—his attitude toward his subject—in paragraph 20?

8. In paragraph 25, Rodriguez uses the term "revolutionary fighters" to describe some of the founders of the National Organizing Committee. How do you interpret this term—negatively or positively? Explain the reasons for your answer.

RESPONDING TO IMAGES

Our country has been plagued with the problem of graffiti for decades. Write an essay in which you explain why graffiti artists do what they do. Also explain what might be done to stop them.

WRITING ASSIGNMENTS

Assignment 1: Writing a Paragraph

In paragraph 20, Rodriguez says that "every child has value and every child can succeed." Think about a time when you failed at a subject or activity in or out of school. Then, explain one thing your teacher or coach could have done better to help you succeed. Finally, explain what you could have done to succeed.

Assignment 2: Writing a Paragraph

Another proposal Rodriguez puts forward is that we should "rapidly and thoroughly integrate young people into the future, into the new technology." This essay was written in the 1990s. Do you think we have done that? For example, do you think high schools are doing enough to help students learn new technology? If so, explain how. If not, explain what high schools should be doing.

Assignment 3: Writing an Essay

Rodriguez implies that youths join gangs seeking to find the direction and sense of belonging that their families do not provide them. If we are to save such young people, we need to provide opportunities through which they can find this direction and sense of belonging.

What can schools, religious groups, the police, and other organizations do to help keep young people out of gangs? What might the media do? Write an essay that discusses services such groups could offer at-risk youths.

Take your lead from Rodriguez. In paragraphs 25–29, he explains how he and others helped organize retreats and conferences in which gang members themselves discussed solutions. Remember that your focus should be on offering ways in which potential gang members can attain the direction and sense of belonging that they need. You may want to discuss services that are already in existence and that you know about. For example, you might write about the after-school tutoring center established by your church or the job program sponsored by your local chamber of commerce. Of course, you can also offer your own new ideas.

If you want, begin your essay by discussing one or more young people you know who might profit from such opportunities. You can also begin by explaining how serious a problem youth gangs in your town have become. End your essay by explaining what you think will happen in the future if the problem of youth gangs is not addressed now.

Reclaiming Our Home Place

Maya Angelou

PREVIEW		**WORDS TO WATCH**
Maya Angelou is a playwright, actor, poet, and civil rights activist. She is the author of twelve best-selling books, including her acclaimed autobiography *I Know Why the Caged Bird Sings*. In the following selection, Angelou discusses the fact that many African Americans, whose ancestors moved to large northern cities after the Civil War, are returning to the South.		capitulated (4) affluent (5) mythic (7) perspicacity (13) venialities (16)

With liberation comes choices. One of America's worst race riots 1 occurred in Atlanta, in 1906, yet today it is home to many African Americans who choose to live there happily.

To understand the phenomenon, one could say if there is that much 2 evil in the history, there is bound to be that much good.

The Civil War was fought all over the South, and alas it is still being 3 fought in some people's hearts. But the fight for Atlanta was particularly fierce and particularly ongoing. I do not know the impact *Gone with the Wind* had on the resistance to change, but I suspect that many people whose ancestors were white sharecroppers fell in love with the romance in the novel and imagined that if we returned to slavery days, they could be served mint juleps by grinning butlers and hotcakes by loving nannies. The people, black and white, who fought to liberate Atlanta from her prison of ignorance were equal to the task. The organization the Southern Christian Leadership Conference, Martin Luther King, Maynard Jackson, Septima Clark, Andrew Young, Joe Lowery, C. T. Vivian, and others white and black won victory for Atlanta and for all people.

Martin Luther King told a story that after the Montgomery bus boycott 4 ended and the companies capitulated,• a black woman got onto the bus and walked all the way back and sat in the backseat. A young man who had been so adamant about voter registration, so adamant, and about the boycotting, went back and he said, "Ma'am, excuse me, we have walked eighteen miles so that you don't have to sit here." And she said, "Son, I walked with you, but now that I can sit anywhere, I'm sitting in the back. It's much more comfortable. I can relax, put my bags down, and stretch my legs out." Then she smiled.

With choices comes a different kind of criticism. There is surprise that 5 in some affluent• neighborhoods in Atlanta, black people have chosen to live with other affluent black people. But if your neighbor likes the same kind of music you like, and pretty much the same food and maybe goes to the same church, it's easier to go over and ask, excuse me, do you have some pinto beans, or have you got some Mahalia Jackson records, some Tabasco sauce? Most folks live in the same neighborhood with others like them and have very fine homes there where they choose to live. That should be unremarkable.

I can't imagine having a city place that wouldn't be Atlanta. After I 6 moved from California, the first place I bought outside North Carolina was in Atlanta. I'm a country soul—not way rustic, but small town. I love my town, but 140,000 other people do so as well. But I need the city too; from time to time I need its vitality. There are city souls and country souls. I think a country soul could have been born in Times Square, but when he sees the country he says, this is where I'm supposed to live. And a city soul could have been born in the mountains of West Virginia, but when she sees the city she says, hm-mm, this is me. Wherever home is, the closer one gets to it, the more one relaxes. That's even if you're walking. If you've been on a trek, a few blocks or a few miles, you can almost spot your house. You start to breathe differently. I think this is true for all people.

The federal census for the year 2000 tells us that far more African 7 Americans are now choosing to migrate south than the other way around. This reverse migration has its roots, I believe, in the first move north.

Not the very first, because obviously slaves were escaping slavery going north. The move in the late nineteenth and twentieth centuries to the place Robert Hayden called the "mythic• northern city" was caused by people who hoped they could find a better place. People thought if they could get away north, get away from the cotton, the worn-out South, get away from all the hatred, from the mean sharecropping days, they would find milk and honey in the streets of Chicago and New York and even St. Louis, and certainly Los Angeles. However, if the North did promise that, it never lived up to its promise, although many black people remained there.

So when the people sent their children back to the South, to the 8 grandmothers, to the grandfathers, to Sister and Bubba, they sent them to be looked after, I believe, because of the northern disappointment. It was thanks to the Civil Rights Movement and the leveling of the playing field that we had the possibility of Maynard Jackson and Andrew Young as mayors of the great southern city. Then the congressmen and -women began coming from the South to Washington, D.C., to plan a better world. I believe that those events freed people from the painful memories of southern treatment. They began to look south again and see it as they want it to be.

Something basic and earth-shattering happened with the Civil Rights 9 Movement. The fabric of old belief was shattered. The belief that in the South you're black get back, if you're white you're all right. That was structurally shaken so that black people in Detroit and Philadelphia and Tucson began to look back at the South. They began to remember not only the South's beauty, but that our people's bodies and sweat and tears and blood have enriched this soil, and thought, wait a minute, maybe I belong there too.

I am saying our people have been in exile in the North for three-10 quarters of a century. In exile, and in many cases, not realizing it but terribly uncomfortable. There's a wonderful cartoon by the great Ollie Harrington, who drew the character Bootsie for the *Chicago Defender*. In the 1950s, in a particularly relevant drawing, he showed Bootsie and his friend standing atop a mountain in Maine. They are outfitted in ski gear with the ski poles and this heavy, heavy, heavy clothing. Bootsie turns to his friend and asks, "Do you think Martin Luther King really wanted us to do this? Is this part of our liberation?"

Our people are coming home. The South is rich with memories of 11 kindness and courage and cowardice and brutality. It is beautiful physically, and spiritually rich.

I live in the South because it's the best place to live. It's beautiful beyond 12 the weight and even the ecstasy of my memories. If you come as far south as North Carolina, you see the lush, almost tropical growth and the fireflies and hear the birds in the morning and the cicadas in the evening.

Come south, walk along honeysuckled paths, and listen carefully to 13 the sounds of good southern music that will play so easily on your ears. You will be happy that you had the nerve and perspicacity• to travel on a southern train.

We can reclaim our home place.   14

We can stand for the good. That's why we risk our lives.   15

I see the work, the art and the music, and the lyrics of the poets, and 16 the sculpture and the paintings, and I see that the culture is healthy. I do not believe that drugs and criminalities and venialities• have total power over our youth. There is a core of health in our culture. Still we rise, out of the huts of history's shame, we rise. From a past rooted in pain, we rise. Bringing the gifts that our ancestors gave, we are the hope and the dream of the slave.

VOCABULARY IN CONTEXT

1. The world *capitulated* in "Martin Luther King told a story that after the Montgomery bus boycott ended and the companies capitulated, a black woman got onto the bus and walked all the way back and sat in the backseat" (paragraph 4) means

   a. won.

   b. went out of business.

   c. started running again.

   d. gave up.

2. The word *mythic* in "The move in the late nineteenth and twentieth centuries to the place Robert Hayden called the "mythic northern city" was caused by people who hoped they could find a better place" (paragraph 7) means

   a. real.

   b. distant.

   c. fictional.

   d. large.

READING COMPREHENSION QUESTIONS

1. Which of the following would be the best alternative title for this selection?

   a. Exile in the North

   b. Coming Home

   c. African Americans: North and South

   d. The South after the War

2. Which sentence best expresses the main idea of this selection?

   a. "Wherever home is, the closer one gets to it, the more one relaxes."

   b. "Something basic and earth-shattering happened with the Civil Rights Movement."

   c. "Our people are coming home."

   d. "Our people have been in exile. . . ."

3. Angelou claims that, in some ways, the Civil War

   a. is still being fought.

   b. devastated the South.

   c. drove African Americans north.

   d. has been largely forgotten.

4. We can infer that Angelou believes the novel *Gone with the Wind*
    a. helped bring blacks and whites together.
    b. helped heal wounds between the North and the South.
    c. took place only in Atlanta.
    d. had a negative effect on race relations.

5. For Angelou, the fact that affluent black people want to live with other affluent black people is
    a. remarkable.
    b. not surprising.
    c. unbelievable.
    d. illogical.

6. *True or false?* _____ According to this selection, more African Americans today are moving to the South than to the North.

7. Angelou lives in the South because
    a. she dislikes the North.
    b. she works in the South.
    c. she grew up there.
    d. she believes it is the best place to live.

DISCUSSION QUESTIONS

About Content

1. Why, according to Angelou, did blacks migrate north in great numbers after the Civil War?

2. What was the "earth-shattering" effect of the Civil Rights Movement that the author talks about? Why did it influence increasingly more African Americans to relocate in the South?

3. What was the Montgomery, Alabama, bus boycott? Find information about this event on the Internet.

About Structure

4. Part of Angelou's introduction concerns the story of a black woman who wanted to sit in the back of the bus even after the bus boycott had given her the right to sit in the front. Is this story appropriate to the essay's thesis? Explain why.

5. Where in this essay does Angelou use description? How does what she describes make this essay—which discusses causes and effects, among other things—more effective?

About Style and Tone

6. Is Angelou happy about African Americans returning to the South? What does she say in paragraphs 10, 11, and 12 to make this clear?

7. Where does Angelou reveal her pride in the accomplishments of African Americans?

WRITING ASSIGNMENTS

Assignment 1: Writing a Paragraph

Think of a place in which you once lived and in which you were happy. You might focus on a city or a town. Then again, you might think about the particular neighborhood or area you once lived in, or you could consider a specific house or apartment. What was the most wonderful thing about this place? Was it the place itself   the building, the natural surroundings, the nearby buildings and attractions? Was it the people who lived in or near it? Was it the fact that it offered a number of interesting and entertaining things to do? Did you love this place because your grandparents lived close by? Or did it have to do with the nearby lake where you fished in summer and ice-skated in winter?

Once you have decided on the most important reason you liked the place, state that reason in a topic sentence. Then develop that idea in detail using illustration (examples), description, narration, cause/effect, or other methods of development.

Assignment 2: Writing a Paragraph

Angelou reminds us that "Wherever home is, the closer one gets to it, the more one relaxes." Do you agree? Write a paragraph that expresses how you feel whenever you are approaching your home. You might write about what it is like to come home after a long absence, or you could simply explain how you feel when you come home after a long day at school or work. Do you feel safer? More relaxed? More self-confident? Or is the opposite true? Is there something about home that makes you sometimes want to stay away?

Assignment 3: Writing an Essay

"I live in the South because it's the best place to live," writes Angelou. What might be the best place for you to live?

Look to the future and think about a time when you will have started your career and begun to put down roots (if you haven't done so already). In what kind of place would you like to put down those roots: a large city, the suburbs, a small town or village, or a setting that is open and wild?

Write an essay in which you describe this "mythic" location. Explain where it might be, what it might look like, and what kinds of people might live there. Also, discuss the quality and type of lifestyle you would experience in this place. To gather even more information for this essay, consider answering questions such as following:

a. Does the place offer entertainment and cultural opportunities such as museums, concert halls, and theaters?

b. Is it close to major sports arenas or stadiums?

c. How does its school system rate? Will your children get a good education there?

d. How do other public services rate? How are the roads? Are there public parks nearby? Does the place have a low crime rate?

e. Are there opportunities to pursue outdoor activities such as camping and hiking?

f. What kind of shopping opportunities does the place offer?

g. Will you be able to commute easily to a job from this place?

h. How would you rate the quality of the air and water in this area?

i. Is the population diverse?

Of course, the questions that you ask will be appropriate to your own interests and desires. For example, if you are really interested in cultural offerings, such as theater and ballet, you might not care whether or not your city offers camping facilities.

Remember that you are trying to describe an ideal place. Your essay doesn't have to be realistic. You are simply trying to tell your readers about a place that you wish existed. So, don't be afraid to dream a little. Just fill your essay with enough detail about your subject to enable readers to imagine it and feel as if they are in it.

Consume Less, Conserve More
Al Gore

PREVIEW	WORDS TO WATCH
Al Gore was vice president of the United States under President Clinton from 1993 to 2001. Soon after losing the presidential election of 2000, Gore increased his efforts to make people become more environmentally conscious. This selection is taken from the conclusion to Gore's book *An Inconvenient Truth* (2006), which was made into a motion picture.	intrinsic (1) extraneous (4) aerate (8) decomposition (8) ferments (8) cooperatives (13) carbon offsets (14) sequestering (15)

In America, we have grown used to an environment of plenty, with 1 an enormous variety of consumer products always available and constant enticement to buy "more," "new," and "improved." This consumer culture has become so intrinsic° to our worldview that we've lost sight of the huge toll we are taking on the world around us. By cultivating a new awareness of how our shopping and lifestyle choices impact the environment and directly cause carbon emissions, we can begin to make positive changes to reduce our negative effects. Here are some specific ideas on how we can achieve this.

Consume less

Energy is consumed in the manufacturing and transport of everything 2 you buy, which means there are fossil-fuel emissions at every stage of production. A good way to reduce the amount of energy you use is simply to buy less. Before making a purchase, ask yourself if you really need it. Can you make do with what you already have? Can you borrow or rent? Can you find the item secondhand? More and more Americans are beginning to simplify their lives and choose to reduce consumption.

▶ For ideas on how to pare down, visit www.newdream.org

Buy things that last

"Reduce, reuse, and recycle" has become the motto of a growing move- 3 ment dedicated to producing less waste and reducing emissions by buying less, choosing durable items over disposable ones, repairing rather than discarding, and passing on items that are no longer needed to someone who can make use of them.

▶ For more information about the three Rs, visit www.epa.gov/msw/reduce.htm

▶ To learn how to find a new home for something you no longer need, visit www.freecycle.org

Pre-cycle—reduce waste before you buy

Discarded packaging materials make up about one-third of the waste clog- 4 ging our landfills. Vast amounts of natural resources and fossil fuels are consumed each year to produce the paper, plastic, aluminum, glass, and Styrofoam that hold and wrap our purchases. Obviously, some degree of packaging is necessary to transport and protect the products we need, but all too often manufacturers add extraneous• wrappers over wrappers and layers of unnecessary plastic. You can let companies know your objection to such excess by boycotting their products. Give preference to those products that use recycled packaging or that don't use excess packaging. When possible, buy in bulk and seek out things that come in refillable glass bottles.

▶ For more ideas about how to pre-cycle, visit www.environmentaldefense.org/ article.cfm?contentid=2194

Recycle

Most communities provide facilities for the collection and recycling of 5 paper, glass, steel, aluminum, and plastic. While it does take energy to gather, haul, sort, clean, and reprocess these materials, recycling takes far less energy than does sending recyclables to landfills and creating new paper, bottles, and cans from raw materials. It has been suggested that if 100,000 people who currently don't recycle began to do so, they would collectively reduce carbon emissions by 42,000 tons per year. As an added benefit, recycling reduces pollution and saves natural resources, including precious trees that absorb carbon dioxide. And in addition to the usual materials, some facilities are equipped to recycle motor oil, tires, coolant, and asphalt shingles, among other products.

▶ To learn about where you can recycle just about anything in your area, visit www.earth911.org/master.asp?s=ls&a=recycle&cat=1 or www.epa.gov/epaoswer/ non-hw/muncpl/recycle.htm

Don't waste paper

Paper manufacturing is the fourth-most energy-intensive industry, not to 6 mention one of the most polluting and destructive to our forests. It takes an entire forest—more than 500,000 trees—to supply Americans with their Sunday newspapers each week. In addition to recycling your used paper, there are things you can do to reduce your overall paper consumption. Limit your use of paper towels and use cloth rags instead. Use cloth napkins instead of disposables. Use both sides of paper whenever possible. And stop unwanted junk mail.

▶ For information about how to remove your name from mailing lists, visit www.newdream.org/junkmail or www.dmaconsumers.org/offmailinglist.html

Bag your groceries and other purchases in a reusable tote

Americans go through 100 billion grocery bags every year. One estimate 7 suggests that Americans use more than 12 million barrels of oil each year just to produce plastic grocery bags that end up in landfills after only one use and then take centuries to decompose. Paper bags are a problem too: To ensure that they are strong enough to hold a full load, most are produced from virgin paper, which requires cutting down trees that absorb carbon dioxide. It is estimated that about 15 million trees are cut down annually to produce the 10 billion paper bags we go through each year in the United States. Make a point to carry a reusable bag with you when you shop, and then when you're asked, "Paper or plastic?" you can say, "Neither."

▶ To purchase reusable bags, learn more bag facts, and find out about actions you can take, visit www.reusablebags.com

Compost

When organic waste materials, such as kitchen scraps and raked leaves, 8 are disposed of in the general trash, they end up compacted deep in landfills. Without oxygen to aerate● and assist in their natural decomposition,● the organic matter ferments● and gives off methane, which is the most potent of the greenhouse gases—23 times more potent than carbon dioxide in global-warming terms. Organic materials rotting in landfills account for about one-third of man-made methane emissions in the United States. By contrast, when organic waste is properly composted in gardens, it produces rich nutrients that add energy and food to the soil—and of course also decreases the volume added to our landfills.

▶ For information about how to compost, visit www.epa.gov/compost/index.htm or www.mastercomposter.com

Carry your own refillable bottle for water or other beverages

Instead of buying single-use plastic bottles that require significant 9 energy and resources to produce, buy a reusable container and fill it up yourself. In addition to the emissions created by producing the bottles themselves, imported water is especially energy inefficient because it has to be transported over long distances. If you're concerned about the taste or quality of your tap water, consider using an inexpensive water purifier or filter. Also consider buying large bottles of juice or soda and filling your own portable bottle daily. Using your own mug or thermos could also help reduce the 25 billion disposable cups Americans throw away each year.

▶ For more information about the benefits of using refillable beverage containers, visit www.grrn.org/beverage/refillables/index.html

Modify your diet to include less meat

Americans consume almost a quarter of all the beef produced in the world. 10
Aside from health issues associated with eating lots of meat, a high-meat
diet translates into a tremendous amount of carbon emissions. It takes
far more fossil-fuel energy to produce and transport meat than to deliver
equivalent amounts of protein from plant sources.

In addition, much of the world's deforestation is a result of clear- 11
ing and burning to create more grazing land for livestock. This creates
further damage by destroying trees that would otherwise absorb carbon
dioxide. Fruits, vegetables, and grains, on the other hand, require 95%
less raw materials to produce and, when combined properly, can provide
a complete and nutritious diet. If more Americans shifted to a less meat-
intensive diet, we could greatly reduce CO_2 emissions and also save vast
quantities of water and other precious natural resources.

▶ For more information about cows and global warming, visit www.earthsave.org/
globalwarming.htm and www.epa.gov/methane/rlep/faq.html

Buy local

In addition to the environmental impact that comes from manufacturing 12
the product you are buying, the effects on CO_2 emissions from transport-
ing those goods at each and every stage of production must also be calcu-
lated. It is estimated that the average meal travels well over 1,200 miles
by truck, ship, and/or plane before it reaches your dining room table.
Often it takes more calories of fossil-fuel energy to get the meal to the
consumer than the meal itself provides in nutritional energy. It is much
more carbon efficient to buy food that doesn't have to make such a long
journey.

One way to address this is to eat foods that are grown or produced 13
close to where you live. As much as possible, buy from local farmers' mar-
kets or from community-supported agriculture cooperatives.• By the same
token, it makes sense to design your diet as much as possible around foods
currently in season in your area, rather than foods that need to be shipped
from far-off places.

▶ To learn more about eating local and how to fight global warming with your knife and fork,
visit www.climatebiz.com/sections/news_detail.cfm?NewsID=27338

Purchase offsets to neutralize your remaining emissions

So many things we do in our day-to-day lives—driving, cooking, heating 14
homes, working on our computers—result in greenhouse-gas emissions.
It is virtually impossible to eliminate our personal contributions to the
climate crisis through reducing emissions alone. You can, however, reduce
your impact to the equivalent of zero emissions by purchasing carbon
offsets.•

When you purchase carbon offsets, you are funding a project that 15
reduces greenhouse-gas emissions elsewhere by, for example, increasing energy efficiency, developing renewable energy, restoring forests, or
sequestering• carbon in soil.

▶ For more information and links to specific carbon offsetting organizations, visit
www.NativeEnergy.com/climatecrisis

VOCABULARY IN CONTEXT

1. The word *intrinsic* in "This consumer culture has become so intrinsic to our worldview that we've lost sight of the huge toll we are taking on the world around us" (paragraph 1) means
   a. harmful.
   b. beneficial.
   c. related to.
   d. fundamental.

2. The word *extraneous* in "all too often manufacturers add extraneous wrappers over wrappers and layers of unnecessary plastic" (paragraph 4) means
   a. additional.
   b. helpful.
   c. protective.
   d. essential.

READING COMPREHENSION QUESTIONS

1. Which of the following would make the best alternative title for this selection?
   a. The Climate Crisis: What One Person Can Do
   b. Why Everyone Should Recycle
   c. Our Carbon Footprint: It's Just Too Big
   d. A Planet in Jeopardy

2. Which of the following best captures the central point of the selection?
   a. Each person can help reduce civilization's harmful effects on the natural world and its climate.
   b. It is not hard to save energy.
   c. Recycling can reduce pollution and eliminate landfills.
   d. We need to encourage the use of alternative fuels.

3. Which of the following is not one of the questions Gore suggests you ask yourself before making a purchase?
   a. Can you find the item secondhand?
   b. Can you find the item for less online?
   c. Can you make do with what you already have?
   d. Can you borrow or rent the item?

4. Each week, it takes an entire forest to supply Americans with
   a. paper towels.
   b. unwanted junk mail.
   c. Sunday newspapers.
   d. napkins.

5. According to this selection, if organic waste is not properly composted it can

   a. increase the spread of disease.

   b. result in the emission of harmful methane.

   c. pollute groundwater with toxic chemicals.

   d. give off more emissions than cars and trucks.

6. *True or false?* _____ Americans consume almost a quarter of all the beef produced in the world.

7. Gore believes we should eat less meat because

   a. vegetable farmers are finding it hard to earn a living.

   b. cows, pigs, and other livestock have rights too.

   c. it takes more energy to provide protein from meat than from fruits and vegetables.

   d. eating too much meat is bad for our health.

DISCUSSION QUESTIONS

About Content

1. What does Gore mean by "greenhouse-gas emissions" (paragraph 14)? If necessary, look up this term on the Internet.

2. In your own words, summarize three ways Gore says we can reduce emissions:

   a. _____

   b. _____

   c. _____

3. Using what you have learned from this selection, take an energy inventory of the way you shop, the kinds of food you eat, or the way you recycle at home, in your dormitory, or anywhere else. How might you be able to save energy and reduce carbon emissions?

4. Is Gore optimistic about the future? How can you tell?

About Structure

5. One of the reasons this essay is easy to read is that Gore uses many subheadings to introduce various topics. Write a scratch outline using these major headings and subheadings as a way to create a visual of this essay's structure.

6. The author includes notes for further research after various subsections of the essay. How does doing this help him increase the persuasiveness and usefulness of the selection?

About Style and Tone

7. The author is aiming at a very wide audience. What is it about the kinds of words he uses that shows this? What do his frequent references to the Internet tell us about his intended readers?

8. At times, Gore uses technical terms such as "carbon offsets" without defining them. Should he have? Why or why not?

9. How would you describe the author's tone—his attitude toward his subject? Is it objective, passionate, skeptical?

10. The purpose of this essay is to get us to help solve the climate crisis and, therefore, save the planet. One of the ways Gore tries to persuade us is to appeal to our self-interest. Find places in which he does this.

WRITING ASSIGNMENTS

Assignment 1: Writing a Paragraph

Discuss ways in which you might conserve energy or reduce greenhouse gases by changing one thing in your daily routine. For example, you might buy in bulk and only use items that come in refillable glass bottles. You might use cloth rags instead of paper towels. You might carry a reusable bag with you when you shop. You might choose to only eat foods that are grown or produced where you live. Or you might follow another suggestion contained in the essay you just read.

In any event, be as detailed as you can in showing how what Gore advises might apply to your daily life.

Assignment 2: Writing a Paragraph

Thinking about the topics Gore addresses in his essay, take an audit of any area of your college campus: the student center, the gymnasium, a dormitory, or the college dining facility, for example. How effective is the college in producing less waste and reducing carbon emissions in this area of the campus? Write a paragraph in which you explain how the college might have a more positive effect on the environment in this area of the campus.

Assignment 3: Writing an Essay

Gore's essay is quite persuasive in that it shows us practical and relatively easy ways to address the crisis. Write an essay in which you persuade your reader that it is necessary we address the need to reduce the amount of nonbiodegradable garbage we produce.

However, instead of discussing what we might do to address the problem, as Gore does, paint a verbal picture of what might happen if we don't take action. For example, you might describe what our countryside, lakes, and oceans might look like if we continue to use plastic containers that do not degrade naturally. You might explain what our lifestyles will be like if we run out of fossil fuels and don't develop renewable sources of energy to replace them. Will we be able to generate electricity and heat for our homes? Will we be able to power our cars? Or will we go back to living as people did in the Middle Ages?

In other words, create a scene that a futurist or science fiction writer might dream up. If you need to gather information for this project, research some of the Internet sites Gore recommends in his essay. At any rate, remember that your purpose is to get your readers to see that there is real need to plan for the future—a future in which our lives and our relationship to the earth will be better, not worse, than they are now.

A Grand Unified Theory of YouTube and MySpace

Point-and-Click Sites That Don't Tell You What to Do

Paul Boutin

PREVIEW	WORDS TO WATCH
Paul Boutin is a journalist who writes primarily on matters concerning computers and the Internet. He is the former editor of *Wired* magazine, and his writing has appeared in the *Wall Street Journal*, the *New York Times*, *Slate*, and other well-known newspapers and magazines. In this selection, Boutin explains why YouTube and MySpace have become so popular so quickly.	skeptical (1) vague (1) collaborative (3) automate (4) predictable (9) deterrent (10) aggressively (10) budding (10) enthralled (13) genres (13) templates (13)

1   I was skeptical• when I heard how huge video-sharing hub YouTube and social-networking hotspot MySpace have become. YouTube claims 40 million plays a day, up from 35 million just a week ago. The *Washington Post* recently reported that MySpace pulls more monthly visitors than Amazon and is closing in on AOL and eBay. Both sites are vague• about their traffic details, though, so I ran them through Alexa, the traffic report generator favored by techies who don't trust press releases. I nearly fell out of my chair. On Alexa's charts, MySpace is an order of magnitude bigger than Friendster. YouTube will pass CNN any day now.

2   Both YouTube and MySpace fit the textbook definition of Web 2.0, that hypothetical next-generation Internet where people contribute as easily as they consume. Even self-described late adopters like *New York*'s Kurt Andersen recognize that by letting everyone contribute, these sites have reached a critical mass where "a real network effect has kicked in."

3   But the focus on the collaborative• nature of these sites has been nagging at me. Sites like Friendster and Blogger that promote sharing and friend-making have been around for years with nowhere near the mainstream success. I've got a different theory. YouTube and MySpace are runaway hits because they combine two attributes rarely found together in tech products. They're easy to use, and they don't tell you what to do.

4   There are two design requirements for technology meant for the masses. First, you need to automate• all the techie parts so people can just press Play. To watch television online, I shouldn't have to install extra video software, figure out my bandwidth setting (100K? 300K?), and sign up for an account with the player's maker. Second, Web moguls shouldn't presume to foresee what 100 million people will want to do with their site. I'm one of many who stopped using Google's Orkut social network because its hardwired page designs made everyone look like they were there to find a date and/or a job.

The guys behind YouTube hit the sweet spot. Most important, they 5 made it head-slappingly easy to publish and play video clips by handling the tricky parts automatically. Given up on BitTorrent because it feels like launching a mission to Mars? If you've sent an e-mail attachment, you've got the tech skills to publish on YouTube.

To post your own video, sign up for a free account and go to the Upload 6 page. Select your file, click the Upload Video button, and you're done! YouTube's servers convert your vid to a standardized format, but you don't need to know what that format is. If you send the URL to your aunt, it'll play in her browser without spraying the screen with pop-ups and errors.

You don't have to upload video to use YouTube. If you just like to 7 watch, it's even easier. There's no software to install, no settings to muck with. The video auto-plays as soon as you load the page, without launching more windows—why can't CNN do that?

Three months ago, I predicted Google Video would become the hot- 8 test thing on the Net. I was wrong, and I think Google has failed to take off for the simple reason that it's more annoying to use than YouTube. To begin with, you have to install Google's special uploading application. When I tried to upload the same clips I'd posted to YouTube, Google's app wouldn't let me. I combed through the FAQ and found this: "While we also support other digital formats such as QuickTime, Windows Media, and RealVideo . . . submitting your files in these formats may significantly delay us from using them on Google Video." Come on, guys. Whatever happened to "I'm Feeling Lucky?"

Google Video lets you google videos (of course) by their titles and a 9 brief description of each. Each page links to other matches. That's OK, but predictable.• YouTube lets posters tag each clip themselves. For example, I tagged [a] clip of my 12 seconds on *Good Morning America* with "boutin wired slate gma." Whenever you play a YouTube clip, the page shows a half-dozen potential matches. A tag like "slate" could mean all sorts of things, so each page mixes perfect matches with what-the-huh results. A documentary on Scientology links to a *South Park* episode, which links to comedian Pablo Francisco. A few clicks later I'm watching some merry prankster get an unexpected smackdown. In Web 2.0-speak, this is a "folksonomy." In English, it means YouTube is a mix of every video genre imaginable.

Judging by the number of *South Park* episodes and music videos avail- 10 able for viewing, it's fair to say that YouTube's warnings not to post copy-righted material aren't much of a deterrent.• The site removes porn much more aggressively• than it does copyright violations. That makes a lot of sense: There are more than enough places to browse for porn online, but the presence of easily downloadable mainstream fare among YouTube's home movies is a huge draw. I hope the site's budding• deals with Hollywood work out and the networks don't launch their own sites. If they do, it's a sure bet they won't be user-friendly. Just look at CNN's recent redesign, which just now threw a giant "PLUGIN WARNING!" onto my screen.

When trying to rope in the movie and TV studios, YouTube should point 11 to MySpace, where A-listers like Eminem peddle their wares alongside unsigned bands and lip syncers. MySpace makes it easy for musicians, kids, and grandparents to post their own pages by removing the technical hurdles. I created a profile page in three minutes, complete with an auto-play jingle.

I'd planned to upload an MP3 of a band I used to play in, until I found they already have their own MySpace page. Clicking "Add" instantly copied the song from their page onto mine. Another one-click tool imported my Gmail and Hotmail address books so I could mass-invite everyone to join me.

MySpace isn't that much easier to use than Friendster, or than other 12 shared-user-content sites like Flickr (photo sharing), del.icio.us (bookmarks), or Digg (tech news). But it mixes multiple publishing models—blogs, photos, music, videos, friend networks—into one personal space. Most important, it doesn't presume to know what your goals are. The site's management ditched their early focus as a home for musicians when they realized Margaret Cho and my crazy friend Kenny wanted spaces of their own. Next, MySpace may let marketers set up profiles for brands. That's a great idea—the same people who'll bitch about Snickers having a page will add Wikipedia as their friend.

I think MySpace's popularity has to do with its puppy-like accessibility. 13 A typical page looks like something a Web-enthralled• high schooler might have put up in 1996, but with more pics and a soundtrack. I agree with design guru Jesse James Garrett, who says the site's untrained layout sends a "we're just like you" message to newcomers. That encourages them to experiment with content genres• the site's designers didn't build into templates.• If tech builders want to hand the controls over to their users, shouldn't they presume they haven't thought of everything? Apple's iWeb publishing system is easy to use and way more attractive than MySpace, but we'd have gotten old waiting for Apple to invent a Lip Sync Video template.

The secret to success is to make everything one-button easy, then get 14 out of the way. If you think collaborative architecture matters more, click the charts: The same Alexa plots that show MySpace and YouTube obliterating top sites reveal that Flickr, Digg, and del.icio.us have plateaued with audiences barely bigger than *Slate*'s. Photos, news, and other people's bookmarks just aren't as interesting as bootleg TV and checking out the hotties. The easier it gets to use, the less geeky the Net becomes, and the more it starts to look like real life.

VOCABULARY IN CONTEXT

1. The word *skeptical* in "I was skeptical when I heard how huge video-sharing hub YouTube and social-networking hotspot MySpace have become" (paragraph 1) means
   a. trusting.
   b. bored.
   c. doubtful.
   d. impressed.

2. The word *predictable* in "That's OK, but predictable" (paragraph 9) means
   a. surprising.
   b. expected.
   c. uninteresting.
   d. unnecessary.

READING COMPREHENSION QUESTIONS

1. Which of the following would make the best alternative title for this selection?
   a. YouTube and MySpace: Why They're So Popular
   b. The Growth of YouTube and MySpace
   c. The Internet and Social Networking
   d. Publishing Your Stuff on the Net

2. Which of the following best expresses the selection's main point?
   a. The growth of YouTube and MySpace is hard to believe.
   b. YouTube and MySpace are successful because they are easy to use.
   c. YouTube and MySpace will be successful for years to come.
   d. YouTube and MySpace allow more choices than Google Video.

3. In your own words, list two reasons why, according to Boutin, YouTube and MySpace are so popular.

   a. _____

   b. _____

4. *True or false?* _____ The author agrees with Kurt Andersen, who believes that these sites have become popular because anyone can contribute to them.

5. *True or false?* _____ No sites other than YouTube and MySpace offer the possibility of collaboration to users.

6. *True or false?* _____ YouTube is more diligent about removing pornography than about removing copyrighted material.

7. We can infer from this essay that
   a. knowing how the Internet works is needed if you want to post on YouTube and MySpace.
   b. posting on these sites is hardly more difficult than sending an e-mail.
   c. special equipment or software is needed to post on these sites.
   d. YouTube and MySpace charge a fee to post on their sites.

8. Why does the author prefer YouTube over Google Video?
   a. Google Video provides fewer options.
   b. YouTube is easier to use.
   c. Google's answer to its FAQs are annoying.
   d. Google Video is no longer the "hottest thing on the Net."

DISCUSSION QUESTIONS

About Content

1. Boutin illustrates how easy it is to use YouTube by explaining how to post a video. Summarize the three steps of his instructions here.

a. _____

b. _____

c. _____

2. In paragraph 4, Boutin claims that "there are two design requirements for technology meant for the masses." Explain them in your own words.

   a. _____

   b. _____

3. Why is it that YouTube's "warnings not to post copyrighted material aren't much of a deterrent"?

About Structure

4. To make this essay easier to read, Boutin maintains coherence between paragraphs. Identify the transitional words and phrases he uses between

   a. paragraphs 1 and 2 _____

   b. paragraphs 2 and 3 _____

   c. paragraphs 7 and 8 _____

   d. paragraphs 8 and 9 _____

5. The author contrasts YouTube with Google Video in paragraphs 8 and 9. Where else does he use contrast? What do those passages reveal about his subjects?

6. In what way does the conclusion of this essay make reference to its introduction?

About Style and Tone

7. Who is the intended audience for this essay? Is it written for people with little knowledge of the Internet? If not, how can you tell?

8. How would you describe Boutin's style? Is it formal and scholarly? Or is it more relaxed and conversational? What does a sentence such as "there's no software to install, no settings to muck with" reveal about it?

9. Even people new to YouTube and MySpace can learn much from this essay because Boutin sometimes stops to define terms. Find one example of a definition in this selection.

WRITING ASSIGNMENTS

Assignment 1: Writing a Paragraph

Do you ever use YouTube, MySpace, Facebook, or any of the other sites that Boutin mentions? If so, pick the site you use most often, and explain why you use the site, what information it provides, or why you find it helpful or interesting.

In other words, tell your reader what you like about the site—why you use it over and over. You might provide details about how easy it is to use. Then again, you can give examples of the kinds of things it lets you to do—things you wouldn't be able to do if this site didn't exist.

Assignment 2: Writing a Paragraph

Do you agree with Boutin that YouTube and MySpace are the best at what they do? Write a paragraph in which you contrast

1. MySpace with any other social-networking site

-OR-

2. YouTube with any other video sharing site.

You might contrast either of these with any one of the other sites Boutin mentions. Or you might contrast them with any other site of your choice. In any event, judge both sites according to the *same* standards or principles. Here are three suggested standards you might want to use:

a. Quality of layout

b. Ease of use or navigation

c. Amount and quality of information or services provided.

Assignment 3: Writing an Essay

If you use the Internet often, you may have a favorite Web site. Write an essay that recommends it to the reader. You might discuss aspects such as

a. quality of layout.

b. amount and quality of information provided.

c. links to other sites.

d. tools that allow you to search or use the site easily.

However, you should spend most of your time discussing aspects or functions of the site that relate to the reason it was created in the first place. For example, if you are writing about a video-sharing hub such as YouTube, you might discuss how easy it is to upload your own videos. If you are talking about a social-networking site such as MySpace, you might explain how the site helps you meet new people or keep in contact with old friends, things that would otherwise be impossible or at least more difficult.

Assume that your reader is someone who uses the Internet for e-mailing and researching but not necessarily a college student who is familiar with the jargon or language of the Internet and with sites such as YouTube and MySpace. Therefore, make sure to define technical terms, at least when you first mention them.

In addition to definition, try using comparison and contrast. For example, point out similarities and differences between your favorite site and another that covers the same subject or that provides the same service.

Begin your essay with a clearly stated central idea. State your preference for the site or service and recommend it to your reader. Conclude the essay by pointing out at least one weakness in the site or service you are recommending. Then, however, reaffirm your recommendation by summarizing each of the reasons behind it.

Five appendixes follow. Appendix A consists of parts of speech, and Appendix B is a series of ESL pointers. Appendixes C and D consist of a diagnostic test and an achievement test that measure many of the sentence skills in this book. The diagnostic test can be taken at the outset of your work; the achievement test can be used to measure your progress after you have studied these topics. Finally, Appendix E supplies answers to the introductory activities and practice exercises in Part 3. The answers, which you should refer to only after you have worked carefully through each exercise, give you responsibility for testing yourself. (To ensure that the answer key is used as a learning tool only, answers are not given for the review tests. These answers appear only in the Instructor's Manual; they can be copied and handed out at the discretion of your instructor.)

Parts of Speech

Words—the building blocks of sentences—can be divided into eight parts of speech. *Parts of speech* are classifications of words according to their meaning and use in a sentence.

This appendix explains the eight parts of speech:

nouns	prepositions	conjunctions
pronouns	adjectives	interjections
verbs	adverbs	

Nouns

A *noun* is a word that is used to name something: a person, a place, an object, or an idea. Here are some examples of nouns:

NOUNS			
woman	city	pancake	freedom
Alice Walker	street	diamond	possibility
George Clooney	Chicago	Hummer	mystery

Most nouns begin with a lowercase letter and are known as *common nouns.* These nouns name general things. Some nouns, however, begin with a capital letter. They are called *proper nouns.* While a common noun refers to a person or thing in general, a proper noun names someone or something specific. For example, *woman* is a common noun—it doesn't name a particular woman. On the other hand, *Alice Walker* is a proper noun because it names a specific woman.

| ACTIVITY 1 | **Using Nouns** |

Insert any appropriate noun into each of the following blanks.

1. The shoplifter stole a(n) _____ from the department store.

2. _____ threw the football to me.

3. Tiny messages were scrawled on the _____ .

4. A _____ crashed through the window.

5. Give the _____ to Keiko.

Singular and Plural Nouns

A *singular noun* names one person, place, object, or idea. A *plural noun* refers to two or more persons, places, objects, or ideas. Most singular nouns can be made plural with the addition of an *s*.

Some nouns, like *box*, have irregular plurals. You can check the plural of nouns you think may be irregular by looking up the singular form in a dictionary.

SINGULAR AND PLURAL NOUNS	
Singular	**Plural**
goat	goats
alley	alleys
friend	friends
truth	truths
box	boxes

- For more information on nouns, see "Subjects and Verbs," pages 150–161.

Identifying Nouns	**ACTIVITY 2**

Underline the three nouns in each sentence. Some are singular, and some are plural.

1. Two bats swooped over the heads of the frightened children.

2. The artist has purple paint on her sleeve.

3. The lost dog has fleas and a broken leg.

4. Tiffany does her homework in green ink.

5. Some farmers plant seeds by moonlight.

Pronouns

A *pronoun* is a word that stands for a noun. Pronouns eliminate the need for constant repetition. Look at the following sentences:

The phone rang, and Malik answered the phone.

Lisa met Lisa's friends in the music store at the mall. Lisa meets Lisa's friends there every Saturday.

The waiter rushed over to the new customers. The new customers asked the waiter for menus and coffee.

Now look at how much clearer and smoother these sentences sound with pronouns.

> The phone rang, and Malik answered it.
>
> (The pronoun *it* is used to replace the word *phone*.)
>
> Lisa met her friends in the music store at the mall. She meets them there every Saturday.
>
> (The pronoun *her* is used to replace the word *Lisa's*. The pronoun *she* replaces *Lisa*. The pronoun *them* replaces the words *Lisa's friends*.)
>
> The waiter rushed over to the new customers. They asked him for menus and coffee.
>
> (The pronoun *they* is used to replace the words *the new customers*. The pronoun *him* replaces the words *the waiter*.)

Following is a list of commonly used pronouns known as *personal pronouns*:

PERSONAL PRONOUNS						
I	you	he	she	it	we	they
me	your	him	her	its	us	them
my	yours	his	hers		our	their

ACTIVITY 3	**Using Personal Pronouns**

Fill in each blank with the appropriate personal pronoun.

1. André feeds his pet lizard every day before school. _____ also gives _____ flies in the afternoon.

2. The reporter interviewed the striking workers. _____ told _____ about their demand for higher wages and longer breaks.

3. Students should save all returned tests. _____ should also keep _____ review sheets.

4. The pilot announced that we would fly through some air pockets. _____ said that we should be past _____ soon.

5. Adolfo returned the calculator to Sheila last Friday. But Sheila insists that _____ never got _____ back.

There are several types of pronouns. For convenient reference, they are described briefly in the following box:

TYPES OF PRONOUNS

Personal pronouns can act in a sentence as subjects, objects, or possessives.

> *Singular:* I, me, my, mine, you, your, yours, he, him, his, she, her, hers, it, its
>
> *Plural:*   we, us, our, ours, you, your, yours, they, them, their, theirs

Relative pronouns refer to someone or something already mentioned in the sentence.

> who, whose, whom, which, that

Interrogative pronouns are used to ask questions.

> who, whose, whom, which, what

Demonstrative pronouns are used to point out particular persons or things.

> this, that, these, those

> **Note:** Do not use *them* (as in *them* shoes), *this here, that there, these here,* or *those there* to point out.

Reflexive pronouns are those that end in *-self* or *-selves*. A reflexive pronoun is used as the object of a verb (as in *Cary cut **herself***) or the object of a preposition (as in *Jack sent a birthday card to **himself***) when the subject of the verb is the same as the object.

> *Singular:* myself, yourself, himself, herself, itself
>
> *Plural:*   ourselves, yourselves, themselves

Intensive pronouns have exactly the same forms as reflexive pronouns. The difference is in how they are used. Intensive pronouns are used to add emphasis. (*I **myself** will need to read the contract before I sign it.*)

Indefinite pronouns do not refer to a particular person or thing.

> each, either, everyone, nothing, both, several, all, any, most, none

Reciprocal pronouns express shared actions or feelings.

> each other, one another

- For more information on pronouns, see pages 252–274.

Verbs

Every complete sentence must contain at least one verb. There are two types of verbs: action verbs and linking verbs.

Action Verbs

An *action verb* tells what is being done in a sentence. For example, look at the following sentences:

> Mr. Jensen *swatted* at the bee with his hand.
>
> Rainwater *poured* into the storm sewer.
>
> The children *chanted* the words to the song.

In these sentences, the verbs are *swatted*, *poured*, and *chanted*. These words are all action verbs; they tell what is happening in each sentence.

- For more about action verbs, see "Subjects and Verbs," pages 150–161.

| ACTIVITY 4 | **Using Action Verbs** |

Insert an appropriate word in each blank. That word will be an action verb; it will tell what is happening in the sentence.

1. The surgeon _____ through the first layer of skin.

2. The animals in the cage _____ all day.

3. An elderly woman on the street _____ me for directions.

4. The boy next door _____ our lawn every other week.

5. Our instructor _____ our papers over the weekend.

Linking Verbs

Some verbs are *linking verbs*. These verbs link (or join) a noun to something that is said about it. For example, look at the following sentence:

The clouds *are* steel gray.

In this sentence, *are* is a linking verb. It joins the noun *clouds* to words that describe it: *steel gray*.

Other common linking verbs include *am, is, was, were, look, feel, sound, appear, seem,* and *become*.

- For more about linking verbs, see "Subjects and Verbs," pages 150–161.

| ACTIVITY 5 | **Using Linking Verbs** |

In each blank, insert one of the following linking verbs: *am, feel, is, look, were*. Use each linking verb once.

1. The important papers _____ in a desk drawer.

2. I _____ anxious to get my test back.

3. The bananas _____ ripe.

4. The grocery store _____ open until 11:00 p.m.

5. Whenever I _____ angry, I go off by myself to calm down.

Helping Verbs

Sometimes the verb of a sentence consists of more than one word. In these cases, the main verb will be joined by one or more *helping verbs*. Look at the following sentence:

The basketball team *will be leaving* for their game at six o'clock.

In this sentence, the main verb is *leaving*. The helping verbs are *will* and *be*.

Other helping verbs include *do, has, have, may, would, can, must, could,* and *should*.

- For more information about helping verbs, see "Subjects and Verbs," pages 150–161, and "Irregular Verbs," pages 220–230.

Using Helping Verbs	ACTIVITY 6

In each blank, insert one of the following helping verbs: *does, must, should, could, has been.* Use each helping verb once.

1. You _____ start writing your paper this weekend.

2. The victim _____ describe her attacker in great detail.

3. You _____ rinse the dishes before putting them into the dishwasher.

4. My neighbor _____ arrested for drunk driving.

5. The bus driver _____ not make any extra stops.

Prepositions

A *preposition* is a word that connects a noun or a pronoun to another word in the sentence. For example, look at the following sentence:

A man *in* the bus was snoring loudly.

In is a preposition. It connects the noun *bus* to *man*. Here is a list of common prepositions:

PREPOSITIONS				
about	before	down	like	to
above	behind	during	of	toward
across	below	except	off	under
after	beneath	for	on	up
among	beside	from	over	with
around	between	in	since	without
at	by	into	through	

The noun or pronoun that a preposition connects to another word in the sentence is called the *object* of the preposition. A group of words beginning with a preposition and ending with its object is called a *prepositional phrase*. The words *in the bus,* for example, are a prepositional phrase.

Now read the following sentences and explanations:

An ant was crawling *up the teacher's leg.*

The noun *leg* is the object of the preposition *up. Up* connects *leg* with the word *crawling.* The prepositional phrase *up the teacher's leg* describes *crawling.* It tells just where the ant was crawling.

The man *with the black moustache* left the restaurant quickly.

The noun *moustache* is the object of the preposition *with.* The prepositional phrase *with the black moustache* describes the word *man.* It tells us exactly which man left the restaurant quickly.

The plant *on the windowsill* was a present *from my mother.*

The noun *windowsill* is the object of the preposition *on.* The prepositional phrase *on the windowsill* describes the word *plant.* It describes exactly which plant was a present.

There is a second prepositional phrase in this sentence. The preposition is *from,* and its object is *mother.* The prepositional phrase *from my mother* explains *present.* It tells who gave the present.

- For more about prepositions, see "Subjects and Verbs,"
  pages 150–161, and "Sentence Variety II," pages 304–317.

ACTIVITY 7	**Using Prepositions**

In each blank, insert one of the following prepositions: *of, by, with, in, without.* Use each preposition once.

1. The letter from his girlfriend had been sprayed _____ perfume.

2. The weedkiller quickly killed the dandelions _____ our lawn.

3. _____ giving any notice, the tenant moved out of the expensive apartment.

4. Donald hungrily ate three scoops _____ ice cream and an order of French fries.

5. The crates _____ the back door contain glass bottles and old newspapers.

Adjectives

An *adjective* is a word that describes a noun (the name of a person, place, or thing). Look at the following sentence:

The dog lay down on a mat in front of the fireplace.

Now look at this sentence when adjectives have been inserted:

The *shaggy* dog lay down on a *worn* mat in front of the fireplace.

The adjective *shaggy* describes the noun *dog;* the adjective *worn* describes the noun *mat.* Adjectives add spice to our writing. They also help us to identify particular people, places, or things.

Adjectives can be found in two places:

1. An adjective may come before the word it describes (a *damp* night, the *moldy* bread, a *striped* umbrella).

2. An adjective that describes the subject of a sentence may come after a linking verb. The linking verb may be a form of the verb *be* (he *is* **furious,** I *am* **exhausted,** they are **hungry**). Other linking verbs include *feel, look, sound, smell, taste, appear, seem,* and *become* (the soup *tastes* **salty,** your hands *feel* **dry,** the dog *seems* **lost**).

- For more information on adjectives, see "Adjectives and Adverbs," pages 275–282.

Using Adjectives   ACTIVITY 8

Write any appropriate adjective in each blank.

1. The _____ pizza was eaten greedily by the _____ teenagers.

2. Melissa gave away the sofa because it was _____ and _____.

3. Although the alley is _____ and _____, Jian often takes it as a shortcut home.

4. The restaurant throws away lettuce that is _____ and tomatoes that are _____.

5. When I woke up in the morning, I had a(n) _____ fever and a(n) _____ throat.

Adverbs

An *adverb* is a word that describes a verb, an adjective, or another adverb. Many adverbs end in the letters *-ly*. Look at the following sentence:

The canary sang in the pet store window as the shoppers greeted each other.

Now look at this sentence after adverbs have been inserted:

The canary sang *softly* in the pet store window as the shoppers *loudly* greeted each other.

The adverbs add details to the sentence. They also allow the reader to contrast the singing of the canary and the noise the shoppers are making.

Look at the following sentences and the explanations of how adverbs are used in each case:

The chef yelled **angrily** at the young waiter.

(The adverb *angrily* describes the verb *yelled.*)

My mother has an **extremely** busy schedule on Tuesdays.

(The adverb *extremely* describes the adjective *busy.*)

The sick man spoke **very** faintly to his loyal nurse.

(The adverb *very* describes the adverb *faintly*.)

Some adverbs do not end in *-ly*. Examples include *very, often, never, always,* and *well*.

- For more information on adverbs, see "Adjectives and Adverbs," pages 275–282.

ACTIVITY 9	**Using Adverbs**

Fill in each blank with any appropriate adverb.

1. The water in the pot boiled _____.

2. Carla _____ drove the car through _____ moving traffic.

3. The telephone operator spoke _____ to the young child.

4. The game show contestant waved _____ to his family in the audience.

5. Wes _____ studies, so it's no surprise that he did _____ poorly on his finals.

Conjunctions

A *conjunction* is a word that connects. There are two types of conjunctions: coordinating and subordinating.

Coordinating Conjunctions

Coordinating conjunctions join two equal ideas. Look at the following sentence:

Kevin *and* Steve interviewed for the job, *but* their friend Anne got it.

In this sentence, the coordinating conjunction *and* connects the proper nouns *Kevin* and *Steve*. The coordinating conjunction *but* connects the first part of the sentence, *Kevin* and *Steve interviewed for the job,* to the second part, *their friend Anne got it.*

Following is a list of all the coordinating conjunctions. In this book, they are simply called *joining words.*

COORDINATING CONJUNCTIONS (JOINING WORDS)			
and	so	nor	yet
but	or	for	

- For more on coordinating conjunctions, see information on joining words in "Run-Ons," pages 179–194, and "Sentence Variety I," pages 195–208.

| **Using Coordinating Conjunctions** | **ACTIVITY 10** |

Write a coordinating conjunction in each blank. Choose from the following: *and, but, so, or, nor.* Use each conjunction once.

1. Either Jerome _____ Alex scored the winning touchdown.

2. I expected roses for my birthday, _____ I received a vase of plastic tulips from the discount store.

3. The cafeteria was serving liver and onions for lunch, _____ I bought a sandwich at the corner deli.

4. Marian brought a pack of playing cards _____ a pan of brownies to the company picnic.

5. Neither my sofa _____ my armchair matches the rug in my living room.

Subordinating Conjunctions

When a *subordinating conjunction* is added to a word group, the words can no longer stand alone as an independent sentence. They are no longer a complete thought. For example, look at the following sentence:

Karen fainted in class.

The word group *Karen fainted in class* is a complete thought. It can stand alone as a sentence. See what happens when a subordinating conjunction is added to a complete thought:

When Karen fainted in class

Now the words cannot stand alone as a sentence. They are dependent on other words to complete the thought:

When Karen fainted in class, we propped her feet up on some books.

In this book, a word that begins a dependent word group is called a *dependent word.* Subordinating conjunctions are common dependent words. The following are some subordinating conjunctions:

SUBORDINATING CONJUNCTIONS			
after	even if	unless	where
although	even though	until	wherever
as	if	when	whether
because	since	whenever	while
before	though		

Following are some more sentences with subordinating conjunctions:

After she finished her last exam, Irina said, "Now I can relax."

(*After she finished her last exam* is not a complete thought. It is dependent on the rest of the words to make up a complete sentence.)

Lamont listens to audiobooks **while** he drives to work.

(*While he drives to work* cannot stand by itself as a sentence. It depends on the rest of the sentence to make up a complete thought.)

Since apples were on sale, we decided to make an apple pie for dessert.

(*Since apples were on sale* is not a complete sentence. It depends on *we decided to make an apple pie for dessert* to complete the thought.)

- For more information on subordinating conjunctions, see information on dependent words in "Fragments," pages 162–178; "Run-Ons," pages 179–194; "Sentence Variety I," pages 195–208; and "Sentence Variety II," pages 304–317.

ACTIVITY 11	**Using Subordinating Conjunctions**

Write a logical subordinating conjunction in each blank. Choose from the following: *even though, because, until, when, before.* Use each conjunction once.

1. The bank was closed down by federal regulators _____ it lost more money than it earned.

2. _____ Paula wants to look mysterious, she wears dark sunglasses and a scarf.

3. _____ the restaurant was closing in fifteen minutes, customers sipped their coffee slowly and continued to talk.

4. _____ anyone else could answer it, Leon rushed to the phone and whispered, "Is that you?"

5. The waiter was instructed not to serve any food _____ the guest of honor arrived.

Interjections

An *interjection* is a word that can stand independently and is used to express emotion. Examples are *oh, wow, ouch,* and *oops.* These words are usually not found in formal writing.

"*Hey!*" yelled Maggie. "That's my bike."

Oh, we're late for class.

A Final Note

A word may function as more than one part of speech. For example, the word *dust* can be a verb or a noun, depending on its role in the sentence.

I *dust* my bedroom once a month, whether it needs it or not. (verb)

The top of my refrigerator is covered with an inch of *dust*. (noun)

ESL Pointers

This section covers rules that most native speakers of English take for granted but that are useful for speakers of English as a second language (ESL or ESOL).

Articles

Types of Articles

An *article* is a noun marker—it signals that a noun will follow. There are two kinds of articles: indefinite and definite. The indefinite articles are *a* and *an.* Use *a* before a word that begins with a consonant sound:

a *d*esk, **a p**hotograph, **a u**nicycle

(*A* is used before *unicycle* because the *u* in that word sounds like the consonant *y* plus *u*, not a vowel sound.)

Use *an* before a word beginning with a vowel sound:

an error, **an o**bject, **an h**onest woman

(*Honest* begins with a vowel sound because the *h* is silent.)

The definite article is *the.*

the sofa, **the** cup

An article may come right before a noun:

a magazine, **the** candle

Or an article may be separated from the noun by words that describe the noun:

a popular magazine, **the** fat red candle

> **TIP** There are various other noun markers, including quantity words (*a few, many, a lot of*), numerals (*one, thirteen, 710*), demonstrative adjectives (*this, these*), adjectives (*my, your, our*), and possessive nouns (*Raoul's, the school's*).

Articles with Count and Noncount Nouns

To know whether to use an article with a noun and which article to use, you must recognize count and noncount nouns. (A *noun* is a word used to name something—a person, place, thing, or idea.)

597

Count nouns name people, places, things, or ideas that can be counted and made into plurals, such as *pillow, heater,* and *mail carrier* (*one pillow, two heaters, three mail carriers*).

Noncount nouns refer to things or ideas that cannot be counted and therefore cannot be made into plurals, such as *sunshine, gold,* and *toast.* The following box lists and illustrates common types of noncount nouns:

COMMON NONCOUNT NOUNS

Abstractions and emotions: justice, tenderness, courage, knowledge, embarrassment

Activities: jogging, thinking, wondering, golf, hoping, sleep

Foods: oil, rice, pie, butter, spaghetti, broccoli

Gases and vapors: carbon dioxide, oxygen, smoke, steam, air

Languages and areas of study: Korean, Italian, geology, arithmetic, history

Liquids: coffee, kerosene, lemonade, tea, water, bleach

Materials that come in bulk or mass form: straw, firewood, sawdust, cat litter, cement

Natural occurrences: gravity, sleet, rain, lightning, rust

Other things that cannot be counted: clothing, experience, trash, luggage, room, furniture, homework, machinery, cash, news, transportation, work

---

The quantity of a noncount noun can be expressed with a word or words called a *qualifier,* such as *some, more, a unit of,* and so on. In the following two examples, the qualifiers are shown in *italic* type, and the noncount nouns are shown in **boldface** type:

How *much* **experience** have you had as a salesclerk?

Our tiny kitchen doesn't have *enough* **room** for a table and chairs.

Some words can be either count or noncount nouns depending on whether they refer to one or more individual items or to something in general:

Three **chickens** are running around our neighbor's yard.

(This sentence refers to particular chickens; *chicken* in this case is a count noun.)

Would you like some more **chicken?**

(This sentence refers to chicken in general; in this case, *chicken* is a noncount noun.)

Using a *or* an *with Nonspecific Singular Count Nouns*

Use *a* or *an* with singular nouns that are nonspecific. A noun is nonspecific when the reader doesn't know its specific identity.

A photograph can be almost magical. It saves a moment's image for many years.

(The sentence refers to any photograph, not a specific one.)

An article in the newspaper today made me laugh.

(The reader isn't familiar with the article. This is the first time it is mentioned.)

Using the with Specific Nouns

In general, use *the* with all specific nouns—specific singular, plural, and noncount nouns. A noun is specific—and therefore requires the article *the*—in the following cases:

- When it has already been mentioned once:

  An article in the newspaper today made me laugh. **The** article was about a talking parrot who frightened away a thief.
  (*The* is used with the second mention of *article*.)

- When it is identified by a word or phrase in the sentence:

  The song that is playing now is a favorite of mine.
  (*Song* is identified by the words *that is playing now*.)

- When its identity is suggested by the general context:

  The service at Joe's Bar and Grill is never fast.
  (*Service* is identified by the words *at Joe's Bar and Grill*.)

- When it is unique:

  Some people see a man's face in **the** moon, while others see a rabbit.
  (Earth has only one moon.)

- When it comes after a superlative adjective (for example, *best, biggest, or wisest*):

  The funniest movie I've seen is *Superbad*.

Omitting Articles

Omit articles with nonspecific plurals and nonspecific noncount nouns. Plurals and noncount nouns are nonspecific when they refer to something in general.

Stories are popular with most children.

Service is almost as important as food to a restaurant's success.

Movies can be rented from many supermarkets as well as video stores.

Using *the* with Proper Nouns

Proper nouns name particular people, places, things, or ideas and are always capitalized. Most proper nouns do not require articles; those that do, however, require *the*. Following are general guidelines about when not to use *the* and when to use *the*.

Do not use *the* for most singular proper nouns, including names of the following:

- *People and animals* (Tom Cruise, Fluffy)

- *Continents, states, cities, streets, and parks* (South America, Utah, Boston, Baker Street, People's Park)

- *Most countries* (Cuba, Indonesia, Ireland)

- *Individual bodies of water, islands, and mountains* (Lake Michigan, Captiva Island, Mount McKinley)

Use *the* for the following types of proper nouns:

- *Plural proper nouns* (the Harlem Globetrotters, the Marshall Islands, the Netherlands, the Atlas Mountains)

- *Names of large geographic areas, deserts, oceans, seas, and rivers* (the Midwest, the Kalahari Desert, the Pacific Ocean, the Sargasso Sea, the Nile River)

- *Names with the format* "the _____ of _____ " (the king of Morocco, the Strait of Gibraltar, the University of Illinois)

ACTIVITY 1	**Using Articles**

Underline the correct word or words in parentheses.

1. (Map, The map) on the wall is old and out of date.

2. To show (affection, the affection), a cat will rub against you and purr.

3. This morning my daughter sang (a song, the song) I had not heard before.

4. She had learned (a song, the song) in her kindergarten class.

5. When Javier takes a test, he always begins by answering (the easiest, easiest) questions.

6. (Nile River, The Nile River) has been used for irrigation in Egypt since 4,000 BC.

7. Although (Sahara Desert, the Sahara Desert) is very hot during the day, it can get terribly cold at night.

8. The reason we don't fall off the Earth is the pull of (gravity, the gravity).

9. (Patience, The patience) is not always a virtue.

10. Don't forget to put the (garbage, garbages) out to be picked up Wednesday morning.

Subjects and Verbs

Avoiding Repeated Subjects

In English, a particular subject can be used only once in a word group with a subject and a verb (that is, a clause). Don't repeat a subject in the same word group by following a noun with a pronoun.

Incorrect: My *parents they* live in Miami.

Correct: My **parents** live in Miami.

Correct: **They** live in Miami.

Even when the subject and verb are separated by several words, the subject cannot be repeated in the same word group.

Incorrect: The *windstorm* that happened last night *it* damaged our roof.

Correct: The **windstorm** that happened last night **damaged** our roof.

Including Pronoun Subjects and Linking Verbs

Some languages omit a subject that is a pronoun, but in English, every sentence other than a command must have a subject. In a command, the subject *you* is understood: (You) Hand in your papers now.

Incorrect: The soup tastes terrible. *Is* much too salty.

Correct: The soup tastes terrible. **It is** much too salty.

Every English sentence must also have a verb, even when the meaning of the sentence is clear without the verb.

Incorrect: The table covered with old newspapers.

Correct: The table **is** covered with old newspapers.

Including *There* and *Here* at the Beginning of Sentences

Some English sentences begin with *there* or *here* plus a linking verb (usually a form of *to be: is, are,* and so on). In such sentences, the verb comes before the subject.

There are ants all over the kitchen counter.

(The subject is the plural noun *ants,* so the plural verb *are* is used.)

Here is the bug spray.

(The subject is the singular noun *spray,* so the singular verb *is* is used.)

In sentences like those above, remember not to omit *there* or *here.*

Incorrect: *Are* several tests scheduled for Friday.

Correct: **There are** several tests scheduled for Friday.

Not Using the Progressive Tense of Certain Verbs

The progressive tenses are made up of forms of *be* plus the *-ing* form of the main verb. They express actions or conditions still in progress at a particular time.

The garden **will be blooming** when you visit me in June.

However, verbs for mental states, the senses, possession, and inclusion are normally not used in the progressive tense.

Incorrect: I **am knowing** a lot about auto mechanics.

Correct: I **know** a lot about auto mechanics.

Incorrect: Gerald **is having** a job as a supermarket cashier.

Correct: Gerald **has** a job as a supermarket cashier.

Common verbs not generally used in the progressive tense are listed in the following box:

COMMON VERBS NOT GENERALLY USED IN THE PROGRESSIVE

Verbs relating to thoughts, attitudes, and desires: agree, believe, imagine, know, like, love, prefer, think, understand, want, wish

Verbs showing sense perceptions: hear, see, smell, taste

Verbs relating to appearances: appear, look, seem

Verbs showing possession: belong, have, own, possess

Verbs showing inclusion: contain, include

Using Gerunds and Infinitives after Verbs

Before learning the rules about gerunds and infinitives, you must understand what they are. A *gerund* is the *-ing* form of a verb that is used as a noun:

Reading is a good way to improve one's vocabulary.

(*Reading* is the subject of the sentence.)

An *infinitive* is *to* plus the basic form of the verb (the form in which the verb is listed in the dictionary), as in **to eat.** The infinitive can function as an adverb, an adjective, or a noun.

On weekends, Betsy works at a convenience store **to make** some extra money.

(*To make some extra money* functions as an adverb that describes the verb *works.*)

My advisor showed me a good way **to study** for a test.

(*To study for a test* functions as an adjective describing the noun *way.*)

To forgive can be a relief.

(*To forgive* functions as a noun—it is the subject of the verb *can be.*)

Some verbs can be followed by only a gerund or only an infinitive; other verbs can be followed by either. Examples are given in the following lists. There are many others; watch for them in your reading.

Verb + gerund (*enjoy + skiing*)
Verb + preposition + gerund (*think + about + coming*)

Some verbs can be followed by a gerund but not by an infinitive. In many cases, there is a preposition (such as *for, in,* or *of*) between the verb and the gerund. Following are some verbs and verb-preposition combinations that can be followed by gerunds but not by infinitives:

admit	deny	look forward to
apologize for	discuss	postpone
appreciate	dislike	practice
approve of	enjoy	suspect of
avoid	feel like	talk about
be used to	finish	thank for
believe in	insist on	think about

Incorrect: The governor *avoids to make* enemies.

Correct: The governor **avoids making** enemies.

Incorrect: I *enjoy to go* to movies alone.

Correct: I **enjoy going** to movies alone.

Verb + infinitive (*agree + to leave*)

Following are common verbs that can be followed by an infinitive but not by a gerund:

agree	decide	manage
arrange	expect	refuse
claim	have	wait

Incorrect: I *arranged paying* my uncle's bills while he was ill.

Correct: I **arranged to pay** my uncle's bills while he was ill.

Verb + noun or pronoun + infinitive
(*cause + them + to flee*)

Following are common verbs that are first followed by a noun or pronoun and then by an infinitive, not a gerund:

cause	force	remind
command	persuade	warn

Incorrect: The flood *forced them leaving* their home.

Correct: The flood **forced them to leave** their home.

Following are common verbs that can be followed either by an infinitive alone or by a noun or pronoun and an infinitive:

ask	need	want
expect	promise	would like

Rita **expects to go** to college.

Rita's parents **expect her to go** to college.

Verb + gerund or infinitive (*begin* + *packing* or *begin* + *to pack*)

Following are verbs that can be followed by either a gerund or an infinitive:

begin	hate	prefer
continue	love	start

The meaning of each verb in the previous box remains the same or almost the same whether a gerund or an infinitive is used.

I love **to sleep** late.

I love **sleeping** late.

With the following verbs, the gerunds and the infinitives have very different meanings.

forget	remember	stop

Yuri **forgot putting money** in the parking meter.
(He put money in the parking meter, but then he forgot that he had done so.)

Yuri **forgot to put money** in the parking meter.
(He neglected to put money in the parking meter.)

ACTIVITY 2	**Using Subjects and Verbs**

Underline the correct word or words in parentheses.

1. The coffee table (wobbles, it wobbles) because one leg is loose.

2. The firewood is very dry. (Is, It is) burning quickly.

3. (Are knives and forks, There are knives and forks) in that drawer.

4. Olivia (seems, is seeming) sad today.

5. Our instructor warned us (studying, to study) hard for the exam.

6. When the little boy saw his birthday presents, he (very excited, became very excited).

7. Do you (feel like walking, feel like to walk) home?

8. A vegetarian (refuses eating, refuses to eat) meat.

9. The alarm on my watch (it started beeping, started beeping) in the middle of the church service.

10. I like small parties, but my boyfriend (prefers, is preferring) large, noisy ones.

Adjectives

Following the Order of Adjectives in English

Adjectives describe nouns and pronouns. In English, an adjective usually comes directly before the word it describes or after a linking verb (a form of *be* or a "sense" verb such as *look, seem,* or *taste*), in which case it modifies the subject of the sentence. In each of the following two sentences, the adjective is **boldfaced** and the noun it describes is *italicized*.

Marta has **beautiful** *eyes.*

Marta's *eyes* are **beautiful.**

When more than one adjective modifies the same noun, the adjectives are usually stated in a certain order, though there are often exceptions. Following is the typical order of English adjectives:

TYPICAL ORDER OF ADJECTIVES IN A SERIES

1. Article or other noun marker: a, an, the, Helen's, this, seven, your

2. Opinion adjective: rude, enjoyable, surprising, easy

3. Size: tall, huge, small, compact

4. Shape: triangular, oval, round, square

5. Age: ancient, new, old, young

6. Color: gray, blue, pink, green

7. Nationality: Greek, Thai, Korean, Ethiopian

8. Religion: Hindu, Methodist, Jewish, Islamic

9. Material: fur, copper, stone, velvet

10. Noun used as an adjective: book (as in *book report*), picture (as in *picture frame*), tea (as in *tea bag*)

Here are some examples of the order of adjectives:

an exciting new movie

the petite young Irish woman

my favorite Chinese restaurant

Greta's long brown leather coat

In general, use no more than two adjectives after the article or another noun marker. Numerous adjectives in a series can be awkward: **that comfortable big old green velvet** couch.

Using the Present and Past Participles as Adjectives

The present participle ends in *-ing*. Past participles of regular verbs end in *-ed* or *-d;* a list of the past participles of many common irregular verbs appears on pages 221–223. Both types of participles may be used as adjectives. A participle used as an adjective may come before the word it describes:

There was a **frowning** *security guard.*

A participle used as an adjective may also follow a linking verb and describe the subject of the sentence:

The *security guard* was **frowning.**

While both present and past participles of a particular verb may be used as adjectives, their meanings differ. Use the present participle to describe whoever or whatever causes a feeling:

a **disappointing** *date*

(The date *caused* the disappointment.)

Use the past participle to describe whoever or whatever experiences the feeling:

the **disappointed** *neighbor*

(The neighbor *is* disappointed.)

Here are two more sentences that illustrate the differing meanings of present and past participles.

The waiter was **irritating.**

The diners were **irritated.**

(The waiter caused the irritation; the diners experienced the irritation.)

The following box shows pairs of present and past participles with similar distinctions:

annoying / annoyed	exhausting / exhausted
boring / bored	fascinating / fascinated
confusing / confused	surprising / surprised
depressing / depressed	tiring / tired
exciting / excited	

Using Adjectives

ACTIVITY 3

Underline the correct word or wording in parentheses.

1. When my grandfather died, he left me his (big old oak, old big oak) seaman's chest.

2. The guest lecturer at today's class was a (young Vietnamese Buddhist, Vietnamese Buddhist young) nun.

3. Yolanda's family lives in a (gray huge stone, huge gray stone) farmhouse.

4. Doesn't working all day and studying at night make you very (tired, tiring)?

5. The (fascinated, fascinating) children begged the magician to tell them how he made a rabbit disappear.

Prepositions Used for Time and Place

The use of a preposition in English is often not based on its common meaning, and there are many exceptions to general rules. As a result, correct use of prepositions must be learned gradually through experience. Following is a chart showing how three of the most common prepositions are used in some customary references to time and place:

USE OF *ON*, *IN*, AND *AT* TO REFER TO TIME AND PLACE

Time

On a specific day: on Wednesday, on January 11, on Halloween

In a part of a day: in the morning, in the daytime (but *at* night)

In a month or a year: in October, in 1776

In a period of time: in a second, in a few days, in a little while

At a specific time: at 11:00 p.m., at midnight, at sunset, at lunchtime

Place

On a surface: on the shelf, on the sidewalk, on the roof

In a place that is enclosed: in the bathroom, in the closet, in the drawer

At a specific location: at the restaurant, at the zoo, at the school

---

Using Prepositions

ACTIVITY 4

Underline the correct preposition in parentheses.

1. May I come see you (on, at) Saturday?

2. We will eat dinner (on, at) 7:00 p.m.

3. I found this book (on, in) the library.

4. Alex will be leaving for the army (in, at) a week.

5. David and Lisa met each other (on, at) the post office.

REVIEW TEST

Underline the correct word or words in parentheses.

1. I had to pull off the road because of the heavy (hail, hails).

2. (Are, There are) fresh cookies on the kitchen table.

3. Theresa does not like living alone—she becomes (frightening, frightened) at every little sound.

4. Have you gotten used to working (in, at) night?

5. Carla (practiced to give, practiced giving) her speech at least ten times.

6. What a (pretty red, red pretty) scarf you are wearing today!

7. That antique car (belongs to, is belonging to) my cousin.

8. Fireworks are set off (on, in) the Fourth of July to commemorate the American Revolution.

9. The newlyweds' apartment does not contain much (furnitures, furniture).

10. Paul's favorite pastime is going to (the rock concerts, rock concerts).

Sentence-Skills Diagnostic Test

Part 1

This diagnostic test will help check your knowledge of a number of sentence skills. In each item below, certain words are underlined. Write *X* in the answer space if you think a mistake appears at the underlined part. Write *C* in the answer space if you think the underlined part is correct.

The headings within the text ("Fragments," "Run-Ons," and so on) will give you clues to the mistakes to look for. However, you do not have to understand the heading to find a mistake. What you are checking is your own sense of effective written English.

Fragments

_____ 1. Because I didn't want to get wet. I waited for a break in the downpour. Then I ran for the car like an Olympic sprinter.

_____ 2. The baby birds chirped loudly, especially when their mother brought food to them. Their mouths gaped open hungrily.

_____ 3. Trying to avoid running into anyone. Cal wheeled his baby son around the crowded market. He wished that strollers came equipped with flashing hazard lights.

_____ 4. The old woman combed out her long, gray hair. She twisted it into two thick braids. And wrapped them around her head like a crown.

Run-Ons

_____ 5. Irene fixed fruits and healthy sandwiches for her son's lunch, he traded them for cupcakes, cookies, and chips.

_____ 6. Angie's dark eyes were the color of mink they matched her glowing complexion.

_____ 7. My mother keeps sending me bottles of vitamins, but I keep forgetting to take them.

_____ 8. The little boy watched the line of ants march across the ground, he made a wall of Popsicle sticks to halt the ants' advance.

Standard English Verbs

_____ 9. When she's upset, Mary tells her troubles to her houseplants.

_____ 10. The street musician counted the coins in his donations basket and pack his trumpet in its case.

_____ 11. I tried to pull off my rings, but they <u>was</u> stuck on my swollen fingers.

_____ 12. Belle's car <u>have</u> a horn that plays six different tunes.

Irregular Verbs

_____ 13. I've <u>swam</u> in this lake for years, and I've never seen it so shallow.

_____ 14. The phone <u>rung</u> once and then stopped.

_____ 15. Five different people had <u>brought</u> huge bowls of potato salad to the barbecue.

_____ 16. The metal ice cube trays <u>froze</u> to the bottom of the freezer.

Subject-Verb Agreement

_____ 17. The songs in my iPod <u>is</u> arranged in alphabetical order.

_____ 18. There <u>was</u> only one burner working on the old gas stove.

_____ 19. My aunt and uncle <u>gives</u> a party every Groundhog Day.

_____ 20. One of my sweaters <u>have</u> moth holes in the sleeves.

Consistent Verb Tense

_____ 21. After I turned off the ignition, the engine <u>continued</u> to sputter for several minutes.

_____ 22. Before cleaning the oven, I lined the kitchen floor with newspapers, <u>open</u> the windows, and shook the can of aerosol foam.

Pronoun Reference, Agreement, and Point of View

_____ 23. All visitors should stay in <u>their</u> cars while driving through the wild animal park.

_____ 24. At the library, <u>they</u> showed me how to use the microfilm machines.

_____ 25. As I slowed down at the scene of the accident, <u>you</u> could see long black skid marks on the highway.

Pronoun Types

_____ 26. My husband is more sentimental than <u>me</u>.

_____ 27. Andy and <u>I</u> made ice cream in an old-fashioned wooden machine.

Adjectives and Adverbs

_____ 28. Brian drives so <u>reckless</u> that no one will join his carpool.

_____ 29. Miriam pulled <u>impatiently</u> at the rusty zipper.

_____ 30. I am <u>more happier</u> with myself now that I earn my own money.

_____ 31. The last screw on the license plate was the <u>most corroded</u> one of all.

Misplaced Modifiers

_____ 32. I stretched out on the lounge chair <u>wearing my bikini bathing suit</u>.

_____ 33. I replaced the shingle on the roof <u>that was loose</u>.

Dangling Modifiers

_____ 34. <u>While doing the dishes</u>, a glass shattered in the soapy water.

_____ 35. <u>Pedaling as fast as possible</u>, Todd tried to outrace the snapping dog.

Faulty Parallelism

_____ 36. Before I could take a bath, I had to pick up the damp towels on the floor, gather up the loose toys in the room, and <u>the tub had to be scrubbed out</u>.

_____ 37. I've tried several cures for my headaches, including drugs, meditation, exercise, and <u>massaging my head</u>.

Capital Letters

_____ 38. This <u>fall</u> we plan to visit Cape Cod.

_____ 39. Vern ordered a set of tools from the <u>sears</u> catalog.

_____ 40. When my <u>aunt</u> visits us, she insists on doing all the cooking.

_____ 41. Maureen asked, "<u>will</u> you split a piece of cheesecake with me?"

Numbers and Abbreviations

_____ 42. Before I could stop myself, I had eaten <u>6</u> glazed doughnuts.

_____ 43. At <u>10:45</u> a.m., a partial eclipse of the sun will begin.

_____ 44. Larry, who is now over six <u>ft.</u> tall, can no longer sleep comfortably in a twin bed.

End Marks

_____ 45. Jane wondered if her husband was telling the truth<u>.</u>

_____ 46. Does that stew need some salt<u>?</u>

Apostrophes

_____ 47. <u>Elizabeths</u> thick, curly hair is her best feature.

_____ 48. I tried to see through the interesting envelope sent to my sister but <u>couldnt</u>.

_____ 49. Pam's heart almost stopped beating when Roger jumped out of the closet.

_____ 50. The <u>logs'</u> in the fireplace crumbled in a shower of sparks.

Quotation Marks

_____ 51. <u>Someone once said, "A lie has no legs and cannot stand."</u>

_____ 52. <u>"This repair job could be expensive, the mechanic warned."</u>

_____ 53. <u>"My greatest childhood fear," said Sheila, "was being sucked down the bathtub drain."</u>

_____ 54. <u>"I was always afraid of everybody's father, said Suzanne, except my own."</u>

Commas

_____ 55. The restaurant's "sundae bar" featured bowls <u>of whipped cream chopped nuts and chocolate sprinkles.</u>

_____ 56. My <u>sister, who studies karate, installed</u> large practice mirrors in our basement.

_____ 57. When I remove my thick <u>eyeglasses the world</u> turns into an out-of-focus movie.

_____ 58. Gloria wrapped her son's presents in pages from the comics <u>section, and</u> she glued a small toy car atop each gift.

Spelling

_____ 59. When Terry <u>practices</u> scales on the piano, her whole family wears earplugs.

_____ 60. I wondered if it was <u>alright</u> to wear sneakers with my three-piece suit.

_____ 61. The essay test question asked us to describe two different <u>theorys</u> of evolution.

_____ 62. A <u>thief</u> stole several large hanging plants from Marlo's porch.

Omitted Words and Letters

_____ 63. <u>After dark, I'm afraid to look in the closets or under the bed.</u>

_____ 64. I turned on the television, but <u>baseball game had been rained out.</u>

_____ 65. <u>Polar bear cubs stay with their mother for two year.</u>

Commonly Confused Words

_____ 66. Before <u>your</u> about to start the car, press the gas pedal to the floor once.

_____ 67. The frog flicked <u>it's</u> tongue out and caught the fly.

_____ 68. I was to lonely to enjoy the party.

_____ 69. The bats folded their wings around them like leather overcoats.

Effective Word Choice

_____ 70. If the professor gives me a break, I might pass the final exam.

_____ 71. Harry worked like a dog all summer to save money for his tuition.

_____ 72. Because Monday is a holiday, sanitation engineers will pick up your trash on Tuesday.

_____ 73. Our family's softball game ended in an argument, as usual.

_____ 74. As for my own opinion, I feel that nuclear weapons should be banned.

_____ 75. This law is, for all intents and purposes, a failure.

Part 2 (Optional)

Do the following at your instructor's request. This second part of the test will provide more detailed information about skills you need to know. On a separate piece of paper, number and correct all the items that you marked with an X in Part 1. For example, suppose you had marked the word groups below with an X. (Note that these examples are not taken from the actual test.)

4. When I picked up the tire. Something in my back snapped. I could not stand up straight.

7. The phone started ringing, then the doorbell sounded as well.

15. Marks goal is to save enough money to get married next year.

29. Without checking the rearview mirror the driver pulled out into the passing lane.

Here is how you should write your corrections on a separate sheet of paper:

4. When I picked up the tire, something in my back snapped.

7. The phone started ringing, and then the doorbell sounded as well.

15. Mark's

29. mirror, the driver

There are more than forty corrections to make in all.

Sentence-Skills Achievement Test

Part 1

This achievement test will help you check your mastery of a number of sentence skills. In each item below, certain words are underlined. Write *X* in the answer space if you think a mistake appears at the underlined part. Write *C* in the answer space if you think the underlined part is correct.

The headings within the test ("Fragments," "Run-Ons," and so on) will give you clues to the mistakes to look for.

Fragments

_____ 1. When the town's bully died. Hundreds of people came to his funeral. They wanted to make sure he was dead.

_____ 2. Suzanne adores junk foods, especially onion-flavored potato chips. She can eat an entire bag at one sitting.

_____ 3. My brother stayed up all night. Studying the rules in his driver's manual. He wanted to get his license on the first try.

_____ 4. Hector decided to take a study break. He picked up *TV Guide.* And flipped through the pages to find that night's listings.

Run-Ons

_____ 5. Ronnie leaned forward in his seat, he could not hear what the instructor was saying.

_____ 6. Our television obviously needs repairs the color keeps fading from the picture.

_____ 7. Nick and Fran enjoyed their trip to Chicago, but they couldn't wait to get home.

_____ 8. I tuned in the weather forecast on the radio, I had to decide what to wear.

Standard English Verbs

_____ 9. My sister Louise walks a mile to the bus stop every day.

_____ 10. The play was ruined when the quarterback fumble the handoff.

_____ 11. When the last guests left our party, we was exhausted but happy.

_____ 12. I don't think my mother have gone out to a movie in years.

Irregular Verbs

_____ 13. My roommate and I <u>seen</u> a Broadway show this weekend.

_____ 14. My nephew must have <u>growed</u> six inches since last summer.

_____ 15. I should have <u>brought</u> a gift to the office holiday party.

_____ 16. After playing touch football all afternoon, Al <u>drank</u> a quart of Gatorade.

Subject-Verb Agreement

_____ 17. The cost of those new tires <u>are</u> more than I can afford.

_____ 18. Joe and Julie <u>give</u> a New Year's Eve party every year.

_____ 19. There <u>was</u> only two slices of cake left on the plate.

_____ 20. Each of the fast-food restaurants <u>have</u> a breakfast special.

Consistent Verb Tense

_____ 21. After I folded the towels in the basket, I <u>remembered</u> that I hadn't washed them yet.

_____ 22. Before she decided to buy the wall calendar, Joanne <u>turns</u> its pages and looked at all the pictures.

Pronoun Reference, Agreement, and Point of View

_____ 23. All drivers should try <u>their</u> best to be courteous during rush hour.

_____ 24. When Bob went to the bank for a home improvement loan, <u>they</u> asked him for three credit references.

_____ 25. I like to shop at factory outlets because <u>you</u> can always get brand names at a discount.

Pronoun Types

_____ 26. My brother writes much more neatly than <u>me</u>.

_____ 27. Vonnie and <u>I</u> are both taking Introduction to Business this semester.

Adjectives and Adverbs

_____ 28. When the elevator doors closed <u>sudden</u>, three people were trapped inside.

_____ 29. The homeless woman glared <u>angrily</u> at me when I offered her a dollar bill.

_____ 30. Frank couldn't decide which vacation he liked <u>best</u>, a bicycle trip or a week at the beach.

_____ 31. I find proofreading a paper much <u>more difficult</u> than writing one.

Misplaced Modifiers

_____ 32. The car was parked along the side of the road <u>with a flat tire</u>.

_____ 33. We bought a television at our neighborhood discount store <u>that has stereo sound</u>.

Dangling Modifiers

_____ 34. <u>While looking for bargains at Target</u>, an exercise bike caught my eye.

_____ 35. <u>Hurrying to catch the bus</u>, Donna fell and twisted her ankle.

Faulty Parallelism

_____ 36. Before she leaves for work, Agnes makes her lunch, does fifteen minutes of yoga, and <u>her two cats have to be fed</u>.

_____ 37. Three remedies for insomnia are warm milk, <u>taking a hot bath</u>, and sleeping pills.

Capital Letters

_____ 38. Every <u>Saturday</u> I get up early, even though I have the choice of sleeping late.

_____ 39. We stopped at the drugstore for some <u>crest</u> toothpaste.

_____ 40. Rows of crocuses appear in my front yard every <u>spring</u>.

_____ 41. The cashier said, "<u>sorry</u>, but children under three are not allowed in this theater."

Numbers and Abbreviations

_____ 42. Our train finally arrived—<u>2</u> hours late.

_____ 43. Answers to the chapter questions start on page <u>293</u>.

_____ 44. Three <u>yrs</u>. from now, my new car will finally be paid off.

End Marks

_____ 45. I had no idea who was inside the gorilla suit at the Halloween <u>party</u>.

_____ 46. Are you taking the makeup <u>exam</u>.

Apostrophes

_____ 47. My <u>fathers</u> favorite old television program is _Star Trek_.

_____ 48. I <u>couldnt</u> understand a word of that lecture.

_____ 49. My <u>dentist's</u> recommendation was that I floss before brushing my teeth.

_____ 50. Three <u>house's</u> on our street are up for sale.

Quotation Marks

_____ 51. Garfield the cat is fond of saying, "I never met a carbo-hydrate I didn't like."

_____ 52. "This restaurant does not accept credit cards, the waiter said."

_____ 53. Two foods that may prevent cancer," said the scientist, "are those old standbys spinach and carrots."

_____ 54. "I can't get anything done," Dad complained, if you two insist on making all that noise."

Commas

_____ 55. The snack bar offered overdone hamburgers rubbery hot dogs and soggy pizza.

_____ 56. My sister, who regards every living creature as a holy thing, cannot even swat a housefly.

_____ 57. When I smelled something burning I realized I hadn't turned off the oven.

_____ 58. Marge plays the musical saw at parties, and her husband does Dracula imitations.

Spelling

_____ 59. No one will be admitted without a valid student identification card.

_____ 60. Pat carrys a full course load in addition to working as the night manager at a supermarket.

_____ 61. Did you feel alright after eating Ralph's special chili?

_____ 62. My parents were disappointed when I didn't enter the family busines.

Omitted Words and Letters

_____ 63. Both high schools in my hometown offer evening classes for adults.

_____ 64. I opened new bottle of ketchup and then couldn't find the cap.

_____ 65. Visiting hour for patients at this hospital are from noon to eight.

Commonly Confused Words

_____ 66. Shelley has always been to self-conscious to speak up in class.

_____ 67. Its not easy to return to college after raising a family.

_____ 68. "Thank you for <u>you're</u> generous contribution," the letter began.

_____ 69. Nobody knew <u>whose</u> body had been found floating in the swimming pool.

Effective Word Choice

_____ 70. My roommate keeps <u>getting on my case</u> about leaving clothes on the floor.

_____ 71. Karla decided to <u>take the bull by the horns</u> and ask her boss for a raise.

_____ 72. Although Lamont <u>accelerated his vehicle,</u> he was unable to pass the truck.

_____ 73. When the movie <u>ended suddenly,</u> I felt I had been cheated.

_____ 74. <u>In light of the fact that</u> I am on a diet, I have stopped eating between meals.

_____ 75. <u>Personally, I do not think</u> that everyone should be allowed to vote.

Part 2 (Optional)

Do the following at your instructor's request. This second part of the test will provide more detailed information about which skills you have mastered and which skills you still need to work on. On a separate piece of paper, number and correct all the items that you marked with an X in Part 1. For example, suppose you had marked the word groups below with an X. (Note that these examples were not taken from the actual test.)

4. <u>When I picked up the tire.</u> Something in my back snapped. I could not stand up straight.

7. The phone started <u>ringing, then</u> the doorbell sounded as well.

15. <u>Marks</u> goal is to save enough money to get married next year.

29. Without checking the rearview <u>mirror the</u> driver pulled out into the passing lane.

Here is how you should write your corrections on a separate sheet of paper:

4. When I picked up the tire, something in my back snapped.

7. The phone started ringing, and then the doorbell sounded as well.

15. Mark's

29. mirror, the driver

There are more than forty corrections to make in all.

Answers to Activities in Part 3

APPENDIX E

This answer key can help you teach yourself. Use it to find out why you got some answers wrong—to uncover any weak spot in your understanding of a given skill. By using the answer key in an honest and thoughtful way, you will master each skill and prepare yourself for many tests in this book that have no answer key.

CHAPTER 6: Subjects and Verbs

Introductory Activity (*page 153*)

Activity 1: Finding Subjects and Verbs (*page 155*)

1. Rachel poured
2. company offered
3. host introduced
4. Taryn adjusted
5. butt burned
6. bathroom is
7. Royden tripped
8. drink quenched
9. trimmer tossed
10. Volunteers collected

Activity 2: Subject and Linking Verbs (*page 156*)

1. parents are
2. I am
3. Tri Lee was
4. dog becomes
5. Liz seems
6. hot dog looks
7. people appear
8. students felt
9. cheeseburger has
10. phone seemed

Activity 3: Subjects and Verbs (*page 156*)

1. rabbits ate
2. father prefers
3. restaurant donated
4. Stanley looks
5. couple relaxed
6. Lightning brightened
7. council voted
8. throat kept
9. sister decided
10. I chose

Activity 4: Subjects and Prepositional Phrases (*page 157*)

1. ~~By accident~~, my girlfriend dropped her set ~~of keys into the toilet at the public restroom~~.
2. ~~Before the trial~~, the defense attorney quickly read ~~through her trial notes~~.
3. My two-year-old daughter Olivia sleeps ~~in my bed on stormy nights~~.
4. I applied ~~for a pre-approved credit card from my bank~~.
5. ~~On Friday nights~~, my family watches movies ~~on our newly purchased LCD TV~~.
6. ~~Over the weekend~~, Patrice wrote a five-page research paper ~~on indigenous rights for her political science class~~.
7. The wireless connection ~~from my neighbor's apartment~~ allows me access ~~to the Internet free~~.
8. ~~On Thursday~~, several foreign-born soldiers received U.S. citizenship ~~during the naturalization ceremony at the Federal Building~~.
9. All my friends, ~~except Nino~~, play the video game *Grand Theft Auto* ~~on their home computers~~.
10. The spicy horseradish ~~beneath the raw tuna in my nigiri sushi roll~~ burned the back ~~of my tongue~~.

Activity 5: Verbs of More than One Word (*page 159*)

1. Ellen has chosen
2. You should plan
3. Felix has been waiting
4. We should have invited
5. I would have preferred
6. Classes were interrupted
7. Sam can touch
8. I have been encouraging
9. Joe has agreed
10. students have been giving

Activity 6: Compound Subjects and Verbs (*page 160*)

1. Boards and bricks make
2. We bought and finished
3. fly and bee hung
4. twins look, think, act, and dress
5. salmon and tuna contain
6. I waited and slipped

619

7. girl waved and smiled
8. bird dived and reappeared
9. Singers, dancers, and actors performed
10. magician and assistant bowed and disappeared

CHAPTER 7: Fragments

Introductory Activity (page 162)

1. verb
2. subject
3. subject . . . verb
4. express a complete thought

Activity 1: Correcting Dependent-Word Fragments (page 165)

Activity 2: Combining Sentences to Correct Dependent-Word Fragments (page 166)

1. When the waitress coughed in his food, Frank lost his appetite. He didn't even take home a doggy bag.
2. Our power went out during a thunderstorm.
3. Tony doesn't like going to the ballpark. If he misses an exciting play, there's no instant replay.
4. After the mail carrier comes, I run to our mailbox. I love to get mail even if it is only junk mail.
5. Even though she can't read, my little daughter likes to go to the library. She chooses books with pretty covers while I look at the latest magazines.

Activity 3: Correcting -ing Fragments (page 168)

1. Desmond looked anxiously at his cell phone, waiting for his supervisor to return his call. He needed to call in sick to work.
2. Using one of the computers at the library, Hari could not access several Web sites, which he later learned were blocked.
3. A virus infected my computer. As a result, it destroyed data.

Activity 4: Correcting -ing or to Fragments (page 169)

1. Some workers dug up the street near our house, causing frequent vibrations inside.
2. I therefore walked slowly into the darkened living room, preparing to look shocked.
   or: I was preparing to look shocked.
3. Dribbling skillfully up the court, Luis looked for a teammate who was open.

4. Wanting to finish the dream, I pushed the Snooze button.
5. To get back my term paper, I went to see my English instructor from last semester.

Activity 5: Identifying and Correcting Fragments (page 171)

1. For example, she waits until the night before a test to begin studying.
2. My eleventh-grade English teacher picked on everybody except the athletes.
3. For example, he bought an air conditioner in December.

Activity 6: Identifying and Correcting Added-Detail Fragments (page 171)

1. My daughter faithfully watches the programs on the Disney Channel, including *Hannah Montana*, *Wizards of Waverly Place*, and *The Suite Life of Zack and Cody*.
2. There are certain snacks I love to eat when I watch TV, especially microwave popcorn.
3. For example, the ink-jet printer often needs a new printer cartridge.
4. By noon, the stadium parking lot was packed with tailgaters, with some of them grilling barbeque ribs and drinking ice-cold beer.
5. For example, free online game sites are filled with distracting marketing messages.

Activity 7: Correcting Missing-Subject Fragments (page 173)

1. Jack tripped on his shoelace and then looked around to see if anyone had noticed.
   or: Then he looked around to see if anyone had noticed.
2. I started the car and quickly turned down the blaring radio.
   or: And I quickly turned down the blaring radio.
3. Its orange-red flames shot high in the air and made strange shadows all around the dark room.
4. She also forgot to take my name.
5. She places herself in front of a seated young man and stands on his feet until he gets up.
   or: And she stands on his feet until he gets up.

Activity 8: Editing and Rewriting (page 174)

1. 2–3   If you think that these kids will simply outgrow their "baby fat," you're wrong.
2. 4–5   The number of overweight children in this country has doubled in the past twenty years, creating a health epidemic.

3. 6–7   Too many children spend hours watching television and playing video games when they should
be outside playing.

4. 8–9   They consume sugary, high-calorie snacks when
they should be eating fresh fruits and low-fat
yogurt.

5. 15–16 For example, everyone can be a positive role
model.

Activity 9: Creating Sentences (*page 174*)

CHAPTER 8: Run-Ons

Introductory Activity (*page 179*)

1. period
2. *but*
3. semicolon
4. *Although*

Activity 1: Correcting Fused Sentences (*page 181*)

1. month. Its
2. porch. They
3. make. It
4. do. He
5. shirt. A
6. B.C. The
7. cheaply. She
8. desk. She
9. fireplace. The
10. traffic. Its

Activity 2: Correcting Run-Ons: Fused Sentences and Comma Splices (*page 182*)

1. man. He
2. mailbox. Then
3. common. The
4. tiny. A
5. greyhound. It
6. Chinese. She
7. working. Its
8. lovely. It
9. drink. One
10. times. For

Activity 3: Writing the Next Sentence (*page 183*)

Activity 4: Connecting Two Thoughts (*page 184*)

1. , but
2. , and
3. , and
4. , so
5. , but
6. , so
7. , for
8. , but
9. , so
10. , for

Activity 5: Using Commas and Joining Words (*page 185*)

Activity 6: Using Semicolons (*page 186*)

1. Denny's; the
2. wedding; it
3. class; her
4. decreased; auto
5. ancient; it

Activity 7: Using Logical Transitions (*page 187*)

1. drive; however, the
2. art; otherwise, it
3. gasoline; as a result, spectators (*or* thus *or* consequently *or* therefore)
4. started; however, all
5. feelers; consequently, they (*or* as a result *or* thus *or* therefore)

Activity 8: Using Semicolons and Commas (*page 188*)

1. store; nevertheless, she
2. candy; as a result, he
3. strangers; however, he
4. schedule; otherwise, he
5. children; furthermore, she

Activity 9: Using Dependent Words (*page 189*)

1. since
2. Unless
3. because
4. After
5. although

Activity 10: Using Subordination (*page 189*)

1. Although I want to stop smoking, I don't want to gain weight.
2. Because it was too hot indoors to study, I decided to go down to the shopping center for ice cream.
3. Although he had hair implants, it looked very natural.
4. When Professor Williams scowled at the class, her facial expression told the story.
5. Although this world map was published only three years ago, the names of some countries are already out of date.

Activity 11: Editing and Rewriting (*page 190*)

1. When Mark began his first full-time job, he immediately got a credit card. A used sports car was his first purchase.
2. Then the began to buy expensive clothes that he could not afford. He also bought impressive gifts for his parents and his girlfriend.
4. To make matters worse, his car broke down, and a stack of bills suddenly seemed to be due at once.
5. Although Mark tried to cut back on his purchases, he soon realized he had to cut up his credit card to prevent himself from using it.
6. He also began keeping a careful record of his spending, for he had no idea where his money had gone till then.

Activity 12: Creating Sentences (*Page 191*)

CHAPTER 9: Sentence Variety I

Activity 1: The Simple Sentence (*page 195*)

Activity 2: The Compound Sentence (*page 196*)

1. I am majoring in digital media arts, for I hope to find a job doing video-game animation.
2. My children were spending too much time in front of the TV and computer, so I signed up my entire family for a one-year gym membership.
3. Nicole's skin was blemished and sun damaged, so she consulted with a plastic surgeon about a chemical face peel.
4. Riley insists on buying certified-organic fruits and vegetables, but I cannot distinguish organic from conventionally grown produce.
5. I was recently promoted to shift manager at work, so I need to drop down to part-time status at school next semester.

Activity 3: Writing Compound Sentences (*page 197*)

Activity 4: Creating Complex Sentences (*page 198*)

1. Lydia read the quarterly reports while her assistant drove them to the regional sales meeting.
2. When Keiko heard the punch line to the joke, she laughed hysterically.
3. Although I wanted to order the chef's seafood special, the kitchen ran out of fresh prawns.
4. Raymond refuses to drink from a public water fountain because he is afraid that he will catch an infectious disease.
5. Before I can register for a calculus class, I need to take the math placement exam.

Activity 5: Using Subordination (*page 199*)

1. As Carlo set the table, his wife finished cooking dinner.
2. Although Maggie could have gotten good grades, she did not study enough.
3. After I watered my drooping African violets, they perked right up.
4. Though the little boy kept pushing the "down" button, the elevator didn't come any more quickly.
5. I never really knew what pain was until I had four impacted wisdom teeth pulled at once.

Activity 6: Using *Who, Which,* or *That* (*page 200*)

1. Karen, who is an old friend of mine, just gave birth to twins.

2. The tea, which was hotter than I expected, burned the roof of my mouth.
3. I dropped the camera that my sister had just bought.
4. Ashaki, who is visiting from California, brought us some enormous oranges.
5. Liz used a steam cleaner to shampoo her rugs, which were dirtier than she had expected.

Activity 7: Writing Complex Sentences (*page 201*)

Activity 8: Using Joining Words and Dependent Words (*page 201*)

1. After . . . for
2. When . . . but
3. when . . . and
4. Because . . . so
5. but . . . because

Activity 9: Writing Compound-Complex Sentences (*page 202*)

Activity 10: Using Subordination or Coordination (*page 202*)

1. Though Jaylen likes loud music, his parents can't stand it, so he wears earphones.
2. After the volcano erupted, the sky turned black with smoke. Nearby villagers were frightened, so they clogged the roads leading to safety.
3. After Min-Yeng had a haircut today, she came home and looked in the mirror. Then she decided to wear a hat for a few days because she thought she looked like a bald eagle.
4. When I ran out of gas on the way to work, I discovered how helpful strangers can be. A passing driver saw I was stuck, so he drove me to the gas station and back to my car.
5. Our dog often rests on the floor in the sunshine while he waits for the children to get home from school. As the sunlight moves along the floor, he moves with it.
6. Because my father was going to be late from work, we planned to have a late dinner. But I was hungry before dinner, so I secretly ate a salami and cheese sandwich.
7. A baseball game was scheduled for early afternoon, but it looked like rain, so a crew rolled huge tarps to cover the field. Then the sun reappeared.
8. Cassy worries about the pesticides used on fruit, so she washes apples, pears, and plums in soap and water. Because she doesn't rinse them well, they have a soapy flavor.
9. Charlene needed to buy stamps, so she went to the post office during her lunch hour, when the line was long. After she waited there for half an hour, she had to go back to work without stamps.

10. After the weather suddenly became frigid, almost everyone at work caught a cold, so someone brought a big batch of chicken soup. She poured it into one of the office coffeepots, and the pot was empty by noon.

CHAPTER 10: Standard English Verbs

Introductory Activity (*page 210*)

played . . . plays
hoped . . . hopes
juggled . . . juggles

1. past time . . . *-ed* or *-d*
2. present time . . . *-s*

Activity 1: Using Standard Verb Forms (*page 211*)

1. drives
2. gets
3. practices
4. makes
5. brushes
6. falls
7. *C*
8. comes
9. watches
10. buzzes

Activity 2: Using Present Tense *-s* Verb Endings (*page 212*)

My little sister wants to be a singer when she grows up. She constantly hums and sings around the house. Sometimes she makes quite a racket. When she listens to music on the radio, for example, she sings very loudly in order to hear herself over the radio. And when she takes a shower, her voice rings through the whole house because she thinks nobody can hear her from there.

Activity 3: Using Standard Verb Forms: *-d* and *-ed* Endings (*page 213*)

1. spilled
2. jailed
3. burned
4. tied
5. measured
6. *C*
7. smashed
8. constructed
9. leveled
10. realized

Activity 4: Using Past Tense Verb Endings (*page 214*)

Brad hated working long hours, but he needed money to support his growing family and to pay for school. He started working at the auto body shop when he graduated from high school because he liked cars, but now the job bored him. He wished that he could spend more time at home with his wife and new baby girl. He also wanted to dedicate more time to his homework. Brad knew that he had made his own choices, so he decided to appreciate his job, his family, and his chance to move ahead in life.

Activity 5: Standard Forms of Irregular Verbs (*page 216*)

1. is
2. do
3. has
4. is
5. have
6. are
7. has
8. do
9. were
10. does

Activity 6: Identifying and Correcting Nonstandard Verbs (*page 216*)

1. ~~does~~ do
2. ~~be~~ is
3. ~~be~~ are
4. ~~has~~ have
5. ~~were~~ was
6. ~~have~~ had
7. ~~was~~ were
8. ~~done~~ did
9. ~~do~~ does
10. ~~have~~ has

Activity 7: Using Standard Forms of *be, have,* and *do* (*page 217*)

My cousin Rita has decided to lose thirty pounds, so she has put herself on a rigid diet that does not allow her to eat anything that she enjoys. Last weekend, while the family was at Aunt Jenny's house for dinner, all Rita had to eat was a can of Diet Delight peaches. We were convinced that Rita meant business when she joined an exercise club whose members have to work out on enormous machines and do twenty sit-ups just to get started. If Rita does reach her goal, we are all going to be very proud of her. But I would not be surprised if she does not succeed, because this is her fourth diet this year.

CHAPTER 11: Irregular Verbs

Introductory Activity (*page 220*)

1. *R* . . . talked . . . talked
2. *I* . . . read . . . read
3. *I* . . . sang . . . sung
4. *R* . . . tasted . . . tasted
5. *R* . . . picked . . . picked
6. *I* . . . made . . . made
7. *I* . . . felt . . . felt
8. *R* . . . typed . . . typed
9. *I* . . . became . . . become
10. *R* . . . mailed . . . mailed

Activity 1: Identifying Incorrect Verb Forms (*page 224*)

1. came
2. stood
3. built
4. swum
5. held
6. drove
7. written
8. blew
9. bought
10. knew

Activity 2: Using Present Tense, Past Tense, and Past Participle Verbs (*page 224*)

1. (a) sleeps
   (b) slept
   (c) slept
2. (a) rings
   (b) rang
   (c) rung
3. (a) write
   (b) wrote
   (c) written
4. (a) stands
   (b) stood
   (c) stood
5. (a) swims
   (b) swam
   (c) swum
6. (a) buys
   (b) bought
   (c) bought
7. (a) choose
   (b) chose
   (c) chosen
8. (a) eats
   (b) ate
   (c) eaten
9. (a) freezes
   (b) froze
   (c) frozen
10. (a) give
    (b) gave
    (c) given

Activity 3: Using *lie* and *lay* (*page 227*)

1. lies
2. Lying
3. laid
4. laid
5. lay

Activity 4: Using *set* and *sit* (*page 228*)

1. set
2. set
3. sit
4. set
5. setting

Activity 5: Using *rise* and *raise* (*page 229*)

1. rises
2. raised
3. rose
4. risen
5. raise

CHAPTER 12: Subject-Verb Agreement

Introductory Activity (*page 231*)

Correct: The postings on the college gossip site are very cruel.

Correct: There were many résumés for the supervisor to read.

Correct: Everybody wants wireless Internet access on campus.

1. postings . . . résumés
2. singular . . . singular

Activity 1: Words between Subjects and Verbs (*page 232*)

1. trail ~~of bloodstains~~ leads
2. clothes ~~in the hall closet~~ take
3. basket ~~of fancy fruit and nuts~~ was
4. instructions ~~for assembling the bicycle~~ were
5. Smoke ~~from the distant forest fires~~ is
6. Workers ~~at that automobile plant~~ begin
7. date ~~on any of the cemetery gravestones~~ appears
8. line ~~of cars in the traffic jam~~ seems
9. boxes ~~in the corner of the attic~~ contain
10. bags ~~with the new insulation material~~ protect

Activity 2: Verbs that Precede Subjects (*page 233*)

1. is noise
2. are berries
3. were cans
4. sits cabin
5. were students
6. stands cutout
7. was shape
8. were sneakers
9. are magazines
10. was row

Activity 3: Using Verbs with Indefinite Pronouns (*page 234*)

1. keeps
2. works
3. pays
4. have
5. slips
6. leans
7. expects
8. was
9. stops
10. has

Activity 4: Using Verbs with Compound Subjects (*page 235*)

1. seem
2. is
3. are
4. help
5. impresses

Activity 5: Using *who*, *which*, or *that* with Verbs (*page 236*)

1. has
2. goes
3. become
4. taste
5. are

Activity 6: Editing and Rewriting (*page 236*)

they do not think

there are enough creatures

guests . . . make

Everybody . . . thinks

somewhere that has

Activity 7: Creating Sentences (*page 237*)

CHAPTER 13: Consistent Verb Tense

Introductory Activity (*page 241*)

Mistakes in verb tense: Alex discovers . . . calls . . . present . . . past

Activity 1: Avoiding Unnecessary Tense Shifts (*page 242*)

1. answered
2. grabbed
3. announced
4. worked
5. called
6. allowed
7. showed
8. stopped
9. placed
10. crowded

CHAPTER 14: Additional Information about Verbs

Activity 1: Using the Correct Verb Tense (*page 247*)

1. have occurred
2. had finished
3. have grown up
4. am taking
5. had written
6. were raising
7. is organizing
8. was presenting
9. have testified
10. was playing

Activity 2: Using Infinitives, Participles, and Gerunds (*page 248*)

1. *P*
2. *G*
3. *I*
4. *G*
5. *I*
6. *P*
7. *P*
8. *P*
9. *G*
10. *I*

Activity 3: Making Sentences Active (*page 249*)

1. The paparazzi clamored to photograph the celebrities on the red carpet.
2. A large falling branch broke the stained-glass window.
3. The professor gave students a five-day extension on the research project.
4. A cigarette started the fire that destroyed the hotel.
5. Doctors must face the pressures of dealing with life and death.
6. The phlebotomist drew blood to randomly test employees for illegal drug use.
7. A thick layer of yellowish grease covered the kitchen shelves.
8. A group of volunteers removed trash in the neighborhood park.
9. Keith has gambled away thousands of dollars playing online video poker.
10. Women of all ages donated their "gently used" prom and bridal dresses to high school girls in need of gowns.

CHAPTER 15: Pronoun Reference, Agreement, and Point of View

Introductory Activity (*page 252*)

1. b
2. b
3. b

Activity 1: Pronoun Reference (*page 254*)

1. Sienna removed the blanket from the sofa bed and folded the blanket up.
2. The defendant told the judge, "I am mentally ill."
3. Before the demonstration, the leaders passed out signs for us to carry.
4. Kristy complained to Rachel, "My (*or* Your) boyfriend is being dishonest."
5. Because I didn't rinse last night's dishes, my kitchen smells like a garbage can.
6. A film on endangered species really depressed the students.

   or: Watching a film on endangered species really depressed the students.
7. The veterinarian said that if I find a tick on my dog, I should get rid of the tick immediately.
8. My sister removed the curtains from the windows so that she could wash the curtains.

   or: So that she could wash the curtains, my sister removed them from the windows.

   or: My sister removed the curtains from the windows so that she could wash the windows.

   or: So that she could wash the windows, my sister removed the curtains from them.
9. Richard said his acupuncture therapist could help my sprained shoulder, but I don't believe in acupuncture.
10. I discovered when I went to sell my old textbooks that publishers have put out new editions, and nobody wants to buy my textbooks.

    or: I discovered when I went to sell my old textbooks that nobody wants to buy them because publishers have put out new editions.

Activity 2: Pronoun Agreement (*page 255*)

1. them
2. their
3. they
4. them
5. it

Activity 3: Using Pronouns Correctly (*page 257*)

1. his
2. his
3. its
4. her
5. them
6. his or her
7. her
8. he
9. her
10. his or her

Activity 4: Correcting Inconsistent Pronouns (*page 259*)

1. my blood
2. they know
3. they have
4. they should receive
5. I can avoid

6. their hands
7. she can worry . . . her own
8. we could
9. she can still have . . . her day
10. our rights

CHAPTER 16: Pronoun Types

Introductory Activity (*page 263*)

Correct sentences:

Andy and I enrolled in a Web design course.

The police officer pointed to my sister and me.

Meg prefers men who take pride in their bodies.

The players are confident that the league championship is theirs.

Those concert tickets are too expensive.

Our parents should spend some money on themselves for a change.

Activity 1: Identifying Subject and Object Pronouns (*page 266*)

1. her (*O*)
2. She (*S*)
3. me (*O*)
4. her and me (*O*)
5. he (*S*)
6. I (*am* is understood) (*S*)
7. they (*S*)
8. me (*O*)
9. We (*S*)
10. I (*S*)

Activity 2: Using Subject or Object Pronouns (*page 266*)

1. I
2. him *or* me
3. they
4. I *or* we
5. us
6. I *or* he *or* she *or* they *or* we
7. they *or* he *or* she
8. I *or* he *or* she *or* they *or* we
9. I *or* he *or* she *or* they *or* we
10. us *or* them

Activity 3: Identifying Correct Relative Pronouns (*page 269*)

1. that
2. that
3. who
4. which
5. whom

Activity 4: Using Relative Pronouns (*page 269*)

Activity 5: Correcting Possessive Pronouns (*page 270*)

1. hers
2. mine
3. ours
4. its
5. their

Activity 6: Correcting Demonstrative Pronouns (*page 271*)

1. This town
2. those seats
3. That dress
4. those chocolates
5. those potholes

Activity 7: Using Demonstrative Pronouns (*page 271*)

Activity 8: Using Reflexive Pronouns (*page 272*)

1. themselves
2. herself
3. himself
4. ourselves
5. themselves

CHAPTER 17: Adjectives and Adverbs

Introductory Activity (*page 276*)

adjective . . . adverb . . . *ly* . . . *er* . . . *est*

Activity 1: Using Comparatives and Superlatives (*page 278*)

tougher	toughest
more practical	most practical
quieter	quietest
more aggressive	most aggressive
clearer	clearest

Activity 2: Using the Correct Comparative and Superlative Forms (*page 278*)

1. best
2. dirtier
3. more considerate
4. worse
5. scariest
6. less
7. more stylish
8. sillier
9. slowest
10. most fattening

Activity 3: Using Adjectives or Adverbs (*page 279*)

1. badly
2. harshly
3. steep
4. frequently
5. truthfully
6. peacefully
7. bright
8. loudly
9. carefully
10. nicely

Activity 4: Using *well* or *good* (*page 280*)

1. well
2. good
3. good
4. well
5. well

CHAPTER 18: Misplaced Modifiers

Introductory Activity (*page 283*)

1. Intended: The grocery clerk was working at the supermarket.

   Unintended: The Mega Millions lottery was working at the supermarket.

2. Intended: The social worker works for the hospital.

   Unintended: The terminally ill patient's family works for the hospital.

Activity 1: Fixing Misplaced Modifiers (*page 284*)

1. At the back of his cage, the tiger growled at a passerby.
2. Lee hung colorful scarves made of green and blue silk over her windows.
3. Standing on our front porch, we watched the fireworks.
4. Jason has almost two hundred friends on Facebook.
5. With a smile, the salesclerk exchanged the blue sweater for a yellow one.
6. We all stared at the man with curly purple hair in the front row of the theater.
7. I love the cookies with the chocolate frosting from the bakery.
8. During their last meeting, the faculty decided to strike.
9. Larry looked on with disbelief as his car burned.
10. My cousin sent me instructions in a letter on how to get to her house.

Activity 2: Placing Modifiers Correctly (*page 285*)

1. Using caution, I rolled down my car window only a few inches for the police officer.
2. Tabloids all over the world publish unflattering photos of celebrities who are arrested for drunk driving or possession of illicit drugs.
3. The mongoose, which resembles the ferret, was brought to Hawaii to kill rats but has since destroyed much of the native plant life.
4. Led Zeppelin's fourth album has sold almost 22 million copies.
5. Elisa decided to undergo laser eye surgery at the university medical center to correct her astigmatism.

CHAPTER 19: Dangling Modifiers

Introductory Activity (*page 289*)

1. Intended: The grilled T-bone steak was sizzling.

   Unintended: The customer at the restaurant was sizzling.

2. Intended: Eric arrived home from college.

   Unintended: Eric's parents arrived home from college.

Activity 1: Correcting Dangling Modifiers (*page 291*)

1. A security guard pointed to the priceless painting that was hanging safely on a wall.
2. When I was five, my mother bought me a chemistry set.
3. C
4. Since the milk had turned sour, I would not drink it.
5. While I was updating my Facebook profile, my hot tea turned cold.
6. Pete hated to look at the kitchen sink, which was piled high with dirty dishes.
7. Because I locked my keys in the car, the police had to open it for me.
8. Because the plants were drooping and looking all dried out, the children watered them.
9. After I sat through a long lecture, my foot was asleep.
10. Since I was late, stopping for Starbucks was out of the question.

Activity 2: Placing Modifiers Correctly (*page 292*)

CHAPTER 20: Faulty Parallelism

Introductory Activity (*page 295*)

Correct sentences:

I use my TV remote control to change channels, to adjust the volume, and to turn the set on and off.

One option the employees had was to take a cut in pay; the other was to work longer hours.

The refrigerator has a cracked vegetable drawer, a missing shelf, and a strange freezer smell.

Activity 1: Using Parallelism (*page 296*)

1. (example: fast service)
2. howling dogs
3. rude
4. hiking
5. poor security
6. cleaned the apartment
7. having fun
8. inexpensive desserts
9. on the closet floor
10. sings in the church choir

Activity 2: Creating Nonparallel Sentences (*page 297*)

1. waited
2. cramming
3. illness
4. late buses
5. attracting
6. to suffocate
7. interrupted
8. financial security
9. birds chirping
10. breathed fire

Activity 3: Writing Parallel Sentences (*page 298*)

Activity 4: Editing and Rewriting (*page* 299)

1. Running is an exercise that can be good for you mentally, physically, and emotionallly.
2. A beginning runner should keep three things in mind: the warm-up session, the run, and the cool-down period.
4. Stretching reduces muscle stiffness, decreases the possibility of injury, and gradually increases the heart rate.
6. Your breathing should be steady and deep.
8. An adequate cool-down period allows time for the body to relax and the heart rate to normalize.

Activity 5: Creating Sentences (*page* 299)

CHAPTER 21: Sentence Variety II

Activity 1: Combining Sentences with *-ing* Words (*page* 304)

1. Gathering up their books and backpacks, the students began leaving the lecture hall.
2. Crossing the street with her daughter, Susan was involved in a hit-and-run accident.
3. Rushing to class, Arnold parked his motorcycle on the school lawn.
4. Acting quickly, the nurse brought the patient his pain medication.
5. Knowing that his team would lose the game, the football coach buried his face in his hands.

Activity 2: Using *-ing* Word Groups (*page* 305)

Activity 3: Combining Sentences with *-ed* Words (*page* 305)

1. Mary, startled by thunder, sat up suddenly in bed.
2. Married for fifty years, my parents decided to have a second wedding.
3. Frightened by the large dog near the curb, Erica wouldn't leave her car.
4. Dotted with mold, the old orange felt like a marshmallow.
5. Scott, determined to have plenty to eat during the movie, made a huge sandwich and popped popcorn.

Activity 4: Using *-ed* Word Groups (*page* 306)

Activity 5: Combining Sentences with *-ly* Words (*page* 307)

1. Hungrily, we ordered extra-large pepperoni pizzas and buffalo wings.
2. Suddenly, Nino left the party.
3. Lazily, I watched TV all afternoon.
4. Eagerly, David returned the customer's phone call.
5. Surprisingly, the visiting team won the game in double overtime.

Activity 6: Using *-ly* Words (*page* 308)

Activity 7: Combining Sentences with *to* Word Groups (*page* 308)

1. To make the tub less slippery, Lily put a thick towel on the bottom.
2. To keep raccoons away, we now keep our garbage in the garage.
3. To count his pulse, Bill pressed two fingers against the large vein in his neck.
4. To steam her face, my aunt opens her dishwasher when it begins drying.
5. To help out the homeless, we looked through our closets for unused clothing.

Activity 8: Using *to* (*page* 309)

Activity 9: Combining Sentences by Opening with Prepositional Phrases (*page* 309)

1. About once a week, we have dinner with my parents at a restaurant.
2. Before company came, I put the dirty cups away in the cupboard.
3. During my English exam, my eyes roamed around the room until they met the instructor's eye.
4. For twenty minutes, the little boy drew intently in a comic book without stopping once.
5. At the zoo, a playful young orangutan wriggled in a corner under a paper sack.

Activity 10: Using Prepositional Phrases (*page* 311)

Activity 11: Using Adjectives in a Series (*page* 311)

1. The old, peeling shingles blew off the roof during the blustery storm.
2. The lean, powerful dancer whirled across the stage with his graceful, elegant partner.
3. A large, furry rat scurried into the crowded kitchen of the restaurant.
4. The full, golden moon lit up the cloudy sky like a huge floating streetlamp.
5. The oval plastic doorbell of the large, ornate house played a loud rock tune.

Activity 12: Writing with Adjectives in a Series (*page 313*)

Activity 13: Combining Sentences with Verbs in a Series (*page 313*)

1. The robber scanned the liquor store for a surveillance camera, fidgeted with his dark sunglasses and baseball cap, and signaled to the clerk behind the counter that he had a handgun.
2. In the sports bar, Tanner placed a bet on his favorite basketball team, took a swig from his bottle of Budweiser, and sat back to watch the NBA playoff semi-finals.
3. The phlebotomist pressed down on Logan's forearm, slid the needle into his arm, and let out a heavy sigh as the needle missed his vein.
4. The comedy hypnotist invited a volunteer to the stage, quickly brought her into a trance, and offered her a clove of garlic, which she thought was a cashew nut.
5. The paparazzo stalked the Hollywood actor on vacation, adjusted his telephoto lens, and snapped hundreds of candid photos.

Activity 14: Using Verbs in a Series (*page 314*)

CHAPTER 22: Paper Format

Introductory Activity (*page 319*)

In "A," the title is capitalized and has no quotation marks around it; there is a blank line between the title and the body of the paper; there are left and right margins around the body of the paper; no words are incorrectly hyphenated.

Activity 1: Correcting Formatting Errors (*page 321*)

1. (example: Break words at correct syllable divisions (sis-ter))
2. Do not use quotation marks around the title.
3. Capitalize the major words in the title ("Being a Younger Sister").
4. Skip a line between the title and first line of the paper.
5. Indent the first line of the paper.
6. Keep margins on both sides of the paper.

Activity 2: Writing Titles (*page 321*)

1. Benefits of Pets
2. Learning How to Budget
3. The Value of a Study Group
4. A Special Relationship *or* Grandparents and Grandchildren
5. A Wise Decision

Activity 3: Rewriting Dependent Sentences (*page 322*)

1. Effective communication is often the key to a healthy relationship.
2. Reality TV shows are popular for several reasons.
3. Correct
4. The best vacation I ever had began when my friends from high school booked a one-week trip to Cancun, Mexico.
5. Most professional athletes say that they don't use steroids to enhance athletic performance.

CHAPTER 23: Capital Letters

Introductory Activity (*page 324*)

1–13: Answers will vary, but all should be capitalized.
14–16: On . . . "Let's . . . I

Activity 1: Capitalizing Names and Titles (*page 326*)

1. I . . . Boy Scouts
2. Friday . . . Thanksgiving . . . Target
3. Regal Cinema . . . If
4. New England . . . Republicans . . . Democrats
5. State Farm . . . Nationwide . . . Prudential Building
6. *Time* . . . *Newsweek* . . . California
7. Valentine's Day . . . Mother's Day
8. Pepsis . . . Fritos . . . Macintosh
9. Ford Taurus . . . Saturday
10. Broadway . . . *My Fair Lady*

Activity 2: Where Is Capitalization Needed? (*page 329*)

1. Uncle David
2. Motorola Razr . . . Bluetooth
3. United States President Jimmy Carter . . . Nobel Peace Prize
4. Pacific Islander . . . Samoa . . . East Coast
5. Principles . . . Marketing

Activity 3: Where Is Capitalization Unnecessary? (*page 330*)

1. husband . . . barbeque ribs
2. community college . . . technical writer
3. electronics store . . . televisions . . . players
4. community organizations . . . food drive
5. science teacher . . . tidal pools

Activity 4: Editing and Rewriting (*page 330*)

1. Lincoln, Memorial
2. Thursday, October

3. Uncle, Walt, Smithsonian, Institution
4. Now
5. Lincoln's
6. Potomac, River
7. Gettysburg, Address
9. Kodak

Activity 5: Creating Sentences (*page 331*)

CHAPTER 24: Numbers and Abbreviations

Introductory Activity (*page 334*)

Correct choices:

First sentence: 7:30 . . . 75 percent
Second sentence: Eighty-five . . . fifteen
Second sentence: 9 a.m.
Second sentence: hour . . . minutes

Activity 1: Using Numbers (*page 335*)

1. 2:30
2. five
3. eleven . . . seventy-seven
4. five . . . four
5. 15
6. 206
7. 15
8. two hundred
9. 7 . . . 2007
10. seven

Activity 2: Using Abbreviations (*page 336*)

1. newspaper . . . telephone
2. bushels . . . market . . . Route
3. Monday . . . September
4. psychology . . . England
5. chicken . . . macaroni
6. ounce . . . tablespoon
7. chemistry . . . Sunday . . . hours
8. January . . . company . . . year
9. license . . . medical
10. veteran . . . business . . . college

CHAPTER 25: End Marks

Introductory Activity (*page 339*)

1. depressed.   3. parked.
2. paper?   4. control!

Activity 1: Using End Punctuation (*page 340*)

1. door?   6. "Gotcha!"
2. message.   7. "Got milk?"
3. jerk?   8. storm.
4. shocked.   9. think?"
5. psychology.   10. officer.

CHAPTER 26: Apostrophes

Introductory Activity (*page 342*)

1. In each case, the 's indicates possession or ownership.
2. The apostrophes indicate omitted letters and shortened spellings.
3. In the first sentence, s indicates a plural noun; in the second sentence, 's indicates possession.

Activity 1: Combining Words (*page 343*)

you've	we're	couldn't
haven't	you'll	they'll
he's	we'd	doesn't

Activity 2: Forming Contractions (*page 343*)

1. didn't . . . wasn't   4. isn't . . . you've
2. doesn't . . . she's   5. We'd . . . don't
3. You're . . . can't

Activity 3: Using the Apostrophe (*page 344*)

Activity 4: Using Apostrophes Correctly (*page 345*)

1. Your . . . you're   4. There . . . they're
2. your . . . its   5. It's . . . they're
3. whose . . . Who's

Activity 5: Using 's to Show Possession (*page 346*)

1. singer's voice
2. Dawn's garage
3. Murphy's law
4. computer's memory
5. my wife's mother
6. yesterday's meat loaf
7. My sister's promotion
8. Alexis's bratty little brother
9. the referee's call
10. the tanker's hull

Activity 6: Identifying Possessive Nouns (*page 347*)

1. horse's   3. son's
2. brother's   4. comedian's

5. landlord's
6. Ted's
7. teller's
8. people's
9. studio's
10. girl's

Activity 7: Making Words Possessive (*page 348*)

1. (example: Aaron's)
2. bus's
3. computer's
4. Ross's
5. pizza's

Activity 8: Apostrophes vs. Simple Plurals (*page 349*)

1. parlors: parlor's, meaning "belonging to the parlor"
   aromas: simple plural meaning more than one aroma
   vents: simple plural meaning more than one vent
2. cars: car's, meaning "belonging to the car"
   streets: simple plural meaning more than one street
   buildings: simple plural meaning more than one building
3. Karens: Karen's, meaning "belonging to Karen"
   plants: simple plural meaning more than one plant
   stakes: simple plural meaning more than one stake
4. lakes: lake's, meaning "belonging to the lake"
   officials: simple plural meaning more than one official
5. positions: simple plural meaning more than one position
   exterminators: exterminator's, meaning "belonging to an exterminator"
6. candlelights: candlelight's, meaning "belonging to the candlelight"
   plates: simple plural meaning more than one plate
   goblets: simple plural meaning more than one goblet
7. Crackers: simple plural meaning more than one cracker
   slices: simple plural meaning more than one slice
   fathers: father's, meaning "belonging to my father"
8. insects: insect's, meaning "belonging to the insect"
   eggs: simple plural meaning more than one egg
   worms: simple plural meaning more than one worm
9. Seabirds: simple plural meaning more than one seabird
   oceans: ocean's, meaning "belonging to the ocean"
   surfers: simple plural meaning more than one surfer
10. daughters: daughter's, meaning "belonging to my daughter"
    prayers: simple plural meaning more than one prayer
    schools: simple plural meaning more than one school

Activity 9: Missing Apostrophes (*page 350*)

1. nurses' union
2. sisters' feet
3. lions' keeper
4. The Tylers' new flat screen TV
5. parents' wedding pictures

Activity 10: Editing and Rewriting (*page 351*)

1. My neighbor's dog
2. there's
3. the dog's constant barking . . . can't
5. my landlord's fence
7. I've
8. there's . . . the dog's behavior
9. that's . . . doesn't

Activity 11: Creating Sentences (*page 351*)

CHAPTER 27: Quotation Marks

Introductory Activity (*page 354*)

1. Quotation marks set off the exact words of a speaker.
2. Commas and periods following quotations go inside quotation marks.

Activity 1: Using Quotation Marks (*page 356*)

1. The chilling bumper sticker read, "You can't hug children with nuclear arms."
2. "One day we'll look back on this argument, and it will seem funny," Bruce assured Rosa.
3. "Hey, lady, this is an express line!" shouted the cashier to the woman with a full basket.
4. My grandfather was fond of saying, "Happiness is found along the way, not at the end of the road."
5. "When will I be old enough to pay the adult fare?" the child asked.
6. On his deathbed, Oscar Wilde is supposed to have said, "Either this wallpaper goes or I do."
7. The sign on my neighbor's front door reads, "Never mind the dog. Beware of owner."
8. "I'm not afraid to die," said Woody Allen. "I just don't want to be there when it happens."
9. My son once told me, "Sometimes I wish I were little again. Then I wouldn't have to make so many decisions."
10. "I don't feel like cooking tonight," Eve said to Adam. "Let's just have fruit."

Activity 2: Formatting Quotations (*page 356*)

1. The firefighter asked the neighbors, "Is there anyone else still in the building?"
2. "You'll have to remove your sunglasses," the security guard reminded the customers at the bank.
3. Upon eating a few drops of Horacio's homemade habanero sauce, Trudy yelped, "That's hot!"
4. "Good things come to those who wait," Zhao told himself as he waited in line for hours to buy an iPhone.
5. "If at first you don't succeed," my wife joked, "you should read the directions."

Activity 3: Writing with Quotation Marks (*page 357*)

Activity 4: Using Dialogue (*page 358*)

1. (example: Agnes said to me as we left work, "Henry got a raise.")
2. I said, "That's hard to believe, since Henry is a do-nothing."
3. Agnes replied, "Even so, he's gone up in the world."
4. I told her, "You must be kidding."
5. Agnes laughed and said, "Henry was moved from the first to the fourth floor today."

Activity 5: Converting Quotations into Indirect Statements (*page 359*)

1. Josh muttered that he is so tired of studying for finals.
2. The dental hygienist asked me if I brush and floss regularly.
3. Leona asked Matt if he would mind if she copied his lecture notes.
4. The security guard asked me if I had seen any suspicious activity in the building.
5. The delivery driver asked if I would mind signing for the package.

Activity 6: Using Quotations in Titles (*page 360*)

1. My sister just bought a TiVo so she won't have to miss any more episodes of General Hospital.
2. Rhianna grabbed the National Enquirer and eagerly began to read the article "I Had a Space Alien's Baby."
3. Our exam will cover two chapters, "The Study of Heredity" and "The Origin of Diversity," in our biology textbook, Life.
4. The last song on the bluegrass program was called "I Ain't Broke but I'm Badly Bent."
5. The classic 1980s movie Stand by Me was actually based on "The Body," a short story written by Stephen King.
6. At last night's performance of Annie Get Your Gun, the audience joined the cast in singing "There's No Business Like Show Business."
7. A typical article in Cosmopolitan will have a title like "How to Hook a Man without Letting Him Know You're Fishing."
8. One way Joanne deals with depression is to get out her Man of La Mancha album and play the song "The Impossible Dream."
9. I read the article "How Good Is Your Breakfast?" in Consumer Reports while munching a doughnut this morning.
10. According to a Psychology Today article titled "Home on the Street," there are 36,000 people living on New York City's sidewalks.

Activity 7: Editing and Rewriting (*page 361*)

3. . . . asked, "Has . . . before?"
4. "Once," she said.
5–6. "About . . . long."
8–9. "We're . . . ones."
10. asked, "Is . . . somebody?"
12. read, "Open . . . Emergency."
13. "I . . . there," she said, pointing to the sign.
15. "Can anyone hear me?" he asked.
16–17. "Yes, . . . minutes."
19. "I . . . quickly," he said softly, wringing his hands.
21–22. "Don't . . . time."

Activity 8: Creating Sentences (*page 362*)

CHAPTER 28: Commas

Introductory Activity (*page 365*)

1. a: card, . . . check, . . . ; ants, roaches,
2. b: car, . . . ; hiking,
3. c: leeches, . . . blood, . . . ; Derek, . . . arrested,
4. d: easy, . . . ; trees,
5. e: asked, . . . ; work, . . . said,
6. f: 1,500,000; Newark, New Jersey, . . . August 26, 2009,

Activity 1: Commas between Items in a Series (*page 367*)

1. sunglasses, a bottle of water, and a recent issue of *Every Day with Rachael Ray*
2. e-mail, play games, surf the Internet, download music, and send instant messages
3. igloo-shaped doghouse, several plastic toys, trampled flowers, and a cracked ceramic gnome

Activity 2: Necessary and Unnecessary Commas (*page 367*)

1. pennies, and a sock hidden under the seats
2. Squirrels, . . . and clouds of mosquitoes populate
3. spun to his left, . . . arms of the Panthers' center

Activity 3: Commas after Introductory Clauses (*page 368*)

1. airport,   2. library,   3. others,

Activity 4: More Necessary and Unnecessary Commas (*page 368*)

1. presents, . . . ribbon and tied
2. aisle, I saw a bead of sweat roll from her forehead
3. For example, I wrote a note to remind me that

Activity 5: Commas That Set Off Interruptions (*page 370*)

1. clerk, assisted by no one,
2. Craig, who were engaged for a year,
3. furniture, rusted beyond repair,

Activity 6: More Necessary and Unnecessary Commas (*page 370*)

1. gigantic, . . . the rest is deadwood
2. council, in a rare fit of wisdom
3. presidents of the United States,
4. aunt, a talkative woman,

Activity 7: Commas That Connect Complete Thoughts (*page 371*)

1. spacious, but
2. thunderstorm, so
3. C
4. space, for
5. C
6. supermarket, but
7. C
8. college, but
9. schoolwork, but
10. C

Activity 8: Setting Off Quotations with Commas (*page 372*)

1. speak,"
2. miseducated, " said John F. Kennedy,
3. building," muttered the patrol officer,

Activity 9: More Necessary and Unnecessary Commas (*page 372*)

1. poster in the subway station,
2. fine," . . . forgetting to kick."
3. think," the judge asked the defendant,

Activity 10: Adding Commas (*page 373*)

1. me, madam,
2. 6,000 . . . 15,000
3. 15, 1912.
4. Teresa, . . . Love,
5. Washington, D.C., . . . 50,000 . . . 6,500 . . . 114,000

Activity 11: Eliminating Unnecessary Commas (*page 374*)

1. We grew a pumpkin last year that weighed over one hundred pounds.
2. Anyone with a failing grade must meet with the instructor during office hours.
3. Last weekend a grizzly bear attacked a hiker who got too close to its cubs.
4. After watching my form on the high diving board, Mr. Riley, my instructor, asked me if I had insurance.

5. Rosa flew first to Los Angeles, and then she went to visit her parents in Mexico City.
6. The tall muscular man wearing the dark sunglasses is a professional wrestler.
7. Onions, radishes, and potatoes seem to grow better in cooler climates.
8. Whenever Vincent is in Las Vegas, you can find him at the blackjack table or the roulette wheel.
9. While I watched in disbelief, my car rolled down the hill and through the front window of a Chinese restaurant.
10. The question, sir, is not whether you committed the crime but when you committed the crime.

Activity 12: Editing and Rewriting (*page 375*)

On Tuesday, May 4, 2004, my husband$_x$ and I were unable to sleep because of the loud music coming from your apartment. When I first heard the music, I didn't say anything to you because it was still early. But the music, along with loud$_x$ laughter and talking, continued until around four o'clock in the morning. At midnight, my husband went into the hallway to see what was happening, and he ran into one of your guests. The man, who seemed very drunk, stared at him$_x$ and said, "Go back to bed, old man." The next morning, we found beer cans, pizza boxes, and cigarette butts$_x$ piled outside our door. This is unacceptable. We have written this letter to you as a warning. The next time something like this happens, we will call the police$_x$ and the building manager. We don't want to cause trouble with you, but we will not tolerate another incident like what happened that night.

Activity 13: Creating Sentences (*page 376*)

CHAPTER 29: Other Punctuation Marks

Introductory Activity (*page 379*)

1. list:
2. chocolate-dipped
3. (1994–2008)
4. seriously;
5. abused—but happy

Activity 1: Using Colons (*page 380*)

1. diet:
2. summer:
3. columns:

Activity 2: Using Semicolons (*page 381*)

1. library; consequently,
2. crying; my
3. roommate; Rami . . . boyfriend; and

Activity 3: Using the Dash (*page 381*)

1. sea—shivering
2. —her third in three years—
3. time—eight

Activity 4: Using Hyphens (*page 382*)

1. rabbit-ear . . . high-definition
2. hole-in-the-wall . . . hoity-toity
3. hard-working . . . out-of-towners

Activity 5: Using Parentheses (*page 383*)

1. Americans (80 percent) had
2. hours (3:00 to 4:00 p.m.) are
3. often (1) make a list and then (2) check off items I have done.

CHAPTER 30: Dictionary Use

Introductory Activity (*page 386*)

1. fortutious (fortuitous)
2. hi/er/o/glyph/ics
3. be
4. oc/to/ge/naŕ/i/an (primary accent is on *nar*)
5. (1) identifying mark on the ear of a domestic animal (2) identifying feature or characteristic

Answers to the practice activities are in your dictionary. Check with your instructor if you have any problems.

Activity 1: Using a Dictionary (*page 387*)

arguing . . . friend . . . mortgage . . . reference . . . beautiful . . . marriage . . . achieve . . . tournament . . . ninety . . . appearance . . . representative . . . yesterday . . . unanimous . . . visitor . . . unusual . . . hammer . . . committed . . . vegetable

Activity 2: Marking Syllable Divisions (*page 387*)

2 . . . 3 . . . 4 . . . 5 . . .

Activity 3: Understanding Vowel Sounds (*page 388*)

pet . . . pie . . . pot . . . toe . . . cut . . . boot

Activity 4: Using the Schwa (*page 389*)

Activity 5: Using a Dictionary's Abbreviations Key (*page 390*)

plural . . . singular . . . adjective . . . adverb

Activity 6: Principal Parts (*page 391*)

choose - chose - chosen - choosing
know - knew - known - knowing
speak - spoke - spoken - speaking

Activity 7: Writing Plural Forms (*page 391*)

countries . . . volcanoes . . . curricula . . . women

Activity 8: Using Sentence Context (*page 391*)

Dictionary definitions:

1. Of foremost importance
2. requiring skillful or tactful handling
3. expressed objections or criticisms in bitter, harsh, or abusive language

Activity 9: Etymology (*page 392*)

magazine: from a French word meaning "storehouse"
anatomy: from the Greek anatome, meaning "dissection"
frankfurter: after Frankfurt, Germany

Activity 10: Usage (*page 393*)

informal . . . informal . . . informal . . . nonstandard . . . slang

Activity 11: Synonyms (*page 393*)

desire: covet, crave, want, wish
ask: question, inquire, query, interrogate, examine, quiz
cry: weep, wail, whimper, sob, blubber

CHAPTER 31: Spelling Improvement

Introductory Activity (*page 395*)

Misspellings:

akward . . . exercize . . . buisness . . . worryed . . . shamful . . . begining . . . partys . . . sandwichs . . . heros

Activity 1: Using Correct Endings (*page 397*)

1. hurried
2. admiring
3. denies
4. jabbing
5. magnified
6. committed
7. diving
8. hastily
9. propelling
10. nudges

Activity 2: Using Plural Endings or Forms (*page 398*)

1. buses
2. patches
3. therapies
4. batches
5. reefs
6. avocados
7. fifties
8. knives
9. daughters-in-law
10. theses

CHAPTER 32: Omitted Words and Letters

Introductory Activity (*page 402*)

bottles . . . in the supermarket . . . like a wind-up toy . . . his arms . . . an alert shopper . . . with the crying

Activity 1: Adding Missing Words (*page 403*)

1. I grabbed a metal bar on the roof of the subway car as the train lurched into the station.
2. For most of our country's history, gold was the basis of the monetary system.
3. Maggie made about a quart of French-toast batter—enough to soak a few dozen slices.
4. Several pairs of sneakers tumbled around in the dryer and banged against the glass door.
5. To err is human and to forgive is divine, but never to make a mistake in the first place takes a lot of luck.
6. Raccoons like to wash their food in a stream with their nimble, glove-like hands before eating.
7. When I got to the grocery store, I realized I had left my shopping list in the glove compartment of my car.
8. Reality shows are an inexpensive way for networks to make a high profit.
9. Soap operas, on the other hand, are very expensive to produce because of the high salaries of many cast members.
10. One memorable Friday the thirteenth, a friend of mine bought a black cat and a broken mirror and walked under a ladder. He had a wonderful day!

Activity 2: Using -s Endings (*page 404*)

1. sightseers . . . ghouls
2. sets . . . names
3. Dozens . . . beetles
4. dentists . . . restaurants . . . lines
5. workers . . . departments
6. lights . . . games . . . cars . . . persons
7. games . . . balls
8. shoes . . . jeans . . . months
9. stamps . . . pens
10. Workers . . . logs . . . chunks . . . chips

Activity 3: Writing with Plural Forms (*page 405*)

CHAPTER 33: Commonly Confused Words

Introductory Activity (*page 407*)

1. Incorrect: your   Correct: you're
2. Incorrect: who's   Correct: whose
3. Incorrect: there   Correct: their
4. Incorrect: to   Correct: too
5. Incorrect: Its   Correct: It's

Activity 1: Homonyms (*page 408*)

all ready . . . already
break . . . brake
course . . . coarse
here . . . hear
whole . . . hole
its . . . it's
new . . . knew
know . . . no
pair . . . pear
passed . . . past
peace . . . piece
plane . . . plain
principal . . . principle
right . . . write
then . . . than
there . . . their . . . they're
through . . . threw
two . . . too . . . to
where . . . wear
weather . . . whether
who's . . . whose
you're . . . your

Activity 2: Commonly Confused Words (*page 415*)

an . . . a
except . . . accept
advice . . . advise
affect . . . effect
among . . . between
beside . . . besides
can . . . may
cloths . . . clothes
desert . . . dessert
dose . . . does
fewer . . . less
former . . . latter
learn . . . teach
loose . . . lose
quite . . . quiet
though . . . thought

Activity 3: Incorrect Word Forms (*page* 419)

being that

1. Since (*or* Because) our stove doesn't work
2. since (*or* because) they don't speak to each other
3. since (*or* because) it's my birthday

can't hardly / couldn't hardly

1. I could hardly
2. I can hardly
3. everyone can hardly

could of

1. you could have
2. you could have
3. I could have

irregardless

1. Regardless of your feelings
2. regardless of the weather
3. regardless of age

must of / should of / would of

1. I must have
2. he would have
3. You should have

CHAPTER 34: Effective Word Choice

Introductory Activity (*page* 423)

Correct sentences:

1. After playing basketball with my friends, I quickly drank a soda.
2. Even though my essay was concise, I tried my best.
3. I will try to finish the report after lunch.
4. If my daughter calls while I am in a meeting, please tell her that I am unavailable.

   1 . . . 2 . . . 3 . . . 4

Activity 1: Avoiding Slang (*page* 424)

1. When I confronted my ex-boyfriend about cheating on me, he simply shrugged and said, "It was my fault."
2. My friend thinks that Chantel is attractive, but I think she's too emotional.

3. Rayna is on her cell phone all the time, but that's fine.
4. Joe wanted to quickly leave the family dinner so that he could meet his friends.
5. Everyone at the gym thinks that Gavin is taking steroids, but he swears that he doesn't use steroids to get his well-toned abdominal muscles.

Activity 2: Avoiding Clichés (*page* 426)

1. Substitute In brief for To make a long story short.
2. Substitute Very quickly for As quick as a wink.
3. Substitute is ignored for goes in one ear and out the other.
4. Substitute was delighted for felt like a million dollars.
5. Substitute rare for few and far between.

Activity 3: Avoiding Inflated Words (*page* 427)

1. Please ask one of our salespeople.
2. The weather is terrible today.
3. My parents want me to get a college degree.
4. Do not put your arm out of the car, or an accident might happen.
5. Many fires are caused by the careless use of portable heaters.

Activity 4: Omitting Unnecessary Words (*page* 429)

1. There is no cure for the common cold.
2. My main point is that our state should legalize gambling.
3. Because Chen's car wouldn't start, he took a bus to work.
4. Even when I was a boy, my goal was to be a stockbroker.
5. Susan's daily exercises energize her.

CREDITS

Photo Credits

Part 1

Page 3: © Corbis; p. 4: © Jamie Squire/Getty; p. 15: © Steven Weinberg/Stone/Getty; Chapter Opener 2: © Richard Lord Enterprises/The Image Works; p. 42: © Jeff Greenberg/Photo Edit.

Part 2

Page 45 top: © Photodisc/PunchStock; p. 45 bottom: © Digital Vision/Getty; CO 3: © Tim McGuire/Corbis; p. 51 top: © Darren Hopes/Getty; p. 51 bottom: © Frank May/dpa/Corbis; p. 52 top: © Nick White/Digital Vision/Getty; p. 52 middle: © Amanda Edwards/Getty; p. 52 bottom: © David Young Wolff/Photo Edit; p. 84: Library of Congress; CO 4 Superdome: top © Mario Tama/Getty; bottom © Mark Wilson/Getty; CO 4 Highway: © Mario Tama/Getty; p. 110 right: © David Buffington/Getty; p. 110 left: © McGraw-Hill Companies, Inc./Gary He, photographer; p. 125 both: © Angela Gaul; CO 5: © Reunion des Musees Nationaux/Art Resource, NY; p. 146 top right: © The Bridgeman Art Library/Getty; p. 146 top left: © Jim Zuckerman/Corbis; p. 146 bottom: © Vatican Museums and Galleries, Vatican City, Italy/Getty.

Part 3

Opener: © Owaki/Kulla/Corbis; p. 152 bottom: © Andrew Walsh; p. 152 top: Courtesy of Sheryl Stephen;

Section II Opener: © Natalie Hummel; p. 313: © Peter Adams/Getty; SO IV top: © Oren Levine; SO IV bottom: © Ryan Caiazzo; p. 351: © Nicole Hill/Getty; SO V: © Lisa Beebe.

Part 4

Opener: © Livia Corona/Taxi/Getty; p. 442: Courtesy of the Franciscan Sisters of Little Falls, Minnesota; p. 446: © Ryan McVay/Taxi/Getty; p. 455: © Bob Daemmrich/Photo Edit; p. 466: © BananaStock/PictureQuest; p. 468: Courtesy of Rose Del Castillo Guilbault; p. 473: © Royalty-Free/Corbis; p. 475: Courtesy of Firoozeh Dumas; p. 480: Library of Congress, Prints and Photographs Division; p. 483: © Joe Giza/Reuters/Corbis; p. 492: © Mark Peterson/Corbis; p. 499: © Left Lane Productions/Corbis; p. 501: © Larry Marcus of Minneapolis, MN; p. 508: © Louie Psihoyos/Corbis; p. 521: © Jason LaVeris/FilmMagic/Getty; p. 525: © Kevin S. Moul; p. 529: © BananaStock/PunchStock; p. 535: © Photodisc Red/Getty; p. 545: © ImageSource; p. 546: © Frank Capri/Hulton Archive/Getty; p. 551: © Kelly & Massa; p. 556: © Fabio Cardoso/zefa/Corbis; p. 565: © The McGraw-Hill Companies, Inc./Lars A. Niki, photographer; p. 566: © Eric Neitzel/WireImage/Getty.

Text/Line Art Credits

Chapter 35

p. 442 Sister Helen P. Mrosla, O.S.F., "All the Good Things." Originally, "Good Night, Sister, Thank You For Teaching Me" in *Proteus*, Spring, 1991. Reprinted with permission as edited and published by *Reader's Digest* in October, 1991.

p. 448 Paul Logan, "Rowing the Bus." Copyright © 1997. Reprinted by permission of the author.

p. 455 Rick Bragg, "All She Has—$150,000—Is Going to a University" from *The New York Times*, August 13, 1995. Copyright © 1995 The New York Times. All rights reserved. Used by permission.

p. 462 Mee Her, "Bowling to Find a Lost Father" from *Passages: An Anthology of the Southeast Asian Refugee Experience*, compiled by Katsuyo Howard. California State University, Fresno (1990). Reprinted with permission.

p. 468 Rose Del Castillo Guilbault, "Hispanic USA: The Conveyor-Belt Ladies" in *San Francisco Chronicle*, "This World," April 15, 1990. Reprinted by permission of the San Francisco Chronicle, via Copyright Clearance Center.

p. 475 The "F Word" from *Funny in Farsi: A Memoir of Growing Up Iranian in America* by Firoozeh Dumas.

Chapter 36

Chapter 37

INDEX

A

abbreviations
  achievement test, 616
  diagnostic test, 611
  in formal writing, 336
  practice activity, 336–37
  review test, 337–38
abbreviations key, 390
accent marks, 389
added detail fragments, 170–72
adjectives, 282, 592
  achievement test, 615
  activities using, 593, 607
  adverbs and, 279–80, 610–11
  comparatives and superlatives,
    278–79
  introductory activity, 276
  irregular forms, 278
  to make comparisons, 277
  more and *most*, 277
  present and past participles
    as, 606
  review tests, 281–82
  in series, 311–13, 605–6
adverbs, 593
  achievement test, 615
  activities using, 594
  adjectives *v.*, 279–80, 610–11
  review tests, 281–82
  using *well* or *good*, 280–81
all ready v. already, 408
"All She Has—$150,000—Is Going
    to a University" (Bragg)
  content, 459
  preview, 455
  reading comprehension, 458–59
  structure, 459–60
  style and tone, 460
  vocabulary in context, 458
  words to watch, 455
  writing assignments, 460–62
"All the Good Things" (Mrosla)
  content, 445–46
  preview, 442
  reading comprehension, 444–45
  structure, 446
  style and tone, 446
  visual prompt, 446

  vocabulary in context, 444
  words to watch, 442
  writing assignments, 447
Angelou, Maya ("Reclaiming Our
    Home Place"), 566–72
another v. other, 68
apostrophe, 78, 79, 611–12
  achievement test, 616
  in contractions, 343–45
  introductory activity, 342
  missing, 350–51
  practice writing with, 351–52
  review tests, 352–53
  to show ownership, 345–48
argumentation writing, 87,
    122, 124
  beyond the classroom, 125
  example, 121
  prewriting, 123–24
  revising, 124
  visual prompt for, 122
articles
  activities using, 600
  with count *v.* noncount nouns,
    597–99
  omitting, 599
  with proper nouns, 599–600
  types of, 597
attitude
  toward subject matter, 87
  toward writing, 10–12
audience, in paragraph
    development, 86–87
auxiliaries, 402–3

B

back up (saving your document), 32
"Baking a Cake" (Goldberg)
  content, 528
  preview, 525
  reading comprehension, 527–28
  structure, 528
  style and tone, 528–29
  visual prompt, 529
  vocabulary in context, 527
  words to watch, 525
  writing assignments, 529–30

Barrett, Katherine ("Old Before
    Her Time"), 537–46
Berry, Grant ("A Change of
    Attitude"), 501–10
blogs, 14
boldface, 287
Boutin, Paul ("A Grand Unified
    Theory of YouTube and
    MySpace"), 579–84
"Bowling to Find a Lost Father"
    (Her)
  content, 465
  preview, 465
  reading comprehension, 464
  structure, 466
  style and tone, 466
  visual prompt, 466
  vocabulary in context, 464
  words to watch, 462
  writing assignments, 466–67
Bragg, Rick ("All She Has
    —$150,000—Is Going to a
    University"), 455–62
brainstorming, 21–22
brake v. break, 408

C

capital letters, 78
  achievement test, 616
  correcting run-ons, 181–83
  diagnostic test, 611
  game, 326–27
  introductory activity, 324
  in letter writing, 329
  main uses, 325–27
  review test, 332–33
  unnecessary, 330–31
Carson, Ben ("Do It Better!"), 483–92
cause and effect writing
  beyond the classroom, 108
  checklist for peer review, 108
  example, 105–6
  prewriting, 107
"Change of Attitude, A" (Berry)
  content, 507
  preview, 501
  reading comprehension, 505–7

"Change of Attitude, A" (*contd.*)
  structure, 507
  style and tone, 507–8
  visual prompt, 508
  vocabulary in context, 505
  words to watch, 501
  writing assignments, 508–10
checklists
  cause and effect writing, 108
  classification and division
      writing, 120
  coherence, 148
  comparison and contrast
      writing, 113
  descriptive writing, 96
  exemplification writing, 91
  four bases for revising
      paragraphs, 148–49
  narrative writing, 99
  paragraph writing
      assignment, 83
  process writing, 104
  sentence skills, 134, 148–49
  support, 148
  unity, 148
  writing, 83
citations, 42
class activity/discussion
  blog sharing, 14
  capital letters game, 326–27
  details, 64–65
  details, omitting/grouping, 65–67
  details, providing specific, 60–61
  details, providing supportive, 63
  details, that don't fit, 61–62
  four bases for evaluating
      paragraphs, 80–83
  freewriting, 18
  "How do you feel about
      writing?", 10–12
  ideas, commonality of, 52–54
  ideas, developing specific, 51–52
  ideas, identifying general, 51
  ideas, "What is the general
      idea?", 54–55
  point and support, 8–9
  revising for coherence, 76–77
  revising for sentence skills, 78–79
  revising for support, 75–76
  revising for unity, 74
  support in a paragraph, 58–59
  support, specific *v.* general, 56–58
  topic sentences, 48–49
  transitions: appropriate, 71–73, 76
  transitions: compared to hinges, 76

transitions: listing order, 68–69
transitions: time order, 69–71
understanding paragraphs,
    47–48
"unified" objects, 74
"Web site purpose" sentences, 14
writing as discovery process,
    12–13
classification and division
    writing, 120
  beyond the classroom, 120
  checklist for peer review, 120
  examples, 117–18
  prewriting, 119–20
clichés, 38, 425–26
closing sentence, 38, 83
clustering
  activities for reviewing, 37
  prewriting using, 22–23
coherence, 84
  argumentation writing, 124
  checklist, 148
  classification and division
      writing, 119, 120
  clustering technique, 23
  comparison and contrast
      writing, 113
  definition writing, 116
  descriptive writing, 93
  exemplification writing, 89, 91
  narrative writing, 98
  paragraph, 80–83
  process writing, 104
  revising for, 76–77
  in supporting material, 5
colon, 379–80
  See also semicolon
comma
  achievement test, 617
  around interrupting words,
      368–70
  between complete thoughts,
      370–71
  with direct quotations, 372
  with everyday material, 373
  introductory activity, 366
  after introductory material,
      367–68
  between items in series,
      366–67
  practice activity, 376
  review tests, 377–78
  run-ons correction, 184–85
  sentence skills, 612
  unnecessary, 374–75

comma splice, 180
commonly confused words,
    414–19
  homonyms, 385, 407–14
  incorrect word forms, 419–20
  introductory activity, 407
  review test, 421–22
common prepositions, 233
comparatives, superlatives and,
    278–79
comparison and contrast writing,
    108, 113
  beyond the classroom, 114
  checklist for, 113
  examples, 109–10
  prewriting, 111–12
  visual prompts, 110
complex sentence, 197–201
compound-complex sentences, 201–2
compound sentence, 196–97
compound subject and verb,
    159–60
computer use
  blogs, 14
  editing and proofreading, 34
  first draft, 32, 33–34
  freewriting, 19
  prewriting, 33
  saving your document, 32
  spell-checker, 396
  See also online
concluding paragraph, 132
conjunctions, 296
  coordinating, 594–95
  subordinating, 595–96
"Consume Less, Conserve More"
    (Gore, Al)
  content, 577
  preview, 572
  reading comprehension, 576–77
  structure, 577
  style and tone, 577–78
  vocabulary in context, 576
  words to watch, 572
  writing assignments, 578
content
  writing for, 11
  See also specific essay
contractions, 343–45
"Conveyor-Belt Ladies, The"
    (Guilbault)
  content, 472
  preview, 468

reading comprehension, 471–72
structure, 472
style and tone, 472–73
visual prompt, 473
vocabulary in context, 470
words to watch, 468
writing assignments, 473–75
coordinating conjunctions, 595
coordination (ideas of equal
importance), 202–5
copy and paste, 33–34
Cordoza, Glen, 521–25
Cornell, Mike, 8–10, 20–23, 128
correction symbols, 8, 432
count nouns, 597–99
course v. coarse, 409

D

dangling modifiers, 611
achievement test, 616
correcting, 290–92
introductory activity, 289
review tests, 292–94
dash, 78, 381–82
definition writing, 116
beyond the classroom, 117
example, 114
prewriting, 115–16
revising, 116
Del Castillo Guilbault, Rose ("The
Conveyor-Belt Ladies"), 468–75
demonstrative/possessive pronouns, 269–71, 348, 589
dependent clause, 197
dependent words
fragments, 163–67
usage, 197
descriptive writing, 87
beyond the classroom, 96
checklist for peer review of, 96
example of, 92–93
prewriting, 94–95
revising, 96
unity/support/coherence in, 93
writing, 93–95
details
added detail fragments, 170–72
class activity/discussion, 64–65
classification and division
writing, 119
general *v.* specific support, 56–58
movie script compared to, 56

omitting/grouping, 65–67
providing specific, 60–61, 63–64
providing supportive, 63
recognizing specific, 55–56
that don't fit, 61–63
diagramming, to generate ideas,
17, 22–23
dialogue, quotation marks for,
358–59
dictionary use
abbreviations key, 390
accent marks, 389
correct spelling, 387
electronic/online, 388
etymology, 392
introductory activity, 386
irregular verbs, 390–91
parts of speech, 390
plural forms, 391
pronunciation, 388–90
schwa, 389
spelling improvement, 395
syllable divisions, 387–88
synonyms, 393–94
usage labels, 392–93
discovery process, writing as, 12–13
"Do It Better!" (Carson and Murphy)
content, 490
preview, 483
reading comprehension, 489–90
structure, 490
style and tone, 490–91
vocabulary in context, 488–89
words to watch, 483
writing assignments, 491–92
draft. *See* first draft
Dumas, Firoozeh ("The "F
Word""), 475–78

E

editing and proofreading
activities for reviewing, 39
computer for, 34
first draft, 29–32, 73
paragraph, 29–31
parallelism, 298–99
effective word choice
clichés, 38, 425–26
inflated words, 426–28
introductory activity, 423
omitting unnecessary words,
428–29
review tests, 430–31
slang, 424–25

effective writing, four principles, 5
electronic dictionary, 388
end marks, 339–40, 611
achievement test, 616
review test, 341
essay
assignments, 142–45
concluding paragraph, 132
"Crescent Falls Diner and Truck
Stop" as, 128
diagram of, 127
introductory paragraph, 129–31
methods of introduction, 139–40
model of, 128
paragraph *v.*, 127
planning/outlining, 135–36
revising, 140–42
supporting paragraphs, 131–32,
137–39
thesis statement, 136–37
etymology, 392
even though v. even if, 197
exclamation point, 340
exemplification writing
beyond the classroom, 92
checklist for peer review, 91
examples, 88–89
prewriting, 90–91
unity/support/coherence
in, 89
writing, 90
exposition, 87

F

""F Word", The" (Dumas)
content, 479
preview, 475
reading comprehension, 478–79
structure, 479–80
style and tone, 480
visual prompt, 480
vocabulary in context, 478
words to watch, 475
writing assignments, 481–82
false cognates, 396
faulty parallelism, 611
Feldman, Robert S. ("Why Go to
College?"), 531–36
file, creating, 32
first draft, 25–26
activities for reviewing, 37, 38
computer for, 32, 33–34

first draft (*contd.*)
  editing and proofreading,
      29–32, 73
  revising, 27–29, 73
formal writing, abbreviations in, 336
formatting
  identifying/fixing/avoiding
      errors, 77–78, 321–22
  See also paper format
four bases for revising paragraphs,
    73–79
  checklist, 148–49
  class activity/discussion, 80–83
four steps to writing paragraphs,
    47–72
  leading to four bases for
      revising, 73–79
fragments, 78, 79, 609
  achievement test, 614
  added detail, 170–72
  dependent-word, 163–67
  editing and rewriting activities,
      174–75
  -ing and *to*, 167–69
  introductory activity, 162
  missing-subject, 172–75
  review tests, 175–78
freewriting, 18–20
  activities for reviewing, 37
  computer for, 19
  nonstop writing *v.* "correct," 17, 20
  prewriting, 18–20
fused sentence, 180

G

gerunds, infinitives and, 247, 248,
    602–4
Goldberg, Natalie ("Baking a
    Cake"), 525–30
Gore, Al ("Consume Less,
    Conserve More"), 572–78
grammar, identifying/fixing/
    avoiding errors, 77–78
"Grand Unified Theory of YouTube
    and MySpace, A" (Boutin)
  content, 582–83
  preview, 579
  reading comprehension, 582
  structure, 583
  style and tone, 583
  vocabulary in context, 581
  words to watch, 579
  writing assignments, 583–84

H

have v. be, 215
helping verbs, 590–91
Her, Mee ("Bowling to Find a Lost
    Father"), 462–67
here v. hear, 409
hole v. whole, 409
homonyms, 407
  all ready v. already, 408
  brake v. break, 408
  course v. coarse, 409
  here v. hear, 409
  hole v. whole, 409
  its v it's, 409
  know v. no, 410
  misuse, 385
  new v. knew, 410
  pair v. pear, 410
  past v. passed, 410
  peace v. piece, 411
  plane v. plain, 411
  principal v. principle, 411
  right v. write, 412
  their v. there, 412
  then v. than, 412
  threw v. through, 412–13
  to v. too *v.* two, 413
  where v. wear, 413
  whether v. weather, 413–14
  who's v. whose, 414
  you're v. your, 414
"How do you feel about writing?",
    10–12
"How They Get You to Do That"
    (Scott)
  content, 498–99
  preview, 492
  reading comprehension, 497
  structure, 499
  style and tone, 499
  visual prompt, 499
  vocabulary in context, 497
  words to watch, 492
  writing assignments, 499–500
hyphen, 78, 381–82

I

ideas
  commonality of, 52–54
  developing specific, 51–52
  generating, from journal
      writing, 13–14
  identifying general, 51
  "What ideas have in common,"
      52–54
  "What is the general idea?", 54–55
inconsistent pronouns, 259–60
indefinite pronouns, 256–57, 589
independent clause, 197
inference, 441
infinitives, gerunds and, 247, 248,
    602–4
inflated words, 426–28
-ing and *to* fragments, 167–69
intensive pronoun, 589
interrogative pronoun, 589
introduction, methods of, 139–40
introductory paragraphs, 129–31
irregular adjective forms, 278
irregular verbs, 214–17, 610
  achievement test, 615
  dictionary use for, 390–91
  incorrect forms of, 224
  introductory activity, 220
  list of, 221–23
  past tense, 225–26
  in present/past/past participle
      tenses, 224–25, 248, 606
  regular *v.*, 220–21
  review tests, 229–30
  troublesome, 226–29
  See also verb forms
its v. it's, 409

J

Johnson, Beth ("Let's Get
    Specific"), 511–21
joining words (and, but, for, or, so,
    nor, yet), 197
journal keeping, 13–14

K

know v. no, 410
Kraus, Erich, 521–25

L

"Let's Get Specific" (Johnson)
  content, 517–18
  preview, 511
  reading comprehension, 516–17

structure, 518
style and tone, 518
visual prompt, 519
vocabulary in context, 516
words to watch, 511
writing assignments, 519–21
letter writing, capitalization in, 329
limbering up (prewriting), 19
linking verbs, 590
list making, 21–22
    activities for reviewing, 37
    prewriting, 21–22
listing order, 38, 67–69, 71–73
Logan, Paul ("Rowing the Bus"), 448–51
long vowels, 388

M

Macintosh computer, 33
magazines, quotation marks for, 359–61
main idea (MI), 49
    reading comprehension, 441
    visual image with, 45, 46
mapping, to generate ideas, 22–23
mental block, prewriting v., 17
MI. *See* main idea
Microsoft Word, 34
misplaced modifiers, 611
    achievement test, 616
    correctly placing, 285–86
    fixing, 284–85
    introductory activity, 283
    review tests, 286–88
missing-subject fragments, 172–75
mistakes
    formatting, 77–78
    grammar, 77–78
    ignoring, in freewriting, 13, 17, 20
    punctuation, 77–78
    sentence structure, 77–78
    spelling, 77–78
Mixed Martial Arts: The Book of Knowledge (Penn, Cordoza, Kraus), 521–25
modifiers, 78, 275, 283–88
    See also misplaced modifiers
more and *most*, 277
"Most Hateful Words, The" (Tan)
    content, 549
    preview, 546

reading comprehension, 548–49
structure, 549
style and tone, 550
vocabulary in context, 547–48
words to watch, 546
writing assignments, 550–51
movie script analogy, 56
Mrosla, Helen ("All the Good Things"), 442–44
Murphy, Cecil ("Do It Better!"), 483–92
music CDs, quotation marks for, 359–61
"My Job at the Crescent Falls Diner and Truck Stop" (Cornell)
    as essay, 128
    as paragraph, 8–10, 20–23

N

narrative writing, 87
    beyond the classroom, 100
    checklist for peer review, 99
    example, 97–98
    prewriting, 98–99
    writing, 98
new v. knew, 410
New York Times, 455
newspaper, quotation marks for, 359–61
noncount nouns, 597–99
nonstop writing, 17, 20
nouns
    common v. proper, 586
    possessive, 345–48
    proper, articles with, 599–600
    singular v. plural, 587
    words as both verb and noun, 596
    See also pronouns
numbers, 611
    achievement test, 616
    introductory activity, 334
    practice activities, 335–36
    rules for, 334–35

O

object pronoun, 265–66
"Old Before Her Time" (Barrett)
    content, 544
    preview, 537

reading comprehension, 543–44
structure, 544
style and tone, 544
visual prompt, 545
vocabulary in context, 542
words to watch, 537
writing assignments, 545–46
omitted words and letters
    achievement test, 612, 617
    finding, 402–3
    introductory activity, 402
    review tests, 405–6
    -s endings, 403–5
online
    campus Web site, 125
    dictionary, 388
    homepage v. introductory paragraph, 145
    Web site evaluation, 83
    Web site purpose activity, 14
    writing process Web sites, 42
    See also computer use
organization, pattern of, 87–88, 125

P

pair v. pear, 410
paper format
    correcting errors, 77–78, 321–22
    guidelines, 320
    introductory activity, 319
    review test, 323
    rewriting dependent sentences, 322–23
paragraph development, 86–88
paragraphs, 8–10
    broken down into parts, 49–50
    editing and proofreading, 29–31
    essay v., 127
    four bases for evaluating, 80–83
    four steps to writing, 47–73
    omitting/grouping details in, 65–67
    organizing support in, 67–73
    providing details in, 64–65
    specific v. general support, 56–58
    symbol for, 8
    writing assignment checklist, 83
parallelism, 78, 79
    achievement test, 616
    correcting, 297–98
    creating, 299–300
    editing and proofreading, 298–99
    faulty, 611

parallelism (*contd.*)
    introductory activity, 295
    nonparallelism *v.*, 295–96
    practice activities, 296–97
    prewriting, 298–99
    review tests, 300–303
    writing/editing/rewriting, 298–99
parentheses, 78, 382–83
participles, 224–25, 248, 606
past v. passed, 410
pattern of organization, 87–88, 125
    campus Web site, 125
peace v. piece, 411
peer review
    cause and effect writing, 108
    classification and division
        writing, 120
    descriptive writing, 96
    elements of, 35–36
    exemplification writing, 91
    narrative writing, 99
    process writing, 104
Penn, B. J. ("Stance"), 521–25
period, 339
personal pronoun, 588–589
photographic images. *See* visual
    images
plagiarism, 42
plane v. plain, 411
plural forms, 397–99, 587, 589
    dictionary use for, 391
    -s endings, 403–5
poetry books, quotation marks for,
    359–61
points
    backing up, 50–67
    making, 6, 47–48
    in paragraphs, 8–10
    support and, 7, 8–9
possessive nouns, 345–48
possessive pronouns, 269–71,
    348, 589
prepositional phrase, 232–33
    as sentence opener, 309–11
prepositions, 157–58, 233, 591
    activities using, 592, 607–8
    time and place, 607
    See also subjects and verbs
present and past participles,
    224–25, 248, 606
prewriting
    activities for reviewing, 37

argumentation writing, 123–24
for auditory learners, 19
cause and effect writing, 107
classification and division
    writing, 119–20
clustering, 22–23
comparison and contrast
    writing, 111–12
computer use, 33
definition writing, 115–16
descriptive writing, 94–95
exemplification paragraph, 90–91
freewriting, 18–20
list making, 21–22
mental block *v.*, 17
narrative writing, 98–99
parallelism, 298–99
process writing, 102–3
questioning, 20–21
scratch outline, 23–25
techniques for, 17
principal v. principle, 411
process writing
    checklist for peer review, 104
    example of, 100–101
    prewriting, 102–3
progressive tense
    verbs not used in, 602
pronoun reference, agreement,
    point of view, 610
pronoun subjects, linking verbs
    and, 601
pronouns, 78, 587
    achievement test, 615
    correct use activities, 257–58
    demonstrative, 269–71, 348, 589
    inconsistent, 259–60
    indefinite pronouns, 256–57, 589
    intensive, 589
    interrogative, 589
    introductory activity, 252
    object, 265–66
    personal, 588, 589
    point of view, 258–59
    possessive, 269–71, 348, 589
    pronoun agreement, 255–56
    pronoun reference, 253–55
    pronoun reference, agreement,
        point of view, 610
    pronoun subjects and linking
        verbs, 601
    reciprocal, 589
    reflexive, 272–73, 589
    relative, 267–69, 589
    review tests, 260–62, 273–74

singular *v.* plural, 589
subject, 263–65, 263–67
subject or object practice, 266–67
types of, 263–74, 589, 610
pronunciation, 388–90
proper nouns, 586, 599–600
punctuation, 318
    capital letters, 78, 181–83,
        324–33, 611, 616
    colon, 379–80
    hyphen; dash, 78, 381–82
    identifying/fixing/avoiding
        errors, 77–78
    paper format, 77–78, 319–23
    parentheses, 78, 382–83
    period, 339
    question mark, 339
    review tests, 332–33, 337–38,
        341, 352–53, 363–64, 377–78,
        383–84
    semicolon, 78, 186–88, 380–81
    See also comma; quotation marks

Q

question mark, 339
questioning, 20–21
    activities for reviewing, 37
quotation marks, 78, 612
    achievement test, 617
    dialogue, 358–59
    for exact quotes, 355–58
    indirect *v.* direct quotes, 358
    introductory activity, 354
    practice activities, 361–63
    review tests, 363–64
    titles of short works, 359–61
    underlining *v.*, 359–61

R

reading
    aloud, 39
    backward, 39
    four steps to effective, 439–40
    skimming, 439–40
reading steps
    concentration, 439
    reading with a pen nearby, 440
    skimming first, 439–40
    working with it, 440
"Reclaiming Our Home Place"
    (Angelou, Maya)
    content, 570
    preview, 566

reading comprehension, 569–70
structure, 570
style and tone, 570
vocabulary in context, 569
words to watch, 566
writing assignments, 571–72
reference, pronoun, 253–55
reflective activities
adjectives and adverbs, 282
apostrophes, 352
capital letters, 332
comma, 377–78
correcting fragments, 175
dangling modifiers, 292
end marks, 341
irregular verbs, 229
misplaced modifiers, 286
paragraph development, 124
parallelism, 298, 300
pronouns, 260, 273
quotation marks, 363–64
run-ons, 192
sentence variability, 317
subordination v. coordination, 208
verb forms, 217
verb tense, 251
reflexive pronouns, 272–73, 589
revising
argumentation writing, 124
cause and effect writing, 108
classification and division
writing, 120
comparison and contrast
writing, 113
definition writing, 116
descriptive writing, 96
elements of, 35–36
essay, 140–42
evaluating and, 80–83
exemplification writing, 91
first drafts, 27–29, 73
four bases for, 73–79
narrative writing, 99
paragraphs, 27–29
process writing, 104
for sentence skills, 77–79
right v. write, 412
Rodriguez, Luis J. ("Turning Youth
Gangs Around"), 558–66
"Rowing the Bus" (Logan)
content, 453
preview, 448
reading comprehension, 452–53
structure, 453
style and tone, 453

vocabulary in context, 451
words to watch, 448
writing assignments, 454
rubric for evaluation, peer review, 36
"Rudeness at the Movies" (Wine)
content, 555
preview, 551
reading comprehension, 554–55
structure, 555–56
style and tone, 556
visual prompts, 556
vocabulary in context, 554
words to watch, 551
writing assignments, 556–58
run-ons, 78, 79, 609
achievement test, 614
correcting, via comma and
joining word, 184–85
correcting, via period and
capital letter, 181–83
correcting, via semicolon, 186–88
correcting, via subordination,
188–90
creating sentences with, 191
editing and rewriting, 190–91
introductory activity, 179
review tests, 192–94
words that lead to, 180–81

S

saving your document, 32
schwa, 389
Scott, Janny ("How They Get You
to Do That"), 492–500
scratch outline, 23–25
activities for reviewing, 38
peer review using, 35
SD (supporting details), 49
semicolon, 78, 186–88, 380–81
sentence patterns
complex sentence, 197–201
compound-complex sentences,
201–2
compound sentence, 196–97
review tests, 205–8
simple sentence, 195–96
sentence skills
abbreviations, 611
adjectives and adverbs, 610–11
apostrophes, 611–12
argumentation writing, 124
capital letters, 611
checklists, 134, 148–49

in classification and division
writing, 120
commas, 612
in comparison and contrast
writing, 113
consistent verb tense, 610
dangling modifiers, 611
in definition writing, 116
in descriptive paragraph, 96
diagnostic for, 613
effective word choice, 613
end marks, 611
evaluating paragraphs for,
80–83
in exemplification paragraph, 91
faulty parallelism, 611
fragments, 609
irregular verbs, 610
misplaced modifiers, 611
in narrative paragraph, 99
numbers, 611
in process writing, 104
pronoun reference, agreement,
point of view, 610
pronoun types, 610
quotation marks, 612
revising for, 77–79
run-ons, 609
spelling, 612
subject-verb agreement, 610
verbs, 609–10
words and letters omitted, 612
words confused, 612–13
sentence structure, 77–78
sentence variability
adjectives in series, 311–13
ed word groups, 305–6
ing words, 304–5
-ly openers, 306–8
prepositional phrase openers,
309–11
review tests, 315–17
verbs in series, 313–14
to word groups, 308–9
simple sentence, 195–96
skimming, 439–40
slang, 424–25
spelling, 34, 39, 73, 387, 612
achievement test, 617
basic rules, 396–97
basic word list, 399–401
computer spell-checker, 396
dictionary use for, 395
forming plurals, 391, 397–99,
403–5, 587, 589

spelling (*contd.*)
  identifying/fixing/avoiding
    errors, 77–78
  introductory activity, 395
  personal spelling list, 396
spontaneity, planning ahead *v.*, 12
"Stance" (Penn)
  content, 523–24
  preview, 521
  reading comprehension, 523
  structure, 524
  style and tone, 524
  vocabulary in context, 522
  words to watch, 521
  writing assignments, 524–25
structure. *See* sentence structure;
  specific essay
style and tone. *See specific essay*
subject pronoun, 263–67
subjects and verbs
  activities using, 604–5
  avoiding repeated subjects,
    600–601
  compound, 159
  finding subjects, 154
  finding verbs, 154–55
  gerunds and infinitives, 247,
    248, 602–4
  including pronoun subjects and
    linking verbs, 601
  introductory activity, 153–54, 231
  prepositions, 157–58
  progressive tense, 601–2
  pronoun subjects, 601
  review tests, 160–61
  subjects and linking verbs,
    156, 601
  There and *Here* at beginning of
    sentence, 601
  words between, 232–33
subject-verb agreement, 78, 79, 610
  achievement test, 615
  compound subjects, 235
  indefinite pronouns, 234–35
  practice activities, 237
  review tests, 238–40
  verb before subject, 233–34
  who, which, and *that,* 236
subordinating conjunctions, 595–96
superlatives, comparatives and,
    278–79
support
  argumentation writing, 124
  checklist, 148

classification and division
  writing, 118, 120
comparison and contrast
  writing, 113
definition writing, 116
description (writing pattern),
  92–93
descriptive writing, 93
details that don't fit, 61–63
evaluating paragraphs for, 80–83
exemplification, 89
exemplification paragraph, 91
exemplification writing, 89
general *v.* specific, 56–58
narrative paragraph, 99
narrative writing, 98
process writing, 104
providing specific details,
  60–61, 63–64
recognizing specific details,
  55–56
revising for, 75–76
supporting paragraphs in essay,
  131–32, 137–39
supportive evidence
  logical and detailed, 5
  none/too little, 6
  in paragraphs, 8–10
  specific details, 7–8
syllable divisions, 387–88
synonyms, 393–94

T

talking
  parts of speech, 390
  pronunciation, 388–90
  writing compared to, 5–6
Tan, Amy ("The Most Hateful
  Words"), 546–51
tense. *See* verb forms
their v. there, 412
then v. than, 412
There and *Here* at beginning of
  sentence, 601
thesis statement, 136–37
thinking on paper, 13
threw v. through, 412–13
time order, 67, 69–73
to v. too v. two, 413
tone, 87
  See also specific essay

topic sentence, 89
  class activity, 48–49
  details that don't fit, 61–62
  difficulty with, 8
  providing specific details,
    60–61
  recognizing specific details,
    55–56
  specific *v.* general support for,
    58–59
  topic *v.* support *v.*, 49–50
  where to find, 47
  writing specific details, 63
transition, 89
  appropriate, 71–73, 76
  compared to hinges, 76
  listing order, 38, 67–69, 71–73
  narrative writing, 98
  time order, 38, 69–71
  transitional sentences, 132
"Turning Youth Gangs Around"
  (Rodriguez)
  content, 564–65
  preview, 558
  reading comprehension,
    356–564
  structure, 565
  style and tone, 565
  visual prompts, 565
  vocabulary in context, 563
  words to watch, 558
  writing assignments, 565–66

U

underlining, quotation marks *v.*,
  359–61
unity
  argumentation writing, 124
  checklist, 148
  classification and division
    writing, 118, 120
  comparison and contrast
    writing, 113
  definition writing, 116
  descriptive writing, 93
  evaluating for, 80–83
  exemplification writing,
    89, 91
  narrative writing, 97–98
  process writing, 104
  revising for, 74
usage labels, 392–93
USB drive, 32

V

verb forms, 78
  achievement test, 615
  active and passive, 249–50
  consistent, 241–44, 601–2, 610
  correct practice, 247
  dialect *v.* standard, 210–11, 214–17
  examples, 245
  nonstandard, 209, 210
  past perfect, 246
  past progressive, 246
  past tense, 213–14
  present perfect, 246
  present progressive, 246
  present tense endings, 211–12
  review tests, 218–19, 251
  verbals, 247–48
  verbs not used in progressive tense, 602
  See also irregular verbs; subject-verb agreement
verbs, 609–10
  achievement test, 614
  action, 589–90
  compound subject and verb, 159–60
  have v. be, 215
  helping, 590–91
  linking, 590
  of more than one word, 158–59
  not used in progressive tense, 602
  in series, 313–14
  See also subjects and verbs; verb forms
visual images
  argumentation writing, 122
  clustering technique use of, 22–23
  coherence in, 84
  fried chicken, 151
  homonym misuse, 385
  hug your dog, 152
  Hurricane Katrina, 85
  litter is obscene, 152
  Lover's Leap, 209
  main point, 45, 46
  modifiers, 275
  Mona Lisa, 126
  pattern of development/ purpose in, 125
  pattern of organization, 125
  punctuation, 318
  responding to, 12, 15, 16
  Sistine Chapel, 146
  Tiger Woods, 4

visual clues, 446
  written description *v.*, 42
vocabulary expansion, 390
vowel sounds, 388

W

well or *good*, 280–81
"What is the general idea?", 54–55
where v. wear, 413
whether v. weather, 413–14
who's v. whose, 414
"Why Go to College?" (Feldman)
  content, 534
  preview, 531
  reading comprehension, 533–34
  structure, 534
  style and tone, 535
  visual prompt, 532, 535
  vocabulary in context, 533
  words to watch, 531
  writing assignments, 535–36
Wine, Bill ("Rudeness at the Movies"), 551–58
Woods, Tiger, 4
wordiness, 38, 428–29
word processing, 33–34
words
  achievement test, 617–18
  clichés, 38, 425–26
  confused, 612–13
  inflated, 426–28
  introductory activity, 423
  omitted, 402–6, 612, 617
  omitting unnecessary words, 428–29
  review tests, 430–31
  slang, 424–25
  as verb and noun, 596
  vocabulary expansion, 390
  See also homonyms; spelling
writer's template, across disciplines
  "The Sun's Effect," 147
  "What Do Psychologists Do?", 43
  "Where in the World?", 433
writing
  approach to, 39–40
  attitude toward, 10–12
  effective, principles of, 5
  formal, abbreviations in, 336
  four steps to, 47–72
  goals of effective, 17
  letters, 329
  movie script analogy, 56
  nonstop, 17, 20
  plagiarism, 42

  as process of discovery, 12–13
  as skill, 10, 40
  slang, 424–25
  starting assignments, 17
  as talent or learned skill, 4
  talking compared to, 5–6
  Web sites on, 42
  See also checklists
writing assignments
  "All She Has —$150,000 — Is Going to a University," 460–62
  "All the Good Things," 447
  "Baking a Cake," 529–30
  "Best/worst job" paragraph, 9–10
  "Bowling to Find a Lost Father," 466–67
  "A Change of Attitude," 508–10
  "Consume Less, Conserve More," 578
  "The Conveyor-Belt Ladies," 473–75
  "Do It Better!", 491–92
  essay, 145
  "The "F Word"", 481–82
  "A Grand Unified Theory of YouTube and MySpace," 583–84
  "How They Get You to Do That," 499–500
  "Let's Get Specific," 519–21
  "Major decision" paragraph, 41
  "The Most Hateful Words," 550–51
  "Old Before Her Time," 545–46
  paragraph, 89–92
  personal journal, 14
  "Reclaiming Our Home Place," 571–72
  "Rowing the Bus," 454
  "Rudeness at the Movies," 556–58
  "Stance," 524–25
  "Turning Youth Gangs Around," 565–66
  "Valued possession" paragraph, 82–83
  "Why Go to College?", 535–36
writing patterns, 87–88
writing process, 40–42

Y

you're v. your, 414

Z

zip code, 373